797,885 Books
are available to read at

www.ForgottenBooks.com

Forgotten Books' App
Available for mobile, tablet & eReader

ISBN 978-1-331-18527-7
PIBN 10155516

This book is a reproduction of an important historical work. Forgotten Books uses state-of-the-art technology to digitally reconstruct the work, preserving the original format whilst repairing imperfections present in the aged copy. In rare cases, an imperfection in the original, such as a blemish or missing page, may be replicated in our edition. We do, however, repair the vast majority of imperfections successfully; any imperfections that remain are intentionally left to preserve the state of such historical works.

Forgotten Books is a registered trademark of FB &c Ltd.
Copyright © 2017 FB &c Ltd.
FB &c Ltd, Dalton House, 60 Windsor Avenue, London, SW19 2RR.
Company number 08720141. Registered in England and Wales.

For support please visit www.forgottenbooks.com

1 MONTH OF FREE READING

at

www.ForgottenBooks.com

By purchasing this book you are eligible for one month membership to ForgottenBooks.com, giving you unlimited access to our entire collection of over 700,000 titles via our web site and mobile apps.

To claim your free month visit:

www.forgottenbooks.com/free155516

* Offer is valid for 45 days from date of purchase. Terms and conditions apply.

English
Français
Deutsche
Italiano
Español
Português

www.forgottenbooks.com

Mythology Photography **Fiction**
Fishing Christianity **Art** Cooking
Essays Buddhism Freemasonry
Medicine **Biology** Music **Ancient Egypt** Evolution Carpentry Physics
Dance Geology **Mathematics** Fitness
Shakespeare **Folklore** Yoga Marketing
Confidence Immortality Biographies
Poetry **Psychology** Witchcraft
Electronics Chemistry History **Law**
Accounting **Philosophy** Anthropology
Alchemy Drama Quantum Mechanics
Atheism Sexual Health **Ancient History**
Entrepreneurship Languages Sport
Paleontology Needlework Islam
Metaphysics Investment Archaeology
Parenting Statistics Criminology
Motivational

PRACTICAL TREATISE

UPON THE

Jurisdiction of, and Practice in,

THE

County and Probate Courts

OF ILLINOIS,

EMBRACING

A Collation of Statutes and Authorities

UPON THE

SETTLEMENT OF ESTATES OF DECEASED PERSONS; CORRELATIVE RELATIONS OF GUARDIAN AND WARD; THE ADOPTION OF CHILDREN INQUISITIONS OF LUNACY; APPOINTMENT AND DUTY OF CONSERVATORS OF LUNATICS AND DISTRACTED PERSONS; ASSIGNMENT FOR THE BENEFIT OF CREDITORS; BASTARDY, AND TRIAL OF THE RIGHT OF PROPERTY; CONTESTED ELECTIONS.

BY

WILLIAM C. JONES and JOSEPH O. CUNNINGHAM,
Of the Illinois Bar.

SECOND EDITION.

CHICAGO:
T. H. FLOOD & CO., PUBLISHERS.
1892.

T
J7286 p
1892

Entered, according to Act of Congress, in the year 1882, by
THE ILLINOIS PRINTING COMPANY,
In the Office of the Librarian of Congress, at Washington.

Entered, according to Act of Congress, in the year 1892, by
T. H. FLOOD & CO.,
In the Office of the Librarian of Congress, at Washington.

ILLINOIS PRINTING CO.,
PRINTERS,
DANVILLE, ILLINOIS.

PREFACE TO THE FIRST EDITION.

In offering to the profession this work upon Practice in the County Courts, it is proper for us to say, that we have aimed to bring together in an accurate and concise form the Statutes and decisions of our own State regulating such practice, and also such decisions of other states as we have deemed applicable; added to which are various forms, either adopted from approved precedents or framed by ourselves, which we hope will be found useful and suggestive in practice.

Inaccuracies and redundancies will undoubtedly be found to exist in the work; yet, we trust, not to an extent which will interfere with its practical value to the profession and class of business men whom we have aimed to assist. In citing adjudged cases we have uniformly adopted the language employed by the jurist who delivered the opinion, where to do so would not interfere with the brevity of language with which we have endeavored to clothe the principles set forth, blending the work of the judicial writers together where possible—in all cases citing our authority. If our generalizations are deemed insufficient the cases cited may be consulted for greater accuracy.

The subjects treated comprise almost the entire jurisdiction cognizable in the County Courts of Illinois, (its common law jurisdiction excepted,) as Estates of Decedents, testate and intestate, Guardian and Ward, Insanity, Assignments, voluntary and involuntary, Adoption of Children, Trial of the Right of Property, Bastardy, Contested Elections and Naturalization of Foreigners. It would be too much to claim for the work that it is a complete code under these various heads, and that the student and practitioner need look no farther, for our experience with the best text books and works of practice found in the libraries of the profession, proves that such a claim for any book is too extravagant. It is, perhaps, not too much to say, that in dealing with human affairs, as they develope themselves under these phases of life—often of the most delicate nature—the practitioner will here find precedents and principles cited, which, if followed, will insure the successful consummation of cases in his hands, and avoid that confusion which frequently delays or defeats heirs from coming into the possession of the fortunes justly theirs, and renders the administration of the estates of deceased persons, of infants, of lunatics, and of bankrupts, a system of robbery under the forms of law.

We have been materially assisted by timely and valuable suggestions from several of the distinguished gentlemen who do now, and have formerly occupied the position of Judge of the County Court, as well as from other experienced lawyers of the State, for which we hereby make our grateful acknowledgments.

In the preparation of the various chapters, our work has been about equally divided. The design of the book is that of our Mr. J., while our Mr. C. has had the entire labor of superintending the publication and arrangement of the work, and hereby assumes the responsibility of any imperfections that may be found in the book, due to such agency.

J. O. CUNNINGHAM,	W. C. JONES,
Urbana, Ill.	Robinson, Ill.

DANVILLE, ILL., *January*, 1883.

PREFACE TO THE REVISED EDITION.

The favor with which the first edition of this work was received by the profession has been an incentive to the authors to prepare a second and revised one, bringing citations therein of the decisions and statutes of Illinois down to date. Not only have our references to the decisions and statutes been brought down to the present time, but in addition thereto many new and valuable forms have been added, making the work in every respect complete.

Our Mr. Jones desires to acknowledge the assistance rendered him in the revision of that part of the work assigned to him, of his law partner, Mr. E. E. Newlin, who has aided materially in the revision of the work.

The authors desire here to return thanks to the profession, who have so generously supported the work by its purchase and use, and trust the revised edition may prove equally acceptable, and receive equal favor with the first.

THE AUTHORS.

TABLE OF CONTENTS.

PART I.

CHAPTER I.   PAGE. 3

County Courts of Illinois,

Constitutional provisions—Jurisdiction general—Force of their decrees—Not to be questioned collaterally—Statutory powers—Jurisdiction shared by chancery courts—Jurisdiction continues—May adjudicate upon equitable claims—May enforce their orders—Power to construe will—Probate courts—Sheriff shall attend sessions.

CHAPTER II.   8

Granting and Revoking Letters,

Administration under English laws—What court may appoint—Right of administration under our statute—Next of kin—Statute imperative—Who should not be appointed—When letters may be granted to others than the next of kin—Creditor must be actual—Administration unnecessary — Preference between claimants—Proof of death necessary—Grant may be delayed—Oath of administrator—Oath of executor—Act of granting ministerial—Appointment cannot be questioned collaterally—Acts of one irregularly appointed not void—Letters void in the beginning remain so—Public administrators—Duties of public administrator—Administrator to collect—Bond of same—Limitation on appointment of administrator—Revocation of letters and resignation—Resignation and costs—When action void—Who may administer *de bonis non*—Suits against former administrator.

CHAPTER III.   24

Administrators' and Executors' Bonds,

Bond of executors; form—When no security required—Bond of administrator—Requiring other security—On application of sureties—Form of new bonds—Two bonds may be taken—Giving new bond under Sec. 33 releases old securities—Giving new bond under Sec. 32 does not release old securities—Removal for failure to give new bond—Death of sole executor—Death or disqualification of executor or administrator—Court may take one or more bonds—Court shall examine bonds at January and July terms—Record to be kept—Summons of principals in bonds—When new bond to be required—Failure to give new bond; removal—Liability under new bonds—When not binding on sureties—*Devastavit*—Liability for taking insolvent security—For releasing a debt—For removing property from the State—For exhibiting an untrue account—For failure to file inventory within three months—For suffering judgment on claim barred by statute—For failure to account for debt due from

Administrators' and Executors' Bonds—*Continued.*

himself—For money recovered for causing death—One administrator liable for his co-administrator—As trustee or executor—Extent of liability—Administrator must use diligence; money stolen—Must redeem incumbered property—Must pay to distributees—Of the demand—Suit against part or all of obligors—Sureties liable only for assets of estate—Voluntary bond—Surety not in fiduciary relation to estate—Former bond; liability to administrator *de bonis non*—Security for costs—Irregularities in drafting bonds—Liability where letters are revoked—Where bonds are given by each administrator—Where administrator acts in two capacities—Will set aside and executor continues to administer—Sureties may appeal—Sureties may rely on bar of the statute to a claim—When fiduciary relation ceases—Estoppel—Jurisdiction of a court of chancery over remedies on bond—Form of judgment—Action of account may be maintained.

CHAPTER IV. 44

Duties and Liabilities of Executors and Administrators,

Duties prescribed by law—Grant of letters relates back—Duty of person named as executor in will—Power before probate of will—Administrator an officer—Death of part of executors—Power of one of several executors—Power of administrator with the will annexed—Succeeds to title to personalty—Liable for such as by diligence may be received—Courts to hold them liable for abuse of trust, but not upon slight grounds—For loss by fire—Should collect foreign debts—Must not continue a partnership relation—Power over real estate—When ejectment may be maintained—Rents—Must redeem real estate—Liability to third parties—As garnishee—Can not loan the money of the estate—Not liable for costs—Acting as administrator and guardian—Can not bind heirs by his action—Can not buy an interest in the estate—Good faith protects him—May compound a suit for negligence—Can not be sued with another—When not liable for interest—Must account for profits—May receive real estate on debts—Contracts of decedent may be performed—May assign note due deceased—May sell personal property—Liable for fraud—Not chargeable for mistake—Administrator to collect—His powers—Suits by him—When his powers cease—Administrator *de son tort;* liability—One acting honestly with him—Court no power to compel an account—How he may discharge himself—Widow not liable as administrator *de son tort*—Title to property—Suits between executors.

CHAPTER V. 59

Inventories and Appraisement,

Inventory to be filed—How prepared—Additional inventory—Inventory after discharge—A protection and guide—Should embrace all property of the estate—Appraisement bill; form—Oath of appraisers—Compensation—Return into court—Court may set aside—Inventories, etc.; evidence—Further appraisal—Executors, etc., chargeable—Assets not exceeding widow's allowance.

CHAPTER VI.   64
Collection and Disposition of Assets,

Property of deceased bound for debts—Duty and power to collect assets—Property fraudulently transferred—Actions which survive to the executor or administrator—Administrators and executors must sue and be sued jointly—Where plaintiff or defendant dies; suggestion and substitution—Concealed goods; collection of the same—Jurisdiction of chancery—Books of account—What are personal assets; dividends—Suits by executors and administrators—Title to property vests in legal representative—Actions of covenant—Widow; when liable—Practice—Suit by administrator *de bonis non*—Set-off not allowed—Payment to an acting administrator—Payment by administrator by mistake—Personal estate first liable for debts—Desperate claims—Avails of desperate claims—Claims may be compounded—Removal of property by executor or administrator—Sale of personal property—Rule of *caveat emptor*—Who may not purchase—Growing crops—Sale—Return of sale bill.

CHAPTER VII.   81
Partnership Estates,

Partnership terminated by death of one partner—Must be authority in the will to continue business after such dissolution—Statutory partnership—Proceedings on dissolution - Surviving partner to file inventory—In what county—Survivor continues in possession—Waste by him—Effects must first pay partnership debts—Statute declaratory—Account—Survivor may purchase—When partnership to be settled—Power of administrator to enforce settlement—Final settlement—No compensation to survivor—Real estate of partnership.

CHAPTER VIII.   88
Award to Widow and Children,

Widow's award—Not affected by renunciation—Allowance to children—Policy of the law—Right to award becomes fixed upon the death of the husband—Right can not be cut off by will—Nor by an ante nuptial contract—Widow not justified in seizing and holding money to satisfy claim—Widow's claim need not be presented as other claims—None but widows of *bona fide* residents entitled to it—Definition of "family"—Practice—Power of court over award—Title vests in widow—Widow bound by her relinquishment—Lien upon real estate.

CHAPTER IX.   96
Claims against Estates,

Notice and adjustment—What is a claim—Claim for monument for deceased—Partnership debts—Court may entertain equitable claims—Funeral expenses—Claim of former executor or administrator—Forfeiture enforcible as a claim—Taxes—How and when claims should be presented—Claim presented after two years—Claims presented after administration is completed—Proceedings—Continuance—Costs—Oath of claimant—Judgment as evidence—Offset, judgment for estate—Claims not due—Claimant may choose his forum—How allowed—Can not be submitted to arbitration—Judgments bear interest—Defenses to claims; duty of administrator—Defenses

Claims against Estates—*Continued.*
    to claims; limitations—Practice; judgment cannot exceed the demand—Change of venue—judgment conclusive—Demands of executor or administrater, how allowed—Insolvent estates—Fees to be charged.

CHAPTER X. 116

Classification and Payment of Debts,
    Order of payment at common law—By statute—Order of classification—Conflict of statutes—Preferred claims—Classification may be changed—Payment of claims before allowance—Payment by mistake.

CHAPTER XI. 122

Accounting, Settlement and Distribution,
    Accounts; when to be made—Partial distributions—Form of account—Account may be required at any time—Interest upon balances due to the administrator—Assets to be charged—Administrator, etc., to be allowed for attorneys' fees—Contingent fees not allowed—Expenses allowed—For board of minors—Costs of administration must be paid before distribution—Order approving accounts conclusive—Final settlement—Effect on claims—Chancery jurisdiction to effect settlements and open the same—Settlements to be enforced by county court—Ten per cent. interest—When account should be rejected—Account for monument—Heirs not bound by judgments paid—Order of approval several as to each item of account—Appeal from an order rejecting—Errors in account not evidence of fraud—Failure to pay over as ordered—Enforcement of orders by imprisonment—Duration of imprisonment—Suit cannot be maintained until order of distribution—Payment of legacies—Bond by legatees—When bond should be taken—Citation and proceedings thereunder—Court no power to render a money judgment—Refunding by legatees—What will bar claim for refunding—Suits between joint executors and administrators—Sureties not liable—One administrator or executor may have citation against his associate—Disposition of unclaimed estate—To be deposited—How obtained by claimant—Compensation of executors, etc.—Additional allowances—Equitable principles to govern.

CHAPTER XII. 139

Descent and Distribution,
    Intestacy presumed—Rules of descent—Where will is renounced—Who are next of kin—Meaning of term "children"—Children of the half blood—What will bar distribution—Estate of deceased infant—Administrator must collect—Advancements—Value of real property advanced—Value of personal estate—Evidence of advancements must be written—Death of heir—Advancements do not affect widow—When heirs may have distribution—Illegitimate offspring—How legitimated—Rights before the statute—Bastards under the common law—Posthumous child—Heirs at law—Adopted children—Husband and wife—Ante nuptial contracts—Acceptance under will—Descent not defeated by naked trust—Where heir is indebted to estate—Equalizing legacies—Notice of final settlement and order of distribution—Law in force at time and place of death governs distribution—Debts and charges must be first paid—Order of court necessary—Distribution in kind—Escheats.

CHAPTER XIII. 152

Sale of Real Estate to Pay Debts,

Real estate ultimately liable—When it may be sold—Where executor has exhausted his power in the will—Petition to the court; parties thereto—Proceedings coerced—Form of petition; exhibit of estate—Parties to proceeding under various statutes—Description of premises—Summons—Service of summons—Notice by publication; contents of notice—Affidavit of non-residence; may be made on belief—Where decree shows that notice was given—Parties must be before the court; want of jurisdiction—Practice; docketed as in other cases—Guardian *ad litem;* his duties—Hearing of cause—Assignment of dower—Dower may be assigned together—Homestead—Sale of—Land may be platted—Description of land in decree—Extent of sale—Power of court limited—Power to order sale judicial—Not a chancery proceeding—Administrator no power to remove incumbrance by proceedings in court—Heirs may interfere to prevent loss, but creditors can not—jurisdiction of chancery courts to order sale of land—Decree can not be attacked—Defenses; heirs may attack judgments—Time of payment—Limitations in absence of a statute—Sale, report and confirmation—Title of purchaser; *caveat emptor*—Effect on sale of a reversal of the decree—Forgery; fraud; chancery jurisdiction—Conveyance under decree and sale—Proceeds of sale—Sale of land not fully paid for—Power to sell under a will.

CHAPTER XIV. 180

Wills,

Scope of the chapter—Origin of the testamentary power—Definition—Who may make wills; what may be disposed of—How made and declared; declaration of witnesses—What may be disposed of by will; may totally disinherit children—Probate of will; custodian to produce it—Appeals; evidence on appeal—Custody of probated will—Issue of letters testamentary; refusal of executor—Contesting wills in chancery—Wills proven without the state; admission to probate—Revocation; not revoked by words—Nuncupative wills—Lost will—What law governs bequests—Mortgage of real estate by executors; effect of same—Construction of wills; intention—Where land devised is sold by testator before death—Legacies charged upon real estate—When title vests—Against whom wills are fraudulent—Trustees to receive compensation.

CHAPTER XV. 203

Foreign Executors and Administrators,

Power of executors and administrators in other jurisdictions under the common law—Powers in this state of those holding authority from other states—Exceptions—Authority local—Authentication of letters—Certificate—How right to sue must be questioned—May sue out execution.

CHAPTER XVI. 208

Appeals,

Appeals from order rejecting claim—Who may take appeals, and how—Right extends to all cases; exception—Condition of bond—What may be done upon appeal—Writ of error.

PART II.

CHAPTER I. — 213
Of the various kinds of Guardians,
Definition—Guardians by nature—Guardians by chancery—Guardians by statute—Guardians *ad litem*.

CHAPTER II. — 228
Appointment of Guardians,
Appointment; jurisdiction—Nomination by the court; jurisdiction—Testamentary guardians—Guardian's bond—Letters of guardianship; form—Record of appointment—Review of the appointment.

CHAPTER III. — 245
The Inventory,
Inventory.

CHAPTER IV. — 248
Powers, Duties and Liabilities of Guardians,
Power in the management of his ward's estate—Power to appear for ward in suits—Power to lease his ward's real estate—Power to remove wards—Duty with respect to ward's property—Duty to loan the funds of his ward—Duty to educate his ward—Liability for money received—Liability for ward's property—Liability upon contracts—Liability for negligence.

CHAPTER V. — 264
Rights and Liabilities of the Ward,
Rights in general—Right to disaffirm acts done and contracts made during infancy—Right of action by and against ward—Right of action by ward against guardian—Rights of the infant as to homestead—Rights of the ward as to settlements—Rights of the infant as to the doctrine of estoppel—Right of election by ward—Right to contract marriage—Liability for the debts of the ancestor—Liability of the infant for contracts—Liability of the infant for wrongs.

CHAPTER VI. — 283
Accounting by Guardian,
Duty to render account—Sureties of guardian—Powers of the county court in regard to—Allowances on accounting—Commissions—Opening and reviewing settlements—Form of a guardian's settlement.

CHAPTER VII. 298
Sale of Ward's Real Estate,

Proceedings to sell real estate—Form of petition; when filed—Notice of application; form; service—Practice; form of bond and decree—Notice and terms of sale; form—Return; sale approved; title; form of guardian's report; deed—Proceeds; accounting for; re-investment—Sale of real estate by non-resident guardian—Terms of sale—Deeds; title—Bond for costs—The proceeding—The petition—Jurisdiction—Special bond—Fixing time of sale—Notice of application—Purchaser at sale—Report of sale—Guardian's deed—Confirmation of sale—Purchaser need not see to the application of purchase money—Rule of *caveat emptor*.

CHAPTER VIII. 323
Mortgaging and Leasing Real Estate of Ward,

Statutory power—Petition; forms—Foreclosures—No strict foreclosures—Forms used in foreclosure—Remarks—Leasing ward's real estate.

CHAPTER IX. 332
Non-Resident Guardians,

Non-resident guardians; power to collect—Transfer of estate to non-resident guardians—Conditions—Manner of procedure; forms—Rules governing non-resident guardians.

CHAPTER X. 339
Resignation of Guardians,

Resignation of guardians; forms—Rules.

CHAPTER XI. 342
Removal of Guardians,

Power of court—Notice to guardian; petition, etc.—Successor in office—Rules governing the removal of guardians—Appeals.

CHAPTER XII. 348
Rights and Liabilities of Sureties on Guardians' Bonds,

Defenses to suits upon guardians' bonds—Counter security; petition; order of court—Proceedings under the order.

CHAPTER XIII. 357
The Law of Trusts as Applied to Executors, Administrators and Guardians,

Definition—When a trust is not implied—Duties of trustees—Disabilities of trustees—Duty to act in good faith—Remedy against trustees—Settlements between trustee and *cestui que* trust—Relations of trustee to the court.

CHAPTER XIV.   371

Adoption of Children,

Humane provisions of the law; who may adopt—What the petition shall contain; forms—What must be found by court; decree—When consent of child is necessary; form—Rights of child adopted—Rights of parents of adopted children—Former adoptions—Effect as to natural parents.

CHAPTER XV.   380

Proceedings as Conservator,

Appointment of; form of a petition for the appointment of a conservator—Summons; notice; form of notice to person alleged to be insane—Bond; counter security—Suit on bond—Care of estate; custody of person; children—Inventory—Form of inventory—Settlements—Final settlement—Manner of accounting—Collections—Performance of contracts—Legal proceeding—What contracts void—What contracts voidable—Swindling idiot, lunatic, etc.—Management of estate—Investment of money—Leasing real estate—Mortgaging real estate—Petition to mortgage—No strict foreclosure—Sale of real estate provided for—Petition for sale—Notice of application—Docket; practice—Sale—Return of sale; approval; record; title—Proceeds of sale—Sufficiency of sureties—Counter security—Removal of conservator—Summons to show cause; notice—Resignation—Successor appointed; delivery to successor—Compensation—Restoration to reason; form of petition to remove the conservator—Notice—Trial—judgment; form of order removing conservator—Appeals—Suits, collection, etc., by non-resident conservator—Sale of real estate by non-resident conservator—Notice of petition—Bond—Bond for costs.

CHAPTER XVI.   391

Proceedings in Insanity,

Petition; form of petition—Writ; service; order of the county judge to the clerk; form of writ—Subpœnas; form of precipe for witnesses; form of subpœnas for witnesses—jury; trial; form of a venire for jury—Verdict; form of the verdict of the jury—Verdict recorded; order of committal; application; form of final order—To which hospital; application—Warrant to commit—Form of warrant—Indorsement; return—Who not admitted; idiots discharged—Temporary commitment—Costs—Who to pay expenses; sheriff's fees—Bond to furnish clothing; form of a bond to trustees of hospital—Clothing—Paupers; duty of the county judge in regard to clothing—Discharge of patient; notice; removal—Non-resident patients—Restoration to reason; discharge—County hospital—Trial by jury necessary—Penalty.

CHAPTER XVII.   407

Proceedings in Insanity and as Conservator,

Inquisition of lunacy and appointment of conservator—Can not be questioned collaterally—Liability when appointed—Liability for interest—How insanity is ascertained—Who are deemed insane—Evidence—Effect of finding—Powers—Custody and support—

Proceedings in Insanity and as Conservator—*Continued.* 407

Claims against the estate of the insane—Commissions—Voluntary support—Suits affecting the person and property of lunatics—Sale of real estate by conservator—Contracts—Criminal responsibility—Liability for torts.

CHAPTER XVIII. 428

Assignment for the Benefit of Creditors,

Definition—How made—Notice to creditors to present claims—Assignee to file inventory under oath—Report of claims made and list of creditors—How claims may be contested—Dividends; final account and settlement—Power of court over assignee—Want of list or inventory not to avoid assignment—When additional inventory and bond—When claim not due; limitation—Power of assignee to sell property, collect debts, etc.—Death or failure of assignee to act—Preferences void—jurisdiction of county courts—Discontinuance of proceedings—Forms of a deed of assignment and schedules—Inventory of the estate of assignor; bond—Assignee's notice to creditors; form—List of creditors and their claims to be filed—Manner of presenting claims; form—Exceptions to claim; forms and service of notice—Order of distribution—Final report of assignee—Who may make assignments—Construction given to deeds— What assignments are fraudulent—Modifications subsequently made—Preference of creditors—Trustees; rights of creditors.

CHAPTER XIX. 462

Proceedings in Insolvency--Involuntary Assignment,

Jurisdiction—Release of debtor—Notice of intended application required—Duty of officer—Traverse of fraud or refusal; jury; forms—Schedule—Contesting schedule—Adjournments; bond—Assignment; assignee; exemption; bond—Effect of assignment; form—Discharge of debtor; form of discharge—Liberation by officer—Recording assignment—Proving demands; notice—What proof required—Further assignment—Collection and disposition of estate—Conveyances—Keeping account—Removal; new assignment—Settlement; dividends—Compensation of assignee—Fees—Insolvency of judge—Effect of discharge; evidence—Appeal; bond—Filing record—Proceedings on appeal—Stay during appeal—jail fees—Further jail fees; unexpended fees—jail fees as costs—Effect of discharge of debtor—Satisfaction by imprisonment—False oath; penalty therefor—Rules governing; sufficiency of affidavit—Effect of arrest—Debtor can not be compelled to schedule—Fraud; presumption as to—Jurisdiction—Appeal—Bond on appeal.

CHAPTER XX. 486

Bastardy,

Complaint by mother; form—Warrant; form—Examination; bail; forms—Trial in the county court—Continuance; form of recognizance—Parties may testify—When judgment is for the defendant—When judgment is against defendant; forms—Refusal to give security—Money; how used—Quarterly installments; default in pay-

Bastardy-- *Continued.* 486

ment; forms—Contempt; lien of judgment—Custody of child—Child not born alive, or dying—Marriage of parents—Limitation—Rules governing the action of bastardy—Pleadings—Annuity—Birth of twins--Escape of defendant—Acquittal of defendant—Marriage of mother—Venue—By next friend—Exceptions—Instructions—Defendant as witness—New trial—Verdict—Fees of State's Attorney—Period of gestation—Evidence—Continuance—Depositions—Action on bond—Appeals and writ of error.

CHAPTER XXI. 516

Trial of the Right of Property,

Proceedings for; jurisdiction; forms—Trial in county court; form of judge's entry—Notice to plaintiff in execution—Service of notice; continuance—Notice by publication—Affidavit of complaint—Time of giving notice; forms—Entering appearance—Trial; pleadings; jury—Trial by jury; forms of venire, etc.—Subpœnas for witnesses—judgment; exempt property; costs—Appeal; bond; trial *de novo*—judgment; indemnity—Apportionment of costs; fees; form—Rules governing the action of the trial of the right of property.

CHAPTER XXII. 532

Contested Elections,

jurisdiction of county courts—Powers of chancery courts to inquire into elections--Who may contest elections in the county court—Manner of proceeding; pleading—Matters to be considered on trial—Custody of ballots; examination—Intention of voter to govern—Bribery by candidates—In case of a tie vote—Void election—judgment of the court—Certified copy of judgment—Appeal.

CHAPTER XXIII. 554

Naturalization of Foreigners,

Definition—Who are subjects of this jurisdiction—How an alien may be admitted to citizenship—Congress alone may prescribe rules of naturalization—jurisdiction of county courts—Aliens who have served in the army of the United States—Aliens who have resided within the United States—Widow and children of one who has declared his intention—African aliens—Term of residence—Subjects of countries at war with the United States—Children of naturalized citizens—Foreign seamen—Power to admit to citizenship judicial—Declaration—Perjury—Record not to be contradicted by parol—Effect upon children.

TABLE OF CASES CITED.

	PAGE.
Abbott vs. Coburn, 28 Vt., 663	16
Achey vs. Stephens, 8 Ind , 411	411
Adams' Appeal, 38 Conn., 304	243
Ætna Ins. Co. vs. Swayze, 30 Kansas, 118.	76
Albert vs. Perry, 15 N J. Eq., (1 McCart.)	233
Alexander vs. Alexander, 8 Ala., 796....290,	412
Alexander vs. Masonic Aid Association, 126 Ill., 558 71,	136
Allen, *Ex parte*. 89 Ill., 474	138
Allen vs. Gaillard, 1 S. C., 279	255
Allen vs. Peete, 25 Miss., 29	233
Allen vs. Shepherd, 87 Ill., 314......174,	175
Allison vs. Allison, 46 Ill., 61	184
Allison vs. People, 45 Ill., 37	493
Allman vs. Taylor, 101 Ill., 185..............169, 222, 320,	387
Alsop vs. Barbee, 14 B. Mon. (Ky.)....585,	285
Alsop vs. Mather, 8 Conn., 584.... .23,	82
Alston vs. Alston, 34 Ala , 15	240
Ambre vs. Weishaar, 74 Ill., 109	184
American Board vs Nelson, 72 Ill., 564....	196
Ames vs. Downing, 1 Bradf., 321	62
Ammons vs People, 11 Ill., 6.....126, 239,	348
Amoskeag Manf. Co. vs. Barnes, 49 N. H , 312	239
Anderson vs. Anderson, 42 Vt., 330	412
Anderson vs Darby, 1 Mott & M. (S. C.), 369	215
Anderson vs. Foster, 2 Bailey, 501	508
Anderson vs. Foulke, 2 Harris & Gill, 346..	318
Anderson vs. Gregg, 44 Miss., 170.....149,	204
Anderson vs. Thompson, 11 Leigh (Va.), 439	289
Andrews vs. Bernhardi, 87 Ill., 365	160
Andrews vs. Black, 43 Ill , 256 188,	209
Andrews vs. Hunneman, 6 Pick., 128	144
Andrews vs Jones, 10 Ala., 400	270
Antouidus vs. Walling, 4 N. J. Eq. (3 Green), 42	310
App vs. Dresbach, 2 Rawle, 287	42
Arenz vs. Reihle, 1 Scam., 340	5.8
Armistead vs. Bozman, 1 Ired. (N. C. Eq.), 117	349
Armstrong vs. Armstrong, 1 Oregon, 207..	150
Armstrong vs. Cooper, 11 Ill., 560	6
Armstrong vs. Lear, 12 Wheat., 169	252
Armstrong vs. Mill, 6 Ohio, 119	217
Armstrong vs. Walkup, 12 Gratt. (Va.), 608.	290
Arnett vs. Arnett, 27 Ill., 247 197,	198
Arnold vs. Brown, 24 Pick. (Mass.), 89....	362
Arnott vs. Friel, 50 Ill., 174	42
Arthur's Appeal, 1 Grant (Pa.), 55	230
Asay vs. Allen, 124 Ill., 391	453
Ashley vs. Martin, 50 Ala., 297	255
Ashulot R. R. vs. Elliott, 57 N. H., 397...	360
Askew vs. Hudgens, 99 Ill., 468........137,	138
Atcheson vs. Robertson, 3 Rich. Eq., 132	136
Atiridge vs. Billings, 57 Ill., 489....72, 253,	290
Atkinson vs. Whitehead, 66 N. C., 296.240,	256
Aurentz vs. Anderson, 3 Pittsb. (Pa.), 310.	411
Austin vs Charlestown Female Sem., 8 Met. (Mass), 196	233
Austin vs. Lamar, 23 Miss , 189	290
Ayers vs. Baumgarten, 15 Ill., 444....314,	317
Ayers vs. Clinefelter, 20 Ill., 465	16

	PAGE.
Bacon vs. Taylor, Kirby (Conn.), 368.....	251
Badenhoof vs. Johnson, 11 Nev., 87	230
Bahe vs. Jones, 132 Ill, 134	549
Bailey's Ex'rs vs. Staley, 5 Gill & Johnson, 432	171
Bailey vs. Bailey, 115 Ill., 651	261
Bailey vs. Dilworth, 10 Smedes & M., 404 5,	51
Bailey vs. Miller, 5 Iredell's Law, 444	56
Bailey vs. Rodgers, 1 Me. (1 Greenlf.), 186..	350
Baird vs. Chapman, 120 Ill., 537	101
Baker. *Ex parte*, 3 Humph. (Tenn.), 592..	337
Baker vs. Bradsby, 23 Ill., 632	174
Baker vs. Brown, 18 Ill., 91............109, 2	9
Baker vs. Hunt, 40 Ill., 264	275
Baker vs. Lafitte, 4 Rich. (S. C.) Eq., 392..	291
Baker vs. Ormsby, 4 Scam., 325........73,	253
Baker vs. Richards, 8 Sergt. & R , 12	256
Baker vs. Roberts, 14 Ind., 552..............	499
Baker vs. Strahorn, 33 Ill. Ap., 59	379
Baldwin vs. Allison, 4 Minn., 25	358
Bales vs. Elder, 118 Ill , 436............145,	150
Ballance vs. Frisbie, 2 Scam., 63........73,	207
Ballance vs. Samuel, 3 Scam., 380	113
Ballard vs Spoor, 2 Cow. (N. Y.), 430....	220
Ballew vs. Clark, 2 Ired. (N. C.) L., 23....	418
Ball vs. Bryce, 21 Ill., 161	250
Bank of Orleans vs. Torrey, 7 Hill (N. Y.), 260	358
Barbero vs. Thurman, 49 Ill., 284	102
Barbour vs. White, 37 Ill., 164	67
Barger vs. Hobbs, 67 Ill., 592	142
Barker vs. Kunkel, 14 Legal News, 175....	125
Barnaby vs. Barnaby, 1 Pick. (Mass.), 221.	272
Barnard vs. Barnard, 119 Ill., 92.5, 108, 180,	378
Barnes vs. Brown, 32 Mich., 146	366
Barnes vs. Compton, 8 Gill (Md.), 391....	217
Barnes vs. Hardeman, 15 Texas, 366......	309
Barnes vs. Hazelto , 50 Ill., 430..............143, 265, 266, 267,	319
Barnes vs. Maring, 23 Ill. Ap., 68	88
Barnes vs. Powers, 12 Ind., 341	345
Barnett vs. Churchill, 18 B. Mon., 387	310
Barnett vs. Monroe, 4 Dev. & B. (N. C.) L., 194	349
Barnett vs. Wolf, 70 Ill., 76............4,	5
Barney vs. Sanders, 16 How., 535	361
Barney vs Seeley, 38 Wis., 381 250,	252
Barnum vs. Gilpin, 27 Minn., 426..........	543
Barnum vs. Reed, 136 Ill., 388........69,	108
Barrett vs. Churchill, 18 B. Monroe, 387...	310
Bartell vs Bauman, 12 Ill Ap , 450........	50
Bartlett, *Ex parte*, 4 Bradf. (N. Y.), 221 ..	252
Bassett vs. Abbott, 4 Gray (Mass), 69	503
Bassett vs Noble, 15 Ill. Ap., 360.........	114
Bates, *In re*., 118 Ill., 524	454
Bates vs. Woodruff, 123 Ill., 205...........	170
Batton vs Allen. 1 Halst. Ch., 99	149
Batson vs. Murrall, 10 Hump., 301.........	114
Baxter vs. Costiu, 1 Busb., 262...........	51
Beall vs. Hilliary, 1 Md., 186............	34
Beals vs. Furbish, 19 Me., 496...........	499
Beardstown vs. Virginia, 76 Ill., 34....543,	557
Bearss vs. Montgomery, 46 Ind , 544.	414
Beaubien vs. Cicotte, 12 Mich., 459.........	411
Bedell vs. Janey, 4 Gilm., 193	38

b

TABLE OF CASES CITED.

	PAGE.
Beebe vs. Saulter, 87 Ill., 518	168, 169
Beeler vs. Dunn, 3 Head (Tenn.), 87	287
Beeler vs. Young, 1 Bibb., 519	289
Beller vs. Jones, 22 Ark., 92	410, 418
Bell vs. People, 94 Ill., 230	42, 293, 350
Belton vs. Fisher, 44 Ill , 32	84
Bendall vs. Bendall, 24 Ala., 295	101, 125
Bennett vs. Albert, 132 Ill., 665	322
Bennett vs. Bradford, 132 Ill., 269	282
Bennett vs. Byrne, 2 Barb. (N. Y) Ch., 216.	230
Bennett vs. Hanifin, 87 Ill , 32	284, 285
Bennett vs. State, Mart. & Y. (Tenn.), 13 i.	421
Bennett vs. Whitman, 22 Ill., 448	156, 167
Bensell vs. Chancellor, 5 Whart. (Pa.), 371.	418
Benton vs. Pope, 5 Hump. (Tenn.), 392.267,	268
Berry vs. Hamilton, 12 B. Monroe, 191	16
Berry vs. Powell, 18 Ill., 98	85
Berry vs. Young, 15 Texas, 369	309
Berryhill's Appeal, 35 Pa. St., 245	367
Bice vs. Hall, 120 Ill., 597	182, 188
Bigelow vs. Bigelow, 4 Ohio, 138	7, 28, 34
Biggs vs. Postlewait, Breese, 154	33
Bingham vs. Maxcey, 15 Ill , 295	79, 176
Bird vs. Bird, 21 Gratt. (Va.), 712	413
Birely's Heirs vs. Staley, 5 Gill & Johns., 432	275
Bishop vs. Davenport, 58 Ill., 105.14', 143,	267
Bishop vs. O'Connor, 69 Ill., 432.172, 176,	275
Black vs. Hills, 36 Ill., 376	266
Black vs. Whital, 1 Stockton's Ch., 572	61
Blacklaws vs. Milne, 82 Ill., 505	142, 145
Blair vs. Sennott, 134 Ill., 78	4, 69
Blake vs. Pegram, 109 Mass., 541	290
Blake vs. People, 80 Ill., 11	133
Blakeney vs. Blakeney, 6 Porter, 109	66
Blanchard vs. Williamson, 70 Ill., 607	6, 60, 103, 108, 128, 129
Blanck vs. Pausch, 113 Ill., 60	548
Bland vs. Muncaster, 24 Miss., 62	175, 318
Blankenship vs. Stout, 25 Ill., 132	265
Blankenstrip vs. Israel, 132 Ill., 314	549
Blattner vs. Weis, 19 Ill., 246	184
Blauvelt vs. Ackerman, 5 C. E Gr. Ch., 117.	361
Blauvelt vs. Ackerman, 20 N. J. Eq , 141	361
Bliss vs. Perryman, 1 Scam., 484	265, 266
Blodgett vs. Am. Nat. Bank (Conn.), 14 Legal News, 112	82
Bloomer vs. Bloomer, 2 Bradf. Surr., 341.	215
Blow vs. Gage, 44 Ill., 208	448, 449, 535
Board of Supervisors vs. Keady, 34 Ill., 293.	535
Bochlest vs. McBride, 48 Mo., 505	367
Bogert vs. Furman, 10 Paige, 466	72
Bond vs. Lockwood, 33 Ill., 212	249, 254, 255, 256, 258, 272, 284, 289, 290
Bond vs. Ramsey, 89 Ill., 29	176
Bond vs. Zeigler, 1 Ga., 324	79
Bonham vs. People, 102 Ill., 439	42, 238, 239
Bonnell vs. Holt, 89 Ill., 71	203, 221, 273
Border vs. Murphy, 125 Ill., 577	174, 370
Boren vs. Smith, 47 Ill., 482	535
Bosler vs. Banks, 4 Pa. St., 32	75
Bostwick vs. Atkins, 3 Comst., 53	317
Bostwick vs. Skinner, 80 Ill., 147	5, 156
Boswell vs. State, 63 Ala., 307	420
Botsford vs. O'Connor, 57 Ill., 72	146, 158, 159, 160, 174
Bowden vs. Bowden, 75 Ill., 143	481, 482
Bowen vs. Allen, 113 Ill., 53	200
Bowen vs. Bond, 80 Ill., 351	160, 175
Bowen vs. Parkhurst, 24 Ill., 257	447
Bowen vs. Reed, 103 Mass., 46	504
Bowen vs. Shay, 105 Ill., 132	78
Bower vs. G. & M. R. R. Co., 92 Ill., 223.67,	209
Bowers vs. Block, 129 Ill., 424	155, 158, 168
Bowers vs. Bowers, 26 Pa. St., 74	11
Bowie vs. Puckett, 7 Humph. (Tenn), 169	239
Bowles vs. Rouse, 3 Gilm., 409	18, 156, 167
Boyce vs. Warren, 2 Dev. & B. (N. C.) L., 152	412

	PAGE.
Boyd vs. Clements, 14 Ga., 639	363
Boyd vs. Hawkins, 2 Ired. (N. C.) Eq., 304	358, 363
Boyd vs. Strahan, 36 Ill., 355	185, 200
Boyden vs. Boyden, 5 Mass., 427	412
Boyden vs. Frank, 20 Ill. Ap., 169	458
Boyer vs. Boyer, 89 Ill., 447	223
Boyett vs. Hurst, 1 Jones (N. C.) Eq., 166.	270
Boyles vs. Murphy, 55 Ill., 236	148
Boys vs. Rogers, 21 Ill. Ap., 534	93
Bozza vs. Rowe, 30 Ill., 198	178
Bradford vs. Abend, 89 Ill., 78	415
Bradford vs. Jones, 17 Ill., 93	102, 103
Bradley vs State, 31 Ind., 492	421
Branch vs. Branch, 108 Ill., 444	206
Branch vs. Rankin, 108 Ill., 444.18, 30, 31,	204
Brand vs. Abbott, 42 Ala., 499	256
Brandon vs. Brown, 106 Ill., 519	100, 138, 176, 295
Branger vs. Lucy, 82 Ill., 91	273, 277
Brantley vs. Key, 5 Jones (N. C.) Eq., 332	361
Brassfield vs. French, 59 Miss., 632	83
Brazier vs. Clark, 5 Pick. (Mass.), 96	35
Breckinridge vs. Ostrom, 79 Ill., 71	85, 207
Bree vs. Bree, 51 Ill., 367	157
Breed vs. Pratt, 18 Mass., 115	411
Brenner vs. Gauch, 85 Ill., 368	91
Brewer vs. Vanarsdale, 6 Dana (Ky.), 204	270
Brewster vs. Kilduff, 15 Ill., 492	542
Bricks' Estate, 15 Abb. (N. Y.) Pr., 12	317
Bridges vs. Rice, 99 Ill., 414	169, 201
Brigham vs. Brigham, 12 Mass., 505	408
Brigham vs. Tillinghast, 15 Barb. (N. Y.), 618	445
Brinkerhoff vs. Everett, 38 Ill., 2 3	270
Brisbane vs. The Bank, 4 Watts (Pa.), 92	264
Brisbin vs. Cleary, (Sup. Ct. Minn.), 11 Legal News, 365	541
Brock vs. Slaten, 82 Ill., 283	101
Brockman vs. Sieverling, 6 Ill. Ap., 512	102
Bromwell vs. Schubert, 28 N. E. Rep., 1057.	109
Brooklyn Industrial School vs. Kearney, 31 Barb. (N. Y.), 430	219
Brooks vs. Brooks, 3 Ired. (N. C.) L., 389.	414
Brooks vs. People, 15 Ill. Ap., 570	356
Broughton vs. Bradley, 34 Ala., 694	9
Brower vs. Fisher, 4 Johns. Ch , 441	410
Brown vs. Anderson, 2 Md., 111	248
Brown vs. Chase, 4 Mass., 436	266
Brown vs. Christie, 27 Texas, 73	313
Brown vs. Cowell, 116 Mass., 461	359
Brown vs Lynch, 2 Bradf. (N. Y.), 214	230
Brown vs. McWilliams, 29 Ga., 194	292
Brown vs. Mullins, 24 Miss., 2.4	287, 290
Brown vs. Parker, 15 Ill., 307	68
Brown vs. Pitney, 39 Ill., 470	149
Brown vs. Riggin, 94 Ill., 560	182
Brown vs. Sullivan, 22 Ind , 359	56
Brownfield vs. Brownfield 43 Ill., 163	193
Brubaker's Appeal, 98 Pa. St., 21	14
Bruce vs. Doolittle. 81 Ill., 103	285, 291, 292
Brush vs. Blanchard, 18 Ill., 46	291
Brush vs. Blanchard, 19 Ill., 31	253
Brush vs. Lemma, 77 Ill., 496	533, 536
Bryan vs. Moore, 11 Martin, 26	150
Bryant vs. Craig, 12 Ala., 354	255, 285
Bryant vs. Jackson, 6 Humph. (Tenn.), 199.	421
Bucher vs. Bucher, 86 Ill., 877	74, 128
Buck vs. Eaman, 18 Ill., 529	72
Buckingham vs. Morrison, 136 Ill., 439.82,	87
Buckley vs. Redmond, 2 Bradf. Sur., 281	9
Buckmaster vs. Carlin, 3 Scam , 104	319
Buell vs. Buckingham, 16 Iowa, 284	361
Bullock vs. Babcock, 3 Wend. (N. Y.), 391.	277
Burgen vs. Straughan, 7 J. J. Marsh. (Ky.), 583	499
Burger vs. Potter, 32 Ill., 72	222
Burgess vs. Pollock, 53 Iowa, 273	417

TABLE OF CASES CITED. XIX

	PAGE.
Burnap vs. Dennis, 3 Scam., 478........51,	79
Burnett vs. Commonwealth, 4 T. B. Monroe, 108	501
Burnett vs. Lester, 53 Ill., 325	185
Burnett vs. Meadows, 7 B. Monroe, 277....	11
Burr vs. Wilson, 18 Texas, 367............	347
Burr vs. Wilson, 50 Ind., 587.	5 7
Bursen vs Goodspeed, 69 Ill., 278.....172,	224
Burton vs. Tunnell, 4 Harr. (Del.), 424....	349
Burwell vs. Mandeville, 2 Hav., 579........	82
Bush vs. Sherman, 80 Ill., 160	367
Butler vs. Durham, 3 Ired. (N. C.) Eq., 589............239,	349
Butterworth's Case, Woodb. & M., 323....	560
Bybee vs. Tharp, 4 T. B. Monroe (Ky), 313 257,	287
Byrnes vs. Barr, 86 N. Y., 210............	185
Cagney vs O'Brien, 83 Ill., 72 135,	21
Caldwell vs. Young, 21 Texas, 800	289
Calhoun vs. Calhoun, 41 Ala., 369	287
Call vs. Ruffin, 1 Call (Va.), 333............	350
Call vs. Ward, 4 Watts (Pa.), 118..........	277
Calvert vs. Carpenter, 96 Ill., 63	194
Campbell vs. Campbell, 63 Ill., 462........	221
Campbell vs. Campbell, 130 Ill. 436	182
Campbell vs. harmon, 43 Ill., 19..222, 309,	313
Campbell vs. Johnson, 1 Sandf. (N Y) Ch., 148................	358
Campbell ve. Knights, 26 Me., 244	15
Campbell vs. Sneldon, 13 Pick., 8.	57
Campbell vs. Tousey, 7 Cow., 64..........	56
Campau vs. Gillette, 1 Mich., 416	170
Canatsey vs. Canatsey, 130 Ill., 397........	183
Canfield vs. Fairbanks, 63 Barb. (N. Y.), 461...................	417
Capehart vs. Huey, 1 Hill (S. C.) Ch., 405.	249
Capen vs. Foster, 12 Pick., 485...........	541
Caplinger vs. Stokes, Meigs (Tenn.), 175..	272
Carlile vs. Tuttle, 30 Ala., 613.............	337
Carlysle vs. Carlysle, 10 Md., 440.....	255
Carmichael, In re , 36 Ala., 514............	411
Carmichael, In re, 6 Daily (N. Y.), 51....	4 8
Carow vs Mowatt, 2 Edw., 57	21
Carpenter vs Calvert, 83 Ill., 62 182,	192
Carpenter vs. Carpenter, 8 Busb. (Ky.), 283.	411
Carpenter vs. McBride, 3 Fla., 292........	269
Carpenter vs. Sloane, 20 Ohio, 327........	237
Carroll vs. Bosely, 6 Yerger, 220..........	42
Cartwright vs. Wise. 14 Ill., 417............	222
Casey vs. Casey, 14 Ill., 112............358,	365
Cassell vs Williams, 12 Ill., 387............	528
Castleman vs. Castleman, 6 Dana (Ky.), 55.	407
Castner vs. Walrod, 83 Ill., 171.............	226
Carroll vs. Bonham, 42 N. J. Eq., 625	198
Caskie vs. Harrison, 76 Va., 85...........	85
Carter vs. Tice, 120 Ill., 277	255
Cavanaugh vs. McConochie, 134 Ill., 516 ..	549
Chaffin vs. Heirs of Kimball, 23 Ill., 36....	221
Chamberlain vs. Bates, 2 Porter (Ala.), 550.	39
Chambers vs. Jones, 72 Ill., 275........174,	321
Chambers vs. Howill, 11 Beav., 13	85
Champion vs. Brown, 6 Johns. Ch., 398.72,	99
Chapin vs. Hastings, 2 Pick., 71	13
Chapman vs. Chapman, 32 Ala., 106	269
Chappell vs. McKnight, 108 Ill., 570	179
Chapple vs. Cooper, 13 M. & W, 259.....	277
Charles vs. Charles, 8 Gratt., 486	12
Charles vs. Jacobs, 9 Rich, 205............	34
Chase vs. People, 40 Ill., 352	421
Cheney vs. Roodhouse, 135 Ill., 257....261,	296
Chicago & Alton R. R. Co. vs. Gregory, 58 Ill., 226	. 265
Chicago & N. W. R. R. Co. vs. Chisholm, 79 Ill., 584	92
Chicago & Pacific R. R. Co. vs. Munger, 78 Ill., 300	414
Chicago & R. I. and P. R. R. Co. vs. Kennedy, 70 Ill., 350..................267,	268

	PAGE.
Chicago Mut. Life Indemnity Ass'n vs. Hunt, 127 Ill., 257......................	28
Chicago West. Div R. R. Co. vs. Mills, 91 Ill., 39	411
Chickering vs. Raymond, 15 Ill., 362......	447
Child vs. Brace, 4 Paige 309	358
Child vs. Gratiot, 41 Ill., 357 ....12, 20,	21
Childers vs. Bennett, 10 Ala., 751	204
Chilton vs. Parks, 15 Ala., 671............	348
Chilton vs. People, 66 Ill., 501 507,	508
Chirac vs. Chirac, 2 Wheaton, 259	557
Choteau vs. Jones, 11 Ill., 300 168,	169
Christmas vs. Mitchel, 3 Ired. (N. C.) L., 535 362,	410
Christy vs McBride, 1 Scam., 75.36, 48, 63,	206
Church vs. People, 26 Ill. Ap., 232........	515
City of Alton vs. County of Madison, 21 Ill., 115	413
City of Beardstown vs. City of Virginia, 81 Ill., 541 .... 537, 539, 540, 557,	561
Clark vs. Board of Supervisors, 27 Ill., 3 5.	537
Clark vs. Burnside, 15 Ill., 62........60, 72,	254
Clark vs. Deveaux, 1 S. C., 172............	358
Clark vs. Hogle, 52 Ill, 427 ....6, 107,	172
Clark vs. Ga field, 8 Allen (Mass.), 427....	255
Clark vs. Groom, 24 Ill., 316............	448
Clark vs. Knox, 70 Ala., 607	114
Clark vs Montgomery, 23 Barb. (N.Y.),461.	289
Clark vs. Robinson, 88 Ill , 498 ... .539, 541, 542, 543,	544
Clark vs. Thompson, 47 Ill., 27.159, 161, 163,	221
Clark vs Trail, 1 Metc. (Ky.), 35..........	408
Clark, In re, 18 Barb. (N. Y.), 444........	560
Clay vs. Clay, 3 Metc. (Ky). 548	255
Clayton vs. Johnson, 36 Ark., 40..........	448
Cleland vs. Porter, 74 Ill., 76	538
Clelland vs. Fish, 43 Ill., 282............	357
Clinch vs. Eckford, 8 Paige, 412	138
Clinefelter vs. Ayers. 16 Ill., 329 .. 16, 47,	179
Clingman vs. Hopkie, 78 Ill., 152..........	111
Clubb vs. Wise, 64 Ill., 157................	209
Coat vs. Coat, 63 Ill., 73	174
Coates vs. Mackey, 56 Md., 416..........	105
Cochran vs. McDowell, 15 Ill., 10.........	265
Cockrell vs. Cockrell, 36 Ala., 673..........	345
Coffey vs. Home Life Ins. Co , 44 How. (N. J.) Pr., 481	410
Coffin vs. Argo, 134 Ill., 236..............	281
Cohen vs. Shyer, 1 Tenr. Ch., 192........	287
Colah, Matter of, 6 Daily (N. Y.), 51......	413
Colby vs. O'Donnell, 17 Ill. Ap , 473	458
Cole vs. Marple, 98 Ill., 58. 71,	119
Cole vs. Pennoyer, 14 Ill., 158 265,	266
Coleman vs Commissioners, 6 B. Monroe (Ky) 239................	408
Coleman vs. Frum, 3 Scam., 378......499,	507
Collins vs Ayers, 13 Ill., 358........73, 74,	207
Colton vs. Field, 131 Ill., 398..... 51, 82,	119
Combs vs. Janiver, 31 N. J L., 240	409
Comer vs. Comer, 120 Ill., 420........149,	183
Commissioners vs. Gilbert, 2 Strobh. (S. C.), 152	507
Common vs. People, 28 Ill. Ap., 230...... ..	515
Commonwealth vs. Heath, 11 Gray (Mass.), 303.....................	419
Commonwealth vs. Henshaw, 2 Bush. (Ky), 286......................	216
Commonwealth vs. Moore, 3 Pick. (Mass.), 194	504
Commonwealth vs. Mosler, 4 Pa. St., 264............................	4 1
Commonwealth vs. Pearce, 7 Mon, 317....	508
Commonwealth vs. Rodgers, 7 Metc. (Mass.), 500....................	421
Commonwealth vs. Sherman, 6 Pa. St , 346	313
Commonwealth vs. Thompson, 3 Litt (Ky.), 284..................501,	509
Compton vs. Compton, 3 Gill. (Md.), 241.	230

TABLE OF CASES CITED.

Case	Page
Fry's Election Case, 71 Pa St., 302	540
Fryrear vs Lawrence, 5 Gilm., 335....108,	126
Fuller vs. Hilliard, 29 Ill., 413	535
Funk vs. Eggleston, 92 Ill., 515	201
Fuqua, Succession of, 27 La. Aun., 271	230
Furlong vs. Riley, 103 Ill., 629........90,	172
Furmau vs. Coe, 1 Csi. C., 96	36
Gage vs. Shroeder, 73 Ill., 44... 163,	223
Gammage vs. Noble, 24 Miss., 150	249
Gardner vs Commercial National Bank, 95 Ill., 298.................4 6,	407
Gardner vs. Hyer, 19 Johns., 187	84
Gardner vs. Ladue, 47 Ill., 211	184
Gardner vs. Maroney, 95 Ill., 552	409
Garland, *Ex parte*, 10 Vesey. Jr., 119	81
Garrett vs. Moss, 20 Ill, 550	318
Garvin vs. Stewart, 59 Ill., 229 6,	1 0
Gauch vs. Harvey, 36 Ill., 313	163
Gauch vs. St. Louis Ins. Co., 88 Ill., 251	147
Gay vs Ballou, 4 Wend., 403	290
Gay vs. Du Uprey, 16 Cal , 195	277
Genet vs. Tallmadge, 1 Johns. Ch., 3	215
Georgetown College vs. Brown, 34 Md., 450	12
Gibson vs. Gibson, 81 Ill , 61 171,	275
Gibson vs. Rees, 50 Ill , 383	449
Gibson vs. Roll, 27 Ill., 88....157, 160, 309,	3 8
Gilbert vs. Bone, 64 Ill., 518	273
Gilbert vs. Bone, 79 Ill., 341	273
Gilbert vs. Guptill, 34 Ill., 112.72, 255, 285,	348
Gilbert vs. McEachen, 38 Miss., 469	287
Gilkey vs. Hamilton, 22 Mich., 283	46
Gill vs. Mining Co., 92 Ill., 249.......149,	201
Gillett vs. Wiley, 126 Ill., 310.........281,	356
Gilliland vs. Rea. 9 Paige, 66	170
Gilman C. & S. R. R. Co. vs. Kelley, 77 Ill , 426 360,	368
Gilmore vs. Rodgers, 41 Pa. St., 120	312
Gilmore vs. Gilmore, 109 Ill., 277	279
Gilmore vs. Sapp, 100 Ill., 297	313
Glenn vs. Smith, 2 Gill & Johns., 493....57,	206
Glidden vs. Nelson, 15 Ill. Ap., 297	511
Glinwater vs. M. & A. R. R Co., 13 Ill., 1	29
Goeppner vs. Leitzelmann, 98 Ill., 409 ....94, 170,	171
Gold vs Bailey, 44 Ill., 491.......34, 107,	131
Goltra vs. People, 53 Ill., 224.........35,	72
Gooch vs. Green, 102 Ill., 507	319
Goodall vs. Marshall, 35 Am. Dec., 483	207
Goodbody vs. Goodbody, 95 Ill , 456 ..170,	175
Goodwin vs Jones, 3 Mass., 514 203,	204
Gore vs. Clisby, 8 Pick, 555	450
Gotts vs. Clark, 78 Ill., 229	215
Gottsberger vs. Taylor, 2 Bradf., 86	20
Goudy vs. Hall, 36 Ill., 313 ....160, 161, 163, 176,	223
Grabill vs. Barr, 5 Pa St. R., 441	410
Graff vs. Castleman, 5 Rand. (Va.), 195	364
Graff vs. Fitch, 58 Ill., 373	526
Graham vs. Commonwealth, 16 B. Mon. (a y., 587	419
Graham vs. Pub. Adm'r, 4 Bradf., 127	204
Grand Tower Mining Co. vs. Gill, 111 Ill., 541	189
Granger vs. Granger, 6 Ohio, 35	112
Granjang vs. Merkle, 22 Ill., 250	113
Grant vs. Green, 41 Iowa, 88.... 408, 413	
Grant vs. Thompson, 4 Conn., 203	410
Grattan vs. Grattan, 18 Ill., 167 ... 5, 144,	218
Green vs. Massie, 13 Ill., 363.........50,	71
Green vs. Phoenix Ins. Co., 134 Ill., 310	425
Green vs Winter, 1 Johns. (N. Y.) Ch., 27.	363
Greenbaum vs. Greenbaum, 81 Ill., 367	311
Greene vs. Grimshaw, 11 Ill., 389	125
Greenman vs. Harvey, 53 Ill., 386.....163,	241
Greenwood vs. Murphy, 131 Ill., 604	548
Greenwood vs. Spiller, 2 Scam., 502	51
Greer vs. Walker, 42 Ill., 401	128
Greer vs. Wheeler, 1 Scam., 554	268
Gregg vs. Gregg, 15 N. H., 190	286
Gridley vs. Watson, 53 Ill., 186	168
Griffith vs. Frazier, 8 Cranch, 9	17
Grimsley vs. Klein, 1 Scam., 346	527
Griswold vs. Butler, 3 Conn., 227	417
Griswold vs. Griswold, 4 Bradf., 216	101
Griswold vs. Miller, 15 Barb. (N. Y.), 520.	4.6
Griswold vs. Waddington, 15 Johns. (N. Y.), 57	81
Grover vs. Wakeman. 11 Wend. (N. Y.), 187............445,	448
Guardianship of Feegan, 45 Cal., 176	415
Guernsey, *Ex parte*, 21 Ill., 443......317,	318
Guinea vs. People, 37 Ill Ap., 450	512
Guitteau vs. Wiseley, 47 Ill., 433	176
Guthrie vs. Murphy, 4 Watts (Pa), 80	277
Guy vs. Gericks, 85 Ill., 428........61, 109,	273
Hadnul vs. Wilder, 4 McCord (S. C.), 294	362
Haines vs. Hewitt, 129 Ill., 347	281
Haines vs. People, 97 Ill , 162............131, 133, 209, 210,	509
Hale vs. Brown, 11 Ala., 87	418
Hales vs. Holland, 92 Ill., 494.....5, 98, 112,	128
Hall vs. Commonwealth, Hard. (Ky.), 479.	500
Hall vs. Cone, 5 Day (Conn.), 543	270
Hall vs. Davis, 44 Ill., 494	221
Hale vs. Hale, 125 Ill., 399 179,	184
Hall vs. Hall, 3 Atk. Ch., 721	264
Hall vs. Hoxey, 84 Ill., 616	106
Hall vs. Irwin, 2 Gilm., 176 ....30, 47,	179
Hall vs. Pratt, 5 Ohio, 72	34
Hall vs. Unger, 2 Abb. (U. S.), 507	410
Halleck vs. Guy, 9 Cal., 181	317
Hallowell vs. Saco, 5 Greenlf., 143	252
Halstead vs. Hyman, 3 Bradf., 426	38
Hamilton vs. Gilman, 12 Ill , 260	265
Hamilton vs. Hamilton, 98 Ill., 254	179
Hamilton, *In re*, 17 Serg. & R. (Pa.), 144.	264
Hammer vs. Swift, 7 Legal News, 167	541
Hanchett vs. Weber, 17 Ill. Ap., 114	485
Hancock vs. Titus, 39 Miss., 224	364
Hanford vs. Prouty, 133 Ill., 339	457
Hanford Oil Co. vs. First Nat. Bank, 126 Ill., 584..........455, 456, 458,	460
Hanifan vs. Needles, 108 Ill., 403.......22,	39
Hanna vs. Reed, 102 Ill., 596	423
Hanna vs. Yocum, 17 Ill., 387	4
Hannahs vs. Sheldon, 20 Mich., 278	418
Hannum vs Speer, 2 Dallas, 291	179
Hardin vs. Osburn, 94 Ill., 571	454
Harding vs. Le Moyne, 114 Ill., 65..49, 156,	168
Harding vs. Shepherd, 107 Ill., 264...6, 75,	112
Hardy vs. Thomas, 23 Miss., 544	57
Harrer vs. Wallner, 80 Ill., 197....... 265,	266
Harring vs. Coles, 2 Bradf (N. Y.), 343	287
Harrington vs. Stees, 82 Ill., 51	198
Harris vs. Douglas, 64 Ill , 466 6,	186
Harris vs. Lester, 80 Ill , 30 ..157, 160, 163,	175
Harris vs. Millard, 17 Ill. Ap., 513	101
Harris vs. Schryrock, 82 Ill., 119	534
Harrison vs. Rowan, 4 Wash., 202	414
Harrison vs. Singleton, 2 Scam., 21	527
Harrod vs. Norris, 11 Martin, 297	79
Hart vs. Ten Eyck, 2 Johns. Ch., 62	34
Harter vs. Johnson, 16 Ind., 271	499
Hartman vs. Hartman, 59 Ill., 103	217
Hartman vs. Schultz, 101 Ill., 437	166
Hartwell vs. McDonald, 69 Ill., 293	166
Harvey vs. Harvey, 87 Ill., 54........134,	286
Harvey vs. Hobson, 55 Me., 256	417
Harvey, In the Matter of, 16 Ill., 127	315
Harvey vs. Thornton, 14 Ill., 217	139
Harward vs. Robinson, 14 Ill. Ap., 56	36
Hasler vs. Hasler, 1 Bradf., 248	125
Hatcher vs. Hatcher, 80 Va., 169	184
Hauskins vs. People, 82 Ill., 193 ..500, 501,	509
Hawe vs. State, 11 Neb., 537	410
Hawkins' Appeal, 32 Pa. St., 263	270

TABLE OF CASES CITED.

	PAGE.
Hawkins vs. Hawkins, 54 Iowa, 443	190
Hawkins vs. Johnson, 4 Blakf., 21	56
Hawley vs. Maucius, 7 Johns. Ch., 274	363
Hawley, Matter of, 1 Daley, 531	557
Hayes vs. Mass. Life Ins. Co., 125 Ill., 256	261, 262, 281
Haynes vs. Swann, 6 Hask. (Tenn.), 56	411
Hays vs. Jackson. 6 Mass., 149	47
Hays vs. Thomas, Breese. 134	142
Hayward vs. Ellis, 13 Pick. (Mass.), 272	207
Heacock vs. Durand, 42 Ill., 230	407
Heard, *Ex parte*, 2 Hill (S. C.) Eq , 54	337
Hehn vs. Hehn, 23 Pa. St., 415	413
Helm vs. Cantrell, 59 Ill., 524	170, 171
Helm vs. Van Vleet, 1 Blackf. (Ind.), 34 ! 73,	74
Hemmer vs. Wolfer, 124 Ill., 435	289
Hemphill vs. Lewis, 7 Bush. (Ky.), 2..	249
Hempstead vs. Dickson, 20 Ill., 193	201
Henchey vs. Chicago, 41 Ill., 136	52, 72
Hendrix vs. People, 9 Ill. Ap., 42	514
Henson vs. Moore, 104 Ill., 403	148
Herdman vs. Short, 18 Ill., 59	161, 163, 272
Herrick vs. Grow, 5 Wend., 579	49
Hertel vs. Bogart, 9 Paige, 52	47
Heslop vs. Gatton, 71 Ill., 528	200, 201
Hess vs. Voss, 52 Ill., 472	223, 224, 319
Hestor vs. Wilkinson, 6 Hump.(Tenn.), 215.	367
Hetfield vs. Fowler, 60 Ill., 45	134, 185
Heuer vs. Schaffner, 30 Ill. Ap., 337	456, 460
Heustis vs. Johnson, 84 Ill., 61	6
Heward vs. Slagle, 52 Ill., 336.	12, 129
Hewitt vs. School District, 94 Ill., 528	366
Hexter vs. Loughry, 6 Ill. Ap., 262	451
Hickox vs. Frank, 102 Ill., 660	9, 25, 48
Hicks vs. Hotchkiss, 7 Johns. Ch., 742	429
Hickenbotham vs. Blackledge, 54 Ill., 3:6	173, 221
Hide & Leather Nat. Bank vs. Kahm, 126 Ill., 461	456
Hier vs. Kaufman, 134 Ill., 215	455, 457
Higgins vs. McClure, 7 Bush. (Ky.), 379.	286
Higgins vs. Whitson, 20 Barb. (N .Y.), 141.	367
Hill vs. Cooper, 8 Oregon, 254	362
Hill vs. McIntyre, 39 N. H., 410	348
Hill vs. Reitz, 24 Ill. Ap., 391	531
Hill vs Tucker, 13 Howard, 458	105
Hines vs. State, 10 Miss., 532	252
Hinton vs. Dickerson, 19 Ohio St., 583	500
Hirsch vs. Trainer, 3 Abb. (N. Y.) Cas., 274	408
Hitchcock vs. Watson, 18 Ill., 289	326, 358, 361, 363
Hitt vs. Ormsby, 12 Ill., 166	265
Hitt vs. Scammon, 82 Ill., 519	71
Hoare vs. Harris, 11 Ill., 24	267
Hobson vs. Ewan, 62 Ill., 146	16, 156, 157, 160, 161, 177
Hobson vs. Payne, 45 Ill., 158	105, 160, 161, 170, 210
Hoch vs. Lord, Thach. Mass. Cr. Cas	507
Hodges vs. Wise, 16 Ala., 509	221
Hodgin vs. Toler, 70 Iowa, 21	46
Holcomb vs. People, 79 Ill., 409	498, 499, 501, 502, 503, 509
Holland vs. State, 48 Ind., 391	293
Holley vs. Chamberlain, 1 Redf. (N.Y.), 333.	230
Holloway vs. Galloway, 51 Ill., 159	184
Holman vs. Blue, 10 Ill Ap., 130	263
Holmes vs Fields, 12 Ill., 424. 218, 219, 250,	347
Holmes vs. Remsen, 4 Johns. Ch., 460	150
Holmes vs. Seele, 17 Wend., 75	251
Holyoke vs. Haskins, 5 Pick. (Mass.), 20.18,	252
Home Nat. Bank vs. Sanchez & Haya, 131 Ill., 330	457
Hooper vs. Hooper, 26 Mich., 435	307
Hooper vs. Royster, 1 Mump. (Va.), 119	287
Hopkins vs. McCann, 19 Ill., 113	107, 113, 171
Hopps vs. People, 31 Ill., 385	420, 421
Hopson vs. Boyd, 6 B. Mon. (Ky.), 296	408

	PAGE.
Horine vs. Horine, 11 Mo , 649	249
Horner vs. Goe, 54 Ill., 285	210
Horskins vs. Williamson, 1 T. U. P. Charlton (Ga.), 145	73
Hosack vs. Rogers, 6 Paige, 415	150
Hoskins vs. Wilson, 4 Dev. & B. (N. C.) L., 243	317
Hough vs. Doyle, 8 Black, 300	222
Hough vs. Harvey, 71 Ill., 72	52, 125, 137
House vs. Trustees, 83 Ill., 368	118
Housh vs. People, 66 Ill., 181	4, 114, 126
Howard vs. Crawford, 15 Ga., 424	481
Howell vs. Edgar, 3 Scam , 417	449
Howell vs. Edmonds, 47 Ill., 79	99
Howell vs. Moores, 127 Ill., 67. 117, 455, 459,	460
Howlett vs Mills, 22 Ill., 341	449
Hoyt vs. Hilton, 2 Edw. (N.Y.), 202	220
Hoyt vs Swar, 53 Ill., 134	266
Hubbard vs. McNaughton, 43 Mich., 220.	448
Hudson vs. Maze, 3 Scam., 578	447
Huff vs. Walker, 1 Ind , 193	251
Huffer's Appeal, 2 Grant (Pa.) Cas., 341	256
Hughes' Minor's Appeal, 5 Pa. St., 5 .0	251
Hughes vs. People, 111 Ill., 457. 262, 263, 295,	369
Huie vs. Nixon, 6 Port. (Ala.), 77	234
Huls vs. Buntin, 47 Ill., 396	267, 268
Hulse vs. Mershon, 125 Ill., 52	456, 457
Hume vs. Beale, 17 Wall., 336	363
Hungate vs Reynolds, 72 Ill., 425	50
Hunt vs. Thompson, 3 Scam., 179	215, 276
Bunter vs. Bryson, 5 Gill & Johnson, 483.	195
Hunter vs. Postlewa t, 10 Martin, 456	73
Hurd vs. Slaten, 43 Ill., 348	160
Hurdle vs. Leath, 63 N. C., 507	259
Huson vs. Wallace, 1 Rich. (S. C) Eq., 1..	206
Hutchinson vs. Mudd, 6 J. J. Marsh. (Ky.), 580	285
Hyde vs. Stone, 7 Wend. (N. Y.), 354	214
Ice vs. McLean, 14 Ill., 62	526, 527
Ide vs. Sayre, 129 Ill., 23	408
Illinois Central R. R. Co. vs Cragin, 71 Ill., 177	13, 16, 17
Illinois Central R. R. Co. vs. Latimer, 28 Ill. Ap., 552	226
Illinois Central R. R. Co. vs. Latimer, 128 Ill. Ap., 163	226
Illinois Land & Loan Co. vs. Bonner, 75 Ill., 315	142, 266
Inferior Court vs. Cherry, 14 Ga., 594	230
Ingelow vs. Douglas, 2 Stark, 36	197
Insurance Co vs Aspinwall, 44 Mich., 33 ,	198
Irby vs. Kitchel, 42 Ala., 438	61
Isham vs. Gibbons, 1 Bradf., 69	15, 252
Isom vs. First Nat. Bank, 52 Miss , 902	362
Iverson vs. Loberg, 26 Ill., 179	156, 161
Jackson vs. Jackson, 1 Gratt. (Va), 143	287
Jackson vs. Ryan, 3 J. J. Marshall, 308	80
Jackson vs. Sears, 10 Johns. (N. Y.), 435.	249
Jackson vs. Todd, 25 N. J. L. (1 Dutch), 121.	310
Jackson vs. Van Duesen, 5 Johns, 154	410
Jacobs vs. Allen, 18 Barb. (N. Y.), 549	445
Jacobs vs. Bull, 1 Watts, 370	35
James vs. Langdon, 7 B. Monroe (Ky.), 193.	418
Jamison vs. Glasscock, 29 Mo., 191	361
Jarrett vs. Andrews, 7 Bush. (Ky.), 311	287
Jeffries vs. Decker, 42 Ill., 519	158
Jenkins vs. Drane, 121 Ill., 217	145
Jenkins vs. Pierce, 98 Ill., 646	754
Jenkins vs. Waters, 8 Gill. & J. (Md.), 218.	257
Jenners vs. Howard, 6 Blackf. (Ind.), 240.	419
Jennings vs. Joyce, 116 Ill., 179	548
Jennings vs. Kee, 5 Ind., 277	264
Jennings vs. McConnell, 17 Ill., 14	6, 100
Jennings vs. Teague, 14 S. C., 229	46
Jenuison vs. Hapgood, 10 Pick., 77	252
Jessup vs Jessup, 102 Ill., 480	53, 291
Johnson vs. Baker, 38 Ill., 98.	159

XXIV TABLE OF CASES CITED.

	PAGE.
Johns vs. Norris,	
12 C. E. Green (N. J.) Ch., 485	362
Johnson vs. Carter, 19 Mass., 443	347
Johnson vs Chadwell,	
8 Humph. (Tenn), 145	418
Johnson vs. Corpenning, 4 Ired. Eq., 2 6.	9
Johnson vs. Gillett, 52 Ill., 358....112, 114,	128
Johnson vs. Johnson, 30 Ill., 215	159
Johnson vs. Miller, 33 Miss., 553	291
Johnson vs. Rockwell, 29 Barb. (N. Y., 16..	276
Johnson vs. Von Kettler, 66 Ill., 63.....70,	132
Johnson vs. Von Kettler, 84 Ill., 315...132,	133
Johnston vs. Maples, 49 Ill., 101........50,	126
Jones vs. Brewer, 1 Pick. (Mass.), 314	258
Jones vs. Cooper, 2 Aikens, 54	108
Jones vs. Jones, 15 Texas, 463	206
Jones vs. Knox, 46 Ala., 53	239
Jones vs. People, 19 Ill. Ap., 300	531
Jones vs. People, 53 Ill., 366.....499, 5 01,	505
Jones vs. Perkins, 5 B. Mon. (Ky.), 221. ,11,	418
Jones vs. Smith, 33 Miss., 215	261
Judge of Probate vs. Cook, 57 N. H., 450...	348
Judy vs. Kelley,	
11 Ill., 211.60, 72, 101, 103, 105, 113, 171, 2 3,	206
Julliard vs. May, 130 Ill., 87	461
Karr vs. Karr, 6 Dana (Ky), 3.......215,	257
Keefer vs. Mason, 36 Ill., 406......... 68,	207
Keegan vs. Gerahty, 101 Ill., 26.......147,	376
Keegan, In re , 13 Legal News, 161 & 328..	147
Keible vs. Cummings, 5 Hayw. (Tenn.), 43.	418
Keil vs. Healey, 84 Ill., 104.........265,	266
Keith vs. Funk, 47 Ill., 272	448
Keith vs. Jolly, 26 Miss., 131	249
Kelley vs. Davis, 49 N. H.. 187	215
Kelley vs. People, 29 Ill., 287..498, 499, 500,	502
Kelley vs. Smith, 15 Ala , 647	230
Kellogg vs. Holley, 29 Ill., 437	90
Kellogg vs Wilson, 89 Ill., 357	177
Kaster vs. Pearson, 27 Iowa, 90	34
Keating vs. Stack, 116 Ill., 91	549
Kellers' Appeal, 8 Pa. St., 288	76
Kelley vs. Kelley, 9 Ala., 908	39
Kelley vs. Viggs, 112 Ill , 242	146
Kendall vs. Miller, 9 Cal., 591	214
Kenedy vs. Gaines, 51 Miss., 625	311
Keniston vs. Rowe. 18 Me., 38	503
Kenley vs. Bryan, 110 Ill., 652....155, 165,	174
Kennedy vs. Kennedy, 105 Ill., 350	5
Kennedy vs. Shepley, 15 Mo., 640	48
Kershaw vs Kershaw, 102 Ill., 307	142
Kesler vs. Penninger, 59 Ill., 134.....221,	267
Kester vs. Stark, 19 Ill., 328	224
Ketteltas vs. Gardner, 1 Paige, 488	346
Ketteltas vs. Ketteltas, 72 N. Y., 312	146
Kevan vs. Waller, 41 Leigh (Va.), 414	235
Kidd vs. Chapman. 2 Barb. Ch., 414	131
Kilber vs. Myrick, 12 Fla , 419	417
Kilgour vs. Gockley, 83 Ill., 109.... 161,	266
Kimball vs. Mulhern, 15 Ill., 205	450
Kimmel vs. Kimmel, 48 Ind., 203	345
King vs. Collins, 21 Ala., 363	222
King vs Cushman, 41 Ill., 31........358,	362
King vs. Goodwin, 130 Ill., 102	91
King vs. Green, 2 Stewart, 133	34
King vs. King, 15 Ill., 187	218
King vs. King, 3 Johns. Ch., 552	33
King vs. Morphew, 2 Maule & Sel., 602	506
Kingery vs. Berry, 94 Ill., 515 543,	545
Kingsbury vs. Buckner, 134 U. S., 650	282
Kingsbury vs. Burnside, 58 Ill., 311	195
Kingsbury vs. Hutton, 40 Ill. Ap., 424	297
Kingsbury vs. Powers,	
131 Ill., 182............131, 281, 295, 296,	330
Kingsbury vs. Sperry, 119 Ill., 279	330
Kinne vs Johnson, 50 Barb., 70	183
Kinney vs. Knoebel, 51 Ill., 114	155
Kirby vs. Taylor, 6 Johns. Ch. (N. Y.), 242.	270
Kirby vs. Turner, Hopk. (N. Y.), 309..257,	270

	PAGE.
Kirby vs. Wilson, 98 Ill., 240	119
Kirkham vs. Boothe, 11 Beav., 273	82
Kitson vs. Farwell, 132 Ill., 327.......484,	485
Kline vs. Beebe, 6 Conn., 494	214
Klingensmith vs. Beau, 2 Watts, 486	5
Klokke, vs. Dodge, 103 Ill., 125	7
Knickerbocker vs. Knickerbocker,	
58 Ill., 399	311
Knowles, Ex parte, 5 Cal., 300	560
Knowton vs. Bradley,	
17 N. H., 458...............256, 258,	367
Knox Co. vs. Davis, 63 Ill., 405...535, 542,	557
Kolbe vs People, 85 Ill., 336	500
Kreitz vs. Behrensmeyer,	
125 Ill., 141...............548, 549,	561
Kreitz vs. Behrensmeyer, 131 Ill., 239	549
Kreuchi vs. Dehler, 50 Ill., 176.......527,	528
Kruse vs. Steffens, 47 Ill., 112	174
Kuchenbeiser vs. Beckert,	
41 Ill., 172.....................266, 267,	319
Kurtz vs. Hibner, 55 Ill., 514	200
Kuykendall vs. Harker, 89 Ill., 126	541
Kyle vs. Barnett, 17 Ala , 306	272
Labadie vs. Hewitt, 85 Ill., 341	162
Labouchere vs. Tupper,	
11 Moore Priv. Coun., 221	82
Ladd vs. Griswold, 4 Gilm., 25......29, 85,	99
Laiable vs. Fetry, 32 N. J. Eq., 791	83
Lamar vs Micou, 112 U. S., 452....244, 261,	338
L'Amoureaux vs. Crosby,	
2 Paige (N. Y.), 422	416
Larker vs. Kunkel, 14 Legal News, 75	125
Lane vs. Dorman, 3 Scam., 239	107
Lane vs Soulard. 15 Ill., 123	266
Langdon vs. Potter, 11 Mass., 313	150
Langworthy vs. Baker,	
23 Hill , 484..12, 17, 32, 107, 110, 171, 210,	276
Laughlin vs. Heer, 89 Ill., 119........275,	276
Lawrence vs. Elmendorf, 5 Barb., 73 ...	204
Lawrence, Matter of, 2 N. J. Eq., 331	408
Laycock vs. Oleson, 60 Ill., 30........73,	74
Leamon vs. McCubbin, 82 Ill., 263 65,	142
Lee vs. Fox, 6 Dana (Ky.), 171.......264,	287
Lee vs. Havens, Brayt., 92	204
Lee vs. People, 30 N. E. Rep., 690	515
Lee vs. People, 40 Ill. Ap., 79	515
Lefever vs. Lefever, 6 Md. 472	346
Lehman vs Rothbarth, 111 Ill., 457	369
Leiper's Appeal, 35 Pa. St., 420	73
Leland vs. Felton, 1 Allen, 531	34
Le Moyne vs. Harding, 132 Ill., 23.....154,	177
Le Moyne vs. Quimby, 70 Ill., 400....6, 49,	168
Lent vs. Howard, 2 Probate Reports, 109..	138
Lentz vs. Pilert, 60 Md., 296	13
Leonard vs. Leonard, 14 Pick (Mass), 280.	411
Leonard vs. Putman, 51 N. H., 247....203,	249
Lesher vs. Wirth. 14 Ill.. 39	89
Lessley vs. Lessley, 44 Ill., 527	148
Lester vs. Abbott, 28 How. (N. Y.) Pr., 488.	443
Letcher vs. Morrison, 27 Ill., 209	68
Lewis vs. Lusk, 35 Miss., 696	49
Lewis vs. Lyons, 13 Ill , 117	74
Lew s vs. People, 82 Ill., 104..498, 501, 506,	509
Liddell vs. McVicker, 6 Halstead, 44....125,	127
Lieb vs. Pierpont, 14 Reporter, 77	445
Lill vs. Brant, 1 Ill. Ap , 266	111
Lill vs. Brant, 6 Ill. Ap., 366 ...6, 446, 448,	449
Lilly vs. Wagoner, 27 Ill , 395.....182, 417,	418
Linegar vs. Rittenhouse, 94 Ill., 208...533,	534
Linnard's Appeal, 93 Pa. St., 313	195
Linton vs. Walker, 8 Fla., 144	269
Lipman vs. Link, 20 Ill. Ap., 359	461
Lippincott vs. Town of Pana, 92 Ill., 24..537,	538
Littlefield vs. Brooks, 50 Me., 475	252
Livingston vs. Jones,	
Harr. Ch. (Mich.), 165............258,	272
Lloyd vs. Kirkwood, 112 Ill., 329	279
Lochenmyer vs. Fogarty, 112 Ill., 572	99

TABLE OF CASES CITED.   XXV

	PAGE.
Lockhart vs. Phillips, 1 Ired. (N. C.) Eq., 342	269
Lockwood vs. Mills, 39 Ill., 602....358,360,	361
Lockwood vs. Stradley, 1 Delaware Ch., 298 47,	179
Long vs. Long, 132 Ill., 72........127, 143,	194
Long vs. Norcum, 2 Ired. (N. C.) Eq., 354.	287
Long vs. Thompson, 60 Ill., 27........128,	150
Longworth vs. Riggs, 123 Ill., 258	200
Lott vs. Sweet, 33 Mich., 308	421
Lovell vs. Minot, 20 Pick., 116	255
Lowe vs. Bartlett, 8 Allen, 259 170,	171
Lowe vs. Mitchell, 18 Me., 372 503,	5 4
Lowry vs. McMillan, 35 Miss., 147	150
Loyd vs. Malone, 23 Ill., 43 ..222, 310, 318,	319
Lucas vs. Perkins, 23 Ga., 267	408
Lund vs. Skanes Enskilda Bank, 96 Ill., 181.	451
Lunt vs. Lunt, 108 Ill., 307...........184,	2 0
Lupton vs. Cutter, 8 Pick., 298	450
Luscom's vs. Ballard, 5 Gray, 403	13
Luther vs. Luther, 122 Ill., 558	131
Lynch vs. Hickey, 13 Ill. Ap , 139	94
Lynch vs. Rotan, 39 Ill., 14 .....5, 142,	217
Lyndon vs. Lyndon, 69 Ill., 43	273
Lyon vs. Kain, 36 Ill., 3 2	139
Lyon vs. Vanatta, 35 Iowa, 521...	311
Lyttle, Matter of, 3 Paige (N. Y.), 251.....	412
Mack vs. Woodruff, 87 Ill., 570.....65, 85,	112
Maconnehey vs. State, 5 Ohio St., 77......	421
Madden vs. Cooper, 47 Ill., 359	160
Magee vs. Toland, 8 Port. (Ala.), 36	264
Magruder vs Peters, 11 Gil. & J.(Md.) 217.	215
Mahar vs O'Hara, 4 Gil., 424 136,	150
Maher vs. Huette, 89 Ill., 495	483
Mahill vs. Mahill, 113 Ill., 465	91
Mahler vs. Siusheimer, 20 Ill. Ap., 401.484,	485
Makepeace vs. Moore, 5 Gilm., 476 ....48, 53, 54,	70
Malcom vs. Rogers, 5 Cowan, 188.... .	20
Maloney vs. Dewey, 127 Ill., 395........4 5,	426
Maloney vs. People, 38 Ill , 62	4 8
Mann vs People, 35 Ill., 467..........498,	5 4
Manson vs. Felton, 13 Pick. (Mass.), 206..	248
Mapps vs. Sharpe, 32 Ill., 13	360
Maraman vs. Trunnell, 3 Met., 146	40
Mariner vs. Dyer, 2 Greenl. (2 Me.), 172...	506
Markillie vs. Ragland, 77 Ill., 98	200
Markle vs. Markle. 4 Johns Ch. (N.Y.), 168.	410
Marks vs. Whitkouski, 16 La. Ann., 341...	345
Marlatt vs. Wilson, 30 Ind., 240	507
Marsh vs. People, 15 Ill., 284..21, 22, 35, 39,	40
Marsh vs. Scarborough, 2 Deveraux Eq., 551	134
Marshall Co. vs. Cook, 38 Ill., 44........	537
Marshall vs. Cunningham, 13 Ill., 20.....	526
Marshall vs. Rose, 86 Ill., 374.....94, 157,	171
Marshall vs Silliman, 61 Ill., 218	537
Marston vs. Wilcox, 1 Scam , 60.........	20
Martin vs. Martin, 1 Vt., 91	168
Martin vs. McDonald, 14 B. Mon. (Ky), 544.	3 7
Martin vs. Railroad, 92 N. Y., 70.........	19
Marvin vs. Collins, 98 Ill., 510	141
Marvin vs. Schilling, 12 Mich., 356.......	249
Mason vs. Bair, 33 Ill., 194.. .....107, 113,	171
Mason vs. Caldwell, 5 Gilm., 196..51, 259,	315
Mason vs. Johnson, 24 Ill., 159...........	209
Mason vs State Bank, Breese, 141.........	526
Mason vs Tiffany, 45 Ill., 392..........99,	100
Mason vs. Wait, 4 Scam., 127. ....177, 248, 249, 309, 310,	319
Mason vs Whitthorne, 2 Coldw. (Tenn.), 242	256
Massey vs. Massey, 2 Hill (S. C.) Ch., 492.	257
Masterson vs Cheek, 23 Ill., 72..........	266
Mather vs. Bush., 16 Johns., 233	429
Mathes vs. Bennett, 21 N. H. (1 Foster), 204..............	290
Mathews vs Cowan, 59 Ill., 341	278

	PAGE.
Matthews vs. Hoff, 113 Ill., 90.....4, 159,	160
Mattock vs. Rice, 1 Heisk. (Tenn.), 33	292
Maxson vs. Sawyer, 12 Ohio, 195.....230,	238
Maxwell, Ex parte, 37 Ala., 362...........	27
May vs. Calder, 2 Mass., 55	215
May vs. First Nat. Bank, 122 Ill., 551.....	461
May vs. May, 109 Mass., 252 365,	413
May vs. May, 7 Fla., 207.................	365
Maybin, In re., 15 Bank. Reg., 468.......	258
Maynard vs. People, 135 Ill., 416.....512,	513
Means vs. Earls, 15 Ill. Ap., 273	262
Means vs. Harrison, 136 Ill., 49............	77
Means vs Means, 42 Ill., 50	173
Meek vs. Allison, 67 Ill., 46. ...17, 20, 28,	52
Meek vs. Perry, 36 Miss., 190...........	270
Meeker vs. Meeker, 75 Ill., 260....182, 183,	194
Melia vs. Simmons, 45 Wis., 334..........	14
Melvin vs. Lisenby, 72 Ill., 63	539
Menkins vs. Lightner, 18 Ill., 282..410, 411,	419
Merch vs. Russell, 136 Ill., 22...........	534
Meredith vs. Wait, 14 Allen (Mass.), 155...	500
Merricks vs. Davis, 65 Ill., 319...........	527
Merrill vs. Atkin, 59 Ill., 19.............	147
Merriman vs Cunningham, 11 Cush., 40..	279
Merritt vs. Simpson, 41 Ill., 391......199,	329
Mersinger vs. Yager, 16 Ill. Ap., 26	453
Meyer vs. Rives, 11 Ala., 769.	348
Meyer vs Temme, 72 Ill., 574............	291
Meyres vs. Meyres, 2 McCord (S. C.), 214.	362
Meyers vs. Meyers, 32 Ill. Ap., 189.......	379
Michoud vs. Girod, 4 How., 503......357,	366
Mickle vs. Hicks, 19 Kansas, 578......160,	168
Miene vs. People, 37 Ill. Ap.. 589	512
Milburn vs. Milburn, 60 Iowa, 411........	196
Miles vs. Boyden, 3 Pick. (Mass.), 213. 214,	215
Miles vs. Wheeler, 43 Ill., 123..79, 174, 358,	360
Milk vs. Moore, 39 Ill., 588..............	194
Millard vs. Harris, 119 Ill., 367........120, 131, 138, 165, 178,	210
Millard vs. Marmon, 116 Ill., 649..........	280
Miller vs. Anderson, 3 N. E. Rep., 605....	511
Miller vs. Craig, 36 Ill., 109 416,	417
Miller vs. Jones, 39 Ill., 54..........83, 85,	86
Miller vs. Kingsbury, 128 Ill., 45........84,	91
Miller vs. Miller, 3 Sergt. & R., 269.......	193
Miller vs. Miller, 82 Ill., 463..62, 92, 93, 94,	210
Miller vs. Receiver, 1 Paige, 444	19
Miller vs. Williams, 66 Ill., 91............	146
Milligan vs. O'Connor, 19 Ill. D., 487	453
Milliken vs. Welliver, 37 Ohio, 460	141
Mills vs. Fogal, 4 Edw., 559	198
Mills vs. McCabe, 44 Ill , 194	557
Miner vs. Miner, 11 Ill., 43 214,	218
Mings vs. People, 111 Ill., 98	511
Mitchell vs. Lunt, 4 Mass., 554...........	56
Mitchell vs. Mayo, 16 Ill., 83........4, 107,	112
Mitchell vs. Reynolds, 10 Mod., 85........	277
Mock's Heirs vs. Steele, 134 Ala., 193	133
Modin vs. Steward, 5 Ill. Ap., 533........	277
Moffat vs. Hill, 131 Ill., 239	549
Moffit vs. Thompson, 5 Richardson's Eq., 155	85
Moffitt vs. Moffitt, 69 Ill., 641..........5, 157, 169, 172,	175
Mohr vs. Tulip, 40 Wis., 66..............	417
Moline Water Power Co. vs. Webster, 26 Ill., 234...........6, 99, 100, 167,	171
Mollins vs. Cottrell, 41 Miss., 291	411
Monahan vs. Vandyke, 27 Ill., 154.....156,	160
Monk vs. Horne, 38 Miss., 100	160
Monroe vs. People, 102 Ill., 406..........	22
Montgomery vs. Dunning, 2 Bradf., 220..	88
Montgomery vs. Smith, 3 Dana (Ky.), 599.	346
Montsinger vs. Wolf, 16 Ill., 71..........	107
Moore vs. Bruner, 31 Ill. Ap., 400........	356
Moore vs. Chapman, 2 Stewart, 466.......	41
Moore vs. Ellsworth, 51 Ill., 308......172,	276
Moore vs. Holsington, 31 Ill., 243.........	534
Moore vs. Hood, 9 Rich. (S. C.) Eq., 311..	310

XXVI   TABLE OF CASES CITED.

Case	Page
Moore vs. Neil, 39 Ill., 257....160, 161, 173,	176
Moore vs. People, 13 Ill. Ap., 248	514
Moore vs. Philbrick, 32 Me., 102	9
Moore vs. Rogers, 19 Ill., 347............6,	100
Moore vs. Shields, 69 N. C., 50	287
Moore vs. Smith, 11 Richardson's Law, 569.	14
Moore vs. Wallis, 18 Ala., 458	348
Mootrie vs. Hunt, 4 Bradf., 176	20
Morehouse vs. People, 18 Ill., 472	71
Morey's Appeal, 57 N. H., 54	408
Morgan vs. Griffin, 1 Gilm., 565	5 0
Morgan vs. Hannas, 49 N. Y., 667	290
Morgan vs. Hoyt, 69 Ill., 489	413
Morgan vs. Johnson, 68 Ill., 190	253
Morgan vs. Morgan, 83 Ill., 196.....98, 99,	131
Morgan vs. Morgan, 39 Barb. (N. Y.), 20..	291
Morgan vs. Stevens, 78 Ill., 287	198
Morrell vs. Dickey, 1 Johns. Ch., 153..203,	252
Morris vs. Hogle, 37 Ill., 150....157, 161,	167
Morris vs. Joseph, 1 W. Va., 256	361
Morrison, Matter of, 22 How., 99	561
Morse vs Crawford, 17 Vt., 499	421
Mortimer vs People, 49 Ill., 473	258
Morton vs. Bailey, 1 Scam., 213	112
Moses vs. Murgatroyd, 1 Johns. Ch., 119 .	72
Motsinger vs. Coleman, 16 Ill., 71. 101, 171,	209
Mott vs. Mott, 11 Barb., 127	74
Moulton vs. Holmes, 57 Cal., 337	76
Mozely vs. Lane, 27 Ala., 62	362
Muir vs. Stewart, 1 Murph. (N. C.), 410....	224
Mulford vs. Beveridge, 78 Ill., 455...........310, 314, 316, 317,	318
Mulford vs. Stalzenbach, 46 Ill., 303....................311, 318,	319
Muller vs. Benner, 69 Ill., 108	251
Mullin, In re., 118 Ill., 551	485
Mulvey vs. Johnson, 90 Ill., 457	111
Munson vs. Newson, 9 Texas, 109	230
Murphy, In re., 109 Ill., 31.........484,	485
Murphy vs. Boyles, 49 Ill., 110	148
Murray vs. Carlin, 67 Ill., 286	419
Murray vs. Riggs, 15 Johns., 571	449
Myatt vs Myatt, 44 Ill., 473	12
Myatt vs. Walker, 44 Ill., 485 411,	417
Myer vs. Fales, 12 Ill. Ap., 351	453
Myer vs. McDougal, 47 Ill., 278....154, 172,	177
Myers vs. Kinzie, 25 Ill., 26	415
Myers vs. Wade, 6 Rand. (Va.), 444	287
McAllister vs. Moye, 30 Miss., 258	222
McAllister vs. Olmstead, 1 Humph. (Tenn.), 210	219, 209
McAnnulty vs. McAnnulty, 120 Ill., 26..90,	196
McApee vs. Commonwealth, 3 B. Mon. (Ky., 305	407
McBeth vs. Smith, 2 Brevard, 565	23
McCabe vs. Fowler, 84 N. Y., 314	36
McCagg vs. Woodman, 28 Ill., 84	449
McCahan's Appeal, 7 Pa. St., 56	290
McCall vs. Lee, 120 Ill., 261..........100, 102, 113, 117,	119
McCall vs. Parker, 13 Met (Mass.), 372.507,	515
McCampbell vs McCampbell, 5 Littell, 92.	75
McCauts vs. Bee, 1 McCord (S. C.)Ch., 383.	363
McCarty vs. Carter, 49 Ill., 53	276
McClanahan vs. Henderson, 2 A. K. Marsh (Ky.), 388	361
McClay vs. Norris, 4 Gilm., 370....221, 267,	309
McCleary vs. Menke, 109 Ill., 294....3, 142,	338
McClennan vs. Kenedy, 8 Md., 230	270
McClure vs. Miller, 1 Bailey Eq., 107	365
McClure vs. People, 19 Ill. Ap., 105	45
McConnell vs. Hodson, 2 Gilm., 640.54, 79,	304
McConnell vs. McConnell, 94 Ill., 296	57
McConnell vs Smith, 23 Ill., 611......146,	171
McConnell vs. Smith, 39 Ill., 279......146,	176
McCord vs. McKinley, 92 Ill., 11........93,	94
McCormick vs. Littler, 85 Ill., 62.....415,	418
McCoy vs. Morrow, 18 Ill..519.34, 107, 172,	276
McCoy vs. People, 65 Ill., 439	505
McCoy vs. Scott, 2 Rawle, 222	50
McCracken vs. Milhous, 7 Ill. Ap., 169..................438,	446
McCreary vs. Newberry, 25 Ill., 496	39
McCreedy vs. Mier, 64 Ill., 495........6, 37,	50
McCullum vs. Chidister, 63 Ill., 477 ...65,	198
McDaniel vs. Correll, 19 Ill., 226.......163,	222
McDermaid vs. Russell, 41 Ill., 490	221
McDermed vs. McCartland, Hardin, 18....	49
McDonald vs. Fithian, 1 Gilm., 269	365
McDonald vs. Meadows, 1 Metc. (Ky.), 507.	239
McDonald vs. White, 130 Ill., 493	192
McDougald vs. Maddox, 17 Ga., 52	349
McDowell vs. Caldwell, 2 McCord. (S. C.) Ch., 43	290
McDowell vs. Cochran, 11 Ill., 31	169
McEldery vs. McKinzie, 2 Porter (Ala.), 33.	51
McElhaney vs. People, 1 Ill. Ap., 550..488,	499
McElheny vs. Music, 63 Ill., 328........36,	251
McFadden vs. Vincent, 21 Texas, 47	418
McFarland vs. People, 72 Ill., 368	506
McGarvey vs. Darnall, 134 Ill., 367....23, 75, 105, 131, 171, 203,	206
McGary vs. Lamb, 3 Texas. 342	290
McGee vs. McGee, 91 Ill., 548	91
McIntyre vs. Benson, 20 Ill., 500	446
McIntyre vs. People, 103 Ill., 142..............295, 349, 354,	358
McIntyre vs. Sholty, 121 Ill., 660	422
McKanna vs. Merry, 61 Ill., 177....253, 257,	289
McKean vs. Vick, 108 Ill., 373	172
McKinley vs. Braden, 1 Cam., 64......73,	207
McKinley vs. Irwin, 13 Ala., 681	358
McKillip vs. McKillip, 8 Barb. (N. Y.), 552.	414
McKim vs. Aulbach, 130 Mass., 481	35
McKinnon vs. People, 110 Ill., 305	549
McLean Coal Co. vs. Long, 91 Ill., 617.48, 67,	143
McLean vs. Hosea, 14 Ala., 194	259
McLean vs. McBean, 74 Ill., 134	275
McLeod vs. First Nat. Bank, 42 Miss., 99.	362
McMahon vs. Allen. 4 E. D. Smith, 519...	126
McMillan vs. Lee, 78 Ill., 443	215
McMillan vs. McNeill, 4 Wheat., 209....428,	477
McNabb vs. Wixon, 7 Nev., 163	62
McNail vs. Zeigler, 68 Ill., 224	529
McNamara vs. Dwyer, 7 Paige Ch., 239....	204
McNees vs. Thompson, 5 Bush. (Ky.), 686.	411
McNeil vs. McNeil, 36 Ala., 109 ....6, 50,	120
McNickle vs. Henry, 4 Brews. (Pa.), 150...	287
McNish vs. Pope, 8 Rich. (S. C.) Eq., 112.	358
McSorley vs. McSorley, 4 Sand. Ch., 414 .	35
McVickar vs. Constable, Hopk. (N. Y.), 102.	2 4
McWilliams vs. McWilliams, 15 La. An., 88.	287
Nance vs. Nance, 1 S. C., 209........255,	257
National Bank vs. Gage, 93 Ill., 172	119
National Bank vs. Hyde Park, 101 Ill., 595.	362
Nease vs. Capehort, 8 W. Va., 95	362
Neff's Appeal, 57 Pa. St., 91	367
Neil vs. Morgan, 28 Ill., 524	41
Neill vs. Neill, 31 Miss., 36	247
Neilson vs. Cook, 40 Ala., 498	290
Nelson vs. Hayner, 66 Ill., 488......79, 84,	85
Nettleton vs. State, 13 Ind., 159	345
Neubright vs. Santmeyer, 50 Ill., 74....48,	138
Newcomb vs. State, 37 Miss., 383	419
Newell vs Montgomery, 129 Ill., 58... 162,	168
Newhall vs. Turney, 14 Ill., 339 . 39, 73, 74,	75
Newman vs. Newman, 4 Maule & Sel., 70..	507
Newman vs. Reed, 50 Ala., 297	255
Newman vs. Willetts, 52 Ill., 98	195
Newson vs. Newson, 5 Ired. (N.C.) Eq., 122.	254
Nichol vs Thomas, 53 Ind., 42 ..	417
Nichols vs. Mitchell, 70 Ill., 258	3 1
Nichols vs. Pool, 89 Ill., 491	451
Nichols vs. Sargent, 125 Ill., 309	281
Nicholson vs. Spencer, 11 Ga., 607	289
Nicholson's Appeal, 20 Pa St., 50	346
Nickerson vs. Gilliam, 29 Mo., 456	414

TABLE OF CASES CITED.

	PAGE.
Nicoll vs. Scott, 99 Ill., 535 ....30, 47, 179	
Nimmo vs. Kuykendall, 85 Ill., 476........	448
Noble, In the Matter of,	
124 Ill., 266 ....187, 188, 190	
Nolan vs. Jackson, 16 Ill., 272	174
Norris's Appeal, 71 Pa. St., 106....	361
Northern Line Packet Co. vs. Shearer,	
61 Ill., 263	529
Northy vs. Johnson, 8 Ga , 236..........	367
Norton vs. Cook, 9 Conn., 314.	429
Norwood vs. Hardy, 17 Ga., 595..........	408
Nutz vs. Rutter, 1 Watts (Pa.), 229........	269
Oakley, Matter of, 2 Edw. (N. Y.), 478	363
Obert vs. Hammel, 18 N. J. L. (3 Har.), 73.	358
O'Brien vs. State, 14 Ind., 469..........	505
O'Connor vs. O'Connor, 52 Ill., 316.......	108
Offutt vs. Offutt, 3 B. Monroe, 16 !.......	197
Ogden vs. Saunders, 12 Wheat., 212.......	477
Oglesby Coal Co., vs. Pasco, 79 Ill., 164 .	142
O'Halloran vs Fitzgerald, 71 Ill., 53	361
O'Hara vs. Jones, 46 Ill., 288	454
Oliver vs. Forrester, 96 Ill., 315..........	81
O'Neil's Case, 1 Tuck. (N. Y. Sur.), 34...	345
Orcutt vs. Orms, 3 Paige, 459	33
Ordronoux vs. Helie, 3 Sand. Ch., 512.....	204
O' Bear vs. Crum, 135 Ill., 294..........	12
Orthwein vs. Thomas, 127 Ill., 554....142, 145	
Osborn vs. Bank, 120 Ill., 111............	196
Osborn vs. Moss, 7 Johns., 161....	66
Osborn vs. Rabe, 67 Ill., 108	71
Osborne vs. Gibbs, 27 Ill. Ap., 246	458
Osborne vs. Williams, 34 Ill. Ap., 422..453, 458	
Osgood vs Manhattan Co., 3 Cow., 612....	71
Owens vs. Peebles, 42 Ala., 338..........	287
Owens vs.Walker, 2 Strobh.(S. C.) Eq., 289.	289
Paddock vs. Bates, 19 Ill. Ap., 471.......	454
Paddock vs. Stout, 121 Ill., 571........454, 469	
Padfield vs. Padfield, 78 Ill., 16..........	91
Padfield vs. Pierce, 72 Ill., 500 ....270, 272	
Page vs. Dennison, 1 Grant, 577	511
Page, In the Matter of, 118 Ill., 576.126, 188, 193	
Page vs. Naglee, 6 Cal., 241.............	361
Pahlman vs. Graves, 26 Ill., 405. . .....6, 190	
Pahlman vs Smith, 23 Ill., 448.........47, 179	
Painter vs. Henderson, 77 Pa. St., 48......	358
Palmer vs. Oakley,	
2 Dougl. (Mich.), 433.....................	316
Parcher vs. Russell,	
11 Cush. (Mass.), 107 ....126, 127	
Parker vs. Lincoln, 12 Mass., 16	281
Parker vs. Way, 15 N H., 45............	511
Parmele vs. McGinty, 52 Miss., 476......	319
Parmele vs. Smith, 21 Ill., 620 ....21 , 250	
Parris vs. Cobb, 5 Rich. (N. C.) Eq., 450..	418
Parsons vs. Ely, 45 Ill., 232..............	142
Parsons vs. Lyman, 4 Bradf., 269.........	150
Paschall vs. Hailman, 4 Gilm., 285.116, 117, 150	
Patten vs. Pearson, 60 Me., 220	360
Patterson vs. Johnson, 113 Ill., 559.......	280
Patterson vs. Patterson,	
59 N. Y., 574.................75, 100, 203	
Patterson vs. Pullman, 104 Ill., 80........	225
Patton vs. Thompson,	
2 Jones' (N. C.) Eq., 285................	317
Paulin vs. Howser, 63 Ill., 312............	278
Faulk vs. State, 52 Ala., 427 ....499, 503	
Payne vs. Stone,	
15 Miss. (7 Smeed & M.), 367............	259
Paytou vs. Freet, 1 Ohio St., 544.........	222
Peacock vs. Haven, 22 Ill., 23.....103, 109, 113	
Peak vs. People, 76 Ill., 289...498, 501, 502, 509	
Peak vs. Pricer, 24 Ill., 164 ....222, 224	
Peak vs. Shasted, 21 Ill., 137......221, 223, 267	
Pearce vs. Swan, 1 Scam., 266...........	527
Pearl vs. McDowell,	
3 J. J. Marsh (Ky.), 658	419
Pease vs. Hubbard, 37 Ill., 257........ 487, 500	

	PAGE.
Pease vs. Roberts, 16 Ill. Ap., 634.........	244
Peaslee vs. Robbins, 3 Metcf. (Mass.), 164.	410
Peck vs. Bonman, 2 Blackf. (Ind.), 141....	286
Peck vs. Botsford, 7 Conn., 172...........	111
Peck vs. Peck, 9 Yerger, 304..............	144
Pedan vs. Robb, 8 Ohio, 227..............	252
Peebles vs. Watts, 9 Dana, 102............	27
Pelham vs. Taylor, 1 Jones' Eq., 121......	134
Pendlay vs. Eaton, 130 Ill., 69	192
Pendleton vs. Trueblood,	
3 Jones (N. C.), 96	310
Penn vs. Brewer, 12 Gill & J. (Md.), 113...	368
Penn & Wife vs. Heisey, 19 Ill., 295....271, 318	
Pensoneau vs. Bleakley, 14 Ill., 15.....358, 360	
People vs. Abbott, 1 5 Ill., 588...........	13
People vs. Admire, 39 Ill , 251..........38, 134	
People vs. Allen, 86 Ill., 167	35
People vs. Allen, 8 Ill Ap., 17...........	41
People vs. Brooks, 123 Ill., 246....106, 110, 141	
People vs. Brooks. 22 Ill. Ap., 594.........	356
People vs. Christnan, 66 Ill., 162.........	498
Peeple vs. Circuit Judge, 19 Mich., 296....	314
People vs. City of Galesburg, 48 Ill., 485..	534
People vs. Clute, 50 N. Y., 451...........	543
People vs. Coffman, 24 Cal., 230	419
People vs. Cole, 84 Ill., 327..........4, 17, 75	
People vs. Curry, 59 Ill , 35..............	30
People vs. Falconer, 5 Sand., 81	42
People vs. Garbutt, 17 Mich., 9...........	420
People vs Gilbert, 115 Ill., 59.........406, 427	
People vs. Gray, 72 Ill., 343..........4, 109 118	
People vs. Green, 58 Ill., 236....	508
People vs Greer, 33 Ill., 213..............	482
People vs. Hamilton, 14 Reporter, 46.....	420
People vs. Hanchett, 111 Ill., 90..........	485
People vs. Housh, 66 Ill., 178............	37
People vs. Hunter, 89 Ill., 392 .....33, 126, 150	
People vs. Jane, 27 Barb. (N Y.), 58......	508
People vs. Jennings, 44 Ill., 488...........	200
People vs. Knickerbocker, 114 Ill., 539....	189
People vs. Lewis, 36 Cal., 531............	421
People vs. Lott, 27 Ill., 215......29, 41, 43, 129	
People vs. Lott, 36 Ill , 447..............	99
People vs. Matteson, 17 Ill., 167	544
People vs. McGowan, 77 Ill., 644......557, 561	
People vs. McKee, 105 Ill., 588...........	70
People vs. Miller, 1 Scam., 85............	38
People vs. Mitchell,	
44 Barb. (N. Y.), 245	214
People vs. Montgomery,	
13 Abb. (N. Y. Pr.) N. S., 207............	421
People vs. Nixon, 45 Ill., 253............	500
People vs. Noxon, 40 Ill., 30.............	498
People vs. Ogden, 10 Ill. Ap , 226	514
People vs. Peck, 3 Scam., 118..........68, 206	
People vs. Phelps,	
78 Ill., 148..............7, 108, 119, 120, 131	
People vs. Pine, 2 Barb. (N. Y.), 566......	421
People vs. Randolph, 24 Ill., 324.......32, 43	
People vs Smith, 17 Ill. Ap , 597	515
People vs. Smith, 31 Cal., 466............	421
People vs. Smith, 51 Ill., 177..............	535
People vs. Starr, 50 Ill., 52............49 , 5 2	
People vs. Steele. 7 Ill. Ap., 20...	259
People vs. Stevens, 19 Ill. Ap., 405........	512
People vs. Stewart, 29 Ill. Ap., 441... ...	355
People vs. Summers, 16 Ill., 173....... 32, 43	
People vs. Turner, 55 Ill , 280........214, 278	
People vs. Volksdorf, 112 Ill., 292........	511
People vs. Waite, 70 Ill., 26..............	537
People vs. White,	
11 Ill., 341.....6, 83, 85, 86, 101, 103, 106, 109	
People vs. Williamson, 13 Ill., 660........	482
People vs. Woodside, 72 Ill., 407 .....499, 500	
Peoria & R. I. R. R. Co. vs. Rice, 75 Ill., 329.	69
Pepper vs Stone, 10 Vt., 427..........346, 347	
Perkins vs. Fairfield, 11 Mass., 227.......	176
Perkins vs. Finnegan, 105 Mass., 501......	345
Perry vs. Carmichael, 95 Ill., 519.......35, 214

XXVIII TABLE OF CASES CITED.

	PAGE.
Peters vs. Pub. Admr., 1 Bradf., 200	12
Peters vs. Spellman, 18 Ill., 370	181, 185
Pfershing vs. Falsh, 87 Ill., 260	209
Phelps vs. Funkhouser, 39 Ill., 401	49, 168
Phelps vs. Phelps, 72 Ill., 545	90, 91
Phelps vs. Reeder, 39 Ill., 172	363
Phillips vs. Davis, 2 Sneed. (Tenn.), 520	257, 287
Phillips vs. State, 5 Ohio, 122	134
Phipps vs Jones, 20 Pa. St., 260	53
Phœnix Ins. Co. vs. Gudery, 20 Ill. Ap., 161	1 2
Piatt vs. People, 29 Ill., 54	5 8
Pickens vs. Clayton, 7 Blackf. (Ind.), 321	345
Pierce vs. Brewster, 32 Ill., 268	447, 449
Pierce vs. Carleton, 12 Ill., 364	314
Pierce vs. McKeehan, 3 Watts & S. (Pa.), 280	364
Piggott's Case, 11 Coke, 27	507
Piggott vs. Ramey, 1 Scam., 145	132, 134, 135
Pike vs. People, 34 Ill. Ap., 112	513
Pile vs. McBratney, 15 Ill., 314	139
Pim vs. Downing, 11 Sergt. & R. (Pa.), 66	257
Pinckard vs Smith, 6 Litt. (Ky.), 331	264
Pinkstaff vs. People, 59 Ill., 148	29, 43
Pinneo vs. Goodspeed, 120 Ill., 524	71
Piper vs. Moulton, 72 Me., 155	190
Platt vs. Robbins, 1 Johnson's Cases, 276	112
Plimptou vs. Richards, 59 Me., 115	50
Porter vs. Tudor. 9 Conn., 411	254
Poston vs. Young, 7 J. J. Marsh. (Ky.), 501	233
Potter vs. Hiscox, 30 Conn, 508	260
Potter vs. Potter, 41 Ill., 80	193
Potts vs Davenport, 79 Ill., 455	71
Potts vs. Smith, 2 Rawle, 361	39
Pratt vs. McJunkin, 4 Rich. (S. C.), 5	290
Pratt vs Trustees, 93 Ill., 475	99
Pratt vs. Wright, 13 Gratt. (Va.), 175	240
Preble vs. Longfellow, 48 Me., 279	288
Prentice vs. Dehon, 10 Allen, 353	101
Prescott vs. Cass, 9 N H., 93	277
Preston vs. Hodgen, 50 Ill., 56	265
Preston vs. Spaulding, 120 Ill., 208, 454, 456,	459
Prevo vs. Walters, 4 Scam., 35	362
Price vs. Crone, 44 Miss., 571	221
Price vs. Evans, 36 Mo., 30	365
Price vs. Johnson, 1 Ohio St., 390	312
Price vs. Mace, 47 Wis, 23	105, 206
Priest vs. Cummings, 16 Wend., 616	558
Priest vs. Watkins, 2 Hill, 225	45
Pritchett vs. People, 1 Gilm., 525	16, 17, 38
Probate Court vs. Strong, 27 Vt., 202, 238,	240
Proctor vs. Wanamaker 1 Barb. Ch., 302	20
Propst vs. Meadows, 13 Ill., 157	4, 104, 107
Pub. Admr , vs. Watts, 1 Paige, 347	11
Pugh vs. Pugh, 9 Ind., 132	363
Pursley vs. Hays, 22 Iowa, 11	512
Putnam vs. Richie, 6 Paige (N. Y.), 390	251
Pusey vs. Clemson, 9 Serg. & R., 208	34
Puzey vs. Senier, 9 Wis., 370	359
Quigley vs. Roberts, 44 Ill., 503	221, 222, 265
Rabb vs. Graham, 43 Md., 9	193
Racouillat vs. Requeena, 36 Cal., 651	287
Rafferty vs. McGowan, 136 Ill., 621	535, 536
Railsback vs. Williamson, 88 Ill., 494, 270,	292
Ralston vs. Wood, 15 Ill., 159	37, 42, 107, 114, 126, 208, 348
Ramsdell vs. Siegerson, 2 Gilm., 78	449
Randolph vs. People, 130 Ill., 533	209
Rankin vs. Barcroft, 114 Ill., 441	369
Rankin vs. Miller, 43 Iowa, 11	311
Rankin vs. Porter, 7 Watts (Pa.), 387	365
Rankin vs. Rankin, 36 Ill., 293	197
Rapalje vs. Norseworthy, 1 Sandf. (N. Y.) Ch., 399	291
Rapp vs. Phœnix Ins. Co., 113 Ill., 390	99
Rappelyea vs. Russell, 1 Dailey, 214	100
Rattoon vs. Overacker, 8 Johns., 126	45, 57

	PAGE.
Rawlings vs. Bailey, 15 Ill., 178	314
Rawlings vs. People, 102 Ill., 475	498, 509, 512
Rawson vs Rawson, 52 Ill., 62	146, 148
Ray vs. Haines, 52 Ill., 485	276
Ray vs. Virgin, 12 Ill., 216	54, 79
Raymond vs. Vaughn, 128 Ill., 356	427
Raymond vs. Wyman, 8 Me., 385	412
Raynor vs. Pearsoll, 3 Johns. Ch., 578	36
Reagan vs. Long, 21 Ind , 264	57
Ream vs. Lynch, 7 Bradwell, 161	348
Rebham vs. Mueller, 114 Ill., 343	20, 186
Rector vs. Reavill, 5 Ill. Ap., 242	93, 94
Rector vs Rector, 3 Gilm., 105	268
Reddick vs. State Bank, 27 Ill., 148	265
Redmond vs. Collins, 4 Deveraux, 430	189
Reed vs. Colby, 89 Ill., 104	276
Reed vs. Emery, 8 Paige Ch., 417	447
Reed vs. Railroad Co., 18 Ill., 403	66
Reed vs. Ryburn, 23 Ark., 47	29
Reed vs. Wilson, 13 Mo., 28	414
Reeves vs. Stipp, 91 Ill., 609	101
Reid vs. Morton, 119 Ill , 118	321, 322
Reitz vs. Cover, 83 Ill., 29	110
Reitz vs. People, 72 Ill., 435	239
Reitzel vs. Miller, 25 Ill., 67	102, 107, 110
Remick vs. Butterfield, 31 N H.(2 Frost),70	358
Remick vs Emig, 42 Ill., 342	85
Renew vs. Butler, 30 Ga., 954	358
Reynolds vs. Lamont, 45 Ind., 308	499
Reynolds, Matter of, 18 N. Y. Sup. Ct., 41	220
Reynolds vs. McCurry, 100 Ill., 356	319
Reynolds vs. People, 55 Ill., 328. 7, 116, 134,	144
Reynolds vs. Walker, 29 Mass. (7 Cushing), 250	256
Reynolds vs. Wilson, 15 Ill., 394	171, 172, 174, 317
Rhett vs. Mastin, 43 Ala., 86	221
Rhoads vs. Rhoads, 43 Ill., 239	163, 164, 184, 221, 222, 223
Rhyne vs. Hoffman, 6 Jones' Eq., 335	511
Ricaud, In re., 13 Legal News, 326	144
Rice vs. Parkman, 16 Mass., 326	309
Rice vs Rice, 108 Ill., 199	355, 369
Ricer vs. Snoddy, 7 Ind., 442	16
Rich vs. People, 66 Ill., 514	493, 499
Richards vs. Dutch, 8 Mass., 506	204
Richards vs. Griggs, 16 Mo., 416	50
Richards vs. Miller, 62 Ill., 417	146
Richards vs. Nightengale, 9 Allen, 149	120
Richardson vs. People, 85 Ill., 495	383, 414
Richardson vs. People, 31 Ill., 170	506, 507
Richardson vs. State, 55 Ind., 381	253
Richardson vs. Spencer, 18 B. Mon. (Ky.), 450	361
Rietz vs. Coyer, 83 Ill., 29	110
Rigg vs. Wilton, 13 Ill., 15	192, 193
Riley vs. Loughrey, 22 Ill., 98	56
Riley vs Morely, 44 Miss., 37	204
Riley vs. Riley, 3 Day, 74	203
Ringhouse vs. Keever, 49 Ill., 470	14, 148
Ringo vs. Binns, 10 Peters, 266	358
Risley vs. Fellows, 5 Gilm., 531	67, 68
Robbins vs. Butler, 24 Ill., 387	358
Robbins vs. Robbins, 2 Ind., 74	221
Roberts vs. Adams, 2 S. C., 337	33
Roberts vs. Roberts, 2 Bulst., 130	199
Robertson vs. Roberson, 1 Root (Conn.), 51	269
Robinson vs. Brewster, 30 N. E. Rep., 683 (Ill.)	188
Robinson vs. Nye, 21 Ill., 592	466
Robnett vs. People, 16 Ill. Ap., 209	513
Rock vs. Haas, 110 Ill., 528	92
Rockwell vs. Young, 60 Md., 563	57
Rodgers' Appeal, 16 Pa. St., 36	257
Rodgers vs. Higgins, 48 Ill., 211	266, 267
Rodgers vs. McLean, 31 Barb. (N. Y.), 304	412
Rodgers vs. People, 34 Ill. Ap., 448	515
Rodrigas vs. East River Savings Inst., 63 N. Y., 469	14

TABLE OF CASES CITED.

		PAGE.
Rodrigas vs. East River Savings Inst., 76 N. Y., 316		16, 46, 51, 75
Roe vs. Taylor, 45 Ill., 485		182, 193
Roland's Heirs vs. Barkley, 1 Brock, 356		261
Roodhouse vs. Roodhouse, 132 Ill., 360		281
Rooseboom vs. Whitaker, 132 Ill., 81		370
Roosevelt vs. Roosevelt, 6 Abb. (N. Y. N. Cas., 447		367
Root, In the Matter of, 5 N. Y. Leg. Obs., 449		11
Rorback vs. Van Blarcom, 20 N. J. Eq., 4 I.		242
Rosenthal vs. Prussing, 108 Ill., 128		18
Rosenthall vs. Magee, 41 Ill, 370		104, 106
Rosenthall vs. Rennick, 44 Ill., 202		105, 170, 171, 276
Ross vs. Cobb, 9 Yerg. (Tenn.), 463		215
Ross vs. Gill, 1 Wash. (Va.), 87		251
Ross vs. People, 34 Ill. Ap., 21		513
Ross vs. Sutton, 1 Bailey Law, 126		75
Roth vs. Jacobs, 21 Ohio, 646		500
Roth vs. Roth, 104 Ill., 35		149
Rountree vs. Talbott, 89 Ill., 246		199
Rowan vs. Kirkpatrick, 14 Ill., 1		36, 39, 48, 52, 61, 62, 63, 101, 256
Rowand vs. Carroll, 81 Ill., 224		160, 165, 174
Rowe vs. Bowen, 28 Ill., 117		529
Rowth vs. Howell, 3 Ves., 565		36
Royers' Appeal, 11 Pa. St., 36		260, 291
Rozier vs. Fagan, 46 Ill., 404		167
Rubottom vs. Morrow's Admr., 24 Ind, 202		48
Rucker vs. Moore, 1 Heisk. (Tenn.), 726		221
Rucker vs. Redmond, 67 Ill., 187		36
Ruffin vs. Farmer, 72 Ill., 6.5		17, 71
Russell vs. Hoar, 3 Met. (Mass.), 187		11
Russell vs. Hubbard, 59 Ill., 335		51, 101, 102, 103, 105, 111
Russell vs. Madden, 95 Ill., 485		149, 150
Ruston vs. Ruston, 2 Dallas, 243		65
Rutherford vs. Morris, 77 Ill., 397. 132, 193, 194		
Rutter vs. Puckhofer, 9 Bosw. (N. Y.), 638		223
Ryan vs. Duncan, 88 Ill., 144		168
Ryan vs. Jones, 15 Ill., 1		202, 275
Sabin vs. Gilman, 1 N. H., 193		252
Sabines vs. Jones, 119 Mass., 167		504
Sackett vs. Mansfield, 26 Ill., 21		446, 447, 449
Sadler vs. Rose, 18 Ark., 600		242
Sale vs. Crutchfield, 8 Bush. (Ky.), 636		503
Saltmarsh vs. Beene, 4 Port. (Ala.), 283		358
Samuel vs. Thomas, 5 Wis., 549		101
Sandford vs. Bliss, 12 Pick., 116		450
Sanford vs. Waggaman, 14 La. Ann., 852		288
Saukey's Appeal, 55 Pa. St., 496		5
Sargeant vs. Courier, 66 Ill., 245		528
Saurez vs. Mayor, 2 Sand. Ch., 173		150
Savage vs. Dickson, 16 Ala., 256		259
Saxton vs. Chamberlain, 6 Pick., 422		127
Say vs. Barnes, 4 Serg. & R. (Pa.), 112		257
Scanlan vs. Cobb, 85 Ill., 296		416
Scharf vs. People, 134 Ill., 240		511
Scheel vs. Eidman, 68 Ill., 193		111, 286
Scheel vs. Eidman, 77 Ill., 301		116, 239, 286
Schneider vs. Manning, 121 Ill., 376		182
Schnell vs. Chicago, 38 Ill., 382		11, 16, 18, 158, 162, 174, 271, 318
Schofield, Estate of, 99 Ill., 513		52, 123, 130
Schwartz vs. Wendell, Walk. Ch. (Mich.), 267		359
Schweizer vs. Tracy, 76 Ill., 345		448
Sconce vs. Whitney, 12 Ill., 150		164
Scott vs. Freeland, 15 Miss. (7 Smeed & M.), 409		272
Scott, In the Matter of, 5 N. Y. Legal Obs., 378		76
Scott vs. Searles, 7 Smedes & M., 498		53
Scott vs. White, 71 Ill., 287		268
Scoville's Estate, In re., 20 Ill. Ap., 426.8		93
Sengo vs. People, 21 Ill. Ap., 283		356
Searle vs. Galbraith, 73 Ill., 269		416
Sebastian vs. Johnson, 72 Ill., 282		49, 168, 174
Seegar vs. State, 6 Harris & Johnson, 162		51
Selb vs. Montague, 102 Ill., 446		319
Selectmen of Boston vs. Boyleston, 2 Mass., 384		205
Seeleye vs. People, 40 Ill. Ap., 449		356
Sellews' Appeal, 10 Am. Law Reg., 708		128
Selz vs. Evans, 6 Ill. Ap., 466		448
Sessions vs. Kell, 30 Miss., 458		216, 230
Sever vs. Russell, 4 Cush., 513		126
Sewell vs. Slingluff, 13 Reporter, 526		196
Shaefer vs. Gates, 2 B. Mon. (Ky.), 453		221
Shanks vs. Seamonds, 24 Iowa, 13		310
Shaw vs. Berry, 35 Me., 279		46
Shaw vs. Burney, 1 Ired. (N. C.) L., 148		414
Shaw vs. Moderwell, 104 Ill., 64		192
Shelburn vs. Robinson, 3 Gilm., 597		135
Sheldon vs. Estate of Rice, 30 Mich., 296. 293, 368		
Sheldon vs. Reihle, 1 Scam., 519		527, 529, 530
Sheldon vs. Wright, 7 Barb., 89		15
Shellabarger vs. Wyman, 15 Mass., 322		57
Shepherd vs. Bank, 87 Ill., 292		103
Shepherd vs. Carriel, 19 Ill., 313		184, 195
Shepherd vs. Rhodes, 60 Ill., 301		17, 101, 109
Shepherd vs. Speer, 29 N. E. Rep., 718 (Ill.)		138
Shepherd vs. Spremont, 111 Ill., 631		165
Sherman vs. Dutch, 16 Ill., 283		50
Sherman vs. Lehman, 137 Ill., 94		202
Sherry vs. Sansbury, 3 Ind., 320		255
Sherwood vs. Wooster, 11 Paige, 441		150
Shevalier vs. Seager, 121 Ill., 254		191
Shewell vs. Keen, 2 Wharton, 322		50
Shibla vs. Ely, 2 Hals. (N. J.) Ch., 181		362
Shields vs. Smith, 8 Bush. (Ky.), 601		38
Shiff vs. Shiff, 20 La. Ann, 269		258
Shockley vs. Fisher, 14 Reporter, 89		445
Shoemate vs. Lockridge, 53 Ill., 504		157, 160, 168
Short vs. Johnson, 25 Ill., 489		51, 126
Shultz's Appeal, 30 Pa. St., 397		286
Shultz vs. Pulver, 3 Paige, 182		48, 60, 72, 150
Shutt vs. Carloss, 1 Ired. (N. C.) Eq., 232		291, 347
Silms vs. Norris, 5 Ala, 42		258
Simmons vs. Adams, 15 Vt., 677		508
Simons vs. People, 18 Ill. Ap., 588		549
Simpson vs. Gonzales, 15 Fla., 9		345
Simpson vs. Simpson, 114 Ill., 603		142
Sims vs. McClure, 8 Rich. (S. C.) Eq., 286		419
Sinclair vs. Jackson, 8 Cowen (N. Y.), 543		317
Sisk vs. Smith, 1 Gilm., 503		148
Skidmore vs. Romaine, 2 Bradf. (N. Y.) 122		419
Skinner vs. Newberry, 51 Ill., 203		148
Slaughter vs. Froman, 5 T. B. Monroe, 19		39, 41, 136, 150
Sloan vs. Graham, 85 Ill., 26		161, 175
Sloo vs. Law, 3 Blatchf., 459		361
Sloo vs. Poole, 15 Ill., 47		61, 101, 103
Smith vs. Bean, 8 N. H., 15		290
Smith vs. Bell, 2 Peters, 74		199
Smith vs. Brittingham, 109 Ill., 540		176
Smith vs. Dennison, 94 Ill., 582		208, 209
Smith vs. Dennison, 101 Ill., 531		430
Smith vs. Dennison, 112 Ill., 367		200
Smith vs. Denny, 34 Mo., 219		291
Smith, Ex p rte, 8 Blackf., 395		501
Smith, Ex parte, 1 Hill (S. C.) Ch., 140		337
Smith vs. Fortescue, Burbee's Eq., 127		53
Smith vs. Frost, 70 N. Y., 63		366
Smith vs. Hileman, 1 Scam., 323		171, 177
Smith vs. Hutchinson, 108 Ill., 662		49, 198
Smith vs. Kramer, 5 Pa Law. J. Rep., 226		410
Smith vs. Lawrence, 11 Paige, 206		136
Smith vs. McConnell, 17 Ill., 135		49, 50, 146, 168
Smith vs. McLaughlin, 77 Ill., 596		108
Smith vs. People, 44 Ill., 16		252, 540
Smith vs. People, ex. rel., 66 Ill., 375		413
Smith vs. Race, 27 Ill., 387		222, 339
Smith vs. Sackett, 5 Gilm, 534		320
Smith vs. Smith, 55 Ill., 204		72

XXX   TABLE OF CASES CITED.

	PAGE.
Smith vs. Smith, 69 Ill., 308	224
Smith vs. Smith, 13 Grant Ch., 81	82
Smith vs. Smith, 4 Johns Cb.(N.Y., 281.	255
Smith vs. Warden, 7 Pa. St., 424	318
Smith vs. Whitaker, 11 Ill., 417	42
Smith vs. Wilmington Coal Co., 83 Ill., 498 ... 53,	99
Smyley vs. Reese, 53 Ala., 89 ... 125,	131
Smythe vs. Taylor, 21 Ill. 296	200
Sneed vs. Hiely, 29 Ga., 587	287
Snook vs. Sutton, 5 Halst., 133	251
Snow vs. Benton, 28 Ill., 3 6 ... 410,	411
Snydam vs. Broadnax, 14 Peters, 75	477
Somerset vs. Dighton, 12 Mass., 38	214
Southhall vs. Clark, 3 Stew. & P. (Ala.), 388.	292
Speers vs. Sewell, 4 Bush. (Ky.), 239	417
Speight vs. Knight, 11 Ala., 461 ... 242,	345
Spellman vs. Dowse, 79 Ill., 66 ... 310, 312,	315
Spellman vs. Mathewson, 65 Ill.; 3:6	314
Spencer vs. Boardman, 118 Ill., 553	94
Spencer vs. Langdon, 21 Ill., 192	207
Sperry vs. Fanning, 80 Ill., 371 ... 258,	259
Spivey vs. State, 8 Ind, 405	502
Spratt vs. Spratt, 4 Peters, 406	560
Spring vs. Kane, 86 Ill., 580..312, 313, 315,	316
Staats vs. Bergen, 7 N.J. Eq, 554	359
Stacey vs. Thrasher, 6 Howard, 44 ... 105,	171
Stafford, Matter of, 11 Barb. (N.Y.), 353..	256
Stamper vs. Hooks, 22 Ga., 603	197
Stanley's Appeal, 8 Pa. St., 431	258
Stanley vs. People, 84 Ill., 212	509
Stark vs. Brown, 101 Ill., 395..49, 164, 168,	218
Stark vs. Gamble, 43 N.H., 465	256
State vs. Baker, 8 Md., 44	291
State vs. Brandon, 8 Jones (N.C.) Law, 463.	421
State vs. Brinyea, 5 Ala., 241	419
State vs. Broadwell, 69 N.C., 411	503
State vs. Christmas, 6 Jones (N.C.) L., 471.	421
State vs Church, 5 Oregon, 375	544
State vs. Clark, 16 Ind, 97	288
State vs. Collier, 72 Mo., 13	544
State vs. Crawford, 11 Kansas, 32	420
State vs. Hall, 53 Miss., 626	348
State vs. Herman, 13 Ired, 502	511
State vs. Humphreys, 7 Ohio. 223	238
State vs. Hyde, 29 Conn., 564	412
State vs. Ingram, 4 Hayw. (Tenn.), 221	501
State vs. Klinger, 43 Mo., 127	420
State vs. Lawrence, 57 Me., 574	419
State vs. Lean, 9 Wis., 279	541
State vs. Marler, 2 Ala., 43	419
State vs. Martin, 69 N.C, 175	240
State vs. Mason, 2 Nott & M. (1 S.C.), 425.	5 7
State vs. McCoy, 34 Miss., 13	418
State vs. Newell, 36 Wis., 213	544
State vs. Palin, 63 N.C., 471	490
State vs. Penney, 10 Ark., 621	559
State vs. Perkins, 1 Jones (N.C.), 325	240
State vs. Pratt, 40 Iowa, 631	505
State vs. Reddick, 7 Kansas, 143	411
State vs. Romaine, 58 Iowa, 48	511
State vs. Sewell, 3 Jones (N.C) L., 245	421
State vs. Shoemaker, 62 Iowa, 353	511
State vs. Smith, 54 Iowa, 104	511
State vs. Smith, 55 Ind., 3 5	501
State vs. Strange, 1 Ind., 538 ... 291,	349
State vs. Thorn, 28 Ind., 3 6	3 0
State vs. Ueland, 30 Minn., 277 ... 7,	141
State vs. Wilson, 21 Ind., 273	499
State vs. Wilson, 10 Ired., 131	511
State vs. Whittemore, 50 N.H, 245	561
Stebbins vs. Palmer, 1 Pick., 71	13
Steele, In re., 65 Ill., 322 ... 100, 272, 284, 286,	315
Steele vs. Steele, 89 Ill., 51 ... 174.	208
Steinman vs. Steinman, 105 Ill., 348	69
Stephens vs. People, 89 Ill., 338 ... 535,	5 6
Stephenson's Appeal, 22 Pa. St., 318	292
Stevens vs. Gage, 55 N.H., 175	36

	PAGE.
Stevens vs. Gaylord, 11 Mass., 256..34,203,	204
Stewart vs. Crabbin. 6 Mumf. (Va.), 280	218
Stewart vs. Howe, 17 Ill., 71	268
Stewart vs. Kearney, 6 Watts, 453	65
Stewart vs. Morrison, 38 Miss., 417	233
Steyer vs. Morris, 39 Ill. Ap., 382	282
Stiger vs. Bent, 111 Ill., 336 ... 50,	37
Stigers vs. Brent, 50 Md., 214	413
Stiles vs. Burch, 5 Paige, 132	127
Stillman vs. Young, 16 Ill.,318.51, 101, 113,	131
Stillwell vs. Melrose, 15 Hun., 378, 381	49
Stillwell vs. Mills, 19 Johns (N.Y.), 304	349
Stires vs. Stires, 1 Halstead's Ch, 224	65
Stockdale vs. Conway, 14 Md., 99	11
Stokes vs. Goodykoontz, 26 N.E. Rep., 391 (Ill.)	121
Stolz vs. Doering, 112 Ill., 234 ... 145,	146
Story, In re., 120 Ill., 244 ... 189,	190
Stone vs. Clark, 40 Ill.. 411 ... 103,	110
Stone vs. Damon, 12 Mass, 488	411
Stone vs. Scripture, 4 Laus. (N.Y.), 186	204
Stone vs. Wood, 16 Ill, 177 ... 49, 113, 114, 170, 171,	448
Stose vs. People, 25 Ill., 600	39
Stowe vs. Kimball, 28 Ill., 94 ... 156, 157, 16, 166, 173, 175,	177
Strawn vs. Strawn, 53 Ill., 263 ... 90, 92,	93
Strode vs. Broadwell, 36 Ill., 409	481
Stroug vs. Lord, 107 Ill., 25	87
Strong vs. Lord, 107 Ill, 26	99
Strong vs. Strong, 131 Ill., 210	94
Stubblefield vs. McRaven, 5 Smedes & M., 130	39
Strubher vs. Belsey, 79 Ill., 307	200
Stumph vs. Pfeiffer, 58 Ind., 472 ... 409,	412
Sturgis vs. Crowningshield, 4 Wheat, 125..	428
Sturges vs. Ewing, 18 Ill., 176	148
Sullivan vs. Blackwell, 28 Miss., 737	270
Sullivan vs. Sullivan, 42 Il., 315	221
Sumner vs. Williams, 8 Mass., 165	176
Sunday vs. Gordon, Blatchf. & H, 569	414
Sunderland's Estate, 60 Iowa, 732	147
Suppiger vs. Seybt, 23 Ill. Ap., 468	453
Sutherland vs Harrison, 86 Ill., 363 ... 60, 75, 103, 129,	148
Swayzee vs. Miller, 17 B. Mon (Ky.), 564..	337
Swearingen vs. Gulick, 67 Ill., 208	156
Sweet vs. Jacobs, 6 Paige (N.Y., 355	364
Sweet vs. Sherman, 20 Vt., 23	5
Sweet vs. Sweet, Spear's (S C) Ch., 309..	316
Sweezey vs. Willis, 1 Bradf., 495	11
Swifts, In the Matter of, 47 Cal., 629	346
Swinton vs. Bailey, 33 L.T. Rep. (English), 564 ... 184,	195
Switzer vs. Skiles, 3 Gilm, 529 ... 358, 361,	366
Tabb vs. Boyd, 4 Call (Va.), 451	291
Tilkington vs. Turner, 71 Ill., 234 ... 533, 535, 536,	544
Tauner vs. Skinner, 11 Bush. Ky.), 120	292
Tate vs. Tate, 89 Ill., 42	192
Tatum vs. McLillan, 50 Miss., 1	358
Taubenham vs. Dunz, 125 Ill., 524	199
Taylor vs. Delancy, 2 Cai C., 143	11
Taylor vs. Dudley, 5 Dana (Ky.), 308	418
Taylor vs. Fickas, 64 Ind., 167	66
Taylor vs. Hite, 16 Mo., 142	260
Taylor vs. Hopkins, 40 Ill., 442	174
Taylor vs. Kilgore, 33 Ala., 214	290
Taylor's Will, In re, 55 Ill., 252 ... 147,	148
Teague vs. Dendy, 2 McCord Ch., 207	126
Telford vs. Boggs, 63 Ill., 498	94
Tenny vs. Evans, 14 N.H., 343	258
Terwilliger vs. Brown, 5 Hand (N.Y.), 237.	175
Teyn, Matter of, 2 Redf. (N.Y.), 306	257
Thomas vs. Adams, 59 Ill., 223	265
Thomas vs. Burrus, 23 Miss., 550 ... 22,	238
Thomas vs. Minot, 10 Gray, 263	100
Thomas vs. People, 107 Ill., 515	14

TABLE OF CASES CITED. XXXI

	PAGE.
Thompson vs. Brown,	
4 Johns. Ch., 619 ....36, 48, 51	
Thompson vs. Reed, 48 Ill., 118............	109
Thompson vs. Thompson, 1 Bradf., 24...	6
Thompson vs. Wilhite, 81 Ill , 356... .527,	528
Thorn vs. Watson, 5 Gilm., 26........101,	103
Thornley vs. Moore, 106 Ill., 496..........	68
Thornton vs. Bradshaw, Breese, 13	50
Thornton vs Heirs of Henry, 2 Scam , 218.	2 7
Thornton vs Mehring, 117 Ill , 55	57
Thorp vs. Goewey, 85 Ill , 612	73
Thorp vs. McCullum,	113
1 Gilm., 614 ....174, 358, 360, 361,	366
Thorpe vs. Starr, 17 Ill., 199..............	67
Tibbs vs. Allen, 27 Ill., 119................	223
Tilley vs. Bridges, 105 Ill., 336............	176
Tioga Co. vs. South Creek Tp.,	
75 Pa St., 433......................	511
Titcomb vs. Vantyle, 84 Ill., 371....410, 417,	418
Tobey vs. Miller, 54 Me., 480	57
Tobin vs. Addison, 2 Strobh. (S. C.), 3....	258
Toug vs. Marvin, 26 Mich., 35............	243
Torrey vs. Black, 65 Barb. (N. Y.), 417....	249
Townsend vs. Kendall, 4 Minn., 413...216,	252
Townsend vs. Ratcliff, 44 Ill., 446.	5
Townsend vs. State, 13 Ind., 357..........	504
Tracey vs. Hadden, 78 Ill., 30.............	110
Tracey vs. Howe, 119 Mass., 228	506
Trammell vs. Trammell, 20 Texas, 406....	252
Traver vs. Rogers, 16 Ill. Ap., 372........	461
Treadwell vs. McKeon,	
7 Baxter (Tenn.), 201...............362,	363
Treat vs. Fortune, 2 Bradf., 116	114
Trenton Banking Co. vs. Woodruff,	
1 Gr, Ch., 117........................	361
Trimble vs. Dodd, 2 Tenn. Ch., 500.......	346
Trish vs. Newell, 62 Ill., 196........182,	192
Trogdon vs. Murphey, 85 Ill., 119.........	185
Troupe vs. Rice, 55 Miss., 278............	52
Trueman vs. Hurd, 17 Rep., 40..........	277
Tucker vs. Clisby, 12 Pick., 22	450
Tucker vs. People, 87 Ill., 76...........	33
Tulter, In re., 79 Ill., 99...............182,	196
Tunison vs. Chamblin, 88 Ill., 378........	266
Turley vs. Logan Co , 17 Ill., 151..........	535
Turner vs. Egerton, 1 Gill & Johnson, 430.	129
Turner vs. Jenkins, 79 Ill., 229...........	223
Turner vs. Mason. 14 M. & W., 111.......	216
Turney vs. Gates, 12 Ill., 141 106,	119
Turney vs. Turney, 24 Ill., 625........112,	157
Turney vs. Young, 22 Ill., 253	112
Tuttle vs. Garrett, 16 Ill , 354...	265
Tuttle vs. Garrett, 74 Ill , 444............	223
Tuttle vs. Wilson, 24 Ill., 553.............	481
Tutorship of Hughes, 13 La. Ann., 380....	242
Tyler vs. Daniel, 65 Ill., 316	92
Tyler vs. Tyler, 19 Ill., 151..............	196
Tyson vs. Postlewait, 13 Ill., 727	148
Underwood vs. Brockman, 4 Dana (Ky.), 309.	259
United States vs. Brown, Gilpin's Rep., 178.	508
United States vs. Collins,	
1 Cranch. (Ct.), 592	503
United States vs. Nichols,	
4 Cranch. (Ct.), 290....................	346
United States Mortgage Co. vs. Sperry,	
138 U. S., 313	330
Union National Bank vs. Bank of Com.,	
94 Ill., 271	446
Union R. R. Co. vs. Shacklet, 119 Ill., 332.	73
Unknown Heirs of Langworthy vs. Baker,	
23 Ill., 484........12, 18, 34, 107, 110, 172,	210
Upstone vs. People, 109 Ill., 169.....423, 424,	425
Van Alstine vs. Lemons, 19 Ill., 394......	109
Van Auken, Ex parte,	
10 N. J. Eq. (2 Stock.), 186	407
Van Dusen vs. Sweet, 51 N. Y., 378........	417
Van Epps vs. Douser, 4 Paige, 71.........	283

	PAGE.
Van Horn vs. Fonda,	
5 Johns. Ch., 388..................52,	364
Van Meter vs. Love, 33 Ill., 260 275,	276
Van Patton vs. Beals, 46 Iowa, 62........	418
Van Steinwyck vs. Washburn, 59 Wis., 483.	141
Vansyckle vs. Richardson, 13 Ill., 171....6,	154
Van Uxen vs. Hazelhurst,	
1 Southard (N. J), 192	429
Van Wickle vs. Calvin, 23 La. Ann., 205...	168
Vaughn vs. Barrett. 5 Vt., 333............	203
Veasey vs. Graham, 17 Ga., 99.	358
Veile vs Koch, 27 Ill., 129 90,	92
Vetten vs. Wallace, 39 Ill. Ap., 390........	511
Vick vs. Vicksburg, 1 Howard, 379........	5
Villard vs. Chovin, 2 Strobh. (S C., Eq , 40.	287
Vincent vs. Morrison, Breese 175	176
Von Kettler vs. Johnson, 57 Ill., 109 4,	132
Voris vs. Sloan, 68 Ill., 588...............	14
Voris vs. Steele, 47 Ind., 345..............	318
Vroom vs. Ex'r of Smith,	
2 Green (N. J.), 480	508
Vroom vs. Van Horne, 2 Paige, 549....45,	150
Wade vs. Carpenter, 4 Iowa, 361	317
Wade vs. Pritchard, 69 Ill., 280..........	69
Wadhams vs. Gay, 73 Ill., 415 266,	267
Wadsworth vs. Connell,	
104 Ill., 369..5, 50, 51, 100, 126, 138, 165, 225,	226
Wadsworth vs. Sherman,	
14 Barb. (N. Y.), 169...................	416
Waite vs. Maxwell, 5 Pick. (Mass.), 217....	417
Walbridge vs. Day, 31 Ill., 379..........	49
Walden vs. Gridley, 36 Ill., 523..........	176
Waldo vs. Cummings, 45 Ill., 423.....184,	185
Walker vs. Alexander, 24 N. E. Rep., 557..	98
Walker vs. Craig, 18 Ill., 115..........53,	79
Walker vs. Crowder,	
2 Ired. (N. C.) Eq., 478................	287
Walker vs. Diehl, 79 Ill., 473.49, 101, 120, 156,	170
Walker vs. Doane, 108 Ill., 336..........	164
Walker vs. Douglas, 70 Ill., 445	276
Walker vs. Ellis, 12 Ill., 470..............	265
Walker vs. Hallett, 1 Ala., 379. 220,	224
Walker vs. McKay, 2 Met. (Ky.), 294.....	112
Walker vs. Ray, 111 Ill., 315............	279
Walker vs. State, 6 Blackf. (Ind.), 1...503,	504
Walker vs. Walker, 2 Scam., 291..........	188
Walker vs. Walker, 101 Mass., 169........	318
Wall vs. Wall, 123 Pa. St., 545..........5,	188
Wallace vs. Gatchel, 106 Ill., 315........4,	104
Wallace vs. Gatchel, 106 Ill., 316........	102
Wallace vs. Marss, 5 Hill (N. Y.), 391....	277
Wallace vs. Rappelye, 103 Ill., 229.145, 379,	514
Wallace vs. Reddick, 119 Ill., 151........	143
Walter vs. Kirk, 14 Ill., 55...............	53
Walters vs. People, 32 N. Y., 147........	419
Walters vs. People, Ex. rel Bradley,	
21 Ill., 178	270
Walton vs. Develing, 61 Ill., 201..........	535
Wann vs. People, 57 Ill., 2 2 ....2 8, 269,	349
Ward vs. Armstrong, 84 Ill., 151..........	359
Ward vs. Bevill, 10 Ala., 197..............	57
Ward vs. Brewer, 19 Ill., 291..............	158
Ward vs. Durham,	
134 Ill., 195....98, 102, 107, 112, 114, 170,	171
Ward vs. Roper, 7 Humph. (Tenn.), 111....	220
Ward vs. Ward, 134 Ill., 417.........141,	196
Wardwell vs McDowell, 31 Ill., 364..16, 47,	179
Ware vs. Coleman, 6 J. J. Marsh. (Ky.), 198	230
Ware vs. Murph, Rice's Law Rep.(S. C.), 54.	179
Warnecke vs. Lembca, 71 Ill., 91......50,	71
Warner vs. Thornton, 98 Ill., 156..... 48,	179
Warner vs. Wilson, 4 Cal., 310...........	409
Warren vs. Ball, 40 Ill., 117.............	67
Warren vs. Hofer, 13 Ind., 167..........	337
Washington vs. L. & N. Ry. Co.,	
136 Ill., 49 52,	76
Waterman vs. Alden, 115 Ill., 83..........	151
Watson vs. Sherman, 84 Ill., 263........ ..	367

XXXII   TABLE OF CASES CITED.

	PAGE
Weaver vs. Weaver, 109 Ill., 225	91
Webber vs. Brown, 38 Ill., 87	527
Weber vs. Mick, 131 Ill., 520	452
Webster vs. Byrnes, 34 Cal., 274	543
Webster vs. Conley, 46 Ill., 13....199, 251,	329
Webster vs. Gilmore, 91 Ill., 324..539, 543,	545
Webster vs. Judah, 27 Ill. Ap., 294....458,	461
Weeks vs. Gibbs, 9 Mass., 74	57
Weer vs. Gand, 88 Ill., 490...........119,	209
Weir vs. People, 78 Ill., 192............42,	134
Welch vs. Hoyt, 24 Ill., 117............54,	79
Weld vs. Sweeney, 85 Ill., 50..........189,	190
Wellman vs. Lawrence, 15 Mass., 326	317
Wells vs. Cowherd, 2 Metc. (Ky.), 514	310
Wells vs. Cowles, 4 Conn., 182	71
Wells vs. Miller, 45 Ill., 382........61, 102,	106
Wells vs. Smith, 44 Miss., 296	281
Wenn r vs. Thornton, 98 Ill., 156.....48,	179
Wernse vs. Hall, 101 Ill., 423..........20,	171
West vs. Krebaum, 88 Ill., 263	111
West vs. West, 8 Paige, 433	561
Westbrook vs. Comstock, Walk. Ch. (Mich), 314	272
Wever vs. Marvin, 14 Barb., 376	57
Whedbe vs. Whedbe, 5 Jones (N. C.) Eq., 392	292
Wheeler vs. Dawson, 63 Ill., 54.............112, 113, 125, 126,	162
Wheeler vs. Wheeler, 9 Cowan, 34	47
Whipple vs. Pope, 33 Ill., 334........446,	447
White vs. Bailey, 10 Mich., 155	411
White vs. Dance, 53 Ill., 414	148
White vs. Glover, 59 Ill., 459	216
White vs. Murtland, 71 Ill., 250.....250,	269
White vs. Parker, 8 Barb. (N. Y.), 48..249,	290
White vs. Russell, 79 Ill., 155	169
Whitenack, Matter of, 3 N. J. Eq. (2 Green), 252	407
Whiteside vs. Jennings, 19 Ala., 784	49
Whitford vs. Daggett, 84 Ill., 144	108
Whiting vs. Dewey, 15 Pick. (Mass.), 428	315
Whiting vs. Nichol, 46 Ill., 230	14
Whitledge vs. Callis, 2 J. J. Marsh. (Ky.), 403	287
Whitlock vs. McClusky, 91 Ill., 582	177
Whitlock's Case, 32 Barb. (N Y.), 48	309
Whitman vs. Fisher, 74 Ill., 147......169,	200
Whitman vs. State, 34 Ind., 360	505
Whitney vs. Peddecord, 63 Ill., 249....36,	51
Whitney vs. Porter, 23 Ill., 445	158
Whitney vs. Whitney, 15 Miss., 740	345
Wilbur vs. Wilbur, 129 Ill., 392	192
Wilburn vs. Shell, 59 Miss., 205	198
Wickiser vs. Cook, 85 Ill., 68..267, 270, 272,	368
Wickliff vs. Robinson, 18 Ill., 145....358,	360
Wiggle vs. Owen, 45 Miss., 691	257
Wight vs. Walbaum, 39 Ill., 554......17,	18
Wilcox vs. Smith, 26 Barb., 316	51
Wilcox vs. Wilcox, 14 N. Y., 575	218
Wild vs. Sweeney, 84 Ill., 213	5
Wile vs. Wright, 32 Iowa, 451	103
Wilhite vs. Pearce, 47 Ill., 413	265
Wilkins vs. Elliott, 9 Wal., 740	150
Wilkinson vs. Demming, 80 Ill., 342	220
Willard vs. Bassett, 27 Ill., 37.........125,	137
Willenborg vs. Murphy, 36 Ill., 344	61
Williams vs. Conley, 20 Ill., 643	70
Williams vs. Johnson, 112 Ill., 61	185
Williams vs. Morton, 38 Me., 47	312
Williams vs. Powell, 1 Ired.(N. C.) Eq., 460	270
Williams vs. Rhodes, 81 Ill., 572...........79, 132, 170,	174
Williams vs. Stein, 38 Ind., 89	541
Williams vs. Stratton, 10 Sm. & M. (Miss.), 418	223
Williams vs. Walker, 62 Ill., 517......79,	174
Williams vs. Wiggand, 53 Ill., 233	51
Williamson vs. Gordon, 1 Bush. (N. C.) Eq., 46	220

	PAGE
Williams vs. Williams, 55 Wis., 300	36
Willis vs. Fox, 25 Wis., 646	292
Willis vs. Watson, 4 Scam., 64......185,	199
Wilson's Estate, 2 Pa. St., 325	412
Wilson vs. Aaron, 132 Ill., 238	458
Wilson vs. Gerard, 59 Ill., 151	277
Wilson vs. Kirby, 88 Ill., 566	119
Wilson vs. Oldham, 12 B. Mon, 55	418
Wilson vs. Pearson, 20 Ill., 81........445,	448
Wilson vs. Robertson, 21 N. Y., 587	448
Winch vs. Tobin, 107 Ill., 212	31
Wing vs. Dodge, 80 Ill., 564.........409,	415
Wingate vs. Pool, 25 Ill, 118........52, 101,	103
Winship vs. Bass, 12 Mass., 198	34
Winslow vs. Leland, 128 Ill., 304...........6, 7, 85, 138, 142,	165
Winslow vs. People, 17 Ill. Ap, 222	355
Winslow vs. People, 117 Ill., 152	355
Winslow vs. People, 117 Ill., 649..280, 295,	355
Winter vs. Thistlewood, 101 Ill., 450	533
Wisdom vs. Becker, 52 Ill., 342..47, 51, 75,	150
Wiser vs. Blachly, 1 Johns. Ch. (N. Y.), 607	238
Wiswall vs. Stewart, 32 Ala., 433	363
Withers vs. Hickman, 6 B. Mon., 292	257
Woelper's Appeal, 2 Pa. St., 71	358
Wolf vs. Beard, 123 Ill., 585..100, 134, 120,	126
Wolf vs. Bollinger. 62 Ill., 368........184,	192
Wolf vs. Griffin, 13 Ill. Ap., 559	135
Wolf vs. Ogden, 66 Ill., 224.........168,	172
Wood vs. Byington, 2 Barb. Ch, 387	170
Wood vs. Gale, 10 N. H., 247	250
Wood vs. Stafford, 5 Miss., 370	362
Wood vs. Vanderburg, 6 Paige, 277	101
Wood vs. Washburne, 2 Pick., 24	32
Woodberry vs. Hammond, 54 Me., 332	285
Woodruff vs. Young, 43 Mich., 548	6
Woodside vs. Woodside, 21 Ill., 207	194
Woodward vs. Brooks, 128 Ill., 222	461
Woodward vs. Donally, 27 Ala., 198	254
Woodworth vs. Payne. Breese, 294	117
Work vs. Cowhick, 81 Ill., 317	177
Wormley vs. Wormley, 98 Ill., 544	143
Worth vs. Curtiss, 15 Me., 228	310
Worthy vs. Johnson, 8 Ga., 256	358
Wrm vs. Kirton, 11 Vesey, 577	252
Wright's Appeal, 8 Pa. St., 57	413
Wright vs. Arnold, 14 B. Mon. (Ky.), 638	270
Wright vs. Campbell, 27 Ark., 637	364
Wright vs. Conley, 14 Ill. Ap., 551	261
Wright vs. Gay, 101 Ill., 233	319
Wright vs. Minshall, 72 Ill., 584	201
Wright vs. Smith, 123 N. J. Eq., 106	365
Wright vs. Williams, 5 Cowen, 501	71
Wright vs Wright, 2 Mass., 109	214
Wyatt vs. Mansfield, 18 B. Mon. (Ky.), 779	221
Wyman vs. Campbell, 6 Porter (Ala.), 219............26, 28,	175
Wyman vs. Hooper, 2 Gray (Mass.), 141	317
Wynne vs. Always, 1 Murph. (N. C.), 38	242
Wyse vs. Dandridge, 35 Miss., 672	362
Yates vs Dodge, 123 Ill., 50	454
Yoe vs. McCord, 74 Ill., 33...........182,	184
York vs. York, 38 Ill., 522..............91,	92
Young vs. Adam, 74 Ill., 480	533
Young vs. Dowling, 15 Ill., 481....158, 314,	316
Young vs. Keogh, 11 Ill., 642	314
Young vs. Lorain, 11 Ill., 624....230, 310, 311, 315, 316, 341,	345
Young vs. Makepeace, 103 Mass., 50	503
Young vs. Wittenmyre, 123 Ill., 303............118, 156, 157, 170,	204
Young vs. Young, 5 Ind., 513	346
Zeigler vs. McCormick, (Sup. Ct. Neb.) 14 Legal News, 375	528
Zimmerman vs. Cowan, 107 Ill., 631	547

TABLE OF STATUTES CITED.

HURD'S REVISED STATUTES.

Chapter.	Section.	Page.	Chapter.	Section.	Page.	Chapter.	Section.	Page.	Chapter.	Section.	Page.
1	10	67	3	65	105	3	117	135	22	6	220
2	1	43	3	66	105	3	118	58	22	12	520
3	1	191	3	67	106	3	118	136	22	13	520
3	2	46	3	68	208	3	118	150	24	34	533
3	3	191	3	69	113	3	119	198	24	57	533
3	4	46	3	69	114	3	119	329	33	1	40
3	5	46	3	70	103	3	120	199	33	2	41
3	9	179	3	70	116	3	121	199	33	3	41
3	11	19	3	70	117	3	122	66	38	237	27
3	15	55	3	71	117	3	124	208	38	283	278
3	16	55	3	72	114	3	125	209	39	1	141
3	17	55	3	73	120	3	126	53	39	2	145
3	18	10	3	74	89	3	127	70	39	3	145
3	18	12	3	75	90	3	128	115	39	6	144
3	19	13	3	75	93	3	129	155	39	7	144
3	20	14	3	76	90	3	130	7	39	8	144
3	22	15	3	77	90	3	131	7	39	9	146
3	23	27	3	78	149	3	132	137	39	10	196
3	23	37	3	79	74	3	134	137	39	12	141
3	24	31	3	80	69	3	135	137	41	1	147
3	25	32	8	82	76	3	136	202	41	12	141
3	25	38	8	83	77	3	137	49	41	36	16
3	26	20	3	84	77	4	1	147	41	37	165
3	27	20	3	85	33	4	1	371	41	39	165
3	28	20	3	85	78	4	2	372	46	60	542
3	29	20	3	86	83	4	3	373	46	65	541
3	30	21	3	87	84	4	4	375	46	66	539
3	31	21	3	88	84	4	5	376	46	97	533
3	32	28	3	89	84	4	7	377	46	98	533
3	33	29	3	89	86	4	8	377	46	112	535
3	34	29	3	90	78	10a	1	430	46	113	536
3	35	28	3	91	151	10a	2	431	46	114	536
3	36	30	3	92	151	10a	3	431	46	115	536
3	37	30	3	93	79	10a	4	431	46	116	537
3	38	31	3	94	80	10a	5	431	46	119	543
3	39	39	3	95	80	10a	6	432	46	120	544
3	40	22	3	96	179	10a	7	432	46	121	545
3	41	22	3	97	155	10a	8	433	46	122	544
3	42	205	3	98	155	10a	9	432	46	123	545
3	43	206	3	98	156	10a	11	434	49	1	151
3	44	18	3	98	157	10a	12	434	49	2	151
3	45	18	3	99	156	10a	13	435	52	8	166
3	46	18	3	100	162	10a	13	449	52	9	166
3	47	18	3	100	168	10a	14	435	54	66	115
3	49	337	3	101	158	10a	15	437	59	10	201
3	50	19	3	102	158	17	1	486	59	12	274
3	51	34	3	103	159	17	2	486	59	13	274
3	51	59	3	104	159	17	4	489	59	14	275
3	52	60	3	105	163	17	5	490	59	15	106
3	53	61	3	106	164	17	6	491	59	15	275
3	54	62	3	107	177	17	7	491	59	16	275
3	55	62	3	108	173	17	8	491	59	17	275
3	56	61	3	108	174	17	9	510	64	2	228
3	56	62	3	109	178	17	10	494	64	3	230
3	57	48	3	110	178	17	11	494	64	4	230
3	57	63	3	111	123	17	12	498	64	4	256
3	58	63	3	111	150	17	13	498	64	5	219
3	59	62	3	112	123	17	14	498	64	6	234
3	59	63	3	112	150	17	15	498	64	7	236
3	60	98	3	113	130	17	16	498	64	8	219
3	61	104	3	114	37	17	17	511	64	9	219
3	62	104	3	114	132	17	17	514	64	10	227
3	63	104	3	115	133	22	5	218	64	10	236
3	64	105	3	116	134	22	6	522	64	11	239

HURD'S REVISED STATUTES.

Chapter.	Section.	Page.	Chapter.	Section.	Page.	Chapter.	Section.	Page.	Chapter.	Section.	Page.
64	12	245	72	6	467	85	18	402	86	39	390
64	13	245	72	7	467	85	19	402	86	40	391
64	14	283	72	8	468	85	20	403	86	41	392
64	15	283	72	9	469	85	21	403	86	42	392
64	16	284	72	10	470	85	22	403	86	43	392
64	17	253	72	11	471	85	23	403	86	44	393
64	18	250	72	12	471	85	24	404	86	45	393
64	19	253	72	13	471	85	30	405	89	3	273
64	20	256	72	14	472	85	31	406	89	8	273
64	21	256	72	15	473	85	32	406	89	14	273
64	22	254	72	16	474	86	1	382	103	5	31
64	23	251	72	17	474	86	2	382	103	7	31
64	24	323	72	18	474	86	3	383	103	8	31
64	25	323	72	19	475	86	4	383	103	9	31
64	26	325	72	20	476	86	5	383	103	13	33
64	27	325	72	21	476	86	6	383	110	21	37
64	28	299	72	22	476	86	7	384	140a	1	517
64	29	299	72	26	478	86	8	384	140a	2	517
64	30	301	72	27	479	86	9	384	140a	3	518
64	31	302	72	28	479	86	10	384	140a	4	519
64	32	304	72	29	479	86	11	384	140a	5	519
64	33	305	72	30	480	86	12	384	140a	7	522
64	34	308	72	31	480	86	13	385	140a	8	521
64	35	284	72	32	480	86	14	385	140a	9	523
64	36	350	72	33	480	86	15	385	140a	10	523
64	37	342	72	34	480	86	16	385	140a	11	524
64	38	342	72	34	484	86	17	385	140a	12	525
64	39	339	77	18	37	86	18	386	140a	13	525
64	40	345	77	18	50	86	19	386	148	1	182
64	44	332	77	37	68	86	20	386	148	2	183
64	45	332	77	38	53	86	21	386	148	3	186
64	46	333	77	39	68	86	22	386	148	4	187
64	47	309	85	1	394	86	23	386	148	5	187
64	48	309	85	2	395	86	24	387	148	6	188
64	49	309	85	3	396	86	25	387	148	7	192
64	50	309	85	4	397	85	26	387	148	8	199
64	53	226	85	5	397	86	27	387	148	9	194
64	53	226	85	6	398	86	28	387	148	10	195
64	54	226	85	7	399	86	29	388	148	11	186
64	55	227	85	8	399	86	30	388	148	12	185
64	56	227	85	9	399	86	31	388	148	13	190
64	57	227	85	10	399	86	32	388	148	14	190
70	1	35	85	11	400	86	33	388	148	15	197
72	1	463	85	12	400	86	34	388	148	16	197
72	2	463	85	13	400	86	35	389	148	17	195
72	3	463	85	14	400	86	36	389	148	18	190
72	4	465	85	16	401	86	37	389	148	19	191
72	5	465	85	17	402	86	38	390	148	20	190

PART I.

SETTLEMENT OF ESTATES,

Testate and Intestate.

SETTLEMENT OF ESTATES,

TESTATE AND INTESTATE.

CHAPTER I.

COUNTY COURTS OF ILLINOIS AND THEIR JURISDICTION IN PROBATE.

1. Constitutional provisions.
2. Jurisdiction general.
3. Force of their decrees.
4. Not to be questioned collaterally.
5. Statutory powers.
6. Jurisdiction shared by chancery courts.
7. Jurisdiction continues.
8. May adjudicate upon equitable claims.
9. May enforce their orders.
10. Power to construe will.
11. Probate courts.
12. Sheriff shall attend sessions.

1. The constitution of 1848 established county courts,[1] and provided that their jurisdiction should extend to all probate and such other jurisdiction as the general assembly may confer in civil cases, and such criminal cases as may be prescribed by law, where the punishment is by fine only, not exceeding $100.[2] Their existence was perpetuated by the constitution of 1870,[3] and their office somewhat more specifically declared to be courts of record, which shall have original jurisdiction in all matters of probate, settlement of estates of deceased persons, appointment of guardians and conservators, and settlements of their accounts, etc.[4]

[1] Art. 5, § 1.
[2] Art. 5, § 18.
[3] Art. 6, § 1.
[4] Art. 6, § 18.
But this jurisdiction is not exclusive: Shaw vs. Moderwell, 104 Ill., 64.

The statute more particularly prescribes their powers:

PROBATE JURISDICTION.—County courts shall have jurisdiction in all matters of probate, settlements of estates of deceased persons, appointment of guardians and conservators, and settlements of their accounts; all matters relating to apprentices; proceedings for the collection of taxes and assessments; and in proceedings by executors, administrators, guardians and conservators for the sale of real estate for the purposes authorized by law, and such other jurisdiction as is or may be provided by law. All of which, except as hereinafter provided, shall be considered as probate matters, and be cognizable at the probate terms hereinafter mentioned.[1]

This jurisdiction is not exclusive.[2]

PROBATE TERMS, ETC.—The terms of county courts for all probate business shall commence on the first Monday of each month, and shall be always open for the transaction of all probate business, and for hearing applications for the discharge of insolvent debtors from arrest or imprisonment, and all matters cognizable at such probate terms shall also be cognizable at the law terms of such courts.[3]

2. JURISDICTION GENERAL.—Thus established and invested with a jurisdiction, these courts have been recognized by the supreme court as courts whose jurisdiction, although of limited is not, strictly speaking, inferior, and certainly not of special jurisdiction. It has said, when speaking of one of these courts, that it is a court of general jurisdiction of unlimited extent over a particular class of subjects, and when acting within that sphere its jurisdiction is as general as the circuit court; that when adjudicating upon the administration of estates over which it has general jurisdiction, as liberal intendments will be granted in its favor as would be extended to the proceedings of the circuit court; and that it is not necessary that all the facts and circumstances which justify its action should affirmatively appear upon the face of its proceedings.[4]

3. FORCE OF THEIR DECREES.—Their decrees and findings, when exercising the jurisdiction conferred by statute, and where the record

---

(1) Hurd's R. S., Chap. 37, § 93.
(2) Shaw vs. Moderwell, 104 Ill., 64.
(3) Hurd's R. S., Chap. 37, § 94; Wallace vs. Gatchel, 106 Ill., 315.
(4) Hanna vs. Yocum, 17 Ill., 387; Propst vs. Meadows, 13 Ill., 157; Mitchell vs. Mayo, 16 Ill., 83; Barnett vs. Wolf, 70 Ill., 76; People vs. Gray, 72 Ill., 343; Von Kettler vs. Johnson, 57 Ill., 109; Housh vs. People, 66 Ill., 181; People vs. Cole, 84 Ill., 327; Matthews vs. Hoff, 113 Ill., 90; Blair **vs.** Sennott, 134 Ill., 78.

shows jurisdiction of the persons of those to be affected, are entitled to the same force and the same presumptions as if such decrees had been rendered by the circuit court, which is of unlimited original jurisdiction. Like other courts of record, their records cannot be contradicted, varied or explained by evidence beyond or outside of the record itself; but one part of their records may limit, qualify or explain another part.([1])

4. DECREES AND JUDGMENTS NOT QUESTIONED.—Likewise, the judgments and decrees of this court, when adjudicating within its jurisdiction, may not be questioned in any collateral proceeding.([2])

5. STATUTORY POWERS.—The statute has conferred upon the county court the power to grant letters of administration, to admit to probate the wills of deceased persons, and to enforce the settlement of estates; and in these matters its jurisdiction is exclusive, although courts of equity may take jurisdiction of the administration of estates, and thus, in the particular case, supersede the jurisdiction of the probate court. But a court of equity will not exercise this jurisdiction except in extraordinary cases, where some special reasons are shown to exist why the administration should be withdrawn from the probate court.([3])

6. HOW FAR THIS JURISDICTION IS SHARED BY EQUITY COURTS.—While this jurisdiction is given to our county courts by the statute, courts of equity have long exercised the right of a paramount jurisdiction in cases of administration and the settlement of estates, and in this, control courts of law in their action in the settlement and distribution of estates of decedents;([4]) yet a court of equity will never take jurisdiction to admit a will to probate, nor to appoint an executor, that being peculiarly the office of a probate court;([5]) nor will it assume jurisdiction of a claim against an estate until it has

---

(1) Barnett vs. Wolf, 70 Ill., 76; Moffatt et al. vs. Moffatt, 69 Ill., 641; Barnard vs. Barnard, 119 ., 92.
(2) Bostwick et al. vs. Skinner et al., 80 Ill., 147; Klingensmith vs. Bean, 2 Watts, 486; Sankey's Ap., 55 Pa. St., 496; Bailey vs. Dilworth, 10 Smedes and M., 404. . But when acting without its jurisdiction its acts are void: Vick vs. Vicksburg, 1 Howard, 379; Fisk vs. Norvell, 9 Texas, 13; Wall vs. Wall, 123 Pa. St., 545; Wadsworth vs. Connell, 104 Ill., 369.
(3) Freeland vs. Dazey et al., 25 Ill., 294.
(4) Story's Eq. Jurisp., Chap. 9: Grattan vs. Grattan et al., 18 Ill., 167. Townsend vs. Radcliff et al., 44 Ill., 446; Freeland vs. Dazey, 25 Ill., 294, Lynch et al vs. Rotan et al., 39 Ill., 14.
(5) Wild vs. Sweeney et al., 84 Ill., 213; Hales vs. Holland, 92 Ill., 494; Kennedy vs. Kennedy, 105 Ill., 350.

been allowed in probate, that also being peculiarly the office of that court, and some special reasons shown why its aid should be granted;([1]) nor unless all parties in interest as creditors are before it.([2]) Some cases present a complication of circumstances under which a court of equity alone can do full justice.([3])

7. JURISDICTION CONTINUES.—Where a court of one county acquires jurisdiction over an estate, it retains it until it is fully administered.([4]) Whenever, by the division of any county, or the removal of the executor or administrator to whom letters have been granted, he is, by such removal or division, beyond the limits of the county in which said letters were granted, and in some other county of this state, the county court of the county in which the letters were or are granted shall proceed and settle the estate in the same manner as if no removal or division had occurred.([5])

8. MAY ENTERTAIN JURISDICTION OF EQUITABLE CLAIMS.— Where claims against estates are purely of an equitable nature, this court is not ousted of its jurisdiction thereby, but may proceed to adjudicate thereon as if they were of a legal nature;([6]) but where third parties are to be brought in, and conflicting interests are to be composed and settled, this court may not act.([7]) Nor has it power to adjudicate in case of a resulting trust.([8])

9. POWER OF COURT.—County courts shall have power to enforce due observance of all orders, decisions, judgments and decrees made by them in discharge of their duties under this act; and they may issue attachments for contempt offered such courts or their processes, by any executor, administrator, witness or other person; and may fine and imprison, or either, all such offenders, in like manner as the

---

(1) Garvin et al. vs. Stewart, 59 Ill., 229; Le Moyne vs. Quimby, 70 Ill., 400; Heustis et al. vs. Johnson, 84 Ill., 61; Crain vs. Kennedy et al., 85 Ill., 340; Harris vs. Douglas, 64 Ill., 466; Blanchard vs. Williamson, 70 Ill., 647; Armstrong et al. vs. Cooper, 11 Ill., 560; Clark et al. vs. Hogle et al., 52 Ill., 427; Winslow vs. Leland, 128 Ill., 304; Harding vs. Shepherd, 107 Ill., 264; Cowdrey vs. Hitchcock, 103 Ill., 264; McNeil vs. McNeil, 36 Ala., 109.
(2) Vansyckle et al. vs. Richardson et al., 13 Ill., 171; 1 Story's Eq., 536.
(3) McCreedy vs. Meier et al., 64 Ill., 495; Jennings et al. vs. McConnell et al., 17 Ill., 148.
(4) People vs. White et al., 11 Ill., 341; Woodruff vs. Young, 43 Mich., 548.
(5) Hurd's R. S., Chap. 3, § 9.
(6) Moline Water Power Co. vs. Webster, 26 Ill., 234; Moore et al. vs. Rogers, 19 Ill., 347; Dixon et al. vs. Buell, 21 Ill., 203.
(7) Pahlman et al. vs. Graves, 26 Ill., 405.
(8) Lill vs. Brant, 6 Ill. Ap., 366.

circuit courts may do in similar cases.(¹) In all matters pertaining to the administration of the estates of deceased persons, the county court has unlimited general jurisdiction; and the statute must be so construed as to give to this court power to require of administrators and executors prompt and honest discharge of all their duties, for the interest of those interested in the estates committed to their care.(²)

10. POWER TO CONSTRUE WILLS, ETC.—These courts, by virtue of their probate jurisdiction, have power, in the first instance, to construe wills, whenever such construction is involved in the settlement and distribution of the estate of a testator. Their jurisdiction over the estates of persons under guardianship includes not only the appointment of guardians and the control over their official actions, but the care and protection of the estates of the wards, formerly vested in the court of chancery.(³)

11. PROBATE COURTS.—Section 20, Art. 6 of the constitution of 1870, provides, that the general assembly may establish probate courts in counties having a population of over 50,000. Said courts, when established, to have original jurisdiction of all probate matters, the settlement of estates of deceased persons, the appointment of guardians and conservators, and settlement of their accounts. Upon the establishment of such court in any particular county, the county court of any such county is at once, by operation of law, deprived of its jurisdiction in matters of probate, and in all matters over which probate courts have jurisdiction.(⁴)

12. SHERIFF'S DUTIES—FEES.—The sheriff shall, when required by the court, attend all sessions of said court, either by himself or deputy, and shall preserve good order in the court, and execute all writs of attachment, summonses, subpœnas, citations, notices and other processes which may, at any time, be legally issued by such court, and make return thereof. And such sheriff shall be entitled to the same fees as he is allowed for similar services in the circuit court.(⁵)

(1) Hurd's R. S., Chap. 3, § 130.
(2) Reynolds vs. People, 55 Ill., 328; Winslow vs. Leland, 128 Ill., 304; Spencer vs. Boardman, 118 Ill., 553.
(3) State vs. Ueland, 30 Minn., 277.
(4) Klokke vs. Dodge, 103 Ill., 125.
(5) Hurd's R. S., Chap. 3, § 131.

CHAPTER II.

GRANTING AND REVOCATION OF LETTERS TESTAMENTARY AND ADMINISTRATION.

1. Administration under English laws.
2. What court may appoint.
3. Right of administration under our statute.
4. Next of kin.
5. Statute imperative.
6. Who should not be appointed.
7. When letters may be granted others than the next of kin.
8. Creditor must be actual.
9. Administrator unnecessary.
10. Preference between several.
11. Proof of death necessary.
12. Grant may be delayed.
13. Oath of administrator.
14. Oath of executor.
15. Act of granting ministerial.
16. Appointment cannot be questioned collaterally.
17. Acts of one irregularly appointed not void.
18. Letters void in the beginning remain so.
19. Public administrators.
20. Duties of public administrator.
21. Administrator to collect.
22. Bond of same.
23. Limitation on appointment of administrator.
24. Revocation of letters and resignation.
    a. False pretenses—costs.
    b. When will is discovered.
    c. When will is set aside.
    d. For violating order of paying claims.
    e. For refusal to perform duties.
    f. Where minor or non resident is appointed.
    g. Where appointee becomes unsound of mind
    h. Where administrator removes.
25. Resignation and costs.
26. When action void.
27. Who to administer *de bonis non*.
28. Suits against former administrator.

1. When a person died intestate in the early periods of the English history, his goods went to the king, as the general trustee or guardian of the state. This right was afterward conceded by the crown to the clergy, for, as was quaintly said, "the law presumes that he who had the care of his soul in his lifetime would, after his death, have care of his temporal goods, to see them well disposed of,"(1) but the sequel did not justify the confidence of the fathers in the probity of the clergy, who, by rapidly absorbing all the property of the kingdom into the church, under the pretense of pious uses, so flagrantly abused the right so confidingly given, that the parliament was obliged to interfere, and take the power of administration entirely from the church, and confer it upon those more disposed to a faithful execution of the trust. This produced the statutes of 31 Edward III. (1358), Chap. 11, and 21 Henry VIII. (1530), Chap. 5, which are the models from which we have copied our statutes of administration. While in England this reform still left the power of granting administration, and of superintending the process of administration, in the hands of the bishop, or ordinary in each diocese, our law assigns it to the civil courts, which are the successors of these ecclesiastical courts.(2)

2. WHAT COURT MAY APPOINT.—The county court of the county in which a decedent had his residence at the time of his death alone has jurisdiction to appoint an administrator of his estate, though ancillary administration may be granted, when necessary, in another state. Whether a given appointment is void or voidable, depends upon whether the court had or had not jurisdiction to make the appointment. If the court has such jurisdiction, any irregularity in the appointment can make it voidable and revocable only, and not void.(3)

3. Administration shall be granted upon the goods and chattels of decedent to the surviving husband or wife, or to the next of kin to the intestate, or some of them, if they will accept the same, or the court may grant letters of administration to some competent person who may be nominated to the court by either of them; but in

---

(1) 2 Bl. Com., 494; Wentworth on Executors, 473.
(2) 2 Kent's Com., 499.
(3) Broughton vs. Bradley, 34 Ala., 694; Moore vs. Philbrick, 32 Maine, 102; Johnson vs. Corpenning. 4 Iredell's Eq., 216; Hickox vs. Frank, 102 Ill., 660: Buckley vs. Redmond, 2 Bradf. Sur., 281.

all cases the surviving husband or wife, or the person so nominated by him or her, respectively, shall have the preference, and if none of the persons hereinbefore mentioned applies within sixty days from the death of the intestate, the county court may grant administration to any creditor who shall apply for the same. If no creditor applies within fifteen days next after the lapse of sixty days, as aforesaid, administration may be granted to any person whom the county court may think will best manage the estate. In all cases where the intestate is a non-resident, or without a widow, next of kin or creditors in this state, but leaves property within the state, administration shall be granted to the public administrators of the proper county: *Provided*, That no administration shall, in any case, be granted until satisfactory proof be made before the county court, to whom application for that purpose is made, that the person in whose estate letters of administration are requested is dead and died intestate; *And provided, further*, That no non-resident of this state shall be appointed administrator or allowed to act as such.([1])

4. WHO ARE NEXT OF KIN.—The rule for determining who are "next of kin," long in use in England and this country, is derived from the civil law, and makes the intestate himself the point from whence the degrees are numbered. The children and parents of any intestate are equally near, being all related to him in the first degree; but in determining the right to administer, preference is given to children, if not otherwise disqualified. From the children and parents the next degree embraces the brothers or sisters and grand parents, and so on in the same order—in the case of collaterals always counting back to the common ancestor, and then down to the claimant, to determine the degree of relationship. The law and course, in those states which follow the English law, must be to grant administration,

  I. To the husband or wife;
  II. To the children, sons or daughters;
  III. To the parents, father or mother;
  IV. To the brothers or sisters of the whole blood;
  V. To the brothers or sisters of the half blood;
  VI. To the grand parents.
  VII. To the uncles, aunts and nephews and neices, who stand in equal degree.
  VIII. To cousins.

(1) Hurd's R. S., Chap. 3, § 18.

Grand parents are preferred to aunts, as nearer of kin; for the grand parent stands in the second degree to the intestate, and the aunt in the third.(¹) In case of a claim by two or more whose relationship to the intestate entitles them to claim administration, the court will exercise a wise discretion, and after excluding such as are disqualified by statute, notwithstanding their relationship, confer letters upon those whose interest or qualifications best fit them for the trust. It will not be error to grant letters to any one of the next of kin to the exclusion of all others in equal degree.(²)

5. STATUTE MANDATORY.—The requirements of the statute in relation to the grant of letters of administration are mandatory, and it is error to disregard the rights thereby given.(³) It specifically points out who may be appointed. The rule there laid down must not be departed from except for some cause specified in the statute. Nor can the right be delegated,(⁴) nor sold.(⁵)

In a contest between relatives for letters, whose priority is not settled by statute, the single point to be ascertained is, who will be entitled to the surplus of the personal estate.(⁶) Being nearer of kin to the decedent than any other person in the United States, does not give a right to administer. If the next of kin is not within the state, or is legally disqualified, a creditor or the public administrator, as the case may require, is entitled to administer.(⁷) Before letters are granted to one, before whom others are preferred, the renunciation of all so preferred must be produced before the court,(⁸) and this, too, although the person seeking the appointment may be nominated by one having priority of right (⁹) Letters *de bonis non* may be granted without the observance of these restrictions, but only by the court which granted administration.(¹⁰)

It is stated in the English books, that administration is granted

(1) 2 Kent's Com., 505.
(2) Taylor vs. Delancy, 2 Cai. C., 143.
(3) Schnell vs. City of Chicago, 38 Ill., 382; Coope vs. Lowerre, 1 Barb., Ch. 45.
(4) Stockdale vs. Conway, 14 Md., 99.
(5) Bowers vs. Bowers, 26 Pa. St., 74.
(6) Sweezey vs. Willis, 1 Bradf., 495.
(7) Public Administrator vs. Watts, 1 Paige, 347.
(8) In the matter of Root, 5 N. Y. Leg. Obs., 449. A renunciation cannot be withdrawn: Stocksdale vs. Conway, *supra*.
(9) *Ib.*
(10) Russell vs. Hoar, 3 Met., 187; Burnett vs. Meadows, 7 B. Monroe, 277.

to the next of kin on account of his interest, and, therefore, if that cease, the reason ceases, and it is to be granted to the residuary legatee, if there be one, whether there be any present residue or not; but the husband is entitled to administer on the estate of his wife, though by a post-nuptial contract he relinquished all right to her property.([1])

6. WHO SHOULD NOT BE APPOINTED.—A non-resident of Illinois should not be appointed administrator of an estate situated in this state.([2]) He being beyond the reach of any process issued in this state, cannot be compelled by the court appointing him to render an account and make settlement of the estate committed to him.([3]) A surviving partner should never be appointed administrator of the estate of his deceased partner, because, as such survivor, he becomes accountable to the estate, and could not well account to himself as its representative.([4]) Administration should be refused to the husband, wife, next of kin or creditor, if it should appear to the court that there is anything in the character or qualifications of the applicant which would "disqualify" him for a proper discharge of the high trust.([5])

Letters cannot be granted to a corporation, though it be the legatee and the executor appointed in the will.([6]) Nor have the illegitimate children of an intestate a right as next of kin to letters of administration upon the estate of their father.([7])

The court has no right to join with one who has a right to administer, a person not entitled, without the consent of the former.([8])

Before a court can obtain jurisdiction of a case to appoint a stranger or the public administrator, it should affirmatively appear of record that application for the appointment of an administrator has been made by some person interested in the estate, and that there is no relative within the state or creditor possessing qualifications to whom administration may be committed.([9])

(1) 1 Dane's Ab., 580; O'Rear vs. Crum, 135 Ill., 294; Charles vs. Charles, 8 Grattan, 486.
(2) Hurd's R. S., Chap. 3, § 18.
(3) Child vs. Gratiott, 41 Ill., 357.
(4) Heward vs Slagle et al., 52 Ill., 336.
(5) Hurd's R. S., Chap. 3, § 18; O'Rear vs. Crum, *supra*.
(6) Georgetown College vs. Browne, 34 Md., 450.
(7) Myatt vs. Myatt, 44 Ill., 473.
(8) Peters vs. Public Administrator, 1 Brad., 200.
(9) Unknown Heirs of Langworthy vs. Baker, 23 Ill., 484.

7. WHEN LETTERS MAY BE GRANTED TO OTHERS.—Letters of administration upon the goods and chattels, rights and credits of a person dying intestate shall not be granted to any person not entitled to the same, as husband, widow, next of kin, creditor or public administrator, within seventy-five days after the death of the intestate, without satisfactory evidence that the persons having the preference have relinquished their prior right thereto; but if application is made after the expiration of seventy-five days, the county court may proceed to grant letters to the applicant or any other person, as he may think fit.([1])

8. CREDITOR.—To entitle a creditor of the deceased to a grant of administration, his claim upon the estate of the intestate must be such as survives against the legal representative of a deceased person.([2]) A mere legatee is not entitled to administration as a creditor;([3]) nor one having claim for causing death.([4]) But one who has paid funeral expenses is.([5])

9. ADMINISTRATOR UNNECESSARY.—When the appointment of an administrator is not necessary to the proper settlement of an estate, letters of administration may properly be refused—as where the surviving husband is the sole heir of his deceased wife as to her personal estate, has paid all her debts and liabilities, and has reduced her personal estate to his possession, the appointment of an administrator is unnecessary; and if one is appointed, he will not, as a matter of right, be entitled to the possession of her personal estate.([6]) And the heir, by tendering to a creditor the amount of his debt, deprives him of his right to administer.([7])

10. PREFERENCE BETWEEN SEVERAL.—Where the class primarily entitled to administration consists of several persons, it is the duty of the court to grant letters to such one or more of them as he shall judge will best administer the estate. Letters may thus be granted to them all jointly, if they so desire; or, in the discretion of the court, one of them may be selected, and administration committed

---

(1) Hurd's R. S., Chap. 3, § 19.
(2) Stebbins vs. Palmer, 1 Pick., 71.
(3) Chapin vs. Hastings, 2 Pick., 71.
(4) I. C. R. R. Co. vs. Cragin, 71 Ill., 177.
(5) Lentz vs. Pilert, 60 Md., 296.
(6) People vs. Abbott, 105 Ill., 588; 46 Am. Dec., 438; McCleary vs Menke, 109 Ill., 294.
(7) Culley vs. Mohlnbrock, 36 Ill. Ap., 84.

to him alone, to the exclusion of the others. This discretion, when properly exercised, is not subject to review. Primogeniture gives no preference to the older over the younger; yet, if things are precisely equal, being the elder brother would incline the balance. And the same principle applies to the elder of two sisters.([1])

11. PROOF OF DEATH.—Before letters of administration shall hereafter be issued, the person applying for the same, or some other credible person, shall make and file an affidavit with the proper clerk, setting forth, as near as may be, the date of the death of the deceased, the probable amount or value of the personal estate, and the names of the heirs and widow, or surviving husband, if known.([2])

The *fact* of death must exist, otherwise, by no proofs deduced, can the court obtain jurisdiction of the estate, and all it or its appointees can do will be void absolutely.([3])

When a person goes abroad, and has not been heard of for a long time, the presumption of the continuation of life ceases at the expiration of seven years from the period when he was last heard from.([4]) The ordinary rule is, that it is general reputation among the kindred only of a deceased person that is admissible in proof of death, but that rule is relaxed from necessity in cases where the deceased left no kindred that are known, in which case reputation among the acquaintances of deceased is received in proof of death.([5])

Proof of the death of the person whose estate is to be administered is necessary to give jurisdiction to the court; and where letters are granted upon the estate of a living person, such letters are void.([6]) In New York it was held that letters granted upon the estate of a person then living, but upon proof of death deemed sufficient by the surrogate, were not void, but only voidable, and that acts done by the administrator so appointed were conclusive upon the person supposed to be dead.([7]) An affidavit of death made " according to the best of the petitioner's knowledge and belief," without alleging

---

(1) Brubaker's appeal, 98 Pa. St., 21 ; 1 Williams on Executors, 374.
(2) Hurd's R. S., Chap. 3, § 20.
(3) Melia vs. Simmons, 45 Wis., 334, and note 30, Am. Rep., 748; Thomas vs. People, 107 Ill., 517.
(4) Whiting vs. Nichol, 46 Ill., 230; Moore vs. Smith, 11 Richardson's Law, 569.
(5) Ringhouse vs Keever, 49 Ill., 470.
(6) Melia vs. Simmons, *supra*.; Ringhouse vs. Keever, 49 Ill., 470. See note 30, Am. Rep., 748.
(7) Rodrigas vs. East River Savings Institution, 63 N. Y., 469.

any knowledge or means of knowledge, in the petition, or reason for the belief, was held colorable proof, sufficient to vest jurisdiction in the court to act, and that the grant of letters could not be impeached collaterally.(1)

12. GRANT MAY BE DELAYED.—It will be proper, upon an allegation of the existence of an unproven will of the deceased, to stay proceedings, and so afford an opportunity to have it proven in due course.(2)

13. OATH.—The county court shall, in all cases, upon granting administration of the goods and chattels, rights and credits of any person having died intestate, require the administrator (public administrators excepted) to take and subscribe and file with the clerk of the court an oath, in substance following, to-wit:

I do solemnly swear (or affirm) that I will well and truly administer all and singular the goods and chattels, rights, credits and effects of A. B., deceased, and pay all just claims and charges against his estate, so far as his goods, chattels and effects shall extend, and the law charge me; and that I will do and perform all other acts required of me by law, to the best of my knowledge and abilities.(3)

14. OATH OF EXECUTOR—FORM.—Every executor or administrator with the will annexed shall, at the time of proving the will and granting letters testamentary, or of administration, take and subscribe the following oath, to-wit:

I do solemnly swear (or affirm) that this writing contains the true last will and testament of the within named A. B., deceased, so far as I know or believe; and that I will well and truly execute the same, by paying first the debts and then the legacies mentioned therein, as far as his goods and chattels will thereunto extend, and the law charge me; and that I will make a true and perfect inventory of all such goods and chattels, rights and credits as may come to my hands or knowledge belonging to the estate of the said deceased, and render a fair and just account of my executorship, when thereunto required by law, to the best of my knowledge and ability; so help me God.

Which said oath shall be administered by the clerk of the county court, and be attached to and form a part of the probate of said will.(4)

(1) Sheldon vs. Wright, 7 Barb., 39.
(2) Isham vs. Gibbons, 1 Brad., 69.
(3) Hurd's R. S., Chap. 3, § 22: Campbell vs. Knights, 26 Me., 224.
(4) Hurd's R. S., Chap. 3, § 23.

If the person nominated by a testator as executor of his will is not disqualified by law from being executor, the court has no power to refuse to permit him to qualify, or to refuse to grant him letters testamentary.(¹)

15. ACT OF GRANTING LETTERS.—The acts of granting letters of administration, approving bonds of administrators and executors, and of admitting to probate the wills of deceased persons, under the old probate system in force in this state until the adoption of the constitution of 1848, were ministerial only, and not judicial, and where performed by one who was a *defacto* probate justice, were effectual and binding;(²) but as the county court is now organized, these acts, when performed by the court duly organized, must be held to be judicial and beyond inquiry in any collateral proceeding.(³) Where letters were granted by a clerk of the surrogate, in the absence of that officer, the clerk having no authority under the law to pass upon the sufficiency of the proof of the death of the intestate, which is a judicial function, the letters so granted were held absolutely void, and no protection to those debtors of the supposed decedent who had paid debts due to the decedent to the acting administrator.(⁴)

16. APPOINTMENT CANNOT BE QUESTIONED COLLATERALLY.— The regularity of the appointment of an administratar cannot be questioned in a collateral proceeding, as in a petition to sell land, or in a suit to enjoin an ejectment proceeding, for the recovery of lands sold at administrator's sale, nor in an action against a stranger to recover a debt due the estate ; they can only be questioned by appealing from the order of the court making the appointment.(⁵) Where, however, the act of granting is the act of the clerk, and not of the judge, it is a ministerial act, and not judicial, and may be

---

(1) Berry vs. Hamilton, 12 B. Monroe, 191 ; See Brief 54, Am. Dec., 518.

(2) Pritchett et al. vs. People, 1 Gil., 525; Ferguson et al. vs. Hunter, 2 Gil., 657 ; Wardwell vs. McDowell et al., 31 Ill., 364 ; Clinefelter et al. vs. Ayers, 16 Ill., 329 ; Ayers vs. Clinefelter, 20 Ill., 465.

(3) I. C. R. R. Co. vs. Cragin, 71 Ill., 177.

(4) Rodrigas vs. East River Savings Institution, 76 N. Y., 316. See also a full collation of authorities upon the subject of granting administration upon estates of living persons, 30 Am. Rep., 748.

(5) Schnell vs. City of Chicago, 38 Ill., 382; Duffin et al. vs. Abbott et al., 48 Ill., 17 ; Hobson et al. vs. Ewan, 62 Ill., 146 ; Emery vs. Hildreth, 2 Gray (Mass.), 228 ; Riser vs. Snoddy, 7 Ind., 442 ; Abbott vs. Coburn, 28 Vt., 663.

enquired of collaterally.(¹) Where a stranger (not the husband or wife, next of kin or a creditor of the intestate) is appointed administrator, the record of the court making the appointment should show that seventy-five days have elapsed since the death, or that there is no widow or next of kin.(²) If the court, by a proper petition, has jurisdiction to appoint an administrator, but errs by appointing one not entitled to letters, the letters are not void, but voidable.(³)

17. ACTS OF ADMINISTRATOR NOT VOID.—All acts of an administrator regularly appointed are binding upon all persons interested in the estate, though the letters should be afterward revoked.(⁴) So, where, after letters of administration were granted upon the estate of a deceased person as of an intestate's estate, and afterward a will of the deceased person was discovered and admitted to probate, the letters of administration were held not void, but voidable.(⁵) In an action of ejectment, where one party claims under a deed made by an administrator, the regularity of the appointment cannot be called in question.(⁶) Where a court has jurisdiction of the subject matter and of the parties, its judgment in the appointment of an administrator, as in any other case, is held conclusive in all trials except in a direct proceeding to reverse it.(⁷) Where letters are granted to a wrong person, they are voidable; where in a wrong county, they are void.(⁸)

A judgment recovered against and revived against an administrator whose appointment is void, is a nullity; and a *scire facias* issued thereon and sale of lands of the intestate thereunder are also null and void, and the heirs of the deceased can recover in trespass against a *bona fide* purchaser under him who purchased of the sheriff at such sale.(⁹)

18. LETTERS VOID IN THE BEGINNING REMAIN SO.—A grant

(1) I. C. R. R. Co. vs. Cragin, 71 Ill., 177.
(2) Schnell vs. City of Chicago, *supra*.
(3) Flinn vs. Chase, 4 Denio, 85.
(4) Meek vs. Allison et al., 67 Ill., 46; People vs. Cole, 84 Ill., 327; Foster vs. Brown, 1 Bailey's Law, 221; Bigelow vs. Bigelow, 4 Ohio, 138; Pritchett et al. vs. People, *supra*.
(5) Shepherd vs. Rhodes, 60 Ill., 301.
(6) Wight vs. Wallbaum, 39 Ill., 554; Ruffin vs. Farmer, 72 Ill., 615.
(7) Wight vs. Wallbaum, *supra*.
(8) 1 Dane's Ab., 561.
(9) Griffith vs. Frazier, 8 Cranch, 9.

of administration originally void, and not merely voidable, acquires no validity by acquiescence for any period of time.(¹)

19. PUBLIC ADMINISTRATOR.—A public administrator is appointed by the Governor for each county,(²) who, before entering upon his duties, takes an oath, which is filed in the office of the county court, to support the constitutions of the United States and of Illinois, and to faithfully discharge the duties of public administrator to the best of his ability.(³) In cases where a deceased person has estate in Illinois, but no relative or creditor within the state who will administer upon the estate of such deceased person, it is made the duty of the county court, upon the application of any person interested therein, to commit the administration of such estate to the public administrator of the proper county.(⁴) Such public administrator is required to give bond in each case, conditioned the same as other administrators' bonds.(⁵)

The proper county in case of non-residents dying, leaving lands in this state, is the county where such lands or a part of them lie, and in such county administration is to be granted.(⁶)

Before the county court can get jurisdiction of the estate of a deceased person to commit it to the public administrator, it should affirmatively appear to the court that there is no relative within the state, or creditor, to whom administration may be committed, and it should further appear that the application for the appointment of an administrator on the estate is made by a party interested ;(⁷) but the failure of the court to require such proof cannot be called in question collaterally.(⁸)

20. DUTIES OF PUBLIC ADMINISTRATOR.—Upon the death of any person intestate, not leaving a widow, or next of kin, or creditor within this state, the public administrator of the county wherein such person may have died, or, when the decedent is a non-resident,

---

(1) Holyoke vs. Haskins, 5 Pick., 20.
(2) Hurd's R. S., Chap. 3, § 44.
(3) Hurd's R. S., Chap. 3, § 45.
(4) Hurd's R. S., Chap. 3, § 46; Branch vs. Rankin, 108 Ill., 444.
(5) Hurd's R. S., Chap. 3, § 47 ; But a creditor in this state is entitled to preference over the public administrator: Rosenthal vs. Prussing, 108 Ill., 128.
(6) Bowles et al. vs. Rouse, 3 Gil., 409.
(7) Unknown Heirs of Langworthy vs. Baker, 23 Ill., 484; Schnell et al. vs. Chicago, 38 Ill., 382.
(8) *Ib.;* Wight vs. Wallbaum, *supra.*

the public administrator of the county wherein the goods and chattels, rights and credits of such decedent shall be, may take such measures as he may deem proper to protect and secure the effects of such intestate from waste or embezzlement, until administration thereon is granted to the person entitled thereto—the expenses whereof shall be paid to such public administrator, upon the allowance of the county court, in preference to all other demands against such estate, funeral expenses excepted.(¹)

The public administrator does not administer by virtue of his office as public administrator, but by virtue of letters issued to him in each particular case.(²)

21. ADMINISTRATOR TO COLLECT.—During any contest in relation to the probate of any will, testament or codicil, before the same is recorded, or until a will which may have once existed, but is destroyed or concealed, is established, and the substance thereof committed to record, with proof thereupon taken, or during any contest in regard to the right of executorship, or to administer the estate of any person dying either testate or intestate, or whenever any other contingency happens which is productive of great delay before letters testamentary or of administration can be issued upon the estate of such testator or intestate, to the person or persons having legal preference to the same, the county court may appoint any person or persons as administrators, to collect and preserve the estate of any such decedent, until probate of his will, or until administration of his estate is granted, taking bond and security for the collection of the estate, making an inventory thereof, and safe keeping and delivering up the same, when thereunto required by the court, to the proper executor or administrator, whenever they shall be admitted and qualified as such.(³)

22. BOND, ETC.—Such administrators are required to give bonds similar in form to those of other administrators,(⁴) and also to take a similar official oath.(⁵)

The appointment of such an administrator is in the discretion of the county court, and neither of the parties litigant should, in

---

(1) Hurd's R. S., Chap. 3, § 50.
(2) Miller vs. Receiver of Franklin Bank, 1 Paige, 444.
(3) Hurd's R. S., Chap. 3, § 11; Martin vs. Railroad, 92 N. Y., 70; Fisk vs. Norvell, 9 Texas, 13.
(4) Hurd's R. S., Chap. 3, § 13.
(5) Hurd's R. S., Chap. 3, § 14.

general, be appointed.(¹) When so appointed, the authority of the court over such an administrator is the same as that over any other appointee.(²)

23. LIMITATION.—Letters of administration should not be granted after the lapse of seven years from the death of the intestate, unless the delay is explained.(³)

24. REVOKING LETTERS AND RESIGNATION.—The county court is given by statute full and ample power over its appointees, and for good cause may remove administrators for fraud in obtaining letters, or where it appears that a will was executed by the deceased.

(*a.*) FALSE PRETENSES.—County courts shall revoke letters of administration in all cases where the same were granted to any person upon the false and fraudulent pretense of being a creditor of the estate upon which administration is granted, or upon any other false pretense whatever.(⁴)

When it appears that such letters were fraudulently obtained by such administrator, the court revoking the same shall give judgment against the administrator for all costs of suit.(⁵)

(*b.*) WHEN WILL IS PRODUCED.—If, at any time after letters of administration have been granted, a will of the deceased shall be produced, and probate thereof granted according to law, such letters of administration shall be revoked.(⁶)

In such a case the letters of administration are not void, but voidable, and their previous existence was valid for the purposes of a due administration of the estate.(⁷)

(*c.*) WHEN WILL IS SET ASIDE.—In all cases where a will, testament or codicil shall have been proved and letters granted thereon, as aforesaid, and such will shall thereafter be set aside by due course of law, the letters granted thereon shall be revoked.(⁸)

(*d.*) Where an administrator shows by his report that he has

---

(1) Mootrie vs. Hunt, 4 Brad., 173.
(2) Gottsberger vs. Taylor, 2 Brad., 86.
(3) Child vs. Gratiot, 41 Ill., 357; Fitzgerald vs. Glancy, 49 Ill., 465.
(4) Hurd's R. S., Chap. 3, § 26; Marston vs. Wilcox, 1 Scam., 60; Proctor vs. Wanamaker, 1 Barb., Ch. 302; Wernse vs. Hall, 101 Ill., 424.
(5) Hurd's R. S., Chap. 3, § 27.
(6) Hurd's R. S., Chap. 3, § 28.
(7) Meek vs. Allison, 67 Ill., 46; Rebhan vs. Mueller, 114 Ill., 343.
(8) Hurd's R. S., Chap. 3, § 29.

given an unauthorized preference to creditors in the payment of assets, it is sufficient to justify his removal.(¹)

(e.) The refusal of an administrator to perform any of the duties of his trust imposed by law is sufficient cause for revoking his authority and appointing another administrator.(²)

(f.) Should a minor or a non-resident, by inadvertence, be appointed administrator of an estate in this state, it is the duty of the court to revoke the appointment, on proper application being made.(³)

(g.) LUNACY, ETC.—The county court may revoke all letters testamentary, or of administration, granted to persons who become insane, lunatic or of unsound mind, habitual drunkards, are convicted of infamous crimes, waste or mismanage the estate, or who conduct themselves in such manner as to endanger their co-executors, co-administrators or securities, in all which cases the court shall summon the person charged to be in default or disqualified, as aforesaid, to show cause why such revocation should not be made. When revocation is made, the reason therefor shall be stated at large upon the record.(⁴)

(h.) DUTY OF COURT TO REVOKE LETTERS ON REMOVAL.— When it shall come to the knowledge of the county court, by affidavit or otherwise, that any executor or administrator of an estate is about to remove or has removed beyond the limits of this state, it shall be the duty of such court to cause a notice to be published in some newspaper in the county where letters testamentary or of administration were granted, for four weeks successively; and if no newspaper is published in said county, then by posting up a notice at the court house door, notifying the said executor or administrator to appear before him within thirty days after the date of such notice, and make a settlement of his accounts as required by law. If the executor or administrator neglects or refuses to make such settlement, it shall be the duty of said county court to remove him from office.(⁵) As has already been said, the laws of this state

(1) Foltz vs. Prouse, 17 Ill., 487.
(2) Marsh et al. vs. People, 15 Ill., 284.
(3) Child vs. Gratiot, 41 Ill., 357; Carow vs. Mowatt, 2 Edw., 57.
(4) Hurd's R. S., Chap. 3, § 30; Estate of Pike, 45 Wis., 391; See 1 Probate Reports, 336, for brief.
(5) Hurd's R. S., Chap, 3, § 31.

will not tolerate the appointment of a non-resident as administrator, (¹) so, when an administrator becomes a non-resident of the state, it is undoubtedly the duty of the court, even upon informal knowledge coming to the judge of that fact, to proceed under the foregoing section to his removal.

25. RESIGNATION—SETTLEMENT.—An executor or administrator may, upon his petition and upon giving such notice to the legatees, devisees or distributees, as the court shall direct, be allowed to resign his trust when it appears to the county court to be proper; and upon such resignation the court shall grant letters of administration, with the will annexed, or *de bonis non*, to some suitable person, to administer the goods and estate not already administered. But no administrator or executor shall be discharged till he shall have made full settlement with the court and complied with its orders, and shall deliver over to his successor all money, chattels and effects of the estate in his hands not paid over according to the orders of the court.(²)

The acceptance of the resignation of an administrator amounts to a removal.(³)

An administrator who resigns is required by statute to pay all costs caused by the proceeding, and judgment may be rendered against him for the same, to be collected by execution.(⁴)

26. WHEN ACTION VOID.—Until a valid revocation of letters of administration already granted upon an estate is made, or a voluntry resignation of the same has been tendered and accepted, the county court has no power or jurisdiction to appoint another as administrator *de bonis non* of the same estate; and an order for such appointment under such circumstances is absolutely void.(⁵)

27. WHO TO ADMINISTER DE BONIS NON.—The statute is silent as to the right to letters *de bonis non*, except that letters shall be granted "to some suitable person."(⁶) The rule of precedence laid

---

(1) Ante page 10.
(2) Hurd's R. S., Chap. 3, § 40.
(3) Marsh et al. vs. People, 15 Ill., 284.
(4) Hurd's R. S., Chap. 3, § 41.
(5) Munroe vs. People, 102 Ill., 406; Hanifan vs. Needles, 108 Ill., 403; Thomas vs. Burrus, 23 Miss., 550; See 24 Am. Dec., 379, for brief of authorities.
(6) Hurd's R. S., Chap. 3, § 40.

down in section 18 *ante* (¹), if rights thereunder have not already been renounced, would seem to be a safe guide.(²)

28. Suit cannot be maintained against an administrator *de bonis non* on a contract made by a former administrator, for the reason that no privity of contract exists between them (³)

(1) Ante page 9.
(2) See brief of authorities, 24 Am. Dec., 382; McGarvey vs. Darnall, 134 Ill., 367.
(3) McBeth vs. Smith, 2 Brevard, 565; Alsop vs. Mather, 8 Conn., 584; Luscomb vs. Ballard, 5 Gray, 403.

CHAPTER III.

ADMINISTRATORS' AND EXECUTORS' BONDS AND LIABILITIES THEREUNDER.

1. Bond of executors—form.
2. When no security required.
3. Bond of administrator.
4. Requiring other security.
5. On application of sureties.
6. Form of new bonds.
7. Two bonds may be taken.
8. Giving new bond under Sec. 32 releases old securities.
9. Giving new bond under Sec. 32 does not release old securities.
10. Removal for failure to give new bond.
11. Death of sole executor.
12. Death or disqualification of executor or administrator.
13. Court may take one or more bonds.
14. Court shall examine bonds at January and July terms.
15. Record to be kept.
16. Summons of principals in bonds.
17. When new bond to be required.
18. Failure to give new bond—removal.
19. Liability under new bonds.
20. When not binding on sureties.
21. *Devastavit*.
22. Liability for taking insolvent security.
23. For releasing a debt.
24. For removing property from the State.
25. For exhibiting an untrue account.
26. For failure to file inventory within three months.
27. For suffering judgment on claim barred by statute.
28. For failure to account for debt due from himself.
29. For money recovered for causing death.
30. One administrator liable for his co-administrator.
31. As trustee or executor.
32. Extent of liability.
33. Administrator must use diligence—money stolen.
34. Must redeem incumbered property.
35. Must pay to distributees.
36. Of the demand.
37. Suit against part or all of obligors.

38. Sureties liable only for assets of estate.
39. Voluntary bond.
40. Surety not in fiduciary relation to estate.
41. Former bond—liability to administrator *de bonis non*
42. Security for costs.
43. Irregularities in drafting bonds.
44. Liability where letters are revoked.
45. Where bonds are given by each administrator.
46. Where administrator acts in two capacities.
47. Will set aside and executor continues to administer.
48. Sureties may appeal.
49. Sureties may rely on bar of the statute to a claim.
50. When fiduciary relation ceases.
51. Estoppel.
52. Jurisdiction of a court of chancery over remedies on bonds.
53. Form of judgment.
54. Action of Account may be maintained.

1. BOND OF EXECUTOR—FORM.—All executors hereafter appointed, unless the testator shall otherwise direct in his will, and all administrators with the will annexed, shall, before entering upon their duties, enter into bond, with good and sufficient security, to be approved by the county court, and in counties having a probate court, by the probate court, in a sum double the value of the personal estate, and payable to the people of the State of Illinois for the use of the parties interested, in the following form, to-wit:

Know all men by these presents, that we, A B, C D and E F, of the county of......, and State of Illinois, are held and firmly bound unto the People of the State of Illinois, in the penal sum of......dollars, current money of the United States, which payment, well and truly to be made and performed, we and each of us bind ourselves, our heirs, executors and administrators, jointly, severally and firmly by these presents. Witness our hands and seals, this...day of..., A. D. 18...

The condition of the above obligation is such, that if the above bounden A B, executor of the last will and testament of G H, deceased, (or administrator with the will annexed, of G H, deceased, as the case may be,) do make, or cause to be made, a true and perfect inventory of all and singular the goods and chattels, rights and credits, lands, tenements and hereditaments, and the rents and profits issuing out of the same, of the said deceased, which have, or shall come to the hands, possession or knowledge of the said A B, or into the possession of any other person for him, and the same so made do exhibit in the county court (or probate court) for said county of......, as required by law; and also make and render a fair and just account of his actings and doings as such executor, (or administrator) to said court, when thereunto lawfully required; and do well and truly fulfill the duties enjoined on him in and by the said will; and shall, moreover, pay and deliver to the persons entitled thereto, all the legacies and bequests contained in said will, so far as the estate of the said testator will thereunto extend, according to the value thereof, and as the law shall charge him; and shall, in general, do all other acts which may, from time to time, be required of him by law—then this obligation to be void: otherwise to remain in full force and virtue.

Which said bond shall be signed and sealed by the said executor (or administrator) and his securities, and filed in the office of the clerk of the county court, or office of the clerk of the probate court in counties having a probate court, and spread upon the records; and that where it becomes necessary to sell the real estate of any intestate, for the payment of debts against his estate, under the provisions of this act, or in case real estate is to be sold under the provisions of a will, the court shall require the executor (or administrator) to give further and additional bond, with good and sufficient security, to be approved by the court, in a sum double the value of the real estate of the decedent sought to be sold, and payable to the people of the State of Illinois, for the use of the parties interested, in form above prescribed.(¹)

2. WHEN SECURITY NOT REQUIRED.—When any testator leaves visible estate more than sufficient to pay all his debts, and by will shall direct that his executors shall not be obliged to give security, in that case no security shall be required, unless the county court shall see cause, from its own knowledge, or the suggestions of creditors and legatees, to suspect the executors of fraud, or that the personal estate will not be sufficient to discharge all the debts, in which case such court may require security, and the same shall be given before or after letters testamentary are granted, notwithstanding any directions to the contrary in the will.(²)

3. BOND OF ADMINISTRATOR.—Every administrator, except as hereinbefore in Sec. eight (8) provided, shall, before entering upon the duties of his office, enter into bond, with good and sufficient security, to be approved by the county court, and in counties having a probate court, by the probate court, in double the value of the personal estate, and payable to the people of the State of Illinois,

---

(1) Hurd's R. S., Chap. 3 § 7, as amended by act of 1881; Wyman vs. Campbell, 6 Porter, 219.
(2) Hurd's R. S., Chap. 3, § 8.

for the use of the parties interested, substantially in the following form, to-wit:

Know all men by these presents, that we, A B, C D and E F, of the county of......, and State of Illinois, are held and firmly bound unto the People of the State of Illinois in the penal sum of......dollars, current money of the United States, which payment, well and truly to be made and performed, we and each of us bind ourselves, our heirs, executors and administrators, jointly, severally and firmly by these presents. Witness our hands and seals, this...day of...,18...

The condition of the above obligation is such, that if the said A B, administrator of all and singular the goods and chattels, rights and credits of J K, deceased, do make, or cause to be made, a true and perfect inventory of all and singular the goods and chattels, rights and credits of the said deceased, which shall come to the hands, possession or knowledge of him, the said A B, as administrator, or to the hands of any person or persons for him; and the same so made, do exhibit, or cause to be exhibited, in the county court (or probate court) of the said county of......, agreeably to law; and such goods and chattels, rights and credits, do well and truly administer according to law, and all the rest of the said goods and chattels, rights and credits, which shall be found remaining upon the account of the said administrator, the same being at first examined and allowed by the court, shall deliver and pay unto such person or persons, respectively, as may be legally entitled thereto; and further, do make a just and true account of all his actings and doings therein, when thereunto required by the said court; and if it shall appear that any last will and testament was made by the deceased, and the same be proved in court, and letters testamentary or of administration be obtained thereon, and the said A B do, in such case, on being required thereto, render and deliver up the letters of administration granted to him as aforesaid, and shall in general do and perform all other acts which may at any time be required of him by law, then this obligation to be void: otherwise to remain in full force and virtue. *

Which said bond shall be signed and sealed by said administrator and his securities, attested by the clerk of the county court or probate court, and filed in his office, and that where it becomes necessary to sell real estate of any intestate for the payment of debts against his estate, under the provisions of this act, the court shall require the administrator to give further and additional bond, with good and sufficient security, to be approved by the court, in a sum double the value of the real estate of the decedent sought to be sold, and payable to the people of the State of Illinois, for the use of the parties interested, in the form above prescribed. And in all cases where bonds shall be taken from any administrator *de bonis*

---

* NOTE.—The failure of an administrator to give bond renders his appointment void, but a defect in the bond makes the appointment voidable only. *Exparte Maxwell*, 37 Ala., 362; *Peebles vs. Watts*, 9 Dana, 102.

non, or in any other case where a form shall not be prescribed in this act, the same shall be made, as nearly as may be, in conformity with the form above prescribed, with corresponding variations to suit each particular case.([1])

4. REQUIRING OTHER SECURITY—DUTY OF COURT.—One of the most important duties of a court having probate jurisdiction, is the taking and approval of the securities upon the bonds of administrators, executors and guardians. A bond ample for the security of those interested when taken, may, under the mutations of fortune incident to this day, soon become in part or wholly inadequate for their protection. The statute requires the county court at the January and July terms to inform itself of the condition and sufficiency of each bond.([2])

When any court grants letters, testamentary or of administration, of the estate of any person deceased, without taking good security as aforesaid, or when any security heretofore or hereafter taken becomes insufficient, the court may, on the application of any person entitled to distribution, or otherwise interested in such estate, require such executor or administrator to give other and sufficient security; and in default thereof the letters, testamentary or of administration, shall be revoked, and administration *de bonis non* granted; but all acts done according to law by the executor or administrator so removed prior to such revocation, shall be valid.([3])

5. PETITION OF SECURITY FOR RELEASE.—Whenever any surety on the bond of any executor or administrator desires to be released from further liability upon any such bond, he may petition the court in which said bond is filed for that purpose, and upon notice being given to the executor or administrator, as the court may direct, the court shall compel such executor or administrator, within a reasonable time, to be fixed by the court, to settle and adjust his accounts, and pay over whatever balance may be found in his hands, and file in such court a new bond, in such penalty and security as may be approved by the court—which being done, the surety may be discharged from all liability on such bond.([4])

---

(1) Hurd's R. S., Chap. 3, § 23, as amended by act of 1881; Wyman vs. Campbell, 6 Porter, 219.
(2) Hurd's R. S., Chap. 103, § 4.
(3) Hurd's R. S., Chap. 3, § 32; Meek vs. Allison, et al., 67 Ill., 46; Foster vs. Brown, 1 Bailey's Law, 221; Bigelow vs. Bigelow, 4 Ohio, 138.
(4) Hurd's R. S., Chap. 3, § 35.

When a surety for an executor or an administrator, or his representatives, may conceive himself or themselves in danger of suffering by the mismanagement of such executor or administrator, and shall petition the county court for relief, in writing, setting forth the cause of such apprehension, the said court shall examine such petition, and if the court shall deem the causes therein set forth sufficient to entitle such petitioner or petitioners to relief, if true, he shall summon such executor or administrator to show cause against such petition; and may dismiss the same, or direct such executor or administrator either to give good counter security to save such petitioner or petitioners harmless, or to give a new bond in the like penalty as the first; and upon refusal or neglect to give such counter security or new bond, the letters granted to such executor or administrator, may be revoked.[1] The word *may*, although seeming to authorize the use of a discretion by the court, inasmuch as the rights of the securities are imperiled, should, under an accepted rule of construction, always be construed to be *shall*.[2]

6. FORM OF NEW BOND.—Should a new bond be required by the court, under either of the above sections, the condition of such new bond will require him to keep and to have kept and performed the condition of his former bond in all respects according to law, and in all respects perform and have performed his duty as administrator, according to law. Which bond shall have relation back to the time of granting letters of administration.[3]

7. TWO NEW BONDS MAY BE TAKEN.—If, instead of taking one bond, the administrator or executor elects to give two bonds, the aggregate amount of whose penalties equals that of the first bond, this will be a compliance with the law.[4]

8. RELEASE OF SECURITIES ON OLD BOND.—The execution and approval of a new bond as required in the foregoing section of the statute, (Sec. 33) operates as a release of the securities upon the old bond from all liability for past as well as for the subsequent acts of the principal.[5]

(1) Hurd's R. S., Chap. 3, § 33.
(2) Glinwater vs. M. & A. Railroad Co., 13 Ill., 1; Ladd vs. Griswold et al., 4 Gilman, 25; Malcom vs. Rogers, 5 Cowan, 188.
(3) Hurd's R. S., Chap. 3, § 34.
(4) People vs. Lott et al., 27 Ill., 215.
(5) *Id;* Pinkstaff et al. vs. People, 59 Ill., 148.

9. DOES NOT RELEASE OLD BOND.—A bond given by an executor or administrator, under section 32 above given, upon a requirement originating with the court, does not discharge the securities upon the former bond.(¹)

10. REMOVAL FOR FAILURE TO COMPLY.—If such executor or administrator shall fail to comply with such order within the time fixed by the court, the court shall order that such executor or administrator be removed from his office, and shall appoint some other fit person as administrator, with the will annexed, or *de bonis non*, who shall give a bond as required by law. And in case of the failure of the former executor or administrator to settle his accounts and to pay over to the person so appointed all moneys, effects or choses in action in his hands by reason of his said office, then such successor shall proceed to collect the same by suit against such executor or administrator, or by suit upon his bond; and upon collection thereof such surety shall be discharged.(²)

11. DEATH OF SOLE EXECUTOR, ETC.—When a sole or surviving executor or administrator dies, without having fully administered the estate, if there is personal property not administered, or are debts due from the estate, or is anything remaining to be performed in the execution of the will, the county court shall grant letters of administration, with the will annexed, or otherwise, as the case may require, to some suitable person, to administer the estate of the deceased not already administered: *Provided*, that when there is still a surviving executor or administrator, he may proceed to administer the estate, unless otherwise provided.(³)

By the enactment of the above section, the legislature did not intend to confer upon the administrator with the will annexed, all the powers given to the executor by the will of the testator.(⁴)

12. DEATH OR DISQUALIFICATION OF EXECUTOR, ETC.—Where the letters of one of several executors or administrators is revoked, or one or more of the executors or administrators die or become disqualified, the court may join others in their place, and require additional bonds from the new administrator or administrators, or

(1) People vs. Curry, 59 Ill., 35.
(2) Hurd's R. S., Chap. 3, § 36; Branch vs. Rankin, 108 Ill., 444.
(3) Hurd's R. S. Chap. 3, § 37.
(4) Nicoll vs. Scott et al., 99 Ill., 536; Hall vs. Irwin, 2 Gil., 176.

the survivor or survivors, or such as shall not have their powers revoked, shall proceed to manage the estate. When the letters of all of them are revoked, or all of such executors or administrators die before final settlement and distribution of the estate, administration, with the will annexed or *de bonis non,* shall be granted to the person next entitled thereto.(¹)

13. JOINT AND SEVERAL BONDS.—When two or more persons are appointed executors or administrators of the same estate, the court may take a separate bond, with sureties, from each, or a joint bond, with sureties, from all.(²)

14. BONDS FILED WITH COUNTY CLERK OR CLERK OF COUNTY COURT—JUDGE TO EXAMINE, ETC.—It shall be the duty of the judge of the county court of each county, at the terms of said court to be held in the months of January and July of each year, on the first day of the term, in open court, to examine and inquire into the sufficiency of all official bonds required by law to be filed in the office of the county clerk, or of the clerk of the county court, including bonds of executors, administrators, guardians and conservators.(³)

15. RECORD TO BE MADE.—It shall be the duty of the said judges to cause to be entered upon the records of their respective courts, at the times hereinbefore prescribed for the making of such examinations, that an examination and inquiry into the sufficiency of the official bonds within their cognizance has been made, and that they are severally deemed sufficient, or insufficient, as the facts may justify.(⁴)

16. SUMMONS TO SHOW CAUSE.—If, upon any examination by either of said judges, he is of opinion that for any reason the bond of any officer is insufficient, he shall cause to be issued from his court a summons to such officer to appear before said court on a day fixed therein, to show cause why he should not be required to give a new bond with sufficient surety.(⁵)

17. WHEN NEW BOND TO BE REQUIRED.—Unless it is shown to the court that such bond is insufficient, the court should require a new bond to be given with sufficient sureties, within such time as the court may direct, not to exceed thirty days.(⁶)

(1) Hurd's R. S., Chap. 3, ?? 38; Branch vs. Rankin, 108 Ill., 444.
(2) Hurd's R. S., Chap. 3, ? 24.   (5) Hurd's R. S., Chap. 103, ? 7.
(3) Hurd's R. S., Chap. 103, ? 4.   (6) Hurd's R. S., Chap. 103, ? 8.
(4) Hurd's R. S., Chap. 103, ? 5.

18. FAILURE TO GIVE.—A failure to comply with any order of the court requiring a new bond, works a removal of such executor or administrator from his office.(¹)

19. LIABILITY UNDER BONDS.—All bonds which may at any time be given by any executor or administrator, either with or without the will annexed, or *de bonis non*, to collect, or public administrator, may be put in suit and prosecuted against all or any one or more of the obligors named therein, in the name of the People of the State of Illinois, for the use of any person who may have been injured by reason of the neglect or improper conduct of any such executor or administrator, and such bonds shall not become void on the first recovery thereon, but may be sued upon, from time to time, until the whole penalty shall be recovered: *Provided*, that the person for whose use the same is prosecuted, shall be liable for all costs which may accrue in the prosecution of the same, in case the plaintiffs fail in their suit; and certified copies of all such bonds, under the seal of the clerk of the county court, shall be received as evidence to authorize such recovery in any court of law or equity of competent jurisdiction.(²)

20. A bond not signed by the administrator is not binding on the sureties.(³)

21. DEVASTAVIT.—A *devastavit* is a mismanagement and waste by an executor or administrator of the estate and effects trusted to him, as such, by which a loss occurs—such as the selling, embezzling or conversion to his own use by the executor or administrator, of the moneys or goods of the estate. The payment of claims not owing by the estate, or the payment of claims out of their order, or paying legacies before debts, are each recognized as instances of a *devastavit*. The selling of goods at private sale at inadequate prices, suffering the effects of the estate to become wasted, and the neglect to collect a debt due the estate, whereby it is lost, are each recognized by the common law as a *devastavit*. The law requires of these officers, as of all who act in a fiduciary character, due diligence, the want of which and consequent loss to those interested

(1) Hurd's R. S., Chap. 103, § 9.
(2) Hurd's R. S., Chap. 3, § 25; People vs. Randolph, 24 Ill., 324; People vs. Summers, 16 Ill., 173.
(3) Wood vs. Washburne, 2 Pick., 24.

in the estate, is punished by making them responsible for the losses which may be sustained; when, therefore, an administrator or executor has been guilty of a *devastavit*, he is required to make up the loss out of his own estate.([1])

At common law, in order to charge the sureties on an administrators' bond, it was first necessary to establish a *devastavit*.([2]) In Illinois it is provided that in order to a recovery upon the bonds of administrators or executors, it shall not be necessary to establish a *devastavit* against the principal; but whenever such administrator or executor has violated any condition in his bond, the sureties become liable to answer for the damages.([3])

22. FOR TAKING INSOLVENT SECURITY.—Where an administrator, on sale of personal property belonging to the estate, received the notes of the purchaser with security, and it resulted that the principals and sureties were insolvent, this will show *prima facie*, that the administrator had neglected his duty, and was guilty of a *devastavit*.([4])

If an administrator neglects to take good security, or if he takes as sureties those who live beyond the jurisdiction of the courts of this state, and a loss thereby occurs, he will become liable.([5])

23. FOR RELEASING A DEBT.—If an administrator or executor compounds or releases a debt, he is responsible at law for the whole amount which was due.([6])

24. FOR REMOVAL OF PROPERTY WITHOUT THE STATE.—The statute([7]) forbids the removal beyond this state, by an executor or administrator, of any property of his testator or intestate, wherewith he is charged, and authorizes the summary removal of the offender and a suit upon his bond, as a penalty for such removal.

25. UNTRUE ACCOUNT.—If an administrator exhibits an untrue account of the personal estate to the court, and so fraudulently obtains a sale of the real estate, he must not only account for the

---

(1) Bouvier's Law Dictionary, Vol. 1, p. 417; Curry vs. People, 54 Ill., 263; Estate of Corrington, 124 Ill., 363.
(2) Biggs vs. Postlewait, Breese, 154.
(3) Hurd's R. S., Chap. 103, § 13; Tucker vs. People, 87 Ill., 76.
(4) Curry et al. vs. People, *supra*.
(5) Roberts vs. Adams, 2 S. C., 337; King vs. King, 3 Johns., Ch. 552; Orcutt vs. Orms, 3 Paige, 459.
(6) DeDiemar vs. Van Wagenen, 7 Johns., 404; 1 Dane's Ab., 590.
(7) Hurd's R. S., Chap. 3, § 85.

personal property omitted in the account, but for the value of the real estate at the time of bill filed.(¹)

26. FAILURE TO FILE INVENTORY WITHIN THREE MONTHS.—An administrator failing to file an inventory as provided by law(²) within three months from the date of letters, he becomes liable in a suit on his bond, alleging such failure as one of the breaches; but to recover more than nominal damages, the plaintiff must allege and prove substantial injury.(³) In such a suit, evidence tending to prove any particular failure on the part of the administrator to perform the duty imposed upon him by the law, is inadmissible, unless the declaration contains a breach averring such neglect of duty.(⁴)

27. FOR SUFFERING JUDGMENT ON CLAIM BARRED.—It is the duty of an administrator to interpose the statute of limitations and all known defenses to claims presented against the estate in his charge;(⁵) and failing to do so, he is liable upon his bond.(⁶)

28. WHERE ADMINISTRATOR FAILS TO ACCOUNT FOR A DEBT DUE FROM HIMSELF TO DECEASED.—Where a debtor of the deceased becomes administrator or executor of such decedent, his debt is considered paid, and from that time becomes assets in the hands of the administrator or executor, for the proper application of which the securities on the bond become liable;(⁷) and a subsequent removal of such administrator or executor, and the appointment of an administrator *de bonis non* will not revive the debt so as to enable the maintenance of a suit on the original cause of action.(⁸)*

(1) Hart vs. Ten Eyck, 2 Johns., Ch. 62.
(2) Hurd's R. S., Chap. 3, § 51.
(3) People vs. Hunter et al., 89 Ill., 392.
(4) *Id.*
(5) McCoy vs. Morrow, 18 Ill., 519; Unknown Heirs of Langworthy vs. Baker, 23 Ill., 484; Dawes vs. Shed, 15 Mass., 6.
(6) Gold et al. vs. Bailey, 44 Ill., 491.
(7) Bigelow vs. Bigelow, 4 Ohio, 138; Winship vs. Bass, 12 Mass., 198: King vs. Green, 2 Stewart, 133; 1 Dane's Ab., 562; Beall vs. Hilliary, 1 Md., 186.
(8) Hall vs. Pratt, 5 Ohio, 72.

*NOTE.—An Iowa decision, rendered in 1869, denounces the above rule as "arbitrary, unjust in its effects, and unsupported by reason, and ought certainly to be received with little favor by the courts of the present day."(1) The decision further holds the rule to be, that the liability of the executor is not released or discharged, but the debt is, in his hands, general assets of the estate, for the benefit of creditors, legatees, and all other parties interested, upon which a subsequent administrator coming into possession of the evidence of the debt, may maintain a suit. The court cites authorities (2) in support of its position, but the rule laid down in *Bigelow vs. Bigelow, supra.*, seems to be the better rule.

(1) Kaster vs. Pearson, 27 Iowa, 90.
(2) Stevens vs. Gaylord, 11 Mass., 256; Winship vs. Bass et al., 12 Id., 202; Pusey vs. Clemson, 9 Serg., and Rawle, 208; Leland vs. Felton, 1 Allen, 531; Eichelberger vs. Morris, 6 Watts, 43; Hall vs. Pratt, 5 Hammond, 72; Gardner vs. Hyer, 19 Johnson, 187; Charles vs. Jacobs, 9 Richardson, (S. C.), 295; see American Probate Reports, 85, for brief.

29. For money recovered for causing death.—Where money is paid into the hands of an administrator in settlement of a claim made by the administrator for negligently causing the death of his intestate, under the statute,([1]) such money becomes assets in the hands of the administrator, to be distributed according to law among the widow and next of kin, and sureties must respond for any failure to so distribute such money.([2])

30. One administrator liable for co-administrator.— One of several administrators is liable for the acts done by either while the relation continues; but this liability ceases to attach to such of them as are removed from office, for all acts done after the removal.([3]) The administrator is liable, if at all, as principal, and not as surety for his co-administrator.([4]) But in no case is one liable for the torts or waste of the other.([5])

31. Liability as trustee or executor.—Where executors are made trustees of a fund arising from the estate, and have received the fund in contemplation of law as trustees, it is demandable from them only in that capacity.([6]) As trustees over real estate, although made so by the will of a deceased person, they are not within the power of the probate court, but of a court of chancery. Where, however, the accounts of such trustees have been received and adjusted in the court of probate, the court of chancery will adopt such action, provided it appears that the rights of infant parties have been properly protected.([7])

32. Extent of liability.—Where the administrator of an estate dies, and his surety on his bond succeeds him, and he is sued as such surety on the bond, he will be liable in such suit only for the acts of the deceased administrator, and not for moneys that came into his hands as such successor.([8])

33. Administrator must use diligence.—If an administrator, when acting for the estate, uses proper diligence, and acts

(1) Hurd's R. S., Chap. 70, § 1.
(2) Goltra et al. vs. People, 53 Ill., 224, Perry vs. Carmichael, 95 Ill., 519.
(3) Marsh et al. vs. People, 15 Ill., 284; McKim vs. Aulbach, 130 Mass., 481.
(4) *Id.* Crofts vs. Williams, 88 N. Y., 384.
(5) Brazier vs. Clark, 5 Pick., 96; see 2 Probate Reports, 256.
(6) Jacobs vs. Bull, 1 Watts, 370.
(7) McSorley vs. McSorley, 4 Sand., Ch. 414.
(8) People vs. Allen, 86 Ill., 167.

with ordinary care and circumspection in the discharge of his trust, he should not be held answerable for losses which could not have been foreseen, and which ordinary precaution might not guard against. The general principle which seems to run through all the authorities as to his liability, recognizes the doctrine that if he acts in good faith, honestly and prudently, though there be a loss to, and a diminution of, the estate, he will not be liable.([1]) Where money belonging to an estate was stolen by burglars from the safe of the administrator, the court, upon being satisfied that the administrator had been guilty of no want of due care, held, that he should be discharged as to the money so lost.([2]) Where a testator had trusted a banker, and at the time of his death had stocks deposited with him, which the executor afterwards allowed to remain with him on deposit, and which stocks were lost on account of the subsequent insolvency of the banker, it was held that the executor should not be chargeable on account of such loss.[3]

The deposit of funds in the name of the administrator in a bank outside of the state is illegal, and loss, if any, falls on him.([4])

On the other hand, if an administrator fails to make use of that degree of diligence in collecting and caring for the assets of the estate, which a reasonably prudent man would exercise in the care and management of his own affairs, and loss to the estate thereby occurs, he will be held to make good such loss.([5])

Where an administrator held money belonging to the estate long after he should have reported it to the court and distributed it, and until the banker holding it as a deposit had failed and gone into bankruptcy, he cannot charge such loss to the estate, although the credit of the bank was good at the time of the deposit.([6])

34. REDEEM MORTGAGED LANDS.—Where the real estate of the intestate is mortgaged, or has been sold under execution, the administrator, if he have assets sufficient in his hands to effect a redemption thereof, or if he could have raised money upon the assets of the estate, should redeem from such mortgage, and failing

(1) Christy et al. vs. McBride, 1 Scam., 75; Rowan vs. Kirkpatrick, 14 Ill., 1; Thompson vs. Brown, 4 Johns., Ch., 619.
(2) Stevens vs. Gage, 55 New Hampshire, 175; Furman vs. Coe, 1 Cai. C. 96; Raynor vs. Pearsall, 3 Johns., Ch., 578.
(3) Rowth vs. Howell, 3 Ves., 565; McCabe vs. Fowler, 84 N. Y., 314; see 2 Probate Reports, 130, for brief: Spaulding vs. Wakefield, 53 Vt., 660.
(4) Harward vs. Robinson, 14 Ill. Ap., 560.
(5) Whitney et al. vs. Peddecord et al., 63 Ill., 249; McElheney vs. Musick, *Id.* 328; see 75 Am. Dec., 799, for brief.
(6) Rucker vs. Redmon, 67 Ill., 187; Williams vs. Williams, 55 Wis., 300.

to do so, becomes liable to those interested who may suffer loss.(¹)

35. FOR FAILURE TO PAY OVER.—The statute also provides, that if any executor or administrator shall fail or refuse to pay over any moneys or dividend to any person entitled thereto, in pursuance of the order of the county court lawfully made, within thirty days after demand made, such failure or refusal shall be deemed a *devastavit*, and an action upon such executor's or administrator's bond, and against his securities, may be forthwith instituted and maintained, and such failure to pay, shall be a sufficient breach to authorize a recovery thereon.(²)

Since the adoption of these provisions, waiving the requirement of the common law, it is no longer necessary to aver and prove a technical *devastavit*, but, after reciting the appointment, the execution of the bond and the condition thereof, the pleader may assign such breaches of the condition of the bond as the nature of his case will admit.(³)

Under the authority of Section 114 above quoted, it has been held that an order of the county court directing an administrator to pay over money in his hands to the heir or to the administrator *de bonis non*, the court at the time having jurisdiction of the person of the administrator, is conclusive upon the sureties upon the bond in a suit to recover against them for a failure of the administrator to comply with such order, and may not be questioned.(⁴) No reason is perceived why this rule should not apply to all orders made upon administrators and executors to pay money in their hands to claimants, legatees, &c. By the terms of the condition of the bond, the sureties undertake that the administrator "shall deliver and pay unto such person or persons respectively, as may be legally entitled thereunto," whatever property or money "shall be found remaining upon the account of the said administrator, the same being first examined and allowed by the court."(⁵)

36. DEMAND.—As a general rule, a demand for the payment of any sum claimed from the administrator as such, is necessary

---

(1) McCreedy vs. Mier et al., 64 Ill., 495; Hurd's R. S., Chap. 77, § 18; Evartson vs. Tappan, 5 Johns., Ch. 497; *contra*, Stiger vs. Bent, 111 Ill. 336.
(2) Hurd's R. S., Chap. 3, § 114.
(3) Hurd's R. S. Chap. 110, § 21.
(4) Ralston et al. vs Wood, 15 Ill., 159; People vs. Housh, 66 Ill., 178; see 58 Am. Dec., for brief of authorities.
(5) Hurd's R. S., Chap. 3, § 23; State vs. Holt, 27 Mo., 340.

before bringing suit;(¹) but where the administrator is dead,(²) or has removed from the state,(³) a demand being impossible or impracticable, need not be averred.

37. SUIT AGAINST PART OF THE OBLIGORS.—Suit may be maintained against a portion or all of the obligors upon the bond of an administrator or executor, at the option of the plaintiff, and it is no irregularity or error to omit joining all,(⁴) as in ordinary suits upon contracts.

38. LIABILITY OF SURETIES.—The sureties on the bond of an administrator or executor, are liable only to the extent of such assets as properly belong to the estate, which came to the hands of the principal, or might have come to his hands, by the exercise of proper vigilance; so, where funds come to his hands which are not legal assets, though he charges himself with them, his sureties are not liable for their loss.(⁵)

39. VOLUNTARY BOND.—Any obligation entered into voluntarily and for good consideration is valid at common law, unless it contravenes the policy of the law, or is repugnant to some provision of the statute. So, where a bond was entered into informally, by which one received the appointment of administrator and the custody of property, neither he nor his securities could plead such informalities as a defense.(⁶)

40. SURETY NOT IN FIDUCIARY RELATION.—A surety occupies no fiduciary relation to the estate, and may buy up claims against it at a discount for his own advantage.(⁷)

41. BOND OF FORMER EXECUTOR, ETC.—LIABILITY.—In all cases where any such executor or administrator shall have his letters revoked, he shall be liable on his bond to such subsequent administrator, or to any other person aggrieved, for any mismanagement of the estate committed to his care; and the subsequent administrator may have and maintain actions against such former executor or administrator for all such goods, chattels, debts and credits as shall

(1) Bedell vs. Janney, 4 Gilm., 193.
(2) People vs. Admire, 39 Ill., 251.
(3) County of Warren vs. Jeffrey, 18 Ill., 329.
(4) People vs. Miller et al., 1 Scam., 85; Hurd's R. S., Chap. 3, § 25; Curry vs. People, 54 Ill., 263.
(5) Shields vs. Smith, 8 Bush., (Ky.) 601.
(6) Pritchett et al. vs. People, 1 Gil., 525.
(7) Halstead vs. Hyman, 3 Brad., 426.

have come to his possession, and which are withheld or have been wasted, embezzled or misapplied, and no satisfaction made for the same.([1])

At the common law no action could be maintained by an administrator *de bonis non* against a former administrator or executor, nor his legal representatives, for an account for any part of the estate sold, converted or wasted. Such goods as remained in specie, and debts due to the testator or intestate, alone came to the hands of the administrator *de bonis non*. The right of action for money converted or wasted by the former administrator or executor, was in the creditor or heir of the deceased.([2]) In *Rowan* vs. *Kirkpatrick*,([3]) and in *Newhall* vs. *Turney*,([4]) where the right of the administrator *de bonis non* to recover from the legal representatives of the former administrator, for assets of the estate converted by him in his lifetime was involved, the court decided, without discriminating between cases where the administrator was removed by the court, and where he died, that in no case could the administrator *de bonis non* recover from a prior administrator or his representatives, assets converted by him. In *Marsh et al.* vs. *People*,([5]) the court, citing the above section of the statute, say that it changes the common law so far as to permit the administrator *de bonis non* to recover the assets of the estate from a former administrator, where he had been removed by order of the court, leaving the common law in force so far as it applies to deceased administrators and their legal representatives. The same court in *Stose* vs. *People*,([6]) and in *McCreary* vs. *Newberry*,([7]) ignoring the above statute, and the decision in *Marsh* vs. *People*, *supra*, held the common law above quoted still in force. The case of *Stose* vs. *People*, was specially overruled in *Duffin et al.* vs. *People*,([8]) citing the case of *Marsh et al.* vs. *People*, and the distinction made between cases where the administrator dies, and where he resigns. ([9])

(1) Hurd's R. S., Chap. 3, § 39.
(2) 4 Bacon's Abridgement, 24; Slaughter vs. Froman, 5 T. B. Monroe, 19; Chamberlain vs. Bates, 2 Porter, (Ala.), 550; Potts vs. Smith, 3 Rawle, 361; Stubblefield vs. McRaven, 5 Smedes & M., 130; Kelley vs. Kelley, 9 Ala., 908.
(3) 14 Ill., 1.
(4) 14 Ill., 339.
(5) 15 Ill., 284.
(6) 25 Ill., 600.
(7) 25 Ill., 496.
8 Ill 1 .

It may now be said, that upon the revocation of letters and the appointment of an administrator *de bonis non*, the law requires the former administrator or executor to fully account to the court, and place the new administrator in possession of all assets of whatever nature remaining in his hands, belonging to the estate, and upon his failure to do so, after demand and the expiration of thirty days, suit may be maintained upon his bond.

An administrator *de bonis non* may maintain an action in his own name as such on notes executed to a former administrator as such, and which have come to the hands of the administrator *de bonis non* as assets of the estate.(¹)

As it has been held, that the acceptance by the court of the resignation of an administrator, is equivalent to a removal,(²) the same rule would apply to cases of resignation followed by the appointment of a successor. But in cases where the executor or administrator dies, the administrator *de bonis non* can only recover such assets as have not been reduced to money, while the unpaid creditor, legatee or heir, may call upon the legal representatives of the deceased executor or administrator for an account of such assets as have been reduced to money or converted.

42. SECURITY FOR COSTS.—That in all actions in any court of record on official bonds for the use of any person, actions on the bonds of executors, administrators or guardians, *qui tam* actions, actions on a penal statute, and in all cases in law or equity, where the plaintiff, or person for whose use an action is to be commenced, shall not be a resident of this state, the plaintiff, or person for whose use the action is to be commenced, shall, before he institutes such suit, file, or cause to be filed, with the clerk of the court in which the action is to be commenced, security for costs, substantially in the following form:

A B, *vs.* C D—(Title of Court.)

I, (E F,) do enter myself security for all costs which may accrue in the above cause.

Dated this...day of..., A. D. 18... (Signed) E F.

Such instrument shall be signed(³) by some responsible person, being a resident of this state, to be approved by the clerk, and shall bind such person to pay all costs which may accrue in such action, either to the opposite party or to any of the officers of the court in

(1) Maraman vs. Trunnell, 3 Metcalf, 146.
(2) Marsh et al vs. People, 15 Ill., 284.
(3) Hurd's R. S., Chap. 33, § 1.

which the action is commenced, or to which it is removed by change of venue or appeal.(¹)

If any such action shall be commenced without filing such instrument of writing, the court, on motion, shall dismiss the same, and the attorney of the plaintiff shall pay all costs accruing thereon, unless the security for costs shall be filed within such time as shall be allowed by the court, and when so filed, it shall relate back to the commencement of the suit; the right to require security for costs shall not be waived by any proceeding in the cause.(²)

Any person who may have been injured by reason of the negligence or improper conduct of the administrator, may sue upon the bond in the name of the People of the State of Illinois for his use, and one recovery will not bar a future suit by any other person who has suffered injury; but he may maintain his suit, and so on, until the entire penalty of the bond shall have been recovered,(³) when a plea of such recovery would bar future suits.

To entitle an injured creditor to maintain a suit on such a bond, his claim must have been allowed in some court of competent jurisdiction, and it need not be in a court of probate.(⁴)

43. IRREGULARITIES IN DRAFTING BONDS.—The omission of the names of the sureties from the blanks left for them in the body of the bond, will not invalidate it as to such sureties,(⁵) nor will any mistake therein apparent on its face, vitiate such bond.(⁶)

44. REVOCATION OF LETTERS.—Where the letters of an executor or administrator are revoked by the court, the sureties are released from all future, but not the past liabilities.(⁷)

45. WHERE THERE ARE TWO ADMINISTRATORS.—Where a joint bond is given by two administrators, the sureties are not liable to one administrator for property of the estate converted by the other.(⁸)

46. ACTING IN TWO CAPACITIES.—Where the same person acts as administrator of an estate, and at the same time as executor or guardian of the deceased heir or distributee, after the debts and liabilities of the estate have been settled, or the expiration of the two years allowed for administration, he will be regarded as hold-

(1) Hurd's R. S., Chap. 33, § 2.
(2) Hurd's R. S., Chap. 33, § 3.
(3) Hurd's R. S., Chap. 3, § 25; People vs. Randolph et al., 24 Ill., 324.
(4) People vs. Allen, 8 Ill. Ap., 17.
(5) Neil vs. Morgan et al., 28 Ill., 524.
(6) Moore vs. Chapman, 2 Stewart, 466.
P   le vs. Lott et al, 2 Ill

ing the excess in his capacity of executor or guardian of the distributee, although he may not have rendered his final account as administrator, and the order of distribution was never made. In such a case, the sureties upon his bond as administrator, are discharged from their liability,([1]) and the sureties upon his bond as guardian, become liable for a waste or diminution of the fund.([2])

47. WILL BEING SET ASIDE.—Where by a decree of the circuit court, the will of a deceased person was set aside, and the administrator with the will annexed, was directed by the decree to administer the property as intestate property, such proceedings will not operate to discharge the securities on the bond, if the administrator continues to act as such.([3])

48. RIGHT OF SURETIES TO APPEAL.—Sureties upon the bonds of administrators and executors, may appeal from any order of the county court which may ultimately effect their liability, in the same manner that the principal may do.([4])

49. STATUTE OF LIMITATIONS.—Where an administrator suffers a judgment on a claim due from his decedent, barred by the statute of limitations, to be rendered against him, and suit is brought by the owner of such judgment against the bond of such administrator, the securities thereon may insist upon the defense the administrator might have made.([5])

50. RELATION CHANGES.—After the settlement of the accounts of an executor or administrator, and an order of distribution, the fiduciary capacity of the officer ceases, and the statute of limitation begins to run,([6]) but not until then.([7])

51. ESTOPPEL.—One who has signed the bond of an executor or administrator, containing a clause reciting such an official character, is estopped from denying the appointment to and acceptance of the office.([8]) So, both the principal and sureties, in an administrator's bond, are estopped from denying the jurisdiction of the court to grant the letters.([9])

(1) Weir vs. People, 78 Ill., 192; Bell et al. vs. People, 94 Ill., 230.
(2) Carroll vs. Bosley, 6 Yerger, 220; See other authorities in note on page 461, 27 Am. Dec.; State vs. Hearst, 12 Mo., 365.
(3) Bell et al. vs. People, *supra.*
(4) Rawlston vs. Wood, 15 Ill., 159.
(5) Dawes vs. Shed, 15 Mass., 6.
(6) App vs. Dreisbach, 2 Rawle, 287.
(7) Bonham vs. The People, 102 Ill., 439.
(8) Arnott et al. vs. Friel, 50 Ill., 174; Smith vs Whittaker, 11 Ill., 417.
(9) People vs. Falconer, 2 Sand., 81.

52. JURISDICTION OF CHANCERY.—Where administrators have given several bonds, and there is a complication of interests, resulting from the death of one of the administrators and of some of the sureties, whose legal representatives cannot be made parties in a joint action at law upon the bonds, a court of equity will entertain jurisdiction at the suit of any party interested. In such a case, all the securities on all bonds or their representatives if deceased, should be made parties, and upon a final hearing, if anything in the nature of damages be found due the complainant, the same should be apportioned for payment among the different classes of sureties, as would appear equitable and just.(1) The section of the statute, (Sec. 25, Chap. 3,) giving an action against all or any of the obligors, has reference only to actions at law.(2)

If an administrator makes fictitious reports to the county court, falsely charging himself with money not in fact due from him, for the fraudulent purpose of making his surety liable, a court of equity would, doubtless, interfere at the suit of the surety on the bond, to correct such reports, and make them conform to the truth as to the amount of money actually owing by the principal.(3)

53. FORM OF JUDGMENT.—Where judgment for the plaintiff is rendered in a suit upon bonds ordinarily, the judgment should be for the full penalty of the bond, to be discharged by the payment of the damages and costs;(4) but it has been held, under the peculiar wording of our statute, giving a right of action upon bonds of administrators to any person injured, that this technicality of the common law practice is done away with, and that judgment in debt may be rendered for the entire or a part only of the penalty, to be discharged upon the payment of the damages, or judgment may be rendered for the damages only as in assumpsit.(5)

54. ACTION OF ACCOUNT MAY BE MAINTAINED.—The action of account may be maintained by and against executors and administrators, to recover legacies and debts due from the estate of the intestate.(6)

---

(1) People vs. Lott et al., 27 Ill., 215.
(2) Id.
(3) Fogarty et al. vs. Ream et al., 100 Ill., 366.
(4) Eggleston et al. vs. Buck, 31 Ill., 254; 1 Chitty's Pleadings, 115.
(5) Pinkstaff et al. vs. People, 59 Ill., 148; People vs. Summers, 16 Ill., 173; People vs. Randolph et al., 24 Ill., 324.
(6) Hurd's R. S., Chap. 2, § 1.

CHAPTER IV.

DUTIES AND LIABILITIES OF EXECUTORS AND ADMINISTRATORS.

1. Duties prescribed by law.
2. Grant of letters relates back.
3. Duty of person named as executor in will.
4. Power before probate of will.
5. Administrator an officer.
6. Death of part of executors.
7. Power of one of several executors.
8. Power of administrator with the will annexed.
9. Succeeds to title to personalty.
10. Liable for such as by diligence may be received.
11. Courts to hold them liable for abuse of trust, but not upon slight grounds.
12. For loss by fire.
13. Should collect foreign debts.
14. Must not continue a partnership relation.
15. Power over real estate.
    a. How available.
    b. No power to put one in possession.
16. When ejectment may be maintained.
17. Rents.
18. Must redeem real estate.
19. Liability to third parties.
20. As garnishee.
21. Cannot loan the money of the estate.
22. Not liable for costs.
23. Acting as administrator and guardian.
24. Cannot bind heirs by his action.
25. Cannot buy an interest in the estate.
26. Good faith protects him.
27. May compound a suit for negligence.
28. Cannot be sued with another.
29. When not liable for interest.
30. Must account for profits.
31. May receive real estate on debts.
32. Contracts of decedent may be performed.
33. May assign note due deceased.
34. May sell personal property.

35. Liable for fraud.
36. Not chargeable for mistake.
37. Administrator to collect.
38. His powers.
39. Suits by him.
40. When his powers cease.
41. Administrator *de son tort*—liability.
42. One acting honestly with him.
43. Court no power to compel an account.
44. How he may discharge himself.
45. Widow not liable as administrator *de son tort.*
46. Title to property.
47. Suits between executors.

1. DUTIES PRESCRIBED BY LAW.—Those accepting the important duties incident to the settlement of estates, both testate and intestate, should not forget the governing fact, that they are in all cases to be controlled by the law; or, in case of testate estates, by the will of the deceased, so far as its provisions may go, and the law as applicable to the same. The wishes of friends of the deceased, the oral "request" of the deceased, and also the oral instructions of the probate judge himself, when improperly wrung from him by the importunities of executors and administrators seeking advice, are alike to be disregarded, except so far as they are justified by the provisions of the statute, for neither will justify a disregard of the plain provisions of the law.

2. GRANT OF LETTERS RELATES BACK.—The grant of administration has relation to the death of the intestate, and it legalizes all intermediate acts of the administrator.[1]

3. DUTY OF PERSON NAMED AS EXECUTOR.—It shall be the duty of any person knowing that he is named or appointed as the executor of the last will and testament of any person deceased, within thirty days next after the decease of the testator, to cause such will to be proved and recorded in the proper county; or to present the will and declare his refusal to accept of the executorship; and every such executor neglecting so to do, without just excuse for such delay, shall forfeit the sum of twenty dollars per month from and after the expiration of said term of thirty days, until he shall cause probate of said will to be made, or present the same as aforesaid, to be recovered by action of debt, for the use of the estate,

(1) Vroom vs. Van Horne, 10 Paige, 549; Rattoon vs. Overacker, 8 johns., 126; Priest vs. Watkins, 2 Hill, 225; Matter of Faulkner, 7 Hill, 181; see 51 Am. Dec., 523, for brief; McClure vs. People, 19 Ill. Ap., 105.

by any person who will sue for the same in any court having jurisdiction thereof.(¹)

4. POWER OF EXECUTOR BEFORE PROBATE OF WILL.—The power of the executor over the testator's estate, before probate of the will and obtaining letters testamentary, shall extend to the burial of the deceased, the payment of necessary funeral charges, and the taking care of the estate; but in all such cases, if the will is rejected when presented for probate, and such executor thereby never qualifies, he shall not be liable as an executor of his own wrong, unless upon refusal to deliver up the estate to the person authorized to receive the same: *Provided*, that this section shall not be construed to exempt any person claiming to be executor as aforesaid, for any waste or misapplication of such estate.(²)

5. ADMINISTRATOR AN OFFICER.—An administrator is a mere officer of the law; his title relates back to the death of the intestate, and cannot be affected by any acts of his own prior to his appointment.(³) But, while it is true, that executors and administrators are officers of the law, they are not such in the sense that the *de facto* principle applies to their official character, and protects those doing business with them to the same extent as the official acts of *de facto* public officers are protected. Where there is an utter want of jurisdiction in the court appointing them, their *de facto* character will not give efficiency to their acts.(⁴)

6. DEATH, ETC., OF PART OF EXECUTORS.—Where two or more executors are appointed in and by the same will, and one or more of them dies, refuses to take upon himself the executorship, or is otherwise disqualified, letters testamentary shall be granted thereon to the other person or persons so named, not renouncing as aforesaid, and not disqualified.(⁵)

7. POWER OF ONE OF SEVERAL EXECUTORS.—At the common law, where one of two executors named in a will as trustees or merely as executors of the will, died or refused to act, the remaining executor might not execute alone the powers given by the will. By the

(1) Hurd's R. S., Chap. 3 § 2.
(2) Hurd's R. S., Chap. 3, § 4.
(3) Gilkey vs Hamilton, 22 Mich., 283.
(4) Rodrigas vs. East River Savings Institution, 76 N. Y., 316.
(5) Hurd's R. S., Chap. 3, § 5; Shaw vs. Berry, 35 Me., 279; Jennings vs. Teague, 14 S. C., 229; Hodgin vs. Toler, 70 Iowa, 21.

act of 21, Henry VIII., where lands are devised to be sold by executors, and part of them refuse, those who qualify may sell; and by Sec. 93, of Chap. 109, Revised Statutes of 1845, (*Sec.* 96, *supra*) where a part of the executors die, the survivor or survivors, may execute the power bestowed by the will. Under the authority of these statutes, the English statute having been adopted in this state, it has been held that, where one of two or more executors named in a will refuses to act or dies, the remaining executor may make conveyances, authorized in the will, and otherwise execute the will of the testator.([1])

In order to sustain a conveyance made under a will, by one of two persons nominated in the will as executors or trustees, it must be shown that those not joining, have refused to accept the trust and qualify as executors; or that they were deceased at the time of the execution of the conveyance; and a recitation in the record of the court granting letters, that one of those nominated by the will declined to act, was held insufficient to prove the fact. The proof of refusal or death, should be satisfactory and conclusive.([2]) In the matter of the personal estate, one of two executors or administrators may sell or transfer, acting alone, and the act of one is the act of both.([3]) Where a portion of the estate of a testator was intestate estate by reason of not being disposed of by the will, it was held that the executor should administer thereon *ex officio*.([4])

8. POWER OF AN ADMINISTRATOR WITH THE WILL ANNEXED.— Where a testator by his will invests his executor with power to convey the real estate of the testator for any purpose, the power is a personal trust, and cannot be executed by an administrator with the will annexed, either at common law or under the statutes of this state. In such a case, should the person named in the will as executor or trustee, refuse to accept and perform the trust, or die, not having performed it, a court of equity may be resorted to, for the appointment of a trustee.([5]) In such a case, the administrator,

---

(1) Clinefelter vs. Ayers, 16 Ill., 329; Pahlman vs. Smith, 23 Ill., 448; Wardwell vs. McDowell et al., 31 Ill., 364; Wisdom et al. vs. Becker, 52 Ill., 342.
(2) Clinefelter vs. Ayers, *supra*.
(3) Wheeler vs. Wheeler, 9 Cow., 34; Hertell vs. Bogert, 9 Paige, 52.
(4) Hays et al. vs. Jackson, 6 Mass., 149; 1 Dane's Ab., 579.
(5) Hall vs. Irwin, 2 Gill, 176; Lockwood vs. Stradley, 1 Delaware Ch., 298; Nicoll vs. Scott, 99 Ill., 529.

with the will annexed, has such an interest in the execution of the will, as to be heard in a court of equity, upon application for the appointment of a trustee, empowered to make the conveyances provided for in the will.(¹)

9. SUCCEEDS TO THE TITLE TO PERSONALTY.—The administrator succeeds to the title to the personal estate, and the title takes effect by relation from the death of the intestate;(²) and the title remains in such administrator until there is an order of distribution.(³)

10. LIABLE FOR SUCH AS BY DILIGENCE MAY BE RECEIVED.—Executors and administrators shall be chargeable with so much of the estate of the decedent, personal or real, as they, after due and proper diligence, might or shall receive.(⁴)

In the prosecution and defense of claims, the administrator is deemed the full representative of the creditors of the estate.(⁵)

11. COURTS TO HOLD THEM LIABLE FOR ABUSE OF TRUST, BUT NOT UPON SLIGHT GROUNDS.—While care must be taken to guard against an abuse of their trusts by administrators, courts ought not to hold them personally liable upon slight grounds, lest suitable persons be deterred from undertaking these offices.(⁶)

12. FOR LOSS BY FIRE.—An administrator must be held to adopt such precautions against the loss of property by fire, as prudent men are, under similar circumstances, accustomed to exercise.(⁷)

13. FOREIGN DEBTS.—It is the duty of the personal representative appointed in this state, to endeavor to collect debts due from solvent persons in other states, by procuring himself, if necessary, or some proper person to be appointed administrator there; and where such a debt was lost by his refusal to take steps in the matter, he was held accountable for the amount.(8)

14. PARTNERSHIP.—If an administrator of a deceased partner, puts assets of the estate of his decedent into the hands of the surviving partner to trade with, he will be anwerable for the loss.(⁹)

(1) Wenner vs. Thornton et al., 98 Ill., 156.
(2) Makepeace vs. Moore, 5 Gill., 476; 1 Blackstone's Com., 510; 4 Bacon's Abridgement, 74; McLean Co. Coal Co. vs. Long. 91 Ill., 617.
(3) Neubricht vs. Santmeyer et al., 50 Ill.,75; Hickox vs. Frank,102 Ill.,660.
(4) Hurd's R. S., Chap. 3, ? 58 ; Christy et al., vs. McBride, 1 Scam., 75; Spaulding vs. Wakefield, 53 Vt., 660 ; People vs. Brooks, 123 Ill., 246.
(5) Kennedy vs. Shepley, 15 Mo., 640.
(6) Rowan vs. Kirkpatrick, 14 Ill., 1.
(7) Rubottom vs. Morrow's Admr., 24 Ind., 202.
(8) Shultz vs. Pulver, 3 Paige, 182.
(9) Thompson vs. Brown, 4 johns., Ch. 619.

15. POWER OVER REAL ESTATE.—The administrator of an intestate estate, as such, has no power over the real estate of his decedent, unless upon failure of the personal estate to pay the debts and liabilities of the estate.([1]) He is not bound to pay taxes thereon, which, having accrued after the death of the decedent are, therefore, not a lien upon the personal estate in his hands;([2]) it would, however, seem to be a proper exercise of the discretion of the court, to permit the payment of taxes accruing after death, where it is apparent that by reason of a failure of the personal estate, such real estate must be relied upon to furnish the means for paying the residue of debts and liabilities after the exhaustion of the personal estate, otherwise such payment might be defeated.([3])*

a. To make such power available, he must proceed in the manner pointed out in the statute hereafter treated of, and has no power to make a binding private sale of the real estate of his decedent, in contemplation of an order of the court authorizing the sale. Such a sale would be void.([4]) But he may be bound personally.([5]) The estate cannot be estopped by his conduct.([6])

b. Nor has the administrator any power to deal with the possession of the land sold by him, and a party taking possession of such land by consent of the administrator cannot be considered as put in possession by any one authorized to do so. Such an act by the administrator is a violation of trust, from which no one privy thereto can take any benefit.([7]) Nor can he mortgage the real estate.([8]

The administrator of a trustee under a trust deed, authorizing a sale by the trustee or his "legal representative," to pay the debt of

---

(1) Walker et al. vs. Diehl, 79 Ill., 473: Walbridge vs. Day et al., 31 Ill,, 379; Le Moyne et al. vs. Quimby et al., 70 Ill., 400; Harding vs. Le Moyne, 114 Ill., 65.
(2) Phelps vs. Funkhouser et al., 39 Ill.,401; Smith et al. vs. McConnell et al., 17 Ill., 135; Stone et al. vs. Wood, 16 Ill., 177; Walker et al. vs. Diehl, *supra*; Stark vs. Brown, 101 Ill., 396.
(3) Stillwell vs. Melrose, 15 Hun., 378, 381.
(4) Herrick vs. Grow, 5 Wend., 579; McDermed vs. McCartland, Hardin, 18; 1 Hilliard on Vendors, 62.
(5) *Ib.*; Whiteside vs. Jennings, 19 Ala., 784.
(6) Lewis vs. Lusk, 35 Miss., 696.
(7) Sebastian vs. Johnson, 72 Ill., 282.
(8) Smith vs. Hutchinson, 108 Ill., 662.

Be it enacted, &c., That when it shall appear to the county or probate court that it is for the interest of any estate being administered upon, that the taxes on the real estate of such estate should be paid out of any moneys on hand, the court may enter an order authorizing the executor or administrator of such estate to pay such taxes.—Hurd's R. S., Chap. 3, § 137.

the grantor, is not authorized thereby to make such sale, and a sale by such administrator will not bar the equity of redemption (¹)

16. MAY MAINTAIN EJECTMENT.—An executor or administrator of a tenant for a term of years may maintain ejectment where he has a right of entry.(²)

17. RENTS.—Nor has the administrator any control over rents upon the real estate accruing after the death of his decedent, such rents being chattels real, and descend to the heir.(³)

18. MUST REDEEM REAL ESTATE.—The administrator is, however, not entirely a stranger to the real estate of the deceased, even where not needed to pay debts and liabilities. The statute(⁴) authorizes him to redeem from sales under executions and decrees, and where he has money of the estate in his hands sufficient to enable him to do so, or can get money by reasonable exertion on his part, to redeem from such sales or from mortgages, and such redemptions will advance the interests of the estate in his care, he should do so.(⁵)

19. LIABILITY TO THIRD PARTIES.—Where an administrator or his agent, under color of acting for the estate, fraudulently injures a third party, the administrator will be personally liable to the party so injured;(⁶) but the estate represented by him will not be rendered liable by his torts (⁷)

20. AS GARNISHEE.—Until there has been an order of distribution to claimants or heirs, an administrator is not liable as the garnishee of one of those parties.(⁸) But not so of a legacy.(⁹)

21. CAN NOT LOAN MONEY OF ESTATE.—The money in the hands of an administrator, as such, should not be loaned; and if loaned, he is guilty of a *devastavit*.(¹⁰)

(1) Warnecke et al. vs. Lembca, 71 Ill., 91.
(2) 2 Archibold's Nisi Prius, 113.
(3) Green vs. Massie, 13 Ill., 363; Foltz vs. Prouse, 17 Ill., 487; Dixon vs. Nichols, 39 Ill., 372; Smith vs. McConnell, 17 Ill., 135; Sherman vs. Dutch, 16 Ill., 283; McCoy vs. Scott, 2 Rawle, 222.
(4) Hurd's R. S., Chap. 77, § 18.
(5) McCreedy vs. Mier et al., 64 Ill., 497; Evertson vs. Tappan, 5 Johns.. Ch. 497; *Contra*, Stiger vs. Bent, 111 Ill., 336; McNeil vs. McNeil, 36 Ala., 109.
(6) Hungate et al. vs. Reynolds, 72 Ill., 425.
(7) Plimpton vs. Richards, 59 Me., 115.
(8) Crownover vs. Bamburg et al., 2 Ill. Ap., 162; Bartell vs. Bauman, 12 Id., 450; Richard vs. Griggs, 16 Mo., 416.
(9) Shewell vs. Keen, 2 Wharton, 322.
(10) Thornton vs. Bradshaw, Breese, 13; Johnston vs. Maples et al. 49, Ill., 102; Wadsworth vs. Connell, 104 Ill., 370.

22. NOT LIABLE FOR COSTS.—An administrator is not personally liable for costs when prosecuting or defending a suit as such,([1]) although should he act *mala fide*, or be guilty of gross negligence, he may be made personally liable.([2])

23. ACTING IN TWO CAPACITIES.—One who, at the same time, acts as administrator and guardian of the heirs, has no right to apply the funds of one capacity to the interests of the other. Accounts for each should be kept carefully and separately.([3]) Where the same person is administrator and guardian of the heir, the balance upon final settlement of his account as administrator, shall be considered as in his hands as guardian.([4])

24. CAN NOT BIND THE HEIRS.—An administrator can not bind the heirs of an intestate of whose estate he is the representative, by any settlement he can make with another.([5]) Nor can he make the estate liable for his contracts in its behalf—he is personally liable for such undertakings ([6])

Where an administrator accepts a draft drawn on him as such, it does not bind the estate, although it may bind him.([7])

25. CAN NOT BUY AN INTEREST IN THE ESTATE.—An administrator, as such, has no power to buy a distributive share of the estate,([8]) nor to purchase interests in it of any kind.([9])

26. ACTS IN GOOD FAITH.—If an administrator settles a claim against a debtor in good faith, his action can not be called in question by a subsequent administrator,([10]) unless it should appear that the appointment of the first administrator was void.([11])

27. SUIT FOR NEGLIGENCE.—An administrator may compound

(1) Greenwood vs. Spiller, 2 Scam., 502; Dye vs. Noel et al., 85 Ill., 299.
(2) Burnap vs. Dennis, 3 Scam., 478; Russell vs. Hubbard et al., 59 Ill., 335; Colton vs. Field et al., 131 Ill., 398; Estate of Corrington, 124 Ill., 363.
(3) Stillman et al. vs. Young et al., 16 Ill., 318; Wadsworth vs. Connell, 104 Ill., 370.
(4) Seegar vs. The State, 6 Harris & Johnson, 162.
(5) Williams et al. vs. Wiggand et al., 53 Ill., 233.
(6) McEldery vs. McKenzie, 2 Porter (Ala.), 33; See also note on page 645, 27 Am. Dec.; Mason vs. Caldwell, 5 Gilm., 196; Fitzhugh vs. Fitzhugh, 11 Gratton, 300; Davis vs. French, 20 Me., 21, and note, 37 Am. Dec., 37.
(7) Wisdom vs. Becker, 52 Ill., 342.
(8) Wilcox vs. Smith, 26 Barb., 316.
(9) Baxter vs. Costin, 1 Busb., 262; 1 Hilliard on Vendors, 387.
(10) 2 Kent's Com., 505; Thompson vs. Brown, 4 Johns. Ch., 619; Short et al. vs. Johnson, 25 Ill., 489.
(11) Rodrigas vs. East River Savings Institution, 76 N. Y., 316; Bailey vs. Dilworth, 10 Smedes & M., 404.

a pending suit for negligently causing the death of his decedent, for a sum less than the maximum amount given by statute.(¹)

28. CAN NOT BE JOINED IN A SUIT WITH ANOTHER.—An administrator or executor can not be sued as such jointly with another person.²

29. NOT LIABLE FOR INTEREST.—Where, after the grant of administration upon the estate of a deceased person, the will of the deceased was offered for probate and allowed, after several years' litigation, and letters testamentary issued to the executor, and it appeared that the money of the estate, in the hands of the administrator, was always ready to be paid, whenever a proper person was appointed to receive it, the administrator was held not liable to pay interest on such sum,(³) although if he detains money belonging to his intestate unreasonably, he is liable for interest.(⁴)

30. MUST ACCOUNT FOR PROFITS.—An administrator, as to money in his hands as such, is a trustee of the same, and must be held amenable to the law governing such a relation; accordingly he should be required to account for all profits realized by him or interest received by loaning the money or otherwise. It is his duty to act for the best interest of the estate, and to discharge the debts of the estate with the smallest amount possible.(⁵) If he retains money unreasonably, he should be charged interest thereon.(⁶)

31. MAY RECEIVE REAL ESTATE.—An administrator may take real estate in payment of a debt due the intestate, and, failing to do so when offered him, he will become liable if the debt be lost thereby.(⁷)

When it is necessary, in order to secure the collection of a judgment or decree belonging to any estate, it shall be the duty of the executor or administrator to bid for, and become the purchaser of real estate, at the sale thereof by the sheriff, master in chancery, or other officer. The premises so purchased shall be assets in his

---

(1) Henchey vs. Chicago, 41 Ill., 136; Washington vs. L. & N. Ry. Co., 136 Ill., 51.
(2) Eggleston et al. vs. Buck, 31 Ill., 254.
(3) Meek vs. Allison et al., 67 Ill., 47.
(4) Hough vs. Harvey et al., 71 Ill., 72; Field et al. vs. Colton, 7 Ill. Ap., 379; Estate of Schofield, 99 Ill., 513; Troup vs. Rice, 55 Miss., 278.
(5) Wingate vs. Pool, 25 Ill., 118; Hough vs. Harvey, 71 Ill., 72; Rowan vs. Kirkpatrick, 14 Ill., 1; Van Horn vs. Fonda, 5 Johns. Ch., 388.
(6) Hough vs. Harvey et al., *supra.*
(7) Whitney et al. vs. Peddecord et al., 63 Ill., 249.

hands, and may be again sold by him, with the approval of the county court, and the moneys arising from such sale shall be accounted for and paid over as other moneys in his hands.([1])

32. CONTRACTS OF DECEDENT.—All contracts made by the decedent may be performed by the executor or administrator, when so directed by the county court.([2])

By the common law, the death of one party to an executory contract does not necessarily terminate it. If the thing to be performed, is of such a nature, that the personal representative of the deceased can fairly and sufficiently execute all that the deceased might have done, he may do so, and enforce the contract. When the contract is of a personal character, or requires in its execution, the exercise of peculiar taste or skill, the rule is otherwise. But when the administrator undertakes to perform the contract of his intestate, it is upon his own personal responsibility, and if losses are sustained, he must bear them, and if profits are realized, they inure to the benefit of the estate. This statute changes the common law in one particular only. Under its provisions, when directed by the court to perform the contract, the estate may be charged with all losses that may be incurred, as well as receive all benefit of any profits that may be realized, and in that way the executor or administrator may be relieved from all personal responsibility.([3])

33. MAY ASSIGN NOTE DUE DECEASED.—The administrator or executor of a deceased person, or one of several administrators, may assign a note made payable to his decedent, so as to transfer the title thereof to an assignee.([4]) But the sale must be for the benefit of the estate.([5])

34. MAY DISPOSE OF PROPERTY.—As a general principle, an administrator has power to dispose of the personal effects, and they can not be followed into the hands of the alienee. There are exceptions to the rule, as where the purchaser knows, or has reason to

---

(1) Hurd's R. S., Chap. 77, ¿ 38.
(2) Hurd's R. S., Chap. 3, ¿ 126; Phipps vs. Jones, 20 Pa. St., 260; See 3 Probate Reports, 107, for brief of authorities; also 68 Am. Dec., 758.
(3) Smith vs. Wilmington Coal Co., 83 Ill., 498; Jessup vs. Jessup, 102 Ill., 485.
(4) Makepeace vs. Moore, 5 Gil., 474; Dwight vs. Newell, 15 Ill., 333; Walker et al. vs. Craig, 18 Ill., 116; Walter vs. Kirk et al., 14 Ill., 55; 2 Archibold's Nisi Prius, 44.
(5) Smith vs. Fortescue, Burbees Eq., 127; Scott vs. Searles, 7 Smedes & M., 498.

believe, that the sale is made with a design to misapply the funds; or where the property is transferred by the administrator in payment of a private debt; or where it is sold at a grossly inadequate price. In such cases, those interested in the estate, may treat the administrator as personally liable, or pursue the property in the hands of the purchaser.(¹)

35. FRAUD MAY BE PLEAD AGAINST HIM.—Where an administrator at a sale of the personal property, fraudulently represented the goods to be sound, such fraud may be pleaded as a defense to a suit on a note given for such property; the rule, *caveat emptor*, applies to such sales, but that rule is never so applied as to excuse a fraud. Nor can an administrator bind the estate he represents, by his warranty.(²)

36. MISTAKE, ETC.—No executor or administrator, or his security, shall be chargeable beyond the assets of the testator or intestate, by reason of any omission or mistake in pleading, or by false pleading of such executor or administrator.(³)

37. ADMINISTRATOR TO COLLECT.—As before seen, it is proper for the county court, pending the contest over any will or codicil, to appoint an administrator during any preliminary litigation. The duties of such an administrator are similar to those of a permanent incumbent, so far as is consistent with his temporary character, and cease with the appointment of a permanent executor or administrator. The following sections of the statute specifically point out the duties of such administrators:

38. POWERS—COMMISSION.—Every collector so appointed shall have the power to collect the goods, chattels and debts of the said deceased, according to the tenor of the said letters, and to secure the same at such reasonable and necessary expense as shall be allowed by the court; and the said court may authorize him, immediately after the inventory and appraisement of such estate, to sell such as are perishable, or may depreciate by delay, and to account for the same; and for the whole trouble incurred by such collector, the court may allow such commission on the amount of the said personal

---

(1) Makepeace vs. Moore, 5 Gil., 474; McConnell vs. Hodson et al., 2 Gil., 640; 2 Williams on Ex'rs. 796.
(2) Ray vs. Virgin, 12 Ill., 216; Welch et al vs. Hoyt, 24 Ill., 117.
(3) Hurd's R. S., Chap. 103 ? 125.

estate, as shall be actually collected and delivered to the proper executor or administrator, as aforesaid, as said court may deem just and reasonable: *Provided*, the same shall not exceed six per cent. on the amount stated in such inventory or bill of appraisement.(1)

39. SUITS TO COLLECT.—Every such collector may commence suits for debts due to the decedent, and release the same on payment thereof; and no such suit shall abate by the revocation of his letters, but the same may be prosecuted to a final decision, in the name of, and by the executor or administrator, to whom letters testamentary or of administration may be granted.(2)

40. WHEN POWERS CEASE—PENALTY.—On the granting of letters testamentary or of administration, the power of any such collector, so appointed, shall cease, and it shall be his duty to deliver, on demand, all property and money of the deceased, which shall have come to his hands or possession, (saving such commission as may be allowed by the court, as aforesaid,) to the person or persons obtaining such letters; and in case any such collector shall refuse or neglect to deliver over such property or money to his successor, when legal demand is made therefor, such person so neglecting or refusing, shall be liable to pay twenty per cent. over and above the amount of all such property or money as comes to his hands by virtue of his administration, and is not paid or delivered over as aforesaid, and shall forfeit all claim to any commission for collecting and preserving the estate—which said twenty per cent., together with all damages which may be sustained by reason of the breach of any bond which may at any time be given by any such collector, may be sued for and recovered by the person or persons to whom letters testamentary or of administration may be granted, for the use of the estate of such decedent.(3)

41. ADMINISTRATOR DE SON TORT.—If a stranger takes upon himself to act as executor or administrator, without any just authority, as by intermeddling with the goods of the deceased, he is called in law an administrator (or executor) *de son tort*, (of his own wrong), and thereby becomes liable as the true administrator or executor, without any of the profits or advantages; but merely doing acts of necessity or humanity, as locking up the goods or burying the

---

(1) Hurd's R. S., Chap. 3, § 15.
(2) Hurd's R. S., Chap. 3, § 16.
(3) Hurd's R. S., Chap. 3, § 17.

corpse of the deceased, will not amount to such an intermeddling as will charge a man as administrator of his own wrong;(¹) nor will an intermeddling with the lands of the deceased operate to charge the wrong-doer as such.(²)

Where a person improperly intermeddles with the property of an estate, he becomes a trustee *de son tort*, and is liable at the suit of those beneficially interested.(³)

Regularly there can not be an executor or administrator *de son tort*, where there is a rightful executor, or when administration has been duly granted; for, if, after probate or administration-granted, a stranger gets possession of the goods of the deceased, he is a trespasser to such executor or administrator, and may be sued as such. But if a stranger get possession of the goods of the deceased before probate of the will, he may be charged as executor *de son tort*, because the lawful executor can be no further charged than the assets that came to his hands (⁴)

An executor *de son tort* should be sued as executor generally, and if he plead *ne unques executor*, and it be found against him, the judgment is *de bonis propriis*.(⁵) Though an executor *de son tort* is liable to the creditors of the deceased, he is not liable to his legatees.(⁶)

42. ONE ACTING HONESTLY WITH HIM.—Whatever is honestly done by one acting in the capacity of administrator, although he may be an administrator *de son tort*, and not contrary to law, is binding between the parties. A settlement made in good faith with such an administrator is valid. So, where notes made payable to a person afterwards deceased, came to the hands of his widow, who, as administrator *de son tort*, assumed to accept a renewal to herself, surrendering the old notes to the maker, it was held that the transaction was proper, and the new note binding upon the maker.(⁷)

43. COURT NO POWER TO COMPEL AN ACCOUNT.—The county court has no power over an administrator *de son tort* to compel him

---

(1) 1 Tomlin's Law Dictionary, 721; Brown vs Sullivan, 22 Ind., 359.
(2) Mitchell vs. Lunt, 4 Mass., 654; 1 Dane's Ab., 570.
(3) Perry on Trusts, 245; Bailey vs. Miller, 5 Irdell's Law, 444.
(4) 1 Lomax on Executors, 78.
(5) Campbell vs. Tousey, 7 Cow., 64.
(6) 1 Lomax on Executors, 80.
(7) Riley vs. Loughrey, 22 Ill., 98; 4 Bacon's Abridgement, 31; Hawkins vs. Johnson, Blackf. 21.

to account ;(¹) nor can such an administrator sue for and collect a debt, or do anything toward settling the estate.(²)

44. HOW ADMINISTRATOR DE SON TORT MAY DISCHARGE HIMSELF.—The administrator *de son tort* of a solvent estate may discharge himself from the liability imposed by his intermeddling, even against the demand of the rightful executor, by showing that he has paid debts of the deceased to the amount of the value of the goods belonging to the estate, which came to his hands.(³)

He may pay the debts of the deceased due to others, but may not retain property of the deceased to pay his own debt.(⁴)

If an administrator *de son tort* take out letters of administration, it makes legal all acts which were before tortious, but will not operate to discharge him from any personal liability previously incurred by reason of an unlawful intermeddling in the affairs of the estate.(⁵)

45. WIDOW AS ADMINISTRATOR DE SON TORT.—The widow of a decedent does not render herself liable as administrator *de son tort* by continuing to reside where the family lived at the time of her husband's death, nor by taking care of the property of the estate until a legal representative has been appointed (⁶)

46. TITLE TO PROPERTY.—A valid title to the property of a decedent can not be obtained from an administrator *de son tort* as against a subsequently appointed administrator.(⁷)

47. SUITS BETWEEN EXECUTORS, ETC.—Where there are two or more executors or administrators of an estate, and any one of them takes all or a greater part of such estate and refuses to pay the debts of the decedent, or refuses to account with the other executor or administrator, in such case the executor or administrator so aggrieved may have his action of account or suit in equity against such delinquent executor or administrator, and recover such proportionate share of said estate as shall belong to him; and every

(1) Wever vs. Marvin, 14 Barb., 376.
(2) Campbell vs. Sheldon, 13 Pick., 8.
(3) McConnell vs. McConnell, 94 Ill., 296; Weeks vs. Gibbs, 9 Mass., 74; Reagan vs. Long, 21 Ind., 264; Tobey vs. Miller, 54 Me., 480; 1 Williams on Executors, 267; *Contra*, Hardy vs. Thomas, 23 Miss., 544.
(4) Glenn vs. Smith, 2 Gill & Johnson, 493.
(5) Shellaber vs. Wyman, 15 Mass., 322; Rattoon vs. Overacker, 8 Johns., 126.
(6) Ward vs. Bevill, 10 Ala., 197.
(7) Rockwell vs. Young, 60 Md., 563.

executor, being a residuary legatee, may have an action of account or suit in equity against his co-executor or co-executors, and recover his part of the estate in his or their hands. Any other legatee may have the like remedy against the executors: *Provided*, that before any action shall be commenced for legacies as aforesaid. the court shall order them to be paid.([1])

([1]) Hurd's R. S., Chap. 3, § 118.

CHAPTER V.

INVENTORIES AND APPRAISEMENT.

1. Inventory to be filed.
2. How prepared.
3. Additional inventory.
4. Inventory after discharge.
5. A protection and guide.
6. Should embrace all property of the estate.
7. Appraisement bill—form.
8. Oath of appraisers.
9. Compensation.
10. Return into court.
11. Court may set it aside.
12. Inventories, etc.—evidence.
13. Further appraisal.
14. Executors, etc., chargeable.
15. Assets not exceeding widow's allowance.

1. INVENTORY TO BE FILED.—Whenever letters testamentary, of administration, or of collection, are granted, the executor or administrator shall make out a full and perfect inventory of all such real and personal estate, or the proceeds thereof, as are committed to his superintendence and management, and as shall come to his hands, possession or knowledge, describing the quantity, situation and title of the real estate, and particularly specifying the nature and amount of all annuities, rents, goods, chattels, rights and credits and money on hand, and whether the credits are good, doubtful or desperate; which said inventory shall be returned to the office of clerk of the county court, within three months from the date of the letters testamentary or of administration.([1])

2. HOW PREPARED.—The first, and among the more important duties of an executor or administrator, is the careful preparation and filing with the clerk by him, of an inventory of all the real and personal property of his decedent, of whatever name or nature. The inventory need not affix values to real estate or chattels. Money on hand at decease, and notes and accounts should be described by the amounts; and in the case of notes and accounts,

---
(1) Hurd's R. S., Chap. 3, § 51.

a statement of their character, as "good," "doubtful," or "desperate," should be attached to each entry; for without being otherwise designated, all debts inventoried are, *prima facie*, collectible.(¹)

As administration extends only to the assets of the intestate lying within this state, it would seem to follow, that such real and personal property as lies beyond the limits of this state, need not be inventoried.(²) But debts due from non-resident debtors, should be inventoried.(³) It has not been usual to make a specific inventory of co-partnership assets, in inventorying the estate of a deceased partner, but it has always been deemed sufficient to note generally the co-partnership interest, as an interest in an unascertained balance—the balance, when found, being the only thing in which the administrator has any individual right of property for the exclusive benefit of the estate of his intestate.(⁴)

3. ADDITIONAL INVENTORY.—If, after making the first inventory, any other real or personal estate of the deceased comes to his possession or knowledge, he shall file a similar additional inventory thereof.(⁵)

4. INVENTORY AFTER DISCHARGE OF ADMINISTRATOR.—The final discharge of an administrator, after having fully administered the assets which came to his hands, during the two years elapsing, next after the grant of letters, may not terminate his duties in respect to inventorying the estate of his decedent. Should estate, either real or personal, not before inventoried, be discovered belonging to the deceased, it would still be his duty to make and return an inventory of the same to the court; and if it be personal chattels, to cause the same to be appraised.(⁶)

5. A PROTECTION AND GUIDE.—The inventory when so prepared and filed, is a guide, check and protection to the officer filing it, as well as to those interested in the estate. It is admissible

---

(1) 2 Redfield on Wills, 204.
(2) Doolittle vs. Lewis, 7 Johns. Ch., 45; Judy et al. vs. Kelley, 11 Ill., 211.
(3) Shultz vs. Pulver, 3 Paige, 182.
(4) Thompson vs. Thompson, 1 Brad., 24.
(5) Hurd's R. S., Chap. 3, ? 52.
(6) Diversey vs. Johnson, 93 Ill., 547; Blanchard vs. Williamson, 70 Ill., 647; Cuthright et al. vs. Stanford et al., 81 Ill., 240; Sutherland vs. Harrison et al., 86 Ill., 363; Clark et al. vs. Burnside, 15 Ill., 62.

in evidence, as well on behalf of, as against, the party filing it.([1]) Claims inventoried as *doubtful*, or *desperate*, in all proceedings against the administrator or executor, are *prima facie*, uncollectible; and he who charges the contrary must support it by proof, and it should appear that the debtor had property out of which by proper diligence the claim so declared, could have been made.([2]) The inventory may also be an estoppel as to the administrator.([3])

6. ALL PROPERTY SHOULD BE INVENTORIED.—All the property of the deceased in the state, known to the executor or administrator, should be inventoried;([4]) otherwise, the two-year statute of limitation can not be relied upon.([5])

7. APPRAISEMENT—FORM.—On granting letters testamentary or of administration, a warrant shall issue, under the seal of the county court, authorizing three persons of discretion, not related to the deceased, nor interested in the administration of the estate, to appraise the goods, chattels and personal estate of the deceased, known to them, or to be shown by the executor or administrator; which warrant shall be in the following form, to-wit:

The People of the State of Illinois, to A B, C D and E F, of the county of......, and State of Illinois—GREETING:

This is to authorize you, jointly, to appraise the goods, chattels and personal estate of J K, late of the county of......, and state of Illinois, deceased, so far as the same shall come to your sight and knowledge—each of you having first taken the oath (or affirmation) hereto annexed, a certificate whereof you are to return, annexed to an appraisement bill of said goods, chattels and personal estate by you appraised, in dollars and cents; and in the said bill of appraisement, you are to set down, in a column or columns, opposite to each article appraised, the value thereof.

Witness: A B, clerk of the county court of......county, and the seal of said court, this...day of......, 18...   A B, *Clerk.*
[L. S.]

And on the death, refusal to act, or neglect of any such appraiser, another may be appointed in his place.([6])

8. OATH—APPRAISAL.—The appraisers, before they proceed to the appraisement of the estate, shall take and subscribe the following oath (or affirmation), to be annexed or indorsed on the

(1) Rowan vs. Kirkpatrick, 14 Ill., 1; Hurd's R. S., Chap. 3, § 56: Willenborg et al. vs. Murphy, 36 Ill., 344.
(2) *Id.*
(3) Irby vs. Kitchel, 42 Ala., 438; Bigelow on Estoppel, 425; but in case of mistate in the inventory, the equitable powers of the court will enable it to correct the error and do complete justice. Black vs. Whitall, 1 Stockton's Ch., 572; Dunham vs. Chatham 21 Texas, 231.
(4) Wells et al. vs. Miller, 45 Ill., 382.
(5) Sloo vs. Pool, 15 Ill., 47; Guy et al. vs. Gericks, 85 Ill., 428.
(6) Hurd's R. S., § 53.

said warrant, before any person authorized to administer an oath, viz:

We, and each of us, do solemnly swear (or affirm) that we will well and truly, without partiality or prejudice, value and appraise the goods, chattels and personal estate of J K, deceased, so far as the same shall come to our sight and knowledge; and that we will, in all respects, perform our duties as appraisers to the best of our skill and judgment.

After which the said appraisers shall proceed, as soon as conveniently may be, to the discharge of their duty, and shall set down each article, with the value thereof, in dollars and cents, as aforesaid. All the valuations shall be set down on the right-hand side of the paper, in one or more columns, in figures, opposite to the respective articles of property, and the contents of each column shall be cast up and set at the foot of the respective columns.([1])

9. COMPENSATION.—Every appraiser appointed under this act, shall be entitled to the sum of two dollars per day, for each day's necessary attendance in making all such appraisements, to be allowed by the county court, and paid upon its order by the executor or administrator.([2])

10. RETURN.—When the bill of appraisement is completed, the appraisers shall certify the same under their hands and seals; and shall deliver the same into the hands of the executor or administrator, to be, by him, returned into the office of the clerk of the county court, within three months from the date of his letters.([3])

11. COURT MAY SET ASIDE.—The county court may, for cause shown, set aside the appraisement bill.([4])

12. INVENTORIES, ETC., EVIDENCE.—Inventories and bills of appraisement and authenticated copies thereof, may be given in evidence in any suit by or against the executor or administrator, but shall not be conclusive for or against him, if any other testimony be given that the estate was really worth, or was *bona fide* sold for more or less than the appraised value thereof.([5])

An inventory filed by an administrator, is not conclusive evidence for or against the administrator or his sureties, but is open to denial or explanation.([6])

(1) Hurd's R. S., Chap. 3, § 54.
(2) Hurd's R. S., Chap. 3, § 59.
(3) Hurd's R. S., Chap. 3, § 55.
(4) Miller vs. Miller, 82 Ill., 463.
(5) Hurd's R. S., Chap. 3, § 56; Rowan vs. Kirkpatrick, *supra*.
(6) McNabb vs. Wixon, 7 Nev., 163; Ames vs. Downing, 1 Brad., 321.

13. FURTHER APPRAISAL.—Whenever personal property of any kind, or assets, shall come to the possession or knowledge of any executor or administrator, which are not included in the first bill of appraisement as aforesaid, the same shall be appraised, and return thereof made to the office of the clerk of the county court in like manner, within three months after discovery of the same.([1])

14. LIABILITIES OF EXECUTORS, ETC.—Executors and administrators shall be chargeable with so much of the estate of the decedent, personal or real, as they, after due and proper diligence, might or shall receive.([2])

15. WHEN ASSETS DO NOT EXCEED WIDOW'S ALLOWANCE—NEW ASSETS.—If the administrator or executor of an estate discovers, at any time after an inventory and appraisement of the property is made, that the personal property and assets of the estate do not exceed the amount of the widow's allowance, after deducting the necessary expenses incurred, such administrator or executor shall report the facts to the court, and if the court finds the report to be true, he shall order said property and assets to be delivered to the widow by the administrator or executor, and discharge the executor or administrator from further duty; but such executor or administrator shall first pay out of the property and assets the costs and expenses of administration. After the court orders the delivery of such property and assets to the widow, the clerk of said court shall make and deliver to her a certified copy of the order, under seal, which shall vest her with complete title to said property and assets, and enable her to sue for and recover the same in her own name and for her own use. Such widow shall not be liable for any of decedent's debts or liabilities, excepting the funeral expenses of the deceased. If, upon affidavit being filed with the clerk of said court, that such administrator or executor fails or refuses to report in any case provided for in this section, the court may order a citation and attachment to issue, as in other cases of a failure of administrators to report. And on a discovery of new assets, administration may be granted as in other cases, and charged to the account of the estate.([3])

(1) Hurd's R. S., Chap. 3, § 57.
(2) Hurd's R. S., Chap. 3, § 58; Rowan vs. Kirkpatrick, *supra;* Christy et al., vs. McBride, 1 Scam., 75.
(3) Hurd's R. S., Chap. 3, § 59.

CHAPTER VI.

COLLECTION AND DISPOSITION OF ASSETS.

1. Property of deceased bound for debts.
2. Duty and power to collect assets.
3. Property fraudulently transferred.
4. Actions which survive to the executor or administrator.
5. Administrators and executors must sue and be sued jointly.
6. Where plaintiff or defendant dies—suggestion and substitution.
    - a. Continuance.
    - b. Heirs and legatees.
    - c. Void proceedings.
    - d. Death of plaintiff after judgment
    - e. Foreign administrators included.
    - f. Void sales.
    - g. Lien not defeated by death.
    - h. Death of defendant—copy of letters.
    - i. Attachment suit does not abate.
    - j. Condemnation proceedings.
7. Concealed goods—collection of the same.
8. Jurisdiction of chancery.
9. Books of account.
10. What are personal assets—dividends.
    - a. Rents.
    - b. Legacies.
    - c. Insurance policy.
    - d. Certificate of sale
    - e. Mesne profits.
    - f. Nursery stock.
    - g. Money due from guardian.
    - h. Money paid for causing death.
    - i. Real estate partially paid for.
    - j. Surplus money arising from sale under mortgage
    - k. Foreign effects.
    - l. Rails in a pen.
    - m. Real estate taken by administrator.
    - n. Leasehold.
11. Suits by executors and administrators.
    - a. Proof of official character.
12. Title to property vests in legal representative
13. Actions of covenant.
14. Widow—when liable.
15. Practice.

CH. VI.]   COLLECTION AND DISPOSITION OF ASSETS.   65

 16. Suit by administrator *de bonis non.*
 17. Set-off not allowed.
 18. Payment to an acting administrator.
 19. Payment by administrator by mistake.
 20. Personal estate first liable for debts.
 21. Desperate claims.
 22. Avails of desperate claims.
 23. Claims may be compounded.
 24. Removal of property by executor or administrator.
 25. Sale of personal property.
 26. Rule of *caveat emptor.*
 27. Who may not purchase.
 28. Growing crops.
 29. Sale.
 30. Return of sale bill.

1. PROPERTY OF DECEASED BOUND FOR DEBTS.—On the death of a party and the grant of letters of administration, the statute imposes a lien, incomplete it may be, on all of his property and credits, in favor of, and for the payment of all his debts, according to the class, and in the manner it prescribes;([1]) but where there is a will, the testator can substitute other funds in place of the personal estate.([2]) And where, by will, the entire personal estate is disposed of, leaving the realty intestate estate, the personalty will be held exempt from the payment of debts, until all the realty has been exhausted.([3])

2. ADMINISTRATOR SHOULD COLLECT.—The administrator should collect all the goods and chattels inventoried: and to that end, he has very large powers and interests conferred upon him by law; being the representative of the deceased, and having the same property in his goods, as the principal had when living, and the same remedies to recover them.([4])

According to a decision in Pennsylvania,([5]) he has greater rights, in some cases. For example, where a person parted with the possession of his property for the purpose of defrauding his creditors, he cannot maintain trover to recover it back; but, after

 (1) Mack vs. Woodruff, 87 Ill., 570.
 (2) Ruston vs. Ruston, 2 Dallas, 243.
 (3) McCullom vs. Chidester, 63 Ill., 477; Stires vs. Stires, Halstead's Ch. 224.
 (4) 1 Blackstone's Com., 510; Leamon et al. vs. McCubbin et al., 82 Ill., 263.
 (5) Stewart vs. Kearney, 6 Watts, 453.

his death, if his estate be otherwise insufficient to pay his debts, the action of trover survives to his representatives, who may prosecute it for the benefit of his creditors.

3. PROPERTY FRAUDULENTY TRANSFERRED.—Where one confessed a judgment in fraud of his creditors, under which goods were sold to the plaintiff in said judgment, in satisfaction of an execution issued thereon, after which the defendant in the judgment died, it was held that, while the administrator of the defendant could not lawfully take the goods himself, the plaintiff might be held responsible as an administrator *de son tort,* to any creditor of the estate.([1])

4. ACTIONS WHICH SURVIVE.—In addition to the actions which survive by the common law, the following shall also survive: Actions of replevin, actions to recover damages for an injury to the person, (except slander and libel,) actions to recover damages for an injury to real or personal property, or for the detention or conversion of personal property, and actions against officers for misfeasance, malfeasance or nonfeasance of themselves or their deputies, and all actions for fraud or deceit.([2])

In the case of a mere personal contract, or of a covenant not running with the land, if it were made only with one person, and he be dead, the action for the breach of it, must be brought in the name of his executor or administrator, in whom the legal interest in such contract is vested;([3]) but in case of torts, where the action must be in form *ex delicto,* for the recovery of damages, and the plea of not guilty, the rule at common law was otherwise.([4])

Until the passage of Sec. 122, *supra,* actions for trespass to realty did not survive.([5])

Action for the seduction of a daughter, does not survive.([6])

The action of trover survives.([7])

5. ADMINISTRATORS AND EXECUTORS MUST SUE AND BE SUED JOINTLY.—Administrators must be sued jointly and plead jointly,

(1) Osborne vs. Moss, 7 johns., 161.
(2) Hurd's R. S., Chap. 3, Sec. 122; Blakeney vs. Blakeney, 6 Porter, 109.
(3) 1 Chitty's Pl., 19.
(4) *Id.,* 68.
(5) Reed vs. Railroad Co., 18 Ill., 403; Taylor vs. Fickas, 64 Ind., 167.
(6) 2 Hilliard on Torts, 522.
(7) *Id.*

and no several judgment can be taken against any one of them: such a judgment is wholly void.(¹) But where one of two executors died, having in his hands trust funds belonging to the estate represented by himself and his executor, it was held proper for the surviving executor to probate a claim against the estate of the deceased executor, for the funds so held by him.(²)

6. DEATH OF SOLE PLAINTIFF—REVIVING SUIT.—When there is but one plaintiff, petitioner or complainant in an action, proceeding or complaint, in law or equity, and he shall die before final judgment or decree, such action, proceeding or complaint shall not on that account abate, if the cause of action survive to the heir, devisee, executor or administrator of such decedent, but any of such to whom the cause of action shall survive, may, by suggesting such death upon the record, be substituted as plaintiff, petitioner or complainant, and prosecute the same as in other cases.(³)

a. Upon the death of the plaintiff and the substitution of the name of the personal representative, either party is entitled to a continuance, and neither party can be forced into a trial at that term.(⁴)

b. Where, during the pendency of an action for trespass to real property, the plaintiff died, it was held that the action must proceed, if at all, in the name of the personal representative of the deceased plaintiff, and that such action could not be maintained in the name of the sole legatee of the plaintiff.(⁵)

c. Judicial proceedings commenced and prosecuted in the name of a person deceased, are a nullity, and would constitute no bar to another proceeding in the name of the personal representatives of the deceased, for the same cause.(⁶)

d. The collection of a judgment or decree of a court of record shall not be delayed or hindered, or the lien created by law abate, by reason of the death of any person in whose favor such judgment or decree shall be; but the executor or administrator, or, if the

---

(1) Dickerson vs. Robinson, 1 Halstead, 195.
(2) Fitzsimmons vs. Cassell, 98 Ill., 332.
(3) Hurd's R. S., Chap. 1, § 10; Thorpe vs. Starr, 17 Ill., 199.
(4) Warren vs. Ball, 40 Ill., 117.
(5) McLean Co. Coal Co. vs. Long, 91 Ill., 617; Bower vs. G. & M. R. R. Co., 92 Ill., 223.
(6) Risley vs. Fellows, 5 Gil., 531; Barbour et al. vs. White et al., 37 Ill., 164.

decedent was an executor or administrator, the administrator *de bonis non*, or with the will annexed, may cause his letters testamentary or of administration, to be recorded in such court, after which execution may issue and proceeding be had, in the name of the executor or administrator as such, in the same manner as if the judgment or decree had been recovered in his name.(1)

e. This section is construed to authorize foreign administrators, upon complying with the requirements of Sec. 42, Chap. 3, to sue out executions upon judgments in favor of their decedents in the courts of this state.(2) But an administrator cannot file a transcript in the circuit court under section 95, chapter 79.(3)

f. Sales in the name of a deceased plaintiff are void.(4)

g. The lien created by law in favor of a judgment, is not defeated by the death of the plaintiff, unless no execution has been issued within a year; but the executor or administrator of the deceased plaintiff, may have execution thereon, by filing his letters of administration in the court for record. The failure of the clerk to record the letters, as required by law, will not defeat a sale made under such execution.(5)

h. When a person shall die after the rendition of a judgment or decree for the payment of money against him is obtained in a court of record, execution may issue against the real estate of such deceased person, or sale may be made under such decree without reviving the judgment or decree against his heirs or legal representatives: *Provided*, that no execution shall issue or sale be made, until after the expiration of twelve months from the death of such deceased person, nor shall any sale be had on any such execution or decree, until the person in whose favor the judgment or decree is sought to be enforced, shall give to the executor or administrator, or, if there is neither, the heirs of the deceased, at least three months' notice in writing of the existence of such judgment or decree, before issuing execution or proceeding to sell.(6)

i. An attachment proceeding does not abate upon the death of the defendant(7)

---

(1) Hurd's R. S., Chap. 77, § 37; Letcher et al. vs. Morrison, 27 Ill., 209.
(2) Keefer vs. Mason, 36 Ill., 406; Contra, People vs. Peck, 3 Scam., 118.
(3) Thornley vs. Moore, 106 Ill., 496.
(4) Brown vs. Parker, 15 Ill., 307; Risley vs. Fellows, 5 Gil., 531.
(5) Durham et al. vs. Heaton, 28 Ill., 264; Fitts et al. vs. Davis, 42 Ill., 391.
(6) Hurd's R. S., Chap. 77, § 39; Doe *ex dem* vs. Hamilton, 23 Miss., 496.
(7) Davis et al. vs. Day, 19 Ill., 386.

j. This section does not justify the substitution of the name of an administrator in a proceeding under the statute for condemning a right of way for a railroad, where the owner of the real estate dies. Upon his death, the title vests in his heirs, and the name of the administrator is improperly substituted.([1])

7. CONCEALED GOODS, ETC.—If any executor or administrator, or other person interested in any estate, shall state upon oath to any county court, that he believes that any person has in possession, or has concealed or embezzled any goods, chattels, moneys or effects, books of account, papers, or any evidences of debt whatever, or titles to lands, belonging to any deceased person, the court shall require such person to appear before it by citation, and may examine him on oath, and hear the testimony of such executor or administrator, and other evidence offered by either party, and make such order in the premises as the case may require.([2]) If such person refuses to answer such proper interrogatories as may be propounded to him, or refuses to deliver up such property or effects, or in case the same has been converted, the proceeds or value thereof, upon a requisition being made for that purpose by an order of the said court, such court may commit such person to jail, until he shall comply with the order of the court therein.([3])

Where a party appears in the county court and goes to trial on the merits, in this proceeding, this will be a waiver of any defects in the affidavit, by which the proceeding is commenced.([4])

In such a case, the court is not confined to the examination of the defendant, but either party has a right to introduce any evidence pertinent to the issue. The court is not even bound to examine under oath, but may do so in its discretion.([5])

Where a party is cited under such a proceeding, to reach property in his hands belonging to an estate, denies the charge, and is discharged by the court, it seems that such a trial and discharge, will be a bar to a recovery in another action in respect to the same property.([6])

(1) P. & R. I. R. R. Co. vs. Rice, 75 Ill., 329.
(2) Hurd's R. S., Chap. 3, § 80.
(3) Hurd's R. S., Chap. 3, § 80; Blair vs. Sennott, 134 Ill., 78. Steinman vs. Steinman, 1 5 Ill., 348; Barnum vs. Reed, 136 Ill., 388.
(4) Wade vs. Pritchard, 69 Ill., 280.
(5) *Id.*
(6) *Id.*

This proceeding was not designed to aid in the collection of debts due to the deceased; but for the purpose of obtaining possession of specific articles. So, where one was cited to appear and answer as to the possession of money belonging to the estate of a deceased person, it was held error to order the payment of a sum of money equal to that received, or any sum, unless the evidence showed the possession of the identical money received.([1])

It does not follow, when another party is in possession of goods and chattels of an estate, that the court *shall* order that they be delivered to the administrator under the above section. If the order can accomplish no substantial good, it should not be made. The court is invested with a discretion, and is not compelled, as a matter of arbitrary law, to make any specific order. This discretion is not unlimited, but should be exercised so as best to preserve the estate, and promote the honest, complete and prompt administration of assets.

A court would not require the equitable owner of promissory notes, made payable to a deceased person, to deliver them to the administrator of the estate when not required for the payment of debts of the estate, or for the purpose of distribution.([2])

8. JURISDICTION OF CHANCERY.—Where the husband of an administratrix obtains possession and control of the assets of the estate represented by her, and refuses to pay over to claimants, when an order is legally made upon her to do so, it is quite clear that equity would compel him to deliver up the trust funds in his hands for the benefit of the creditors; or, perhaps, the same end might be attained, by a proceeding against him in the county court under the 80th section.([3])

9. BOOKS OF ACCOUNT.—The books of account of any deceased person shall be subject to the inspection of all persons interested therein.([4])

10. WHAT ARE PERSONAL ASSETS.—Dividends in a turnpike company, declared after the death of the testator or intestate, are personal estate, and may be collected by the executor or adminis-

---

(1) Williams vs. Conley, 20 Ill., 643.
(2) People vs. McKee, 105 Ill., 588.
(3) Johnson vs. Von Kettler, 66 Ill., 63.
(4) Hurd's R. S., Chap. 3, § 127.

CH. VI.]   COLLECTION AND DISPOSITION OF ASSETS.   71

trator; so, also, are damages for opening a public road, ordered before, but not paid until after death.([1])

a. Rent for the use of realty, falling due before the death of the decedent, is personal estate, and goes to the administrator; otherwise if it falls due after the death of the owner.([2])

On the other hand, if the tenant make an under-lease, reserving rent, the rent accruing to the tenant after his death will go to his executor or administrator, and not to his heirs. Where no estate or reversion is left in the landlord, and the rent is reserved to his executors and administrators, it will go to them, and not to the heirs.[3]

b. A legacy to the deceased is personal property, and goes to his administrator, who has a right to it under the terms imposed by the testator.([4])

c. A life insurance policy, payable to one's "legal representatives,"* when collected, is assets in the hands of the administrator for the payment of debts or for distribution; but when payable to the widow or heirs, it is otherwise.([5])

d. Where the deceased held a certificate of sale under execution sale, it descends to his heirs, and the deed must be made to them.([6])

e. Mesne profits due a widow for the use of her dower are personal assets, and go to her administrator; but the right to recover dower must be established in the lifetime of the widow.([7])

f. Nursery trees growing upon real estate at the time of the death of the owner will descend to the heir, and do not go to the administrator.[8]

g. The administrator of a minor may compel a settlement by

(1) Welles vs. Cowles, 4 Conn., 182.
(2) Green vs. Massie, 13 Ill., 372; Foltz vs. Prouse, 17 Ill., 487; Dixon vs. Nichols, 39 Ill., 372; Wright vs. Williams, 5 Cow., 501; Evans vs. Hardy, 76 Ind., 527; Cowdrey vs. Hitchcock, 103 Ill., 262.
(3) 3 Cruise's Digest, 321; Swan's Manual, 63.
(4) Ruffin vs. Farmer, 72 Ill., 615.
(5) People vs. Phelps, 78 Ill., 148; See 6 Probate Reports, 547, for authorities; Alexander vs. Masonic Aid Association, 126 Ill., 558; Pinneo vs. Goodspeed, 120 Ill., 524; Cole vs. Marple, 98 Ill., 58.
(6) Potts vs. Davenport et al., 79 Ill., 455.
(7) Hitt vs. Scammon et al., 82 Ill., 519.
(8) Osborn vs. Rabe, 67 Ill., 108.

---

*The term "legal representatives," means executors, administrators, children, heirs, assignees or grantees, according to the intention of the parties using it.—*Warnecke et al* vs. *Lembca*, 71 Ill., 91; *Morehouse* vs. *People*, 18 Ill., 472.

the guardian of such minor, and receive from him any balance found due.(¹)

h. Money paid an administrator for wrongfully causing the death of the deceased is assets in his hands for certain purposes.(²)

i. Where the deceased has made partial payment for a piece of land, the interest therein goes to the heirs, and if entitled to recover back money paid on the purchase, it must go to the heir.(³)

Where there is a contract for the purchase of land, it descends in equity to the heir.(⁴)

A claim occupied by deceased and family is not assets which the administrator is bound to sell and account for.(⁵)

j. Surplus money, arising from the sale of real estate under a mortgage made by the deceased in his lifetime, is considered a part of the realty, and goes to the heirs, and not to the administrator of the mortgagor.(⁶)

k. Property of an intestate situated in another state or country than that granting letters, is not assets for the payment of debts and distribution—the administrator has no authority over, nor is he responsible for any effects of the decedent that may be beyond the jurisdiction.(⁷) Debts due the decedent from those resident in other states are not included in the term " property," as above used, and should be collected as other debts.(⁸)

l. Rails used in a stack-pen are personal property, and may be recovered by the administrator. It is otherwise where the rails are laid up in a fence.(⁹)

m. Where real estate is taken by an administrator in payment of a debt due to the deceased, or where land sold by him in his lifetime and not paid for is recovered back under a power of forfeiture, such

---

(1) Gilbert vs. Guptill, 34 Ill., 112.
(2) Goltra vs. People, 53 Ill., 224; Henchey vs. City of Chicago, 41 Ill., 136.
(3) Buck vs. Eaman, 18 Ill., 529; Smith vs. Smith et al., 55 Ill., 204.
(4) Smith vs. Smith et al., *supra;* Champion et al. vs. Brown, 6 Johnson's Ch., 398.
(5) Attridge et al. vs. Billings et al., 57 Ill., 489.
(6) Moses vs. Murgatroyd, 1 johns. Ch., 119; Bogert vs. Furman, 10 Paige, 466.
(7) Judy et al. vs. Kelley, 11 Ill., 211.
(8) Shultz vs. Pulver, 3 Paige, 182.
(9) Clark et al. vs. Burnside, 15 Ill., 62.

real estate partakes of the nature of personalty, and will be distributed as such.(¹)

n. A leasehold interest in land for a term of years is personal estate, and on the death of the owner passes to his executor or administrator, and not to the heir.(²)

11. SUITS BY EXECUTORS AND ADMINISTRATORS.—When the nature of a debt originally due an intestate is changed by contract with the administrator, the latter must sue for the new debt in his own name ; and where the plaintiff styles himself administrator in the declaration on a note, but takes judgment in his own name, such designation will be deemed merely a description of the person.(³) An executor or administrator need not sue, as such, upon a contract made by him in his fiduciary capacity, after the death of his decedent, and if he does so, he need not prove that he is executor or administrator.(⁴)

a. An administrator, suing as such, is not required to produce his letters and prove his official capacity, unless his right so to sue is denied by the defendant. In a court of record, the proper manner of denying it is by plea of *ne unques* administrator. Before a justice of the peace, an oral objection should be interposed.(⁵) A plea of the general issue admits his official capacity.(⁶)

Where an administrator sues upon a contract made by himself, although in his official capacity, as upon a note made to himself, as administrator, he need not prove his official character, although his right so to sue is denied by special plea. The description given to himself in making the contract, or in bringing the suit, will be regarded as immaterial, and need not be proven.(⁷)

12. TITLE TO PROPERTY VESTS IN LEGAL REPRESENTATIVE.— The legal title of a note payable to A. B., administrator, upon the death of the payee, passes to his administrator.(⁸)

(1) Leiper's Ap., 35 Pa. St., 420.
(2) Thornton, et al., vs. Mehring, 117 Ill., 55 ; Doe, *ex dem.*, vs. Peters, Burbee's Law, 457.
(3) Helm vs. Van Vleet, 1 Blackf., 342.
(4) Hunter vs. Postlewaite, 10 Martin, 456.
(5) Ballance vs. Frisby et al., 2 Scam., 63 ; Collins vs. Ayers, 13 Ill., 358; Union R. R. Co. vs. Shacklet, 119 Ill., 232.
(6) McKinly vs. Braden, 1 Scam., 64.
(7) Laycock vs. Oleson, 60 Ill., 30 ; Baker vs. Ormsby, 4 Scam., 325.
(8) Newhall vs. Turney, 14 Ill., 338; Horskins vs. Williamson, 1 T. U. P. Charlton (Ga.), 145.

A devisee or heir of realty cannot be called upon to account for rents to be used in paying the debts of the testator or ancestor.([1])

The executor of a trustee who died in possession of a trust fund, takes it, if at all, not as executor, but as a trustee.([2])

13. ACTION OF COVENANT.—An administrator or executor may maintain an action for covenant broken in the lifetime of the testator or intestate, though it were a covenant real running with the land; and the damage shall be recovered by the legal representative, though not named in the deed, as he personally represents the deceased.([3])

14. WIDOW LIABLE.—If the widow commits waste in the lands and tenements, or the personal estate of the deceased, she shall be liable to an action by the heir or devisee, or his or her guardian, if of real estate, or by the executor or administrator, if of personal estate; and if she marry a subsequent husband, he shall be answerable with her, in damages, for any waste committed by her, or by the husband himself, after such marriage.([4])

15. PRACTICE.—A note given to A. B., administrator, may be sued by A. B., in his own name.([5])

A court of equity will not require an heir to pay over to an administrator money due from him to an intestate, when such estate owes no debts, unless it exceeds his distributive share.([6])

An administrator bringing suit must plead his appointment with profert, which, if questioned, should be by a plea of *ne unques* administrator; otherwise, he will not be required to make proof of his representative character.([7])

In an action by an administrator *de bonis non*, to recover the value of goods sold by the intestate to the defendant, the admissions of the former administrator are proper in support of a plea of payment to him.([8])

16. SUIT BY ADMINISTRATOR DE BONIS NON.—An administrator *de bonis non* cannot maintain a suit against a purchaser at a

---

(1) Bucher et al. vs. Bucher, 86 Ill., 377.
(2) Dias vs. Brunell, 24 Wend., 9.
(3) 4 Bacon's Abridgement, 126; Mott vs. Mott, 11 Barb., 127.
(4) Hurd's R. S., Chap, 3, § 79.
(5) Newhall vs. Turney, 14 Ill., 338; Lacock vs. Oleson, 60 Ill., 30; Helm vs. Van Fleet, 1 Blackford, 342.
(6) Lewis vs. Lyons et al., 13 Ill., 117.
(7) Collins vs. Ayers, 13 Ill., 358.
(8) Eckert vs Triplett, 48 Ind., 174.

sale of personal property made by a former administrator. There is no privity of contract between the two administrators.(¹)

17. SET-OFF.—In an action by an executor upon a cause of action arising after the testator's death, the defendant cannot set-off a debt due him from the testator in his lifetime ;(²) so, in a suit upon a debt accruing to the administrator, as such, after the death of the deceased, the defendant cannot offset a debt due to him from the intestate in his lifetime.(³) To allow this to be done, would interfere with the proper order of distribution.(⁴)

A claim against an administrator personally cannot be offset against a debt due the estate he represents.(⁵)

18. PAYMENT TO AN ACTING ADMINISTRATOR.—The receipt of an acting administrator of an estate, under authority of law, regularly appointed by a court of competent jurisdiction, is a sufficient acquittance of a debt due the estate, and will bar any action for the recovery of the same, subsequently brought, notwithstanding some irregularities may have intervened in the appointment of the administrator, which would be fatal on appeal or error.(⁶) But if it subsequently appear that, at the time of the issue of such letters, the alleged decedent was not in fact dead, but alive, then such payment will not acquit a party so paying to an acting administrator.(⁷)

19. PAYMENT BY MISTAKE.—Where an administrator, by mistake, makes a payment out of the assets which ought not to have been made, he may recover it back in his representative character; and this, although such payment amount to a *devastavit*.(⁸)

20. PERSONAL ESTATE PRIMARILY LIABLE.—The personal property of a deceased person is the primary fund for the payment of debts and legacies not charged upon the real estate;(⁹) and this, whether such debts are secured by mortgage or not, and heirs and devisees have the right to compel the payment of a mortgage debt out of the personalty, and thereby relieve real estate of the lien.(¹⁰)

(1) Ross vs. Sutton, 1 Bailey Law, 126; McGarvey vs. Darnall, 134 Ill., 367.
(2) Patterson vs. Patterson, 59 N. Y., 574; Harding vs. Shepard, 107 Ill., 264.
(3) Newhall vs. Turney, 14 Ill., 338.
(4) *Id.;* Bosler vs. Bank, 4 Pa. St., 32.
(5) Wisdom et al., vs. Becker, 52 Ill., 342.
(6) People vs. Cole, 84 Ill., 327.
(7) Rodrigas vs. East River Savings Institution, 79 N. Y., 307.
(8) 4 Bacon's Ab., 127.
(9) McCampbell vs. McCampbell, 5 Littell, 92.
(10) Sutherland vs. Harrison et al., 86 Ill., 363; Diversey vs. Johnson, 93 Ill., 547.

21. DESPERATE CLAIMS.—Upon suggestion made by an executor or administrator to the county court, that any claim, debt or demand whatever belonging to the estate in his hands to be administered, and accruing in the lifetime of the decedent, is desperate on account of the insolvency or doubtful solvency of the person or persons owing the same, or on account of the debtor having availed himself of the bankrupt law of the United States, or on account of some legal or equitable defense, which such person or persons may allege against the same, or for the cause that the smallness of such claim, debt or demand, and the difficulty of finding the debtors, owing to the remoteness of their residence, or such executor's or administrator's ignorance of the same, the said court may order such claim, debt or demand to be compounded or sold, or to be filed in the said court, for the benefit of such of the heirs, devisees or creditors of such decedent, as will sue for and recover the same, giving the creditors the preference, if they or any of them apply for the same before the final settlement of such estate: *Provided*, that no order for the sale or compounding of any such debts, claims or demands, or any of them, shall be made until two weeks' public notice shall have been given, to all whom it may concern, of the time and place when the said order will be applied for—which notice shall be given by the administrator or executor, in a newspaper published in the county where such application is to be made, or if no such newspaper is published in such county, then by posting up such notices in not less than three public places in the county, of which one shall be at the office of the clerk of the county court—which notice shall be so posted at least two weeks previous to the time of said application. The executor or administrator shall report to the said county court, for its approval, the terms upon which he has settled or disposed of any such claim, debt or demand.[1]*

An executor has authority at common law to compound and release a debt due to the estate, and one who settles a debt due the estate in good faith and discreetly, although for less than the whole sum due, is accountable only for the amount received.[2] He has

(1) Hurd's R. S., Chap. 3, § 82; Kellar's appeal, 8 Pa. St., 288.
(2) In the matter of Scott, 5 N. Y., Leg. Obs., 378; Moulton vs. Holmes, 57 Cal., 337; See 2 Probate Reports, 552, for brief; *Contra*, Ætna Ins. Co. vs. Swayze, 30 Kansas, 118.

*NOTE.—This section does not apply to claims for the death of the deceased. The administrator may compromise such claims without consent of the court — *Washington vs. Louisville R. R. Co.*, 136 Ill., 49.

no authority to receive anything but money in payment of notes due the deceased.(¹)

22. AVAILS OF DESPERATE CLAIMS.—And if such claim is compounded or sold, such executor or administrator shall be chargeable with the avails of such compounding, and if the same is taken by any of the creditors, heirs or devisees, he or they may maintain an action for the recovery thereof, in the name of such executor or administrator, for the use hereinafter mentioned; and upon recovering the same, or any part thereof, he or they shall be chargeable therewith, after deducting his claim or distributive share, with reasonable compensation for collecting the same; and upon such suits the executor or administrator shall not be liable for costs (²)

23. COURT MAY ORDER CERTAIN CLAIMS COMPOUNDED.—The county court may order claims, debts and demands, due at so remote a period as to prevent their collection within the time required for the final settlement of estates, and the collection or disposition of which is necessary to the payment of the debts against the estate, to be compounded or sold in the same manner and upon like conditions as though such claims, debts or demands, were desperate or doubtful: *Provided*, that no such claim, debt or demand shall be sold or compounded for less than ten per cent. below the value thereof.(³)

24. REMOVAL OF PROPERTY BY EXECUTOR, ETC.—PENALTY.— No executor or administrator shall, without the order of the court, remove any property wherewith he is charged, by virtue of his letters, beyond the limits of this state. And in case any such executor or administrator shall remove such property without such order, the court shall, on notice, forthwith revoke his letters and appoint a successor, and cause a suit to be instituted on his bond against him and his security, for the use of the person interested in the estate; and if it shall appear, upon the trial of such cause, that the executor or administrator has so removed such property, judgment shall be rendered against the offender and his securities, for

---

(1) Means vs. Harrison, 114 Ill., 248; see 2 Probate Reports, 552, for brief of authorities.
(2) Hurd's R. S., Chap. 3, § 83.
(3) Hurd's R. S., Chap. 3, § 84.

the full value thereof, and such other damages as the parties interested may have sustained by reason thereof.(¹)

25. SALE OF PERSONAL PROPERTY.—When it is necessary for the proper administration of the estate, the executor or administrator shall, as soon as convenient, after making the inventory and appraisement, sell at public sale, all the personal property, goods and chattels of the decedent, when ordered to do so by the county court, (not reserved to the widow, or included in specific legacies and bequests, when the sale of such legacies and bequests is not necessary to pay debts,) upon giving three weeks' notice of the time and place of such sale, by at least four advertisements, set up in the most public places in the county where the sale is to be made, or by inserting an advertisement in the nearest newspaper published in this state, to the place of such sale, at least four weeks successively, previous thereto. The sale may be upon a credit of not less than six nor more than twelve months time, by taking note with good security of the purchasers at such sale. The sale may be for all cash, or part cash and part on time: *Provided*, that any part or all of such personal property may, where so directed by the court, be sold at private sale.(²)

This statute requires that security be taken for the payment of deferred payments, whether the property be sold at public or private sale; and the court has no power to direct otherwise.(³)

As a general principle, an administrator has power to dispose of the personal effects of his decedent, and the alienee obtains a perfect title thereto by such sale. He has to sell the property in order to pay debts against the estate, and make distribution of the surplus among the heirs, and purchasers would not be disposed to deal with an administrator in the assets of an estate, if they were liable to be afterwards called to account. The statute points out the manner of making a sale, but it is only directory, and a sale of personal property in any other manner by the administrator, if not tinctured by fraud, and in good faith, would convey a good title to the

(1) Hurd's R. S., Chap. 3, § 85.
(2) Hurd's R. S., Chap. 3. § 90.
(3) Bowen vs. Shay, 105 Ill., 132.

purchaser.(¹) Should an administrator take the responsibility of selling the personal property of the deceased in a manner different from that pointed out by the statute, he takes upon himself the responsibility of answering to those interested for all damages to the estate which may follow.(²)

26. CAVEAT EMPTOR.—Purchasers at the sales made by administrators and executors in pursuance of the statute, act at their peril, both as to title and quality of the articles sold. They must inquire into the title, and ascertain the quality before purchasing, for the administrator only sells the interest that was vested in the intestate, and makes no warranty either for himself or the estate which he represents. The rule of *caveat emptor* strictly applies to all such sales, whether of personal property or real estate.(³) Notwithstanding this inflexible rule, where fraud is made use of by the administrators, to effect sales of property of the estate at prices in excess of its value, such fraud may be shown to defeat recovery upon notes given for property sold at such sales.(⁴)

27. WHO MAY NOT PURCHASE.—An administrator cannot purchase at his own sale,(⁵) nor can a firm, of which he is a member.(⁶)

28. GROWING CROPS.—If any executor or administrator is of opinion that it would be of advantage to the estate of the decedent, to dispose of the crop growing, and not devised at the time of his decease, the same shall be inventoried, appraised and sold, in like manner as other personal property; but the executor or administrator may, if he believes it would be of more advantage to the estate, cultivate such crop to maturity, and the proceeds of such crop, after deducting all necessary expenses for cultivating, gathering and making sale of the same, shall be assets in his hands, and subject to the payment of debts and legacies, and to distribution as aforesaid.(⁷)

Crops growing upon lands of a testator which are devised by

---

(1) Makepeace vs. Moore, 5 Gil., 474; Walker et al. vs. Craig, 1 Ill. 116; McConnell vs. Hodson, 2 Gil., 640; Bond vs. Zeigler, 1 Ga., 24.
(2) Burnap vs. Dennis, 3 Scam., 478.
(3) Bingham et al. vs. Maxey, 15 Ill., 295.
(4) Welch et al. vs. Hoyt, 24 Ill., 117; Ray vs. Virgin, 12 Ill., 216; liamson vs. Walker, 24 Ga., 257.
(5) Nelson vs. Hayner et al., 66 Ill., 488; Miles et al. vs. Wheeler e al., 43 Ill., 123; Williams vs. Rhodes et al., 81 Ill., 572.
(6) Harrod vs. Norris, 11 Martin, 297.
(7) Hurd's R. S., Chap. 3, § 93.

will, pass to the devisee, and the executor of the will has no interest in, nor control over them.(¹)

An administrator who sells property exempt from sale is liable in trover at the suit of the widow and heirs.(²)

29. CLERK—CRIER.—In all public sales of such property, the executor or administrator may employ necessary clerks, who shall receive such compensation as the court may deem reasonable for their services, not exceeding five dollars per day, and also a crier or auctioneer, who shall receive such compensation as the court may deem reasonable, not exceeding ten dollars per day, to be paid by such executor or administrator and charged to the estate.

All such sales shall be made between the hours of ten o'clock in the forenoon and five o'clock in the afternoon of each day; and any sale made before or after the time herein limited shall be voidable at the instance of heirs, devisees or creditors prejudiced thereby.(³)

30. BILL OF SALES—RETURN.—All executors and administrators shall, immediately after making such sales, make, or cause to be made, a bill of the sales of said estate, under oath, describing particularly each article of property sold, to whom sold, and at what price; which sale bill, when thus made and certified by the clerk of such sale and the crier thereof, if any such was employed, as true and correct, shall be returned into the office of the clerk of the county court, in the like time as is required in cases of inventories and appraisements.(⁴)

(1) Creel vs. Kirkham, 47 Ill., 344.
(2) Jackson vs. Bryan, 3 J. J. Marshall, 308.
(3) Hurd's R. S., Chap. 3, § 94.
(4) Hurd's R. S., Chap. 3, § 95.

CHAPTER VII.

PARTNERSHIP ESTATES.

1. Partnership terminated by death of one partner.
2. Must be authority in the will to continue business after such dissolution.
3. Statutory partnership.
4. Proceedings on dissolution.
5. Surviving partner to file inventory.
6. In what county.
7. Survivor continues in possession.
    a. Survivor must sue alone.
8. Waste by him.
9. Effects must first pay partnership debts.
    a. How balance disposed of.
10. Statute declaratory.
11. Account.
12. Survivor may purchase.
13. When partnership to be settled.
14. Power of administrator to enforce settlement.
15. Final settlement.
16. No compensation to survivor.
17. Real estate of partnership.

1. PARTNERSHIP TERMINATED BY DEATH OF ONE PARTNER.— It has long been the law, that the death, insanity or bankruptcy of one partner in a partnership, independent of statutory provisions, immediately and inevitably dissolves and terminates such partnership.([1]) Some authorities hold that, by a stipulation in the articles of co-partnership, the relation may be perpetuated beyond the death of one of the constituent members, the heirs or personal representatives of the deceased, meantime representing him therein; but the partner being dead—not in existence—he can have no representative. His death has vested the title to his property in others, and if the firm is perpetuated under the agreement that his heirs or representatives shall represent him, it becomes to all intents a new

---

([1]) Remick vs. Emig et al., 42 Ill., 342; Oliver vs. Forrester, 96 Ill., 315; Griswold vs. Waddington, 15 Johns., (N. Y.) 57; Parsons on Partnership, 466–473; Nelson vs. Hayner et al., 66 Ill., 487.

firm, organized under a bargain made for that purpose in the old articles of co-partnership (¹)

Although upon this question there is a conflict of authorities, the better conclusion is consistent with the rule, long observed, laid down above. In this case, where the heirs or personal representatives, in pursuance of the agreement for perpetuating the business, made by the old firm, assent thereto and continue the joint relation, a new firm is thereby created, consisting of the surviving members and personal representatives, the new members becoming liable as the old, to all creditors of the firm.(²)

An executor or administrator entering into such a relation, as to outside parties, loses his trust capacity, and becomes personally liable for the contracts of the new firm.(³)

2. MUST BE AUTHORITY IN THE WILL.—It is a rule, without exception, that to authorize executors to carry on a trade, or to permit it to be carried on with the property of the testator held by them in trust, there ought to be the most distinct and positive authority and directions given by the will itself for that purpose.(⁴) A testator's directions to his partner to continue to carry on his business with his surviving partners does not authorize the executors to embark any new capital in the business.(⁵) But where articles of co-partnership provide that the death of one of the co-partners shall not terminate the partnership, but the same shall continue, the executor of the deceased partner to act for him, the general estate of the deceased partner is bound by the obligations of the partnership contracted in the regular course of business, and a pledge of the assets of the estate for firm debts is valid.(⁶)

Whatever powers of this kind are given to an executor, either

---

(1) Burwell vs. Mandeville, 2 Hav., 579; Ex Parte Garland, 10 Vesey, Jr., 119; Story on Partnership, 438; Forrester vs. Oliver, 1 Ill. Ap., 259; Buckingham vs. Morrison, 136 Ill., 439.
(2) Colton vs. Field et al., 131 Ill., 398.
(3) Alsop vs. Mather, 8 Conn., 584; Edgar vs. Cook, 4 Ala., 588; Labouchere vs. Tupper, 11 Moore, Priv. Coun., 221, Creagh vs. Creagh, 13 Irish Ch., 46; See 2 Probate Reports, 613 for authorities.
(4) Kirkman vs. Booth, 11 Beav., 273.
(5) Smith vs. Smith, 13 Grant Ch., 81.
(6) Blodgett vs. Am. National Bank, Sup. Court of Connecticut, 14 Legal News, 112. This decision was made in a case where the executor had pledged assets of a testator to secure partnership debts, and legatees brought action to recover the assets. In a case where personal creditors should, in like manner, attempt to assert their rights, a different rule might be announced.

to become a partner, or, being partner, to carry on the business for the benefit of the representatives of the deceased, or to leave the estate of the deceased in the partnership and in the business on any terms, and for any purpose, these powers would probably be strictly pursued; at least they would never be enlarged by implication. Thus it is clear that the deceased may limit the amount or proportion of his estate which shall remain in the partnership, or go into it, at his own pleasure, and the executors or appointees can no more enlarge this than they can violate any other of his directions. Nor will such a disposition or limitation in any way affect the rights of the creditors of the partnership.([1])*

3. STATUTORY PARTNERSHIP.—The statute of Illinois([2]) makes provisions for the formation of what is termed *limited partnerships*, under prescribed formalities, under which, when those provisions have been complied with, the rule that the death of one partner dissolves the partnership, may be avoided. What is said above, relates to general partnerships, and not to those formed under this statute.

4. PROCEEDINGS ON DISSOLUTION.—Upon the dissolution of a firm by the death of one partner, the survivor, before the statute and now, succeeds to the effects of the firm as a trustee.([3]) The relation of trustee and *cestui que trust*, is at once raised by law between the survivor and the legal representatives of the deceased; the terms of the trust being, that he will close up the business of the firm as required by law.([4])

5. SURVIVING PARTNER.—In case of the death of one partner, the surviving partner or partners shall proceed to make a full, true and complete inventory of the estate of the co-partnership within his knowledge; and shall also make a full, true and complete list of all the liabilities thereof at the time of the death of the deceased partner. He or they shall cause the said estate to be appraised in like manner as the individual property of a deceased person.([5])

6. RETURN OF INVENTORY.—He or they shall return, under oath, such inventory, list of liabilities and appraisement, within sixty days after the death of the co-partner, to the county court of

(1) Parsons on Partnership, 453; Davis vs. Christian, 15 Gratt., 37; Burnett vs. Rhodes, 58 Md., 78.
(2) Chap. 84.
(3) Miller et al. vs. Jones, 39 Ill., 54; People vs. White, 11 Ill., 342.
(4) Forrester vs. Oliver, 1 Ill. Ap., 259; *Ib.*, 96 Ill., 315.
(5) Hurd's R. S., Chap. 3, § 86.

*NOTE.—Where a testator orders his partnership business carried on after his death, unless by clear and unambiguous language it is otherwise directed, only the fund employed in the business before his decease is answerable to a subsequent creditor.—*Laiable* vs. *Fetry*, 32 N. J. Eq., 791; *Brasfield* vs. *French*, 59 Miss., 632.

the county of which the deceased was a resident or carried on the partnership business at the time of his death; if the deceased shall have been a non-resident, then such return shall be made to the county court granting administration upon the effects of the deceased. Upon neglect or refusal to make such return, he shall, after citation, be liable to attachment.([1])

7. RIGHTS OF SURVIVING PARTNER.—Such surviving partner or partners shall have the right to continue in possession of the effects of the partnership, pay its debts out of the same, and settle its business, but shall proceed thereto without delay, and shall account with the executor or administrator, and pay over such balances as may, from time to time, be payable to him in the right of his testator or intestate. Upon the application of the executor or administrator, the county court may, whenever it may appear necessary, order such surviving partner to render an account to said county court, and in case of neglect or refusal may, after citation, compel the rendition of such account by attachment.([2])

a. The administrator can not join the survivor in a suit to collect partnership debts—the survivor alone must sue.([3])

8. WASTE AND REMEDY THEREFOR.—Upon the committal of waste by the surviving partner or partners, the court may, upon proper application, under oath, setting forth specifically the facts and circumstances relied on, protect the estate of the deceased partner, by citing forthwith the surviving partner or partners to give security for the faithful settlement of the affairs of the co-partnership, and for his accounting for and paying over to the executor or administrator of the deceased, whatever shall be found to be due, after paying partnership debts and costs of settlement, within such time as shall be fixed by the court. The giving of such security may be enforced by attachment, or, upon refusal to give such security, the court may appoint a receiver of the partnership property and effects, with like powers and duties of receivers in courts of chancery—the costs of proceedings under this section to be paid by the executor or administrator, out of the estate of the deceased or surviving partner, or partly by each, as the court may order.([4])

(1) Hurd's R. S., Chap. 3, § 87.
(2) Hurd's R. S., Chap. 3, § 88; Miller vs. Kingsbury, 128 Ill., 45.
(3) Belton vs. Fisher, 44 Ill., 32.
(4) Hurd's R. S., Chap. 3, § 89; Miller vs. Kingsbury, *supra*.

A surviving partner cannot purchase of himself the assets of the firm.(¹)

9. PARTNERSHIP DEBTS.—The surviving partner retains the property of the firm, and settles up affairs of the partnership. The effects are first to be applied to the payment of the joint debts: the surplus divided between the survivor and the personal representatives of the deceased.(²)

a. The surviving partner has not the right, in the adjustment of accounts between himself and the administrator of a deceased partner, to have his individual account against the deceased deducted from any balance which may be found in his hands as surviving partner, although such debt may be secured by a mortgage.(³)

10. STATUTE DECLARATORY.—The statute in relation to partnership is but declaratory—providing some additional remedies, but does not change the rights and duties of parties.(⁴) Nor does it affect the right of a court of equity to entertain suits for the adjustment of partnership affairs.(⁵)

11. TAKING ACCOUNT.—In taking account of partnership assets, the state of stock is to be taken as at the death of the deceased partner.(⁶)

The remedy given by statute, to compel a surviving partner to account to the county court with the administrator, is to be governed by the same equitable rules and principles as a proceeding in equity.(⁷)

12. SURVIVORS MAY PURCHASE OF LEGAL REPRESENTATIVES.—In the absence of all fraud, the survivors of a partnership may purchase from the executor or administrator, the interest of the decedent in the partnership, so as to bind all persons interested in the estate.(⁸)

13. WHEN SETTLED.—No time is prescribed by the statute within which the affairs of partnership estates must be closed and

---

(1) Nelson vs. Hayner et al., 66 Ill., 487.
(2) People vs. White et al., 11 Ill., 341; Ladd vs. Griswold et al., 4 Gil., 25; Miller et al. vs. Jones, 39 Ill., 54; Winslow vs. Leland, 128 Ill, 304; Moffatt vs. Thomson, 5 Richardson Eq., 155.
(3) Berry et al. vs. Powell, 18 Ill., 98; Caskie vs. Harrison, 76 Va., 85.
(4) Forrester vs. Oliver, 1 Ill. Ap., 259; Nelson vs. Hayner et al., *supra*.
(5) Breckinridge et. al. vs. Ostrom, 79 Ill., 71.
(6) Remick vs. Emig, 42 Ill., 342.
(7) Mack vs. Woodruff, 87 Ill., 570; Parsons on Partnership, 347; Nelson vs. Hayner, *supra*.
(8) Davies vs Davies, 15 Eng. Ch., 538; Chambers vs. Howill, 11 Beav., 13; Cook vs. Collinridge, 3 Eng. Ch., 520.

the final accounting had with the administrator; yet, by analogy, to the two years allowed for the presentation of claims against the estates of deceased persons, it is probably safe to say, that, except in extreme cases, requiring more time for an economical administration of partnership estates, surviving partners should be required by courts, to finally account within two years from the dissolution.([1]) This will enable unpaid creditors of the firm, to avail themselves of their rights against the estates of deceased partners, and offer no obstruction in the way of the final accounting of the representatives of the deceased.

14. POWER OF ADMINISTRATOR.—Any dereliction, mismanagement or misapplication, on the part of the surviving partner, may be promptly restrained on the application of the personal representatives of the deceased;([2]) or, such survivors may be compelled to give security, upon the motion of the administrator;([3]) or, the survivor may be required to make sale of partnership effects, as the only certain way of ascertaining their value and making a fair division;([4]) or, he may be compelled to file an account of the partnership, in which respect the power of the administrator is as complete as the right of the deceased while he lived and was partner.([5])

15. FINAL SETTLEMENT.—In rendering an account of partnership assets, the surviving partner may properly set-off in his favor the amount of any debts due to the firm from the estate of the deceased partner, without having had them first allowed in probate, the account being stated under equitable rules.([6])

If partnership property has come to the hands of an administrator, he is responsible only for the interest of the decedent in the property of the firm, after the settlement of the partnership accounts. A fair settlement, made by him with the other partner, will be sustained.([7])

16. NO COMPENSATION TO SURVIVOR.—A survivor of a partnership has no right to demand compensation for his services in settling

(1) Miller vs. Jones, 39 Ill., 54.
(2) People vs. White, 11 Ill., 341; Miller et al. vs. Jones, *supra*.
(3) Sec. 89, *supra*.
(4) Parsons on Partnership, 446.
(5) *Id.;* McKean vs. Vick, 108 Ill., 373.
(6) Parsons on Partnership, *supra*.
(7) Montgomery vs. Dunning, 2 Brad., 220.

the affairs of a partnership, unless under the terms of the articles of copartnership it is provided that compensation shall be paid for such services.(¹)

17. REAL ESTATE OF A PARTNERSHIP.—Where the money of a partnership has been invested in real estate, such property will, for the purposes of the partnership, be treated as personal property, and may be sold by the survivor, like any other property, when necessary, for the payment of partnership debts. What may be left after the payment of debts is treated like other lands held in common.(²)

(1) Buckingham vs. Morrison, 136 Ill., 437.
(2) Strong vs. Lord, 107 Ill., 25; See 73 Am. Dec., for authorities.

CHAPTER VIII.

AWARD TO WIDOW OR CHILDREN.

1. Widow's award.
2. Not affected by renunciation.
3. Allowance to children.
4. Policy of the law.
5. Right to award becomes fixed upon the death of the husband.
6. Right cannot be cut off by will.
7. Nor by an ante nuptial contract.
8. Widow not justified in seizing and holding money to satisfy claim.
9. Widow's claim need not be presented as other claims.
10. None but widows of *bona fide* residents entitled to it.
11. Definition of "family."
12. Practice.
    a. Duty of administrator to set-off.
    b. Legal title to specific articles vests in widow upon death of husband.
    c. New rule of preference.
    d. Appraisers to consider her social condition.
13. Power of court over award.
14. Title vests in widow.
15. Widow bound by her relinquishment.
16. Lien upon real estate.

1. WIDOW'S AWARD.—The widow, residing in this state, of a deceased husband whose estate is administered in this state, whether her husband died testate or intestate, shall, in all cases, in exclusion of debts, claims, charges, legacies and bequests, except funeral expenses, be allowed, as her sole and exclusive property forever, the following, to-wit:*

First—The family pictures and the wearing apparel, jewels and ornaments of herself and her minor children.

Second—School books and family library of the value of $100.

Third—One sewing machine.

Fourth—Necessary beds, bedsteads and bedding for herself and family.

Fifth—The stoves and pipe used in the family, with the necessary cooking utensils; or, in case they have none, $50 in money.

---
* NOTE.—The widow's award is barred in 20 years.—*Barnes vs. Maring*, 23 Ill. App., 68.

Sixth—Household and kitchen furniture to the value of $100.

Seventh—One milch cow and calf, for every four members of her family.

Eighth—Two sheep for each member of her family, and the fleeces taken from the same, and one horse, saddle and bridle.

Ninth—Provisions for herself and family for one year.

Tenth—Food for the stock above specified, for six months.

Eleventh—Fuel for herself and family for three months.

Twelfth—$100 worth of other property suited to her condition in life, to be selected by the widow.

Which shall be known as the widow's award; or the widow may, if she elect, take and receive, in lieu of the foregoing, the same personal property, or money in place thereof, as is or may be exempt from execution or attachment against the head of a family residing with the same.[1]

The appraisers shall make out and certify to the county court an estimate of the value of each of the several items of property allowed to the widow; and it shall be lawful for the widow to elect whether she will take the specific articles set apart to her, or take the amount thereof out of other personal property at the appraised value thereof, or whether she will take the amount thereof in money, or she may take a part in property and a part in money, as she may prefer; and in all such cases, it shall be the duty of the executor or administrator to notify the widow as soon as such appraisement shall be made, and to set apart to her such article or articles of property, not exceeding the amount to which she may be entitled, and as she may prefer or select, within thirty days after written application shall be made for that purpose by such widow. And if any such executor or administrator shall neglect or refuse to comply with the above requisition, when application shall be made for that purpose, he shall forfeit and pay for the use of such widow the sum of twenty dollars per month for each month's delay to set apart said property so selected, after the said term of thirty days shall have elapsed, to be recovered in the name of the People of the State of Illinois, for the use of such widow, in any court having jurisdiction of the same. When there is not property of the

---

[1] Hurd's R. S., Chap. 3, § 74; Lesher vs. Wirth, 14 Ill., 39.

estate, of the kinds mentioned in the preceding section, the appraisers may award the widow a gross sum in lieu thereof, except for family pictures, jewels and ornaments.(1)

2. RIGHT NOT AFFECTED BY RENUNCIATION.—The right of a widow to her award shall in no case be affected by her renouncing or failing to renounce the benefit of the provisions made for her in the will of her husband, or otherwise.(2)

3. ALLOWANCE TO CHILDREN.—When the person dying is at the time of his death a housekeeper, the head of a family, and leaves no widow, there shall be allowed to the children of the deceased, residing with him at the time of his death (including all males under eighteen years of age, and all females), the same amount of property as is allowed to the widow by this act.(3)

The allowance to the widow or children is strictly limited to cases where the deceased resided in this state.(4) Where one sojourned temporarily in this state in company with his children, but had a permanent home in another state, and died here, his children were not entitled to the allowance.(5)

4. POLICY OF THE LAW.—The provisions made for the wife of a deceased resident of this state, is a benefit created in her favor by positive law, and adopted for reasons deemed wise and politic.(6)

The allowance is as much for the benefit of the children as for the wife, and where there are children of the deceased residing with the widow, she has no power by an ante nuptial agreement or otherwise, to deprive them of this means of support for their tender years, which the law has given.(7)

The design of the law was to furnish the necessary sustenance for such household for one year after the death of the husband, and to enable the widow to keep her domestic circle, as respects the remaining members, unbroken during that time; and the allowance of bedding, furniture and provisions, should be made upon this basis.(8)

---

(1) Hurd's R. S., Chap. 3, § 75; Furlong vs. Riley, 103 Ill., 628.
(2) Hurd's R. S., Chap. 3, § 76; Kellogg vs. Holley, 29 Ill., 437; Deltzer vs. Sheuster, 37 Ill., 301.
(3) Hurd's R. S., Chap. 3, § 77; Lesher vs. Wirth, 14 Ill., 39.
(4) Sec. 74, *supra*. See post p. 92.
(5) Veile vs. Koch, 27 Ill., 129.
(6) Phelps vs. Phelps, 72 Ill., 545.
(7) *Id.* McAnnulty vs. McAnnulty, 120 Ill., 26.
(8) Strawn et al. vs. Strawn, 53 Ill., 263.

5. HER RIGHT TO THE AWARD.—The right of the widow to her award is fixed upon the death of the husband, and is not lost by her death before appraisers are appointed. Should she die before the value of her award is determined by the appraisers, her administrator may sue for and recover the value from the husband's estate.([1]) A creditor of the widow cannot have allowance set off.([2])

6. RIGHT CANNOT BE CUT OFF BY WILL.—The husband cannot, by his will, deprive his wife or children of this allowance,([3]) but may, by giving away all of his estate before his death,([4]) or by encumbering it by a valid lien.([5])

7. NOR BY AN ANTE NUPTIAL CONTRACT.—The right of a widow, having in her care dependent children of the deceased, to the widow's award out of the estate of her husband, and to the estate of homestead provided by the statute, cannot be released by her, nor is it affected by an ante nuptial contract entered into between herself and the deceased ;([6]) but where the deceased left no children dependent upon the wife, and previous to her marriage she had entered into an ante nuptial contract with him, that at his death she shall receive $1,500 in lieu of dower and all other rights to his property, the payment of that sum by the administrator will be a complete defense to her claim upon the estate for the award.([7]) Where an ante nuptial contract providing that the widow should accept a sum named in lieu of the allowance was acted upon by the widow by accepting the sum named, it was held that she was bound thereby, though there were children.([8])

8. WIDOW NOT JUSTIFIED IN SEIZING AND HOLDING MONEY TO SATISFY CLAIM.—While the right of a widow of a deceased resident of Illinois to the award provided by statute is fixed and absolute, yet she is not justified in seizing and holding, as against the heirs of her husband, a sum of money on hand at the time of his death, when there has been no administration upon the estate

(1) York vs. York, 38 Ill., 522.
(2) Miller vs. Kingsbury, 28 Ill. Ap., 532.
(3) Phelps vs. Phelps, 72 Ill., 545.
(4) Padfield vs. Padfield et al., 78 Ill., 16.
(5) King vs. Goodwin, 130 Ill., 102.
(6) Phelps vs. Phelps, *supra;* McGee et al. vs. McGee, 91 Ill., 548.
(7) Brenner vs. Gauch, 85 Ill., 368; Mahill vs. Mahill, 113 Ill., 465, Spencer vs. Boardman, 118 Ill., 553.
(8) Weaver vs. Weaver, 109 Ill., 225.

and no ascertainment of the value of the award in her case, under her statutory right to such award.([1])

9. WIDOW'S CLAIM NEED NOT BE PRESENTED AS OTHER CLAIMS.—The widow's award, although in one sense a demand against the estate of her husband, is not such a demand as is required to be exhibited against the estate within two years or be forever barred.([2])

10. NONE BUT WIDOWS OF BONA FIDE RESIDENTS ENTITLED TO IT.—None but the widows or children of decedents who, at the time of death, were *bona fide* residents of this state are entitled to the statutory allowance provided for in section 74.([3])

11. FAMILY.—The word "family," as used in this statute, does not include alone the widow and minor children of the deceased, but includes such persons as constituted the family of the deceased at the time of his death, whether servants or children who had attained their majority. In this is not to be included boarders, but only the persons constituting the private household of the deceased.( )

A son or daughter residing with the father does not cease to be a member of his family when he or she arrives at the age of twenty-one or eighteen years, respectively, by reason of that fact alone.([5])

The above definitions of the word "family," as used in this connection, may be considered somewhat restricted by the enactment of section 77, *supra*.

12. PRACTICE.—The law does not require the appraisers to set apart to the widow the articles of specific property; they are only to fix a value upon such articles as are not given a value by the statute, and certify the same to the court.([6])

a. It is the duty of the administrator to set off to the widow the specific articles of personal property, and failing to do so would be evidence of a conversion.([7])

b. The legal title to specific articles does not vest in the administrator, but vests in the widow upon the death of the husband, and the title does not depend upon the action of the appraisers.([8])

(1) Tyler et al. vs. Daniel et al., 65 Ill., 316.
(2) Miller vs. Miller, 82 Ill., 463.
(3) Veile vs. Koch, 27 Ill., 129; Rock vs. Haas, 110 Ill., 528.
(4) Strawn et al. vs. Strawn, 53 Ill., 263.
(5) Chicago & N. W. R. R. Co. vs. Chisholm, 79 Ill., 584
(6) York vs. York, 38 Ill., 552.
(7) *Ib.*
(8) *Ib.;* Cross vs. Carey, 25 Ill., 562.

c. The statute of 1872, *supra*, makes an exception to the above rule, which prevailed in this state up to that date. The widow now takes her allowance subject to funeral expenses. So, where her award exceeds the value of the personal property which she elects to take, the title thereto becomes vested in her as her sole and separate property forever, subject only to the payment of funeral expenses.([1])

Where the widow's claim is not paid by the application of the personal property, she cannot claim preference over other creditors of the estate, in the distribution of the proceeds of the sale of the real estate.([2])

It is held that, under the law of 1872, the above rule, which prevailed under the old statute, is changed, so far as to make the widow a preferred creditor over all except funeral expenses, in the distribution of the proceeds of the real estate, where her award is not met by the personal property.([3])

d. In fixing the allowance, the appraisers should take into consideration the condition and mode of life in which the widow and family were left by the deceased husband—and regard as necessary that furniture which is the ordinary and appropriate furniture for such homesteads.([4])

Where there are no stoves in use in the family, $50 should be allowed—where there are stoves, no estimate is to be made for that item. No estimate is to be made for family jewels and ornaments.([5])

13. POWER OF THE COURT OVER THE AWARD.—The county court, from its general powers in supervising the administration of estates, has the power, for cause shown, to set aside a report of appraisers, making out and certifying to that court an estimate of the value of the items of property mentioned in the statute as the widow's award;([6]) but while the court has this supervisory power, it has no power to revise and modify the estimate, and substitute the judgment of the court for the judgment of the appraisers.([7])

(1) McCord vs. McKinley, 92 Ill., 11
(2) Cruce vs. Cruce, 21 Ill., 46.
(3) Rector vs. Reavill, 3 Ill. Ap., 232.
(4) Strawn et al. vs. Strawn, 53 Ill., 663.
(5) Hurd's R. S., Chap. 3, § 75.
(6) Miller vs. Miller, 82 Ill., 463; *In re* Scoville's estate, 20 Ill. Ap., 426; Boys vs. Rogers, 21 Ill. Ap., 534.
(7) *Ib.*

Upon the hearing of a petition of an administrator for leave to sell lands of the deceased to pay debts and liabilities, the allowance to the widow was held not to be final and conclusive as to the legatees who were made parties thereto, but that in such proceeding it might be shown to be fraudulent, too large, oppressive or unjust.(¹) Unless impeached for fraud, the award as made by the appraisers is conclusive upon the widow.(²)

In such a proceeding, upon cause shown, the court may set aside the award and appoint other appraisers to make a new one.(³)

On appeal to the circuit court from an order of the county court approving the appraisers' estimate of the value of property allowed as widow's award, the circuit court can only exercise such power as the county court might have done.(⁴)

14. TITLE OF PROPERTY VESTS IN WIDOW—The title to property taken by the widow, whether they be the specific articles named in the statute or others taken in lieu thereof, upon being receipted for by her, vest in her as her separate property, subject, in cases where the estate is unable to pay funeral expenses, to a lien for the payment of such expenses.(⁵) The amount of the award will not draw interest.(⁶)

15. WIDOW RELINQUISHING.—Where a widow relinquishes her right to the specific articles allowed by law, and elects to receive others in lieu thereof, she is bound by such action.(⁷)

16. LIEN UPON REAL ESTATE.—As we have seen above, in cases where the widow's award is not paid out of the personal estate, the amount remaining unpaid, after the application of the personalty to the payment of funeral expenses and the award, becomes a lien upon the real estate of the decedent, whether he died testate or intestate, and the widow becomes a preferred creditor to the extent of her unpaid allowance, entitled to be first paid from the proceeds of the sale of real estate.(⁸) To this end, like any other creditor, she

---

(1) Marshall et al. vs. Rose, 86 Ill., 374; Spencer vs. Boardman, 118 Ill., 553; Goeppner vs. Leitzelman, 98 Ill., 409.
(2) Telford et al. vs. Boggs, 63 Ill., 498.
(3) *Ib.*
(4) Miller vs. Miller, 82 Ill., 463.
(5) McCord vs. McKinley, 92 Ill., 11.
(6) Strong vs. Strong, 131 Ill., 210; Lynch vs. Hickey, 13 Ill. Ap., 139.
(7) Telford et al. vs. Boggs, 63 Ill., 498.
(8) Cruce vs. Cruce, 21 Ill., 46; Rector vs. Reavill, 3 Ill. Ap., 232; Telford vs. Boggs, *supra.*

may compel a sale of the real estate to meet her demand, and such sale will, in cases of intestacy, operate only upon the real estate of the heir, leaving her homestead and dower exempt; but in the case of a testate estate, where the wife took real estate under her husband's will, it was held inequitable to sell the lands devised in the will to others, for the purpose of realizing money out of which to pay the award, leaving the real estate devised to the widow to bear no part of the burden, which should be common to all the real estate of the deceased, except the homestead right.[1]

(1) Deltzer et al. vs. Scheuster, 37 Ill., 301.

CHAPTER IX.

CLAIMS AGAINST ESTATES.

1. Notice—adjustment.
2. What is a claim.
3. Claim for monument for deceased.
4. Partnership debts.
    a. Not to be allowed until partnership assets are exhausted.
    b. Individual creditors first to be paid.
    c. Excess of individual estate may be applied to pay partnership debts.
    d. Partnership debts joint and several.
    e. Allowance of partnership debt evidence of want of partnership assets.
5. Court may entertain equitable claims.
6. Funeral expenses.
7. Claim of former executor or administrator.
8. Forfeiture enforcible as a claim.
9. Taxes.
10. How and when claims should be presented.
    a. Surety discharged if note be not probated against principal's estate.
    b. Filing claim at adjustment term is commencement of a suit
11. Claim presented after two years.
12. Claims presented after administration is completed
13. Proceedings.
14. Continuance.
15. Costs.
16. Oath of claimant.
17. Judgment as evidence.
18. Offset—judgment for estate
19. Claims not due.
20. Claimant may chose his forum.
21. How allowed.
22. Cannot be submitted to arbitration.
23. Judgments bear interest.
24. Defenses to claims—duty of administrator.
    a. Any one interested may defend and prosecute appeals or *certiorari*.
    b. Equity will interfere only in cases of fraud.
    c. Gift cannot be enforced.
    d. *Post mortem* charges not enforcible.

   e. Wife may insist on claim.
   f. There must be a present debt.
   g. Claims of foreign administrator.
   h. Claim not presented to deceased.
 25. Defenses to claims—Limitations.
   a. General statute.
   b. Filing after adjustment day does not arrest the general statute.
   c. Six months' statute may be insisted on against material man.
   d. Claim on guardian's bond not barred by five years.
   e. Long delay.
   f. Contingent claim barred.
   g. In foreclosures.
 26. Practice—judgment can not exceed the demand.
   a. Prosecution of claim not governed by technical rules.
   b. Judgment which is not a lien has no preference.
   c. Claims should be proven as alleged.
   d. Allowance of a claim a judgment, and draws six per cent. interest regardless of what it drew before judgment.
   e. No particular form necessary.
   f. Set-offs must be mutual.
   g. In *scire facias* the usual judgment should be rendered.
   h. Plene Administravit—burden.
   i. Allowance without notice—void.
   j. Debtor can not buy up claims and offset
   k. Administrator need not offset.
   l. Writ of attachment—abatement.
   m. Plene administravit not good plea.
   n. Claim barred by two-year statute may be offset.
   o. Judgment against estate not a specific lien.
   p. Claim of administrator for money overpaid.
   q. No pleadings are necessary.
 27. Change of venue.
 28. Judgment conclusive.
 29. Demands of executor or administrator, how allowed
 30. Insolvent estates.
 31. Fees not to be charged.

  1. NOTICE — ADJUSTMENT. — Every administrator or executor shall fix upon a term of the court, within six months from the time of his being qualified as such administrator or executor, for the adjustment of all claims against such decedent, and shall publish a notice thereof for three successive weeks in some public newspaper published in the county, or if no newspaper is published in the county, then in the nearest newspaper in this state, and also by putting up a written or printed notice on the door of the court house, and in five other of the most public places in the county,

notifying and requesting all persons having claims against such estate to attend at said term of court for the purpose of having the same adjusted, (the first publication of said notice to be given at least six weeks previous to said term,) when and where such claimant shall produce his claim, in writing; and if no objection is made to said claim by the executor, administrator, widow, heirs or others interested in said estate, and the claimant swears that such claim is just and unpaid, after allowing all just credits, the court may allow such claim without further evidence, but if objection is made to such claim, the same shall not be allowed without other sufficient evidence. The court may allow either party further time to produce evidence in his favor, and the case shall be tried and determined as other suits at law. Either party may demand a jury of either six or twelve men, to try the issue, and it shall be the duty of the county clerk, when a jury is demanded, to issue a *venire* to the sheriff of the county to summon a jury, to be composed of the number demanded.(¹)

An administrator gives the court jurisdiction of his person by giving notice for the presentation of claims against the estate, and will be bound to take notice of the orders of the court continuing claims filed on or before the day named in his notice.(²)

An order for the payment of a claim filed after the adjustment day, where the personal representative has no notice of the proceeding, is a nullity.(³)

2. WHAT IS A CLAIM AGAINST A DECEDENT'S ESTATE.—No claims are properly chargeable against the estate of a deceased person, except such as arise out of some contract, express or implied, entered into by him during his lifetime; therefore, a contract entered into by the widow of a deceased person for the erection at his grave of a monument, is not a proper charge for allowance against the administrator.⁴ Nor does the fact that the administrator knew of the contract and of the work being done, without any objection on his part, make the estate liable.(⁵)

---

(1) Hurd's R. S., Chap. 3, § 60; Walker vs. Alexander, 24 N. E. Rep., 557.
(2) Ward vs. Durham, 134 Ill., 195.
(3) Hales vs. Holland, 92 Ill., 494.
(4) Foley vs. Bushway, 71 Ill., 386; Morgan vs. Morgan, 83 Ill., 196.
(5) *Ib.*

The death of a party does not terminate any contract he may have entered into.(¹) But it terminates an agency.(²)

A judgment released without having been paid by the defendant, at his request, is a proper claim for allowance against the estate of the deceased defendant.(³)

Breaches of covenant running with the land, accruing before the death of the covenantor, render the estate of the covenantor liable.(⁴)

Where there is a contract for the purchase of land, it descends to the heirs of the vendee as real estate, and they may call on the executor or administrator to discharge the contract out of the personal estate of the vendee, so as to enable the heirs to demand a conveyance from the vendor.(⁵)

3. CLAIM FOR MONUMENT TO DECEASED.—Where the widow of an intestate made a contract for the erection of a monument over the grave of her husband, to be paid for from his estate, the administrator cannot be required to pay it.(⁶)

4. PARTNERSHIP DEBTS.—Debts against the firm of which the intestate was a member, after the partnership assets have been exhausted in the payment of the firm debts, become an equitable claim against the estate, subject to the individual debts against the estate, all of which must be first paid, before any payment can be allowed upon the firm debts, and this should be provided for in the order of the probate court, in allowing the claim against the estate, or, by order of the circuit court ordering the sale of real estate for the payment of claims against the estate.(⁷)

a. No claim should be allowed against the estate for a partnership debt till it is shown that all the partnership assets have been exhausted, except the order provide for a preference to individual creditors.(⁸)

---

(1) Smith vs. Coal Mining Co., 83 Ill., 498; Rapp vs. Phœnix Ins. Co., 113 Ill., 390.
(2) Rapp vs. Phœnix Ins. Co., *supra;* Pratt vs. Trustees, 93 Ill., 475; Lochenmyer vs Fogarty, 112 Ill., 572.
(3) Howell vs. Edmonds, 47 Ill., 79.
(4) 1 Archibold's Nisi Prius, 356.
(5) Champion et al., vs. Brown, 6 Johnson's Ch., 398; Strong vs. Lord, 107 Ill., 26.
(6) Foley vs. Bushway, 71 Ill., 386; Morgan vs. Morgan, 71 Ill., 386.
(7) Ladd vs. Griswold et al., 4 Gil., 25.
(8) Moline Water Power Manf. Co. vs. Webster, 26 Ill., 239; People vs. Lott et al., 36 Ill., 447; Mason vs. Tiffany et al., 45 Ill., 392; Doggett vs. Dill, 108 Ill., 560.

b. Individual creditors of the deceased may insist upon the full payment of their claims before any payment is made upon claims due from a partnership of which he was a member; but heirs may not object (¹)

c. Where a partnership and its members are in insolvency under one commission, and the separate estate of one partner is more than enough to pay his separate debts, the surplus of that estate over such debts is to be added to the partnership estate, and applied to the payment of joint debts, before paying interest on the separate debts.(²)

d. Every partnership debt is joint and several, and in all such cases resort may be primarily had for the debt to the surviving partners, or, as above stated, to the estate of the deceased.(³)

e. The allowance of a partnership claim against the estate of a deceased member of the firm is *prima facie* evidence that partnership assets were before then exhausted.(⁴)

5. EQUITABLE CLAIMS.—The county court may entertain and adjudicate upon claims against the estates of deceased persons of a purely equitable character, and is not restricted in its adjudications to those of a legal nature. In the adjustment of equitable claims, the courts may adopt the forms of procedure in equity; but where third parties are interested in the subject matter, the county court has not jurisdiction.(⁵)

6. FUNERAL EXPENSES.—The reasonable and necessary expenses of the burial of a deceased person are a charge against his estate; the duty of burial is upon the executor, and, in the absence or neglect of the executor, the law implies a promise from the executor to remunerate one who incurs the expense of such burial; and if he have assets he may be compelled to do so.(⁶) Funeral expenses

(1) *Id;* See 77 Am. Dec., 114, for brief of authorities.
(2) Thomas vs. Minot, 10 Gray, 263.
(3) Mason vs. Tiffany, 45 Ill., 392.
(4) *Ib.;* McCall vs. Lee, 120 Ill., 261.
(5) Pahlman et al. vs. Graves, 26 Ill., 405 ; Moore et al. vs. Rogers, 19 Ill., 347; Dixon vs. Buel, 21 Ill., 203; In Re Steele, 65 Ill., 322 ; Garvin et al. vs. Stewart, 59 Ill., 229; Moline Water Power Co. vs. Webster, 26 Ill., 239; Hurd vs. Slaten et al., 43 Ill., 348; Jennings et al. vs. McConnel et al., 17 Ill., 148; Doggett vs. Dill, 108 Ill., 560; McCall vs. Lee, *supra;* Brandon vs. Brown, 106 Ill., 519; Wadsworth vs. Connell, 104 Ill., 369; Wolf vs. Beard, 123 Ill., 585.
(6) Patterson vs. Patterson, 59 N. Y., 574; Rappelyea vs. Russell, 1 Daily, 214.

and expenses of administration, need not be presented to the court for allowance, but may be paid by the executor or administrator, without being first presented and allowed.

The erection of a suitable headstone at the decedent's own grave, may properly be considered as a part of his funeral expenses, in a case where the rights of creditors cannot be defeated thereby.([1])

7. CLAIM OF A FORMER EXECUTOR OR ADMINISTRATOR.—One who has been an executor or administrator of an estate and resigned his trust, can not maintain a suit either at law or in equity against his successor, to recover a balance due to him from the estate. His remedy is in the settlement of the accounts of administration in the court of probate.([2])

8. FORFEITURE ENFORCIBLE.—Where the deceased in his lifetime executed a promissory note, with a clause providing for the payment of ten per cent. interest from date if not paid at maturity, the clause of forfeiture is enforcible against his estate, and this, although his death occurred before the maturity of the note.([3]) The death of one who contracts to pay a penalty for the non-performance of a legal contract before the time of performance, will not operate to excuse the non-performance, and relieve the estate of such person from the penalty. [4]

9. TAXES due at the death of the owner are payable from the personal estate, and subsequent taxes are chargeable upon the land.([5])

Taxes, insurance and court costs paid in an ejectment suit are not legitimate charges against an estate.([6])

10. HOW AND WHEN PRESENTED.—Claims should be presented against an estate within two years from the date of letters, whether notice for presentation is given or not, or be barred from participating in assets previously inventoried;([7]) and claims presented to

---

(1) Wood vs. Vandenburgh, 6 Paige, 277; Samuel vs. Thomas, 5 Wis., 549; Harris vs. Millard, 17 Ill. Ap., 512; See 2 Probate Reports, 104, for brief of authorities; Bendall vs. Bendall, 24 Ala., 295.
(2) Prentice vs. Dehon, 10 Allen, 353.
(3) Reeves vs. Stipp, 91 Ill., 609.
(4) Id.
(5) Griswold vs. Griswold, 4 Brad., 216.
(6) Walker et al. vs. Diehl, 79 Ill., 473.
(7) Rowan vs. Kirkpatrick, 14 Ill., 1; Sloo vs. Pool, 15 Ill., 47; Stillman vs. Young et al., 16 Ill., 318; Thorn vs. Watson, 5 Gil., 26; Judy et al. vs. Kelley, 11 Ill., 211; People vs. White, 11 Ill., 341; Wingate vs. Pool, 25 Ill., 118; Russell vs. Hubbard et al., 59 Ill., 336; Shepherd vs. Rhodes et al., 60 Ill., 301; Blanchard vs. Williamson, 70 Ill., 647; Baird vs. Chapman, 120 Ill., 537.

the court for allowance after the expiration of that limit, when properly proven, should be ordered paid out of property belonging to the estate which has not been inventoried, whether found previously or subsequently to the judgment.([1]) The judgment of the court allowing such a claim should be special, and not general.([2]) If an administrator does not present an inventory of the real estate within two years from the date of his letters, any creditor filing his claim with the clerk before the presentation of such inventory is entitled to enforce the payment of the same out of such real estate.([3])

Formerly a presentation of a copy of the claim to the administrator within two years was a sufficient exhibition of the claim,([4]) but it is otherwise under the statute of 1872.

A claim filed with the clerk on the day fixed by the administrator for the adjustment of claims, and within two years from the grant of letters, is a sufficient "exhibiting" of the claim within the meaning of the statute, although such claim was not regularly continued from term to term; and when more than three years after such filing, a trial was had, it was held that such claim was entitled to be paid generally out of the personal assets of the estate, as though allowed at the adjustment term.([5])

a. Where the principal in a note dies, the note must be presented as a claim against his estate within two years of date of letters, or the surety will be discharged to the extent of what might have been received on distribution of the estate.([6])

b. Filing a claim is not regarded as the commencement of a suit, unless it be at the term fixed by the administrator for adjustment of claims and continued from term to term.([7])

11. CLAIMS PRESENTED AFTER TWO YEARS.—To facilitate the settlement of estates, the statute provides that all demands not exhibited to the court within two years from the granting of letters shall be forever barred, unless the creditor shall find other estate of

---

(1) Bradford vs. Jones, 17 Ill., 93.
(2) Russell vs. Hubbard et al., 59 Ill., 336.
(3) Sloo vs. Pool, 15 Ill., 47.
(4) Wells vs. Miller, 45 Ill., 33.
(5) Barbero vs. Thurman, 49 Ill., 284; Wallace vs. Gatchel, 106 Ill., 316; McCall vs. Lee, 120 Ill., 261; Ward vs. Durham, 134 Ill., 195; Phœnix Ins. Co. vs. Gudery, 20 Ill. Ap., 161.
(6) Hurd's R. S., Chap. 132, § 3, Brockman vs. Sieverling et al., 6 Ill. Ap., 512.
(7) Reitzel et al. vs. Miller, 25 Ill., 67.

the deceased not inventoried or accounted for by the executor or administrator, in which case the claim shall be paid *pro rata* out of such subsequently discovered estate.(¹) This statute is not construed by the courts in a manner to absolutely bar any recovery whatever upon claims exhibited after the expiration of two years, but only so as to prevent the application to their payment of any of the assets of the estate previously inventoried, while, if not otherwise objectionable, the claims are allowed by the court, by special judgment, directing payment to be made from assets discovered and inventoried after the lapse of two years from the granting of letters of administration. And it makes no difference whether such assets are found before or after the judgment is rendered.(²)

If a claim is filed within the two years, that statute does not run against it, though it was not sworn to until after the two years.(³)

Where the cause of action, as for covenant broken, does not accrue until more than two years after the death of the debtor and the grant of letters and settlement of the estate, the two years limitation of the statute, as to claims against estates, will not apply to an action brought by the creditor against the administrator and heirs of the deceased debtor.(⁴)

12. CLAIMS PRESENTED AFTER ADMINISTRATION COMPLETED.—The right to present claims to the probate court and have them allowed, if found to be valid, with such a judgment as the time of filing the claim shows it entitled to, is not cut off by the approval of the final account, and discharge of the administrator. Although he may have been finally discharged, he may be again summoned into court to answer to some one holding a claim against his decedent. If the claim is proven to be a valid claim, the claimant is entitled to a judgment, to be paid in due course of administration, or, out of assets thereafter discovered, according as it was presented before or after the expiration of two years from the date of letters.(⁵)

(1) Hurd's R. S., Chap. 3, § 70.
(2) Thorn vs. Wilson, 5 Gil., 26; Bradford vs. Jones, 17 Ill., 93; Shepherd vs. Bank, 67 Ill., 292; Russell vs. Hubbard et al., 59 Ill., 335; Stone vs. Clarke, 40 Ill., 411; Sloo vs. Pool, 15 Ill., 47; Peacock vs. Haven et al., 22 Ill., 23; Judy et al., vs. Kelley, 11 Ill., 211; People vs. White, *Ib.* 342; Wingate vs. Pool, 25 Ill., 118.
(3) Wile vs. Wright, 32 Iowa, 451.
(4) Duggar et al. vs. Oglesby, 99 Ill., 405.
(5) Diversey vs. Johnson, 93 Ill., 547; Blanchard vs. Williamson, 70 Ill., 647; Sutherland vs. Harrison et al., 86 Ill., 363.

13. CLAIMS AFTERWARDS PRESENTED—PROCESS.—Whoever has a claim against an estate, and fails to present the same for adjustment at the term of court selected by the executor or administrator, may file a copy thereof with the clerk of the court; whereupon, unless the executor or administrator will waive the issuing of process, the clerk shall issue a summons, directed to the sheriff of the county, requiring such executor or administrator to appear and defend such claim at a term of the court therein specified, which summons, when served, shall be sufficient notice to the executor or administrator of the presentation of such claim.([1])

Claims should be presented to the probate court, either on adjustment day or on notice by the claimant; and if not allowed, should be continued to a day certain, or withdrawn, so as not to be allowed without giving the administrator notice, that he may have the opportunity to appear and contest the claim.([2])

14. CONTINUANCE.—If the summons is not served ten days before the first day of the term to which it is returnable, the cause shall be continued until the next term of the court, unless the parties shall, by consent, proceed to trial at the return term.([3])

15. TRIAL—COSTS.—Upon the trial of such cause, the same proceedings may be had as if the claim had been presented at the time fixed for the adjustment of claims against the estate, but the estate shall not be answerable for the cost of such proceeding: *Provided*, that when defense is made, the court may, if it shall deem just, order the whole or some part of the costs occasioned by such defense, to be paid out of the estate.([4])

This only applies to such costs as might have been avoided by an appearance at the adjustment term.([5])

This section has reference to costs, which accrue in the prosecution of claims presented to the county court for probate or upon appeal therefrom. Where the claimant chooses to litigate the claim before another forum, as he may do, the costs follow the result of the suit as between other suitors, even though the suit is commenced after the adjustment term;([6]) but the above rule, that estates

(1) Hurd's R. S., Chap. 3, § 61.
(2) Propst vs. Meadows, 13 Ill., 157.
(3) Hurd's R. S., Chap. 3, § 62.
(4) Hurd's R. S., Chap. 3, § 63.
(5) Wallace vs. Gatchel, 106 Ill., 315.
(6) Rosenthall vs. Magee, 41 Ill., 370.

are not liable for extra costs accruing in the allowance of claims filed after the adjustment term, is an inflexible one.(¹)

16. OATH OF CLAIMANT.—The court may, in its discretion in any case, before giving judgment against any executor or administrator, require the claimant to make oath that such claim is just and unpaid: *Provided*, that the amount of such judgment shall not in such case be increased upon the testimony of the claimant.(²)

17. JUDGMENT AS EVIDENCE.—A judgment regularly obtained, or a copy thereof duly certified and filed with the court, shall be taken as duly proven; and all instruments in writing, signed by the testator or intestate, if the hand-writing is proven and nothing is shown to the contrary, shall be deemed duly proved.(³)

An authenticated judgment from another state or country, rendered against the deceased in his lifetime, makes a *prima facie* case against his estate. But such a judgment rendered against an administrator of the deceased in another state, will not sustain an action against the administrator appointed in this state, but to maintain such action, resort must be had to original evidence.(⁴) Where an administrator appointed in one state goes into another state, and is there served with process, he will be bound by the judgment which may be rendered.(⁵)

18. OFFSET—JUDGMENT FOR ESTATE.—When a claim is filed or suit brought against an executor or administrator, and it appears on trial that such claimant or plaintiff is indebted to such executor or administrator, the court may give judgment therefor, and execution may issue thereon in favor of the executor or administrator.(⁶)

19. CLAIMS NOT DUE.—Any creditor, whose debt or claim against the estate is not due, may, nevertheless, present the same for allowance and settlement, and shall, thereupon, be considered as a creditor under this act, and shall receive a dividend of the said

---

(1) Russell vs. Hubbard et al., 59 Ill., 335.
(2) Hurd's R. S., Chap. 3, § 64.
(3) Hurd's R. S., Chap. 3, § 65.
(4) Stacey vs. Thrasher, 6 Howard, 44; Hobson et al. vs. Payne, 45 Ill., 158; Rosenthall vs. Renick et al., 44 Ill., 202; Judy et al. vs. Kelley, 11 Ill., 211; Hill vs. Tucker, 13 Howard, 458; As to manner of authentication, see U. S. Rev. Statutes, 1874, title 13, Chap. 17; McGarvey vs. Darnall, 134 Ill., 367.
(5) Evans vs. Tatem, 9 Sergeant & Rawle, 252; See note 11, Am. Dec., 723; Coates vs. Mackey, 56 Md., 416; Price vs. Mace, 47 Wis., 23.
(6) Hurd's R. S., Chap. 3, § 66.

decedent's estate, after deducting a rebate of interest for what he shall receive on such debt, to be computed from the time of the allowance thereof to the time such debt would have become due, according to the tenor and effect of the contract.([1])

Under the provisions of a prior section of the statute, (Sec. 70) all debts against an estate are required to be exhibited against an estate within two years from the grant of letters, and all demands not so exhibited, shall be barred, unless assets of the estate, not inventoried, are discovered out of which such demands may share in the settlement of the estate. If a claim could not be allowed, until due, and it happened not to become due until the expiration of the two years from the grant of letters, it might be in the power of the administrator by inventorying all the estate, to defeat the collection of the claim.([2])

20. CLAIMANT MAY CHOOSE HIS FORUM.—A creditor is not compelled to present his claim to the probate court, but may choose his forum, and resort in the first instance to the circuit court.([3])

It is a sufficient exhibition of a claim against an estate to file it in the probate court.([4])

And it has been held, under the provisions of the statute of frauds of this state,([5]) that if no person administers on the estate of a deceased person, within one year after his death, a separate suit may be maintained against the heirs or devisees of such deceased, on all his contracts and undertakings.([6])

21. HOW ALLOWED.—Where it is sought to revive a judgment rendered against a deceased person in his lifetime, against his administrator, the judgment of the court should be that the amount of such judgment should be paid in due course of administration, and it is error in such a case to award execution against the goods and chattels, lands and tenements of the deceased.([7])

22. ARBITRATION.—An administrator can not submit a claim against his intestate to arbitrators for their decision, so as to bind the estate. Claims allowed upon an award made by arbitrators, are

---

(1) Hurd's R. S., Chap. 3, § 67; Dunnigan vs. Stevens, 122 Ill., 397.
(2) Hall vs. Hoxey, 84 Ill., 616.
(3) Rosenthall vs. McGee, 41 Ill., 371; Wells vs. Miller, 45 Ill., 33; Darling vs. McDonald, 101 Ill., 370.
(4) People vs. White et al., 11 Ill., 341.
(5) Hurd's R. S., Chap. 59, § 15.
(6) Dodds et al. vs. Walker et al., 9 Ill. Ap., 37; People vs. Brooks, 123 Ill., 246.
(7) Turney vs. Gates, 12 Ill., 141.

void.(¹) And where, on appeal to the circuit court from the allowance of a claim in probate, the case was by the court referred to arbitrators, and judgment entered upon their award, to be paid in due course of administration, it was held that such proceedings in the circuit court were void, but did not affect the allowance of the claim in probate from which the appeal was taken.(²)

23. INTEREST.—When allowed, a claim bears six per cent. interest, like any other judgment.(³)

24. DEFENSES TO CLAIMS.—It is the duty of administrators and executors to be vigilant in interposing against claims presented against the estates committed to their care, all legal defenses thereto known to them, or which may be ascertained upon investigation; and to this end they should interpose the presumptions and limitations of the law against such claims,(⁴) and cannot waive the benefit thereof.(⁵) Failing to interpose all lawful defenses to claims, an administrator becomes liable on his bond.(⁶)

a. Their omission to perform their duty in this respect, will not preclude others affected thereby from doing so; but both the heirs and other creditors of the decedent may appear and defend in the probate court, or prosecute appeals from the allowance of a claim.(⁷) No reason is seen why they may not also prosecute writs of *certiorari.*

b. Equity will not interfere to relieve against a judgment in probate, at the suit of an heir, where it appears from the bill that the grounds upon which the impeachment was sought, constituted a good defense, and might have been interposed before the probate judge, and no fraud or collusion is shown in obtaining the judgment.(⁸) But where a judgment in probate has been obtained by fraud, the jurisdiction of a court of equity to grant relief is unquestioned (⁹) A claimant is not bound to disclose a defense to his claim (¹⁰)

(1) Reitzel et al. vs. Miller, 25 Ill., 67; Clark et al. vs. Hogle et al., 52 Ill., 428.
(2) *Id.*
(3) Mitchel vs. Mayo, 16 Ill., 83.
(4) McCoy vs. Morrow, 18 Ill., 519; Unknown Heirs of Langworthy vs. Baker et al., 23 Ill., 484.
(5) Dawes vs. Shed, 15 Mass., 6.
(6) Ward vs. Durham et al., 134 Ill., 195.
(7) Rawlston vs. Wood, 15 Ill., 159; Motsinger vs. Wolf, 16 Ill., 71; Mason et al. vs. Bair, 33 Ill., 194; Hopkins vs. McCan, 19 Ill., 113.
(8) Gold et al. vs. Bailey, 44 Ill., 491.
(9) Probst vs. Meadows, 13 Ill., 157.
(10) Ward vs. Durham, *supra.*

c. A promissory note, executed by a party as a gift, but not delivered in his lifetime, is not enforceable against the maker's estate.([1]) And so of any other verbal gift.([2])

d. The charges of a physician for a *post mortem* examination made on a coroner's inquest is not a proper claim against the estate of the deceased.([3])

e. Since the married woman's act of 1861, a married woman may insist upon her claim for money loaned to her husband, either before or after the marriage.([4]) But she must file her claim as any other claimant.([5])

f. There must be a present debt or duty, or a demand *in presenti*, payable, or to be satisfied at all events *in futuro*. Where there is no subsisting debt or duty, or where the claim, if payable, or to be satisfied at a future day, rests in a contingency, and it is uncertain whether or not any demand will accrue, it cannot be allowed.([6])

g. Where an administrator of another state had concluded his administration in that state, and upon final settlement a balance was found in his favor, the findings of that court were held *res adjudicata* in this state, in a suit between such administrator and the heirs of the deceased.([7])

h. Where a claim was never presented to the deceased in his lifetime, and not presented for allowance until three years after his death, these circumstances cast suspicion upon it as a meritorious claim.([8])

i. It is no objection to the allowance and payment of a claim against an estate, that it is secured by mortgage on real estate of the deceased. The personalty is the primary fund out of which all claims must be paid, and it must first be exhausted.([9])

25. DEFENSES TO CLAIMS—TWO YEARS' LIMITATIONS.—Where no inventory is filed by the executor or administrator, the two

---

(1) Blanchard vs. Williamson, 70 Ill., 647; Williams vs. Forbes, 114 Ill., 167.
(2) Barnum vs. Reed, 136 Ill., 388.
(3) Smith vs. McLaughlin et al., 77 Ill., 596.
(4) Whitford et al., vs. Daggett, 84 Ill., 144.
(5) Barnard vs. Barnard, 119 Ill., 92.
(6) Jones vs. Cooper, 2 Aikins, 54; See 2 Probate Reports, 180, for brief authorities.
(7) Fryrear vs. Lawrence et al., 5 Gil., 325.
(8) O'Connor vs. O'Connor, 52 Ill., 316.
(9) People vs. Phelps, 78 Ill., 147.

years' statute does not run against claims existing against the deceased.(¹)

Where letters of administration are granted upon the estate of a deceased person, supposed to have died intestate, and afterwards upon the discovery and probate of a will of deceased, such letters are revoked, the two years limitation will run from the date of the first letters, and it is error to order a claim, presented after the expiration of two years from the first grant of letters, to be paid generally out of the assets of the estate;(²) but such a claimant is entitled to a judgment, if the claim is not otherwise barred, to be satisfied out of subsequently inventoried estate.(³)

Where the judgment does not provide for its payment from assets of the estate not then inventoried, the presumption is, that the claim was exhibited within two years from the grant of letters.(⁴)

a. When a statute of limitations begins to run, it will continue to run until it operates as a complete bar, unless there is some saving or qualification in the statute itself.(⁵) The statute begins to run whenever there is a right capable of being enforced, and is not arrested from running by the death of the debtor.(⁶) Part payment upon a bond, by the administrator of one of the obligors, before the statute of limitations has run against it, will prevent the running of the statute as to the other obligors.(⁷)

Where a claim for several years' labor was presented against an estate, and the statute of limitations was interposed as a defense, only such services as were rendered within five years were allowed.(⁸)

In the defense of claims against estates, it is not necessary that the statute of limitations be specially pleaded, although it should be relied on as a defense.(⁹)

b. The filing of a claim with the clerk of the court after the adjustment day is not the commencement of a suit, and does not

(1) Guy et al. vs. Gerricks, 85 Ill., 428.
(2) Shepherd vs. Rhodes et al., 60 Ill., 301.
(3) Peacock vs. Haven et al., 22 Ill., 23; and see ante page 102.
(4) People vs. Gray, 72 Ill., 343.
(5) People vs. White, 11 Ill., 342.
(6) Baker vs. Brown, 18 Ill., 91; Van Alstine vs. Lemons, 19 Ill., 394: Thompson vs. Reed, 48 Ill., 118.
(7) County of Vernon vs. Stewart, 64 Mo., 408.
(8) Freeman vs. Freeman, 65 Ill., 106; Wernse vs. Hall, 101 Ill., 423.
(9) Thompson vs: Reed, *supra;* Bromwell vs. Schubert, 28 N. E. Rep., 1057.

arrest the running of the general statute of limitations which had previously begun to run, nor prevent it from afterward running upon a claim not due at the time of its presentation.(¹)

c. A material man, who has furnished lumber for the erection of a building, cannot enforce his lien against the estate of the owner of the building, after the expiration of six months from the time payment is due, so as to cut off the lien of other creditors who have proved their claims, where the personal estate is insufficient for their payment.(²)

d. Where a joint claim was presented by certain persons against the estate of their deceased guardian, for a balance of money in his hands, more than five years after the youngest child became of mature age, the claim was held not to be barred by the five years statute, so long as an action might be brought upon the guardian's bond, to enforce a recovery of the same money.(³) Such a claim may be probated against the estate of the deceased guardian, or suit may be brought upon the bond—the ward has a choice of remedies.(⁴)

e. It will be presumed that a debt of twenty-seven years' standing has been paid, without a plea of the statute of limitations.(⁵)

f. Under our statute, requiring all claims to be presented to the court for allowance, within two years from the granting of letters, it has been held, that where the intestate in her lifetime, executed a bond of indemnity, the damages depending upon a contingency which did not happen until after the lapse of two years from the granting of letters upon the obligor's estate, that the obligee's claim did not accrue within the two years, and no suit could be instituted upon the bond within that time, and, consequently, the claim was barred, except as to future discovered property.(⁶) In *Payson* vs *Hadduck,*(⁷) decided in the U. S. court for the Northern District of Illinois, where, by bill in equity, it was sought to recover on a similar

(1) Reitzel et al. vs. Miller, 25 Ill., 67.
(2) Rietz et al. vs. Coyer et al., 83 Ill., 29.
(3) Scheel et al. vs. Eidman et al., 77 Ill., 301.
(4) Tracey et al. vs. Hadden, 78 Ill., 30.
(5) Heirs of Langworthy vs. Baker, 23 Ill., 484.
(6) Stone vs. Clarke's Admr., 40 Ill., 411.
(7) 11 Legal News, 57; Duggar vs. Oglesby, 99 Ill., 405 ; People vs. Brooks, 123 Ill., 246.

claim against the widow and heirs of a deceased obligor, Blodgett, J., held that, in such a case, a recovery could be had against distributees under the 12th section of the statute of frauds, notwithstanding no claim had been, or could have been presented in probate.

g. When the administrator is made a party to a suit to foreclose a mortgage made by intestate, and on sale of the premises, a sum insufficient to pay the debt is realized, it is error to decree the payment of the residue by the administrator in due course of administration—two years having elapsed after the grant of letters and before the filing of the bill (¹) In such case, the decree should have directed the payment of the deficiency out of assets subsequently discovered.(²)

Whether or not an acknowledgment by a personal representative, of a debt due from the deceased, which is barred by the statute of limitations, will take it out of the statute, has been the subject of much discussion, and of contradictory decisions. The weight of authority justifies the conclusion, that no recognition of the debt or promise to pay by the administrator or executor of an estate, will relieve the claim of the presumption of payment imposed by the statute of limitations.(³)

26. PRACTICE.—A claimant cannot recover judgment for more than the amount claimed.(⁴)

a. The prosecution of a claim against an estate is not to be governed by all the technical rules which apply to a suit at law ;(⁵) hence, where a claim was docketed and a judgment rendered against "the estate of J. S., deceased," without naming the administrator, the proceeding was held good in the supreme court.(⁶)

b. A judgment against the deceased, which is not a lien upon his property, can only be collected as other claims in due course of administration.(⁷)

c. Claims should be proven as alleged, and carefully scrutinized by juries.(⁸)

d. The allowance of a claim against an estate is a judgment,

(1) Mulvey et al. vs. Johnson, 90 Ill., 457.
(2) *Id.*
(3) Fritz vs. Thomas, 1 Wharton, 66; Peck vs Botsford, 7 Conn., 172.
(4) Russell vs. Hubbard et al., 59 Ill., 335.
(5) Scheel et al. vs. Eidman, 68 Ill., 193.
(6) *Id.;* West vs. Krebaum, 88 Ill., 263.
(7) Clingman et al. vs. Hopkie, 78 Ill., 152.
(8) Brock et al. vs. Slaten, 82 Ill., 283; Lill vs. Brant, 1 Ill. Ap., 266.

which draws six per cent. interest, without regard to what interest the debt drew.(¹)

e. No particular form is required in rendering judgment in probate.(²)

f. In a suit brought by an administrator against a debtor to the estate, the latter cannot set off a claim for money which the debtor has paid as surety of deceased after his death.(³)

g. Where a judgment is revived by *scire facias* against an administrator, the judgment should direct its payment in due course of administration, and it is error to award execution.(⁴)

h. On a plea of *plene administravit*, the burden of proof lies on the defendant.(⁵)

i. Where a claim was presented to the county court and allowed against an estate, without notice to the personal representative, as required by statute, and without an appearance by the personal representative, the court will have no jurisdiction, and any order made under such circumstances will be a nullity.(⁶) But it is otherwise where a claim is filed on or before the day of adjustment, and long after that term is allowed. The record failing to show the presence of the administrator, or objection on his part, it will, in the absence of proof to the contrary, be presumed the case was regularly continued from term to term.(⁷)

j. A debtor, after the death of his creditor, cannot purchase outstanding claims against the deceased, and offset the same against his liabilities to the estate, to the prejudice of other claimants where the estate proves insolvent.(⁸)

k. An administrator is not compelled to offset a demand of the deceased against a claim presented, but may maintain a separate suit therefor.(⁹)

l. Where a writ of attachment is levied upon the lands of one

---

(1) Wheeler vs. Dawson, 63 Ill., 54; Mitchell vs. Mayo, 16 Ill., 83.
(2) Johnson vs. Gillett, 52 Ill., 358.
(3) Granger vs. Granger, 6 Ohio, 35; Walker vs. McKay, 2 Met. (Ky.), 294; Harding vs. Shepard, 107 Ill., 264.
(4) Turney et al. vs. Young, 22 Ill., 253.
(5) Platt vs. Robbin et al., 1 Johnson's cases, 276.
(6) Hales vs. Holland, 92 Ill., 494.
(7) Ward vs. Durham, 134 Ill., 195; McCall vs. Lee, 120 Ill., 261.
(8) Mack vs. Woodruff, 87 Ill., 570.
(9) Morton vs. Bailey et al., 1 Scam., 213.

partner and he dies, no levy being made as to the other, the suit abates as to both.([1])

m. The plea of *plene administravit* is not a good plea to an action brought against an administrator upon a debt due by his intestate.([2])

n. Although a claim may be barred by the two year limitation, it may be plead as an offset to a suit against the holder by the administrator for money due from such claimant to the estate.([3])

o. A judgment against an estate is not a specific lien to be enforced by execution against the real and personal property of the deceased in the hands of the administrator;( ) and such a judgment is only *prima facie* evidence of the existence of the debt as to the heir.[5]

p. A claim allowed an administrator for money paid for the estate becomes an equitable lien on real estate, and on bill for dower and partition the widow, who was administrator, was held entitled to a decree for payment of such claim out of the proceeds of the sale.([6])

q. The statute does not require written pleadings where a claim is presented for allowance in the county court, and, if an appeal is taken from the judgment to the circuit court, the trial is *de novo*, and no written pleadings are there necessary.([7]) Amendments may be allowed as in other cases.([8])

27. CHANGE OF VENUE.—In all cases or matters pending in the county court, where the judge of that court shall be interested in the same, or is a material and necessary witness, the case shall be transmitted to the circuit court of the proper county, and there determined as in the county court; and the papers, with the order or judgment of the circuit court thereon, shall be duly certified and

---

(1) Ballance vs. Samuel et al., 3 Scam., 380.
(2) Judy et al. vs. Kelley et al., 11 Ill., 211.
(3) Peacock vs. Haven et al., 22 Ill., 23.
(4) Granjang vs. Merkle, 22 Ill., 250; Stillman et al. vs. Young et al., 16 Ill., 318.
(5) Stone vs. Wood, 16 Ill., 177; Mason et al. vs. Bair, 33 Ill., 194; Hopkins et al. vs. McCan, 19 Ill., 113.
(6) Wheeler vs. Dawson, 63 Ill., 55.
(7) Thorp vs. Goewey, 85 Ill., 612.
(8) McCall vs. Lee, 120 Ill., 261.

filed in the county court, and have the same effect as if determined in the county court.(¹)

28. ALLOWANCE OF A CLAIM A JUDGMENT.—The order of the county court allowing the debt of a creditor against the estate, is a judgment of a court of competent jurisdiction in favor of the creditor against the administrator, and, as between those parties, it is necessarily conclusive, till reversed by a superior tribunal, unless impeached for fraud.(²) The converse of this would be equally true, and where a claim is disallowed by the court, that order becomes as conclusive between the claimant and the executor or administrator, as any other judgment. Such judgments, as before seen, are not conclusive against the heir.(³)

29. DEMANDS OF EXECUTOR, ETC.—When an executor or administrator has a demand against his testator or intestate's estate, he shall file his demand as other persons; and the court shall appoint some discreet person to appear and defend for the estate, and, upon the hearing, the court or jury shall allow such demand, or such part thereof as is legally established, or reject the same, as shall appear just. Should any executor or administrator appeal in such case, the court shall appoint some person to defend as aforesaid.(⁴)

An administrator or executor having a claim against the estate under his charge, accruing in the lifetime of the deceased, may prove the same under this statute, and subject the real estate of the deceased to sale for its satisfaction, the same as if the claim was due to another.(⁵)

The next of kin or other person interested may set up the statute of limitations as a bar to the administrator's private account.(⁶)

An administrator *pro tem.*, appointed to defend against a claim of the executor or administrator, is entitled to fair and reasonable allowance for his services in conducting such defense.(⁷)

30. INSOLVENT ESTATE.—If, after the expiration of two years

(1) Hurd's R. S., Chap. 3, § 69.
(2) Stone et al. vs. Wood, 16 Ill., 177; Ralston et al. vs. Wood, 15 Ill., 159; Housh vs. People, 66 Ill., 178; Ward vs. Durham, 134 Ill., 195; Finley vs. Carrothers, 9 Texas, 517.
(3) Ante page 113.
(4) Hurd's R. S., Chap. 3, § 72. Administrators *pro tem.* may appeal: Bassett vs. Noble, 15 Ill. Ap., 360.
(5) Johnson vs. Gillett, 52 Ill., 358.
(6) Treat vs. Fortune, 2 Brad., 116; Batson vs. Murrall, 10 Humphreys, 301.
(7) Clark vs. Knox, 70 Ala., 607.

from the time administration is granted on an estate, such estate is found to be insolvent, it shall be so entered of record by the county court, and such order [being] made, no action shall be maintained against the executor or administrator of such estate, except at the costs of the party suing; but persons entitled thereto shall receive their proportions of such estate as herein provided.(¹)

31. FEES NOT TO BE CHARGED.—In all cases, in counties of the first and second class, where, by the death of any person, there shall be left surviving such person a widow or children, resident of this state, who are entitled out of said estate to a widow's or child's award, and the entire estate, real and personal, of such deceased person shall not exceed one thousand dollars, and in case of any minor whose estate, real and personal, does not exceed the sum of five hundred dollars, and whose father is dead, and in all cases of any idiot, insane person, lunatic or distracted person, drunkard or spendthrift, when such person has a wife or infant child dependent on such person for support, and the entire estate of such person shall not exceed the sum of one thousand dollars, the county or probate judge shall, by an order to be entered of record, remit and release to such estate all of the county or probate clerk's costs now provided for by law.(²)

(1) Hurd's R. S., Chap. 3, § 128.
(2) Hurd's R. S., Chap. 54, § 66.

CHAPTER X.

CLASSIFICATION AND PAYMENT OF DEBTS.

1. Order of payment at common law.
2. By statute.
3. Order of classification.
    a. Order not specifying.
4. Conflict of statutes.
5. Preferred claims.
6. Classification may be changed.
7. No preference among claimants of same class.
8. Payment of claims before allowance.
9. Payment by mistake.

1. CLASSIFICATION AT THE COMMON LAW.—At the common law and by the laws of some of the states, the debts of a decedent were, and are classified and paid more with regard to the manner of contracting them, than with regard to their meritorious character. These are some of the requirements:

In payment of debts, he (the administrator) must observe the rules of priority: otherwise, on deficiency of assets, if he pays those of a lower degree first, he must answer those of a higher out of his own estate. And, first, he may pay all funeral charges and expense of proving the will, and the like. Secondly, debts due to the king on record or specialty. Thirdly, such debts as are by particular statutes to be preferred to all others: as the forfeitures for not burying in woolen, money due upon poor rates, for letters to the post office, and some others. Fourthly, debts of record; as judgments, statutes and recognizances. Fifthly, debts due on special contracts; as for rent, or upon bonds, covenants and the like, under seal. Lastly, debts on simple contracts, viz.: upon notes unsealed and verbal promises.([1])

2. BY STATUTE.—Our statute distributes the assets of a decedent upon more humane principles. By it debts of record, debts due upon bonds, covenants, and the like, and debts due upon simple contracts, have equal claims for payment, where all are alike unsecured.([2])

The distribution of the effects of deceased persons, is controlled by the law in force at the time of the death of the testator or intes-

(1) Wentworth on Executors, 261; 2 Blackstone's Commentaries, 511; 2 Kent's Com., 416.
(2) Paschall vs. Hailman, 4 Gilman, 285.

tate, and not by that in force at the time the debt was contracted.(¹)

3. DEMANDS CLASSIFIED.—All demands against the estate of any testator or intestate shall be divided into classes, in manner following, to-wit:

First—Funeral expenses.

Second—The widow's award, if there is a widow; or children, if there are children and no widow.

Third—Expenses attending the last illness, not including physician's bill.

Fourth—Debts due the common school or township fund.

Fifth—All expenses of proving the will, and taking out letters testamentary or of administration, and settlement of the estate, and the physician's bill in the last illness of the deceased.

Sixth—Where the decedent has received money in trust for any purpose, his executor or administrator shall pay out of his estate the amount thus received and not accounted for; the wages due a servant or laborer for labor performed for decedent within six months previous to death.

Seventh—All other debts and demands of whatsoever kind, without regard to quality or dignity, which shall be exhibited to the court within two years from the granting of letters as aforesaid, and all demands not exhibited within two years as aforesaid, shall be forever barred, unless the creditors shall find other estate of the deceased, not inventoried or accounted for by the executor or administrator, in which case their claims shall be paid *pro rata* out of such subsequently discovered estate, saving, however, to *femes covert*, infants, persons of unsound mind, or imprisoned, or without the United States in the employment of the United States or of this state, the term of two years after their respective disabilities are removed, to exhibit their claims.(²)

All claims against estates, when allowed by the county court, shall be classed and paid by the executor or administrator, in the manner provided in this act, commencing with the first class; and when the estate is insufficient to pay the whole of the demands, the demands in any one class shall be paid, *pro rata*, whether the same are due by judgment, writing obligatory, or otherwise, except as otherwise provided.(³) The circuit court may also classify claims allowed by it.(⁴)

(1) Paschall vs. Hailman, 4 Gil., 285; Woodworth vs. Paine, Breese, 294.
(2) Hurd's R. S., Chap. 3, ¿ 70; Dunlap et al. vs. McGhee et al., 98 Ill., 287
(3) Hurd's R. S., Chap. 3, ¿ 71.
(4) Darling vs. McDonald, 101 Ill., 370; McCall vs. Lee, 120 Ill., 261; Howell vs Moores, 127 Ill., 67.

a. When the order of payment made by the court does not provide that it is to be paid from assets not then inventoried, the presumption is, the claim was filed within two years from the grant of administration.([1])

4. CONFLICT OF STATUTES.—Section 60, of the school law, gives debts due the school fund from estates, a preference over all debts, except funeral and other expenses attending the last sickness, not including physician's bill.([2]) As the award is to all intents a debt due from the estate, it would seem that there exists a conflict between the two statutes, to be reconciled by the courts.

A conflict between the laws of the domicil of the deceased and the laws of the state where his personal assets may at the time chance to be situated, concerning distribution among creditors, in cases of ancillary administration, has often arisen and caused no little difficulty. As we have seen, different laws prevail in different jurisdictions, upon the matter of distribution among creditors, and while the law of the domicil may disregard the privileged priority given to bond debts, judgments, etc., as does the law of Illinois, the law prevailing at the place where ancillary administration is had, may adhere to those distinctions of the common law. In such cases, the question often arises: What rule is to govern in the distribution, the law of the domicil, or the law prevailing at the place of ancillary administration? The established rule now is, that the administration of the assets of a deceased person is to be governed altogether by the law of the country where the executor or administrator acts, and from which he derives his authority to collect them, and not by that of the domicil of the deceased.([3])

5. PREFERRED CLAIMS.—Money in the hands of a guardian is, by statute, made a preferred claim of the third (6th) class, as is money which came to the hands of the deceased from his wife, who was guardian.([4])

The clause of the statute relating to the classification of claims against estates of deceased persons, and which gives a preference in cases where the deceased has "received money in trust for any

---

(1) People vs. Gay, 72 Ill., 343.
(2) Hurd's R. S., Chap. 122, § 60; House vs. Trustees of Schools, 83 Ill., 368.
(3) Story's Conflict of Laws, § 524; Story's Eq. Juris., § 585; Young vs. Wittenmyre, 123 Ill., 303.
(4) Cruce vs. Cruce et al., 21 Ill., 46; Davis vs. Harkness, 1 Gil., 173.

purpose," does not necessarily extend to and embrace every kind of a trust. It does not embrace trusts implied by law;(¹) nor does it embrace a case where a party voluntarily places money in the hands of another to control and manage for him as his agent.(²)

A judgment creditor having no lien at the time of the death of the deceased, has no preference in the payment of claims;(³) but where there is an execution in the hands of the officer at the time of the death of the defendant, the lien thereby given upon the goods of the defendant, is not affected by the death.(⁴)

The filing of a creditor's bill gives a lien upon all the property of the judgment debtor owned at the time, from the date of the service of the summons upon the defendant, and this lien is not defeated by the death of the defendant.(⁵)

6. ORDER CLASSIFYING MAY BE CHANGED AT A SUBSEQUENT TERM.—Where a claim has been allowed against an estate and classed, the court may, at a subsequent time, by its order, change the claim to another class, if it appear that it was placed in the wrong class.(⁶) This applies to both the county and circuit courts.(⁷)

7. NO PREFERENCE AMONG CLAIMANTS OF SAME CLASS.—The provisions of the statute requiring a classification of the claims allowed against estates of deceased persons and their payment in such classes, without preference as to creditors of the same class, are mandatory, and binding upon the courts. In the distribution of the assets of an estate, there can lawfully be no preference of one creditor over another of the same class. So, where one creditor, by contesting the final account of an executor, increases the assets liable to distribution, this will give him no preference over other creditors of the same class, as to increased assets.(⁸)

8. PAYMENT BEFORE ALLOWANCE.—The county court shall make an entry of all demands against estates, classing the same as above provided, and file and preserve the papers belonging to the

---

(1) Wilson et al. vs. Kirby, 88 Ill., 566; Kirby vs. Wilson et al., 98 Ill., 240.
(2) Weir vs. Gand, 88 Ill., 490.
(3) Turney vs. Gates, 12 Ill., 141.
(4) Dodge vs. Mack, 22 Ill., 93.
(5) National Bank vs. Gage et al., 93 Ill., 172; Cole vs. Marple et al., 98 Ill., 58.
(6) Weir vs. Gand, *supra*.
(7) Darling vs. McDonald, 101 Ill., 370; McCall vs. Lee, 120 Ill., 261.
(8) Colton vs. Field et al., 131 Ill., 398; People vs. Phelps, 78 Ill., 147.

same. If an executor or administrator pays a claim before the same is allowed as aforesaid, said court shall require such executor or administrator to establish the validity of such claim by the like evidence as is required in other cases, before the same is classed, and he credited therewith.([1])

This section of the statute permits the payment of debts contracted by the deceased by the administrator, without first being allowed by the court; but any such payments are made at the peril of the administrator, who assumes the burden of showing to the court, on presentation of his account, and vouchers of payment, that such claims were liabilities against the estate. Payment can not be made after the expiration of two years from the date of letters, and thus relieve the debt from the bar imposed by the statute; nor can debts be paid in full at the expense of other claimants, who have presented their claims and had them allowed. If the administrator has paid in full, and the assets of the estate are insufficient for the payment in full of claims of the same class, the court will only allow for so much as might have been received upon a proper distribution;([2]) and this, whether the account of the administrator showing the payment of debts not allowed by the court, with proof of their genuineness, is presented within two years from the date of letters or otherwise. The presentation to and payment by the administrator, within the period of two years, prevents the operation of the bar of the two years statute of limitation, not only as to the claimant, but as to the administrator.([3])

9. PAYMENT BY MISTAKE—RECOVERY.—If an administrator pays a claim against the estate of his intestate, in the honest belief that the estate is solvent, and the estate is subsequently declared insolvent, and after due proceedings a dividend is declared from all the available assets, among claimants of the same class as those paid in full, the administrator may sue for and recover back the excess so paid above the amount of the dividend, if not barred by the statute of limitations, which will begin to run against the claim from the date when the dividend was ordered.([4]) So, also, should

---

(1) Hurd's R. S., Chap. 3, § 73.
(2) People vs. Phelps, 78 Ill., 148.
(3) Millard vs. Harris, 119 Ill., 185; Walker vs. Diehl, 79 Ill., 474; McNeil vs. McNeil, 36 Ala., 109.
(4) Richards vs. Nightingale, 9 Allen, 149; Wolf vs. Beaird, 123 Ill., 585.

the administrator, anticipating an order of distribution among heirs, pay to one a sum in excess of what the final order of distribution showed to be his due, the administrator may, by the proper action, recover the excess from such heir.[1]

[1] Stokes vs. Goodykoontz, 26 N. E. Reports, 391. (Ill.)

CHAPTER XI.

ACCOUNTING AND SETTLEMENT.

1. Accounts—when to be made.
2. Partial distributions.
3. Form of account.
4. Account may be required at any time.
5. Interest upon balances due to the administrator.
6. Assets to be charged.
7. Administrator, etc., to be allowed for attorneys' fees.
8. Contingent fees not allowed.
9. Expenses allowed.
10. For board of minors.
11. Costs of administration must be paid before distribution.
12. Order approving accounts conclusive.
13. Final settlement.
14. Effect on claims.
15. Chancery jurisdiction to effect settlements and open the same.
16. Settlements to be enforced by county court.
17. Ten per cent. interest.
18. When account should be rejected.
19. Account for monument.
20. Heirs not bound by judgments paid.
21. Order of approval several as to each item of account.
22. Appeal from an order rejecting.
23. Errors in account not evidence of fraud.
24. Failure to pay over as ordered.
25. Enforcement of orders by imprisonment.
26. Duration of imprisonment.
27. Suit cannot be maintained until order of distribution.
28. Payment of legacies.
29. Bond by legatees.
    a. Liability thereunder.
30. When bond should be taken.
31. Citation and proceedings thereunder.
32. Court no power to render a money judgment.
33. Refunding by legatees.
34. What will bar claim for refunding.
35. Suits between joint executors and administrators.
36. Sureties not liable.
37. One administrator or executor may have citation against his associate.
38. Disposition of unclaimed estate.

39. To be deposited.
40. How obtained by claimant.
41. Compensation of executors, etc.
42. Additional allowances.
43. Equitable principles to govern accounting.

1. ACCOUNTS TO BE MADE.—All executors and administrators shall exhibit accounts of their administration for settlement, to the county court from which the letters testamentary or of administration were obtained, at the first term thereof after the expiration of one year after the date of their letters; and in like manner every twelve months thereafter, or sooner, if required, until the duties of their administration are fully completed: *Provided*, that no final settlement shall be made and approved by the court, unless the heirs of the decedent have been notified thereof, in such manner as the court may direct.(¹)

2. DISTRIBUTION.—Upon every such settlement of the accounts of an executor or administrator, the court shall ascertain the whole amount of moneys and assets belonging to the estate of the deceased, which have come into the hands of such executor or administrator, and the whole amount of debts established against such estate; and if there is not sufficient to pay the whole debts, the moneys aforesaid shall be apportioned among the several creditors *pro rata*, according to their several rights, as established by this act; and thereupon the court shall order such executor or administrator to pay the claims which have been allowed by the court, according to such apportionment. And the court, upon every settlement, shall proceed in like manner until all the debts are paid, or the assets exhausted.(²)

It is the duty of the county court to enforce annual settlements by executors and administrators, and to declare dividends among heirs or creditors, as the case may justify.(³)

3. FORM OF ACCOUNTING.—The following form of account, with such variations as may be found necessary in each individual case, may be used for the first account current made to the court by an executor or administrator:

(1) Hurd's R. S., Chap. 3, § 111. (3) Schofield's Estate, 99 Ill., 513.
(2) Hurd's R. S., Chap. 3, § 112.

A B, Administrator, etc.,
In account with the Estate of C D, deceased.

1882.			Dr.
Feb. 1.	To amount of personal property as shown by appraisement bill	$1000	00
Feb. 1.	To cash on hand at decease	500	00
Feb. 1.	To inventory of notes and accounts	1000	00
Feb. 1.	To increase on sale*	50	00
	Total	$2550	00

Contra.

June 14, 1882.	By cash paid J S, Co. Clerk, in part of costs	$5	00
June 14,	" By cash pd. Ill. Printing Co. for adjustment notice	5	00
June 14,	" By cash pd. same for sale bills	5	00
June 14,	" By cash pd. E F, auctioneer	3	00
June 14,	" By cash pd. D L, clerk at sale	2	00
June 14,	" By cash pd. Appraisers	4	50
June 14,	" By property taken by widow	650	00
June 14,	" By cash bal. due widow	350	00
June 14,	" By cash pd. for care of stock	10	00
Dec. 25,	" By amount to balance	1515	50
	Total	$2550	00

4. ACCOUNT MAY BE REQUIRED AT ANY TIME.—An administrator or executor may be required to make either a full or partial account and distribution among the heirs at any time whenever it shall appear that there are assets in excess of the amount required to satisfy all demands against the estate. The statute requiring an accounting at the first term after the expiration of a year from the grant of letters, does not exclude the court from the exercise of power to compel an earlier exhibit.[1] He has no right to hold

(1) Reynolds vs. People, 55 Ill., 328.

*NOTE.—This amount is found by deducting the amount of personal property left in the hands of the administrator after setting off the widow's selection, from the total amount of the public and private sale bills. Should a comparison of these sums show a loss, the amount of such loss will be carried to the credit side of the account as "loss on sale."

Any subsequent account is made by charging upon the debtor side the balance shown in the last account, together with the amount of any new inventory filed, or any interest collected which was not computed at the time of filing the first inventory of notes and accounts, and so accounted for in the first account. The balance shown, of course includes all the assets of the estate, whether good or bad, and they may be so carried, until the administrator is ready to make final settlement, and have a distribution declared among creditors or heirs, of the net assets, when, preparatory to such a step, a petition may be filed, asking for a credit on account of any notes or accounts due the deceased, which have been inventoried as assets, and form a part of the balance shown to be in the hands of the administrator, under the provisions of Section 82, *ante*. At no time should an executor or administrator charge himself in his account current, with separate sums of money paid to him by creditors of the estate. These items form a part of the inventory of notes and accounts, and are properly charged on the debtor side of the account in the third item above charged. To charge each item separately, unnecessarily complicates the account, and leaves the remainder of this class of assets unaccounted for.

The account should be accompanied by the receipts taken upon payment of claims of whatever class.

If, at any time, it is deemed expedient to declare a partial dividend among creditors or heirs, the person rendering the account, may append a statement, showing the uncollected assets in his hands, from which the cash in his hands subject to distribution, may be ascertained.

money of an estate in his hands over and above what is necessary for the payment of debts, and deprive the heirs of its use, and he may be compelled to make a partial distribution within one year from the grant of letters.(¹)

5. INTEREST UPON BALANCES.—Where an account shows a balance due to the administrator, for amounts paid out by him in excess of assets which have come to his hands, he is entitled to interest thereon, until the amount is repaid to him.(²) And where an executor held moneys without investing them and without rendering any account, for several years, he was charged interest at six per cent., although he had put the money to no use whatever.(³) Use of money by the administrator, may be inferred from long delay in settling his account, if unexplained.(⁴)

6. ASSETS.—Money paid to an executor or administrator, by the owners of real estate liable to be sold for the payment of debts, legacies and charges, in order to prevent such sale, is assets of the estate, to be accounted for by him, and paid as assets.(⁵)

7. ATTORNEYS' FEES.—An administrator or executor is entitled to the service and assistance of counsel in the settlement of the estate, whether his accounts and vouchers are litigated or not.(⁶) Should loss accrue to the estate, by reason of not having taken the precaution to employ such, the administrator would, undoubtedly, have to answer for it. But an administrator can not himself act as attorney and charge and receive compensation therefor. If he chooses to exercise his professional skill as a lawyer in the business of the estate, that must be considered a gratuity.(⁷) The employment of an attorney by an administrator to attend to business of the estate represented by him, does not create a personal liability against the administrator, but may be enforced against the estate, for which the services are rendered.(⁸)

(1) Curts vs. Brooks, 71 Ill., 125.
(2) Wheeler vs. Dawson, 63 Ill., 54; Liddell vs. McVickar, 6 Halstead, 44;
(3) Hough vs. Harvey, 71 Ill., 72; Dunscomb vs. Dunscomb 1 Johns. Ch., 508; Field et al. vs. Colton, 7 Ill. Ap., 379.
(4) Hasler vs. Hasler, 1 Brad., 248.
(5) Fay vs. Taylor, 2 Gray, 154.
(6) Greene vs. Grimshaw, 11 Ill., 389,; Smyley vs. Reese, 53 Ala., 89; Bendall vs Bendall, 24 Ala., 295.
(7) Willard vs. Bassett, 27 Ill., 37; Hough vs. Harvey, *Supra*.
(8) Greene vs. Grimshaw, *supra*. *Contra*, see Barker vs. Kunkel, 14 Legal News, 175.

8. ATTORNEYS' FEES—CONTINGENT FEE.—There is no question of the power of an administrator to sue for the recovery of any property of the estate, and, as incidental thereto, he is authorized to retain and employ an attorney, whose fees must be fixed by the court, and allowed to the administrator as a part of the expenses of administration; but the administrator has no power to make a contract with an attorney binding upon the estate, for the transfer or conveyance of an interest in any of the assets of the estate, for the payment of a contingent fee out of the assets of the estate. To give to administrators authority to pay an attorney in property of the estate for services rendered the estate, would be virtually to surrender to them the unrestricted management and disposal of the entire property of the estates they represent.([1]) Nor can an executor give to an attorney or agent employed by him, a lien upon a bond and mortgage of the estate, for services rendered or expenses incurred, in collecting the interest thereon.([2])

9. EXPENSES.—An administrator should only be allowed for expenditures made in employing services which he is not competent to render.([3])

10. FOR BOARD OF MINORS.—Where an executor, not being their guardian, and having no authority in the will, paid the board of the minor children of the testator, his action was approved and account allowed.([4])

11. COSTS.—It should appear that all costs of administration have been paid by the administrator, before an order of distribution is made to creditors.([5])

12. RES ADJUDICATA.—The adjudication of a county court upon a final account of an executor or administrator, like any other judgment of a court, is binding upon all parties affected thereby, until set aside by appeal from the order or on bill to impeach it. It is final and conclusive in all collateral proceedings, and can not be impeached, excep for fraud.([6])

(1) In the matter of the Estate of Page, (Sup. Court of Cal.) 13 Legal
(2) McMahon vs. Allen, 4 E. D. Smith, 519. [News, 270.
(3) Teague vs. Dendy, 2 McCord Ch., 207.
(4) johnston vs. Maples et al., 49 Ill., 101.
(5) People vs. Hunter et al., 89 Ill., 392.
(6) Ralston vs. Wood, 15 Ill., 159; Housh vs. People, 66 Ill., 178; Ammons vs. People, 11 Ill., 6; Wheeler vs. Dawson, 63 Ill., 54; Short et al. vs. johnson, 25 Ill., 489; Dickson et al. vs. Hitt, 98 Ill., 300; Parcher vs. Russell, 11 Cush., 107; Sever vs. Russell, 4 Cush., 513; Fryrear vs. Lawrence, 5 Gil., 325; Wadsworth vs. McConnell, 104 Ill., 369; Wolf vs. Beaird, 123 Ill., 585.

The reasoning upon which the cases cited above were decided would seem to apply with the same force to the judgment of the court upon any interlocutory account approved by the court,(¹) where the parties in interest appear and defend.

Items not charged or credited in an account, when they might have been, are not, for that reason, to be excluded from any future account.(²) And, so it was held, that in the settlement of an account by an administrator, in which he does not charge himself with interest on money received by him, does not preclude a subsequent inquiry as to the propriety of charging him with interest, if the question of interest was not a subject of examination, when the account was passed. But if, when the account was settled, the court inquired into the liability to pay interest, and decided against it, that decision, unless obtained by fraud, is conclusive against the liability.(³) So, also, of a fact alleged in connection with the account.(⁴)

The decree of the court of probate, duly allowing the final account of an administrator, cannot be impeached in an action at law against the administrator. Any objections to such an account should be raised by appeal.(⁵)

The language of the statute quoted above (Section 111, *ante*), and the decisions referred to in the margin, justify the conclusion that the adjudications of the court upon all accounts, interlocutory as well as final, are conclusive upon all parties in all collateral proceedings, until reversed on appeal or impeached for fraud; and further, that while the adjudication upon the final account, notice having been given as required by the court, is final after the adjournment of the term, any interlocutory account may be opened, notice having been given, at any time before the approval of the final account, and the settlement of the estate.

But where an order of distribution of a residue of assets left in the hands of an administrator after all debts and charges were paid, was made, without any notice to the heirs, in which an injustice was done, it was held, that at a subsequent term, notice having been given to the administrator, and it appearing that nothing had been done under the order, it was proper for the county court to vacate such order, and that the heirs were not bound by an order

(1) Stiles vs. Burch, 5 Paige, 132.
(2) Lidell vs. McVickar, 6 Halstead, 44.
(3) Saxton vs. Chamberlain, 6 Pick., 422.
(4) Long vs. Long, 132 Ill., 72.
(Parcher vs. Bussell, 11 Cush. 10

of distribution made in their absence and without notice to them.(¹)*

13. FINAL SETTLEMENT.—Where an administrator received the title to real estate in payment of a debt due the intestate, and conveyed the same to the heirs, it was held that the assets were properly accounted for.(²)

An order declaring an estate finally settled and the administrator discharged, unless cause to the contrary be shown within thirty days, will be considered as final, where no cause is shown within that period.(³)

An order discharging an administrator is a nullity until the estate is fully settled according to law.(⁴)

After a final settlement has been made, it will be presumed he has paid out all the assets in his hands, upon claims and to distributees (⁵) Administration is presumed to be closed at the end of the period fixed by law . ⁶)

Claims of an administrator against an estate should be closely scrutinized by the court.(⁷)

Where a final settlement is in fact made, but not entered of record, the county court is authorized, upon proper proof, to enter and spread of record, *nunc pro tunc*, the preliminary and final settlement of such administrator.(⁸) .

14. EFFECT OF FINAL SETTLEMENT AS TO CLAIMS.—The approval of a final account of distribution and an order discharging the administrator, are inoperative to affect the rights of creditors. Although such final orders may have been entered, and the admin-

(1) Long vs. Thompson, 60 Ill., 27.
(2) Greer et al. vs. Walker, 42 Ill., 401.
(3) Bucher et al. vs. Bucher, 86 Ill., 377.
(4) Blanchard vs. Williamson, 70 Ill., 647.
(5) Hales et al. vs. Holland, 92 Ill., 494.
(6) Easterling vs. Blythe, 7 Texas, 210.
(7) Johnson vs. Gillett, 52 Ill., 358.
(8) Frame vs. Frame et al., 16 Ill., 155.

*NOTE.—The case of *Wheeler* vs. *Dawson*, cited above, where an order of the county court was held *res adjudicata*, and not susceptible of being inquired into in a collateral proceeding, seems to be identical with the case of *Long* vs. *Thompson*, except that in the latter no notice was given, while in the former, the statement of the case is silent upon the matter of notice, and except, also, that the order in the case of *Wheeler* vs. *Dawson*, was in furtherance of the right, while in the case of *Long* vs. *Thompson*, an apparent injustice had been done the heirs. In the latter case, over three years had expired after the order and before the motion was made to set it aside. The motion to vacate the order was not a collateral proceeding; but the order not having been in any matter carried out, and no rights having accrued under it, it was held to be yet in the hands of the court. How far this latter case would have been held *res adjudicata*, in a proceeding strictly collateral, is difficult to determine from the decisions. In the matter of *Sellews' Appeal*, before the supreme court of Connecticut, 10 Am. Law Reg., 708, where an executor's final report showed certain sums of money and articles of personal property in his hands for distribution to the residuary legatees, it was held, in a proceeding before the court of probate, to compel him to turn the property over to the legatees, the executor might show in excuse of his failure to do so, that certain of the property had been lost, and certain other taken from him by a paramount title.

istrator fully discharged from all his duties as to matters embraced in former accounts, yet a creditor may present his claim and have it allowed, upon taking the proper steps, at any time before it is barred by the general statute of limitations. Upon the discovery of assets not before then inventoried, the discharged administrator may be called again to administer and distribute the same, notwithstanding his final discharge. It would be otherwise, in case of a resignation or removal.([1])

15. CHANCERY JURISDICTION.—Where there are conflicting and intricate interests to be adjusted, a bill in chancery is the proper proceeding for effecting the final settlement of an estate; if, however, such a case is heard by a judge in probate, he should proceed as though a bill had been filed and he was sitting as a chancellor.([2])

Before a court of equity will set aside as fraudulent or illegal a settlement of the accounts of an administrator made more than sixteen years before the filing of the bill, and approved by the court, it will require clear proof of the alleged fraud or illegality.([3]) A court of equity will not entertain a bill to impeach a final settlement for mere errors in settlement—such as the allowance by the court of too large compensation, or the failure to account for assets with which the administrator is charged—they being errors which should be corrected by appeal from the order approving the report. The principle of *res adjudicata* applies to such settlements as against attacks through bills in chancery.([4])

Where an administrator, after settlement of an estate and the payment of the balance in his hands to the heirs, is compelled to pay a new claim unknown to him, within two years after the grant of letters, he or his executors may maintain a bill in equity against such heirs, to reimburse him or his estate for the sum so paid, although no refunding bond was taken.([5])

16. SETTLEMENTS ENFORCED.—The county courts of this state shall enforce the settlements of estates within the time prescribed

(1) Diversey vs. Johnson, 93 Ill., 547; Blanchard vs. Williamson, 70 Ill., 647; Cuthright vs. Stanford, 81 Ill., 240; Sutherland vs. Harrison et al., 86 Ill., 363; 2 Redfield on Wills, 411.
(2) Heward vs. Slagle et al., 52 Ill., 336; Russell et al. vs. Madden, 95 Ill., 485.
(3) People vs. Lott, 36 Ill., 447.
(4) Dickson et al. vs. Hitt, 98 Ill., 300.
(5) Cuthright vs. Stanford et al., *supra;* Diversey vs. Johnson, *supra;* Turner vs. Egerton, 1 Gill & Johnson, 430.

by law, and upon the failure of an executor or administrator to make settlement at the next term of the court after the expiration of said time, the court shall order a citation to issue to the sheriff of the county where the executor or administrator resides, or may be found, requiring said executor or administrator to appear at the next term of the court and make settlement of the estate, or show cause why the same is not done; and if an executor or administrator fails to appear at the time required by such citation, the court shall order an attachment requiring the sheriff of the county where the executor or administrator resides, or may be found, to bring the body of said executor or administrator before the court; and upon a failure of an administrator or executor to make settlement under the order of the court after having been so attached, he may be dealt with as for contempt, and shall be forthwith removed by the court, and some discreet person appointed in his stead—the costs of such citation or attachment to be paid by the delinquent executor or administrator, and the court shall enter a judgment therefor, and a fee bill may issue thereon. All moneys, bonds, notes and credits, which any administrator or executor may have in his possession or control, as property or assets of the estate, at a period of two years and six months from the date of his letters testamentary or administration, shall bear interest, and the executor or administrator shall be charged interest thereon from said period at the rate of ten per cent., or, after two years and six months from any subsequent time that he may have discovered and received the same, unless good cause is shown to the court why such should not be taxed.[1]

17. TEN PER CENT. INTEREST.—Where an administrator, by his report, made more than two years after the grant of letters, showed a certain amount in his hands, and no debts remained unpaid, it was held, as it was his duty to have procured an order of distribution, and paid out the same, he was properly chargeable with ten per cent. interest after two years and six months from the date of his letters. In no case should administrators be held liable for interest until after that time, unless it appears that they have received interest on the trust fund before that time.[2]

18. ACCOUNT SHOULD BE REJECTED.—Where an account shows

[1] Hurd's R. S., Chap. 3, § 113; Hanifan vs. Needles, 108 Ill., 403.
[2] In the matter of the Estate of Schofield, 99 Ill., 513.

the payment of some claims in full to the injury of others of the same class, it should be rejected.([1])

19. ACCOUNT FOR MONUMENT TO DECEASED.—A monument contracted for by the administrator, to be erected to the memory of the intestate, is not a proper charge by the administrator against the estate in his account.([2])

20. HEIRS NOT BOUND.—Where the administrator fails to make any known defense to the allowance of a claim, as the statute of limitations, etc., and afterwards pays the claim, the heirs may insist upon the defense on settlement with the administrator, and are not bound by the allowance of the claim by the court.([3])

21. ORDER OF APPROVAL SEVERAL.—An order of the county court allowing in part the account of an administrator, is a complete and distinct judgment from the order rejecting the remainder of the account; and an appeal by him from the order rejecting a portion of his claim, left in full force the order of approval, and it remains binding alike upon the administrator and heirs. If, instead, the heirs appeal, and the administrator does not, the state of the case is reversed. In either case, the county court may proceed to enforce, by proper means, so much of the order as is not appealed from.([4])

22. EFFECT OF AN APPEAL FROM AN ORDER REJECTING.— When some of the items in an administrator's account are rejected by the county court, and he appeals to the circuit court, such appeal does not bring before the circuit court the whole account, but the trial, which is *de novo*, will be confined to the items rejected by the county court.([5]) In such a case, the appeal does not give the circuit court jurisdiction of the whole account, but only of the rejected items, and it can not hear evidence as to any of the items allowed by the county court.([6])

23. ERRORS IN ACCOUNT NOT EVIDENCE OF FRAUD.—Errors

(1) People vs. Phelps, 78 Ill., 147.
(2) Morgan vs. Morgan, 83 Ill., 196; Foley vs. Bushway, 71 Ill., 386; Smyley vs. Reese, 53 Ala., 89.
(3) Stillman et al. vs. Young et al., 16 Ill., 318; Gold et al., vs. Bailey, 44 Ill., 491; Kidd vs. Chapman, 2 Barb. Ch., 414; McGarvey vs. Darnall, 134 Ill., 367.
(4) Curts vs. Brooks, 71 Ill., 125; Millard vs. Harris, 119 Ill., 185; Kingsbury vs. Powers, 131 Ill., 182.
(5) Morgan vs. Morgan, *supra*.
(6) Curts vs. Brooks, *supra*.

in an account made out by an attorney, without the knowledge of the administrator, are not sufficient to show actual fraud.(¹)

24. FAILURE TO PAY OVER.—If any executor or administrator shall fail or refuse to pay over any moneys or dividend to any person entitled thereto, in pursuance of the order of the county court, lawfully made, within thirty days after demand made for such moneys or dividend, the court, upon application, may attach such delinquent executor or administrator, and may cause him to be imprisoned until he shall comply with the order aforesaid, or until such delinquent is discharged by due course of law; and moreover, such failure or refusal on the part of such executor or administrator, shall be deemed and taken in law to amount to a *devastavit*, and an action upon such executor's or administrator's bond, and against his securities, may be forthwith instituted and maintained; and the failure aforesaid to pay such moneys or dividend, shall be a sufficient breach to authorize a recovery thereon.(²)

25. IMPRISONMENT ON FAILURE TO PAY.—The power given to the county court to enforce obedience to its orders by imprisonment, is a special statutory power; and before this extraordinary remedy is resorted to, courts will require a strict and exact compliance with all antecedent conditions prescribed by the statute. There must not only be an order to pay to one lawfully entitled to recover money from the estate, but there must be a failure to comply with the conditions of the order, and a subsequent demand for payment. So, where the order required the administrator to pay within thirty days, a demand on him within that time, was a nullity, and a failure to comply with such demand, conferred no authority on the court to imprison the administrator. In such a case, in order to give the court jurisdiction to make an order of commitment, the creditor should make his demand after the time limited in the order of payment, and even then, the court could not act until thirty days after such demand.(³)

An order made in such a case, acts only upon the person of the administrator, and in no way affects another person, although he

---

(1) Williams vs. Rhodes, 81 Ill., 571
(2) Hurd's R. S., Chap. 3, § 114; People vs. Adm'r, 39 Ill., 251.
(3) Piggott vs. Ramey et al., 1 Scam., 145; Haines vs. People, 97 Ill., 162; Von Kettler vs. Johnson, 57 Ill., 109; Johnson vs. Von Kettler, 66 Ill., 63; Johnson vs. Von Kettler, 84 Ill., 315.

may be present when the order is made and in possession of the assets of the estate sought to be reached, and although he fraudulently withholds such assets. He must be reached by other means, and an imprisonment of such person for a failure to pay, subjects the party instrumental therein to an action of damages.([1])

The demand is one of the necessary elements that enters into the offense, and it cannot be dispensed with or waived by the administrator.([2])

26. DURATION OF IMPRISONMENT.—While this absolute power of imprisonment is given against defaulting executors and administrators, upon a proper case presented, that power is limited by the constitutional prohibition of imprisonment for debt.([3]) Where the neglect or refusal to perform the order of the court is not from mere contumacy, but from want of means, the result of misfortune, the party entitled to payment, will be compelled to adopt some other means than imprisonment to enforce the order, as the courts, in obedience to the constitutional provision, will refuse to imprison; or, having committed the person of the administrator, will discharge him from custody, upon it being made to appear that he is insolvent.([4])

It would, however, appear that it is not sufficient for the imprisoned defendant to show that he has no money with which to pay; but, to purge himself from the contempt, it should appear that the assets which came to his hands, have not fraudulently been converted to his own use.([5])

27. ORDER OF DISTRIBUTION.—Until there has been an order of distribution among the heirs of an intestate, they cannot maintain a suit against a stranger for the recovery of assets of the estate.([6])

28. PAYMENT OF LEGACIES.—Whenever it shall appear that there are sufficient assets to satisfy all demands against the estate, the court shall order the payment of all legacies mentioned in the will of the testator, the specific legacies being the first to be satisfied.([7])

29. BOND FROM LEGATEES.—Executors and administrators shall not be compelled to pay legatees or distributees, until bond

(1) Johnson vs. Von Kettler, 84 Ill., 315.
(2) Haines vs. People. 97 Ill., 162.
(3) Art. 2, § 12.
(4) Dinet vs. People, 73 Ill., 183; Blake vs. People, 80 Ill., 11.
(5) Blake vs. People, *supra*.
(6) Neubrecht vs. Santmeyer et al., 50 Ill., 74.
(7) Hurd's R. S., Chap. 3, § 115.

and security is given by such legatees or distributees, to refund the due proportion of any debt which may afterwards appear against the estate, and the costs attending the recovery thereof; such bond shall be made payable to such executor or administrator, and shall be for his indemnity and filed in the court.([1])

a. No liability can arise under such a bond against the legatee and his sureties, unless it subsequently appears that the executor did not retain enough means of the estate in his hands to pay all liabilities against it, and that the claims unprovided for, were at the time the legacies were delivered, unknown to the executor; or, that there has been a depreciation of the assets retained by him by some unforseen calamity.([2])

30. WHEN A BOND SHOULD BE TAKEN.—Where a life estate in personal property is given to the legatee by the will, with remainder over to another, it is proper that the tenant for life, before coming into possession of such property, be required, by the court, as a condition of his receiving it, to enter into bond and security, to secure the remainder man the full reversion.([3]) There are cases peculiar in themselves, where refunding bonds can not and need not be given.([4])

31. CITATION.—The citation issued by a county court, to an administrator, to show cause why a settlement of an estate is not made, as well as an attachment issued to enforce an order of the court, should run in the name of the people.([5])

Such a proceeding abates on the death of the person against whom it runs, before it is finally disposed of.([6]) Lapse of time may bar it.([7])

No citation can be ordered against the personal representative of a deceased administrator or executor, to enforce a settlement of the estate represented by such deceased officer.([8])

If an administrator or executor fail to pay to distributees as ordered, the remedy is by attachment.([9])

(1) Hurd's R. S., Chap. 3, § 116; Pelham vs. Taylor, 1 Jones' Eq., 121.
(2) Marsh vs. Scarboro et al., 2 Devereux Eq. (N. C.), 551; See, also, note to same case, 27 Am. Dec., 250; Wolf vs. Beaird, 123 Ill., 585.
(3) Hetfield vs. Fowler et al., 60 Ill., 45.
(4) People vs. Admire et al., 39 Ill., 252; Weir vs. People, 78 Ill., 192
(5) Reynolds vs. People, 55 Ill., 328.
(6) Harvey et al., vs. Harvey, 87 Ill., 54.
(7) Phillips vs. State, 5 Ohio, 122; See 64 Am. Dec., 636, for brief of authorities.
(8) Harvey vs. Harvey, *supra.*
(9) Piggott vs. Ramey et al., 1 Scam., 145.

32. No POWER TO RENDER JUDGMENT.—A court of probate has no power to render a money judgment in favor of heirs or devisees, against an executor or administrator, for failing or refusing to pay over to such heirs or devisees, their distributive portions of the estate of the deceased.(¹)

33. REFUNDING BY LEGATEES.—When, at any time, after the payment of legacies or distributive shares, it shall be necessary that the same or any part thereof be refunded for the payment of debts, the county court, on application made, shall apportion the same among the several legatees or distributees, according to the amount received by them, except the specific legacies, which shall not be required to be refunded, unless the residue is insufficient to satisfy such debts; and if any distributee or legatee refuses to refund according to the order of the court, within sixty days thereafter, and upon demand made, such refusal shall be deemed a breach of his bond given to the executor or administrator as aforesaid, and an action may be instituted thereon for the use of the party entitled thereto; and in all cases where there is no bond, an action of debt may be maintained against such distributee or legatee, and the order of the court shall be evidence of the amount due.(²)

A creditor is not a distributee within the meaning of this section.(³)

Where, after the settlement of an estate, and the distribution of the surplus personal estate among the heirs at law of the deceased, the administrator was compelled to pay a claim accruing in the lifetime of the deceased, it was held that the administrator might properly call upon the distributees by bill in chancery, to refund sufficient to reimburse the administrator.(⁴)

34. WHAT WILL BAR CLAIM FOR REFUNDING.—A claim against a distributee for an excess paid upon distribution, like any other money claim, may be barred by the statute of limitations.(⁵)

35. SUITS BETWEEN EXECUTORS AND ADMINISTRATORS.— Where there are two or more executors or administrators of an estate, and any one of them takes all or a greater part of such estate, and refuses to pay the debts of the decedent, or refuses to account with the other executor or administrator, in such case the executor

(1) Piggott vs. Ramey et al., 1 Scam., 145; Cagney vs. O'Brien et al., 83 Ill., 72.
(2) Hurd's R. S., Chap. 103, ¿ 117.
(3) Wolf vs. Griffin, 13 Ill. Ap., 559.
(4) Cuthright et al vs. Stanford et al., 81 Ill., 240; Diversey vs. Johnson, 93 Ill., 547.

or administrator so aggrieved, may have his action of account or suit in equity against such delinquent executor or administrator, and recover such proportionate share of said estate, as shall belong to him; and every executor, being a residuary legatee, may have an action of account or suit in equity against his co-executor, or co-executors, and recover his part of the estate in his or their hands. Any other legatee may have the like remedy against the executors: *Provided*, that before any action shall be commenced for legacies as aforesaid, the court shall order them to be paid.(¹)

The word "action" in the above statute refers only to the action of account.(²)

36. SURETIES NOT LIABLE.—The common sureties of two or more administrators or executors are not liable to one of the principals for the acts or defalcations of the other.(³)

37. ONE ADMINISTRATOR MAY HAVE CITATION.—Executors may cite their co-executor to account before the Surrogate, for personal estate bequeathed by their testator; but such accounting is merely for the purpose of a settlement, and he can not be decreed to pay over to his co-executors.(⁴)

38. DISPOSITION OF UNCLAIMED ESTATE.—If any balance of any such intestate estate as may, at any time, be committed to any public administrator, shall remain in the hands of such administrator, after all just debts and charges against such estate, which have come to the knowledge of such public administrator within two years after the administration of such estate was committed to him, are fully paid, such administrator shall cause the amount thereof, with the name of the intestate, the time and place of his decease, to be published in some newspaper published in his county, or if no newspaper is published in his county, then in the nearest newspaper published in this state, for eight weeks successively, notifying all persons having claims or demands against such estate to exhibit the same, together with the evidence in support thereof, before the county court of the proper county, within six months after the date of such notice, or that the same will be forever barred; and if no such claim is presented for payment or distribution within the said time of six months, such balance shall be paid into the treasury of said county; and the county shall be answera-

(1) Hurd's R. S., Chap. 3, § 118; Crain vs. Kennedy, 85 Ill., 340.
(2) Mahar vs. O'Hara, 4 Gil., 424.
(3) Slaughter vs. Froman, 5 T. B. Monroe, 19; Atcheson vs. Robertson, 3 Rich. Eq., 132.
(4) Smith vs. Lawrence, 11 Paige, 206.

ble for the same, without interest, to such persons as shall thereafter appear to be legally entitled, on order of the county court, to the same, if any such shall ever appear.(¹)

39. UNCLAIMED MONEY TO BE DEPOSITED.—That when any administrator or executor shall have made final settlement with the county court, it shall be the duty of the court to order said administrator or executor to deposit with the county treasurer such moneys as he may have belonging to any non-resident or unknown heir or claimant, taking his receipt therefor, and have the same filed at the office of the county clerk, when such settlement has been made.(²)

40. HOW OBTAINED AFTER DEPOSITED.—When money shall be deposited as aforesaid, the person or persons entitled to the same, may at any time apply to the court making said order, and obtain the same, upon making satisfactory proof to the court of his, her or their right thereto.(³)

41. COMPENSATION OF EXECUTORS, ETC.—Executors and administrators shall be allowed as compensation for their services, a sum not exceeding six per centum on the amount of personal estate, and not exceeding three per centum on the money arising from the sale of real estate, with such additional allowances for costs and charges in collecting and defending the claims of the estate and disposing of the same, as shall be reasonable.(⁴)

42. ADDITIONAL ALLOWANCES.—The provision in the statute for "such additional allowances for costs and charges," means only that the administrator may be reimbursed for moneys and costs actually paid by him to others in and about the collection and disbursement of the assets of the estate, and does not justify the allowance to him of an amount exceeding six per centum on the personal estate and three per centum on the amount arising from the sale of real estate, for his own services as agent or attorney of the estate.(⁵) An administrator is not entitled to compensation for services rendered by himself as attorney for the estate,(⁶) nor for

(1) Hurd's R. S., Chap. 3, ? 49.
(2) Hurd's R. S., Chap. 3, ? 134.
(3) Hurd's R. S., Chap. 3, ? 135.
(4) Hurd's R. S., Chap. 3, ? 132; see 3 Probate Reports, 583 for brief of authorities.
(5) Hough vs. Harvey et al., 71 Ill., 72; Askew vs. Hudgens, 99 Ill., 468.
(6) *Ib.;* Willard vs. Bassett, 27 Ill., 37.

defending a suit brought against him before his appointment as such, even where the money of the estate was involved;([1]) nor is he entitled to a *per diem* in addition to his commissions.([2])

But, under a special authority in a will, an executor may be allowed, by his co-executors, a reasonable salary for extra services in the business of the estate.([3])

43. EQUITABLE PRINCIPLES TO GOVERN THE APPROVAL OF ACCOUNTS.—The county court, in the settlement of estates, is vested with equitable as well as legal powers. In case of mistake or accident, by which an administrator or executor is charged in his report with too much or too little, the court will be authorized to ascertain the true facts, and correct the report as the facts may justify and warrant, and charge the executor or administrator with the amount he justly owes.([4])

The county court may also enjoin parties seeking to interfere with property under its jurisdiction from intermeddling with the same.([5])

(1) Allen, Adm., Ex parte, 89 Ill., 474.
(2) Askew vs. Hudgens, 99 Ill., 468.
(3) Clinch vs. Eckford, 8 Paige, 412; Lent vs. Howard, 3 Probate Reports, 109.
(4) Millard vs. Harris, 119 Ill., 185; Estate of Corrington, 124 Ill., 363; Brandon vs. Brown, 106 Ill., 519; Winslow vs. Leland, 128 Ill., 304; Wadsworth vs. Connell, 104 Ill., 369; Mock's Heirs vs. Steele, 34 Ala., 198; Shepard vs. Speer et al., 29 N. E. Rep., 718, (Ill.)
(5) Farwell vs. Crandall, 120 Ill., 70.

CHAPTER XII.

DESCENT AND DISTRIBUTION.

1. Intestacy presumed.
2. Rules of descent.
3. Where will is renounced.
4. Who are next of kin.
5. Meaning of term "children."
6. Children of the half blood.
7. What will bar distribution.
8. Estate of deceased infant.
9. Administrator must collect.
10. Advancements.
11. Value of real property advanced.
12. Value of personal estate.
13. Evidence of advancements must be written.
14. Death of heir.
15. Advancements do not affect widow.
16. When heirs may have distribution.
17. Illegitimate offspring.
18. How legitimated.
19. Rights before the statute.
20. Bastards under the common law.
21. Posthumous child.
22. Heirs at law.
23. Adopted children.
24. Husband and wife.
25. Rules of descent varied by contract.
26. Acceptance under will.
27. Descent not defeated by naked trust.
28. Where heir is indebted to estate.
29. Equalizing legacies.
30. Notice of final settlement and order of distribution.
31. Law in force at time and place of death governs distribution.
32. Debts and charges must be first paid.
33. Order of court necessary.
34. Distribution in kind.
35. Escheats.

1. INTESTACY PRESUMED.—When the death of the ancestor is shown, until rebutted, the presumption will be indulged that he died intestate, and that his heirs take his estate under the laws of descent.([1])

([1]) Lyon vs. Kain, 36 Ill., 362; Harvey vs. Thornton, 14 Ill., 217; Pile vs. McBratney et al., 15 Ill., 314.

2. RULES OF DESCENT.—That estates, both real and personal, of residents and non-resident proprietors in this state dying intestate, or whose estates or any part thereof shall be deemed and taken as intestate estate, after all just debts and claims against such estates are fully paid, shall descend to and be distributed in manner following to-wit :

First—To his or her children and their descendants, in equal parts; the descendants of the deceased child or grandchild taking the share of their deceased parents in equal parts among them.

Second—When there is no child of the intestate, nor descendant of such child, and no widow or surviving husband, then to the parents, brothers and sisters of the deceased, and their descendants, in equal parts among them, allowing to each of the parents, if living, a child's part, or to the survivor of them if one be dead, a double portion; and if there is no parent living, then to the brothers and sisters of the intestate, and their descendants.

Third—When there is a widow **or surviving** husband, and no child or children, or descendants of a child or children of the intestate, then (after the payment of all just debts) one-half of the real estate and the whole of the personal estate shall descend to such widow or surviving husband, as an absolute estate forever; and the other half of the real estate shall descend, as in other cases, where there is no child or children or descendants of a child or children.

Fourth—When there is a widow or a surviving husband, and also a child or children, or descendants of such child or children of the intestate, the widow or surviving husband shall receive, as his or her absolute personal estate, one-third of all the personal estate of the intestate.

Fifth—If there is no child of the intestate, or descendant of such child, and no parent, brother or sister, or descendant of such parent, brother or sister, and no widow or surviving husband, then such estate shall descend in equal parts to the next of kin to the intestate, in equal degree, (computing by the rules of the civil law,) and there shall be no representation among collaterals, except with the descendants of brothers and sisters of the intestate; and in no case shall there be any distinction between the kindred of the whole and the half blood.

Sixth—If any intestate leaves a widow or surviving husband and no kindred, his or her estate shall descend to such widow or surviving husband.

Seventh—If the intestate leaves no kindred, and no widow or husband, his or her estate shall escheat to and vest in the county in which said real or personal estate, or the greater portion thereof, is situated.([1])

All such estate, both real and personal, as is not devised or bequeathed in the last will and testament of any person, shall be distributed in the same manner as the estate of an intestate; but in all such cases the executor or executors, administrator or administrators, with the will annexed, shall have the preference in administering on the same.([2])

3. IN CASE WILL RENOUNCED—ELECTION TO TAKE IN LIEU OF DOWER.—If a husband or wife die testate, leaving no child or descendants of a child, the surviving husband or wife may, if he or she elect, have, in lieu of dower in the estate of which the deceased husband or wife died seized, (whether the right to such dower has accrued by renunciation as hereinbefore provided, or otherwise,) and of any share of the personal estate which he or she may be entitled to take with such dower, absolutely, and in his or her own right, one-half of all the real and personal estate which shall remain after the payment of all just debts and claims against the estate of the deceased husband or wife. The election herein provided for may be made whether dower has been assigned or not, and at any time before or within two months after notification to the survivor of the payment of debts and claims, and not afterward.([3])

In cases where the widow is insane, the court will make choice for her, and enter such choice of record, being guided by what seems to be for her interest ([4])

4. WHO ARE NEXT OF KIN.—The rule to be followed in determining who are the next of kin of an intestate, in order to determine the fact of descent, is the same as that made use of in determining the right of administration, and to that reference is had.([5])

Computing by the rules of the civil law, the maternal grand-

(1) Hurd's R. S., Chap. 39, § 1; Marvin vs. Collins, 98 Ill., 510; People vs. Brooks. 123 Ill., 246.
(2) Hurd's R. S., Chap. 39, § 12.
(3) Hurd's R. S., Chap. 41, § 12; The renunciation must be in person: Milliken vs. Welliver. 37 Ohio, 460; Cowdrey vs. Hitchcock, 103 Ill., 262; Ward vs. Ward, 134 Ill., 417; Cribben vs. Cribben, 136 Ill., 609.
(4) State vs. Ueland, 30 Minn., 277; Van Steinwyck vs. Washburn, 59 Wis., 483.
(5) See ante page 10.

father is a nearer relative to one than his paternal aunt—the former being related in the second degree, while the latter is related only in the third degree.(¹) And, by the same rule, the father and mother are related to their child in the first degree, while brothers and sisters are related to each other in the second degree.(²)

5. MEANING OF THE WORD CHILDREN.—It is a rule of construction, that the word "children," as used in our statute of descents, means lawful children; and the above use of that term, includes only such children as were born in lawful wedlock, and excludes illegitimate offspring, except as it is modified by Section 2 of this statute.(³)

Every child born in wedlock is presumed to be legitimate.(⁴)

6. CHILDREN OF THE HALF BLOOD.—This term is held to embrace the children of a common mother, who have different fathers, as well as those of a common father, who have different mothers.(⁵)

7. WHAT WILL BAR DISTRIBUTION.—A child and prospective heir, under no disability, may receive from the ancestor a portion of his estate, and by an instrument of writing, agree that such sum or property shall be in full of his share of his ancestor's estate, and thus bar his right to participate in the distribution of the estate.(⁶)

8. ESTATE OF A DECEASED INFANT.—The estate of a deceased infant, who dies at an age at which it is incapable in law of contracting debts, vests immediately in its next of kin, and the appointment of an administrator is unnecessary.(⁷) And in such a case, the mother, being the only surviving parent, will take two shares in such estate.(⁸)

9. ADMINISTRATOR MUST COLLECT.—The personal estate of a person dying intestate, whilst it descends to and is distributed among

---

(1) Barger vs. Hobbs, 67 Ill., 592.
(2) Hays vs. Thomas, Breese, 136.
(3) Blacklaws vs. Milne et al., 82 Ill., 505; Orthwein vs. Thomas, 127 Ill., 554.
(4) Illinois Land and Loan Co. vs. Bonner, 75 Ill., 315; Orthwein vs. Thomas, *supra*.
(5) Oglesby Coal Co. vs. Pasco et al., 79 Ill., 164.
(6) Bishop et al. vs. Davenport et al., 58 Ill., 105, and authorities there cited; Kershaw vs. Kershaw, 102 Ill., 307; Parsons vs. Ely, 45 Ill., 2·2; Galbraith vs. McLain, 84 Ill., 379; Simpson vs. Simpson, 114 Ill., 603; Crum vs. Sawyer, 132 Ill., 443; Winslow vs. Leland, 128 Ill., 304.
(7) Lynch et al. vs. Rotan et al., 39 Ill., 14; McCleary vs. Menke, 109 Ill., 294.
(8) Voris vs. Sloan et al., 68 Ill., 588.

his heirs, after the payment of debts, must pass through due administration, under the direction of the proper court; and an heir can not maintain a suit in his own name, or by virtue of his heirship, upon a debt due to his ancestor.([1])

10. ADVANCEMENTS.—Any real or personal estate given by an intestate in his lifetime as an advancement to any child or lineal descendant, shall be considered as part of the intestate's estate, so far as it regards the divisions and distribution thereof among his issue, and shall be taken by such child or other descendant towards his share of the intestate's estate; but he shall not be required to refund any part thereof, although it exceeds his share.([2])

To be considered as advancements, such sums of money or lands must be charged by the ancestor or received by the heir in writing as such.([3]) But this requirement may be waived.([4])

The value and fact of an advancement to an infant must be proven.([5])

Where a conveyance is made by a man to his wife or child, the presumption of the law is, that such conveyance is intended as an advancement. But that presumption may be overcome by evidence. Whether such a conveyance is an advancement or not, is a question of pure intention, though presumed in the first instance, to be a provision and settlement.([6])

11. VALUE OF REAL ESTATE ADVANCED.—If such advancement is made in real estate, and the value thereof is expressed in the conveyance or in the charge thereof made by the intestate, or in the written acknowledgment thereof by the party receiving it, it shall be considered as of that value in the divisions and distribution of the estate; otherwise, it shall be estimated according to its value when given.([7])

12. VALUE OF PERSONALTY ADVANCED.—If such advancement is made in personal estate of the intestate, the value thereof to be estimated the same as that of real estate; and if, in either

(1) Leamon et al. vs. McCubbin et al., 82 Ill., 263; McLean Co. Coal Co. vs. Long, 91 Ill., 617.
(2) Hurd's R. S., Chap. 39, § 4; Simpson vs. Simpson, 114 Ill., 603.
(3) Bishop et al. vs. Davenport, 58 Ill., 105; Wallace vs. Reddick, 119 Ill., 151; Wilkinson vs. Thomas, 128 Ill., 363.
(4) Long vs. Long, 132 Ill., 72.
(5) Barnes vs. Hazelton et al., 50 Ill., 430
(6) Wormley vs. Wormley, 98 Ill., 544.
(7) Hurd's R. S., Chap. 39, § 5.

case, it exceeds the share of real or personal estate, respectively, that would have come to the heir so advanced, he shall not refund any part of it, but shall receive so much less of the other part of the intestate's estate as will make his whole share equal to the shares of other heirs who are in the same degree with him.([1])

13. EVIDENCE MUST BE WRITTEN.—No gift or grant shall be deemed to have been made in advancement unless so expressed in writing or charged in writing, by the intestate, as an advancement, or acknowledged in writing by the child or other descendant.([2])

14. DEATH OF HEIR.—If a child, or other descendant so advanced, dies before the intestate, leaving issue, the advancement shall be taken into consideration in the division or distribution of the estate of the intestate, and the amount thereof shall be allowed accordingly by the representatives of the heirs so advanced, as so much received towards their share of the estate, in like manner as if the advancement had been made directly to them.([3])

15. ADVANCEMENTS DO NOT AFFECT WIDOW.—Where the intestate has made advancements to some one or more of his heirs in his lifetime, such advancements do not affect the rights of the widow, as she will take her share of the personal estate, and her dower in lands, without regard to advancements.([4])

16. WHEN HEIRS MAY HAVE DISTRIBUTION.—The county court may, at any time, compel a distribution, either entire or partial, to heirs, whenever it shall appear that there are assets to satisfy all demands against an estate.([5]) But where the estate is involved in litigation, and the amount of its net assets is unknown, or whether there are assets in excess of liabilities, the payment to legatees or heirs will not be ordered.([6])

17. ILLEGITIMATES.—An illegitimate child shall be heir of its mother and any maternal ancestor, and of any person from whom its mother might have inherited, if living; and the lawful issue of an illegitimate person shall represent such person, and take, by descent, any estate which the parent would have taken, if living.

(1) Hurd's R. S., Chap. 39, § 6.
(2) Hurd's R. S., Chap. 39. § 7; Wallace vs. Reddick, 119 Ill., 151.
(3) Hurd's R. S., Chap. 39, § 8.
(4) Grattan vs. Grattan et al., 18 Ill., 167.
(5) Reynolds vs. People, 55 Ill., 328.
(6) *In re* Ricaud, Supreme Court of Cal., 13 Legal News, 326; Peck vs. Peck, 9 Yerger, 304; Andrews vs. Hunneman, 6 Pick., 128.

Second—The estate, real and personal, of an illegitimate person, shall descend to and vest in the widow or surviving husband and children, as the estate of other persons in like cases.

Third—In case of the death of an illegitimate intestate leaving no child or descendant of a child, the whole estate, personal and real, shall descend to and absolutely vest in the widow or surviving husband.([1])

Fourth—When there is no widow or surviving husband, and no child or descendants of a child, the estate of such person shall descend to and vest in the mother and her children, and their descendants—one-half to the mother, and the other half to be equally divided between her children and their descendants, the descendants of a child taking the share of their deceased parent or ancestor.

Fifth—In case there is no heir as above provided, the estate of such person shall descend to and vest in the next of kin to the mother of such intestate, according to the rule of the civil law.

Sixth—When there are no heirs or kindred, the estate of such person shall escheat to the state, and not otherwise.([2])

18. CHILD LEGITIMATIZED.—An illegitimate child, whose parents have intermarried, and whose father has acknowledged him or her as his child, shall be considered legitimate.([3])

19. RIGHTS BEFORE THE STATUTE.—Before the passage of the statute of descents of 1872 (the above statute), an illegitimate child could inherit property from its mother only in cases where she remained unmarried.([4]) Where the father of an illegitimate child contracted with the mother to take the child into his own family and raise it as his own, and to give her a portion of his estate in common with his other children, it was held that the legal obligation of the father to support his illegitimate child, would support the contract, and its specific performance was enforced.([5])

(1) Evans vs. Price, 118 Ill., 593.
(2) Hurd's R. S., Chap. 39, ₴ 2; Bales vs. Elder, 118 Ill., 436; Jenkins vs. Drane, 121 Ill., 217; Elder vs. Bales, 127 Ill., 425; See 72 Am. Dec. for brief of authorities.
(3) Hurd's R. S., Chap. 39, ₴ 3; Stolz vs. Doering, 112 Ill., 234.
(4) Blacklaws vs. Milne et al., 82 Ill., 505; Orthwein vs. Thomas, 127 Ill., 554.
(5) Wallace vs. Rappelye, 103 Ill., 229.

20. BASTARDS UNDER THE COMMON LAW.—By the provisions of the common law, bastards could neither inherit nor transmit property, except to direct issue. Where such a person died having no descendants, his property escheated to the crown, although the mother and other near relatives might be living. Such a person was regarded by that law as the child of nobody, entitled to nothing, not even a name, until he acquired it by usage.(1) The statute of Illinois relieves him of these disabilities in part, and enables him to inherit from his mother and her relatives, and to transmit to collateral relatives, the same as other persons.(2)

21. POSTHUMOUS CHILD.—A posthumous child of an intestate shall receive its just proportion of its ancestor's estate, in all respects, as if he had been born in the lifetime of the father.(3)

The true construction of our statute of descents, is, that a posthumous child inherits of an intestate father, precisely as do his children born in his own lifetime. On the death of a father, the title to his real estate vests in the posthumous child, precisely as though such child had been previously born.(4) And such interest will not be divested by a decree against the mother and others, under which a sale was made to satisfy a debt against the relatives and ancestor of such child.(5)

22. HEIRS AT LAW.—An heir at law, is one who takes from another by descent—upon whom the law casts the estate immediately upon the death of the owner. Where property is devised to the heirs of the testator, without any other designation, such a direction is equivalent to a devise or bequest to those who would take the estate under our statute of distribution, if the estate was intestate.(6) In such a case, where the testator died childless, leaving a husband or wife and collateral heirs, such husband or wife, would take, the same as if no will had been made, one-half the real estate, and all the personal property left after the payment of debts

---

(1) 1 Blackstone's Com., 459; Stolz vs. Doering, 112 Ill., 234.
(2) Miller vs. Williams et al., 66 Ill., 91.
(3) Hurd's R. S., Chap. 39, § 9.
(4) Botsford vs. O'Conner et al., 57 Ill., 72.
(5) Detrick vs. Migatt et al., 19 Ill., 146; Smith et al. vs. McConnell et al., 17 Ill., 135; McConnell et al. vs. Smith, 23 Ill., 611; McConnell et al. vs. Smith et al., 39 Ill., 279; Kelley vs. Vigas, 112 Ill., 242; Alexander vs. Masonic Aid Association, 126 Ill., 558.
(6) Rawson et al. vs. Rawson et al., 52 Ill., 62; Richards vs. Miller, 62 Ill, 417; Ketteltas vs. Ketteltas, 72 N. Y., 312.

and specific legacies.(¹) But where a person dies intestate, leaving children capable of inheriting, his wife cannot be considered as being embraced in a provision made for the benefit of his "legal heirs." She would be considered as specially excluded from such a provision.(²) The distinguishing feature seems to be, that one who is entitled to dower out of the lands of an intestate cannot, at the same time, be his heir.(³)

Under the term "heirs" are comprehended the heirs of heirs *ad infinitum*.(⁴)

23. ADOPTED CHILDREN.—The statute provides for the adoption by any resident of this state, by proceedings in the county court, of any child, and when so adopted, the child becomes the legal heir of the person so adopting him, which relation becomes reciprocal, the adopting parents and their heirs taking by descent from the adopted child and his descendants, such property as he may have received from or through the adopting parents, or either of them, either by gift, bequest, devise or descent, with the accumulations, income and profits thereof, but none other.(⁵)

This relation does not extend to the legal heirs of the adopting parents, so as to enable the adopted child to inherit from them.(⁶)

24. RIGHTS OF HUSBAND AND WIFE.—The husband and wife are, by the statutes of Illinois, placed upon an equality as to their rights in each other's property,(⁷) except as to the widow's award. Neither can by will deprive the other of his or her right to dower in the real estate, and one-third of all the personal property, after the payment of debts and costs of administration. And where no provision is made in the will of a decedent leaving descendants, for his or her wife or husband, the estate as to such survivor is intestate, and he or she takes one-third of the personal property after the payment of debts and dower in the lands, according to the provisions of the statute. The right of such surviving husband or wife to one-third of the personal estate remaining, rests on a basis

---

(1) *Id.; In re* Taylor's Will, 55 Ill., 252.
(2) Gauch vs. St. Louis Ins. Co., 88 Ill., 251.
(3) *Id.*
(4) Merrill et al. vs. Atkin, 59 Ill., 19.
(5) Hurd's R. S., Chap. 4.
(6) *In re* Estate of Michael R. Keegan, 13 Legal News, 161–328; Keegan vs. Geraghty, 101 Ill., 26; Estate of Sunderland, 60 Iowa, 732.
(7) Hurd's R. S., Chap. 39, § 1; *Id.*, Chap. 41, § 1.

as solid as the right to dower in the lands.(¹) But the right of the surviving spouse of a person who dies, leaving no descendants, to the statutory provision of "one-half of the real estate and the whole of the personal estate," after the payment of debts, provided for in Section 1 above, does not rest upon such sure foundation; for, the deceased, by making such provision, as he or she pleases in his or her will, may effectually bar the survivor of this right. Where a person having no descendants died, leaving a will, by which certain provisions were made for his wife, which she renounced, and claimed as heir to her husband, one-half of the realty and all of the personal estate, it was held, that she was only entitled to one-half of the realty and one-third of the personal property after the payment of debts, in addition to the award of her specific allowance.(²) This case was decided under the statute as it existed prior to the revision of 1874, when some difficulty was experienced to settle the law, seemingly contradictory,(³) but the enactment of Section 12 of the Dower act, *supra*, settles the rule as there stated.

The personal property being the natural and primary fund for the payment of the debts of the decedent, the widow of a decedent who died without descendants, can only take his personal property with the charge of all his legal liabilities upon it. Though his debts are mortgages upon his real estate, or in that nature, in which the other heirs share equally with the widow, and the payment of such debts will operate to relieve the property of such other heirs therefrom, yet they have the right to insist upon the payment out of the personal property. And this, too, though the estate has been settled, and the personal property paid over to her, freed, as she supposes, from all further charges.(⁴)

25. DESCENT VARIED BY CONTRACT.—It is competent for the widow and heirs of a deceased person to make a different disposition of the personal property left by him from that provided by the

---

(1) *In re* Taylor's Will, 55 Ill., 252; Rawson et al. vs. Rawson, 52 Ill., 62.
(2) Lessley et. al. vs. Lessley, 44 Ill., 527; Henson vs. Moore, 104 Ill., 403.
(3) Tyson vs. Postlewait et al., 13 Ill., 727 ; Sturgis et al. vs. Ewing, 18 Ill., 176 ; Murphy vs. Boyles et al., 49 Ill., 110; Skinner vs. Newberry, 51 Ill., 203, Boyles et al. vs. Murphy, 55 Ill., 236; Rawson et al. vs. Rawson, *supra*; White et al. vs. Dance, 53 Ill., 414 ; Ringhouse vs. Keever, 49 Ill., 470 ; Sisk vs. Smith, 1 Gil., 503.
(4) Sutherland vs. Harrison et al., 86 Ill., 363 ; Young vs. Wittemyre, 123 Ill., 303.

statute of descents, and when they do so by contract duly made, the disposition agreed upon will bind them.(¹)

26. ACCEPTANCE UNDER THE WILL.—A widow, by accepting the provisions of her husband's will, made in her behalf, will afterward be barred from claiming the statutory provisions in favor of widows of persons dying in this state, except as to the specific articles.(²)

27. DESCENT NOT DEFEATED BY A NAKED TRUST.—Where no trust is created by a will, but only a naked power given to sell, and no sale having been made, such would not defeat the right of the heirs to take the property as provided by the statute of descents.(³)

28. DISTRIBUTIVE SHARE OF AN HEIR INDEBTED TO THE ESTATE.—Where one of the distributees of an estate is indebted to the estate, the county court, under its chancery powers, has the right to order sufficient of the share of such debtor paid over to the other heirs, to make the distribution equitable and just, by considering the amount of such indebtedness in the nature of an advancement.(⁴)

One may offset his distributive share against his indebtedness, but such debt must be considered a part of the assets that go to make up the aggregate fund for distribution.(⁵)

29. EQUALIZING LEGACIES.—In all cases where a widow or surviving husband shall renounce all benefit under the will, and the legacies and bequests therein contained to other persons, shall, in consequence thereof, become diminished or increased in amount, quantity or value, it shall be the duty of the court, upon settlement of such estate, to abate from or add to such legacies and bequests in such manner as to equalize the loss sustained or advantage derived thereby, in a corresponding ratio to the several amounts of such legacies and bequests, according to the amount or intrinsic value of each.(⁶)

30. NOTICE.—No final order of distribution should be made

---

(1) Comer vs. Comer, 120 Ill., 420; Roth vs. Roth, 104 Ill., 35.
(2) Brown et al., vs. Pitney, 39 Ill., 470.
(3) Gill vs. Grand Tower Manf. Co., 92 Ill., 250.
(4) 19 Pick., 167; Batton vs. Allen, 1 Halsted's Ch., 99.
(5) Anderson vs. Gregg, 44 Miss., 170.
(6) Hurd's R. S., Chap. 3, § 78.

without notice to those interested, whether they be heirs or creditors; and without notice no one is bound by the order of distribution.(¹)

31. LAW GOVERNING DISTRIBUTION.—Personal estate of a decedent is regarded, for the purposes of succession and distribution, wherever situated, as having no other locality than that of his domicile; and if he dies intestate, the succession is governed by the law of the place where he was domiciled at the time of his decease, and not by the conflicting laws of the various places where the property happens to be situated at the time.(²) So, distribution among either creditors or heirs will be made according to laws in force at the time of the death of the deceased, and not according to laws subsequently passed.(³)

32. ORDER OF PAYMENT AND DISTRIBUTION.—Before a distribution of the personal assets of an estate can be made among the heirs thereto, it must appear that all debts and charges to which it is subject are either paid or otherwise provided for.(⁴)

33. ORDER OF COURT NECESSARY.—Payment of the distributive share of heirs in an estate cannot be enforced by the processes of the county court until there has been an order made by that court, and the distributee has executed a bond to refund the money, if necessary, to pay the debts of the estate.(⁵) Such an order, when made by a court having jurisdiction, is conclusive upon all persons interested.(⁶) Distribution made without an order is at the risk of the administrator.(⁷)

34. DISTRIBUTION IN KIND.—If any testator directs that his estate shall not be sold, the same shall be preserved in kind, and distributed accordingly, unless such sale becomes absolutely neces-

---

(1) Hurd's R. S., Chap. 3, § 111; Long vs. Thompson, 60 Ill., 27; Slaughter vs. Froman, 5 T. B. Monroe, 19.
(2) Hossack vs. Rogers, 6 Paige, 415; Langdon vs. Potter, 11 Mass., 313; Russell et al. vs. Madden, 95 Ill., 485; Holmes vs. Remsen, 4 Johns. Ch., 460; Vroom vs. Van Horne, 10 Paige, 549; Sherwood vs. Wooster, 11 Paige, 441; Shultz vs. Pulver, 3 Paige, 82; Parsons vs. Lyman, 4 Brad., 269; Wilkins vs. Elliott, 9 Wall., 740; Saurez vs. Mayor of N. Y., 2 Sand. Ch., 173.
(3) Pascall vs. Hailman, 4 Gil, 285; Bryan vs. Moore, 11 Martin, 26; See, also, note, 13 Am. Dec., 349; Bales vs. Elder, 118 Ill., 436; Armstrong vs. Armstrong, 1 Ore., 207.
(4) Hurd's R. S., Chap. 3, § 112; People vs. Hunter et al., 89 Ill., 392.
(5) Hurd's R. S., Chap. 3, § 118; Mahar vs. O'Hara, 4 Gilm., 424; Wisdom et al. vs. Becker. 52 Ill., 342.
(6) Bigelow on Estoppel, 159.
(7) Lowry vs. McMillan, 35 Miss., 147.

sary for the payment of the debts and charges against the estate of such testator.([1]) This section is not peremptory.([2])

If the sale of the personal property is not necessary for the payment of debts or legacies, or the proper distribution of the effects of the estate, the court may order that the property be preserved and distributed in kind.([3]) This does not include notes.([4])

35. ESCHEATS.—That if any person shall die seized of any real or personal estate without any devise, and leaving no heirs or representatives capable of inheriting the same, or the devisees thereof be incapable of holding the same, and in all cases when there is no owner of real estate capable of holding the same, such estate, both real and personal, shall escheat to and vest in the county in which said real or personal estate, or greater portion thereof, is situated.([5])

In case said estate shall consist of personal property, letters of administration shall be granted thereon, as in other cases, and the same shall be administered in conformity with the probate laws of this state. Should there be any balance left in the hands of said administrator after the payment of debts and costs of administration, said administrator shall report the same to the probate court, with a statement of all the facts within his knowledge as to the heirship of said decedent, which facts shall constitute a part of his report, and be spread upon the records of said court; and it shall be the duty of said court to enter an order directing said administrator to pay over the balance found in his hands to the county treasurer of said county, taking his receipt therefor, which receipt shall be filed with the county clerk and entered of record, and shall be a good and sufficient voucher to said administrator. The said county clerk shall also charge said amount to the county treasurer as an escheat fund, specially designating from whose estate the same was derived.([6])

(1) Hurd's R. S., Chap. 3, § 91.
(2) Waterman vs. Alden, 115 Ill., 83.
(3) Hurd's R. S., Chap. 3, § 92.
(4) Waterman vs. Alden, *supra*.
(5) Hurd's R. S., Chap. 49, § 1.
(6) Hurd's R. S., Chap. 49, § 2.

CHAPTER XIII.

SALE OF REAL ESTATE TO PAY DEBTS

1. Real estate ultimately liable.
2. When it may be sold.
3. Where executor has exhausted his power in the will.
4. Petition to the court—parties thereto.
5. Proceedings coerced.
6. Form of petition—exhibit of estate.
    a. Must contain averments showing a statutory right to sell.
    b. Jurisdictional facts must be stated.
    c. Statutory averments in the petition invests the court with jurisdiction.
    d. Unnecessary matter will not defeat jurisdiction.
    e. Averment of no personal estate makes exhibit of account unnecessary.
    f. Must be allegation of debts.
    g. Equivalent averment.
    h. just and true account.
7. Parties to proceeding under various statutes.
    a. All parties must be in court.
    b. Failure to name all parties in the petition does not defeat jurisdiction.
8. Description of premises.
9. Summons.
    a. Form immaterial.
10. Service of summons.
    a. Return of sheriff must show legal service
    b. How service must be proven.
11. Notice by publication—contents of notice.
    a. How long published.
    b. Notice must be published for requisite time.
    c. May be given in any paper published at the county seat.
12. Affidavit of non-residence—may be made on belief.
    a. Sufficient if necessary facts are stated.
    b. Whole notice considered together.
13. Where decree shows that notice was given.
14. Parties must be before the court—want of jurisdiction.
    a. Failure to get jurisdiction of parties fatal.
    b. Having jurisdiction decree binds in collateral proceedings.
    c. Presumptions may be rebutted.

CH. XIII.] SALE OF REAL ESTATE TO PAY DEBTS. 153

15. Practice—docketed as in other cases.
    a. Continuance.
    b. Decree to pay debts in partition.
16. Guardian *ad litem*—his duties.
    a. Failure to appoint is error.
    b. Answer not sufficient evidence.
    c. Jurisdiction can not be given by guardian's answer.
    d. Guardian *ad litem* must appear and defend actively.
17. Hearing of cause.
18. Assignment of dower.
19. When dower can not be assigned without injury.
20. Dower may be assigned together.
21. Homestead—sale.
22. Land may be platted
23. Description of land in decree.
24. Extent of sale.
25. Power of court limited.
26. Power to order sale judicial.
27. Not a chancery proceeding.
28. Administrator no power to remove incumbrance by proceedings in court.
29. Heirs may interfere to prevent loss, but creditors can not.
    a. Creditors may maintain bill to set aside fraudulent conveyance.
30. Jurisdiction of chancery courts to order sale of land.
31. Decree can not be attacked.
32. Defenses—heirs may attack judgments.
    a. There must be debts.
    b. Debts barred by statute.
    c. Heirs not bound by judgments against administrator.
    d. Judgments of foreign courts.
    e. Statute must be pursued.
33. Time of payment.
34. Limitations in absence of a statute.
    a. Lapse of time may be explained.
    b. Homestead.
35. Sale, report and confimation.
    a. Attorney no power to sell.
    b. Administrator himself must act.
    c. Successor may make sale.
    d. Failure to advertise.
    e. Decree must be followed.
    f. Sale for less than value.
    g. Requiring deposit.
    h. Sale must be made in separate **tracts.**
    i. Administrator can not purchase.
    j. Irregularity will not vitiate sale.
    k. Time of sale.
    l. Second sale.
    m. Report of sale.

36. Title of purchaser—*caveat emptor.*
37. Effect on sale of a reversal of the decree.
38. Forgery—fraud—chancery jurisdiction.
39. Conveyance under decree and sale.
    a. Must be made by administrator in person.
    b. Formerly must contain copy of decree.
    c. Purchaser need not look back of decree.
    d. Deed to another.
    e. Refusal to consummate sale.
40. Proceeds of sale.
41. Sale of land not fully paid for.
42. Power to sell under a will.

1. REAL ESTATE ULTIMATELY LIABLE.—Under our statute, the lands of an intestate are held subject to the payment of his debts. After the personal estate is exhausted, it is made the duty of the administrator to apply to the proper court, and obtain a license to sell so much of the real estate, as will be sufficient to discharge the residue of the debts. Creditors are not compelled, as at common law, in order to procure satisfaction of their debts, where there is a deficiency of assets for the purpose, to pursue the lands into the hands of the heir; or to charge the heir with its value, in the case of an alienation by him. They have only to establish their demands against the administrator, and he is required to make payment out of the personal estate; and when that proves insufficient, to convert enough of the real estate into assets to meet the deficiency. The statute, in effect, reserves a lien on the lands of an intestate, to secure the payment of any excess of indebtedness beyond the proceeds of the personal estate. This lien is to be enforced by the administrator, for the benefit of the creditors generally. The lien, however, is not perpetual, but may be lost by gross laches or unreasonable delay. The real estate descends to the heir with this charge resting upon it. He can not encumber or aliene it, to the prejudice of the rights of the creditors. He acquires a vested, but not an absolute, interest in the land. He takes a defeasible estate, liable to be defeated by a sale made by the administrator in the due course of administration. He has no just claim to the land, until the indebtedness of the ancestor is fully discharged. He acquires an absolute title only to what remains after the debts are extinguished.([1])

(1) Vansyckle et al. vs. Richardson et al. 13 Ill., 171; Myer et al. vs. McDougal et al., 47 Ill., 278; LeMoyne vs. Harding 132 Ill., 23.

2. When and what may be sold.—When the executor or administrator has made a just and true account of the personal estate and debts to the county court, and it is ascertained that the personal estate of a decedent is insufficient to pay the just claims against his estate, and there is real estate to which such decedent had claim or title, such real estate, or such portion as may be necessary to satisfy the indebtedness of such decedent, and the expenses of administration, may be sold in the manner herein provided.([1])

3. Where executor has exhausted his power under the will.—Where power is given in a will to an executor to sell certain lands of the testator for the payment of debts, and those lands, upon sale, fail to realize a sufficient amount for the payment of all his debts, the executor may apply to the county court for authority to sell other lands.([2])

4. Petition—Parties.—The mode of commencing the proceedings for the sale of real estate in such cases, shall be by the filing of a petition by the executor or administrator in the circuit or county court of the county where letters testamentary or of administration were issued. The widow, heirs and devisees of the testator or intestate, and the guardians of any such as are minors, and the conservator of such as have conservators, and all persons holding liens against the real estate described in the petition, or any part thereof, or having or claiming any interest therein, in possession or otherwise, shall be made parties. If there are persons interested in the premises whose names are not known, then they shall be made parties by the name of unknown owners.([3])

5. Sale to pay debts—coerced.—Whenever real estate is required to be sold for the payment of debts, the court may make all necessary orders to coerce the executor or administrator to make immediate application for an order to sell such real estate.([4])

6. Form of Petition.—The petition shall set forth the facts and circumstances on which the petition is founded, in which shall be stated the amount of claims allowed, with an estimate of the amount of just claims to be presented, and it shall also contain a statement of the amount of personal estate which has come to the hands of the petitioner, and the manner in which he has disposed

[1] Hurd's R. S., Chap. 3, § 97; Kenley vs. Bryan, 110 Ill., 652.
[2] Kinney et al. vs. Knoebel, 51 Ill., 114; 2 Probate Reports, 443.
[3] Hurd's R. S., Chap. 3, § 98; Bowers vs. Block, 129 Ill., 424.
[4] Hurd's R. S., Chap. 3, § 129.

of the same, with a statement of the amount of claims paid, a particular description of the real estate sought to be sold, and the nature and extent of all liens upon said real estate, so far as the same may be known to the petitioner. The petition shall be signed by the executor or administrator and verified by his affidavit, and shall be filed at least ten days before the commencement of the term of court at which the application shall be made.([1])

a. An administrator derives his power to sell lands to pay debts from the statute, and, unless the petition shows, by proper averments, the existence of a state of facts contemplated by the statute to authorize a sale, and those averments are sustained by proof, a decree of sale can not be sustained.([2])

b. County courts acquire jurisdiction in a proceeding by an administrator to sell lands to pay debts, from the death of the party seized of real estate, the grant of letters of administration, his indebtedness in excess of the personal estate, and filing a petition showing these facts.([3])

The record must show that a petition was filed, or the decree will be reversed.([4])

c. Petition need only contain such averments as the statute requires. Followed by such notice to the defendants as the statute requires, the court is invested with jurisdiction, and its decree is binding until reversed, although errors in its proceedings may intervene.([5])

d. Where a petition was addressed to the chancellor, it was held that, while the proceeding was in no sense a chancery proceeding, but strictly one of law, yet as the statute prescribed no particular form for the petition, and as it contained all the required statutory averments, it was sufficient, and would be considered as presented and carried on under the statute.([6])

e. In the same petition there was an averment that there was no personal estate belonging to the deceased, which statement fully met an objection that there was no averment of a just and true account of the personal estate.([7])

(1) Hurd's R. S., Chap. 3, § 99.
(2) Walker et al. vs. Diehl, 79 Ill., 474; Bennett vs. Whitman, 22 Ill., 448.
(3) Bostwick et al. vs. Skinner et al., 80 Ill., 147; Iverson et al. vs. Loberg, 26 Ill., 179; Young vs. Wittenmyre, 123 Ill., 303.
(4) Monahan et al. vs. Vandyke, 27 Ill., 154.
(5) Stow et al. vs. Kimball et al., 28 Ill., 94; Harding vs. LeMoyne, 114 Ill., 65.
(6) Hobson et al. vs. Ewan, 62 Ill., 146; Bowles Heirs vs. Rouse, 3 Gil., 409.
(7) Hobson et al. vs. Ewan, *supra*.

f. There must be some allegation that there are debts against the estate, and that there is no personal property, or there being such, that it is insufficient for the payment of the debts. That more formal allegations may be necessary on demurrer, may be true, but they do not go to the jurisdiction.(¹)

g. In the same case the petition stated that there were debts of the decedent, amounting to——dollars, and that there were no personal assets with which to pay said debts, which was held a sufficient statement of the indebtedness to authorize a decree for the sale of lands.

h. It is not necessary that it should appear from the petition that an appraisement bill was filed by the administrator, to authorize the court to grant a decree of sale. The statute only requires the administrator shall make a just and true account of the personal estate and debts, and he may thereupon file his petition.(²)

7. PARTIES.—Under the statute authorizing this proceeding as it existed up to 1857, it was not necessary to give the names of the heirs of the deceased in the petition, nor need they be made parties;(³) but under the statute as it has existed since 1857, it is necessary to make the widow and heirs of the deceased, together with the guardians of such of the heirs as may be minors, and those in possession of the lands, parties to the proceedings to sell.(⁴) The failure to make a guardian a party, would doubtless be error, but would not vitiate the decree.(⁵) Under the former law, infants not named were bound.(⁶)

a. No decree can be rendered until all the parties interested in the real estate sought to be sold, have been either served with process or have entered their appearance.(⁷)

b. Although only part of the heirs of the intestate are made parties, still, the court having obtained jurisdiction of the subject matter by the filing of the petition, its adjudication will conclude those who are made parties and brought into court by service of

---

(1) Moffatt et al. vs. Moffatt, 69 Ill., 641; Bree et al. vs. Bree, 51 Ill., 367.
(2) Shoemate et al. vs. Lockridge, 53 Ill., 504; Young vs. Wittenmyre, 123 Ill., 303.
(3) Purples Stat., Chap. 110, Sec. 103; Turney et al. vs. Turney et al., 24 Ill., 625; Stowe et al. vs. Kimball et al., 28 Ill., 93; Gibson vs. Roll, 27 Ill., 88; Hobson et al. vs. Ewan, 62 Ill., 147; Swearingen vs. Gulick, 67 Ill., 208; Morris et al. vs. Hogle, 37 Ill., 150.
(4) Hurd's R. S., Chap. 3, § 98.
(5) Harris vs. Lester et al., 80 Ill., 307.
(6) Gibson vs. Roll; *supra.*
(7) Marshall vs. Rose, 86 Ill., 374.

summons.([1]) A posthumous child of the intestate, born after the filing of the petition, will not be concluded by a decree in the case.([2])

8. DESCRIPTION OF PREMISES.—A correct description of the premises sought to be sold is very important, for, where by an error in the petition and subsequent proceedings, the wrong tract was sold, the error is such as cannot be corrected subsequently to the sale by any court.([3])

9. SUMMONS.—Upon the filing of the petition, the clerk of the court where the same may be filed, shall issue a summons, directed to the sheriff of the county in which the defendant resides, if the defendant is a resident of this state, requiring him to appear and answer the petition on the return day of the summons; and where there are several defendants, residing in different counties, a separate summons shall be issued to each county, including all the defendants residing therein. Every summons shall be made returnable to the first term of the county court after the date thereof, unless the petition is filed within ten days immediately preceding any term, in which case the summons shall be returnable to the next term thereafter.([4])

a. In such a proceeding, a mere informality in the summons, which informs the defendants of the nature of the proceedings against them, will not excuse a disregard of it.([5])

10. SERVICE.—The service of summons shall be made by reading thereof to the defendant, or leaving a copy thereof at the usual place of abode, with some member of the family of the age of ten years and upwards, and informing such person of the contents thereof, which service shall be at least ten days before the return of such summons.([6])

a. The return of the sheriff upon the summons, must show such a service as the law requires, or else the court fails to get jurisdiction of the person of the defendant, and no decree can be rendered which will divest him of the title of his property.([7]) The defect in

---

(1) Bowers vs. Block, 129 Ill., 424.
(2) Botsford vs. O'Connor et al., 57 Ill., 72.
(3) Ward vs. Brewer, 19 Ill., 291; Young et al. vs. Dowling, 15 Ill., 481; Schnell et al. vs. Chicago, 38 Ill., 382.
(4) Hurd's R. S., Chap. 3, § 101.
(5) Jeffries et al. vs. Decker et al., 42 Ill., 519.
(6) Hurd's R. S., Chap. 3, § 102.
(7) Whitney vs. Porter et al., 23 Ill., 445.

service is not cured by recitals in the decree, that due service of process was had, when other portions of the same record contradict such recitals.(¹)

b. Where the service is by summons, verbal testimony can not be received to prove or aid it. That can be shown alone by the officer's return. It is otherwise, when the service is by publication.(²)

11. NOTICE BY PUBLICATION.—Whenever any petitioner or his attorney shall file, in the office of the clerk of the court in which his petition is pending, an affidavit showing that any defendant resides or hath gone out of this state, or on due inquiry can not be found, or is concealed within this state, so that process can not be served upon him, and stating the place of residence of such defendant, if known; or that, upon diligent inquiry, his place of residence can not be ascertained, the clerk shall cause publication to be made in some newspaper printed in his county, and if there is no newspaper published in his county, then in the nearest newspaper published in this state, containing notice of the filing of the petition, the names of the parties thereto, the title of the court, and the time and place of the return of summons in the case, and a description of the premises described in the petition; and he shall also, within ten days of the first publication of such notice, send a copy thereof by mail, addressed to such defendant whose place of residence is stated in such affidavit. The certificate of the clerk that he has sent such notice in pursuance of this section, shall be evidence.(³)

a. The notice required in the preceding section may be given at any time after the filing of the petition, and shall be published at least once in each week for four successive weeks, and no default or proceeding shall be taken against any defendant not served with summons, and not appearing, unless forty days shall intervene between the first publication, as aforesaid, and the first day of the term at which such default or proceeding is proposed to be taken.(⁴)

b. It is error to order a sale of land by an administrator, when

---

(1) Botsford vs. O'Connor, 57 Ill., 72; Donlin vs. Hettinger, 57 Ill., 348; Clark vs. Thompson, 47 Ill., 27; Johnson vs. Baker, 38 Ill., 98; Johnson vs. Johnson, 30 Ill., 215; Matthews vs. Hoff, 113 Ill., 90.
(2) Botsford vs. O'Connor et al., *supra*.
(3) Hurd's R. S. Chap. 3 § 103.
(4) Hurd's R. S., Chap. 3, § 104.

the notice has been published only for a period less than the time specified in the statute.(¹)

c. Publication in any newspaper published at the county seat, will meet the requirement of the statute.(²)

12. AFFIDAVIT OF NON-RESIDENCE.—The affidavit required by the statute, showing the non-residence of the defendants, may be made by any person having the requisite knowledge: the affidavit may be made upon information and belief.(³)

a. It is not necessary that the affidavit should be entitled in the case. It will be sufficient if it states the necessary facts, and is filed in the case, even if not entitled at all and without a caption.(⁴)

b. It is not essential that the name of the county in which the court is held, should be named in the notice—the name of the county and state may be inferred from the fact that the notice was published in the county intended.(⁵) Nor is it necessary to specify any particular day of the term upon which the petition will be presented.

In determining the sufficiency of a notice, courts will consider whether a reasonable person, in the exercise of his ordinary faculties, on reading the notice, would be apprized by it, in what court, and at what time the petition would be presented.(⁶)

Where notice does not specify any day of the term, petition may be presented on any day of the term.(⁷)

13. WHERE DECREE SHOWS NOTICE.—Where in the decree it appears that notice of the pendency of the proceedings was given to the defendants, according to the provision of the statute, such a recital will conclude the defendants, unless this recitation is contradicted by other portions of the record.(⁸) And such a recital is not overcome, in a collateral proceeding, by the production of a print-

---

(1) Monahon et al. vs. Vandyke, 27 Ill., 154; Gibson vs. Roll, 30 Ill., 172; Madden vs. Cooper, 47 Ill., 359.
(2) Stowe et al. vs. Kimball et al., 28 Ill., 106.
(3) Rowand et al. vs. Carroll et al., 81 Ill., 224.
(4) Harris vs. Lester et al., 80 Ill., 307.
(5) Moore et al. vs. Neil et al., 39 Ill., 257.
(6) Finch vs. Sink, 46 Ill., 169; Goudy et al. vs. Hall, 36 Ill., 313; Madden vs. Cooper, 47 Ill., 359; Hobson et al. vs. Ewan, 62 Ill., 147.
(7) Cromine vs. Tharp, 42 Ill., 120; Shoemate vs. Lockridge, 53 Ill., 503.
(8) Andrews vs. Bernhardi, 87 Ill., 365; Bowen et al. vs. Bond et al., 80 Ill., 351; Botsford vs. O'Connor, 57 Ill., 72; Harris vs. Lester, *supra;* Mickel vs. Hicks, 19 Kansas, 578; Monk vs. Horne, 38 Miss., 100; Mathews vs. Hoff, 113 Ill., 90.

er's certificate, from the files in the cause, showing defective and insufficient notice. In such a case, it will be presumed that evidence of the publication of a legal notice was before the court.([1])

14. PARTIES MUST BE BEFORE THE COURT.—Unless the mode pointed out by the statute for bringing the parties interested before the court is pursued, there will be such a want of jurisdiction as will vitiate the order of sale.([2])

a. Where the court fails to obtain jurisdiction of the persons of the defendants in some manner known to the law, a decree licensing the administrator to sell lands of the deceased to pay debts, is void, and may be questioned in both direct and collateral proceedings.([3])

b. On the other hand, where by proper averments in the petition filed in court, the court had jurisdiction of the subject matter, and the record showed jurisdiction of the parties by legal service of process or by publication, it matters not how erroneous the findings, judgments and decrees of a court of general jurisdiction may be, when drawn in question collaterally. They can not be questioned collaterally for mere irregularities.([4]) Courts will not overturn titles acquired in good faith upon mere technical grounds.([5])

c. In all collateral proceedings, the presumptions of the law in favor of jurisdiction of the person where courts of general jurisdiction have assumed to adjudicate, are liable to be rebutted; and when the record shows service which was insufficient, and there is no finding by the court, from which it may be inferred that there was other service, or appearance, then the presumption that the court had jurisdiction of the person, is rebutted, and it must be held that the court acted upon the insufficient service.([6])

15. PRACTICE.—Such application shall be docketed as other causes, and the petition may be amended, heard or continued for notice or other cause, and the practice in such cases shall be the same as in cases in chancery. The court may direct the sale of such real estate, disincumbered of all mortgage, judgment or other money

---

(1) Sloan vs. Graham et al., 85 Ill., 26; Hobson et al. vs. Ewan, 62 Ill., 146; Moore vs. Neil, 39 Ill., 256; Kilgour vs. Gockley, 83 Ill., 109.

(2) Herdman et al. vs. Short, 18 Ill., 59; Clark vs. Thompson, 47 Ill., 25; Fell vs. Young, 63 Ill., 106.

(3) Morris et al. vs. Hogle et al., 37 Ill., 150; Herdman et al. vs. Short et al., *supra*.

(4) Hobson et al. vs. Ewan, *supra;* Goudy et al. vs. Hall, 36 Ill. 313; Moore et al vs. Neil et al., *supra;* Iverson et al. vs. Loberg, 26 Ill., 179.

(5) Finch vs. Sink, 46 Ill., 169.

(6) Clark vs. Thompson, *supra;* Donlin vs. Hettinger et al., 57 Ill., 348.

liens that are due, and may provide for the satisfaction of all such liens out of the proceeds of the sale, and may also settle and adjust all equities and all questions of priority between all parties interested therein; and may also investigate and determine all questions of conflicting or controverted titles arising between any of the parties to such proceeding, and may remove clouds from the title to any real estate sought to be sold, and invest purchasers with a good and indefeasible title to the premises sold. The court may, with the assent of any mortgagee of the whole or any part of such real estate, whose debt is not due, sell such real estate disincumbered of such mortgage, and provide for the payment of such mortgage out of the proceeds of such sale; and may also, with the assent of the person entitled to an estate in dower, or by the courtesy, or for life or for years, or of homestead to the whole or in part of the premises, who is a party to the suit, sell such real estate with the rest. But such assent shall be in writing and signed by such person, and filed in the court wherein the said proceedings are pending. When any such estate is sold, the value thereof shall be ascertained and paid over in gross, or the proper proportion of the funds invested and the income paid over to the party entitled thereto during the continuance of the estate.([1])

a. If the administrator files his petition and has the cause docketed at the term named in his notice, there is no doubt it would be competent for the court to continue the cause to a subsequent term, and then grant an order to sell.([2])

b. Where in a partition suit the land was reported by the commissioners not susceptible of a division, and ordered sold, it is proper for the court where the matter is pending, to decree the payment of debts of the ancestor which have been allowed in probate and are a lien upon the land.([3])

16. GUARDIAN AD LITEM APPOINTED.—When it appears that any of the persons required to be made parties defendant, who have been served with summons or notified as aforesaid, are minors, under the age of twenty-one years, if males, or eighteen years, if females, without a guardian resident in this state, or are persons

(1) Hurd's R. S., Chap. 3, § 100; Newell vs. Montgomery, 129 Ill., 58.
(2) Schnell et al. vs. Chicago, 38 Ill., 382.
(3) Labadie et al. vs. Hewitt, 85 Ill., 341; Wheeler vs. Dawson, 63 Ill., 54.

having conservators, or where such guardian, if any, or conservator, shall not be personally served with summons or shall not appear, the court shall appoint a guardian *ad litem*, who shall appear and defend in behalf of such minors, and be allowed such compensation as may be fixed by the court.(¹)

a. The failure to appoint a guardian *ad litem*, and require an answer by him, is such error as, in a direct proceeding by appeal or writ of error, would cause a reversal of the proceedings; yet, if the court had acquired jurisdiction of the subject matter by the filing of a petition containing proper averments, and by such notice to the infant defendants, as the law requires, a sale made under its decree would be sustained in all collateral proceedings.(²)

b. The answer of a guardian *ad litem* is not sufficient foundation for an order of sale. The record should show further that the court heard proof, which satisfied it of the truth of the allegations of the petition.(³)

c. When the service is insufficient, jurisdiction cannot be given of the minors by the appearance and answer of their general guardian, nor by the appointment of a guardion *ad litem*, and his answer for such minors—as to them, a decree in such a case is a nullity.(⁴) Nor can the appearance of the regular guardian for such minors confer jurisdiction of the minors.(⁵) Where sufficient service has been had upon minors, the failure of a guardian *ad litem* to answer for them does not deprive the court of its jurisdiction,(⁶) but it is error for the court to enter a final decree against such minors, without first having on file the answer on their behalf, of the guardian *ad litem*.(⁷)

d. The appointment of a guardian *ad litem* is something more than a mere form. The rule is inflexible in this state, that the guardian *ad litem* shall not only file his answer as required by the rule of the court, but attend at the trial of the cause, and make a

(1) Hurd's R. S., Chap. 3, § 105.
(2) Gage et al. vs. Shroeder, 73 Ill.. 44; McDaniel vs. Correll, 19 Ill., 226; Harris vs. Lester et al., 80 Ill., 308; Herdman et al. vs. Short et al., 18 Ill., 59.
(3) Fridley et al. vs. Murphy, 25 Ill., 146.
(4) Donlin vs. Hettinger et al., 57 Ill., 348; Clark vs. Thompson, 47 Ill., 25; Greenman et al. vs. Harvey, 53 Ill., 386.
(5) *Id.*
(6) Goudy et al. vs. Hall, 36 Ill., 313.
(7) Rhoads vs. Rhoads et al., 43 Ill., 239.

defense of the interests of the infant, as vigorous as the nature of the case will admit. It is his special duty to submit to the court, for its consideration and decision, every question involving the rights of the infant affected by the suit. In no case, can a default be entered against a minor. Nothing can be admitted as against an infant, by the guardian or others, and the record must show that evidence was heard, and it must furnish proof to sustain a decree against him, whether he is defended by his guardian or not.[1]

17. HEARING—DECREE OF SALE—OVERPLUS.—Upon hearing the cause upon the issues formed or taken, the court shall hear and examine the allegations and proofs of the parties and of all other persons interested in the estate, who may appear and become parties; and if, upon due examination, the court shall find that the executor or administrator has made a just and true account of the condition of the estate, and that the personal estate of the decedent is not sufficient to pay the debts against such estate, the court shall ascertain, as nearly as can be, the amount of deficiency, and how much of the real estate described in the petition it is necessary to sell to pay such deficiency, with the expenses of administration then due or to accrue, and make a decree for the sale thereof: *Provided*, that where any houses and lots, or other real estate, are so situated that a part thereof can not be sold without manifest prejudice to the heirs, devisees or owners, the court may order the sale of the whole or such part as it may deem best, and the overplus arising from such sale, shall be distributed among the heirs and devisees, owners, or such other persons as may be entitled thereto.[2]

18. ASSIGNMENT OF DOWER.—Whenever application is made to a county court for leave to sell real estate of a deceased person for the payment of debts, or for the sale of real estate of any ward, as authorized by law, and it appears that there is a dower and homestead, or either, interest in the land sought to be sold, such court may, in the same proceeding, on the petition of the executor, administrator, guardian or conservator, or of the person entitled to dower and homestead, or either, therein, cause the dower and homestead, or either, to be assigned, and shall have the same power and may take like proceedings therefor as hereinbefore provided for the assignment of dower.[3]

(1) Rhoads vs. Rhoads et al., 43 Ill., 239; Sconce et al. vs. Whitney, 12 Ill., 150; Enos vs. Capps, *Ib.*, 255; Stark et al. vs. Brown et al., 101 Ill., 395.
(2) Hurd's R. S., Chap. 3, § 106.
(3) Hurd's R. S., Chap. 41, § 44; Walker vs. Doane, 108 Ill., 236.

19. WHEN DOWER CANNOT BE ASSIGNED WITHOUT INJURY.—When the estate consists of a mill or other tenement, which cannot be divided without damage to the whole, and in all cases where the estate cannot be divided without great injury thereto, the dower may be assigned of the rents, issues and profits thereof, to be had by the person entitled to dower as tenant in common with the owners of the estate; or a jury may be empanneled to inquire of the yearly value of the dower therein, who shall assess the same accordingly, and the court may thereupon enter a decree that said premises be sold free of claim for dower, and that there be paid to the person entitled to dower during life, on a day to be named, by the purchaser at the sale, the sum so assessed as the yearly value of dower, and may make such sum a lien upon the premises, or cause the same to be otherwise secured.(1)

20. DOWER MAY BE ASSIGNED TOGETHER.—The dower need not be assigned in each tract separately, but may be allotted in a body out of one or more of the tracts of land, when the same can be done without prejudice to the interest of any person interested in the premises.(2)

21. HOMESTEAD SALE.—The surviving husband or wife shall have the homestead or dwelling house, if he or she desires, and such allotment shall not affect his or her estate of homestead therein; but if the dower is allotted out of other lands, the acceptance of such allotment shall be a waiver and release of the estate of homestead of the person entitled to such dower, and his or her children, unless it shall be otherwise ordered by the court.(3)

Should the commissioners appointed by the court report that the premises are of such a nature that a homestead of the value of $1,000 cannot be set off, as in case of a building of much greater value than the exemption allowed by law, the county court, in the exercise of its chancery powers in the settlement of estates,(4) may, for the purpose of the enforcement of the lien of creditors of the estate against such real

---

(1) Hurd's R. S., Chap. 41, ¿ 39.
(2) Hurd's R. S., Chap. 41, ¿ 36; Rowand vs. Carroll, 81 Ill., 224; Kenley vs. Bryan, 110 Ill., 652.
(3) Hurd's R. S., Chap. 41, ¿ 37.
(4) Wadsworth vs. Connell, 104 Ill., 369; Winslow vs. Leland, 128 Ill., 304; Millard vs. Harris, 119 Ill., 185; Shepherd vs. Spremont, 111 Ill., 631.

estate, or against so much as exceeds the exemption, order a sale of the whole estate, free from the homestead rights, and the payment of the amount of the exemption to the person entitled thereto. The decree should provide that no sale of the premises should be made unless a greater sum than $1,000 is bid therefor; and should no greater sum be offered at a sale, the decree of the court should be modified, and the premises be released from present claims of creditors.([1])

Any judicial sale of premises in which is an estate of homestead, without the observance of these preliminaries, is void ([2])

22. COURT MAY ORDER LAND PLATTED.—That in any proceeding in any court of record in this state, by executors or administrators, for the sale of lands of deceased persons, or by guardians, for the sale of lands of their wards, or for partition of lands, when such lands are to be sold in parcels, or actual partition thereof shall be made, it shall be competent for the court to order such executor or administrator, guardian, master in chancery, special commissioner, or other officer or person authorized to sell the lands in question in any such proceeding, or commissioners authorized to make partition of such lands, to cause such lands to be surveyed and subdivided, and a map or plat of the same to be made, showing the lots or parcels of such subdivision or partition designated by numbers or letters; which map or plat shall be acknowledged by the person or persons so causing the same to be made, in like manner as is now required by law in cases of plats or maps made by owners of lands, and shall, in like manner, be certified by the surveyor or engineer making the same; which certificate shall contain, among other things, an accurate and definite description of the lands so subdivided or partitioned; and such map or plat shall be submitted to the court for his approval, and if approved by the court, shall be recorded in the recorder's office of the county or counties in which the lands in question in any such proceeding, are situate.([3])

23. DECREE which directs a sale of the land named in the petition is sufficiently certain.([4])

(1) Hurd's R. S., Chap. 52, § 8 & 9.
(2) Hartwell vs. McDonald, 69 Ill., 293; Hartman vs. Schultz, 101 Ill., 437.
(3) Hurd's R. S., Chap. 109, § 11.
(4) Stow et al. vs. Kimball et al., 28 Ill., 93.

24. EXTENT OF SALE.—Under the law, the court is only authorized to license a sale of so much real estate as is necessary to pay the debts not shown to be provided for by the personal estate, and it is error to license the sale of so much as the executor may deem for the best interest of the estate.(¹) A decree which authorized a sale of the whole of the lands of the deceased, or so much thereof as would pay the debts found by the decree to be unprovided for, was held to be correct.(²)

25. POWER OF THE COURT LIMITED.—The power to order a sale of land to pay debts of a decedent, is given by statute, and is therefore limited to the powers expressly delegated by that statute, or given by implication. In such a proceeding, the court has no power to interpret the will of the deceased, to excuse the executors from the performance of any duty imposed by the will, nor to order a sale of real estate for the maintenance of the widow and family.(³) But where the heir has alienated a part of the land, the court may order the residue to be first sold.(⁴)

26. POWER TO ORDER SALE JUDICIAL.—An act of the legislature authorizing the sale of the land of a deceased person to pay debts which are thereby assumed to be due, without providing that such debts shall be judicially ascertained, is an invasion of the powers of government expressly conferred by the constitution, upon the judiciary department of the state government, and unconstitutional. The right of inquiring into and determining facts between debtor and creditor, belongs to the judicial, and not to the legislative department of the government.(⁵)

27. NOT IN CHANCERY.—A proceeding to subject the lands of a decedent to the payment of debts is a statutory, and not a chancery proceeding;(⁶) therefore, in reviewing the decrees rendered in such proceedings, the supreme court will presume there was proof of indebtedness before the court to sustain the decree, although the

---

(1) Morris et al. vs. Hogle et al., 37 Ill., 150.
(2) Bowles et al. vs. Rouse, 3 Gil., 409.
(3) Bennett et al. vs. Whitman et al., 22 Ill., 448.
(4) Eddy vs. Traver et al., 6 Paige Ch., 521.
(5) Cooley's Cont. Lim., 107; Lane et al. vs. Dorman et al., 3 Scam., 238; Rozier vs. Fagan et al., 46 Ill., 404; Davenport vs. Young, 16 Ill., 548.
(6) Moline Water Power Manf. Co. vs. Webster, 26 Ill., 233.

evidence was not preserved in the record.(¹) Such a proceeding is a proceeding *in rem.*(²)

28. ADMINISTRATOR NO POWER TO REMOVE INCUMBRANCES.—An administrator has no power to remove incumbrances he finds upon the lands of the intestate. He must sell them as he finds them.(³)

Nor can an administrator maintain a bill, the purpose of which is to remove a cloud from the title of deceased to the real estate, preparatory to selling the same to pay debts. The lands descend to the heir, subject to the payment of debts, and may afterwards be divested by a decree and sale of the administrator. The administrator therefore takes neither estate, title nor interest, in the realty—he takes simply a power, and nothing more. He must take it as he finds it.(⁴) He derives all his power from the statute, and it only authorizes him to sell the lands of which his intestate died seized. A conveyance in fraud of creditors being binding, *inter parties* leaves no estate, legal or equitable, in the grantor.(⁵)

29. HOW TO PROCEED.—If it becomes necessary to expose the property so incumbered or clouded to sale, for the payment of debts, the administrator should obtain an order to sell it, and, to prevent the anticipated sacrifice, the heir might enjoin the sale until he could make an effort to set aside the incumbrance or cloud. We see no other course, as the law now stands, which could be adopted, to prevent the disastrous consequences likely to result from a sale of property, the title to which is clouded ;(⁶) but a creditor can not maintain such a suit, unless the title to the estate is clouded by fraudulent conveyances.(⁷)*

(1) Shoemate et al. vs. Lockridge, 53 Ill., 503; Wolf et al. vs. Ogden, 66 Ill., 224.
(2) Mickel vs. Hicks, 19 Kansas, 578.
(3) Sebastian vs. Johnson, 72 Ill., 282; Gridley vs. Watson, 53 Ill., 186; Stark vs. Brown, 101 Ill., 395.
(4) Phelps vs. Funkhouser, 39 Ill., 402; Cutter vs. Thompson et al., 51 Ill., 390-531; Le Moyne et al. vs. Quimby et al., 70 Ill., 400; Smith et al. vs. McConnell et al., 17 Ill., 135; Shoemate et al. vs. Lockridge, *supra;* Ryan vs. Duncan, 88 Ill., 144; Choteau vs. jones, 11 Ill., 300.
(5) Beebe et al. vs. Saulter et al., 87 Ill., 518; Martin vs. Martin, 1 Vt., 91; Van Wickle vs. Calvin, 23 La. An., 205; Harding vs. LeMoyne, 114 Ill., 65.
(6) Phelps vs. Funkhouser et al., 39 Ill., 401.
(7) Le Moyne et al. vs. Quimby et al., *supra.*

* NOTE.—By the passage of the amendment of 1887, permitting county courts, upon applications to sell lands for payment of debts, to adjust equities and remove clouds upon title, all questions of conflicting titles affecting lands of decedents may now be settled in the county court —*Hurd's R. S.,* Chap. 3, § 100; *Newell* vs. *Montgomery,* 129 Ill., 58; *Bowers* vs. *Block,* 129 Ill., 424.

a. A creditor of the deceased, who has had his claim allowed in probate, where there is no personal estate with which to discharge such claim, may maintain a bill to set aside a fraudulent and colorable conveyance of real estate made by the deceased in his lifetime.([1])

30. JURISDICTION OF A COURT OF CHANCERY TO ORDER SALE OF LAND.—A court of chancery has no original jurisdiction to order the sale of real estate to pay debts, or for any other purpose, so as to bind the infant's legal estate. The power is derived from legislative authority, and does not exist except in cases where the statute expressly confers it.([2]) The same court which pronounced the above rule, has since, when discussing the same question, said that the doctrine as above stated, has for its support, the best authorities, and its correctness is not to be questioned; but its application is limited to proceedings adverse to the interests of the infants owning the estate.([3])

Courts of chancery, however, having obtained jurisdiction of an estate for any other proper purpose, as for the purpose of construing a will and advising the executors as to their duties, may in the same proceeding, enter a valid decree for a sale of the real estate to pay debts.([4])

31. DECREE OF COUNTY COURT — COLLATERAL PROCEEDINGS.—As the jurisdiction of the county court over the sale of real estate to pay debts of deceased persons, is concurrent with, and as large as that of the circuit court, its decrees, in a collateral proceeding, can only be attacked for want of jurisdiction. Mere errors can only be urged in a direct proceeding to reverse.([5])

32. DEFENSES.—The heirs, devisees or alienees, when called before the court, may show in defense of the application for leave to sell lands to pay debts, that no debts exist; or they may show anything which will reduce the amount of the debt, in order to lessen the quantity of land which it may be necessary to sell. The general rule to direct these inquiries, is the following: Whatever defense an administrator may be allowed to make against the claims or demands of creditors, may be made by any person interested in the realty against an application of this nature. So, if the admin-

---

(1) *Id.;* McDowell vs. Cochran, 11 Ill., 31; Choteau vs. Johnson, *Id.*, 300; Beebe et al. vs. Saulter et al., 87 Ill., 518; White vs. Russell et al., 79 Ill., 155.
(2) Whitman vs. Fisher, 74 Ill., 147.
(3) Allman et al. vs. Taylor et al., 101 Ill., 185.
(4) Bridges vs. Rice, 99 Ill., 414.

istrator has received *mesne* profits enough to pay the debts, it is a good defense.(¹)

a. An order to sell real estate, will not be made, unless it is shown that debts contracted by the deceased in his lifetime, remain unpaid.(²) Where an administrator, there being no debts of the deceased in existence, created debts, by making costs of administration, and obtained an order of sale to meet such only, the order was held to be erroneous and void.(³) The fact that the debts claimed to exist, had not been presented and allowed by the county court, is no ground upon which to impeach a decree of sale: if they are shown to exist and are *bona fide*, it is sufficient. Nor does it matter that such debts were secured.(⁴) But where administration was granted in this state upon the estate of a person who died intestate in the state of Kentucky, where letters of administration had previously been granted, it was not sufficient for the resident administrator to show that debts existed in that state only, to entitle him to an order of sale. The creditors there should have presented their claims to the administrator and court here, and had them allowed. Better evidence of their existence than the certificate of the Kentucky administrator, was held necessary.(⁵)

Where ancillary administration is taken in this state upon the estate of a person domiciled elsewhere, and a petition filed to sell land to pay claims allowed here, it is not necessary to show that the personal estate at the domicil of the deceased is exhausted, to justify a decree to sell the real estate.(⁶)

b. If an administrator having no personal assets, voluntarily pays debts which are barred by the statute of limitations, he can not have a sale of land for his reimbursement.(⁷) But the administrator may pay any just debts due by the intestate, and have lands sold to reimburse himself, even though there be no other debts.(⁸)

(1) Dorman et al. vs. Lane, 1 Gil., 143; Stone vs. Wood, 16 Ill., 177; Helm vs. Cantrell et al., 59 Ill., 524; Goeppner vs. Leitzelmann, 98 Ill., 409; Ward vs. Durham, 134 Ill., 195; Young vs. Wittenmyre, 123 Ill., 303.
(2) Dorman et al. vs. Tost et al., 13 Ill., 127; Wood vs. Byington, 2 Barb. Ch., 387.
(3) Fitzgerald vs. Glancy, 49 Ill., 465; Dorman vs. Tost et al., *supra;* Walker et al., vs. Diehl, 79 Ill., 473; Rhorer on Judicial Sales, 174.
(4) Williams vs. Rhodes et al., 81 Ill., 571.
(5) Hobson et al. vs. Payne, 45 Ill., 158; Lowe vs. Bartlett, 8 Allen, 259.
(6) Rosenthal vs. Remick, 44 Ill., 202.
(7) Gilliland vs. Rea, 9 Paige, 66; Campau vs. Gillett, 1 Mich., 416.
(8) Goodbody et al. vs. Goodbody et al., 95 Ill., 456.

c. The judgment of the county court allowing the debt of a creditor, against an estate, is, as between the creditor and the administrator, conclusive, until reversed or impeached for fraud: but when the administrator applies for leave to sell the real estate for the purpose of paying such judgment, it is not conclusive as against an heir, and he may contest the application, unless he has been made a party to the judgment, by joining in taking an appeal from it. An heir is not privy to a judgment against an administrator. A judgment against an administrator, is only *prima facie* evidence of the existence of a debt against an estate, as against the heir;([1]) but heirs should contest in the name of the administrator.([2])

There is no privity between the heirs of an intestate, and the administrator of his estate.([3])

d. A judgment rendered against the administrator of an estate in a court of the state where he was appointed, to be paid there in due course of administration, is no evidence of indebtedness against another administrator of the same decedent in this state, for the purpose of affecting assets received by the latter under his administration. The administrators are not regarded as in privity with each other; and where it was sought to sell lands in this state to pay a claim allowed upon such a judgment, it was refused.([4])

e. Special statutory powers affecting real estate, must be strictly pursued and so appear upon the face of the proceedings, or the power is not well executed.([5])

A court ordering a sale of real estate, has no power to direct payment to be made in any other than legal currency of the country.([6])

The decree should specify the terms of sale.([7])

33. TIME OF PAYMENT.—The provision in Section 108, per-

(1) Mason et al. vs. Bair, 33 Ill., 194; He]m vs. Cantrell et al., 59 Ill., 524; Stone et al. vs. Wood, 16 Ill., 177; Gibson et al. vs. Gibson et al., 82 Ill., 61; Moline Water Power Manf. Co. vs. Webster, 26 Ill., 233; Hopkins et al. vs. McCan, 19 Ill., 113; Marshall et al. vs. Rose, 86 Ill., 374; McConnell vs. Smith, 23 Ill., 611; Goeppner et al. vs. Leitzelmann, 98 Ill., 409; Osgood vs. Manhattan Co., 3 Cowan, 612; Bailey's Exrs. vs. Staley, 5 Gill & Johnson, 432; McGarvey vs. Darnall. 134 Ill., 367.

(2) Motsinger vs. Coleman, 16 Ill., 71; Gibson vs. Gibson, 82 Ill., 61.

(3) Hopkins et al. vs. McCan, *supra;* McGarvey vs. Darnall, *supra.*

(4) Rosenthall vs. Renick et al., 44 Ill., 202; judy et al. vs. Kelley, 11 Ill., 211; Story's Conflict of Laws, ₴ 522; Stacy vs. Thrasher. 6 Howard, 44; Low vs. Bartlett, 8 Allen, 259; Bigelow on Estoppel, 256; Wernse vs. Hall, 101 Ill., 423; Ward vs. Durham, 134 Ill., 195.

(5) Reynolds vs. Wilson et al., 15 Ill., 394; Donlin vs. Hettinger et al., 57 Ill., 348; Smith et al. vs. Hileman, 1 Scam., 323; Fell vs. Young, 63 Ill., 106.

(6) *Id.*
Moline Water Power Manf. Co. vs. Webster *supra*.

mitting a sale of real estate made by an administrator, to be made upon not less than six nor more than twelve months, applies only to cases where the decree is silent as to the credit to be given. The decree may direct a longer time or require part of the payment to be made for cash.(¹)

34. LIMITATIONS.—There is no statutory limitation of the time beyond which limit decrees for the sale of real estate to pay the debts of a deceased debtor will be refused, yet the supreme court of Illinois has repeatedly held, that by analogy to the statute of limitations relating to judgments, and under certain circumstances to bringing the action of ejectment, the period of seven years should be adopted by the courts, as the time within which the application should be made. But while this is the general rule where the delay is unexplained, every case depends much upon its own circumstances, and if the delay is satisfactorily explained, the mere lapse of time is not a reason why the order of sale should not be made.(²)

a. But if it appears that such lapse of time has been caused by necessary delay in adjusting the claims against the intestate, and the lands remain in the same condition as when the decedent died, the mere lapse of time will not bar the application.(³) The evidence heard by the court to explain the delay, should be preserved in the record.(⁴)

b. Where at the time of the death of the intestate, the real estate was the homestead of the family, and the period of thirteen years elapsed before the particular estate was terminated, this fact was held to sufficiently explain the delay in asking a sale of the real estate, and to avoid the limitation fixed by the supreme court.(⁵)

35. SALE, REPORT AND CONFIRMATION.—No lands or tenements shall be sold by virtue of any such order of the county court, unless such sale is at public vendue, and between the hours of ten o'clock in the forenoon and five o'clock of the afternoon of

---

(1) Reynolds vs. Wilson et al., 15 Ill., 394; Moffitt vs. Moffitt, 69 Ill., 641.
(2) Bursen et al. vs. Goodspeed, 60 Ill., 278; Bishop et al. vs. O'Connor et al., 69 Ill., 432; McCoy vs. Morrow, 18 Ill., 519; Myer et al. vs. McDougal, 47 Ill., 278; Heirs of Langworthy vs. Baker, 23 Ill., 484; Fitzgerald vs. Glancy, 49 Ill., 465; Wolf et al. vs. Ogden, 66 Ill., 224; McKean vs. Vick, 108 Ill., 373; Furlong vs. Riley, 103 Ill., 628.
(3) Moore et al. vs. Ellsworth et al., 51 Ill., 308; Clark et al. vs. Hog'e et al., 52 Ill., 427.
(4) Wolf et al., vs. Ogden, *supra.*
(5) *Id.*

the same day, nor unless the time, place and terms of holding such sale, were previously published for the space of four weeks, by putting up notices thereof in at least four of the most public places in the county where such real estate shall be sold, and also by causing a similar notice thereof to be published four successive weeks prior to the sale, in some newspaper published in such county, or if there be no such newspaper, then in such other newspaper in this state, as the court shall direct, nor unless such real estate shall be described with common certainty in such notices. And if any executor or administrator, so ordered to make sale of any real estate, shall sell the same contrary to the provisions of this act, he shall forfeit and pay the sum of five hundred dollars, to be recovered by an action of debt, in the name of the People of the State of Illinois, for the use of any person interested, who may prosecute for the same: *Provided*, that no such offense shall affect the validity of such sale: *And provided further*, that such executor or administrator may sell the same on a credit of not less than six, nor more than twelve months, by taking notes, with good personal security and mortgage, or sale mortgage, on the premises sold, to secure the payment of the purchase money. It shall be the duty of the executor or administrator making such sale, on or before the first day of the next term of the court thereafter, to file in the office of the clerk of said court, a complete report of said sale, giving a description of the premises sold, to whom, where, and upon what terms sold, and a general statement of the manner in which the terms of the decree were executed. Any person interested in the premises sold, and any creditor of the estate, may file exceptions to such report, and upon the hearing thereof, the court may approve such report and confirm the sale, or disapprove the same, and order the premises to be resold.([1])

Until the passage of the foregoing section, in 1875, no report of the sale to the court, and no confirmation of the sale was necessary, although by the usual practice, sales were generally reported to the court rendering the decree.([2]) A confirmation of a sale of a tract of land not described in the petition, is void, and confers no rights upon the purchaser.([3])

(1) Hurd's R. S., Chap. 3, § 108; Hart vs. Hart, 39 Miss., 221.
(2) Stowe et al. vs. Kimball et al., 28 Ill., 93; Moore et al. vs. Neil et al., 39 Ill., 256.
(3) Means et al. vs. Means, 42 Ill., 50; Higgenbotham et al. vs. Blackledge et al., 54 Ill., 316.

a. An attorney employed by an administrator to procure a decree for the sale of real estate to pay debts, is not, by virtue of such employment, authorized to make a sale under the decree and receive the purchase money.([1])

b. The authority given an administrator to sell real estate to pay debts, is a personal trust, which he cannot delegate to another: while he may employ an auctioneer for that purpose, he must be present at the sale.([2])

c. Where, after a decree had been rendered authorizing a sale, the administrator died, it was held that his successor might complete the sale.([3]) So, where, pending the proceedings to sell land to pay debts, one administrator is removed and another is appointed, the proceeding need not be dismissed, but may proceed in the name of the last administrator.([4])

d. A failure to advertise a sale of real estate by an administrator, will not vitiate the sale.([5])

e. Where an order of court directs the manner of sale, or the time in which the notice shall be published, such directions must be strictly conformed to.([6])

f. The fact that land sold for less than its real value, is no ground for setting aside the sale.([7])

g. Requiring a deposit by the bidder of some part of his bid, is no ground for refusing to approve the sale.([8])

h. As in all judicial sales, lands or lots sold under these decrees, should be offered and sold in separate tracts.([9])

i. The purchase of real estate belonging to the deceased by the administrator, directly, or through another person, at his own sale, is fraudulent *per se*, and it matters not that the sale is made at public auction for a fair price.([10]) This rule is violated, if the administrator

---

(1) Nolan vs. Jackson, 16 Ill., 272.
(2) Sebastian vs. Johnson, 72 Ill., 282; Chambers vs. Jones, 72 Ill., 275; Taylor vs. Hopkins, 40 Ill., 442.
(3) Baker vs. Bradsby et al., 23 Ill., 632.
(4) Steele vs. Steele et al., 89 Ill., 51.
(5) Hurds's R. S., Ch. 3, Sec. 108; Botsford vs. O'Connor et al., 57 Ill., 72.
(6) Reynolds vs. Wilson et al., 15 Ill., 394; Selb vs. Montague, 102 Ill., 446.
(7) Allen et al. vs. Shepherd, 87 Ill., 314.
(8) *Id.*
(9) Schnell et al. vs. Chicago, 38 Ill., 383; Rowand vs. Carroll, 81 Ill., 224; Kenley vs. Bryan, 110 Ill., 652.
(10) Williams vs. Walker et al., 62 Ill., 517; Coat et al. vs. Coat et al., 63 Ill., 73; Thorp et al. vs. McCullum, 1 Gil., 614; Kruse vs. Steffens et al., 47 Ill., 112; Miles et al. vs. Wheeler et al., 43 Ill., 123; Williams vs. Rhodes et al., 81 Ill., 571; Ebelmesser et al., vs. Ebelmesser et al., 99 Ill., 541; Borders vs. Murphy, 125 Ill., 577.

becomes interested at any time before a confirmation of the sale, although not until after the property was struck off.([1])

Such a sale is not void, but voidable only, and if proceedings are not instituted in apt time to set aside the sale, by those having the right to contest the same, a ratification of the sale will be presumed.([2])

j. An irregularity in making an administrator's sale of real estate, by failing to comply with the statute, or a failing to give the further bond required in cases where it is necessary to sell lands to pay debts (ante page 26) will not invalidate the sale. If proper notice is not given of the sale, it can be taken advantage of only on a motion to set aside the sale.([3])

k. A requirement in the decree that the administrator should report the sale at the next term, does not limit the exercise of the power of sale within that time.([4])

l. Where, at the first sale the property named in the decree is not all sold, the power of sale is not thereby exhausted, but another sale may be had;([5]) but where a sale of sufficient lands to pay all the debts, for the payment of which the sale was ordered, is had, and a report thereof made, the decree is satisfied and the case ended, and the court has no power or jurisdiction at a subsequent term, without a new notice, to order a sale of more land for the payment of additional debts which had been proven against the estate.([6])

m. On a motion made to confirm a sale made by an administrator, the court can not consider questions raised upon the appointment of the administrator, the propriety and legality of the decree directing the sale, nor the legality of debts allowed in probate against the estate. The matters before the court upon such a motion, relate solely to the transactions which take place in the attempt to execute the decree. On such a motion, the court can not go behind the order of sale.([7])

(1) Terwilliger vs. Brown, 5 Hand, (N. Y.), 237.
(2) Sloan vs. Graham e. al , 85 Ill., 27; Bland vs. Muncaster, 24 Miss., 62.
(3) Moffatt et al. vs. Moffatt, 69 Ill., 641; Harris vs. Lester et al., 80 Ill., 307; Goodbody et al. vs. Goodbody et al., 95 Ill., 456; Wyman vs. Campbell, 6 Porter, (Ala.) 219.
(4) Bowen et al. vs. Bond et al., 80 Ill., 351.
(5) Stow et al. vs. Kimball et al., 28 Ill., 93.
(6) Cromine vs. Tharp, 42 Ill., 120.
(7) Allen et al. vs. Shepherd, 87 Ill., 314.

The failure of the administrator to report the sale to the court will not invalidate the sale.(¹)

36. TITLE.—In all judicial sales, of which administrators' sales of real estate of deceased persons to pay debts are instances, the rule of *caveat emptor* applies with full force. It is the policy of the law to invest administrators in making sales of real estate under such decrees, with a mere naked power to sell such title as the deceased had, without warranty, or any terms except those imposed by the law. They are the mere instruments of the law to pass such, and only such title as was held by the intestate.(²) A purchaser, who, at such a sale, buys land to which the deceased had no title, is absolutely without any relief, unless a fraud has been practiced upon him.(³) And an administrator who enters into covenants of warranty of the title of his intestate, although they are expressed to be made in his character of administrator, does not thereby bind the estate by the covenant, but becomes personally liable for a breach thereof.(⁴)

37. EFFECT ON THE SALE OF A REVERSAL OF DECREE.—The mere reversal of a decree under which an administrator has sold land, does not divest third persons of the title. If a court has jurisdiction over the parties and subject matter, acts performed and rights acquired by third persons under its judgment or decree, and while it remains in force, must be sustained, notwithstanding a subsequent reversal. If the proceedings are erroneous, the error is not to be corrected at the expense of the purchaser who relied upon the order of a competent court.(⁵)

38. FORGERY — FRAUD — CHANCERY JURISDICTION. — Where letters of administration were obtained for the purpose of enforcing the payment of a forged note purporting to have been made by the intestate—the claimant and the administrator being in collusion—and a sale of real estate made for the payment of such claim, it was held a proper case for the intervention of a court of equity to prevent the payment of the money realized from the sale of real estate

(1) Stow et al. vs. Kimball et al., 28 Ill., 93; Moore et al. vs. Neil et al., 39 Ill., 256.
(2) Bishop et al. vs. O'Connor et al., 69 Ill., 432; Bingham et al. vs. Maxey, 15 Ill., 295; Walden vs. Gridley, 36 Ill., 523, Bond et al. vs. Ramsey, 89 Ill., 29; McConnell vs. Smith, 39 Ill., 279; Brandon vs. Brown, 106 Ill., 519; Tilley vs. Bridges, 105 Ill., 336.
(3) Bond et al. vs. Ramsey, *supra*.
(4) Sumner vs. Williams, 8 Mass., 162; Vincent vs. Morrison, Breese, 175.
(5) Goudy et al. vs. Hall, 36 Ill., 313; Guiteau vs. Wiseley, 47 Ill., 433; Fergus et al. vs. Woodworth et al., 44 Ill., 374; Perkins vs. Fairfield, 11 Mass., 227; Stow et al. vs. Kimball et al., *supra;* Smith vs. Brittenham, 109 Ill., 540.

to the claimant, and direct its payment to the heirs who had been divested of their inheritance.(¹)

39. CONVEYANCES.—All such sales of real estate shall be made and conveyances executed for the same, by the executor or administrator applying for such order, and shall be valid and effectual against the heirs and devisees of such decedent, and all other persons claiming by, through or under him or them. In case of the death of the executor or administrator applying for an order of sale before conveyance is made, the administrator *de bonis non* shall proceed in the premises and make conveyance in the same manner as if he had originally applied for such order—which conveyance shall be good and valid.(²)

a. A person authorized by a decree of court to sell lands and make the conveyance, must execute the power himself. He can not appoint an attorney to execute the deed for him.(³)

b. Conveyances made prior to 1872, which fail to recite the decree of the court, are insufficient, and can not be received in evidence.(⁴)

c. Purchaser at an administrator's sale of real estate under a decree, is only bound to know that the court ordering the sale, had jurisdiction of the subject matter and of the persons of the heirs of the intestate.(⁵)

d. The title of the heirs is divested by the sale, and it is no objection that the deed is made to an assignee of the purchaser.(⁶)

e. Where a purchaser at a sale by an administrator, of real estate, refused to consummate the purchase by giving note with security and mortgage, but did sign a note, the administrator, after having advertised and sold again, recovered the damages caused by such failure to consummate the sale from the first purchaser—the signing of the note by the first purchaser, being held sufficient to take the case out of the statute of frauds.(⁷)

Where, at such a sale, the purchaser refuses to comply with the terms of sale, no memorandum in writing of such sale having been

(1) Whitlock vs. McClusky et al., 91 Ill., 582.
(2) Hurd's R. S., Chap. 3, ¿ 107.
(3) Mason vs. Wait et al., 4 Scam., 127; Kellogg vs. Wilson, 89 Ill., 357.
(4) Smith et al. vs. Hileman, 1 Scam., 323.
(5) Myer et al. vs. McDougal, 47 Ill., 278.
(6) Hobson et al. vs. Ewan, 62 Ill., 146.
(7) Work vs. Cowhick, 81 Ill., 317; Le Moyne vs. Harding, 132 Ill., 23.

signed by him, the administrator can not enforce the verbal contract to purchase, against the purchaser, it being considered within the statute of frauds, as much as if the sale had not been made under the decree of a court competent to render a valid decree of sale.(¹) Due precaution, therefore, on the part of executors or administrators, making such sales, will require a memorandum of the sale to be made and signed by the purchaser immediately upon the fall of the hammer.

40. PROCEEDS OF SALE.—When real estate is sold, the money arising from such sale shall be received by the executor or administrator applying for the order to sell, and the same shall be assets in his hands for the payment of debts, and shall be applied in the same manner as assets arising from the sale of personal property.(²)

41. SALE OF LAND NOT FULLY PAID FOR—COMPLETING THE PURCHASE.—In all cases where a decedent is seized of the legal or equitable title to real estate, the payment whereof has not been completed, and the estate of such decedent is unable to make complete payment therefor, with advantage to such estate, the administrator or executor may sell or dispose of such real estate upon the order of the county court, and the money arising from such sales shall be assets in the hands of such executor or administrator, as in other cases. But in all cases where the estate of any such decedent shall be solvent, and such lands as aforesaid may be paid for without prejudice to the creditors, heirs and devisees of the estate, the executor or administrator shall complete the payment for the same out of the proceeds of the personal property, in the name of the heirs or legal representatives of the decedent entitled thereto; and he shall be allowed a credit for the amount of such payments, and all reasonable expenses incurred in making the same, upon final settlement of such estate : *Provided*, that the provisions of this section shall, in no wise, interfere with the provisions of any last will or testament.(³)

42. POWER TO SELL UNDER A WILL.—Where power is given in a will to the executor to make sale of the lands of the deceased for the purpose of paying debts, or for any other purpose, the executor may make sale and conveyances without first resorting to a

(1) Bozza vs. Rowe, 30 Ill., 198.
(2) Hurd's R. S., Chap. 3, § 109; Millard vs. Harris, 119 Ill., 185.
(3) Hurd's R. S., Chap. 3, § 110.

court. This power may be given by the testator either expressly or by implication. Where the will directed the lands of the testator to be sold, and the executor to distribute the money, it was held, that the executor was invested with power to sell and convey by implication.(¹)

In all such cases, the power of the executor over the real estate of the testator, depends upon the construction of the will of the deceased, which is the measure of his authority.

In all cases, where power is given in any will to sell and dispose of any real estate, or interest therein, and the same is sold and disposed of in the manner and by the persons appointed in such will, the sales shall be good and valid; and where one or more executors shall fail or refuse to qualify, or depart this life before such sales are made, the survivor or survivors shall have the same power and their sales shall be as good and valid as if they all joined in such sales.(²)

An administrator with the will annexed, must procure an order of sale like any other administrator, before he can sell land to pay debts, although there may be express power given in the will to the person nominated as executor to make such sale. Such powers do not pass to the administrator with the will annexed.(³)

If a testator empower his executor to sell lands for the payment of debts, the purchaser holds them discharged against creditors otherwise, if the power be to sell to pay legacies.(⁴)

In such a case the title to the real estate vests in the heir, subject to be defeated by the sale; it is otherwise where the devise is to the executor to sell.(⁵)

---

(1) Rankin et al. vs. Rankin, 36 Ill., 293; Hurd's R. S., Chap. 3, § 96; Bates vs. Woodruff, 123 Ill., 205; Hale vs. Hale, 125 Ill., 399.
(2) Hurd's R. S., *supra;* Wardwell vs. McDowell et al., 31 Ill., 364; Clinefelter vs. Ayers, 16 Ill., 329; Pahlman vs. Smith, 23 Ill., 448; Hamilton vs. Hamilton, 98 Ill., 254; Ely vs. Dix, 118 Ill., 477; Chappell vs. McKnight, 108 Ill., 570.
(3) Hall vs. Irwin, 2 Gil., 176; Lockwood vs. Stradley, 1 De'. Ch., 298; Wenner vs. Thornton et al., 98 Ill., 156; Nicoll vs. Scott, 99 Ill., 529.
(4) Hannum vs. Speer, 2 Dallas, 291.
(5) Ware vs. Murph, Rice's Law Reports (S. C.), 54.

CHAPTER XIV.

WILLS.

1. Scope of the chapter.
2. Origin of the testamentary power.
3. Definition.
4. Who may make wills—what may be disposed of.
    a. Married women.
    b. Of sound mind.
5. How made and declared—declaration of witnesses.
    a. Presence of witnesses.
    b. Publication.
    c. Changes must be witnessed.
    d. Signature of witnesses.
    e. Executed in foreign state.
    f. Joint will.
6. What may be disposed of by will—may totally disinherit children.
    a. Devise may limit the estate to devisee.
    b. Future acquisitions.
7. Probate of will—custodian to produce it.
    a. Place of probate.
    b. Attendance of witnesses.
    c. Necessity of probate.
    d. Non-resident witnesses.
    e. County judge witness.
    f. Handwriting of deceased witnesses.
    g. Character of evidence.
    h. What must concur.
    i. Court without discretion.
    j. When ministerial.
    k. Competency of witnesses.
8. Appeals—evidence on appeal.
9. Custody of probated will.
10. Issue of letters testamentary—refusal of executor.
    a. Who may be executors, etc.
    b. Effect of appointing creditor.
11. Contesting wills in chancery.
    a. Who may contest.
    b. Part only of any will may be contested.
    c. Burden of proof in such a case.
    d. Undue influence.
    e. Practice.
12. Wills proven without the state—admission to probate.
    a. Effect upon property in this state.

13. Revocation—not revoked by words.
    a. Erasure does not revoke.
    b. Declarations.
    c. Birth of child or marriage of testator.
14. Nuncupative wills.
    a. Proof of same—when made.
    b. Statute must be complied with.
    c. Effect on property.
15. Lost will.
16. What law governs bequests.
17. Mortgage of real estate by executors—effect of same.
    a. Foreclosures.
    b. Not in fee simple.
18. Construction of wills—intention.
    a. How intention to be ascertained.
    b. Extrinsic evidence inadmissible.
    c. Whole instrument construed together.
    d. Construction by a court of equity.
19. Where land devised is sold by testator before death.
20. Legacies charged upon real estate.
21. **When title vests.**
22. Against whom wills are fraudulent.
23. Trustees to receive compensation.

1. SCOPE OF THE CHAPTER.—The limits of a single chapter are too contracted to admit of more than a passing notice of the aggregation of legal knowledge which pertains to the execution, probate and construction of wills. Therefore the writer will not essay to enter the field of testamentary jurisprudence any further than may be necessary to present, with conciseness, the statutes and adjudications of Illinois, bearing upon the execution of wills, their admission to probate and contest in the county and circuit courts, leaving the practitioner and student to seek from the able treatises, to be found in every library, for greater details of the branch of the law under consideration in this chapter.

2. FORCE OF THE STATUTE.—The power to dispose of and convey land by will, is a statutory, and not a common law power, and must, therefore, depend for its extent, upon legislative intention as indicated and contained in the frame of the act.[1]

3. WHAT A WILL IS.—A will or testament is the legal declaration of one's intentions of what he wills to be performed after his death.[2] When the will operates upon personal property, it is

---

(1) Peters et al. vs. Spellman, 18 Ill., 370; Evans vs. Price, 118 Ill., 593.
(2) 1 Inst., 111; See 5 Probate Reports, 41, for brief of authorities, as to what instruments have been held to be wills; also, 2 *Ib.*, 24.

sometimes called a testament, and when upon real estate, a devise.(¹)

4. WHO MAY MAKE A WILL.—That every male person of the age of twenty-one years, and every female of the age of eighteen years, being of sound mind and memory, shall have power to devise all the estate, right, title and interest, in possession, reversion or remainder, which he or she hath, or at the time of his or her death shall have, of, in and to any lands, tenements, hereditaments, annuities or rents, charged upon or issuing out of them, or goods and chattels, and personal estate of every description whatsoever, by will or testament.(²)

a. Under the statute as it existed prior to 1861, a married woman could only dispose of her separate property by will; but that law, in effect, made all her estate her separate property, and since that date, married women have possessed the same testamentary power as other citizens.(³)

b. It is not necessary that a testator possess the highest degree of mental capacity to qualify him for the execution of a will. It is enough that he had sufficient understanding to enable him to know and understand the business in which he was engaged at the time he executed the will. If he have such understanding as would enable him to do any binding act, he can execute a will.(⁴) If the testator at the time of the execution of the will, was affected by no morbid or insane delusion, as to some one of those natural objects of his bounty, and understood the nature of the business about which he was engaged, of the kind and value of the property devised, and of the persons who were the natural objects of his bounty, and of the manner in which he wished to dispose of his property, he may be said to have testamentary capacity.(⁵) Want of mental power must be such as to render the testator incapable of acting rationally in the ordinary affairs of life, or incapable of understanding the effects and consequences of his act.(⁶)

Like all other matters relating to the human mind, it is difficult

---

(1) 4 Kent's Com., 555.
(2) Hurd's R. S., Chap. 148, § 1; Freeman vs. Early, 117 Ill., 317; Schneider vs. Manning, 121 Ill., 376; Campbell vs. Campbell, 130 Ill., 466.
(3) *In re* Tuller, Decd., 79 Ill., 99.
(4) Brown vs. Riggin, 94 Ill., 560; Yoe vs. McCord, 74 Ill., 33; Meeker et al. vs. Meeker, 75 Ill., 260; Rutherford et ux. vs. Morris et al., 77 Ill., 397; Carpenter et al. vs. Calvert, 83 Ill., 62; Bice vs. Hall, 120 Ill., 597.
(5) Roe et al. vs. Taylor, 45 Ill., 485; Trish et al. vs. Newell et al,, 62 Ill., 196.
(6) Lilly vs. Waggoner, 27 Ill., 395.

to fix any precise, undeviating rule, by which it can be determined when a person has mind and memory. The law has adopted the rule that, where persons have arrived at full age, the presumption must be indulged, that the party has the requisite capacity to enter into, and bind himself by all lawful engagements, and, among others, may dispose of his property by testament; and to avoid these acts, the presumption must be rebutted by showing a want of sufficient intellectual capacity to make the agreement or disposition of his property by will;(1) but where it is shown that the testator was insane, except at intervals, the proof to establish the will should show that it was executed while the party had a lucid interval.(2)

5. How made and declared.—All wills, testaments and codicils, by which any lands, tenements, hereditaments, annuities, rents or goods and chattels are devised, shall be reduced to writing, and signed by the testator or testatrix, or by some person in his or her presence, and by his or her direction, and attested in the presence of the testator or testatrix, by two or more credible witnesses, two of whom, declaring on oath or affirmation, before the county court of the proper county, that they were present and saw the testator or testatrix sign said will, testament or codicil, in their presence, or acknowledged the same to be his or her act and deed, and that they believed the testator or testatrix to be of sound mind and memory at the time of signing or acknowledging the same, shall be sufficient proof of the execution of said will, testament or codicil, to admit the same to record: *Provided*, that no proof of fraud, compulsion or other improper conduct be exhibited, which, in the opinion of said county court, shall be deemed sufficient to invalidate or destroy the same; and every will, testament or codicil, when thus proven to the satisfaction of the court, shall, together with the probate thereof, be recorded by the clerk of said court, in a book to be provided by him for that purpose, and shall be good and available in law for the granting, conveying and assuring the lands, tenements and hereditaments, annuities, rents, goods and chattels therein and thereby devised, granted and bequeathed.(3)

a. It is not necessary to the proof of a will, that it be signed by the testator in the presence of the attesting witnesses, nor that

(1) Meeker vs. Meeker, 75 Ill., 260.
(2) Emery vs. Hoyt, 46 Ill., 258.
(3) Hurd's R. S., Chap. 148, § 2; Comer vs. Comer, 120 Ill., 420; Canatsey vs. Canatsey, 130 Ill., 397.

they should sign it in the presence of each other. If he acknowledge its execution in their presence, or does some act, without saying anything, which is equivalent to an acknowledgment of the instrument, this will be sufficient.([1])

b. Our statute of wills no where makes the publishing of a will necessary, nor any declaration of the party executing it that it is his will.([2]) The execution of a codicil effects the republication of the will.([3])

c. Any change in a will, after being executed and witnessed, to be effective, must be witnessed with the same formality as the will.([4])

d. If the attestation takes place where the testator might, if he chose, witness the act, though actually in another room, it is to be regarded as taking place in his presence, within the meaning of the statute.([5])

e. Where a will is executed in a foreign state, according to its laws, and there admitted to probate, such will, although not executed according to the laws of this state, will be effective to dispose of estate in this state, when properly certified.([6])

f. There cannot be a joint or mutual will in which two persons unite in disposing of property. Such an instrument is unknown to the law.([7])

6. WHAT MAY BE DISPOSED OF BY WILL.—The right of testators to dispose of their real and personal property as they please, by will, is unlimited, provided no perpetuity is created—by which term it is meant that property can not be so devised as to take the subject out of commerce for a longer period than a life or lives, in being, and twenty-one years beyond. They may pass by their own children, if they choose.([8])

a. A testator has power to bequeath his property, real or personal, to one for life, and to provide that such estate should not be

---

(1) Allison vs. Allison, 46 Ill., 61; Yoe vs. McCord, 74 Ill., 33; Flinn et al. vs. Owen et al., 58 Ill., 111; Blattner vs. Weis et al., 19 Ill., 246.

(2) Dickie vs. Carter, 42 Ill., 376; Holloway et al. vs. Galloway et al., 51 Ill., 159.

(3) Hatcher vs. Hatcher, 80 Va., 169; See 5 Probate Reports, 445, for brief of authorities.

(4) Wolf vs. Bollinger, 62 Ill., 368; Swinton vs. Bailey, 33 L. T. (English) Rep., 695.

(5) Ambre vs. Weishaar, 74 Ill., 109.

(6) Kingsbury vs. Burnside et al., 58 Ill., 311; Shepherd vs. Carriel, 19 Ill., 313; Gardner vs. Ladue, 47 Ill., 211.

(7) Lomax on Executors, 3.

(8) Rhoads vs. Rhoads et al., 43 Ill., 239; Waldo vs. Cummings, 45 Ill., 423; Hale vs. Hale, 125 Ill., 399; Lunt vs. Lunt, 108 Ill., 307.

liable for the debts of the legatee—the probate and record of such a will is notice to all persons of the tenure by which the legatee holds the property, and that no credit is to be given him on account of its possession.(¹)

b. The power of a testator to dispose of his property by will, is not limited to that possessed or owned by him at the time of executing the will, but by the same instrument he may dispose of after acquired property. The question in relation to a bequest in such cases, is one of intention, not of power.(²)

7. CUSTODIAN OF WILL TO DELIVER—PENALTY.—Any person or persons who may have in his or her possession, any last will or testament of another, for safe keeping or otherwise, shall, immediately upon the death of the testator or testatrix, deliver up said will to the county court of the proper county; and upon a failure or refusal so to do, the county court may issue attachment, and compel the production of the same; and the person or persons thus withholding any such will, testament or codicil, as aforesaid, shall forfeit and pay twenty dollars per month, from the time the same shall be thus wrongfully withheld, to be recovered by action of debt for the use of the estate, by any person who will sue for the same, in any court having jurisdiction thereof; and if any person to whom a will, testament or codicil hath been or shall be delivered by the party making it, for safe custody as aforesaid, shall alter or destroy the same without the direction of the said party, or shall wilfully secrete it for the space of six months after the death of the testator or testatrix shall be known to him or her, the person so offending, shall, on conviction thereof, be sentenced to such punishment as is or shall be inflicted by law, in cases of larceny.(³

a. If any testator or testatrix shall have a mansion house or known place of residence, his or her will shall be proved in the court of the county wherein such mansion house or place of residence shall be. If he or she has no place of residence, and lands be devised in his or her will, it shall be proved in the court of the county wherein the lands lie, or in one of them, where there shall be land in several different counties; and if he or she have no such

---

(1) Waldo vs. Cummings et al., 45 Ill., 423; Hetfield vs. Fowler et al., 60 Ill., 45; Boyd et al. vs. Strahan, 36 Ill., 355; Trogdon vs. Murphy et al., 85 Ill., 119; Burnett vs. Lester, 53 Ill., 325.
(2) Willis vs. Watson, 4 Scam., 64; Peters et al. vs. Spellman, 18 Ill., 370; Williams vs. Johnson, 112 Ill., 61; Decker vs. Decker, 121 Ill., 341; Byrnes vs. Barr, 86 N. Y., 210; See 2 Probate Reports, 390, for brief of authorities; Also, 5 *Ib.*, 492.

known place of residence, and there be no lands devised in such will, the same may be proved either in the county where the testator or testatrix shall have died, or that wherein his or her estate, or the greater part thereof, shall lie.(¹)*

b. It shall be the duty of each and every witness to any will, testament or codicil, made and executed in this state, as aforesaid, to be and appear before the county court on the regular day for the probate of such will, testament or codicil, to testify of and concerning the execution and validity of the same; and the said court shall have power and authority to attach and punish, by fine and imprisonment, or either, any witness who shall, without a reasonable excuse, fail to appear when duly summoned for the purpose aforesaid: *Provided,* the said punishment by imprisonment shall in no case exceed the space of twenty days, nor shall a greater fine be assessed, for any such default, than the sum of fifty dollars.(²)

c. A testator has no power to waive the probate of his last will. If it is to be a will at all, it is indispensable that it should be admitted to probate.(³)

d. When any will, testament or codicil shall be produced to the county or probate courts for probate of the same, and any witness attesting such will, testament or codicil, shall reside without the limits of this state, or the county in which such will, testament or codicil is produced for probate, or shall be unable to attend said court, it shall be lawful for such county or probate court, upon application of any person asking for probate thereof, and upon such notice to persons interested as such county or probate court may, by special order, direct, to issue a *dedimus potestatem,* or commission, under the seal of the court annexed to such will, testament or codicil, together with such interrogatories in chief and cross interrogatories as may be filed in said court, or as said court may direct, to be propounded to such witness or witnesses, touching the execution of such will, testament or codicil, which commission shall be directed to any judge, master in chancery, notary public, justice of the peace, mayor or other chief magistrate of a city, United States consul or vice consul, consular agent or secretary of legation,

(1) Hurd's R. S., Chap. 148, § 11.
(2) Hurd's R. S., Chap. 148, § 3.
(3) Harris vs. Douglas et al., 64 Ill., 466.

*Note.—There is no law in this state limiting the time of probating a will to any given number of years.—*Rebhan vs. Mueller,* 114 Ill., 343; *Ha'ock vs. R. R.,* 146 Mass., 155.

authorizing and requiring him to cause such witness or witnesses to come before him at such time and place as he may designate and appoint, and faithfully to take his, her or their depositions on oath or affirmation, upon all such interrogatories as may be enclosed with, or attached to, such commission, and none other, and certify the same, when thus taken, together with the said commission and interrogatories, into the court, out of which such commission issued, with the least possible delay. When so taken and returned unto the court, such deposition or depositions shall have the same operation, force and effect, and such will, testament or codicil, shall be admitted to probate in like manner, as if such oath or affirmation had been made in the court from whence such commission issued.

Whenever a commission shall issue to any officer, above mentioned, not by name, but simply by his official title, then the seal of his office, attached to his certificate, shall be sufficient evidence of his identity and official character.(1)

e. In all cases where a county judge, or such other person as may be authorized by law to grant probate of wills and testaments, may and shall have become a witness to any will or testament which is required by law to be proved before him as such county judge or person authorized to grant probate, as aforesaid, and the testimony of such witness is necessary to the proof of the same, then, and in such case, it shall be his duty to go before the circuit court of the county in which such will is to be admitted to record, and make proof of the execution of the same, in the same manner that probate of wills is required to be made in other cases. And it shall be the duty of the clerk of the circuit court aforesaid, forthwith to certify such will, proven as aforesaid, to the county court of the county; and said will shall, thereupon, have the same force and effect that it would have had if it had been proven by one credible witness before the county court; and if there are other witnesses to said will, the county court shall take their evidence in support of said will, as in other cases.(2)

f. In all cases where any one or more of the witnesses to any will, testament or codicil, as aforesaid, shall die or remove to parts unknown to the parties concerned, so that his or her testimony can

---

(1) Hurd's R. S., Chap. 148, § 4, as amended by act of 1881; In the matter of Noble, 124 Ill., 266.
(2) Hurd's R. S., Chap. 148, § 5.

not be procured, it shall be lawful for the county court, or other court having jurisdiction of the subject matter, to admit proof of the handwriting of any such deceased or absent witness, as aforesaid, and such other secondary evidence as is admissible in courts of justice to establish written contracts generally, in similar cases; and may thereupon proceed to record the same, as though such will, testament or codicil had been proved by such subscribing witness or witnesses, in his, her or their proper persons.(¹)

g. On probate of the will of a deceased person, it is proper to exclude all evidence of the execution of the will and of the state of mind of the testator, except the testimony of the subscribing witnesses; but where probate of the will has been refused in the county court, and upon appeal to the circuit court, a trial *de novo* is had, for the purpose of establishing the sanity of the testator, resort may be had to the same character of evidence as upon a hearing of a bill in chancery, filed under the statute, to set aside a will. Where, however, the will is admitted to probate in the county court, and an appeal is prosecuted by those contesting the will, the rule is different.(²) This rule, however, will not prevent the production of evidence before the county court or on trial upon appeal, by contestants, tending to show fraud, compulsion or improper conduct.(³) Upon appeal to the circuit court from the probate of a will, the trial may be had before a jury.(⁴)

h. To entitle a will to probate, four things must concur—it must be in writing, and signed by the testator or testatrix, or in his or her presence, by some one under his or her direction; it must be attested by two or more credible witnesses; two witnesses must prove that they saw the testator or testatrix sign the will in their presence, or that he or she acknowledged the same to be his or her act or deed; they must swear that they believed the testator or testatrix to be of sound mind and memory at the time of signing and acknowledging the same.(⁵) And where the subscribing witnesses differ as to the mental condition of the testator at the time of

---

(1) Hurd's R. S., Chap. 148, § 6; *In re* Noble, 124 Ill., 266; In the matter of Page, 118 Ill., 576; Robinson vs. Brewster, 30 N. E. Rep., 683, (Ill.)

(2) Hurd's R. S., Chap. 148, § 13; Crowley vs. Crowley, 80 Ill., 469; Andrews vs. Black, 43 Ill., 256; Duncan vs. Duncan, 23 Ill., 364; Walker vs. Walker, 2 Scam., 291; *In re* Noble, *supra;* Bice vs. Hall, 120 Ill., 597.

(3) Andrews vs. Black, *supra.*

(4) Walker vs. Walker, *supra;* Critz vs. Pierce, 106 Ill., 167.

(5) Dickie et al. vs. Carter, 42 Ill., 376; Crowley vs. Crowley, *supra;* Wall vs. Wall, 123 Pa. St., 545.

the execution of the will, one testifying that he was of sound mind, and the other that he was not, it is not competent to permit other witnesses to be examined on the question, and the will can not be admitted to probate.(¹) Also, where neither subscribing witness could write his name, both having signed by a mark, and they could not identify the instrument of writing as that signed by the testator, it was held that the evidence of the witnesses failed to establish the execution of the will, and that probate should be refused.(²)

i. When the proofs touching the execution of a will, bring the case within the rule made by the statute touching the execution of wills, the court having jurisdiction, has no discretion in the matter but to admit the instrument to probate.(³)

j. Under the earlier legislation of this state, the admission to probate of a will was held to be a ministerial act only, which might be questioned;(⁴) but under the legislation which has prevailed since 1847, the act of admitting a will to probate in the county court is held to be a judicial act, which might not be questioned collaterally.(⁵) But where a will was offered for probate by the executors named therein, and upon trial found not to be the will of the deceased, and so rejected, and after many years the heirs of a legatee named in the will, filed their bill in chancery to have the will declared, it was held that courts of probate act *in rem*, and their sentences upon matters within their jurisdiction, are conclusive upon other courts.(⁶)

k. If any beneficial devise, legacy or interest shall be made or given, in any will, testament or codicil, to any person subscribing such will, testament or codicil, as a witness to the execution thereof, such devise, legacy or interest shall, as to such subscribing witness, and all persons claiming under him, be null and void, unless such will, testament or codicil be otherwise duly attested by a sufficient number of witnesses exclusive of such person, according to this act; and he or she shall be compellable to appear and give testimony on the residue of such will, testament or codicil, in like manner as if

---

(1) Weld vs. Sweeney, 85 Ill., 50.
(2) Crowley vs. Crowley, 80 Ill., 469.
(3) Doran vs. Mullen, 78 Ill., 342.
(4) Ferguson et al. vs. Hunter, 2 Gil., 657.
(5) People, &c., vs. Knickerbocker, 114 Ill., 539; Grand Tower Mining Co. vs. Gill, 111 Ill., 541; *In re* Story, 120 Ill., 244.
(6) Redmond vs. Collins, 4 Deveraux, 430; See, also, note to the above case, 27 Am. Dec., 223; Also, 60 *Ib.*, 353.

no such devise or bequest had been made. But if such witness would have been entitled to any share of the testator's estate, in case the will, testament or codicil was not established, then so much of such share shall be saved to such witness as shall not exceed the value of the said devise or bequest made to him or her as aforesaid.(¹)

If any lands, tenements or hereditaments shall be charged with any debts, by any will, testament or codicil, and the creditor whose debt is so secured, shall attest the execution of the same, such creditor shall, notwithstanding, be admitted as a witness to the execution thereof.(²)

8. APPEALS.—Appeals may be taken from the order of the county court, allowing or disallowing any will to probate, to the circuit court of the same county, by any person interested in such will, in the same time and manner as appeals may be taken from justices of the peace, except that the appeal bond and security may be approved by the clerk of the county court; and the trials of such appeals shall be *de novo*.(³)

When the probate of any will and testament shall have been refused by any county court, and an appeal shall have been taken from the order or decision of such court refusing to admit such will to probate, into the circuit court of the proper county, as provided by law, it shall be lawful for the party seeking probate of such will, to support the same, on hearing in such circuit court, by any evidence competent to establish a will in chancery; and in case probate of such will shall be allowed on such appeal, it shall be admitted to probate, liable, however, to be subsequently contested, as provided in the case of wills admitted to probate in the first instance.(⁴)

9. WILLS TO REMAIN WITH CLERK—COPIES EVIDENCE.—All original wills, together with the probate thereof, shall remain in the office of the clerk of the county court of the proper county; and copies of the record of the same, and copies of the record of exemplifications of foreign wills recorded in said office, as in this act provided, duly certified under the hand of the clerk and the seal of said court, shall be evidence in any court of law or equity in this state.(⁵)

(1) Hurd's R. S., Chap. 148, § 8; But the wife of a beneficiary may be a witness: Hawkins vs. Hawkins, 54 Iowa, 443; Piper vs. Moulton, 72 Me., 155.
(2) Hurd's R. S., Chap. 148, § 20.
(3) Hurd's R. S., Chap. 148, § 14; Weld vs. Sweeney, 85 Ill., 50.
(4) Hurd's R. S., Chap. 148, § 13; *In re* Noble, 124 Ill., 266; *In re* Story, 120 Ill., 244; Critz vs. Pierce, 106 Ill., 167.
(5) Hurd's R. S., Chap. 148, § 18.

10. LETTERS TO BE ISSUED.—That when a will has been duly proved and allowed, the county court shall issue letters testamentary thereon to the executor named in such will, if he is legally competent and accepts the trust, and gives bonds to discharge the same; and when there is no executor named in such will, or the executor named therein dies, refuses to act, or is otherwise disqualified, the court shall commit the administration of the estate unto the widow, surviving husband, next of kin or creditor, the same as if the testate had died intestate. In all cases copies of the will shall go out with the letters.[1]

An executor can not in part refuse. He must refuse entirely or not at all.[2]

a. Persons of the age of seventeen years, of sound mind and memory, may be appointed executors; but when a person appointed executor is, at the time of proving the will, under the age of twenty-one years, or of unsound mind, or convicted of any crime rendering him infamous, administration with the will annexed may be granted during his minority or other disability, unless there is another executor who accepts the trust, in which case the estate shall be administered by such other executor until the minor arrives at full age or the other disability is removed, when, upon giving bond as in other cases, he may be admitted as joint executor with the former. When a married woman is executrix her husband may give bond with her for her faithful performance of the trust as in other cases.[3]

b. In no case hereafter, within this state, where any testator or testatrix shall, by his or her will, appoint his or her debtor to be his or her executor or executrix, shall such appointment operate as a release or extinguishment of any debt due from such executor or executrix, to such testator or testatrix, unless the testator or testatrix shall, in such will, expressly declare his intention to devise, bequeath or release such debt; nor even in that case, unless the estate of such testator or testatrix is sufficent to discharge the whole of his or her just debts, over and above the debt due from such executor or executrix.[4]

11. WILL CONTESTED AFTERWARDS.—When any will, testa-

(1) Hurd's R. S., Chap. 3, § 1.   (3) Hurd's R. S., Chap. 3, § 3
(2) 1 Lomax on Executors, 87.   (4) Hurd's R. S., Chap. 148, § 19.

ment or codicil shall be exhibited in the county court, for probate thereof, as aforesaid, it shall be the duty of the court to receive probate of the same without delay, and to grant letters testamentary thereon to the person or persons entitled; and to do all other needful acts, to enable the parties concerned to make settlement of the estate at as early a day as shall be consistent with the rights of the respective persons interested therein : *Provided, however*, that if any person interested shall, within three years after the probate of any such will, testament or codicil in the county court as aforesaid, appear, and by his or her bill in chancery, contest the validity of the same, an issue at law shall be made up, whether the writing produced be the will of the testator or testatrix, or not; which shall be tried by a jury in the circuit court of the county wherein such will, testament or codicil shall have been proven and recorded as aforesaid, according to the practice in courts of chancery in similar cases; but if no such person shall appear within the time aforesaid, the probate as aforesaid shall be forever binding and conclusive on all the parties concerned, saving to infants, *femes covert*, persons absent from the state or *non compos mentis*, the like period after the removal of their respective disabilities. And in all such trials by jury, as aforesaid, the certificate of the oath of the witnesses at the time of the first probate, shall be admitted as evidence, and to have such weight as the jury shall think it may deserve.([1])

a. The right of contesting a will is not confined to the heirs at law of the testator, but is given to "any person interested;" which may embrace a devisee as well as an heir at law.([2])

b. The contest provided for in Section 7, may not extend to the whole will; but may be confined to any part of the writing.([3])

c. On a trial of an issue out of chancery under Section 7, *supra*, the trial is *de novo*, and the burden of proof is on the party affirming the validity of the will.([4]) The subscribing witnesses need not concur in testifying to the sound mind and memory of the testator; and the will may be even established against their testimony. The party sustaining the will is not bound to call them, although a fail-

---

(1) Hurd's R. S., Chap. 148, § 7 ; Luther vs. Luther, 122 Ill., 558; McDonald vs. White, 130 Ill., 493; Shaw vs. Moderwell, 104 Ill., 64; Wilbur vs. Wilbur, 129 Ill., 392; Pendlay vs. Eaton, 130 Ill., 69.
(2) Wolf vs. Bollinger, 62 Ill., 368.
(3) *Ib.*
(4) Rigg et al. vs. Wilton et al., 13 Ill., 15; Tate vs. Tate, 89 Ill., 42; Trish et al. vs. Newell et al., 62 Ill., 196; Carpenter vs. Calvert, 83 Ill., 62.

ure to do so, unexplained, might be regarded as a suspicious circumstance. It is enough that the jury are convinced, from any legitimate testimony, of the sanity and capacity of the testator.(1)

d. The influence to avoid a will must be such as to destroy the freedom of the testator's will, and thus to render his act obviously more the offspring of the will of others, than of his own. It must be an influence specially directed towards the object of procuring a will in favor of particular parties. If any degree of free agency or capacity remained in the testator, so that, when left to himself, he was capable of making a valid will, then the influence which so controls him as to render his making a will of no effect, must be such as was intended to mislead him to the extent of making a will essentially contrary to his duty. This influence, to avoid a will, must be one still operating at the time the will is made, and producing that perversion of mind which made the will.(2)

That fraud or undue influence, to avoid a will, must be directly connected with its execution,(3) and must be of such a nature as to deprive the testator of his free agency specially directed toward the object of procuring a will in favor of particular parties.(4)

Influence and persuasion may be fairly used; and a will procured by honest means, by acts of kindness, attention and importunate persuasion which delicate minds would shrink from, would not be set aside on that ground alone. Influence, to vitiate an act, must not be the influence of affection or attachment; it must not be the mere desire of gratifying the wishes of another, for that would be a very strong ground in support of a testamentary act.(5)

Advice, persuasion or entreaty does not constitute undue influence;(6) nor will love, affection and gratitude afford ground from which undue influence may be inferred.(7)

e. In this State the practice has been for the chancellor, in all cases where there has been a trial of a feigned issue, to act upon it, or reject

---

(1) Rigg et al. vs. Wilton et al., 13 Ill., 15; Potter et al. vs. Potter et al., 41 Ill., 80; *In re* Page, 118 Ill., 576.
(2) 1 Redfield on Wills, 524.
(3) Brownfield vs. Brownfield, 43 Ill., 147.
(4) Roe vs. Taylor, 45 Ill., 485.
(5) Miller vs. Miller, 3 Serg. & Rawle, 269, approved in Rutherford et ux. vs. Morris et al., 77 Ill., 397.
(6) Rabb vs. Graham, 43 Md., 9.
(7) Kinne vs. Johnson, 50 Barb., 70.

it and have it retried, as he might be satisfied or not with the verdict. Where he believes the finding clearly wrong, it is his duty to disregard it, and to have the issue retried, or proceed with the trial of the cause and find the issue himself. This, of course, applies to cases where it is discretionary with the court to have an issue of fact formed, and not where the statute has declared that an issue shall be formed, and tried by a jury. Under such a statutory provision the issue must be found by a jury; but where the finding is manifestly wrong, the court should set it aside and award a retrial of the issue. On a motion for a new trial the court should be governed by the same rules that obtain in granting new trials at law, because the verdict is not supported by the evidence.([1])

Appeals or writs of error will not lie to the supreme court from the feigned issues till the bill in chancery is disposed of.([2])

12. WILLS PROVEN WITHOUT THE STATE, EFFECT OF.—All wills, testaments and codicils, or authenticated copies thereof, proven according to the laws of any of the United States, or the territories thereof, or of any country out of the limits of the United States, and touching or concerning estates within this state, accompanied with a certificate of the proper officer or officers that said will, testament, codicil or copy thereof was duly executed and proved, agreeably to the laws and usages of that state or country in which the same was executed, shall be recorded as aforesaid, and shall be good and available in law, in like manner as wills made and executed in this state.([3])

All wills, testaments and codicils, which heretofore have been, or shall hereafter be made, executed and published out of this state, may be admitted to probate in any county in this state in which the testator may have been seized of lands, or other real estate, at the time of his death, in the same manner, and upon like proof as if the same had been made, executed and published in this state, whether such will, testament or codicil, has first been probated in the state, territory or country in which it was made and declared or not. And all original wills, or copies thereof, duly certified accord-

---

(1) Calvert vs. Carpenter et al., 96 Ill., 63; Meeker et al. vs. Meeker et al., 75 Ill., 260; Rutherford vs. Morris et al., 77 Ill., 397; Milk et al. vs. Moore, 39 Ill., 588; Shevalier vs. Seager, 121 Ill., 564; Long vs. Long, 107 Ill., 210.
(2) Woodside vs. Woodside, 21 Ill., 207.
(3) Hurd's R. S., Chap. 148, § 9.

ing to law, or exemplifications from the records in pursuance of the law of congress in relation to records in foreign states, may be recorded as aforesaid, and shall be good and available in law, the same as wills proved in such county court.([1])

a. Where a will is executed in another state, and probated there, and the record and proceedings in respect thereto are authenticated in conformity with the act of congress providing for the authentication of the public acts, records and judicial proceedings in each state, such will is admissible in evidence in the courts of this state without having been probated here;([2]) and a testator may appoint different executors in different countries in which his effects may lie, or different executors as to different parts of his estate in the same country.([3])

13. REVOCATION OF WILLS.—A will is in all cases revocable, even should it in terms be made irrevocable; the first grant and the last will is always of the greatest force.([4])

No will, testament or codicil shall be revoked, otherwise than by burning, canceling, tearing or obliterating the same, by the testator himself, or in his presence, by his direction and consent, or by some other will, testament or codicil in writing, declaring the same, signed by the testator or testatrix, in the presence of two or more witnesses, and by them attested in his or her presence; and no words spoken shall revoke or annul any will, testament or codicil in writing, executed as aforesaid, in due form of law.([5])

a. Where a testator by his will devised real property to his mother, her heirs and assigns forever, and he subsequently obliterated the words "her heirs and assigns" by striking them out, held, that the words obliterated were not a devise or clause within the meaning of the sixth section of the statute of frauds, and that the obliteration was of no effect and the mother took an estate in fee simple.([6])

b. The declarations of the testator made before or after the exe-

(1) Hurd's R. S., Chap. 148, § 10.
(2) Newman et al. vs. Willets, 52 Ill., 98; Kingsbury vs. Burnside et al., 58 Ill., 311; Sheherd vs. Carriel, 19 Ill., 313.
(3) Hunter vs. Bryson, 5 Gill & Johnson, 483.
(4) 1 Lomax on Executors, 3.
(5) Hurd's R. S., Chap. 148, § 17; See 2 Probate Reports, 208, for brief of authorities.
(6) Swinton vs. Bailey, 33 L. T. Rep. (English), 695; Linnard's Appeal, 93 Pa. St., 313.

cution of the will, cannot be received to invalidate the instrument.(¹)

c. If, after making a last will and testament, a child shall be born to any testator, and no provision be made in such will for such child, the will shall not on that account be revoked; but unless it shall appear by such will that it was the intention of the testator to disinherit such child, the devises and legacies by such will granted and given, shall be abated in equal proportions to raise a portion for such child equal to that which such child would have been entitled to receive out of the estate of such testator if he had died intestate, and a marriage shall be deemed a revocation of a prior will.(²)

Section 10, *supra*, has existed in statutory form in this state only since 1871; but in the case of *Tyler et al.* vs. *Tyler*,(³) the supreme court decided, in 1857, in the absence of any statute like it, that the marriage of a man revoked a former will. That decision was cited and adhered to in *American Board of Foreign Missions* vs. *Nelson*,(⁴) and in *Duryea* vs. *Duryea*;(⁵) but *In the Matter of the Will of Esther Tuller, deceased*,(⁶) the same court refused to apply the rule to the case of Mrs. Tuller, who, having children by a former marriage, executed a will, and afterwards married one Hosmer, from whom she was divorced before her death, qualifying the rule laid down in *Tyler* vs. *Tyler, supra*, so as to apply to childless testators only.

The rule of *Tyler* vs. *Tyler* has now become statutory and is no longer debatable.

14. NUNCUPATIVE WILLS.—A nuncupative will shall be good and available in law for the conveyance of personal property thereby bequeathed, if committed to writing within twenty days after the making thereof, and proven before the county court by two or more credible, disinterested witnesses, who were present at the speaking and publishing thereof, who shall declare on oath or affirmation, that they were present and heard the testator pronounce the said words, and that they believed him to be of sound mind and memory; and that he or she did at the same time, desire the

---

(1) Dickie et al. vs. Carter, 42 Ill., 376; Sewell vs. Slingluff, 13 Reporter, 526.
(2) Hurd's R. S, Chap. 39, § 10; Osborn vs. Bank, &c., 116 Ill., 130; McAnnulty vs. McAnnulty, 120 Ill., 26; Ward vs. Ward, 120 Ill., 111; Crum vs. Sawyer, 132 Ill., 443; Milburn vs. Milburn, 60 Iowa, 411.
(3) 19 Ill., 151.   (5) 85 Ill., 41.
(4) 72 Ill., 564.   (6) 79 Ill., 99.

persons present, or some of them, to bear witness that such was his or her will, or words to that effect; and that such will was made in the time of the last sickness of the testator or testatrix; and it being also proven by two disinterested witnesses, other than those hereinbefore mentioned, that the said will was committed to writing within ten days after the death of the testator or testatrix; and no proof of fraud, compulsion or other improper conduct be exhibited, which, in the opinion of said court, shall be sufficient to invalidate or destroy the same; and all such wills, when proven and authenticated as aforesaid, shall be recorded in like manner as other wills are directed to be recorded by this act: *Provided*, that no letters testamentary shall be granted on such will, until the expiration of sixty days after the death of the testator or testatrix.([1])

a. In all cases where a nuncupative will shall be proved and recorded as aforesaid, the court shall issue a citation to the heirs and legal representatives of the testator or testatrix, if they reside in the county; if not, then said court shall cause an advertisement to be inserted in some one of the newspapers printed in this state, notifying the said heirs and legal representatives of the testator or testatrix, at what time and place letters testamentary will be granted upon such will, requiring them and each of them to appear and show cause, if any they have, why letters testamentary should not be granted; and if no sufficient cause be shown, letters shall be granted thereon, as in other cases.([2])

It is indispensable to the value of a nuncupative will, that the testator should request those present to bear witness that such was his last will, or that he should say or do something equivalent to such an expression.([3]) A writing is not such a will.([4])

b. All the requirements of the statute must be shown to exist to entitle a writing purporting to be a nuncupative will to be admitted to probate. While nuncupative wills were recognized by the common law, the right to dispose of property thereby was confined to two classes of persons, who might make such a will at any time. Our statute has extended the right to all persons, but limited the time in which such a will may be made, to the last sickness of

---

(1) Hurd's R. S., Chap. 148, § 15.
(2) Hurd's R. S., Chap. 148, § 16.
(3) Arnett et al. vs. Arnett, 27 Ill., 247
(4) Stamper vs. Hooks, 22 Ga., 603; See 5 Probate Reports, 391, for brief of authorities; *Contra*, Offutt vs. Offutt, 3 B Monroe, 162; See 36 Am. Dec

the testator. The evidence offered to sustain a nuncupative will, must show a strict conformity to the statute.(¹)

c. Such a will, when reduced to writing and admitted to probate, is as effectual to convey personal property as a written will duly attested.(²)

15. LOST WILL.—Where one dies leaving in existence an unrevoked will, which can not be found to be produced before the court for probate as usual, its loss will not defeat it, but like any other instrument when lost, its contents may be proven, when the court, other proof being sufficient, will admit it to probate and give effect to its provisions as in any other case.(³)

16. BY WHAT LAW GOVERNED.—A bequest of personal property is to be judged by the law of the testator's domicile. It should be proved first at the place of such domicile, and application for letters founded upon the probate, should be made elsewhere where assets chance to be.(⁴)

17. MORTGAGE OF REAL ESTATE OF DECEDENTS.—Real estate may be mortgaged in fee or for a term of years, or leased by executors: *Provided*, that the term of such lease, or the time of the maturity of the indebtedness secured by such mortgage, shall not be extended beyond the time when the heirs entitled to such estate shall attain the age of twenty-one years, if a male, or eighteen years, if a female: *And, provided, also*, that before any mortgage or lease shall be made, the executors shall petition the county court for an order authorizing such mortgage or lease to be made, and which the court may grant, if the interests of the estate may require it: *Provided, further*, that the executor making application as aforesaid, upon obtaining such order, shall enter into bond, with good security, faithfully to apply the moneys to be raised upon such mortgage or lease to the payment of the debts of the testator; and all money so raised, shall be assets in the hands of such executor for the payment of debts, and shall be subject to the order of the court in the same manner as other assets.(⁵)

(1) Morgan et al. vs. Stevens, 78 Ill., 287; Harrington et al. vs. Stees et al., 82 Ill., 51; Arnett vs. Arnett, 27 Ill., 247; Carroll vs. Bonham, 42 N. J. Eq., 625.
(2) McCullom vs. Chidester, 63 Ill., 477.
(3) Foster's Appeal, 87 Pa. St., 67; *In re* Page, 118 Ill., 576.
(4) Mills vs. Fogal, 4 Edw., 559.
(5) Hurd's R. S., Chap. 3, § 119; Smith vs. Hutchinson, 108 Ill., 662; Wilbourn vs. Shell, 59 Miss., 205; Foster's Appeal, *supra;* See 1 Probate Reports, 439, for brief of authorities, and 4 *Ib.*, 90; Ins. Co. vs. Aspinall, 44 Mich., 330.

a. Foreclosures of such mortgages shall only be made by petition to the county court of the county in which the premises, or a major part thereof, are situated; and any sale made by virtue of any order or decree of foreclosure, may, at any time before confirmation, be set aside by the court for inadequacy of price or other good cause, and shall not be binding upon the executor until confirmed by the court.([1])

No decree of strict foreclosure shall be made upon any such mortgage, but redemption shall be allowed as is provided by law in cases of sales under executions issued upon common law judgments.([2])

b. A statute similar to the above in the Revised Statutes of 1845,([3]) was construed by the supreme court to authorize a mortgage which should only affect the title during the minority of the ward, and not to authorize a mortgage of the fee.([4])

18. CONSTRUCTION OF WILLS.—There is no branch of the law in which the student will find greater difficulty in fixing with definiteness rules to guide to correct and satisfactory conclusions, than in this one of the right construction of the language employed by testators in formulating their wills. Upward of two hundred years ago, Lord Coke made the observation, which is nearly as true now as it was then, that "wills and the construction of them do more perplex a man than any other learning; and to make a certain construction of them, exceeds the art of jurisprudence."([5]) The first and great rule in the exposition of wills, to which all others must bend, is, that the intention of the testator, expressed in his will, shall prevail, provided it be consistent with the rules of law. This principle is asserted in the construction of every testamentary disposition. It is emphatically the will of the person who makes it, and is defined to be the legal declaration of a man's intentions, which he wills performed after his death. These intentions are to be collected from his words, and ought to be carried into effect, if they be consistent with law.([6])

a. Generally a will is not to be construed by anything *dehors,*

---

(1) Hurd's R. S., Chap. 3, § 120.
(2) Hurd's R. S., Chap. 3, § 121.
(3) Revised Statutes of 1845, Chap. 109, § 134.
(4) Merritt vs. Simpson et al., 41 Ill., 391; Webster vs. Conley, 46 Ill., 13.
(5) Roberts vs. Roberts, 2 Bulst., 130.
(6 Chief Justice Marshall in Smith vs. Bell, 6 Peters, 74; Rountree vs. Talbott et al., 89 Ill., 246; Willis et al. vs. Watson, 4 Scam., 65; Taubenhan vs. Dunz, 125 Ill., 524.

where there is no latent ambiguity, and parol evidence is not admissible to show the intention of the testator against the construction on the face of the will, and the state of his property can not be resorted to, to explain the intention.(¹)

b. The law requires that all wills of lands be in writing, and extrinsic evidence is never admissible, to alter, detract from, or add to, the terms of a will. To permit evidence, the effect of which would be to take from a will plain and unambiguous language, and insert other language in lieu thereof, would violate the foregoing well established rule.(²)

There is no other class of written instruments known to the law in which so little importance is attached to the technical sense of language, in comparison with that sense in which the apparent object of the writer indicates his words to have been used.(³)

c. It is obvious from the haste in which such instruments are frequently prepared—the fact that they are often written by persons wholly unacquainted with the technical language of the law, and frequently by persons who have an imperfect understanding of the use of language, and unaccustomed to prepare such instruments—that it is frequently a matter of no small difficulty to ascertain that meaning; but it is a rule, that the whole instrument must be considered, in ascertaining the meaning of its various parts; otherwise, in many cases, the intention of the testator would be defeated, rather than effectuated.(⁴)

d. When no trust is created by a will, neither the executor nor the heir or devisee who claims only a legal title in the estate, will be allowed to come into a court of equity for the purpose of obtaining a judicial construction of the provisions of a will. Where purely legal titles are involved and none other relief is sought, a court of equity will not assume jurisdiction to construe the will, but will remit the parties to their remedy at law.(⁵)

But where a trust was imposed by the will of a deceased person upon the executors nominated in the will, in the matter of the sale

---

(1) Heslop vs. Gatton, 71 Ill., 528; People vs. Jennings, 44 Ill., 488; Decker vs. Decker, 121 Ill., 341; Smith vs. Dennison, 112 Ill., 367; Bowen vs. Allen, 113 Ill., 53.

(2) Kurtz et al. vs. Hibner et al., 55 Ill., 514; 10 Law Reg., 97, note by Judge Redfield.

(3) Boyd et al. vs. Strahan et al., 36 Ill., 355.

(4) Markillie vs. Ragland, 77 Ill., 98; Smyth vs. Taylor, 21 Ill., 296; Boyd et al. vs. Strahan et al., *supra;* Lunt vs. Lunt, 108 Ill., 307.

(5) Whitman vs. Fisher, 74 Ill., 147; Strubher et al. vs. Belsey, 79 Ill., 307; Longworth vs. Riggs, 123 Ill., 258.

of certain real estate, it was held proper for the circuit court in chancery to entertain a bill by the executors asking the advice of the court as to the manner in which the trust resting upon them should be performed, the trust being embarrassed by circumstances not foreseen or provided against by the testator.([1])

19. WHERE LAND DEVISED IS SOLD.—Where a testator devises land, the legal title to which is in him, but which he has sold and given to the purchaser a bond for a deed therefor, the purchase money, when paid by the purchaser, will belong to the devisee.([2])

20. CHARGE OF LEGACIES UPON REAL ESTATE.—Unless there appears on the face of a will an intention on the part of a testator to charge his real estate with the payment of legacies bequeathed therein, such real estate will pass to the heir or devisee free from any charge on account of such legacies.([3])

21. TITLE VESTS IN DEVISEE.—Where lands are by will given to trustees during the minority of the children of the testator, then to be divided between the survivors of them, the legal title vests at once in the children named, upon the death of the testator.([4])

22. WILLS, ETC., AGAINST WHOM FRAUDULENT.—All wills and testaments, limitations, dispositions or appointments of, or concerning any lands and tenements, or of any rent, profit, term or charge, out of the same, whereof any person, at the time of his decease, shall be seized in fee simple, in possession, in reversion, or remainder, or have power to dispose of the same by his last will or testament, shall be deemed and taken (only as against the person, his heirs, successors, executors, administrators or assigns, and every of them, whose debts, suits, demands, estates and interests, by such will, testament, limitation, disposition or appointment as aforesaid, shall, or might be in any wise disturbed, hindered, delayed or defrauded,) to be fraudulent, void and of no effect, any pretense, color, feigned or presumed consideration, or any other matter or thing, to the contrary notwithstanding.([5])

Every devise of real estate is fraudulent and void as against the

---

(1) Bridges et al. vs. Rice, 99 Ill., 414.
(2) Wright vs. Minshall, 72 Ill., 584.
(3) Heslop vs. Gatton, 71 Ill., 528; Gill vs. Mining Co., 92 Ill., 249; Funk et al. vs. Eggleston et al., 92 Ill., 515.
(4) Hempstead et al. vs. Dickson, 20 Ill., 193.
(5) Hurd's R. S., Chap. 59, § 10.

existing creditors of the devisor. It is fraudulent in law, without regard to the question of intention. The devisee has no just claim to the lands, until the debts of the testator are fully discharged. Nor has the heir any superior right to the lands of his ancestor. They both acquire the lands subject to the payment of the debts of the former owner, and are only entitled to the surplus that may remain after those debts are discharged.(1)

23. TRUSTEES TO RECEIVE COMPENSATION.—That where a trustee or trustees shall hereafter act under any power or appointment given or created by any will, testament or codicil, and in such will, testament or codicil, except in case of trusts for charitable, religious or educational purposes, shall be contained no provision respecting the compensation to be allowed or paid such trustee or trustees, a reasonable compensation may be charged and allowed, demanded and collected therefor.(2)

(1) Ryan vs. Jones, 15 Ill., 1.
(2) Hurd's R. S., Chap. 3, § 136; Sherman vs. Leman, 137 Ill., 94.

CHAPTER XV.

FOREIGN EXECUTORS AND ADMINISTRATORS.

1. Power of executors and administrators in other jurisdictions under the common law.
2. Powers in this state of those holding authority from other states.
    a. Foreign administrator need not account here.
3. Exceptions.
4. Authority local.
5. Authentication of letters.
6. Certificate.
7. How right to sue must be questioned.
8. May sue out execution.

1. POWER OF EXECUTORS AND ADMINISTRATORS IN OTHER JURISDICTIONS UNDER THE COMMON LAW.—A grant of administration in one state or country, does not, at the common law, confer on an administrator any title to the property of the intestate situated in another state or country.([1]) He has no authority over, nor is he responsible for any effects of the estate that may be beyond the jurisdiction. In administering the estate, he acts only in reference to the effects within the jurisdiction, and the debts that may be there presented against the estate. In his official capacity he can neither sue nor be sued, out of the country from which he derives his authority, and to which he alone is amenable.([2]) If he wishes to reach property, or collect debts belonging to the estate in a foreign country, he must there obtain letters of administration, and give such security, and become subject to such regulations, as its laws may prescribe. So, if a creditor wishes to bring a suit in order to satisfy his debt out of property in another jurisdiction, administration must there be first obtained.([3]) The administration at the domicile of the decedent is the principal, and a foreign administration is, by the laws of nations, merely ancillary and subordinate to it. The foreign administrator, in such a case, may be called to an account here, to

---

(1) Bonnell vs. Holt et al., 89 Ill., 71; Fletcher's Admrs. vs. Sanders, 7 Dana (Ky.), 345; See 76 Am. Dec., 668, for brief of authorities.

(2) Story's Conflict of Laws, § 513; Goodwin vs. Jones, 3 Mass., 514; Riley vs. Riley, 3 Day, 74; Leonard vs. Putnam, 51 N. H., 247.

(3) Judy et al. vs. Kelley, 11 Ill., 211; Sheldon vs. Estate of Rice, 30 Mich., 296; Morrell vs. Dickey, 1 Johns. Ch., 153; Doolittle vs. Lewis, 7 Johns. Ch., 45; Vaughn vs. Barrett, 5 Vermont, 333; Note to same case, 26 Am. Dec., 309; Stevens vs. Gaylord, 11 Mass., 256; McGarvey vs. Darnall, 134 Ill., 367; Patterson vs. Payson, 18 S. C., 584.

the domestic executor or administrator, for the assets received by him abroad, and remaining after the payment of expenses, and the discharge of debts in due course, in the foreign state.([1]) In all cases of double administration, a court of equity will interfere so to marshal the different funds under administration as to produce equality among all creditors, whether foreign or domestic, and also to transmit, if necessary, the residue of assets left in the hands of the foreign administrator to the principal administrator, at the domicile of the deceased, there to be distributed among heirs or creditors.([2])

An administrator can not sue or defend beyond the jurisdiction of the state appointing him, nor can he collect assets of his intestate situated in such jurisdiction, whether they consist of tangible property or choses in action.([3])

So, the release and satisfaction of a mortgage by a foreign administrator, can not avail as a defense to a bill by the domestic administrator, to foreclose.([4])

This regulation can not be evaded by the endorsement and delivery of a note against a citizen of a foreign state, held by an administrator, so as to effect a recovery in the name of a third person.([5]) An ancillary administrator appointed in one state upon the estate of one domiciled in another, is bound to pay the debts of his decedent due to citizens of the state where his letters are granted, but not to pay legacies; the legatees must resort to the state of the testator's domicile.([6])

The county court has power to order funds in the hands of an ancillary administrator to be transmitted to the principal administrator in another state, when the administration here is settled, and there are no heirs, distributees or creditors claiming such fund.([7])

Should the excess of funds in the hands of such administrator arise from the sale of real estate, the court should order distribution under our law of descent.

(1) Ordronoux vs. Helie, 3 Sand. Ch., 512; Graham vs. Pub. Admr., Brad., 127; Branch vs. Rankin, 108 Ill., 444; Young vs. Wittenmyre, 123 Ill., 304
(2) Lawrence vs. Elmandorf, 5 Barb., 73; Story's Eq. Juris., § 588-9; McNamara vs. Dwyer, 7 Paige Ch., 239, and note to same case, 32 Am. Dec., 632.
(3) Riley vs. Morely, 44 Miss., 37; Anderson vs. Gregg, *Id.*, 170; Goodwin vs. Jones, 3 Mass., 514.
(4) Stone vs. Scripture, 4 Lans., (N. Y.) 186; Stevens vs. Gaylord, 1 Mass., 256; See note, 32 Am. Dec., 106; *Contra*, Wilkins vs. Elliott, 9 Wal., 740.
(5) Lee vs. Havens, Brayt., 92.
(6) Richards vs. Dutch, 8 Mass., 506.
(7) Childers vs. Bennett, 10 Ala., 751.

Notwithstanding these regulations, it is competent for an administrator appointed in one state to collect and receive money and personal property and effects within another state, belonging to the intestate, so far as it can be done without the aid of legal process.([1]) And where a power of sale in a mortgage provided that the mortgagee, his executors and assigns, might sell the property in default of payment, it was held, upon default, the mortgagee being dead, that the power of sale was properly executed by his administrator, although he was appointed in another state.([2])

2. POWERS BY STATUTE.—When any person has proved or may prove the last will and testament of any deceased person, and taken on him the execution of said will, or has obtained or may obtain administration of the estate of an intestate in any state in the United States, or in any territory thereof, such person shall be enabled to prosecute suits to enforce claims of the estate of the deceased, or to sell lands to pay debts, in any court in this state, in the same manner as if letters testamentary or of administration had been granted to him under the provisions of the laws of this state: *Provided*, that such persons shall produce a copy of the letters testamentary or of administration, authenticated in the manner prescribed by the laws of congress of the United States for authenticating the records of judicial acts in any one state, in order to give them validity in other states: *And, provided*, that said executor or administrator shall give a bond for costs, as in case of other non-residents.([3])

a. A foreign administrator availing himself of this statute, and making collections here, is not bound to account for any part of the assets of the estate here.([4])

3. EXCEPTIONS.—Nothing contained in the preceding section shall be so construed as to apply to cases where administration is obtained upon the estate of any intestate nor where letters testamentary are granted in this state; and when, after any suit is commenced by any administrator or executor under the provisions of the preceding section, and before final judgment thereon, administration is had, or execution undertaken within this state, under the laws of the same, upon the estate of any decedent, upon suggestion

---

(1) Doolittle vs. Lewis, 7 Johns. Ch., 45; Story's Conflict of Laws, § 515.
(2) *Ib.*
(3) Hurd's R. S., Chap. 3, § 42; Hickox vs. Frank, 102 Ill., 660.
(4) Selectmen of Boston vs. Boylston, 2 Mass., 384.

of such fact, entered of record, the said resident administrator or executor shall, upon motion, be substituted as party to such suit; and thereupon the court shall proceed to hear and determine the same, as if it had been originally instituted in the name of the said resident executor or administrator, and the benefits of the judgment, order or decree shall inure to him, and be assets in his hands.([1])

4. HIS AUTHORITY LOCAL.—An administrator is the officer of the court appointing him; and his power is only commensurate with the state or country from whose court he receives authority to act; therefore, letters granted in another state, give no authority to sue or administer assets in this state.([2])

But for the foregoing statute, administrators and executors holding authority from another state, could have no standing as such in the courts of this state. The statute only including such as receive their appointment in some one of the states or territories of the United States, only such are enabled, by conforming to its provisions, to bring suits in the courts of this state.([3])

5. NO PRIVITY BETWEEN DOMESTIC AND FOREIGN ADMINISTRATORS.—The doctrine is well settled, that if letters of administration are granted in different states to different persons, in respect to the estate left by the same deceased person, there is no privity between such adminstrators; and that, therefore, a judgment against the administrator in one state is not competent testimony to show a right of action against either a domiciliary administrator in another state, or to affect assets in such other state.([4])

6. AUTHENTICATION.—The copy of letters of foreign executors and administrators, to entitle them to credit in the courts of this state, must be authenticated by the attestation of the clerk of the court granting them, and the seal of the court annexed, if there be a seal, together with a certificate of the judge, chief justice or presiding magistrate, that said attestation is in due form.([5])

7. WHAT IS A SUFFICIENT CERTIFICATE.—Letters of adminis-

---

(1) Hurd's R. S., Chap. 3, § 43; Branch vs. Rankin, 108 Ill., 444.
(2) Glenn vs. Smith, 2 Gill & Johnson, 493.
(3) Judy et al. vs. Kelley, 11 Ill., 211; People vs. Peck, 3 Scam., 118; Christy vs. McBride, 1 Scam., 75.
(4) McGarvey vs. Darnall, 134 Ill., 367; Price vs. Mace, 47 Wis., 23; Jones vs. Jones, 15 Texas, 463.
(5) U. S. Revised Statutes, 1874, title 13, Chap. 17; Baker vs. Brown, 18 Ill., 91.

tration granted in one of the United States, authenticated by the attestation of the sole presiding judge, by whom the records are kept, there being no clerk, with the seal of the court annexed, are admissible as evidence in the courts of this state.(1)

8. Issue to be raised by special plea.—The right of a plaintiff to sue in the assumed capacity of administrator must be questioned by the defendant by a special plea of *ne unques administrator*—the general issue admits such right (2)

Suits brought by foreign administrators in the courts of this state are alike subject to the same rules of pleading as in cases where suits are brought by domestic administrators; and the mode of proof, when the official character is questioned, is there prescribed.(3)

9. May sue out execution.—The power given to foreign administrators in the above statute includes the power to sue out an execution on a judgment rendered in favor of the intestate in his lifetime.(4)*

(1) Spencer vs. Langdon, 21 Ill., 192.
(2) McKinley vs. Braden, 1 Scam., 64; Breckinridge et al. vs. Ostrom, 79 Ill., 71; Collins vs. Ayers, 13 Ill., 358; Ballance vs. Frisby et al., 2 Scam., 63.
(3) Collins vs. Ayers, *supra*.
(4) Keefer vs. Mason, 36 Ill., 406.

*Note.—The whole doctrine of domestic and foreign administration is well collated in a note to *Goodall vs. Marshall*, 35 American Decisions, 483.

CHAPTER XVI.

APPEALS.

1. Appeals from order rejecting claim.
2. Who may take appeals, and how.
3. Right extends to all cases—exception.
4. Condition of bond.
5. What may be done upon appeal.
6. Writ of error.

1. APPEALS FROM ORDER ALLOWING OR REJECTING A CLAIM.— In all cases of the allowance or rejection of claims by the county court, as provided in this act, either party may take an appeal from the decision rendered to the circuit court of the same county, in the same time and manner appeals are now taken from justices of the peace to the circuit courts, by appellant giving good and sufficient bond with security to be approved by the county judge; and such appeals shall be tried *de novo* in the circuit court.([1])

2. WHO MAY TAKE APPEAL—HOW ALLOWED.—Appeals shall be allowed from all judgments, orders or decrees of the county court in all matters arising under this act, to the circuit court, in favor of any person who may consider himself aggrieved by any judgment, order or decree of such court, and from the circuit court to the supreme court, as in other cases, and bonds with security to be fixed by the county or circuit court, as the case may be.([2])

This section includes petitions for leave to sell land to pay debts, from which decrees either party may appeal to the circuit court.([3])

Under Section 124, above, it has been decided that a security upon the bond of an administrator, though not a party to the record, may appeal from an order of distribution made by the county court against the principal in the bond, if he feels himself aggrieved by such order.([4])

So, a security upon the bond of a deceased guardian, who died with money in his hands belonging to his ward, may appeal from an order of the county court transferring a claim other than the

---

(1) Hurd's R. S., Chap. 3, ¿ 68; Smith et al. vs. Dennison, 94 Ill., 582.
(2) Hurd's R. S., Chap. 3, ¿ 124.
(3) Steele vs. Steele et al., 89 Ill., 51.
(4) Ralston et al. vs. Wood, 15 Ill., 159.

ward's, allowed as of the 7th class, against the estate of the deceased, and ordering the administrator to pay it as of the 6th class.(¹)

In a proceeding to condemn the right of way for a railroad, where the owner died after the termination of the proceedings in the circuit court, the heirs of the owner are the proper persons to prosecute an appeal, and not the personal representatives.(²)

When the appeal is prosecuted by one aggrieved, who is not a party to the record, it may be prosecuted in the name of the administrator.(³)

3. RIGHT EXTENDS TO ALL CASES—EXCEPTION.—The right of appeal given by Section 124, above quoted, would seem to include in its comprehensive language, every conceivable order of the court, and to extend the right to every person interested, however remotely, and such seems to have been the construction put upon it;(⁴) yet it has recently been held that no appeal lies to the circuit court by an administrator from an order of the county court, under Section 114, Chapter 3, committing him to jail for failure to pay to heirs money in his hands subject to distribution. The same decision holds that the supreme court may only review such a decision, upon a writ of error prosecuted thereto directly from the county court.(⁵)

4. CONDITION OF BOND.—In all cases when an executor or administrator shall take an appeal from the judgment, decree or order of any court or justice of the peace to the county, circuit or supreme court, or when he may prosecute writs of error or *certiorari*, the appeal, *certiorari* or *supersedeas* bond shall be conditioned to pay the judgment or decree, with costs, in due course of administration; in all other respects such bonds shall be in the form prescribed by law in other cases.(⁶)

Where an appeal or *supersedeas* bond is executed by an administrator or executor, it is sufficient if the condition provides for the payment of the debt " in due course of administration," should the appeal be fruitless.(⁷)

5. WHAT MAY BE DONE ON APPEAL.—On an appeal by an

(1) Weer vs. Gand, 88 Ill., 490.
(2) Bower vs. G. & M. R. R. Co., 92 Ill., 223.
(3) Pfershing vs. Falsh, 87 Ill., 260; Motsinger vs. Coleman, 16 Ill., 71.
(4) Andrews et al. vs. Black et al., 43 Ill., 256.
(5) Haines vs. People, 97 Ill., 162; Explained in Randolph vs. People, 130 Ill., 533.
(6) Hurd's R. S., Chap. 3, ₰ 125.
(7) Mason vs. Johnson, 24 Ill., 159; Smith et al. vs. Dennison, 94 Ill., 582.

administrator from an order of the county court rejecting a part of his charges for money paid out, the circuit court does not acquire jurisdiction of the whole account or report, but only of the rejected items, and can not hear evidence as to any of the items allowed by the county court. If the heirs appeal as to the items allowed, the rule is different.(¹) Where both parties appeal, the whole case will come before the court.

On an appeal, the circuit court can only do what the county court might do.(²)

6. WRIT OF ERROR.—Where, by the terms of the statute, no appeal is given from an order or decree of the county court, a writ of error may be prosecuted to the supreme court. But where an appeal may be taken, no writ of error will lie.(³)

As an appeal lies from an order of the county court removing an administrator, no writ of error can be prosecuted from such an order.(⁴)

(1) Curts vs. Brooks, 71 Ill. 126; Millard vs. Harris, 119 Ill., 185.
(2) Cagney vs. O'Brien, 83 Ill., 72; Miller vs. Miller, 82 Ill., 463.
(3) Hobson et al. vs. Payne, 40 Ill., 25; Fitzgerald vs. Glancy, 49 Il., 466; Horner vs. Goe et al., 54 Ill., 285; Unknown Heirs of Langworthy vs. Baker, 23 Ill., 484; Haynes vs. People, 97 Ill., 162; Ennis vs. Ennis, 103 Ill., 95.
(4) Frans vs. People, 59 Ill., 427.

PART II.

GUARDIAN AND WARD.

Adoption of Children; Conservators; Insanity; Assignment; Insolvency; Bastardy; Right of Property.

GUARDIAN AND WARD.

CHAPTER I.

OF THE VARIOUS KINDS OF GUARDIANS.

1. Definition.
    a. Of the various kinds of guardians.
2. Guardians by nature.
    a. Powers of such—custody.
    b. Limitation in chancery.
    c. In case of divorce.
    d. Bastards.
    e. Power over property.
    f. Duty to maintain.
    g. Exception—abandonment.
    h. Exception as to all guardians but the father.
    i. Parent owns clothing of the child.
3. Guardians by chancery.
    a. Unknown to the common law.
    b. Origin of this relation.
    c. Jurisdiction of equity courts.
    d. May direct the action of guardian.
    e. Suits by infants in equity
    f. Peculiar duty of courts of equity.
4. Guardians by statute.
    a. Testamentary.
    b. Statutory.
5. Guardians *ad litem*.
    a. Appointment and power.
    b. Infants the wards of equity courts.
    c. Presumption.
    d. Such guardian may employ counsel.

1. DEFINITION.—A guardian is one that legally has the care and management of the person, or estate, or both, of a child during minority.

At common law such child is denominated a ward.[1]

(1) Reeves' Dom. Rel., 311.

a. There are various kinds of guardianships. First: Guardians by nature. Second: Guardians by chancery. Third: Guardians by statute. Fourth: Guardians *ad litem*.

2. GUARDIAN BY NATURE.—The father is the guardian by nature, and on his death the mother.([1]) This guardianship by the common law extends only to the custody of the person, terminating when the child arrives at the age of legal majority.([2])

The father has the legal right to the custody and control of his children, unless he has forfeited, waived or lost it by misconduct, misfortune or some peculiar circumstances sufficient to deprive him of it. Next to the father the mother has the right.([3])

a. The power of the guardian by nature is limited, and liable to be controled by the court of chancery.([4])

b. It has been held that a court of chancery would deprive him of the custody of the child, if his character rendered him an unfit guardian.([5])

The parent, however, having the natural right to the care and custody of his child, this right should not be abridged by the state, except from a necessity, arising from gross misconduct, or almost total unfitness on the part of the parents.([6])

c. Where a divorce has been granted for the fault or misconduct of the father, the mother will be entitled to the child.([7])

d. The mother of a bastard child is its natural guardian.([8])

e. A guardian by nature is not entitled to the control of his ward's property, either real or personal.([9]) That right, whenever he has it, must be as a guardian, duly appointed, by some competent public authority.([10]) He has no authority to lease the infant's

---

(1) Fields vs. Law, 2 Root, (Conn.) 320.
(2) 2 Kent's Com., 220; Perry vs. Carmichael, 95 Ill., 519.
(3) Miner vs. Miner, 11 Ill., 43.
(4) De Mandeville vs. De Mandeville, 10 Vesey, Jr., (Vt.) 52.
(5) Reeve Dom. Rel., *supra;* 2 Kent's Com., *supra;* Perry vs. Carmichael, *supra*.
(6) The People *Ex. Rel.* Turner, 55 Ill., 280.
(7) Miner vs. Miner, *supra*.
(8) Wright vs. Wright, 2 Mass., 109; Dalton vs. State, 6 Blakf., (Ind.) 357; Somerset vs. Dighton, 12 Mass., 383; People vs. Mitchell, 44 Barb., 245.
(9) Hyde vs. Stone, 7 Wend., (N. Y.) 354; Miles vs. Boyden, 3 Pick., (Mass.) 213; Kline vs. Beebe, 6 Conn., 494; Perry vs. Carmichael, *supra*.
(10) Fonda vs. Van Horne, 15 Wend., (N. Y.) 631; Kendall vs. Miller, 9 Cal., 591; Perry vs. Carmichael, *supra*.

lands;(¹) nor can he give a binding discharge to an executor, on the payment of a legacy belonging to the child.(²)

f. The father, being its natural guardian, must support the ward.(³)

When his means are limited, the court may grant an allowance out of his child's estate.(⁴) But the mother, if guardian, is not obliged to support her child, if it has sufficient estate of its own; nor is she entitled, like the father, when guardian, to its services, unless she is compelled to maintain it.(⁵)

Where the father and mother separate, by mutual consent, and the father permits the mother to take the children with her, then the father constitutes the mother his agent to provide for his children, and is bound by her contracts for necessaries for them.(⁶)

g. There is one exception to the rule that a father, being the natural guardian, is bound for the support of his child; and that is, where the child voluntarily abandons the home of his father and remains abroad against his consent, he thereby forfeits his claim to support; and those who credit him, even for necessaries, must look to him for payment; and it is no excuse that such persons were not aware that the child was acting contrary to the will of the father: for while the father is under a natural obligation to provide for the maintenance of his infant child, an express promise, or circumstances from which a promise by the father can be inferred, are indispensably necessary to bind the parent for necessaries furnished his infant child by a third person.(⁷) For, in order to bind a father for necessaries furnished his infant child, there must be some evidence that he has either sanctioned or ratified the contract. The mere moral obligation resting on the father to maintain his child, affords no legal inference of a promise to pay his debts.(⁸) And courts are

---

(1) Anderson vs. Darby, 1 Mott. & M., (S. C.) 369; Magruder vs. Peter, 11 Gil. & J., (Md.) 217; May vs. Calder, 2 Mass., 55; Ross vs. Cobb, 9 Yerg., (Tenn.) 463.
(2) Genet vs. Tallmadge, 1 Johns. Ch., 3; Miles vs. Boyden, 3 Pick., (Mass.) 213.
(3) Bloomer vs. Bloomer, 2 Bradf. Surr., (N. Y.) 341; Cowls vs. Cowls, 3 Gilm., 435.
(4) Bloomer vs. Bloomer, *supra;* Cowls vs. Cowls, *supra*.
(5) Fonda vs. Van Horne, 15 Wend., (N. Y.) 631.
(6) McMillen vs. Lee, 78 Ill., 443.
(7) Hunt vs. Thompson, 3 Scam., 179; Kelley vs. Davis, 49 N. H., 187; Gotts vs. Clark, 78 Ill., 229; McMillen vs. Lee, *supra*.
(8) Broom's Legal Maxims, 533 to 536.

to decide according to the legal obligations of parties, not mere moral obligations.(¹)

h. No guardian, except a father, is bound to maintain his ward at his own expense, and it is discretionary with a court whether to allow a father anything out of his child's estate for his education and maintenance.(²)

i. The parent of a minor is the owner of the clothing furnished for the use of his child, and may recover for its loss or destruction.(³)

3. GUARDIAN BY CHANCERY.—Courts of chancery have full jurisdiction over the persons and estates of infants, and other persons under legal disabilities, as well as their guardians, trustees or other custodians, alike whether the relationship arise from natural ties, or is created by law.(⁴) The relations of guardian and ward, and the rights and obligations which grow out of it, are peculiarly within the jurisdiction of a court of equity, and its power to afford relief for a breach of trust cannot be questioned, unless taken away by some express statutory enactment.(⁵)

a. This guardianship was unknown to the common law, but it is well established in practice now.(⁶)

b. It grew up in the time of William III., and had its foundation in the royal prerogative of the king as *parens patriæ*.(⁷) This power the sovereign is presumed to have delegated to the chancellor.(⁸) By virtue of it, the chancellor appoints a guardian where there is none, and exercises a superintending control over all guardians however appointed, removing them for misconduct, and appointing others in their stead.(⁹) This power resides in courts of equity in the United States.(¹⁰) The rights of infants will always be guarded by courts of equity, and whenever invaded or endangered, a remedy will be applied.(¹¹)

(1) Turner vs. Mason, 14 M. & W., 111.
(2) Reeve Dom. Rel., 324; Douch vs. Rahner, 6 Ind., 66.
(3) Parmalee vs. Smith, 21 Ill., 620.
(4) Townsend vs. Kendall, 4 Minn., 412; Commonweath vs. Henshaw, 2 Bush, (Ky.) 286.
(5) Crain vs. Barnes, 1 Md. Ch., 151.
(6) Bouvier's Law Dict., 646.
(7) 2 Fonblanque Eq., 5 Ed., 246.
(8) De Mandeville vs. De Mandeville, 10 Vesey Jr., Ch., 63; Reeve Dom. Rel., 317.
(9) 2 Kent's Com., 227.
(10) 2 Kent's Com., *supra;* Cowls vs. Cowls, 3 Gilm., 435; Sessions vs. Kell., 30 Miss., 458; Ex. Parte Dawson, 3 Bradf. Surr., (N. Y.) 133.
(11) White vs. Glover, 59 Ill., 459.

c. The jurisdiction of such courts to superintend the administration of assets, and decree distribution among legatees and distributees, is now firmly established; and a statutory provision giving courts of law power over the same subject, does not deprive chancery of its jurisdiction.(1)

The representatives of a ward may file a bill against the executors of a guardian, in whose hands the estate of the infant remained unaccounted for at his death.(2) And, where a guardian receives a conveyance of the estate of his ward in his own name, in case of his death, a bill in equity may be maintained against his administrator, to enforce a conveyance of the property thus held in trust, and to account for its earnings.(3) So, too, chancery will entertain a bill against a guardian, brought by the heirs of his ward, although the demand be merely for money.(4)

A court of equity has plenary jurisdiction over the persons and estates of infants, and will, in the exercise of that jurisdiction, cause to be done whatever may be necessary to preserve their estate.(5) And where there are infant defendants to a suit for partition, the right of partition of the lands among the several owners, and the consequent sale, if not susceptible of a division, is not absolute in all cases, for in case the court deem it best for the interest of the infant heirs, although such suit may have been instituted in behalf of the minors by their guardian, it will refuse to permit a sale, which a court of chancery, in the exercise of its general supervision over the rights and interests of infants, ought to do, when their interests will be best subserved by it.(6)

d. Where a guardian *ad litem* of infant heirs, puts in an answer to a bill in chancery admitting the allegations, a court of chancery being the general guardian of infants, may doubtless, set aside the answer of the guardian and direct him to put in an answer requiring the complainant to prove the facts set out in his bill.(7)

e. Suits in chancery may be commenced and prosecuted by

(1) Barnes vs. Compton, 8 Gill., (Md.) 391.
(2) *Ib.*
(3) Folger vs. Buck, 66 Me., 205.
(4) Armstrong vs. Mill, 6 Ohio, 119.
(5) Lynch vs. Rotan, 39 Ill., 14.
(6) Hartman vs. Hartman, 59 Ill., 103.
(7) Thornton vs. The Heirs of Henry, 2 Scam., 218.

infants, either by guardian or next friend.(¹) And whenever a suit is instituted in the court of chancery, relative to the person and property of the infant, although he may not be under any general guardian appointed by the court, he is treated as a ward of the court, and as being under its special cognizance and protection.(²)

It is frequently necessary for the infant to file a bill against the guardian; and when that is not the case, there may be reasons for fearing that the guardian is not acting judiciously, or in good faith in relation to the subject of the suit. It is the business of the court of chancery to see that no one stands between the infant and a just protection of its rights; and for this purpose, the court may appoint a person to prosecute or defend for the infant.(³)

A general supervision of the interest of infants is now exercised in courts of chancery, as a branch of general jurisdiction. Indeed, it is one of the peculiar duties of courts of chancery to protect the rights of infants. From the earliest period, courts of chancery have been vested with a broad and comprehensive jurisdiction over the person and property of infants.(⁴) Chancery courts retain a general jurisdiction over every guardian, however appointed.(⁵)

4. GUARDIANS BY STATUTE.—They are divided into two kinds: First—Testamentary guardians, or those appointed by the court by authority in a will. Second—Statutory guardians, or those appointed by the court in pursuance of some statute.

a. First: Testamentary guardians:—The father, being of sound mind and memory, of a child likely to be born, or of any living child, being a minor and unmarried, may, by his last will, dispose of the custody and tuition of such child to continue during its minority, or, for a less time. *Provided*, no such will shall take effect to deprive the mother, during her life, of the custody and tuition of the child, without her consent, if she be a fit and competent person to have such custody and tuition. The mother, being of sound mind and memory, and being sole, or surviving the father

---

(1) Hurd's R. S., Chap. 22, § 5.
(2) 3 Story's Eq. Jur., vol. 2, p. 35.
(3) Holmes vs. Fields, 12 Ill., 424.
(4) Cowls vs. Cowls, 3 Gilm., 435; Grattan vs. Grattan, 18 Ill., 167; K ng vs. King, 15 Ill., 187; Miner vs. Miner, 11 Ill., 43; Stark vs. Brown, 101 Ill., 395.
(5) Durrett vs. Davis, 24 Gratt., (Va.) 302; Cowls vs. Cowls, *supra;* Wilcox vs. Wilcox, 14 N. Y., 575.

of her child, may, in like manner, dispose of the custody and tuition of such child.(¹)

A testamentary guardian shall have the same powers and perform the same duties within the scope of his appointment, as a guardian appointed by the county court.(²)

A testamentary guardian, except for the custody and tuition of the minor, shall, before he can act, be commissioned by the county court of the proper county, and give the bond prescribed in Section 7 of this act. Except, that when the testator has requested in his will that a bond be not required, it shall not be required, unless, from a change in the situation or circumstances of the guardian, or for other sufficient cause, the court shall deem it necessary to require it.(³)

Where a testator, by his will, appointed his wife guardian to his infant daughter, "So long as she should remain his widow," after his decease, his widow took out letters of guardianship for her daughter, from the probate court of the proper county, and subsequently married. The appointment of the probate court was held to be void, for want of jurisdiction, and that the power of the father to name a guardian for his children, is greater than that conferred upon the probate court; and when the former has expressed the right, the latter can not act. That the limitation in the will was strictly legal and should be enforced, and the guardianship of the widow was terminated by her marriage.(⁴)

And where the will of the testator left "The care and custody of his infant children to his wife, so long as she remained his widow," she having married again, the appointment of a new guardian was held to be necessary.(⁵) As the act of the father in disposing of his minor children by deed or will can not be defeated by an appointment of the county court,(⁶) the mere naming a person in a will as guardian, does not constitute him such, unless he qualifies as such, although he may have done some act appropriate to that character.(⁷) So, when a will appoints two persons as "joint guard-

(1) Hurd's R. S., Chap. 64, § 5.
(2) *Ib.*, § 8.
(3) *Ib.*, § 9.
(4) Holmes vs. Fields, 12 Ill., 424.
(5) Corrigan vs. Kiernan, 1 Bradf., (N. Y.) 208.
(6) Brooklyn Industrial School vs. Kearney, 31 Barb., (N. Y.) 430.
(7) McAlister vs. Olmstead, 1 Humph., (Tenn.) 210.

ians" of the person and estate of an infant, and one of them declines to act, all the rights and powers created by the appointment, become vested in the other.([1]) And where the custody of the child is given to the mother by a decree of divorce, for the fault of the father, she may by will appoint a guardian for such child.([2]) But a testamentary guardian can not be appointed by the grandfather of the infant.([3])

A testamentary guardian has the legal right to the custody of the ward; but this right will be controlled, in a case where the interests of the ward obviously require it.([4])

b. Second: of Statutory guardians:—The statute has invested the county court with the power to appoint, "when it shall appear necessary or convenient," guardians for minors, for a consideration of which power the reader is referred to Chapter II, *post.*

5. GUARDIANS AD LITEM.—Guardians *ad litem*, are guardians appointed by the court, to defend the interest of the infant who may be a party defendant to a suit or proceeding, and who has no legal guardian who may answer for him.

a. The appointment of a guardian *ad litem*, is incident to the power of every court to try a case.([5]) And the power of such guardian is then confined to the suit or proceeding in which he is appointed.([6])

In criminal cases no guardian *ad litem* is ever appointed, the court acts as the guardian.([7])

Our statute provides, that in any cause in equity, it shall be lawful for the court in which the cause is pending, to appoint a guardian *ad litem* to any infant or insane defendant in such cause, and to compel the person so appointed to act. By such appointment, such person shall not be rendered liable to pay costs of suit; and he shall, moreover, be allowed a reasonable sum for his charges as such guardian, to be fixed by the court, and taxed in the bill of costs.([8])

(1) Matter of Reynolds, 18 N. Y. Supreme Court, 41.
(2) Willkinson vs. Deming, 80 Ill., 342.
(3) Williamson vs. Gordon, 1 Busb. Eq., (N. C.) 46; Hoyt vs. Hilton, 2 Edw., (N. Y.) 202.
(4) Ward vs. Roper, 7 Humph., (Tenn.) 111.
(5) Ballard vs. Spoor, 2 Cow., N. Y. 430.
(6) Coke, Litt., 89, n. 16.
(7) Reeves' Dom. Rel., 318.
(8) Hurd's R. S., Chap. 22, § 6; Walker vs. Hallett, 1 Ala., 379.

The appointment of a guardian *ad litem* is something more than mere form, although such guardian can not bind the infant by anything he may do or admit in his answer.([1])

A guardian *ad litem* can not be appointed until the infant has been brought before the court in some of the modes prescribed by law.([2]) Infant heirs must be made parties, served personally and be represented by a guardian *ad litem*.([3]) For such a guardian has no power to waive service of process and enter the appearance of the infant.([4]) It is not sufficient that the legal guardian of the infant be served with process to give the court jurisdiction over the person of the minor, even though the infant be named in the bill as a party defendant, and the guardian should enter his appearance and file an answer. To give the court jurisdiction of the person of a minor, there must be notice, actual or constructive, and where no notice has been given a minor, the appointment of a guardian *ad litem* who answered for him, is not sufficient to give the court such jurisdiction.

Infant defendants must be served with process, in order to bind them by a decree.([5]) And where the notice is by publication, which is defective, the appointment of a guardian *ad litem* is void, as the infants are not in court.([6]) So, too, the appointment of a guardian *ad litem* for infants, not naming them, is inoperative, where the record fails to show that any of the defendants were minors.([7])

A minor can only appear and defend a suit by his guardian, and a judgment or a decree in chancery against infant defendants, without the appointment of a guardian *ad litem* for such infants, when they have no general guardians representing them, is erroneous.([8]) And upon an application to sell real estate of a decedent

(1) McClay vs. Norris, 4 Gilm., 370; Cost vs. Rose, 17 Ill., 276; Chaffin vs. Heirs of Kimball, 23 Ill., 36; Rhoads vs. Rhoads, 43 Ill., 239.
(2) Hodges vs. Wise, 16 Ala., 509; Shaefer vs. Gates, 2 B. Mon., (Ky.) 453; Frazier vs. Pankey, 1 Swan, (Tenn.) 75; Clark vs. Thompson, 47 Ill., 25.
(3) Rucker vs. Moore, 1 Heisk., (Tenn.) 726; Bonnell vs. Holt, 89 Ill., 71; Price vs. Crone, 44 Miss., 571.
(4) Robbins vs. Robbins, 2 Ind., 74; Clark vs. Thompson, *supra;* Chambers vs. Jones, 72 Ill., 275; Bonnell vs. Holt, *supra.*
(5) Greenman vs. Harvey, 53 Ill., 386; Hickenbotham vs. Blackledge, 54 Ill., 316; Fischer vs. Fischer, 54 Ill., 231; Campbell vs. Campbell, 63 Ill., 462.
(6) McDermaid vs. Russell, 41 Ill., 490.
(7) Sullivan vs. Sullivan, 42 Ill., 315.
(8) Peak vs. Shasted, 21 Ill., 137; Hall vs. Davis, 44 Ill., 494; Quigley vs. Roberts, 44 Ill., 503; Kesler vs. Penninger, 59 Ill., 134; Rhett vs. Mastin, 43 Ala., 86.

for the payment of debts, infant heirs, who have no guardian appearing for them, must be represented by a guardian *ad litem*.(¹)

It is not, however, necessary, where the general guardian petitions for the sale of his ward's real estate, that the court should appoint a guardian *ad litem*,(²) although it was formerly held to be necessary in this state, and such is now the doctrine in some of the states.(³)

A proceeding which divests a minor of an estate in land, is not, necessarily, against his interest, so that he must, in every possible contingency, be made a defendant, and have a guardian to protect his interest. It is only in those special cases arising under the statute, in which he must be made a defendant, and all the evidence affecting him preserved in the record.(⁴)

Every thing must be proved against an infant, and the record must furnish proof to sustain a decree against him.(⁵) Neither a default nor a decree *pro confesso* can be taken against an infant—a guardian *ad litem* should be appointed, who should file an answer, after which the complainant must make full proof whether the answer admits or denies the allegations of the bill.(⁶) And when so appointed, a guardian *ad litem* can not waive any of the rights of infant defendants whom he represents, and when incompetent and illegal evidence is introduced without objection by the guardian, the court is bound to notice and exclude such evidence.(⁷) And it is the special duty of the guardian *ad litem* to submit to the court every question involving the rights of the infants affected by the suit.(⁸)

It is the duty of the court appointing a guardian *ad litem*, to see that a proper defense is made for the infant; and it is error to permit a guardian *ad litem* to withdraw a plea and allow a judgment by default to be entered against the infant.(⁹) The court should require an answer from such guardian, and to enter a final decree

---

(1) Herdman vs. Short, 18 Ill., 59.
(2) Smith vs. Race, 27 Ill., 387; Campbell vs. Harmon, 43 Ill., 19.
(3) Loyd vs. Malone, 23 Ill., 43; Wyatt vs. Mansfield, 18 B. Mon., (Ky.) 779; King vs. Collins, 21 Ala., 363; McAllister vs. Moye, 30 Miss., 258; Payton vs. Freet, 1 Ohio St., 544.
(4) Burger vs. Potter, 32 Ill., 72.   [Ill., 185.
(5) Rhoads vs. Rhoads, 43 Ill., 239; Allman et al. vs. Taylor et al., 101
(6) Enos vs. Capps, 12 Ill., 255; McDaniel vs. Correll, 19 Ill., 226; Quigley vs. Roberts, 44 Ill., 503; Hough vs. Doyle, 8 Blackf., 300.
(7) Cartwright vs. Wise, 14 Ill., 417.
(8) Rhoads vs. Rhoads, *supra*.
(9) Peak vs. Pricer, 21 Ill., 164.

without so doing, is erroneous.(¹) The fact, however, that the guardian *ad litem* of an infant defendant does not answer for the infant, will not deprive the court of jurisdiction over the infant, and render the subsequent proceedings void, while it may be error:(²) for the omission to appoint a guardian *ad litem* or his failure to answer, only renders the judgment voidable, not void.(³)

b. In chancery, infants are always the wards of the court, and where testimony is taken before a master in chancery without notice to the guardian *ad litem* of the infant defendants, it is not admissible as against the infant defendants for want of such notice, notwithstanding the guardian may make no positive objection on the hearing.(⁴) And where testimony was taken in a chancery suit by a person other than the master, and the record failed to disclose his appointment for that purpose, it was held he had no power to take it, and as against the infant, it was rejected, even though the guardian *ad litem* and the infant should consent to the taking of such testimony.(⁵) Where the record shows the appointment, but no motion for such appointment nor prayer therefor in the bill, it was held the court might, *sua sponte*, make the appointment.(⁶)

It will be presumed where the chancellor received the answer of a person as guardian *ad litem*, that he was regularly appointed, although it does not appear of record.(⁷)

Where a person is sued with certain minor defendants in chancery, as their guardian, and appears, answers and defends in that capacity, procuring a reversal of the decree against the minors, upon a second decree being rendered against the minors, it will not be reversed, because the record shows no appointment of a guardian *ad litem*, or proof that such person was in fact guardian.(⁸) Nor will the fact that an answer of a guardian *ad litem*, neither admitting and waiving nothing, but leaving the complainants to prove their bill, was drafted by the solicitor of the complainant, be sufficient ground for reversing a decree.(⁹)

(1) Rhoads vs. Rhoads, 43 Ill., 239.
(2) Goudy vs. Hall, 36 Ill., 313; Gage vs. Shroder, 73 Ill., 44.
(3) Austin vs. Charlestown Female Seminary, 8 Met., (Mass.) 196; Rutter vs. Puckhofer, 9 Bosw., (N. Y.) 638; Peak vs. Shasted, 21 Ill., 137.
(4) Turner vs. Jenkins, 79 Ill., 229; Boyer vs. Boyer, 89 Ill., 447.
(5) Fischer vs. Fischer, 54 Ill., 231.
(6) Rhoads vs. Rhoads, 43 Ill., 239.
(7) Williams vs. Stratton, 10 Sm. & M., 418; Tibbs vs. Allen, 27 Ill., 119.
(8) Tuttle vs. Garrett, 74 Ill., 444.
(9) Hess vs. Voss, 52 Ill., 472.

An order appointing "the clerk of the court" guardian *ad litem*, is sufficient without designating him by name.([1])

A court of equity may appoint the clerk of the court and master in chancery to appear and answer for an infant defendant.([2]) But in some of the states it is held improper to appoint the same person guardian *ad litem* and master in chancery.([3])

The minority of a female ceases at the age of eighteen, and after that age, it is not necessary to appoint a guardian *ad litem* for a female defendant over the age of eighteen and under twenty-one years of age.([4])

c. The appointment of a guardian *ad litem* for a party to a suit, is conclusive evidence of his infancy for that purpose alone, and does not affect the question of infancy which may be raised subsequently by the proper plea.([5])

d. Where it is necessary, a guardian *ad litem* may employ counsel, and the court will allow a reasonable sum for his charges and expenditures in defending the interest of his wards, infant defendants, and tax the same as costs. Such costs must be taxed against the person at whose instance the appointment was made, and must be taxed in the original suit while it is still pending, and can not be made after the case has been disposed of and gone off the docket. And a guardian *ad litem* appointed to defend the infant, who incurs reasonable expenses, should be reimbursed, and for that purpose, may have a guardian appointed by the county court, and recover the same in the usual mode against such guardian, and collect it out of the minor's estate.([6])

(1) Hess vs. Voss, 52 Ill., 472.
(2) Muir vs. Stewart, 1 Murph., (N. C.) 440.
(3) Walker vs. Hallett, 1 Ala., 379; McVicker vs. Constable, Hopk., (N. Y.) 102.
(4) Kester vs. Stark, 19 Ill., 328; Bursden vs. Goodspeed, 60 Ill., 277.
(5) Peak vs. Pricer, 21 Ill., 164.
(6) Smith vs. Smith, 69 Ill., 308.

ADDITIONAL NOTES.

1. Infant—Who may prosecute and defend suits for infants.
2. Testamentary guardian should give bond and be commissioned, when.
3. Bond for costs in suit in behalf of a minor—When it may be filed.
4. Public guardians—Appointment—Term of office.
5. Oath of a public guardian.
6. Failure of guardian to qualify—Public guardian shall act.
7. Powers and duties of the public guardian.
8. Of the public guardian—Bond.

1. INFANT—WHO MAY PROSECUTE AND DEFEND SUITS FOR INFANTS.—Ordinarily the statutory guardian is the proper person to represent his ward in suits and all legal proceedings, and he should do so unless some good reason shall appear to the contrary. This must be adjudged by the court wherein the proceedings are instituted. But the court may appoint or allow some other person to appear as next friend for a minor. Such person, however, should be one entirely suitable, and there should clearly be no conflicting interests between the infant and the party representing him.(1) A father claiming as tenant by the curtesy is not a proper person to act as the next friend of his infant child.(2)

2. TESTAMENTARY GUARDIAN SHOULD GIVE BOND AND BE COMMISSIONED.—The statute authorizing a parent to appoint a testamentary guardian for the custody and education of the minor, and the custody of the property belonging to the minor's estate, does not dispense with the necessity of entering into a bond, to be approved by the county court, and the receiving a commission to act. This may be dispensed with by will, but unless it is, the appointee will not become the guardian of the minor until bond is approved and the guardian named commissioned. And where one has been named as executor, and also as guardian by the will, until he has been discharged as executor and qualified as guardian by giving bond, and receiving his commission, he will be liable as an executor, and not as a guardian.(3) The county court, however, has equitable jurisdiction in the settle-

(1) Patterson vs. Pullman, 104 Ill., 80.
(2) *Ib.*
(3) Wadsworth vs. Connell, 104 Ill., 369.

ment of claims and of estates, and if one appointed by will as executor and also as testamentary guardian qualifies only in the former capacity, so that he is not the legal guardian, nevertheless acts as the guardian by loaning the funds of the estate, he may in equity be held liable as the guardian, should a loss occur.(¹)

3. BOND FOR COSTS IN SUIT IN BEHALF OF A MINOR—WHEN IT MAY BE FILED.—An action brought by the next friend of an infant without an order of appointment or the filing of a bond for costs, will not be dismissed if such bond be given when ordered by the court. The giving of a bond for costs is not a jurisdictional matter.(²)

4. PUBLIC GUARDIAN—APPOINTMENT—TERM OF OFFICE.— That the governor of this state, by and with the advice and consent of the senate, shall, before the first Monday in December, Eighteen hundred and eighty-nine, and every four years thereafter, appoint in each county in this state, and as often as any vacancies may occur, a suitable person, to be known as public guardian of such county, who shall hold his office for four years from the first Monday of December, Eighteen hundred and eighty-nine, or until his successor is appointed and qualified.(³)

5. OATH.—Every person appointed as a public guardian shall, before entering upon the duties of his office, take and subscribe and file in the office of the clerk of the county court the following oath, to-wit:(⁴)

FORM OF OATH OF A PUBLIC GUARDIAN.

I do solemnly swear [or affirm, as the case may be] that I will support the constitution of the United States and the constitution of the State of Illinois, and that I will faithfully discharge the duties of public guardian of ....county, according to the best of my ability.

6. FAILURE OF GUARDIAN TO QUALIFY—PUBLIC GUARDIAN TO ACT.—Whenever any guardian, appointed under the provisions of section three (3) of the act entitled "An act in regard to guardians and wards," approved April 10th, 1872, in force July 1, 1872, shall fail to qualify as such guardian at the expiration of three months from his or her appointment, it shall be the duty of the court

---

(1) Wadsworth vs. Connell, 104 Ill., 369.
(2) The Ill. Cen. R. R. Co. vs. Latimer, 128 Ill., 163; *Ib.*, 28 Ill. Ap., 552; Kingsbury vs. Buckner, 134 U. S., 650.
(3) Hurd's R. S., § 53, 787.
(4) *Ib.*, § 54.

to appoint the public guardian of the county where the minor resides as guardian of the minor.(¹)

7. POWERS—DUTIES.—The public guardian, when appointed by the court, as provided in this act, shall have the same powers and his duties shall be the same as of guardians appointed under the provisions of section three (3) of the act entitled "An act in regard to guardians and wards," approved April 10, 1872, in force July 1, 1872.(²)

8. BOND.—It shall be the duty of the county court to require of the public guardian, before entering upon the duties of his office, to enter into a bond, payable to the People of the State of Illinois, in a sum of not less than five thousand dollars, with two or more securities, approved by the court, and conditioned that he will faithfully discharge all the duties of his office; and the court may, from time to time, as occasion may require, demand additional security of such guardian, and may require him to give the usual bond required of guardians in other cases; and in default of giving such bond within sixty days after receiving his commission, or in default of giving additional security within such time as the court may fix, after being duly ordered by said court so to do, his office shall be deemed vacant, and upon the certificate of the county judge of such fact, the governor shall fill the vacancy aforesaid.(³)

(1) Hurd's R. S., § 55, 787.
(2) *Ib.*, § 56.
(3) *Ib.*, § 57; Laws of Illinois, 1889, 165.

CHAPTER II.

APPOINTMENT OF GUARDIANS.

1. Appointment—jurisdiction.
    a. Form of a petition for the appointment of a guardian.
    b. Appointment—hearing.
    c. Custody—estate.
2. Nomination by the court—jurisdiction.
    a. Nomination by minor.
    b. Form of a nomination of guardian.
    c. Form of a nomination by minor having attained the age of fourteen, having previously had a guardian appointed by the court.
    d. Representation—minor being over fourteen without guardian—form.
    e. Citation to minor—form.
    f. Service and return.
    g. Who are orphans, and who eligible as guardians.
    h. Parents not being fit and competent—form—hearing.
3. Testamentary guardians.
4. Guardian's bond.
    a. Of its execution.
    b. Form of a guardian's bond.
    c. Filing and approval.
    d. Without bond appointment void.
    e. When appointment void.
    f. Requisites of bond.
    g. Liability of securities—actions thereon.
5. Letters of guardianship—form.
6. Record of appointment.
    a. Final order on petition for appointment—form.
    b. Final order on nomination—form.
7. Review of the appointment.

1. APPOINTMENT—JURISDICTION.—The county courts in their respective counties may, when it shall appear necessary or convenient, appoint guardians to minors, inhabitants of or residents in the same county, and to such as reside out of this state, and have an estate within the same, in the county where the real estate or some part thereof may lie; or if he has no real estate, then in any county where he may have personal property.[1]

(1) Hurd's R. S Chap. 64, § 2.

a. The appointment is made usually upon the petition of some one interested in behalf of the minor; and may be in form as follows:

PETITION FOR THE APPOINTMENT OF A GUARDIAN.

STATE OF ILLINOIS, } ss. *In the County Court,*
...............County. }   *To the........term,* A. D. 18...

To the Hon..........Judge of the County Court of said County:

Your petitioner, A B, of the county of......, and State of Illinois, would respectfully represent that C D, departed this life on the...day of......, A. D. 18..., and that E D, his widow, departed this life on the...day of......, A. D. 18... That the said C D and E D, left surviving them, G D and H D, who are minors, aged respectively as follows, to-wit:

The said G D, being...years of age on the...day of......, A. D. 18..., and the said H D, being aged...years on the...day of......, A. D. 18..., and that said minors are both residents of this county. That said minors have no testamentary or other legal guardian residing in this State.

Your petitioner would further represent, that said minors own the following described real estate, as tenants in common, situate, lying and being in the county of......, and State of Illinois, and known and described as follows, to-wit: [.........] The yearly rental value of which your petitioner believes to be......dollars; and personal estate consisting of notes, mortgages, live stock and other property amounting in value to.........dollars.

Your petitioner would represent that he is the uncle of said minors, and desires the appointment as their guardian upon his giving bond as provided by law. And your petitioner as he is in duty bound will ever pray, etc.

By.........Attorney.   A B.

STATE OF ILLINOIS, } ss.
...............County. }

A B, being duly sworn, deposes and says that the facts averred in the above petition are true, according to the best of his knowledge, information and belief.   A B.

Sworn to and subscribed before me............, Clerk of the County Court of......County, this...day of......, A. D. 18..
                                                    ...., Clerk.

b. Upon application being made for the appointment of a guardian, unless the proper persons are before it, the court shall assign a day for the hearing thereof, and direct such notice of the hearing to be given to the relatives of the minor, residing in the county, as he shall, on due inquiry, think reasonable.([1])

c. The father of the minor if living, and in case of his death, the mother, they being respectively competent to transact their own business, and fit persons, shall be entitled to the custody of the person of the minor and the care of his education. In case the father

---

(1) Hurd's R. S., Chap. 64, § 10.

and mother shall live apart, the court may, for good reason, award the custody and education of the minor to the mother or other proper person.(¹)

2. NOMINATION BY THE COURT—JURISDICTION.—If a minor is under the age of fourteen, the county court may nominate and appoint his guardian.(²) But, in order to give the court jurisdiction, so as to authorize the appointment of a guardian for a minor, such minor must, at the time of the appointment, have an actual or constructive residence in the county.(³) In this case, it was held, that the residence of the mother, (the father being dead,) drew to it in law, that of the minor under fourteen years of age, although he was, at the time in another state, at service, to which the mother had undertaken to bind him.(⁴)

a. After the age of fourteen, the ward is entitled to choose a guardian at common law, and generally by statute.(⁵) His choice is subject, however to the rejection of the court for good reason, when he is entitled to choose again.(⁶) A court should always refuse to sanction an unwise or improvident selection.(⁷) For it is the duty of the court, in appointing a guardian, to consult the interest rather than the wishes of an infant.(⁸) The best interests of the minor alone are to be consulted, and the court is not restricted in his appointment to the relatives. A stranger, who is competent, may be appointed;(⁹) though the parental request is of great weight and ought to prevail, unless good reason to the contrary be shown. But the interest of the minor should be the paramount consideration of the probate court.

If the court appoint one before the age of choice, the infant may appear and choose one at that age, without any notice to the guardian appointed.(¹⁰) And if none be chosen, the old one continues to act.(¹¹)

(1) Hurd's R. S., Chap. 64, § 4.
(2) *Ib.*, § 3.
(3) Maxson vs. Sawyer, 12 Ohio, 195; Ware vs. Coleman, 6 J. J. Marsh.,
(4) *Ib.* [(Ky.) 198.
(5) Brown vs. Lynch, 2 Bradf., (N. Y.) 214; Munson vs. Newson, 9 Texas, 109; Sessions vs. Kell, 30 Miss., 458; Reeve Dom. Rel., 320.
(6) Inferior Court vs. Cherry, 14 Ga., 594.
(7) Arthur's Appeal, 1 Grant, (Pa.) 55; Inferior Court vs. Cherry, *supra.*
(8) Compton vs. Compton, 2 Gill., (Md.) 241.
(9) Holley vs. Chamberlain, 1 Redf., (N. Y.) 333; Bennett vs. Byrne, 2 Barb. (N. Y.) Ch., 216; Badenhoof vs. Johnson, 11 Nev. 87; Succession of Fuqua, 27 La., Ann. 271.
(10) Sessions vs. Kell, *supra;* Kelley vs. Smith, 15 Ala., 687.
(11) Dibble vs. Dibble, 8 Ind., 307; Young vs. Lorain, 11 Ill., 624.

Under our statute, if the ward is above the age of fourteen, he may nominate his own guardian, who, if approved by the court, shall be appointed accordingly; if not approved by the court, or if the minor resides out of the state, or if after being cited, he neglects to nominate a suitable person, the court may nominate and appoint his guardian in the same manner as if he was under the age of fourteen years. *Provided*, that in all cases when a guardian has been appointed by the court while the minor was under the age of fourteen years, such minor, on attaining the age of fourteen years, may at his election nominate his own guardian, who shall be appointed by the court if deemed a suitable person, and the new guardian so appointed, shall supercede the former one, whose functions shall thenceforth cease and determine; and it shall be the duty of the former guardian to deliver up to his successor all the goods, chattels, moneys, title papers and other effects belonging to such minor, in like manner and subject to the same penalties as are provided in the fortieth section of this act, upon the removal, death or resignation of a guardian.([1])

b. The nomination may be in form as follows:

NOMINATION OF GUARDIAN.

State of Illinois, } ss.   *In the County Court,*
...............County. }   *To the......term, A. D. 18...*

To the Hon..........., Judge of said Court:

The undersigned would respectfully represent unto your honor, that he is a minor heir of, and entitled to a distributive share in the estate of........., late of said county, deceased. That said estate consists of the following described personal property, viz.: [*Here describe the personal property,*] and real estate described as follows, to-wit: [*Here describe the real estate.*] The yearly rental value of which is......dollars.

That your petitioner was fourteen years of age on the...day of......, A. D. 18..., and elects to nominate as his guardian......, who has consented to act if appointed, and respectfully prays that his nomination may be confirmed by your honorable court, and the said.........be appointed as his guardian upon entering into bond with good and approved security as provided by law.

Attest :...............   ....

d. Where the minor has a guardian appointed for him previous to his arriving at the age of fourteen, the form of nomination may be as follows:

(1) Hurd's R. S., Chap. 64, § 3.

NOMINATION BY MINOR ON ATTAINING THE AGE OF FOURTEEN.

STATE OF ILLINOIS, } ss.   In the County Court,
............County.   To the......term, A. D. 18...

To the Hon.........., Judge of said Court:

The undersigned respectfully represents that he is a minor, and heir of and entitled to a distributive share in the estate of........., late of said county, deceased, amounting in value to......dollars.

That, heretofore, to-wit: on the...day of......, A. D. 18..., the undersigned being then under the age of fourteen years,.........was by this court appointed as his guardian; that, having now attained the age of fourteen years, and being fourteen years of age on the...day of......, A. D. 18..., he elects to nominate his own guardian, and respectfully prays that.........may be by your honorable court appointed as his guardian.

Dated this...day of......, A. D. 18...
                                                                ....
By.........., his Attorney.

e. If the minor neglects to appear and appoint his guardian, it is the duty of the court, upon proper representation being made in writing, to cause a citation to issue for him.

The representation may be in form as follows:

REPRESENTATION—MINOR BEING OVER FOURTEEN WITHOUT GUARDIAN.

STATE OF ILLINOIS, } ss.   In the County Court,
............County.   To the......term, A. D. 18...

To the Hon.........., Judge of said Court:

Your petitioner would respectfully represent unto your honor, that......... and........., are orphan minors above the age of fourteen years, the said .... being aged...years on the...day of......, A. D. 18..., and the said......being aged...years on the...day of......, A. D. 18...; and that they have no legal guardian residing in this State. That they have an estate amounting, as your petitioner believes, to.........dollars, and that it would be to the interest of the said minors, and their welfare requires a guardian appointed for them: Wherefore your petitioner prays that a citation may issue notifying them to be and appear before the......term, A. D. 18..., of this honorable court, and make choice of a guardian as the law directs, and in case of their refusal or neglect so to do, that your honor will cause some suitable person to be appointed for them. And your petitioner will ever pray, etc.

By..........his Attorney.   ....

Subscribed and sworn to, before me this...day of......, A. D. 18..., by the said.........the petitioner in the above petition.
                                        ...., County Clerk.

f. Upon presentation of the petition to the court, it is his duty to examine the same and cause a citation to issue, which may be in form as follows:

CITATION TO MINOR.

STATE OF ILLINOIS, } ss.
..............County.

The People of the State of Illinois, to..........and.........., minors, etc.:

Whereas, it has been represented by ....upon a petition filed herein to the county court of..........county, at its..........term, A. D. 18..., that you the said..........and.........., are orphan minors over the age of fourteen years respectively and have no guardian; therefore, you are hereby cited to be and appear before the county court, at the..........term, A. D. 18..., to be holden at the court house in.........., in said county, and choose a guardian, in default whereof the court will appoint one for you.

Witness my hand and the seal of said court, at.........., in said county, this...day of......, A. D. 18...

[*Seal.*] ...., Clerk County Court.

g. The citation should be given to the officer whose duty it is to serve the same, and then return the same back into the office of the clerk of the county court.

The return of the officer may be in form as follows:

OFFICER'S RETURN.

STATE OF ILLINOIS, } ss.
..............County.

I have duly served the within citation by reading and delivering to..........and.......... each a copy of the same as I am therein commanded.

Dated this...day of......, A. D. 18...

................, Sheriff of..........County, Illinois.

If the minor be under the age of fourteen, no citation is necessary.

A minor over the age of fourteen, may appear in open court and select his guardian; but the better practice is, to file a petition or nomination.

i. The word orphan, in the statute, giving jurisdiction to the probate court to appoint guardians to minors who are orphans, means a fatherless child.[1]

In the appointment of a guardian, the mother, and after her, the next of kin, are entitled to preference, unless shown to be unsuitable.[2]

Coverture is no incapacity for the office of guardian.[3] It

---

(1) Stewart vs. Morrison, 38 Miss., 417; Poston vs. Young, 7 J. J. Marsh., (Ky.) 501.

(2) Albert vs. Perry, 15 N. J. Eq., 1 McCart., 540; Allen vs. Peete, 25 Miss., 29.

(3) Farrer vs. Clark, 29 Miss.. 195.

would seem, however, that a single woman, by her marriage, loses her guardianship, but she may be reappointed.([1])

The guardianship of the infant's estate may be appointed to one, and the custody and tuition of the minor to another.([2])

Where the father of the minor or the mother are not fit persons, or are not competent to transact their own business, it is the duty of the court, upon petition and proof being made to the court of that fact, to appoint some other person.([3])

The relation of parent forms no exclusive claim to the wardship of a child, and it is competent for the county court to set aside such claim in favor of a stranger, if it appear that the parent is unfit for the trust.([4])

Where the parents are not fit persons to have the care and custody of their children and their property, the petition for the appointment of some other person may be in form as follows:

PETITION FOR THE APPOINTMENT OF GUARDIAN—PARENTS NOT BEING FIT AND COMPETENT PERSONS.

STATE OF ILLINOIS, } ss.   *In the County Court,*
...............County,   *To the......term, A. D. 18...*

To the Hon........., Judge of said Court:

Your petitioner........., would respectfully represent and show unto your honor, that one........., late of said county, deceased, by his last will and testament, now of record in this honorable court, reference being made thereto, bequeathed to one........., his nephew, the sum of......dollars. That said.........is a minor aged...years, on the...day of......, A. D. 18..., and has now living one........., his father; but so it is, may it please your honor, the said......... although legally entitled to be appointed the guardian of the said........., is incapacitated and wholly unfit from accepting said appointment by reason of drunkenness and debauchery, he being thereby rendered unfit and incompetent to transact his own business.

And your petitioner would further show unto your honor, that the mother of the said.........is now deceased, and that it is necessary for the said.........to have some suitable person to be appointed as his guardian, in order that he may receive the legacy aforesaid to which he is entitled:

Wherefore, in consideration of the premises aforesaid, your petitioner prays that one........., an uncle to the said........., may be appointed as his guardian, and that the said........., father of the said........., may be notified of this proceeding, and that your honor will also cause a day to be appointed for the hearing thereof. And your petitioner will ever pray, etc.

By........., Attorney.   ....

(1) 2 Kent's Com., 225; Palmer vs. Oakley, 2 Dougl., (Mich.) 433.
(2) Hurd's R. S., Chap. 64, § 6.
(3) *Ib.*, § 4.
(4) Huie vs. Nixon, 6 Port., (Ala.) 77.

STATE OF ILLINOIS, } ss.
................County.

........., who is the petitioner in the foregoing petition, on oath states, that he has heard the same read over, and that the matters and facts stated therein, are true. ....

Subscribed and sworn to before me this...day of......, A. D. 18...
................, Clerk of the County Court.

Upon the petition being filed and presented, the Judge shall cause a day to be assigned for the hearing, and notify the relative of the minor residing in the county as set out in the petition, as he shall, on due inquiry, think reasonable. This can be done by summons or citation, or by written or printed notice. The more preferable manner of giving notice would be in the form of a citation, and the form given before on page 220, form of citation to minor, may be used; it being varied to suit the case.

3. TESTAMENTARY GUARDIANS.—Where a guardian is appointed by will, the appointment gives him authority to act, and it is the duty of the court to grant to him letters of guardianship. As it is from the will he derives his authority to act, upon the probate of the will, his authority is complete. If two persons are appointed testamentary guardians, the office is joint and several, and either may qualify without the other, and without summoning the other to accept or renounce the guardianship.(¹)

If the will provides that the guardian shall not give bond, no bond will be required, otherwise he must conform to the provisions of the statute in regard to giving bond.

4. GUARDIAN'S BOND.—The county court shall take of the guardian appointed by it, a bond, payable to the People of the State of Illinois, with at least two sufficient sureties, to be approved by the court in a reasonable amount, which shall in no case be less than double the amount of the minor's personal estate, and six times the amount of the gross annual income of the minor's real estate: *Provided*, however, that if such real estate is improved, or is covered in whole or in part with timber, or is improved in part and in part covered with timber, the penal sum in said bond shall be increased by an amount at least double the value of the said improvements, or of said timber, or both as the case may be; and said bond shall be conditioned substantially as follows:

(1) Kevan vs. Waller, 11 Leigh, (Va.) 414.

The condition of this obligation is such, that if the above bounden (*name of the guardian*), who has been appointed guardian of (*name of infant*), shall faithfully discharge the office and trust of such guardian according to law, and shall make a true inventory of all the real and personal estate of the ward, that shall come to his possession or knowledge, and return the same unto the cóunty court of.........county, at the time required by law, and manage and dispose of all such estate, according to law, and for the best interest of said ward, and faithfully discharge his trust in relation thereto, and to the custody, nurture and education of said ward, and render an account, on oath, of the property in his hands and of the management and disposition of all such estate, within one year after his appointment, and at such other times as shall be required by law or directed by the court; and upon removal from office, or at the expiration of his trust, settle his accounts in said court, or with the ward or his legal representatives, and pay over and deliver all the estate, title papers and effects remaining in his hands, or due from him on such settlement, to the person or persons lawfully entitled thereto, then this obligation shall be void, otherwise to remain in full force and virtue.(1)

a. When any person shall at the same time be appointed guardian for several minors, the court may, if the estate shall be so situated as to make it more convenient or advantageous to the interest of the ward, include all in one bond.(2) For example: When a part of the minors are old enough to select their own guardian, while others are under the age necessary to make such selection; the one presents the matter to the court by a nomination, while the other is presented by a petition to the court by some relative or friend, asking for the same person to be appointed guardian for the minors under the age necessary to make choice, that has been selected by those who are of sufficient age, and where the court appoints the same person guardian for all of them, one bond is sufficient, and the court may include all in one bond.

b. The guardian's bond may be in form as follows:

GUARDIAN'S BOND.

KNOW ALL MEN BY THESE PRESENTS, That we..........and..........and.........., of the county of.........., and State of Illinois, are held and firmly bound unto the People of the State of Illinois, for the use of..........and.........., in the penal sum of......dollars, which payment well and truly to be made and performed, we and each of us do hereby bind ourselves, our heirs, executors, administrators and assigns jointly, severally and firmly by these presents. Witness our hands and seals, this...day of......, A. D. 18...

The condition of this obligation is such, that if the above bounden.........,

(1) Hurd's R. S., Chap. 64, § 7.
(2) Hurd's R. S., Chap. 64, § 10.

who has been appointed guardian of..........and........., shall faithfully discharge the office and trust of such guardian according to law, and shall make a true inventory of all the real and personal estate of the ward, that shall come to his possession or knowledge, and return the same unto the county court of..........county, at the time required by law, and manage and dispose of all such estate according to law, and for the best interest of said ward, and faithfully discharge his trust in relation thereto, and to the custody, nurture and education of said ward, and render an account, on oath, of the property in his hands and of the management and disposition of all such estate, within one year after his appointment, and at such other times as shall be required by law or directed by the court; and upon removal from office, or at the expiration of his trust, settle his accounts in said court, or with the ward or his legal representatives, and pay over and deliver all the estate, title papers and effects remaining in his hands, or due from him on such settlement, to the person or persons lawfully entitled thereto, then this obligation shall be void, otherwise to remain in full force and virtue.

Signed, sealed and delivered } in presence of
.... [L. S.]
.... [L. S.]
.... [L. S.]

STATE OF ILLINOIS, } ss.
County of............. }

I,........., in and for said county and State, do hereby certify that.......... and........., who are each personally known to me to be the same persons whose names are subscribed to the foregoing instrument, appeared before me this day in person and acknowledged that they signed, sealed and delivered said instrument as their free and voluntary act, for the uses and purposes as therein set forth.

Given under my hand and...seal, this...day of......, A. D. 18...

.................., ...

This bond examined and approved by me, this...day of......, A. D. 18...

.................., Judge of the County Court.

c. The bond should be filed and presented to the court, and if approved, the judge should indorse his approval thereon, and order that letters of guardianship issue to the guardian named therein, and it will be the duty of the clerk of the court to thereupon issue the letters to the guardian duly appointed.

d. The guardian has no power to act as such, or to control the property of his ward, until he has given the bond required by the statute. Letters of guardianship issued to the guardian before such bond is given, confer no such power and have no legal effect whatever.([1])

(1) Carpenter vs Sloane, 20 Ohio 327.

Letters of guardianship need not in fact issue. The guardian derives his power to act from the appointment and bond.([1])

e. While there is a valid guardianship unrevoked, the appointment of another person as guardian of the same minor is void, and a guardian's bond, executed by him and sureties, is a nullity.([2])

f. If the conditions of a bond, though differing from, are not at variance with the requirements of the statute, the bond is valid.([3])

Where a bond was given payable in the wrong name, as in the name of the people, instead of the infant, the court corrected the mistake, and considered the bond as valid as if taken in the name of the infant.([4])

Where a guardian's sale has been examined and confirmed by the court, and the journal entry shows that a bond has been directed, and securities approved, it will be presumed that a bond was executed.([5])

g. The sureties upon the general bond of a guardian are liable for the rents of the lands of the ward leased by the guardian, notwithstanding the statute requires the guardian to give a special bond before leasing the lands of his ward. The giving of the new bond required by the statute, cannot be construed as a release from the ultimate liability of the sureties on the general bond.([6])

A suit on the bond of a guardian, against the sureties, might be maintained without settlement or liquidation by suit or otherwise ascertaining the amount of the liability of the guardian, as a guardian cannot prevent an action on the bond by refusing or failing to render an account.([7]) Whenever he has committed a breach of any of the conditions of the bond, he is liable to an action.([8])

Where an order of the probate court is made, directing the guardian to pay over to his successor a certain amount found due in his hands belonging to the ward, it is conclusive upon the guardian, unless the order can be impeached for fraud or collusion. And where a guardian was required to give supplemental security on his

---

(1) Maxon vs. Sawyer, 12 Ohio, 195.
(2) Thomas vs. Burrus, 23 Miss., 550.
(3) Probate Court vs. Strong, 27 Vt., 202.
(4) Wiser vs. Blachly, 1 Johns. Ch., (N. Y.) 607.
(5) Maxson vs. Sawyer, *supra.*
(6) Wann vs. The People, 57 Ill., 202.
(7) State vs. Humphreys, 7 Ohio, 223; Wann vs. The People, *supra:*
(8) Wann vs. The People, *supra.*   [Bonham vs. People, 102 Ill., 434.

bond, already executed, and the security signed and sealed the former bond, by so signing, he became liable as an original obligor, and his liability will be the same as if he had signed the bond with the other parties at the same time they signed it.([1])

A claim against a guardian's estate, for moneys coming into his hands belonging to his wards, is not barred within five years after the majority of the wards. The claim will not be barred so long as an action may be brought upon the guardian's bond, to enforce its recovery;([2]) and the limitation runs only from the time the cause of action accrues, and not from the date of the bond.([3])

The liability of a surety upon a guardian's bond, before breach in the condition of the bond, is a conditional liability, within the meaning of the second clause of section 19 of the Bankrupt law of March 2d, 1867, and a discharge in bankruptcy, releases the surety from such liability.([4]) As the liability of a surety upon a guardian's bond is not a debt, created by him whilst acting in a fiduciary character, within the meaning of the exception of the Bankrupt Act, which provides that no debt created by the fraud or embezzlement of the bankrupt, or by his defalcation in a public office, or while acting in a fiduciary capacity, shall be discharged under the act.([5])

Bonds may be put in suit in the name of the people of the State of Illinois, to the use of any person entitled to recover on a breach thereof, and damages assessed and proceedings had thereon, as in other cases of penal bonds.([6])

The bond of a guardian covers property received by him in another state.([7])

Where a bond of the guardian was held void at law on the ground that the sureties were justices of the county, and therefore both obligors and obligees, the bond was enforced in equity.([8])

Until the removal of a guardian from his trust, a suit will not be authorized by his infant wards on his bond for the recovery of money in his hands.([9])

(1) Ammons vs. The People, 11 Ill., 6.
(2) Scheel vs. Eidman, 77 Ill., 301.
(3) Bonham vs. People, 102 Ill., 434.
(4) Reitz vs. The People, 72 Ill., 435; Jones vs. Knox, 46 Ala., 53; Amoskeag Mfg. Co. vs. Barnes, 49 N. H., 312; Bowie vs. Puckett, 7 Humph., (Tenn.) 169.
(5) *Ib.*
(6) Hurd's R. S., Chap. 64, § 11.
(7) McDonald vs. Meadows, 1 Metc., (Ky.) 507.
(8) Butler vs. Durham, 3 Ired., (N. C.) 589.
(9) Ely vs. Hawkins, 15 Ind., 230.

Although an order of the county court appointing a guardian, may by mistake recite the name of the ward incorrectly, yet, a bond taken according to the proper requisitions, with the correct name recited, will be sustained as an official bond.(1)

A probate bond is not to be avoided for slight defects committed through carelessness or error. An instrument intended as a guardian's bond will be sustained, although the names of the wards are recited in the wrong place.(2) So, too, if a guardian's bond contains more than the statute requires, it is not thereby invalidated. And it is valid if it does not recite the fact of his appointment. And if the condition relates to only a part of his duty, it is not void, but is valid to the extent of the condition.(3) And although a guardian's bond be inartificially drawn, it will not thereby be invalidated.(4)

It is made the duty of the judge of the county court, at the January and July terms of the court in each year, to inquire into the sufficiency of guardians' bonds, and to require from such as are found not to have good security, new bonds. Guardians failing to comply with the order, may be removed.(5)

For further authorities on the subject of guardian's bond, see Chapter XII, *post.*, on the rights and liabilities of sureties on a guardian's bond; and Chapter III, part I, upon the liabilities under the bonds of executors and administrators.

5. LETTERS OF GUARDIANSHIP.—The steps necessary to be taken in the appointment of a guardian are few, and usually nothing need be done, but file the petition or nomination; present it to the judge; have it approved; ascertain the amount of bond required; procure and fill out a bond with two good and sufficient securities, sign it and have them sign it; file and present it to the court; have it approved, and then obtain from the clerk of the court your letters of guardianship, which may be in form as follows:

LETTERS OF GUARDIANSHIP.

STATE OF ILLINOIS, } ss. *In the County Court,*
............County. } ss. To the......term, A. D. 18...

The People of the State of Illinois, To..........,of said County—Greeting:

Whereas, at the......term of the county court of said........ county, A. D.

(1) State vs. Perkins, 1 Jones, (N. C.) 325.
(2) State vs. Martin, 69 N. C., 175.
(3) Pratt vs. Wright, 13 Gratt., (Va.) 175.
(4) Probate Court vs. Strong, 27 Vt., 202; Alston vs. Alston, 34 Ala., 15.
(5) Hurd's R. S., Chap. 103, § 4; *ante* page 29.

18..., holden at.........., you were, by order of said court, duly entered of record on the...day of said month duly appointed guardian for.........., aged...years, on the...day of......, A. D. 18..., and.........., aged...years, on the...day of......, A. D. 18...

Trusting in your fidelity, therefore, the said court does, by these presents, constitute and appoint you to be guardian unto said minors, and authorize and empower you to take and have the care of their persons and the custody and management of their property, and frugally, without waste or destruction, to improve and account for the same in all things according to law.

                Witness,..........., Clerk of the County Court of..........County,
[*Seal.*]   and the seal of said court, this...day of......, A. D. 18...
                              ...., Clerk of the County Court.

6. RECORD OF APPOINTMENT.—After issuing the letters of guardianship, the clerk of the court makes up the record of the appointment, which may be in form as follows:

    a.   FINAL ORDER APPOINTING GUARDIAN.

STATE OF ILLINOIS, } *ss.*   *In the County Court, In Probate,*
................County.   ......*term, A. D.* 18...

Present: *Hon..........Judge,*   Attest: ....*Clerk.*

In the matter of the guardianship
    of..........and.........., minor heirs } Appointment of Guardian.
    of........., deceased.

And now on this day, the same being the...judicial day of the present term of this court, comes the said.........., by.........., his attorney, and files and presents his petition herein to the court, and asks that a guardian may be appointed for..........and.........., minor heirs of.........., deceased.

That the said..........is aged...years, on the....day of......, A. D. 18..., and the said..........is aged...years, on the...day of......, A. D. 18..., and that said minors have no guardian residing in this State.

And it appearing to the court from the evidence adduced, that all the facts alleged in said petition are true, and that the said ....is the uncle of the said minors and a suitable person to have the estate, custody, education and maintenance of said minors, It is ordered, That the said..........be appointed guardian of the person and estate of the said..........and.........., upon his entering in bond in the sum of......dollars, with at least two good and sufficient securities to be approved by the court as provided by law.

And now again comes the said........., and presents to the court his bond for the approval of the same, with......, ...and......, as his sureties thereon, and the court having examined the same, and being now sufficiently advised and satisfied in the premises concerning said bond and the sufficiency of the sureties thereon, It is ordered, That the same be approved and filed, and that letters of Guardianship be issued to the said.......... the guardian duly appointed.

b. FINAL ORDER—NOMINATION MADE BY MINOR HAVING ATTAINED THE AGE OF FOURTEEN.

STATE OF ILLINOIS, } ss. *In the County Court, In Probate,*
.... County. ......*term, A. D.* 18...

Present: *Hon..........Judge.* Attest: ....*Clerk.*

In the matter of the guardianship of.........., minor heir of.........., deceased. } Nomination of Guardian.

And now on this day, the same being the...judicial day of the present term, of this court, comes the said.........., by.........., his attorney, and files and presents his nomination herein to the court, nominating.........., to be his guardian, and asks that said nomination may be confirmed.

And the court having examined the same, finds that each and every allegation thereof is true, viz.: That..........is a minor heir of ...., deceased, and entitled to a distributive share in his estate, and that he is aged fourteen years on the...day of......, A. D. 18...; and that..........; the person whom he has nominated to be his guardian, is a suitable person to have the care of the person and estate of the..........

It is therefore ordered, That said nomination be confirmed, and that.......... be required to enter into bond, with at least two good and sufficient sureties, in the penal sum of......dollars, as provided by law.

And now again comes the said.........., ..., and presents to the court his bond for the approval of the same, with......, ...and......, as his sureties thereon, and the court having examined the same, and being now sufficiently advised and satisfied in the premises concerning said bond and the sufficiency of the sureties thereon, It is ordered, That the same be approved and filed, and that letters of guardianship issue to the said.........., the guardian duly appointed.

7. REVIEW.—Error in the appointment of a guardian, can only be reversed in a direct proceeding on the appointment.([1])

The probate judge is invested with a sound legal discretion in the appointment of guardians, and his judgment should not be overruled, except in cases of manifest error, or abuse of such discretion.([2])

A mere stranger, with no allegation of relationship, or present or prospective interest in the property, cannot appeal from an order appointing a guardian.([3]) Where one procured the appointment of

---

(1) Speight vs. Knight, 11 Ala., 461; Tutorship of Hughes, 13 La. An., 380; Fitts vs. Fitts, 21 Texas, 511.
(2) Sadler vs. Rose, 18 Ark., 600; Wynne vs. Always, 1 Murphey, (N. C.) 38.
(3) Rorbuck vs. Van Blarcom, 20 N. J. Eq., 461.

a guardian for the minor, without the consent or knowledge of the father of such minor, for the purpose of secretly obtaining title to the minor's land, for his own benefit, the proceedings were held to be a fraud upon the minor's rights.([1]) Where a minor selects his guardian, and the probate judge in his discretion, refuses to appoint the person so selected, the right of appeal is allowed. For, if the person chosen by the minor, is an unobjectionable person, the minor has a right to have him appointed, and the refusal of the judge to approve the choice made, must be founded on sufficient reason, and his decision is reviewable.([2])

(1) Tong vs. Marvin, 26 Mich., 35.
(2) Adam's Appeal, 38 Conn., 304.

ADDITIONAL NOTES.

1. County court may appoint guardian.
2. Guardian appointed in one state no authority over property in another.
3. County court may remove guardian fraudulently appointed.

1. COUNTY COURT MAY APPOINT GUARDIAN.—The domicile of the infant is the fittest place for the appointment of a guardian of his person and his estate, but for the protection of either, a guardian may be appointed in any state where the person or any property may be found.([1])

2. GUARDIAN APPOINTED IN ONE STATE NO AUTHORITY IN ANOTHER.—But a guardian in one state has no authority over the property in another state, except by the comity of the latter.([2])

3. COUNTY COURT MAY REMOVE GUARDIAN FRAUDULENTLY APPOINTED.—Should there be a fraudulent suppression of facts in making an application for the appointment of a guardian, or any fraud or misrepresentation used, the county court may properly vacate its order, and declare such appointment void *ab initio*, where the rights of third persons have not intervened.([3])

(1) Lamar vs. Micou, 112 U. S., 452.
(2) *Ib.*
(3) Pease vs. Roberts, 16 Ill. Ap., 634.

CHAPTER III.

THE INVENTORY.

1. Inventory.
    a. What it should contain.
    b. Form of an inventory of guardian.
    c. Filing and approval.

1. INVENTORY.—The guardian shall, within sixty days after his appointment, or, if the court is not in session at the expiration of that time, at the next term thereafter, return to the court a true and perfect inventory of the real and personal estate of the ward, signed by him and verified by his affidavit. As often as other estate shall thereafter come to his knowledge, he shall return an inventory thereof, within sixty days from the time the same shall come to his knowledge.([1])

a. The inventory shall describe the real estate, its probable value and rental, and state whether the same is incumbered, and if incumbered, how, and for how much; what amount of money is on hand; and contain a list of all personal property, including annuities and credits of the ward, designating them as "good," "doubtful," or "desperate," as the case may be.([2])

b. The inventory of a guardian may be in form as follows:

INVENTORY BY GUARDIAN.

STATE OF ILLINOIS, } ss.
...............County.

In the matter of the Guardianship of ....., minor heir of......, deceased.

The following is a full, true and perfect inventory of all the Real and Personal estate of the said Minor, so far as the same has come to the possession or knowledge of the undersigned........., by appointment of this Court Guardian of said minor:

Description of Real Estate.	Value.		Probable Rental.	
	Dolls.	Cts.	Dolls.	Cts.
The North-west quarter of Section 8, Township 7, North of Range 10 west, situated in the County of......, State of Illinois, ... Said real estate is incumbered by a mortgage of $1000.00 to........., dated......day of......A. D. 18..., and due in two years after date with interest at......per cent. The interest being paid up to......day of......A. D. 18....	2500	00		00

(1) Hurd's R. S., Chap. 64, § 12.
(2) *Ib.*, § 13.

No.	Chattel Property.	Value.	
	Cash on hand, ...	$600	00
	One horse, five years old, ...	100	00
	One buggy, ...	150	00

ANNUITIES AND CREDITS.

By Whom Owing,	Date.	Interest.	Good.	Doubtful.	Desperate	Amount.	
James Gaines, ... Said note is due in two years after date, and has credited one year's interest. $50.00, the interest payable annually, Balance due, . .	Jan. 1, '77.	10 per ct.	"			$500	00
John Jackson, ... Due one day after date, with a credit of $25.00. Balance due, . .	June 1, '77.	6 per ct.	"			450	00

.........., guardian as aforesaid, being duly sworn, deposes and says, that the above is a true and correct inventory of all the real and personal estate of.........., a minor heir of.........., deceased, so far as the same has come to my possession or knowledge, and that I believe the foregoing to be a fair and just valuation of the same.

............, Guardian of............

Subscribed and sworn to before me this...day of......, A. D. 18...

............, Clerk of the County Court

c. The inventory should be filed in the office of the clerk of the county court, within sixty days from the issuing of the letters of guardianship, and presented to the court for its approval. The court should examine and approve the same, if found in form and correct, and the clerk should enter up an order of its approval; which may be in form as follows:

STATE OF ILLINOIS, } ss.
..............County. }
In the County Court, In Probate,
.. ...term, A. D. 18...

Present: Hon..........Judge. Attest: ....Clerk.

In the matter of the Guardianship
of.........., minor heir of..........,
deceased. } Order on Inventory.

And now on this day, the same being the...judicial day of the present term of this court, comes the said.........., by.........., his attorney, and presents his inventory of the real and personal estate of the said minor, so far as the same has come to his possession or knowledge; and the court having examined the same, and being now sufficiently advised concerning thereof, It is ordered, That the said inventory be approved, filed and recorded.

Where a guardian was indebted to his ward's estate for money received from it prior to his appointment as guardian, he should enter it in his inventory as a part of his ward's estate.(¹) One of the first duties of a guardian judicially appointed, is the filing of an inventory of the estate of his ward.

Much that has herein been said of the inventories of executors and administrators—of their office as evidence for any party interested, and their judicial uses—may be applied with equal force to the inventories of guardians.(²)

(1) Neill vs. Neill, 31 Miss., 36.
(2) See page 58, *ante*.

CHAPTER IV.

POWERS, DUTIES AND LIABILITIES OF GUARDIANS.

1. Power in the management of his ward's estate.
2. Power to appear for ward in suits.
3. Power to lease his ward's real estate.
4. Power to remove wards.
5. Duty with respect to ward's property.
6. Duty to loan the funds of his ward.
7. Duty to educate his ward.
8. Liability for money received.
9. Liability for ward's property.
10. Liability upon contracts.
11. Liability for negligence.

1. POWER IN THE MANAGEMENT OF HIS WARD'S ESTATE.—The relation of a guardian to his wards, is that of a trustee in equity, and bailiff at law.([1]) And it is a trust which cannot be assigned.([2])

The general rule of the law is, that a trust cannot be delegated; and the exception to this rule, that a power coupled with an interest will authorize the delegation of the trust, by making an attorney, does not include a guardian.([3]) He is the mere agent of his ward, having an authority not coupled with an interest.([4])

His possession of the property of his ward is not such as gives him a personal interest, being only for the purpose of agency; but for the benefit of his ward he has a very general power over it. He manages and disposes of the personal property at his own discretion, although it is proper for him to obtain the authority of the court for any important measure.([5])

He is bound to manage in person the estate of his ward;([6]) and it is his duty to get possession and control of his ward's personal property, and the rents and profits of his real estate; to keep and protect the same; to keep it invested, and to render a just and true

---

(1) Brown vs. Anderson, 2 Md., 111.
(2) Parsons on Contracts, 137.
(3) Mason vs. Wait, 4 Scam., 127.
(4) Manson vs. Felton, 13 Pick., (Mass.) 206.
(5) Parsons on Contracts, 134.
(6) Eichelberger's Appeal, 4 Watts, (Pa.) 84.

account thereof, on the ward's becoming of age.(¹) His acts will be sustained if beneficial to his ward, even though they be unauthorized by his guardianship.(²) But he can do no act to the injury of his ward.(³)

He may petition the probate court, in his own name to obtain possession of the estate of his ward;(⁴) or, for distribution to be made of the estate belonging to his ward.(⁵)

He has the right to redeem his ward's estate from a mortgage sale.(⁶)

He has no authority to appoint an attorney to execute a deed,(⁷) nor has he the power to release a debt due to his ward's estate.(⁸)

At common law he was required to take possession of his ward's property, and he was not only liable for such property as actually came into his possession, but for such as he might have taken possession of by the exercise of diligence and without any willful default on his part. So, in regard to the rents and profits of the ward's real estate, and the income from every species of his property, the guardian was chargeable with what he actually received, and with what he might have received had he faithfully discharged his duties.(⁹)

A guardian undertakes to be vigilant, faithful and competent; and these qualifications imply as much knowledge of law as may be necessary for the proper exercise of his duties;(¹⁰) but, he is only bound to use such care and diligence in keeping his trust fund as a prudent man uses in keeping his own funds.(¹¹)

The rights and powers of guardians are purely local, and they are not entitled to exercise any authority over the person or personal property of their wards in other states.(¹²)

Where the ward is in the habit of harboring persons of bad and vicious character about his premises, the guardian is authorized to

(1) White vs. Parker, 8 Barb., (N. Y.) 48.
(2) Capehart vs. Huey, 1 Hill, (S. C. Ch.) 405.
(3) Torrey vs. Black, 65 Barb., (N. Y.) 417; Jackson vs. Sears, 10 Johns., (N. Y.) 435.
(4) Keith vs. Jolly, 26 Miss., 131.
(5) Gammage vs. Noble, 24 Miss., 150.
(6) Marvin vs. Schilling, 12 Mich., 356.
(7) Mason vs. Wait, 4 Scam., 127.
(8) Horine vs. Horine, 11 Mo., 649.
(9) Bond vs. Lockwood, 33 Ill., 212.
(10) Hempbill vs. Lewis, 7 Bush., (Ky.) 214.
(11) Atkinson vs. Whitehead, 66 N. C., 296.
(12) Leonard vs. Putnam, 51 N. H., 247.

warn such persons to leave the premises, and, on their refusal, to cause them to be moved.(¹)

He has authority to accept delivery of a deed of conveyance to his ward.(²)

2. POWER TO APPEAR FOR WARD IN SUITS.—He shall appear for and represent his ward in all legal suits and proceedings, unless another person is appointed for that purpose, as guardian or next friend; but nothing contained in this act shall impair or affect the power of any court or justice of the peace to appoint a guardian to defend the interest of a minor impleaded in such court interested in a suit or matter therein pending, nor their power to appoint or allow any person, as next friend for a minor, to commence, prosecute or defend any suit in his behalf. *Provided*, that any suit or proceeding may be commenced and prosecuted by any minor by his next friend, without any previous authority or appointment by the court, on such next friend entering into bond for costs, and filing the bond in the court in which, or with the justice of the peace, before whom such suit or proceeding is instituted.(³)

An infant is not always bound to appear in a court of chancery by a guardian, although one may be in existence. He may file her bill by his next friend, and if an objection is taken in proper time, that there is a guardian, by whom the bill should have been filed, it may be that the court, in the exercise of a sound discretion, may determine whether the suit shall so proceed, or in the name of the guardian.(⁴)

The right of action for service rendered by a minor, is in the parent or guardian.(⁵)

An action on the case for seduction, may be maintained by the parent, guardian, master, or other person standing in *loco parentis*, for debauching the daughter, ward or servant. And if the person seduced is a minor, the action will be sustained, whether the minor resides with the plaintiff at the time of the seduction or elsewhere, if the minor be legally under the control of, or might be required to perform services for the plaintiff.(⁶)

(1) Wood vs. Gale, 10 N. H., 247.
(2) Barney vs. Seeley, 38 Wis., 381.
(3) Hurd's R. S., Chap. 64, ¿ 18, as amended by act 1881, Sess. Laws, p. 98.
(4) Holmes vs. Fields, 12 Ill., 424.
(5) Dufield vs. Cross, 12 Ill., 397; Parmalee vs. Smith, 21 Ill., 620.
(6) Ball vs. Bruce, 21 Ill., 161; White vs. Murtland, 71 Ill., 250.

3. POWER TO LEASE HIS WARD'S REAL ESTATE.—The guardian may lease the real estate of the ward upon such terms and for such length of time not extending beyond the minority of the ward, as the county court shall approve.([1])

A guardian in socage has the custody of the lands of the infant, and for that reason, may lease it, avow in his own name and bring trespass or ejectment in his own name.([2]) But, under the provisions of our statute, he can not exercise any such power. Where a general guardian has been appointed under our laws, with a defined statutory control over the estate of the wards, there can be no such relation as guardian in socage.([3])

When a guardian, with a view of preserving an estate unimpaired until the heirs become of age, leases for a less sum than could be obtained from ordinary yearly rents, first securing the approval of the probate court, and acts in manifest good faith, he is not liable for having failed to secure higher rent. A rule which would subject a guardian to a sort of a fine for a mere error of judgment, is inapplicable to the character of the office.([4])

While the guardian may lease the real estate of his ward, with the consent of the probate court, not to extend, however, beyond the time of his guardianship,([5]) he cannot be held liable by the lessee upon implied covenants, should he lease the lands of his ward, using the ordinary terms of demise, without complying with the provisions of the statute for the execution of such lease.([6]) A lease of real estate belonging to a minor, by his guardian, for a term not exceeding the date of the ward's majority, is valid, unless disapproved by the county court. The approval of that court is not essential to the validity of the lease.([7])

It is his duty to institute proceedings for the assignment of dower, and after such assignment, to lease whatever portion of the land set apart to his ward.([8])

(1) Hurd's R. S., Chap. 64, § 23.
(2) Hughes' Minor's Appeal, 53 Penn. St., 500; 2 Kent's Com., 228;
(3) Muller vs. Benner, 69 Ill., 108. [Holmes vs. Seele, 17 Wend., 75.
(4) McElheny vs. Mussick, 63 Ill., 328.
(5) Muller vs. Benner, *supra;* Bacon vs. Taylor, Kirby, (Conn.) 368; Huff vs. Walker, 1 Ind., 193; Snook vs. Sutton, 5 Halst., 133; Field vs. Schieffelin, 7 Johns. Ch., 150; Putnam vs. Ritchie, 6 Paige, (N. Y.) 390; Ross
(6) Webster vs. Conly, 46 Mo., 13. [vs. Gill, 1 Wash., (Va.) 87.
(7) Fuld vs. Herrick, 101 Ill., 110.
(8) Clark vs. Burnside, 15 Ill., 62.

4. POWER TO REMOVE WARDS.—He may change the residence of his ward from one state or county to another, if it be beneficial to the ward;(1) but he cannot take advantage of a change in his ward's domicile, brought about by his own illegal acts, if indeed it be any change in law.(2)

Whether he has a right to remove his wards into a foreign jurisdiction, has been a disputed question. By the common law, his authority both over the person and property of his ward, was strictly local.(3) And this view is maintained in many of the states.(4)

The domicile of the parents fixes that of the minors, and should the parent die, his last domicile fixes that of his infant child. And the guardian cannot change the domicile acquired by the ward at the place of his birth, or derived from his parents at their death.(5)

The term domicile has a more extensive signification than the term residence. In addition to residence, it embraces within its meaning, the intention of making the residence the home of the party.(6) And a domicile, when once acquired, continues till a new one is gained. While in transit, the old domicile remains.(7) A conditional removal from one state to another, will not lose the residence of the party removing. There must be intention and acts united to effect a change of domicile.(8) While the weight of authority seems to be that a guardian may change the residence of his ward from one state or county to another if it benefit the ward,(9) the new county may, however, appoint another guardian.(10)

5. DUTY WITH RESPECT TO WARD'S PROPERTY.—The guardian shall manage the estate of his ward, frugally and without waste, and apply the income and profit thereof, so far as the same may be neces-

---

(1) *Ex Parte* Bartlett, 4 Bradf., (N. Y.) 221; Townsend vs. Kendall, 4 Minn., 412; Pedan vs. Robb, 8 Ohio, 227.
(2) Trammell vs. Trammell, 20 Texas, 406.
(3) Morrell et al. vs. Dickey, 1 Johns. Ch., 153; Sabin vs. Gilman, 1 N. H., 193; Armstrong vs. Lear, 12 Wheat., 169; Hines vs. State, 10 Miss., 532.
(4) Story on Conflict of Law, ₰ 540; Holyoke vs. Haskins, 5 Pick., (Mass.) 20; 2 Watts, (Penn.) 548; Dunn vs. Dunn, 8 Ala., 789; Dupree vs. Perry, 18
(5) Daniel vs. Hill, 52 Ala., 430.   [Ala., 34.
(6) Foster vs. Hall, 4 Humph., (Tenn.) 346.
(7) Jennison vs. Hapgood, 10 Pick., 77; Isham vs. Gibbons, 1 Bradf., (N. Y.) 69; Littlefield vs. Brooks, 50 Me., 475.
(8) Hallowell vs. Saco, 5 Greenlf., 143; Crawford vs. Wilson, 4 Barb., 504; Smith vs. People, 44 Ill., 16.
(9) 2 Kent, 227, n. b.; Story on Conflict of Law, ₰ 506.
(10) *Ex Parte* Bartlett, 4 Bradf. Surr., (N. Y.) 221.

sary to the comfort and suitable support and education of his ward.(¹)

The guardian shall settle all accounts of his ward, and demand and sue for, and receive in his own name as guardian, all personal property of and demands due the ward; or, with the approbation of the court, compound for the same, and give a discharge to the debtor upon receiving a fair and just dividend of his estate and effects.(²)

For a guardian to take notes for money belonging to his ward, payable to himself and in his own name, is not in law a conversion,(³) as the word guardian is only *descriptio personæ*, and not necessary to be proved, and therefore can not be put in issue by a plea in abatement. A guardian has an undoubted right to bring a suit in his own name without stating for whom, or in what character he sued.(⁴)

The legal title to a promissory note, taken by a guardian, is in such guardian. He has the right to sue and transfer the same; and a purchaser in good faith, for a valuable consideration, gets an absolutely good title to the paper.(⁵)

The husband of the guardian has no right to possess or control the estate of the ward, and a payment to him on account of such estate is void, unless with the express sanction or direction of the guardian.(⁶)

A guardian, as trustee, may, in a peaceable manner, take the property of his ward or other principal; and if money has been converted into goods, they may be taken in the same manner, so long as the goods can be identified.(⁷)

He may also dispose of the personal estate of his ward, to a *bona fide* purchaser for a valuable consideration, and the contract will be obligatory; but he will not ordinarily be permitted to change the personal property of the infant into real property, or the real property into personalty.(⁸) And, if he should do so, the ward may, upon arriving of age, repudiate the transaction and recover his property.(⁹)

(1) Hurd's R. S., Chap. 64, § 19.
(2) Hurd's R. S., Chap. 64, § 17.
(3) Richardson vs. State, 55 Ind., 381.
(4) Baker vs. Ormsby, 4 Scam., 325.
(5) Fountain vs. Anderson, 33 Ga., 372.
(6) McKanna vs. Merry, 61 Ill., 177.
(7) Brush vs. Blanchard, 19 Ill., 31.
(8) Attridge vs. Billings, 57 Ill., 489.
(9) Morgan vs. Johnson, 68 Ill., 190.

If a guardian severs rails in a fence on the land of his ward, and converts them to his own use, his estate is answerable directly to the heirs for their value.(1)

He may dispose of the personal estate of his ward as he may think most beneficial to the ward, and a person who purchases from the guardian in good faith, with no knowledge of any fraudulent intent on the part of the guardian, is not responsible for the application of the money.(2) And where he *bona fide* transfers to another for a full consideration, a debt due to his wards, the assignee is entitled to the same remedy in equity to recover the debt which the wards would have had.(3) But he cannot transfer bank shares belonging to his ward's estate, who are also his own children, to pay an indebtedness of his own.(4) He has power to exchange the property of his ward, which he thinks hazardous, for other property; and if his discretion has been honestly exercised in the transaction, the courts will not hold him liable for the results.(5)

6. DUTY TO LOAN THE FUNDS OF HIS WARD.—Guardians will not be permitted to make gain to themselves of trust property in their hands. They are therefore required to put on interest the money of their wards.(6)

In this state it is the duty of the guardian to put and keep his ward's money at interest, upon security, to be approved by the court, or to invest the same in United States interest bearing securities. Personal security may be taken for loans not exceeding one hundred dollars. Loans in large amounts shall be upon real estate security. No loan shall be made for a longer time than three years, nor beyond the minority of the ward: *Provided,* the same may be extended from year to year without the approval of the court. The guardian shall be chargeable with interest upon any money he shall wrongfully or negligently allow to remain in his hands uninvested after the same might have been invested.(7)

Where a guardian loans his ward's money without security and

(1) Clark vs. Burnside, 15 Ill., 62.
(2) Field vs. Schieffelin, 7 Johns. (N. Y.) Ch., 156; Woodward vs. Donally, 27 Ala., 198.
(3) Newson vs. Newson, 5 Ired., (N. C. Eq.) 122.
(4) Porter vs. Tudor, 9 Conn., 411.
(5) Freeman vs. Wilson, 74 N. C., 368.
(6) Bond vs. Lockwood, 33 Ill., 212.
(7) Hurd's R. S., Chap. 64, § 22.

without the approval of the court, if the money is thereby lost, he will be chargeable therefor with interest.(¹)

He will not be sustained in loaning the funds of his ward to private individuals without security; nor can the guardian become, himself, surety on such a loan.(²)

It is not reasonable care and prudence in a guardian to invest his ward's money in the note of a single firm, in active business, without security, unless ordinary circumstances are shown to justify such an investment, and if a loss occurs in consequence thereof, he will be responsible for it.(³) For, it is his duty to lend out the surplus money of his ward on bond and mortgage, or on good personal security.(⁴)

Loans to individuals with good collateral security, will be upheld;(⁵) but it is the duty of the guardian, before investing the money of his ward, to obtain the sanction of the proper court to such investment, and if he invests without such sanction, it is at his own risk, and he will be held answerable for loss arising from the investment.(⁶)

And if he take a note with sufficient sureties for money thus loaned, and resign before the note becomes due, he will not be responsible for any loss that may afterwards occur.(⁷)

He should be allowed a reasonable time after the receipt of the money to loan the same out, and can only be required to exercise his best judgment and discretion under all the circumstances of the particular case; and he can not be charged with interest on such surplus funds not loaned out, unless he is shown to have been guilty of culpable negligence in not lending them out.(⁸)

And where the guardian neglects his duty in loaning out the money of his ward, he will be chargeable with interest for such neglect after a reasonable time has elapsed in which to make the

---

(1) Smith vs. Smith, 4 johns. Ch., (N. Y.) 281; Gilbert vs. Guptill, 34 Ill., 112.
(2) Nance vs. Nance, 1 S. C., 209; Allen vs. Gaillard, 1 S. C., 279.
(3) Clark vs. Garfield, 8 Allen, (Mass.) 427; Clay vs. Clay, 3 Metc., (Ky.) 548.
(4) Bond vs. Lockwood, 33 Ill., 212; Newman vs. Reed, 50 Ala., 297.
(5) Lovell vs. Minot, 20 Pick., 116.
(6) Carlysle vs. Carlysle, 10 Md., 440; Bryant vs. Craig, 12 Ala., 354; Sherry vs. Sansbury, 3 Ind., 320; Davis vs. Harris, 21 Miss., 9.
)7) Newman vs. Reed, 50 Ala., 297.
(8) Ashley vs. Martin, 50 Ala., 537; Karr vs. Karr, 6 Dana, (Ky.) 3.

investment, and six months from the receipt of the money has been deemed a reasonable time for that purpose.(¹)

Where he has money in his hands, which he expects to retain for a term of years, it is his duty so to invest it, that the interest will be received, at least annually.(²)

Where he converts money of his ward to his own use, he is chargeable with compound interest.(³) For the trust funds should be kept separate, by distinguishing marks, from the guardian's own private property; and if a guardian deposits money in a bank, to his own account, and the bank afterwards fails, he must bear the consequences.(⁴) But where he has been robbed without his fault, it is otherwise.(⁵)

He may retain on hand a sufficient amount of his ward's money to meet the current and contingent expenses, and also such sums which are too small to be wisely invested.(⁶) And the surplus should never be allowed to lie idle in the guardian's hands. He should loan it out, or otherwise properly invest it for the benefit of his ward, or be chargeable himself with interest upon the same.(⁷)

7. DUTY TO EDUCATE HIS WARD.—The guardian of a minor shall have, under the direction of the court, the custody, nurture and tuition of his ward, and the care and management of his estate.(⁸)

The guardian shall educate his ward, and it is made the duty of all civil officers, to give information to the county court of any neglect of the guardian to educate his ward.(⁹)

And where there is not money of the ward sufficient to teach him to read and write, and the elementary rules of arithmetic, and the guardian fails or neglects to have him so educated, the court shall have the power to put out the ward to any other person for the purpose of having him so educated.(¹⁰)

(1) Bond vs. Lockwood, 33 Ill., 212.
(2) Huffer's Appeal, 2 Grant (Penn.) Cas., 341.
(3) Rowan vs. Kirkpatrick, 14 Ill., 1.
(4) Matter of Stafford, 11 Barb., (N. Y.) 353; Wren vs. Kirton, 11 Vesey, 377; Mason vs. Whitthorne, 2 Coldw., (Tenn.) 242; *ante* pages 33 and 34.
(5) Knowlton vs. Bradley, 17 N. H., 458; Atkinson vs. Whitehead, 66 N. C., 296.
(6) Knowlton vs. Bradley, *supra;* Baker vs. Richards, 8 Serg. & R., 12.
(7) Reynolds vs. Walker, 29 Mass., (7 Cush.) 250; Stark vs. Gamble, 43 N. H., 465; Brand vs. Abbott, 42 Ala., 499.
(8) Hurd's R. S., Chap. 64, § 4.
(9) Hurd's R. S., Chap. 64, § 20.
(10) Hurd's R. S., Chap. 64, § 21.

The guardian should superintend the education and nurture of his ward, and for that purpose, he should first apply the rents derived from his ward's real estate, and next the interest on his money.([1]) If he spend more than the income from his ward's estate, in the maintenance and education of the ward, without permission of the court, he may be held liable for the principal thus consumed.([2]) And it is competent for the probate court to fix the amount to be expended in the maintenance and education of the ward, and to say how far the principal of the funds belonging to the ward shall be encroached upon.([3]) And in a proper case, the profits of the ward's estate may be sometimes anticipated, and an appropriation of the principal be made for the support and education of the ward.([4])

8. LIABILITY FOR MONEY RECEIVED.—A guardian using the money of his ward or neglecting to invest it, is chargeable with interest.([5]) So, too, he is liable for all losses of money belonging to his ward, incurred through culpable indifference and neglect.([6]) And where he deposits money of his ward in a bank, in his own name, although the banking institution was then in good credit, but subsequently failed, and took a certificate thereof payable to himself or order, the loss should fall upon him.([7]) But he is not responsible for a misapplication of the estate of the ward, by a co-guardian, in which he had no agency,([8]) unless he should consent to his co-guardian's misapplication.([9])

Where money is paid by mistake to a guardian, and he pays it over to his ward before notice of such mistake, he is not liable for it.([10])

The guardian is alone responsible for his ward's money, and its proper application;([11]) and he is not protected in an improper or unsafe use of it by the consent of the ward during minority.([12])

(1) McKanna vs. Merry, 61 Ill., 177.
(2) Frelick vs. Turner, 26 Miss., 393; Davis vs. Harkness, 1 Gilm., 173; Phillips vs. Davis, 2 Sneed, (Tenn.) 520; Bybee vs. Tharp, 4 B. Mon., (Ky.) 313.
(3) Wiggle vs. Owen, 45 Miss., 691.
(4) Withers vs. Hickman, 6 B. Mon., (Ky.) 292. [(Ky.) 3.
(5) Say vs. Barnes, 4 Serg. & R., (Penn.) 112; Karr vs. Karr, 6 Dana,
(6) Rodgers' Appeal, 16 Penn. St., 36; Potter vs. Hiscox, 30 Conn., 508.
(7). Jenkins vs. Walters, 8 Gill and J., (Md.) 218.
(8) Kirby vs. Turner, Hopk., (N. Y.) 309.
(9) Pim vs. Downing, 11 Serg. & R., (Penn.) 66.
(10) Massey vs. Massey, 2 Hill (S. C.) Ch., 492.
(11) Nance vs. Nance, 1 S. C., 209.
(12) Matter of Teyn, 2 Redf., (N. Y.) 306.

Where he takes a note payable simply to himself, with no words to indicate that he takes it as guardian, he cannot, after the maker has gone into insolvency, show that it was taken on account of his ward's estate.([1]) And if he should make an investment in bank stock, in his own name, though he be expressly authorized to invest in such stock, it renders him personally liable for the amount invested.([2])

He may receive his ward's money, and when received, he is responsible for its application. If he misapplies it, no new liability is created against the parties from whom it was received, as it is not part of their duty to see that he faithfully applies it.([3])

The guardian of a minor has the right to collect and receive money due to his ward on bond and mortgage, or to sell and assign the bond and mortgage in the exercise of his discretion as guardian.([4])

9. LIABILITY FOR WARD'S PROPERTY.—One who assumes to act for an infant as his guardian, can be held responsible for the property of the infant which may come into his hands and for the management of his estate, even though the appointment be a nullity.([5])

The liability to the ward is not affected by a guardian's discharge in bankruptcy.([6])

At common law, any act or omission which diminished the value of the estate or its income, or increased the burdens upon it, or impaired the evidence of title thereto, was considered waste. Guardians are chargeable for waste committed or suffered by them.([7])

10. LIABILITY UPON CONTRACTS.—A guardian can not, by his contract, bind the person or estate of his ward.([8]) But, if he promises, on a sufficient consideration, to pay the debt of his ward, he is personally bound by it, although he expressly promises as guardian. And a guardian who thus discharges the debt of his ward, may lawfully indemnify himself out of the estate of his ward, or if he be discharged from guardianship, he may have an action

(1) Knowlton vs. Bradley, 17 N. H., 458.
(2) Stanley's Appeal, 8 Penn. St., 431.
(3) Mortimer vs. The People, 49 Ill., 473.
(4) Livingston vs. Jones, Harrington Ch., (Mich.) 165.
(5) Earle vs. Crum, 42 Miss., 165.
(6) Re Maybin, 15 Bank. Reg., 468.
(7) Bond vs. Lockwood, 33 Ill., 212.
(8) Forster vs. Fuller, 6 Mass., 58; Jones vs. Brewer, 1 Pick., (Mass.) 314; Shiff vs. Shiff, 20 La. Ann., 269; Silms vs. Norris, 5 Ala., 42; Tenny vs. Evans, 14 N. H., 343; Tobin vs. Addison, 2 Strobh., (S. C.) 3; Sperry vs. Fanning, 80 Ill., 371.

against the ward for money paid for his use.(¹) For, if a guardian in his representative capacity, makes a contract or covenant which he has no right to make, and which is not binding upon the estate of the ward, he is personally bound to make it good.(²)

A person dealing with a party having by law but a limited authority as a guardian, can have no right beyond what a rightful exercise of the authority would confer;(³) and, if a compromise be made by a guardian, of a groundless and unjust claim against his ward, it will not be upheld in a court of equity, as to either guardian or ward.(⁴)

11. LIABILITY FOR NEGLIGENCE.—A guardian is bound to use ordinary prudence and diligence in managing the estate of his ward.(⁵) And where property is estimated to be worth thirty-five hundred dollars, and he takes a mortgage thereon, to secure a debt due to his ward, of about two thousand dollars, and afterwards permits it to be sold at public sale for five hundred and forty dollars, he will be guilty of such negligence as will make him responsible to his ward, for the loss.(⁶) So, too, he is personally chargeable with costs, where he institutes a suit in his ward's name, where no cause of action exists, even though he acted under the advice of counsel.(⁷) And where he accepts an unsecured note, in payment of a debt due to his ward, he will be guilty of laches, and held personally responsible for the amount of such note, even though he uses due diligence to collect it.(⁸)

The verbal directions of a judge of probate, will not protect a guardian, and are not receivable in evidence in defense of his action.(⁹)

It has been held, that if he loans his ward's money, and takes a bond signed by a principal and surety, and the principal is solvent, but the surety doubtful, he will be liable should the money thus loaned, be lost.(¹⁰) In short, guardians are liable for all losses

(1) Sperry vs. Fanning, 80 Ill., 371.
(2) Mason vs. Caldwell, 5 Gilm., 196; Sperry vs. Fanning, *supra*.
(3) Payne vs. Stone, 15 Miss., 7.Smeed & M., 367.
(4) Underwood vs. Brockman, 4 Dana, (Ky.) 309.
(5) Savage vs. Dickson, 16 Ala., 256.
(6) *Ib.*
(7) McLean vs. Hosea, 14 Ala., 194.
(8) Covington vs. Leak, 65 N. C., 594.
(9) Folger vs. Hudel, 60 Me., 284; *ante* page 43.
(10) Hurdle vs. Leath, 63 N. C., 597.

which may be incurred through culpable indifference and negligence, in the management of the estate of their wards.([1])

The duties and liabilities of guardians, in the collection and disbursement of their trust funds, are much the same as those of executors and administrators as portrayed in Part I.

[1] Taylor vs. Hite, 61 Mo., 142; Royers' Appeal, 11 Penn. St., 36; Potter vs. Hiscox, 30 Conn., 508.

ADDITIONAL NOTES.

1. Authority of guardian—Acting without an order of the county court
2. Chargeable with interests—When.
3. Minors—The domicile of.
4. Failure of guardian to insure ward's property.
5. Investments—Guardian's duty.
6. Custody, etc., estate.
7. Liabilities.

1. AUTHORITY OF GUARDIAN—ACTING WITHOUT AN ORDER OF THE COUNTY COURT.—A guardian may, without the direction of the county court, pay a claim which is secured by a deed of trust or mortgage, which is a direct and immediate charge upon the land of his ward, and which, if left unpaid, would probably destroy the ward's interest.(¹) An order of the court, however, is usually advisable.

2. CHARGEABLE WITH INTERESTS—WHEN.—Where his acts are beneficial to the interests of the ward, they should be allowed, and it would be injustice not to do so, although a guardian doing unauthorized acts, even if done in good faith, does them at his own risk; but if they prove beneficial to the ward, the court will sometimes adopt them. Especially is this so where the court would have directed them on application beforehand.(²)

3. MINORS—DOMICILE OF.—The domicile of an infant is that of his father, if he be living; if not, then that of the mother; if the parents are dead, the guardian has the right to control the domicile of the infant.(³) The guardian has power to collect the arrears of funds for the support of the ward, and secure their proper application.(⁴) In order to compound and release a demand against his ward, he should have the consent and approval of the county court before exercising such powers.(⁵) A guardian has no power to

---

(1) Roland's Heirs vs. Barkley, 1 Brock., 356; Wright vs. Conley, 14 Ill. Ap. 551; Macpherson on Infants, 285.
(2) 9 Am. and Eng. Ency. of Law, 107, 116; Cheney vs. Roodhouse, 135 Ill., 257.
(3) Lamar vs. Micou, 112 U. S., 452.
(4) Bailey vs. Bailey, 115 Ill., 551.
(5) Hayes vs. Mass. Life Ins. Co., 125 Ill., 626.

appear for and enter the appearance of his ward in a suit, where the latter has not been served with process.(¹)

4. FAILURE OF GUARDIAN TO INSURE WARD'S PROPERTY.— If a guardian be guilty of gross negligence in failing to insure the ward's property, he may render himself personally liable, should a loss occur. He is not, however, even where he has trust funds in his hands, personally liable for a failure to insure the property of his ward.(²)

5. INVESTMENTS—GUARDIAN'S DUTY.—It shall be the duty of the guardian to put and keep his ward's money at interest, upon security to be approved by the court, or by investing, on approval of the court, the same in United States bonds, [or in the bonds of any county or city which are not issued in aid of railroads, and where the laws do not permit said counties or cities to become indebted in excess of five per cent. of the assessed valuation of property for taxation therein, and where the total indebtedness of such county or city does not exceed five per cent. of the assessed valuation of property for taxation at the time of such investment.]* Personal security may be taken for loans not exceeding one hundred dollars. Loans upon real estate shall be secured by first mortgage thereon, and not to exceed one-half the value thereof. No mortgage loan shall be made for a longer time than three years, nor beyond the majority of the ward: *Provided*, the same may be extended from year to year without the approval of the court. The guardian shall be chargeable with interest upon any money which he shall wrongfully or negligently allow to remain in his hands uninvested after the same might have been invested.(³)

A guardian who permits his ward's money to lie idle, or who knowingly makes an illegal investment, or loans upon real estate security without the approval of the court, does the same at his own risk, and is liable to be charged compound interest.(⁴) In the absence of evidence to the contrary, it will be presumed that a guardian might have kept funds of his ward at interest.(⁵)

(1) Dickison vs. Dickison, 124 Ill., 483.
(2) Means vs. Earls, 15 Ill. Ap., 273.
(3) Laws of Ill., 1887, 193; Hurd's R. S., 783, § 22.
(4) Hughes vs. The People, for use, etc., 111 Ill., 457; Hayes vs. Mass. Life Ins. Co., 125 Ill., 626; Steyer vs. Morris, 39 Ill. Ap., 382.
(5) Steyer vs. Morris, *supra*.

*NOTE.—Amendment is the original section rewritten, to which was added the matter between the brackets.

6. CUSTODY, ETC., ESTATE.—The guardian of a minor shall have, under the direction of the court, the custody, nurture and tuition of his ward, and the care and management of his estate. But the father of the minor, if living, and in case of his death the mother, they being respectively competent to transact their own business, and fit persons, shall be entitled to the custody of the person of the minor, and the care of his education. In case the father and mother shall live apart, the court may, for good reason, award the custody and education of the minor to the mother, or other proper person: *Provided*, that whenever any person shall make any settlement upon or provision for the support and education of any minor child, it shall be competent for the court, in case either the father or mother of such child be dead, to make such order in relation to the visitation of such minor child by such person or persons so making such settlement or provision as shall to the court seem meet and proper.([1])

7. LIABILITIES.—Guardians of minors must discharge their duties with as much fidelity and care as prudent men ordinarily bestow on their own affairs, and when they have thus acted they are not responsible for a mere error in judgment. So, a guardian is not responsible for a loss occurring through an agent, on account of his dishonesty in collecting a claim belonging to his ward.([2])

(1) Hurd's R. S., 781, § 4, as amended by act approved June 25th, 1883.
(2) Holman vs. Blue, 10 Ill. Ap., 130; Hughes vs. The People, 10 Ill. Ap., 148.

CHAPTER V.

RIGHTS AND LIABILITIES OF THE WARD.

1. Rights in general.
2. Right to disaffirm acts done and contracts made during infancy.
3. Right of action by and against ward.
4. Right of action by ward against guardian.
5. Rights of the infant as to homestead.
6. Rights of the ward as to settlements.
7. Rights of the infant as to the doctrine of estoppel.
8. Right of election by ward.
9. Right to contract marriage.
10. Liability for the debts of the ancestor.
11. Liability of the infant for contracts.
12. Liability of the infant for wrongs.

1. RIGHTS IN GENERAL.—The necessity for guardians results from the inability of infants to take care of themselves, in contemplation of law, until they have attained the age of twenty-one;[1] and wards owe obedience to guardians, which courts will aid in enforcing.[2] The possession of the guardian is the possession of the ward.[3] Real estate purchased by him with the ward's money, will be considered the property of the ward;[4] and if he subscribe for bank stock in the name of his ward, it belongs, with all the proceeds, to his ward on his reaching his majority.[5] He is never allowed to make money out of his ward; what is made must be accounted for;[6] and courts will presume strongly in favor of the ward, and against the guardian, if he has been delinquent or guilty of neglect.[7]

Nothing can be admitted, but everything must be proved against an infant; and a decree cannot be entered against an infant without

---

(1) 2 Kent's Com., 233.
(2) 1 Strange, 167; Hall vs. Hall, 3 Atk. Ch., 721.
(3) Magee vs. Toland, 8 Port., (Ala.) 36.
(4) In re Hamilton, 17 Sergt. & R., (Pa.) 144.
(5) Brisbane vs. The Bank, 4 Watts, (Pa.) 92.
(6) Eberts vs. Eberts, 55 Pa. St., 110; Pinckard vs. Smith, 5 Litt., (Ky.) 331; Lee vs. Fox, 6 Dana, (Ky.) 171.
(7) Jennings vs. Kee, 5 Ind., 257.

proof to sustain the case.(¹) A guardian can not make admissions to bind an infant.(²) Negligence can not be imputable to a child under five years of age, especially to one of less than ordinary capacity; and should a child be injured by the cars, they running with great speed through a town, the corporation operating the train will be liable. Laches are not imputable to an infant.(³) A minor can not bring an advancement received by her mother into hotchpot, nor be charged with latches in omitting to do so.(⁴)

2. DISAFFIRMANCE OF ACTS AND CONTRACTS MADE DURING MINORITY.—Most of the acts of infants are voidable only, and not absolutely void, and it is deemed sufficient if the infant be allowed, when he attains majority, the privilege to affirm or avoid, in his discretion, his acts done and contracts made in infancy.(⁵)

If a minor contracts to sell real estate, the contract can not be enforced, if he refuses, after his majority, to sanction it.(⁶) Conveyances made by an infant in person, are voidable only, to be confirmed or repudiated at his discretion after he arrives at majority;(⁷) but where a party during his infancy, has executed a conveyance of his real estate, he must, if he wishes to disaffirm the same, do so within a reasonable time after attaining his majority;(⁸) and three years is held a reasonable time.(⁹)

An infant female, who is unmarried, may convey her lands before attaining the age of eighteen, and her conveyance will only be voidable, and she will have then a reasonable time after she attains that age, to disaffirm the same;(¹⁰) but deeds made by infant married women are void. Such deeds were void at common law, and have not been authorized by the statute. Under our stat-

---

(1) Hamilton vs. Gilman, 12 Ill., 260; Hitt vs. Ormsbee, 12 Ill., 166; Tuttle vs. Garrett, 16 Ill., 354; Reddick vs. State Bank, 27 Ill., 148; Rhoads vs. Rhoads, 43 Ill., 239; Wilhite vs. Pearce, 47 Ill., 413; Barnes vs. Hazleton, 50 Ill., 429; Preston vs. Hodgen, 50 Ill., 56: Thomas vs. Adams, 59 Ill., 223; Quigley vs. Roberts, 44 Ill., 503.
(2) Cochran vs. McDowell, 15 Ill., 10.
(3) Chicago & Alton R. R. Co. vs. Gregory, 58 Ill., 226.
(4) Barnes vs. Hazleton; *supra*.
(5) 2 Kent's Com., 234; Bliss vs. Perryman, 1 Scam., 484.
(6) Walker vs. Ellis, 12 Ill., 470.
(7) Cole vs. Pennoyer, 14 Ill., 158.
(8) Blankenship vs. Stout, 25 Ill., 132.
(9) Blankenship vs. Stout, *supra*; Harrer vs. Wallner, 80 Ill., 197; Keil vs. Healey, 84 Ill., 104.
(10) Harrer vs. Wallner, *supra*.

ute, a married woman is authorized to convey her land at the age of eighteen years, and if she executes a conveyance before she attains that age, although her husband join her therein, the deed will be void.(¹) But the minority of females ceases at eighteen years, and if she wishes to avoid the effect of the statute of limitations, she must commence her suit within three years after she attains eighteen years;(²) since the passage of the married woman's statute Act of 1861, the statute of limitations runs against a married woman the same as against a *feme sole*.(³)

All gifts, grants or deeds, made by infants by matter in deed, or a writing, which takes effect by delivery of his hand, are voidable by himself, his heirs, or those who have his estates;(⁴) and the heirs of an infant may disaffirm his deed within the same time that the infant might himself, if living.(⁵)

The deed of an infant may be ratified by acts *in pais*, or by long acquiescence. Possession by the first grantee from the infant would be notice, not only of the original deed, but of any acts of ratification.(⁶)

An infant cannot bind himself by bond;(⁷) and where a plaintiff relies upon a new promise made after the defendant became of age, the original contract having been made during infancy, he should declare on the new contract.(⁸) The implied contracts of an infant for necessaries are binding upon him.(⁹)

An infant of any age is capable of being a grantee in a conveyance of land, and a delivery of a deed conveying land to an infant, or one incapable of formally accepting the same, may be shown by facts and circumstances indicating an intention on the part of the grantor to part absolutely with his title and vest it in the grantee, an acceptance will be presumed in such a case from the beneficial nature of the transaction.(¹⁰)

(1) Lane vs. Soulard, 15 Ill., 123; Rodgers vs. Higgins, 48 Ill., 211; Hoyt vs. Swar, 53 Ill., 134; Harrer vs. Wallner, 80 Ill., 197.
(2) Kilgour vs. Gockley, 83 Ill., 109; Keil vs. Healey, 84 Ill., 104.
(3) Castner vs. Walrod, 83 Ill., 171.
(4) Tyler on Infancy, 69; Tunison vs. Chamblin, 88 Ill., 378.
(5) The Illinois Land and Loan Co. vs. Bonner, 75 Ill., 315.
(6) Black vs. Hills, 36 Ill., 376; Ewell's Leading Cases on Infancy, 138; Tunison vs. Chamblin, *supra;* The Illinois Land and Loan Co. vs. Bonner, *supra*.
(7) Bliss vs. Perryman, 1 Scam., 484.
(8) *Ib.*
(9) Cole vs. Pennoyer, 14 Ill., 158.
(10) Masterson vs. Cheek, 23 Ill., 72.

A release by a minor of his full share in the estate of his father is void, nor will it avail anything that such release was executed by a married woman, jointly with her husband, as the husband has no authority to make an agreement of that character which will bind his wife.(¹)

Under the uniform practice in chancery in this state, a decree against an infant is, in the first instance, absolute, and no day is given to show cause after he becomes of age.(²)

The grantees of minor heirs are protected by their disability. Such grantee in asserting his title as against a person defending under the statute of limitations, may show the disability of his grantors at any time within the statutory period, and thus prevent a bar. The statute of limitations does not begin to run until after the disability is removed, and the statutory period must elapse after the disability ceases, before there can be a bar under the statute, and the right of the grantee in this regard is the same as that of the heir.(³)

3. ACTIONS BY AND AGAINST WARD.—An infant can only appear to defend a suit by guardian, and not in person or by attorney.(⁴) He can sue in court only by his guardian or *prochein ami*.(⁵) An order of court appointing the next friend of an infant plaintiff, is unnecessary.(⁶) He may prosecute a writ of error in the supreme court by his next friend. If, however, he prosecute in his own name, and there be a joinder in error, his disability is waived by that proceeding.(⁷) A next friend can only pursue the rights of a minor, and has no power to yield or cede them to others.(⁸) The same is true of an attorney, and where a suit is dismissed on the agreement of the attorneys, the infant's rights will not be affected, nor will he be estopped from instituting a suit on the same cause of action.(⁹)

A minor may maintain an action of trover by his next friend, but he is not entitled to receive the money recovered. It will be

(1) Bishop vs. Davenport, 58 Ill., 105.
(2) Kuchenbeiser vs. Beckert, 41 Ill., 172; Barnes vs. Hazelton, 50 Ill., 429; Wadhams vs. Gay, 73 Ill., 415.
(3) Huls vs. Buntin, 47 Ill., 396.
(4) Peak vs. Shasted, 21 Ill., 137; Kesler vs. Penninger, 59 Ill., 134.
(5) Hoare vs. Harris, 11 Ill., 24.
(6) French vs. Creath, Breese 12.
(7) McClay vs. Norris, 4 Gilm., 370.
(8) Chicago, Rock Island and Pacific R. R. Co. vs. Kennedy, 70 Ill., 350.
(9) Benton vs. Pope, 5 Hump., (Tenn.) 392.

ordered to be paid into court, subject to the demand of a legally constituted guardian.(¹)

In the absence of any positive provision of the law to the contrary, an infant will not be prejudiced or injured by lapse of time, when by reason of his tender years the party is disqualified to prosecute his suit in person ;(²) and a delay of four years after minors have become of age, is not such laches in asserting their rights in bringing a suit and obtaining relief from a fraudulent sale of their real estate where they were ignorant of their rights, and had been wronged by their guardian, and where no rights have been acquired by other persons in the property or material change in the property occurs after they arrived of age and before suit was brought.(³)

Where infant heirs are brought into court by *scire facias* under the statute, to show cause why they should not be made parties to a judgment, it will be necessary to prove up the case *de novo* against them.(⁴)

An infant under the age of ten years may maintain an action by her next friend, for slanderous words, charging her with theft.(⁵)

The plea of infancy is not a dilatory plea, but goes to the foundation of the action,(⁶) and the right to avail of such a plea is personal to the party claiming such disability.(⁷)

An action will not lie against a guardian upon the contract of his ward, but must be brought against the ward, who may defend by his guardian.(⁸) So, too, an action for an assault and battery committed upon an infant, must be brought in the name of the infant, by his guardian, and not in the name of his guardian.(⁹) It will be presumed that the minor was emancipated, by his father, where he worked, and after becoming of age, brought suit to recover for his labor, and the father, who was called as a witness, spoke of the transaction as his son's, and a recovery by the son will be a bar to a recovery by the father.(¹⁰)

(1) Benton vs. Pope, 5 Hump., (Tenn.) 392.
(2) Rector vs. Rector, 3 Gilm., 105.
(3) Chicago, Rock Island and Pacific R. R. Co. vs. Kennedy, 70 Ill., 350.
(4) Cox vs. Reed, 27 Ill., 434.
(5) Stewart vs. Howe, 17 Ill., 71.
(6) Greer vs. Wheeler, 1 Scam., 554.
(7) Huls vs. Buntin, 47 Ill., 396.
(8) Brown vs. Chase, 4 Mass., 436.
(9) Stewart vs. Crabbin, 6 Munf., (Va.) 280.
(10) Scott vs. White, 71 Ill., 287.

A ward will have a right of action against third persons dealing with the guardian, where the guardian has no right to assign an obligation to a third person, for his own private benefit, in which his wards, who are minors, are interested. And where the assignee knew this when taking the obligation, a court of equity will pursue the property into the hands of the assignee, or prevent the payment of the obligation to him.(1)

An infant daughter can not consent to carnal intercourse, so as to bar an action by her father for seduction, because she is incapable of consenting. For the same reason, without regard to the criminal law, she is incapable of consenting to an abortion.(2) So, too, an action on the case will lie to recover damages by a guardian for the seduction of his ward.(3)

4. WARD AGAINST GUARDIAN.—No action is maintainable by a ward against his guardian alone, for the use, income, or profits of the property, which went into the guardian's hands by virtue of his appointment, until there has been a settlement of accounts, and a balance has been struck.(4)

The remedy of a ward against his guardian, is by action of account or bill in equity, in which the equity between the parties may be adjusted and rightfully settled. An action of assumpsit is not maintainable.(5)

The above has no allusion to an action of debt upon the guardian's bond, which may be maintained whenever his guardianship ceases, whether an account has been rendered or not.(6)

5. HOMESTEAD RIGHTS OF THE INFANT.—During the life of the parents, the children have no vested interest in the homestead, and the parents may release the right, or put an end to it by abandonment, and their children can assert no right therein adversely to the acts of their parents; and whatever concludes the parents from asserting the right, and thereby deprives them of it, will, in like manner, affect their children who succeed them.(7) But where

(1) Carpenter vs. McBride, 3 Fla., 292; Lockhart vs. Phillips, 1 Ired., (N. C.) Eq., 342.
(2) White vs. Murtland, 71 Ill., 250.
(3) Fernsler vs. Moyer, 3 Watts & S., (Pa.) 416.
(4) Chapman vs. Chapman, 32 Ala., 106; Robertson vs. Robertson, 1 Root, (Conn.) 51; Nutz vs. Rutter, 1 Watts, (Pa.) 229.
(5) Linton vs. Walker, 8 Fla., 144
(6) Wann vs. People, 57 Ill., 202.
(7) Clubb vs. Wise, 64 Ill., 157.

the homestead has descended to the infants, who are removed therefrom only to place them in charge of their near kindred, and the farm is rented by their guardian for their benefit, it is no abandonment. It is the only occupancy which the circumstances of the case and their interests will admit of. A sale by an execution creditor, of a homestead occupied by a tenant for the benefit of the widow and minor heirs, will be set aside on application by the latter, in a court of equity.[1]

The abandonment of the homestead by the widowed mother, will not prejudice the rights of the infants.[2]

6. SETTLEMENTS BETWEEN GUARDIAN AND WARD.—Courts look upon settlements, made by guardians with wards recently come of age, with distrust, and will not consider them binding, unless made with the fullest deliberation and the most abundant good faith on the part of the guardian;[3] and where a receipt is given by the ward, soon after coming of age, to his former guardian, without a full knowledge of the facts, he is not concluded.[4] But, in the absence of any undue means used on the part of the guardian to obtain it, and with a full knowledge of the facts, a release by the ward after becoming of age, is binding.[5] It is no bar, however, to a bill, filed by the wards, for an account, on the ground of a mistake, which the guardian admits.[6] Advances made by a guardian to his ward, cannot be regarded as a charge upon the ward's land, until an account is presented to the county court and approved.[7]

After the lapse of many years from the final settlement of a guardian with his wards, after their majority, satisfactory evidence will be required to show that he holds funds in his hands not accounted for in his settlement.[8]

7. ESTOPPEL.—Minor heirs, being ignorant of the proceedings

(1) Brinkerhoff vs. Everett, 38 Ill., 263.
(2) Walters vs. People *Ex. Rel.* Bradley, 21 Ill., 178.
(3) Sullivan vs. Blackwell, 28 Miss., 737; Andrews vs. Jones, 10 Ala., 400; Wright vs. Arnold, 14 B. Mon., (Ky.) 638; McClennan vs. Kenedy, 8 Md., 230; Meek vs. Perry, 36 Miss., 190; Williams vs. Powell, 1 Ired. [N. C.) Eq., 460; Boyett vs. Hurst, 1 Jones (N. C.) Eq., 166; Hawkins' Appeal, 32 Pa. St., 263; Wickiser vs. Cook, 85 Ill., 68.
(4) Brewer vs. Vanarsdale, 6 Dana, (Ky.) 204; Hall vs. Cone, 5 Day, (Conn.) 543; Fish vs. Miller, 1 Hoffm., (N. Y.) 267.
(5) Kirby vs. Turner, Hopk.,(N. Y.) 309; Kirby vs. Taylor, 6 Johns. Ch., (N. Y.) 242; Padfield vs. Pierce, 72 Ill., 500.
(6) Felton vs. Long, 8 Ired. (N. C.) Eq., 224.
(7) Wickiser vs. Cook, *supra*.
(8) Railsback vs. Williamson, 88 Ill., 494.

of the administrator at the time, and never having had any settlement with their guardian, would not be estopped from asserting their title by the mere fact that a portion of the consideration received by the guardian from the administrator on the sale, had been applied to their benefit.([1]) Nor will the mere silence, or express assent of an infant to a conveyance of her lands by an administrator, nor standing by in silence, while the purchaser is making improvements on the land, estop an infant from asserting title, any more than they could by their own deed made during infancy.([2]) And where an administrator's sale and deed were adjudged to be void, and the legal title adjudged to be in the minor, a bill in equity can not be filed to restrain the minor from setting up his legal title on the ground that by the acts of the minor, while a minor, and after arriving of age, he was estopped in equity from asserting the same.([3])

Estoppel *in pais* does not result from statements which do no injury.([4])

Where land was regularly sold by the guardian under an authority of law, although the sale was not confirmed, but no complaint appears against the fairness of the transaction, the monies being faithfully applied, part in the acquisition of other lands, which were subsequently conveyed, the minors will be estopped in equity, after long acquiesence, from proceeding in ejectment, to recover the land sold by the guardian, from an innocent purchaser, not immediately connected with the sale.([5])

An infant will not be estopped from asserting his title and claim to real estate, in the estate of his father, because the father in his lifetime, requested certain of his children should have real estate belonging to him, and certain others, who were minors, in lieu of their interest therein, should receive money, though the children who were of age, carried out the request of their father, and the guardian of the infant received the money, and paid it out to the minor upon his arrival at majority, there being no evidence that when the ward receipted for it, he knew or was informed that it was

(1) Schnell vs. City of Chicago, 38 Ill., 382.
(2) Davidson vs. Young, 38 Ill., 145.
(3) *Ib.*
(4) *Ib.*
(5) Penn vs. Heiscy, 19 Ill., 295.

intended to be in lieu of his interest in his father's lands.(¹)

Fraud is necessary to an equitable estoppel ;(²) and the utmost that can be said in this case, is, that the infant disregarded the wishes of his father, and received more money from the estate, than he was entitled to have. This falls far short of an equitable estoppel to title to realty.(³)

8. ELECTION BY WARD.—When the guardian has made profits by the employment of the funds of the ward, the latter may elect to take the profits or charge him with interest, but is not entitled to both.(⁴) And where a guardian invests the personal property of his ward in real estate, without authority, the ward may elect whether to receive the real estate, or to receive the money and interest;(⁵) and if he elects to take the land, within a reasonable time after becoming of age, a court of equity will enforce a conveyance of the legal title to him.(⁶)

The purchase by a guardian of his ward's property, on a sale by him, is voidable at the option of the ward.(⁷)

An award on a submission by the guardian of an infant, is voidable by the infant on his coming of age.(⁸)

Where money was directed to be paid into court, under a decree, for an infant, and her guardian accepted a deed of land in lieu thereof, it was not binding on the infant. The guardian had no right to receive the money, much less the land in lieu of it.(⁹)

Where a ward seeks to avoid a conveyance made by him to his guardian after his majority, on the ground of imposition and misrepresentation of the facts, he will be required to return the whole of the purchase money paid to him, or the land should be ordered to be sold to repay the same, as a condition upon which the sale should be set aside.(¹⁰)

(1) Dorlarque vs. Cress, 71 Ill., 380.
(2) Davidson vs. Young, 38 Ill., 145; Bigelow on Estoppel, 484.
(3) Dorlarque vs. Cress, *supra*.
(4) Bond vs. Lockwood, 33 Ill., 212; *In Re* Steel, 65 Ill., 322; Kyle vs Barnett, 17 Ala., 306.
(5) Eckford vs. Dekay, 8 Paige, (N. Y.) 89; Caplinger vs. Stokes, Meigs, (Tenn.) 175; Padfield vs. Pierce, 72 Ill., 500.
(6) Padfield vs. Pierce, *supra*.
(7) Scott vs. Freeland, 15 Miss., 7 Smed. & M., 409.
(8) Barnaby vs. Barnaby, 1 Pick., (Mass.) 221.
(9) Westbrook vs. Comstock, Walker's Ch., (Mich.) 314; Livingston vs. Jones, Harr. Ch., (Mich.) 165; Bond vs. Lockwood, *supra*.
(10) Wickiser vs. Cook. 85 Ill., 68.

9. RIGHT TO CONTRACT MARRIAGE.—Male persons over the age of seventeen years, and females over the age of fourteen years, may contract and be joined in marriage.(¹) For the purpose of ascertaining the ages of the parties, the county clerk may examine either of them, or any other witness, under oath.(²) And if any county clerk shall issue a license for the marriage of a man under the age of twenty-one years, or of a woman under the age of eighteen years, without the consent of his or her father, (or if he is dead or incapable, or not residing with his family, or his or her mother or guardian, if he or she have one,) first had thereto, he shall forfeit and pay the sum of $300 for each offense, to be recovered by such father, mother or guardian, in an action of debt, in any court of competent jurisdiction.(³)

The statute authorizing the clerk to ascertain the age of those seeking a marriage license, contemplates a personal examination on oath of the parties proposed to be married, or other witnesses.(⁴) The provisions of our statute, requiring the consent of parents or guardians to be had, when parties intending to marry, are in their minority, is founded in justice and in consideration of public policy. In such cases, they are in a state of servitude to their parents, from which they can not be released, except by the consent of the parents.(⁵)

10. DEBTS OF THE ANCESTOR.—Infants are liable for the debts of their ancestors, but only to the extent of what descends to them from such ancestor, and where heirs at law are sued for a debt of their ancestor, who have not sold or aliened any part of the land cast upon them by descent, or received any rents and profits therefrom, or anything from the personal estate, it is erroneous to render a personal judgment against them. No other judgment can be rendered in such a case, than one to be satisfied out of the real estate which descends to them.(⁶)

When any lands, tenements or hereditaments, or any rents or profits out of the same, shall descend to any heir, or be devised to any devisee, and the personal estate of the ancestor of such heir or

(1) Hurd's R. S., Chap. 89, § 3.
(2) Hurd's R. S., Chap. 89, § 8.
(3) Hurd's R. S., Chap. 89, § 14.
(4) Gilbert vs. Bone, 64 Ill., 518; Gilbert vs. Bone, 79 Ill., 341.
(5) Lyndon vs. Lyndon, 69 Ill., 43.
(6) Branger vs. Lucy, 82 Ill., 91; Bonnell vs. Holt, 89 Ill., 71.

devisor of such devisee, shall be insufficient to discharge the just demands against such ancestor, or devisor's estate, such heir or devisee shall be liable to the creditor of their ancestor or devisor to the full amount of the lands, tenements or hereditaments, or rents and profits out of the same, as may descend or be devised to the said heir or devisee; and in all cases where any heir or devisee shall be liable to pay the debts of his executor or devisor, in regard of any lands, tenements or hereditaments, or rent or profit arising out of the same, descending or being devised to him, and shall sell, alien or make over the same before any action brought, or process sued out against him, such heir at law or devisee, shall be answerable for such debts to the value of the said lands, tenements and hereditaments, rents or profits so by him aliened or made over; and executions may be taken out upon any judgment so obtained against such heir or devisee, to the value of said lands, tenements and hereditaments, rents and profits, out of the same, as if the same were his own proper debts, saving and excepting that the lands and tenements, rents and profits, by him *bona fide* aliened, before the action brought, shall not be liable to such execution.([1])

When any action or suit is brought against any heir or devisee, he may plead *riens per descent*, at the time of the commencement of the action or suit, and the plaintiff, in such action, may reply that he had lands, tenements or hereditaments, or rents or profits out of the same, from his ancestor or devisor before the commencement of the action or suit, and if, upon issue joined thereupon, it be found for the plaintiff, the jury shall inquire of the value of the lands, tenements, hereditaments, or rents and profits out of the same, so descended or devised, and thereupon judgment shall be given against such heir or devisee, by confessing of the action without confessing the assets descended or devised, or upon demurrer, or *nil dicit*, or default, said judgment shall be given for the plaintiff, without any writ to inquire of the lands, tenements or hereditaments, or rents and profits out of the same, so descended or devised.([2])

In all cases, where a judgment has been obtained against the executor or administrator of a deceased person, on a contract or undertaking on which a joint action might have been maintained against the executor or administrator, and the heir or devisee of the

(1) Hurd's R. S., Chap. 59, § 12. (2) Hurd's R. S., Chap. 59, § 13.

deceased person, if it shall appear by a judgment of record, or the return of a proper officer, that there is not property of the deceased person in the hands of the executor or administrator to satisfy such judgment, it shall be lawful to bring a separate suit or action against the heir or devisee on such contract or undertaking; and the judgment against the executor or administrator, if not satisfied, shall be no bar to the suit or action against the heir or devisee.(¹)

If no person shall administer on the goods and chattels of a deceased person for the space of one year after his death, a separate suit or action may be maintained against the heirs or devisees, on all the contracts and undertakings of such deceased person.(²)

In all actions or suits commenced under the provisions of the preceding sections, the facts authorizing the suit to be brought separately against the heirs or devisees, shall be distinctly set forth in the declaration.(³)

When any suit or action in law or equity shall be brought against any heir or devisee, who shall be of nonage, it shall be lawful for the court to appoint a guardian *ad litem* for such infant heir or devisee, and may compel the person so appointed, to act: *Provided*, that by such appointment such person shall not be rendered liable to pay any costs of suit.(⁴)

And where a creditor's bill is filed to subject land conveyed by a deceased person to his son, the judgment of the county court allowing the claim in probate, is only *prima facie* evidence, and is not conclusive on the heir. He has the right to contest the indebtedness.(⁵) But heirs are not liable for the debts of their ancestor where the latter leaves personal estate sufficient to discharge all just demands against his estate.(⁶) The facts authorizing such an action must be distinctly set forth in the declaration. No recovery can be had under the common counts.(⁷)

(1) Hurd's R. S., Chap. 59, ¿ 14.
(2) Hurd's R. S., Chap. 59, ¿ 15.
(3) Hurd's R. S., Chap. 59, ¿ 16.
(4) Hurd's R. S., Chap. 59, ¿ 17.
(5) Gibson vs. Gibson, 82 Ill., 61; Birely's Heirs vs. Staley, 5 Gill. & Johns., 432; See Note on p. 313, 25, Am. Decisions.
(6) Ryan vs. Jones, 15 Ill., 1; Vanmeter vs. Love, 33 Ill., 260; Baker vs. Hunt, 40 Ill., 264; Bishop vs. O'Conner, 69 Ill., 431; Forman vs. Stickney, 77 Ill., 575; McLean vs. McBean, 74 Ill., 134; Cutright vs. Stanford, 81 Ill., 240; Branger vs. Lucy, 82 Ill., 91; Guy, admr., vs. Gericks, 85 Ill., 428; Laughlin vs. Heer, 89 Ill., 119.
(7) Ryan vs. Jones, 15 Ill., 1; McLean vs. McBean, *supra*.

A decree against the heirs should not be several, but joint, requiring each to pay pro rata.(¹) Yet, while this is true, no one of the heirs, must be made liable beyond the amount which may have come to him by descent.(²)

An infant heir cannot avail himself of his disability to excuse the non assertion of his rights under an executory contract made with the ancestor, when the immediate performance of his part of the contract is essential to the interest of the other party.(³)

It devolves on those seeking to charge the heir with the ancestor's debt, to allege and prove, not only the descent of real estate from the ancestor, but also, either that there was no personal estate, or that it was not sufficient to pay the just debts and demands against the estate.(⁴) And, after a period of seven years, a creditor of an estate will be considered as having waived his lien upon real estate descended to heirs.(⁵)

11. CONTRACTS OF THE INFANT.—If an infant should contract to work for a certain specified time, and work but a short time and quit, he is not bound by his contract, and can recover from his employer the value of the services rendered.(⁶) But the contract can not be avoided by the adult with whom the infant deals.(⁷)

Where work is done, or materials furnished, under a contract made with a minor, for the improvement of his property, the contract is not binding, and no lien will exist, in favor of the contractor against the infant's property, even though the infant received rents after she became of age.(⁸) The law presumes that one dealing with a person under disability, and knowing the fact, intends to incur the consequences of his acts, and equity will not relieve him against them, or otherwise afford relief,(⁹) as it is the duty of those who give credit to an infant, to know his precise situation, at their peril.(¹⁰)

(1) Cutright vs. Stanford, 81 Ill., 240.
(2) Vanmeter vs. Love, 33 Ill., 260.
(3) Walker vs. Douglass, 70 Ill., 445.
(4) Laughlin vs. Heer, 89 Ill., 119.
(5) McCoy vs. Morrow, 18 Ill., 519; Unknown Heirs of Langworthy vs. Baker, 23 Ill., 484; Rosenthal vs. Renick, 44 Ill., 202; Moore vs. Ellsworth, 57 Ill., 308; Reed vs. Colby, 89 Ill., 104.
(6) Ray vs. Haines, 52 Ill., 485.
(7) Fletcher vs. Holmes, 32 Ind., 537; Johnson vs. Rockwell, 29 Barb.,
(8) McCarty vs. Carter, 49 Ill., 53.   [(N. Y.) 160; 1 Sneed, (Tenn.) 659.
(9) Rodgers vs. Higgins, 48 Ill., 211.
(10) Hunt vs. Thompson, 3 Scam., 179.

A contract with a minor to nurse his child, is good, and can not be avoided by infancy;(¹) so, too, where an infant widow contracted for the burial of her deceased husband, she was held liable, it being held to be for her own personal benefit. But it does not follow, however, from this decision, that an infant child, or more distant relation would be held responsible upon a contract for the burial of his parent or relative.(²)

Evidence that a guardian has permitted his ward to make certain contracts, does not prove a general authority to him to contract.(³)

Where a person with a knowledge of the title and condition of the property, makes improvements upon the land of a ward under a contract with the guardian, which the latter has no authority to make, he has no lien in equity upon the premises for the value of such improvements.(⁴)

An infant who has a guardian or parent, who supplies his wants, can not bind himself for necessaries.(⁵) And where the guardian refuses to supply his ward with necessaries, the remedy is by application to the court to have him discharged, or the ward may purchase necessaries himself, for the recovery of the price of which an action will lie against the minor, but not against the guardian personally.(⁶) And, while the infant is liable for the necessaries furnished, his note given for them, is void, as an infant can not state an account.(⁷)

A contract made by an infant to pay interest, is void.(⁸)

And where he gives his note for necessaries, the reasonable value of the goods must be the basis of a recovery, and not the note.(⁹)

12. LIABILITY FOR TORTS.—Infants are liable for torts and wrongs committed by them, the same as adults.(¹⁰)

Where a minor purchases goods and procures the delivery by

(1) Broom's Legal Maxims, § 533.
(2) Chapple vs. Cooper, 13 M. & W., 259; Broom's Legal Maxims, *supra*.
(3) Prescott vs. Cass, 9 N. H., 93.
(4) Gay vs. Du Uprey, 16 California, 195.
(5) Guthrie vs. Murphy, 4 Watts, (Pa.) 80.
(6) Call vs. Ward, 4 Watts & S., (Pa.) 118.
(7) 1 Parsons on Notes and Bills, 68; 1 Story on Contracts, § 80; Trueman vs. Hurd, 17 Rep., 40; Ingelow vs. Douglass, 2 Stark, 36.
(8) Fisher vs. Mowbray, 8 East., 330.
(9) Mitchell vs. Reynolds, 10 Mod., 85; Modin vs. Steward, 5 Bradwell, 533.
(10) Davidson vs. Young, 38 Ill., 145; Wilson vs. Garrard, 59 Ill., 51; Wallace vs. Marss, 5 Hill, (N. Y.) 391; Bullock vs. Babcock, 3 Wend., (N. Y.) 391; Fitts vs. Hall, 9 N. H., 441.

fraud, he will be liable as in tort. The mere fact that he made the contract, and by fraudulent means obtained possession of the property, will not shield him from liability to suit, in case or trover.(¹)

Infants should not be made to suffer for the trespasses or unauthorized acts of the guardian.(²)

An infant under the age of ten years, shall not be found guilty of any crime or misdemeanor.(³)

Every male person of the age of fourteen years and upwards, who shall have carnal knowledge of any female child, under the age of ten years, either with or without her consent, shall be adjudged to be guilty of the crime of rape.(⁴)

The state has no power to imprison a child, who has committed no crime, on the mere allegation that he is destitute of proper parental care, and is growing up in mendicancy, ignorance, idleness and vice.(⁵)

A father is not, nor can he be held liable for the unauthorized trespass of his minor children. In that respect, the child occupies the same relation to the father as does a servant.(⁶)

An infant who would falsely allege himself to be of age, for the purpose of inducing another person to purchase and take a deed of his lands, would be liable to respond in damages for any injury which might result to the purchaser in consequence of the deceit.(⁷)

(1) Mathews vs. Cowan, 59 Ill., 341.
(2) Cunningham vs. Ill. Central R. R. Co., 77 Ill., 78.
(3) Hurd's R. S., Chap. 38, § 283.
(4) Hurd's R. S., Chap. 38, § 237.
(5) People vs. Turner 55 Ill., 280.
(6) Paulin vs. Howser, 63 Ill., 312.
(7) Davidson vs. Young, 38 Ill., 145.

ADDITIONAL NOTES

1. Estoppel, as applied to infants.
2. Laches—When imputed to an infant.
3. Infants are wards of the court.
4. An infant is bound by the action of his guardian—When.
5. Infancy, as a defense against a judgment rendered without a guardian ad litem having been appointed.
6. Ratification by the ward.
7. Guardian has no power to compromise claims of ward for less sum than is due, without an order of the court.
8. Contracts—Personal liability of guardian upon contracts relating to his ward's estate.
9. A receipt obtained by fraud and circumvention does not bind the ward.
10. Decree against infants—Impeachment thereof.
11. Guardian should not act for the ward, if himself interested.
12. It is error to issue a decree by consent against an infant without hearing evidence.
13. A guardian or next friend cannot stipulate ward's rights away.
14. Attorney's fees.

1. ESTOPPEL, AS APPLIED TO INFANTS.—A defendant is not estopped from setting up infancy as a defense to a contract by his fraudulent representations that he was of full age.(¹)

2. LACHES—WHEN IMPUTED TO AN INFANT.—Laches will not be imputed to an infant during the period of the disability; only from the period of the removal of the disability.(²)

3. INFANTS ARE WARDS OF THE COURT.—A minor is entitled to the protection of the courts, whether his guardian pleads properly or not.(³) If the general guardian or the guardian *ad litem* fails to properly protect the interests of the ward, it is the duty of the court, of its own motion, to compel him to do so, whenever that fact comes to the knowledge of the court.(⁴)

4. AN INFANT IS BOUND BY THE ACTION OF HIS GUARDIAN—WHEN.—On a bill for an accounting filed by a guardian, in respect

---

(1) Merriam vs. Cunningham, 11 Cushing, 40; Wieland vs. Kobick, 110 Ill., 16.
(2) Walker vs. Ray, 111 Ill., 315.
(3) Gilmore vs. Gilmore, 109 Ill., 277.
(4) Lloyd vs. Kirkwood, 112 Ill., 329.

to the income of real property charges and disbursements, where on the hearing the minor was represented by the guardian and his solicitor, the minor was held bound by their action in making up the issues on the accounts.(¹)

5. INFANCY, AS A DEFENSE AGAINST A JUDGMENT RENDERED, ETC.—A judgment rendered by a justice of the peace against a minor without the appointment of a guardian *ad litem* is not void, but voidable, in a case where the court has jurisdiction of the person and the subject matter. A plea to an action of debt on such a judgment, setting up the fact of infancy, that the judgment was not rendered for any tort, or for necessaries furnished to defendant, and that no guardian *ad litem* was appointed, is bad on demurrer.(²)

6. RATIFICATION BY THE WARD.—The fact that a ward, after reaching majority, lived with her father, in a house mortgaged by him to secure a loan from her guardian, is not sufficient to show that she ratified or approved of the act of the guardian in making such loan to her father.(³)

An objection to the competency of a party to testify in his own behalf is not waived by an infant party by failing to object at the proper time.(⁴)

On a bill in chancery, filed by a stepfather against his stepchildren to subject their lands to sale, the service of the summons by delivery of a copy thereof to the complainant, informing him of its contents, will confer no jurisdiction on the court as to the persons of the defendants, and a decree of sale on such service will be void as to them (⁵)

If an infant advances money on a voidable contract, which he afterward rescinds, he cannot recover this money back, because it is lost to him by his own act, and the privilege of infancy does not extend so far as to restore this money, unless it was obtained by fraud.(⁶)

7. GUARDIAN HAS NO POWER TO COMPROMISE CLAIMS OF WARD, ETC.—A guardian has no power to compound or compromise, in

(1) Patterson vs. Johnson, 113 Ill., 559.
(2) Millard vs. Marmon, 116 Ill., 649.
(3) Winslow vs. The People, for use, etc., 117 Ill., 152.
(4) Barnard vs. Barnard, 119 Ill., 92.
(5) Hemmer vs. Wolfer, 124 Ill., 435.
(6) Chicago Mut. Life Indemnity Ass'n vs. Hunt, 127 Ill., 257.

respect to his ward's rights, where a less sum than is due is accepted, except under an order and direction of the county court, and if he does his act will not bind his ward, and his ward may disaffirm it.(1)

8. CONTRACTS—PERSONAL LIABILITY OF GUARDIAN, ETC.— Where a guardian, under the approval of the probate court, leases his ward's property, covenanting in the lease to purchase, at the expiration of the term, the improvements put upon the premises by the tenant, at the valuation of three persons, to be selected as provided in the lease, and the lease is signed by the guardian as such, as such he will be personally liable for a breach of the covenant. In such a case, however, where the guardian discharges the debt of the ward, he may have indemnity out of the ward's estate. If he has been discharged from the guardianship, he may recover off the ward in an action, as for money paid for his use.(2)

9. A RECEIPT OBTAINED BY FRAUD, ETC., DOES NOT BIND THE WARD.—To bind the ward in a transaction with the guardian, it must be shown that he acted, after the termination of his disability, with deliberation, and with a full knowledge of all material facts. A receipt obtained by fraud and circumvention will not bind the ward.(3)

10. DECREE AGAINST INFANTS—IMPEACHMENT THEREOF.—A decree against an infant is absolute in the first instance, but may be attacked and impeached, either for fraud or for error of law apparent upon the face of the record, by original bill filed for the purpose at any time before the infant attains majority, or within a period after majority allowed by law for the prosecution of a writ of error for the reversal of such decree.(4)

11. A GUARDIAN SHOULD NOT ACT FOR THE WARD IF HIMSELF INTERESTED.—A guardian whose interests are hostile to the ward's is incompetent to act for the ward in respect to that interest. In such a case the ward should be made a defendant, and have a guardian *ad litem* appointed, or sue by a next friend, and be represented by separate and distinct counsel from that of his guardian.(5)

---

(1) Hayes vs. Mass. Mut. Life Ins. Co., 125 Ill., 626.
(2) Nichols vs. Sargent, 125 Ill., 309; Kingsbury vs. Powers, 131 Ill., 182.
(3) Gillett vs. Wiley, 126 Ill., 310.
(4) Haines vs. Hewitt, 129 Ill., 347; Coffin vs Argo, 134 Ill., 276.
(5) Roodhouse vs. Roodhouse, 132 Ill., 360; 6 Coldw., 619; Parker vs. Lincoln, 12 Mass., 16; Wells vs. Smith, 44 Miss., 296.

12. Error to issue decree by consent, etc.—It is error to enter a decree by consent against an infant without hearing evidence.(¹)

13. Guardian, etc., cannot stipulate ward's rights away.—Nor can a guardian or next friend stipulate the rights of his ward away.(²)

14. Attorney's fees.—The estate of the ward should not be charged for legal services rendered by guardian in a controversy arising through the guardian's fault.(³)

(1) Bennett vs. Bradford, 132 Ill., 269.
(2) Kingsbury vs. Buckner, 134 U. S., 650.
(3) Steyer vs. Morris, 39 Ill. Ap., 382.

CHAPTER VI.

ACCOUNTING BY GUARDIAN.

1. Duty to render account.
2. Sureties of guardian.
3. Powers of the county court in regard to.
4. Allowances on accounting.
5. Commissions.
6. Opening and reviewing settlements.
7. Form of a guardian's settlement.

1. DUTY TO RENDER AN ACCOUNT.—To the end that the estates of infants which come to the hands of their guardians, may at all times be under the care and scrutiny of a court of competent jurisdiction, it has long been required of guardians, that they render to the court appointing them, accounts of the estate in their hands. And so, even a mere stranger or wrongdoer, who takes possession of the property of an infant, and receives the rents and profits thereof, may, in equity, be considered as the guardian of the infant, and may be compelled to account as such.([1]) To secure such accounts at proper intervals, our statute has provided that the guardian shall, at the expiration of a year from his appointment, settle his accounts as guardian with the county court, and at least once every three years thereafter, and as much oftener as the court may require.([2])

At the expiration of his trust, he shall pay and deliver to those entitled thereto, all the money, estate and title papers in his hands as guardian, or with which he is chargeable as such.([3])

On every accounting and final settlement of a guardian, he shall exhibit and file his account as such guardian, setting forth specifically, in separate items, on what account expenditures were made by him, and all sums received and paid out since his last accounting, and on what account each was received and paid out, and showing the true balance of money on hand, which account shall be

(1) Van Epps vs. Douser, 4 Paige, 71; Davis vs. Harkness, 1 Gilm., 173
(2) Hurd's R. S., Chap. 64, ℈ 14.
(3) Hurd's R. S., Chap. 64, ℈ 15.

accompanied by proper vouchers, and signed by him and verified by his affidavit.(¹)

A guardian's report to the county court, being simply an account of receipts and disbursements, which does not purport to be final, makes no reference to the ward's age, and asks for no discharge nor claims any commissions, with the order of court approving the same, can not be regarded as a final settlement. Any mistake or omission made in a former report, may be rectified on final settlement.(²)

2. SURETIES OF GUARDIAN.—It shall be the duty of the county court, at each accounting of the guardian, to inquire into the sufficiency of his sureties. And if, at any time, it has cause to believe that the sureties of a guardian are insufficient or in failing circumstances, it shall, after summoning the guardian, if he be not before the court, require him to give additional security.(³)

Guardians on final settlement, shall be allowed such fees and compensation for their services as shall seem reasonable and just to the court.(⁴)

3. POWERS OF THE COUNTY COURT.—The county court has power to compel guardians to render an account of their guardianship from time to time.(⁵) The power is co-extensive with that of a court of chancery. In this state the county courts have an equitable jurisdiction, both in the allowance of claims, and in the adjustment of the accounts of guardians, and in such cases may adopt the forms of procedure in equity.(⁶)

Our statute has given a summary power to the county court to oblige guardians to render an account upon oath, touching their guardianship, instead of compelling a resort to a court of equity, as at common law.(⁷) And a citation to a guardian to account, is not a suit at law, but the exercise of a summary power, in the nature of a bill in equity, to compel a discovery against the guardian, and

---

(1) Hurd's R. S., Chap. 64, § 16.
(2) Bennett vs. Hanifin, 87 Ill., 32.
(3) Hurd's R. S., Chap. 64, § 35.
(4) Hurd's R. S., Chap. 64, § 42.
(5) Bond vs. Lockwood, 33 Ill., 212.
(6) Dixon vs. Buell, 21 Ill., 203; *In Re* Steel, 65 Ill., 322; Bennett vs. Hanifin, *supra*.
(7) *In Re* Steel, *supra*.

the statute of limitations can not be pleaded in bar.([1]) He should account annually to the court, unless his settlements are postponed for a longer period, and a failure to render his accounts, indicates negligence or fraud.([2]) In settling the accounts of a guardian, the court should charge him with interest on all money of the ward in his hands, from the time of its receipt, and allow him interest on all disbursements from the time they were made, the interest due from the guardian to extinguish *pro tanto* or in full, as the case may be, the expenditure of the ward.([3])

Transactions between a guardian and ward during his minority, are alone the subject of settlement in a guardianship account.([4]) If he should settle after the ward's majority, it is no objection, provided it embraces only what accrued during minority.([5]) The statute confers express power on county courts to compel guardians to render their accounts upon oath and to require additional security when necessary, and in default thereof, it may remove them.([6]) When a citation has been issued and served, and a return made thereto by the filing of a guardian's account, the correctness of which is assailed by the ward, the guardian should be allowed the privilege of defense, and to submit all legitimate proof, to establish his account.([7]) And for this purpose, he may introduce parol proof to explain a mistake apparent upon the face of his report. He is also competent to testify to any facts occurring after the death of the father of his ward, and therefore competent to explain himself such an error or mistake.([8])

In stating the account of a deceased guardian, for the purpose of establishing a claim against his estate, the rule is to allow compound interest on the sum which came into his hands, up to the time of his death, and simple interest from that time until the allowance of the claim.([9]) The creditors of the estate will be allowed

---

(1) Gilbert vs. Guptill, 34 Ill., 112; *In Re* Steel, 65 Ill., 322; Bruce vs. Doolittle, 81 Ill., 103.
(2) Hutchinson vs. Mudd, 6 J. J. Marsh, (Ky.) 580.
(3) Bryant vs. Craig, 12 Ala., 354; Bennett vs. Hanifin, 87 Ill., 32.
(4) Crowell's Appeal, 2 Watts, (Pa.) 295.
(5) Woodberry vs. Hammond, 54 Me., 332.
(6) Bruce vs. Doolittle, *supra*.
(7) *In Re* Steel, *supra*.
(8) Bruce vs. Doolittle, *supra;* Bennett vs. Hanifin, *supra*.
(9) Alsop vs. Barbee, 14 B. Mon., (Ky.) 525.

to appear and object to the amount to be allowed the ward.(¹)

In stating a guardian's account on final settlement, the court should, at the end of each year, add interest to the principal, and thus compound the interest annually until the final order.(²) An infant after his guardian's death, has a right to compel a settlement of his account, as if he were of age, the guardian's trust being personal, and terminating at his death;(³) but after the death of a guardian, before settlement of his accounts, no citation, under the statute, lies against his administrator to compel him to settle the guardian's account.(⁴). And a proceeding in county court against the guardian, to compel him to account, not being a suit either at law or in equity, abates on the death of the guardian, even after appeal to the circuit court.(⁵)

Where the same person is administrator and guardian, if he charges himself as guardian with his ward's share of the estate, he is no longer liable to account to him as administrator.(⁶)

4· ALLOWANCES ON ACCOUNTING.—He is entitled to be allowed for money furnished his ward for the purpose of completing his medical education.(⁷)

He is allowed to surrender in his account, evidence of a solvent loan.(⁸) He is not bound to go beyond the limits of the state, in the execution of the trust, and upon doing so, is entitled to extra compensation.(⁹)

Where a testator appointed a person permanently residing in another state, guardian for his children, it will be inferred that he expected the guardian would remove the children to that state. And the expense of removing the children will be a proper charge against the estate.(¹⁰)

A guardian who is a merchant, may supply his ward necessaries out of his own store, and charge his ward a reasonable profit

(1) Scheel vs. Eidman, 68 Ill., 193.
(2) *In Re* Steel, 65 Ill., 322.
(3) Peck vs. Bonman, 2 Blackf., (Ind.) 141; Gregg vs. Gregg, 15 N. H., 190.
(4) Harvey vs. Harvey, 87 Ill., 54.
(5) *Ib.*
(6) Crenshaw vs. Crenshaw, 4 Rich. (S. C.) Eq., 14.
(7) Shultz's Appeal, 30 Pa. St., 397.
(8) Higgins vs. McClure, 7 Bush., (Ky.) 379.
(9) Huson vs. Wallace, 1 Rich. (S. C.) Eq., 1.
(10) Cummins vs. Cummins, 29 Ill., 452.

thereon.(¹) He may also claim the allowance of a reasonable fee paid in the protection of their interest, as well as the expenses of a proper defense.(²) He will be allowed for an adverse claim brought in, the purchase being made in good faith, though the claim was in fact worthless.(³) If he advance his own money, in payment of debts or expenses of his ward, he is entitled to interest on the same.(⁴) Where the children are in good circumstances, and their father, who is their guardian, is poor and unable to support them, he will be allowed to charge their estates with the expense of their maintenance.(⁵) Claims against a ward need not be verified by the probate judge, before they are paid by the guardian.(⁶) A guardian, not being the father, should be allowed a reasonable credit for boarding furnished his ward.(⁷) He should be allowed for necessary, proper, and economical disbursements, made for his ward's benefit, without the previous direction of the court.(⁸) But he will not be permitted to break in on the funds of his ward, without showing a necessity therefor, upon proper proceedings, and, it is his duty to either obtain the sanction of the court, in advance, or have his actions subsequently ratified.(⁹)

The allowance to guardians, and those who act as guardians, for the support, maintenance and education of infants, is limited to the amount of interest, rents, hires or other profits of the estate of the infants, unless under very special circumstances.(¹⁰) It is only in very special cases such as could not be foreseen, that the court ought, under any circumstances, to sanction an expenditure by the guard-

---

(1) Moore vs. Shields, 69 N. C., 50.
(2) McWilliams vs. McWilliams, 15 La. Ann., 88; McNickle vs. Henry, 4 Brews., (Pa.) 150.
(3) Lee vs. Fox, 6 Dana, (Ky.) 171.
(4) Hayward vs. Ellis, 13 Pick., (Mass.) 272.
(5) Harring vs. Coles, 2 Bradf., (N. Y.) 349; Cunningham vs. Cunningham, 4 Gratt., (Va.) 43; Walker vs. Crowder, 2 Ired., (N. C.) Eq., 478.
(6) Raconillat vs. Requeena, 36 Cal., 651.
(7) Owen vs. Peebles, 42 Ala., 338.
(8) Jarret vs. Andrews, 7 Bush., (Ky.) 311.
(9) Cohen vs. Shyer, 1 Tenn. Ch., 192; Davis vs. Harkness, 1 Gilm., 173; Bybee vs. Tharp, 4 B. Mon., (Ky.) 313; Villard vs. Chovin, 2 Strobh., (S. C.) Eq., 40; Gilbert vs. McEachen, 38 Miss., 469; Phillips vs. Davis, 2 Sneed, (Tenn.) 520; Brown vs. Mullins, 24 Miss., 204; Beeler vs. Dunn, 3 Head, (Tenn.) 87; Myers vs. Wade, 6 Rand., (Va.) 444.
(10) Jackson vs. Jackson, 1 Gratt., (Va.) 143; Sneed vs. Hiely, 29 Ga., 587; Calhoun vs. Calhoun, 41 Ala., 369; Long vs. Norcum, 2 Ired., (N. C.) Eq., 354; Whitledge vs. Callis, 2 J. J. Marsh., (Ky.) 403; Hooper vs. Royster, 1 Mump., (Va.) 119; Foreman vs. Murray, 7 Leigh, (Va.) 412.

ian beyond the income of his ward, without the previous authorization of the court.(¹) Where he has created an indebtedness, without authority of law, which exceeds the revenues of the minor, the creditor must show that the indebtedness was absolutely necessary for the support of the minor, or the preservation of the property, and that the supplies furnished, inured to his benefit.(²) Nor is he authorized by law to make advances from his own means, for the maintenance of his ward, but he is bound to provide for such maintenance from the income, and if necessary the principal of the ward's personal estate, and if these are insufficient, to obtain license of the court, and sell real estate of the ward to provide the means required.(³)

It is a general rule of the common law, that the expenses of an infant or ward, shall be kept within the income or produce of his estate, although a court of chancery or other proper court, has frequently, in cases of strong necessity, upon proper application, ordered a portion of the principal to be appropriated in that way. But in doing this, they have always proceeded with great caution, and have only done it in urgent cases.(⁴) Guardians should keep their wards employed when able to earn their own support, rather than permit them to consume, in idleness, the principal of their patrimony.(⁵)

In determining what expenditures are necessary or proper, courts are exceedingly jealous of encroachments upon the principal of the ward's estate. It has been repeatedly held that they will not be allowed, except for necessaries, without an order of court is procured before making the expenditure, unless the guardian can show such a state of facts as would have entitled him to the order had he applied for it at the proper time, and a reasonable excuse for his neglect in that regard. A guardian may support his ward without any order of court, and all payments which he can show were necessary for that purpose, will be allowed him. While in this state it has not been usual to procure orders of court for prospective maintenance, yet such orders have been uniformly

(1) Freelick vs. Turner, 26 Miss., 393.
(2) Sanford vs. Waggaman, 14 La. Ann., 852.
(3) Preble vs. Longfellow, 48 Me., 279.
(4) Davs vs. Harkness, 1 Gilm., 173.
(5) State vs. Clark, 16 Ind., 97.

required for expenditures other than for necessaries; and such expenditures, whether from income or principal, should be disallowed, unless a reasonable cause is shown for not obtaining a proper order at the proper time.(¹) He ought to provide necessary support for his infant ward, even though the infant may have a father, provided the father be in needy circumstances and unable to support him.(²)

He may furnish the minor from the income of his estate with such articles as are proper for his condition in life.(³) And, in determining what are necessaries for his ward, according to the estate and social position, a guardian has the same right to judge, that a parent has for a child.(⁴) And they are supplied at the discretion of the guardian, subject to the supervision of the court in passing upon his accounts. Whether articles of a certain class or kind are such as infants would be liable for, or whether certain kinds of expenditures are necessaries, must be judged of by the court, as there is no positive rule in regard to what are necessaries.(⁵) Horses, saddles, bridles, pistols, fiddles, liquors, chronometers and the like, have generally been excluded by courts from the term necessaries. There is no inflexible rule, however, that a riding horse may not be regarded as a necessary for a minor;(⁶) for it has been held, that if riding on horseback, was necessary to the health of an infant, it would be proper to purchase a riding horse.(⁷)

A guardian has the right to judge what are necessaries for his ward, and, if he act in good faith, a third person has no right to usurp his rights and duties. And if a third person, contrary to the wishes of a guardian, advance money to his ward for the purpose of taking a long trip, such person cannot recover for the traveling expenses thus advanced, they being considered not necessaries.(⁸)

(1) Bond vs. Lockwood, 33 Ill., 212; Cummins vs. Cummins, 29 Ill., 452; Davis vs. Roberts, 1 Smeed & M., (Miss.) Ch., 543; Anderson vs. Thompson, 11 Leigh, (Va.) 439.
(2) Clark vs. Montgomery, 23 Barb., (N. Y.) 464.
(3) Owens vs. Walker, 2 Strobh., (S. C.) 289.
(4) Nicholson vs. Spencer, 11 Ga., 607; Caldwell vs. Young, 21 Texas, 800.
(5) Chitty on Contracts, 141—note 2; 1 Parsons on Contracts, 296; Beeler vs. Young, 1 Bibb., 519; 1 Am. Lead. Cases, 248.
(6) McKanna vs. Merry, 61 Ill., 177.
(7) Owens vs. Walker, *supra;* McKanna vs. Merry, *supra.*
(8) McKanna vs. Merry, *supra.*

He will not be charged for the services of his ward.(¹) And where he supported his ward at his own house, under an assurance to the ward that no charge will be made for board, he will not afterwards be permitted to charge for such board.(²) For, if a guardian make a gratuity, he can not afterwards charge the amount to him.(³)

If he erect a building on his ward's land, out of his own money, without an order of the court, he can not recover the amount so expended from his ward's estate.(⁴)

He should be allowed no compensation where he has neglected his duties, and done his ward a positive wrong.(⁵)

Commissions are allowed to guardians for services rendered, and not for neglect of duties.(⁶)

He can not charge his ward's estate with any counsel fees he may choose to pay. It must appear that the services were required, and the compensation such as is usual for such services.(⁷) And in no case will he be allowed to charge attorney's fees where he himself is an attorney, and performs the services himself.(⁸)

He must account for all the property which he receives as belonging to the estate of his ward, and can not be permitted to contest the title of the ward to the property.(⁹) He will not be allowed to charge the estate of his ward with any part of the expense of a controversy on the settlement of his accounts, where such controversy was occasioned by his own fault.(¹⁰)

A step-father is under no obligation to support his wife's children by a former marriage;(¹¹) but it has been held, that a step-father who is also the guardian, is not entitled to compensation for

---

(1) Armstrong vs. Walkup, 12 Gratt., (Va.) 608.
(2) McDowell vs. Caldwell, 2 McCord, (S. C.) Ch., 43.
(3) Pratt vs. McJunkin, 4 Rich., (S. C.) 5.
(4) White vs. Parker, 8 Barb., 48; Royer's Appeal, 11 Penn. St., 36; Austin vs. Lamar, 23 Miss., 189; Brown vs. Mullins, 24 Miss., 204.
(5) Reed vs. Ryourn, 23 Ark., 47; McCahan's Appeal, 7 Pa. St., 56.
(6) Bond vs. Lockwood, 33 Ill., 212.
(7) Alexander vs. Alexander, 8 Ala., 796; Taylor vs. Kilgore, 33 Ala., 214; Neilson vs. Cook, 40 Ala., 498; Smith vs. Bean, 8 N. H., 15; Mathes vs. Bennett, 21 N. H., (1 Foster) 204; *Ex Parte* Dawson, 3 Bradf., (N. Y.) 130; McGary vs. Lamb, 3 Texas, 342.
(8) Morgan vs. Hannas, 49 N. Y., 667.
(9) McAllister vs. Olmstead, 1 Humph., (Tenn.) 210.
(10) Blake vs. Pegram, 109 Mass., 541.
(11) Attridge vs. Billings, 57 Ill., 489; Gay vs. Ballou, 4 Wend., 403; Freto vs. Brown, 4 Mass., 674; Cooper vs. Martin, 4 East., 77.

maintaining the wards, who are his step-children.([1]) The rule would seem to be, that where a man marries a widow with children, if he assume the relation of father to the children, and as such, provides them with board and clothing, and in return has their labor, and has no contract with their guardian, he cannot recover for their support thus furnished.([2])

A guardian will not be allowed compensation for taking care of the trust fund, while he himself is the borrower of it.([3])

5. COMMISSIONS.—The rule is not inflexible that the commissions of the guardian cover every thing which can be allowed him for services respecting the estate of his ward, as we have seen (*ante* page, 129) is the case with executors and administrators.([4]) The time spent by a guardian in the management of his ward's estate, may be considered in fixing his commissions, but can not be charged separately.([5])

He will not forfeit his commissions by failing to make his returns in proper time;([6]) and, where he used in his own business, some of the trust money, expecting to charge no commissions, and to pay no interest thereon, on being charged with interest, he will be entitled to commissions.([7])

6. OPENING AND REVIEWING SETTLEMENTS.—A settlement made by the guardian in the probate court, allowing his accounts, is final as to him, as to all matters before the court, and the court can not re-open the accounts at his instance, although the ward may re-open them by a bill of review, or upon citation to the guardian, where the account is incorrectly stated by him.([8])

Settlements of a guardian, are but *prima facie* evidence of their correctness.([9]) In court, the records of such settlements are evidence, as the vouchers may be lost.([10]) And they may be given in evidence in a suit on a guardian's bond.([11])

(1) Douglas' Appeal, 82 Pa. St., 169.
(2) Meyer vs. Temme, 72 Ill., 574; Brush vs. Blanchard, 18 Ill., 46.
(3) Farwell vs. Steen, 46 Vt., 678.
(4) Morgan vs. Morgan, 39 Barb., (N. Y.) 20.
(5) Shutt vs. Carloss, 1 Ired., (N. C.) Eq., 27.
(6) Baker vs. Lafitte, 4 Rich., (S. C.) Eq., 392.
(7) Rapalje vs. Norsworthy, 1 Sandf., (N. Y.) Ch., 399.
(8) Johnson vs. Miller, 33 Miss., 553; Davis vs. Ford, Wright, (Ohio) 200; Bruce vs. Doolittle, 81 Ill., 103; Jessup vs. Jessup, 102 Ill., 480.
(9) State vs. Strange, 1 Ind., 538; State vs. Baker, 8 Md., 44.
(10) Tabb vs. Boyd, 4 Call., (Va.) 453.
(11) State vs. Strange, *supra*.

They do not, however, bind the ward, when he is able to show that they are erroneous.([1]) But, in the absence of any fraud, and unless the evidence be clear and conclusive, a court of equity will not undertake to control the discretion of the county court therein.([2]) A suit in equity, surcharging a guardian's settlement made with the county court, must specify, particularly, the objectionable items.([3]) For, the law presumes that a guardian has accounted for all the ward's property, in his possession, when he has made a final settlement with the county court.([4]) And after a fair settlement, sanctioned by the ward during many years, and by the court of probate at the time, the court will not re-open the matter, only in a case very clearly calling for new action.([5])

A bill of review is founded on equitable principles, and is never allowed to stand on strict law; and it is against equity, to allow a review of a guardian's account, in order to strike out payments made by him in relief of the estate, when there was no administrator, and in order to save the expense of one.([6]) A receipt given by a ward on final settlement, based upon an erroneous report, for the balance shown by such report to be due the ward, is not conclusive.([7])

If a guardian makes fictitious reports to the county court, falsely charging himself with money not in fact due from him to the ward, for the fraudulent purpose of making his surety liable, a court of equity will, doubtless, interfere at the suit of a surety to correct such reports, and make them conform to the truth.([8])

Where a minor, after arriving at age, settles with his guardian, and receives moneys in his hands, belonging to him, derived from a sale of his lands, under proceedings for partition, it will be presumed that he received the same with a full knowledge of the source from whence it came, and did the act deliberately.([9]) A final settlement, made in a proper court, unless revoked, re-opened

---

(1) Willis vs. Fox, 25 Wis., 646; Douglas' Appeal, 82 Pa. St., 169.
(2) Mattock vs. Rice, 1 Heisk., (Tenn.) 33.
(3) Tanner vs. Skinner, 11 Bush., (Ky.) 120.
(4) Smith vs. Denny, 34 Mo., 219.
(5) Brown vs. McWilliams, 29 Ga., 194; Southall vs. Clark, 3 Stew. & P., (Ala.) 338; Whedbee vs. Whedbee, 5 Jones, (N. C.) Eq., 392; Railsback vs. Williamson, 88 Ill., 494.
(6) Stephenson's Appeal, 22 Pa. St., 318.
(7) Bruce vs. Doolittle, 81 Ill., 103.
(8) Fogarty vs. Ream, 100 Ill., 366.
(9) Corwin vs. Shoup, 76 Ill., 246.

or appealed from, is conclusive upon the parties; it cannot be attacked collaterally, in a suit by the ward, on a guardian's bond.([1])

It may be sometimes important to ascertain the liability where a person sustain the dual relation or trust of administrator and of guardian of the sole distributee—in which capacity he is liable. When the estate is substantially settled, and the person so holding such dual relation, charges himself in a private book as guardian for amount due from the estate to the heir, and pays the necessary expenses of the ward, and collects rents as guardian, a reasonable time having elapsed for completing the administration, he will be chargeable as guardian, and not as administrator.([2])

7.   FORM OF GUARDIAN'S SETTLEMENT.

STATE OF ILLINOIS, } ss.
..............County,

To the Judge of the County Court of.........County,.........Term, A. D. 18...

The undersigned, guardian of........., would respectfully submit to the court the following report of h   acts and doings as such guardian from ....to........., A. D. 18...; ....charge......... with the following, to-wit:

Date.	Items of Receipts.	Amount.	Total Am't.
	Total am't of Moneys rec'd or collected,		

CONTRA.

......ask to be credited with the following sums, paid out per receipts exhibited:

Date.	Items Paid Out.	Amount.	Total Am't.
	Total amount paid out,		

(1) Holland vs. State, 48 Ind., 391.
(2) Bell vs. People, 94 Ill., 230; *ante page* 39.

RECAPITULATION.

	Dols.	Cts.	Dols.	Cts.
Total amount received, " " paid out, Balance due,				

The above balance consists of the following........., which are herewith presented for inspection:

DESCRIPTION.

Kind of Instrument.	Date.	Payor.	Securities.	When Due.	Rate of Int	Am't.

All of which is respectfully submitted.   ....
                                                            ....

STATE OF ILLINOIS, } ss.
.............County,

........., Guardian of........., being duly sworn, say that the foregoing is a full and perfect account of all h   dealings and transactions, and of all moneys and effects received and paid out by h   on account of the said minor , from.........to the...day of......, A. D. 18..., and of all moneys, notes, bonds, accounts and evidences of indebtedness, composing the personal estate of said minor   on hand the...day of......, A. D. 18...

Subscribed and sworn to before me this...day of......, A. D. 18...
                                                            ....
.......................Clerk.   ....

FORM OF GUARDIAN'S FINAL RECEIPT.

N. B.—This receipt, if properly executed, entitles the guardian to a discharge. The ward should be careful not to sign it unless it is in strict accordance with the facts.

STATE OF ILLINOIS, } ss.
.............County.   *In County Court.*

To whom it may concern:

I, ..., of........., in the county of........., and State of Illinois, do hereby certify that I attained the age of......years on the...day of......, A. D. 18.... I do further certify that I have made full and final settlement with........., my former guardian, since I have arrived at said age. And I do hereby acknowledge the receipt of.........dollars and......cents, in full of all demands against........., as such guardian, together with all books, papers and property in...possession belonging to me.

I hereby enter my appearance in the matter of.........application for discharge as such guardian, waiving all further notice.

Witness my hand and seal this...day of......, A. D. 18....
Attest................   .... [L. S.]

ADDITIONAL NOTES.

1. Guardian—Loans must be approved by the county court.
2. Minor repudiating a sale is required to refund what he has received.
3. Expenses incurred for litigation.
4. On appeal—What is to be contested.
5. Jurisdiction of the county court—Possesses chancery powers.
6. Form of the report—As to the mode of computation.
7. Acting without authority of the court.
8. Mode of accounting.
9. Unclaimed money—How claimed and obtained by persons entitled thereto.

1. LOANS—COURT MUST APPROVE.—The loans made by a guardian must be approved by the county court. The requirement of the statute that the security shall be approved by the county court is mandatory, and not merely directory; and should the guardian fail to obtain the approval of loans by him made, the ward may treat the loan as an appropriation by the guardian of money to his own use.(¹)

2. MINOR REPUDIATING SALE MUST REFUND MONEY.—Where a minor repudiates or disaffirms a sale by bill in equity, he will be required to refund what he has received, if it be in his power. Repudiating by action of ejectment is in effect the same as repudiating by bill in equity, and no court possessing equitable powers will permit a party to do this and at the same time receive the proceeds of a sale not yet paid over.(²)

3. EXPENSES INCURRED FOR LITIGATION.—If a guardian incur expense by reason of litigation where he believed it was reasonably necessary, and where it is beneficial to the ward's interests, he will be entitled to be reimbursed out of the ward's estate.(³)

4. ON APPEAL—WHAT IS TO BE CONTESTED.—On appeal from the final order of the probate court, settling the final accounts of the guardian, which were contested by the ward, and such contest was

---

(1) McIntire vs. The People, for the use of Alice Wilkey, 103 Ill., 142; Hughes vs. The People, for use of Kerrick, 111 Ill., 457; Winslow vs. The People, etc., 117 Ill., 152.
(2) Brandon vs. Brown, 106 Ill., 519.
(3) Kingsbury vs. Powers, 131 Ill., 182.

unsuccessful, the attorney's fees paid by the guardian are proper charges against the ward's estate.(¹) An appeal by an administrator or guardian from an order rejecting one or more of his claims against the estate only brings up for review the propriety of the ruling in respect to rejected claims. The same rule applies in case of an appeal by the heir or ward.(²)

5. JURISDICTION OF COUNTY COURT—CHANCERY POWERS.—In the matter of an accounting in the county court by a guardian, in respect to his administration of the trust confided in him, the powers of that court are coextensive with those of a chancery court, and it possesses a similar jurisdiction, and adopts the same forms and mode of procedure.(³)

6. FORM OF REPORT—MODE OF COMPUTATION.—The proper mode of computation of a guardian's accounts of money in his hands used by him is on the principle of annual rests, so that the rights of the ward may be fully protected.(⁴)

7. ACTING WITHOUT AUTHORITY OF COURT.—A guardian should usually act under the authority of the court, but should he make needed repairs which are beneficial to the ward, he should be reimbursed for the same.(⁵)

8. MODE OF ACCOUNTING.—On any accounting and final settlement of a guardian, he shall exhibit and file his account as such guardian, setting forth specifically, in separate items, on what account expenditures were made by him, and all sums received and paid out since his last accounting, [and of all moneys on hand, and an itemized account of all notes, bonds, accounts and evidences of indebtedness, composing the personal estate of his ward, and said guardian shall produce and exhibit to the court the notes, bonds, accounts and evidences of indebtedness, so itemized and held by him; and it is hereby made the duty of the court to inspect the assets so exhibited. Which account shall be accompanied by proper vouchers and [be] signed by him and verified by his affidavit.](⁶)*

(1) Kingsbury vs. Powers, 131 Ill., 182.
(2) Ib.
(3) Cheney vs. Roodhouse, 135 Ill., 257; See Ib., 32 Ill. Ap., 49.
(4) Ib.
(5) Ib.
(6) Hurd's R. S., 783, § 16; Laws of Ill., 1885, 208.

*NOTE.—Amendment substitutes matter enclosed in brackets.

9. UNCLAIMED MONEY—HOW OBTAINED.—When any guardian shall have made final settlement with the county court, it shall be the duty of the court to order such guardian to deposit with the county treasurer such moneys as he may have belonging to any ward whose whereabouts may be unknown, or belonging to the unknown heir or heirs of any deceased ward, or the heirs of any ward whose whereabouts may be unknown, and to take the receipt of such treasurer therefor, and to file such receipt in the office of the clerk of the county court where such settlement has been made.[1]

When money shall be deposited as aforesaid, the person or persons entitled to the same may at any time apply to the court making such order, and obtain the same upon making satisfactory proof to the court of his, her or their right thereto.[2]

An order of the probate court restating a guardian's account, and ordering him to pay to his successor the balance found due from him on such accounting, is not a judgment upon which execution can issue. The order may be enforced by attachment.[3]

(1) Hurd's R. S., 787, § 51; Laws of Ill., 1889, 166.
(2) *Ib.*, § 52.
(3) Kingsbury vs. Hutton, Supreme Court Ill., Vol. 30, No. 7, N. E. Reporter, affirming case in 40 Ill. Ap., 424.

CHAPTER VII.

SALE OF WARD'S REAL ESTATE.

1. Proceedings to sell real estate.
2. Form of petition—when filed.
3. Notice of application—form—service.
4. Practice—form of bond and decree.
5. Notice and terms of sale—form.
6. Return—sale approved—title—form of guardian's report—deed.
7. Proceeds—accounting for—re-investment.
8. Sale of real estate by non-resident guardian.
9. Terms of sale.
10. Deeds—title.
11. Bond for costs.
12. The Proceeding.
13. The Petition.
14. Jurisdiction.
15. Special bond.
16. Fixing time of sale.
17. Notice of application.
18. Purchaser at sale.
19. Report of sale.
20. Guardian's deed.
21. Confirmation of sale.
22. Purchaser need not see to the application of purchase money.
23. Rule of *caveat emptor*.

1. PROCEEDINGS TO SELL REAL ESTATE.—On the petition of the guardian, the county court of the county where the ward resides, or if the ward does not reside in the state, of the county where the real estate, or some part of it is situated, may order the sale of the real estate of the ward, for his support and education, when the court shall deem it necessary, or to invest the proceeds in other real estate, or for the purpose of otherwise investing the same. *Provided*, the said county court shall make no order for a sale under said petition, until the said guardian shall have executed and filed a bond, payable to the People of the State of Illinois, with at least two sufficient sureties to be approved by the court, in double the value of the real estate by said petition sought to be sold, condi-

tioned for the due and faithful accounting for, and disposition of the proceeds of all real estate that may be sold by him, under such order, in the manner provided by law; which bond may be put in suit in the name of the People of the State of Illinois, to the use of any person entitled to recover on a breach thereof, and damages assessed and proceedings had thereon, as in other cases of penal bonds.(¹)

2. FORM OF PETITION—WHEN FILED.—The petition shall set forth the condition of the estate, and the facts and circumstances on which the petition is founded, and shall be signed by the guardian and be verified by his affidavit, and shall be filed at least ten days before the commencement of the term of court at which the application shall be made.(²)

The petition for sale of real estate by guardian, may be in form as follows:

PETITION FOR SALE OF REAL ESTATE BY GUARDIAN.

STATE OF ILLINOIS, } ss. *In the County Court,*
...............County.   *To the..........term, A. D. 18...*

To the Hon.........., sole Judge of the County Court of the County of.........., and State of Illinois:

Your petitioner................., of the county of................., and State of Illinois, guardian by the appointment of this honorable court of..........., minor heir of........., deceased, respectfully represents and shows unto your honor: That your petitioner was, on the...day of......, A. D. 18..., appointed guardian of the person and property of the said........., by the county court of.........county, and State of Illinois, as will more fully appear on a hearing hereof, by the production of his letters of guardianship.

Your petitioner would further represent, that the said.........is the owner in fee simple of the following described real estate, situate, lying and being in the county of........., and State of Illinois, and known and described as follows to-wit: [*Here describe the real estate.*] That said real estate is wholly unimproved and unproductive, and your petitioner is unable to realize anything therefrom, neither has he any funds in his hands belonging to the said........., to improve said lands and bring the same into a state of cultivation. That there is now due on said lands the taxes for the year 18..., ...dollars.

And your petitioner would further represent and show unto your honor, that at the......term of this honorable court, your petitioner made a settlement of his accounts as such guardian to that date, which said settlement was approved and filed in this honorable court, reference being had thereto for greater certainty, and that upon such settlement, there was only the sum of twenty dollars left in the hands of your petitioner, for the support, main-

(1) Hurd's R. S., Chap. 64, § 28.   (2) Hurd's R. S., Chap. 64, § 29.

tenance and education of the said........., and that since said settlement he has been compelled to expend said last mentioned sum for the common necessaries of life, for the support of his said ward........., and your petitioner files herewith a copy of said settlement above referred to, marked exhibit "A," and made a part of this petition.

And your petitioner would further show that funds to the amount of..... dollars are needed and necessary for the support, maintenance and education of said minor, and for the purpose of paying the taxes now due and to accrue on said real estate; wherefore, in consideration of the premises aforesaid, your petitioner believes it will be for the best interest of said minor, to sell a part of said real estate described aforesaid. Your petitioner believes, that the best interest of his ward will be subserved by the sale of that portion of said real estate, described as follows, to-wit: [*Here describe the real estate.*] That said real estate is of the value of......dollars, as your petitioner is informed and verily believes.

And your petitioner would further represent and show unto your honor, that said minor is now of the age of...years, and that your petitioner has been educating him at......, for some time past, and he verily believes that it will be for the best interest of his said ward to still continue him at said school.

Your petitioner therefore prays an order of this court, authorizing him to sell said last above described real estate, or so much thereof as to your honor shall seem meet and proper, for the support, maintenance and education of said ward and the payment of taxes due on his lands, and for such other purposes, as to the court shall seem meet and proper; and that the court will grant your petitioner such other and further relief in the premises as may be necessary and the law will allow; and your petitioner, as he is in duty bound, will ever pray, etc.

By........., his Attorney.   ...., Guardian of.........

STATE OF ILLINOIS, } ss.
..............County.

.........being duly sworn on his oath states, that he is the petitioner in the foregoing petition, and that he has heard the same read over, and that the matters and facts stated therein, are true in substance and in fact, as he verily believes.   ....

Subscribed and sworn to before me, this...day of......, A. D. 18...

........., Clerk County Court.

3. NOTICE OF APPLICATION.—Notice of such application shall be given to all persons concerned, by publication in some newspaper published in the county where the application is made, at least once in each week for three successive weeks, or by setting up written or printed notices in three of the most public places in the county, at least three weeks before the session of the court at which such

application shall be made. The ward shall be served with a copy of such notice at least ten days before the hearing of such application.(¹)

NOTICE OF APPLICATION TO SELL REAL ESTATE BY GUARDIAN.

STATE OF ILLINOIS, } ss.   *In the County Court,*
..............County.   *To the......term, A. D.* 18...

To all persons concerned:

Public notice is hereby given, that the undersigned, guardian of........., minor child of........., deceased, has filed in the office of the clerk of the county court of.........county, and State of Illinois, a petition for an order for the sale of the following described real estate, belonging to said minor, situate, lying and being in the county of........., and State of Illinois, and described as follows, to-wit: [*Here describe the real estate.*] And that said petition will be heard on...the first day of the......term, A. D. 18..., or so soon thereafter as counsel may be heard; at which time and place you can appear and object to said petition if you see fit so to do.

Dated........., ..., 18...

By........., Attorney.   ...., Guardian of.........

The statute provides, in addition to the publishing and posting of the notices aforesaid, the ward shall be served with a copy of the notice, at least ten days before the hearing of such application.(²) The notice may be served by the sheriff, or by some other person. If served by any person other than the sheriff, he should file an affidavit of such service, which may be in form as follows:

STATE OF ILLINOIS, } ss.
..............County.

........being duly sworn, on his oath states, that he personally served........ with a copy of the foregoing notice hereto attached, by reading and delivering to him a true copy of the same, on......, ..., 18...

....

Subscribed and sworn to before me, this...day of......, A. D. 18...

         ...., Clerk County Court.

Where, instead of posting notices as permitted, the notice is published in a newspaper, the guardian should also procure a publisher's certificate, which may be in form as follows:

TOWN OF........., COUNTY OF........., AND STATE OF ILLINOIS.

The undersigned, publisher of the........., a weekly newspaper, of general circulation, published in the town of........., county and state aforesaid,

(1) Hurd's R. S., Chap. 64, § 30.   (2) *Ib.*

hereby certifies that the notice, a true copy of which is hereunto attached, was published in three consecutive numbers of said paper; the first insertion being on the....day of........, A. D. 18...., and the last one on the....day of........, A. D. 18....

Given under my hand, this....day of........, A. D. 18....

.........., Publisher of............

4. PRACTICE.—Such application shall be docketed as other cases, and the petition may be amended, heard or continued for further notice or for other cause. The practice in such cases shall be the same as in other cases in chancery.([1])

GUARDIAN'S BOND IN CASE OF SALE OF REAL ESTATE.

Know all men by these presents, that we........, ...and.........., of the county of..........., and State of Illinois, are held and firmly bound unto the People of the State of Illinois, for the use of..........., in the penal sum of........ dollars, current money of the United States, which payment, well and truly to be made and performed, we, and each of us, do hereby bind ourselves, our heirs, executors and administrators and assigns, jointly, severally and firmly by these presents.

Witness our hands and seals, this....day of........, A. D. 18....

The condition of this obligation is such, that whereas the above bounden..........., guardian of..........., did, on the....day of........, A. D. 18...., file in the county court of............county, his petition for an order to sell certain real estate of his ward in said petition described; and whereas, the said county court is about to make an order directing the sale of said real estate. Now, therefore, if the above bounden..........., guardian as aforesaid, shall duly and faithfully account for and dispose of the proceeds of all real estate that may be sold by him under such order of the county court, in the manner provided by law, then this obligation to be void; otherwise to remain in full force and virtue.

Sealed and delivered in presence of

............., [L. S.]
............., [L. S.]
.... [L. S.]

....

STATE OF ILLINOIS, } ss.
County of................ }

I, ..., in and for said county and State, do hereby certify that..........., who are each personally known to me to be the same persons whose names are subscribed to the foregoing instrument, appeared before me this day in person, and acknowledged that they signed, sealed and delivered said instrument as their free and voluntary act, for the uses and purposes as therein set forth.

Given under my hand and........seal, this....day of........, A. D. 18....

................, ...

Approved by me, this....day of........, A. D. 18....

..........., judge of the County Court.

(1) Hurd's R. S., Chap. 64, § 31.

At the hearing, the court ascertains the value of the real estate to be sold, by competent evidence, and the bond is then fixed at double the amount of the value as ascertained by the court, and it is then the duty of the guardian to file his bond with at least two good and sufficient sureties, to be approved by the court, in the office of the clerk of the county court, when we are ready for the decree of sale, which may be in form as follows:

DECREE FOR THE SALE OF REAL ESTATE BY GUARDIAN.

STATE OF ILLINOIS, ⎫ ss.
.................County.   ⎭

*In the County Court,
Of the.............term, A. D. 18....*

In the matter of............, Guardian ⎫
of............, minor heir of............, ⎬ Decree for the sale of real estate by guardian.
deceased.   ⎭

And now, on this day, the same being the....judicial day of the present term of this court, comes the said petitioner,............, by............, his attorney, and submits to the court proof of the due publication of notice and service of notice in this cause as provided by law. And the court on inspection doth find that notice of petitioner's application for leave to sell the real estate of his ward, has been given to all persons concerned, by [publication in the............, a weekly newspaper, published in............, in the county of............, and State of Illinois, for three successive weeks, commencing on the....day of........., A. D. 18...., and ending on the....day of........, A. D. 18....,]* and that............, petitioner's ward, was served with a copy of said notice on the....day of........, A. D. 18...., the same being more than ten days before the day set for the hearing of this application, and that the notice so published and served, is in all respects in conformity with the statute in such case made and provided.

And this cause coming on now to be heard upon the merits of said petition, exhibits, files, and oral proofs, the petitioner introduced as a witness............, and............ who being duly sworn, testified touching the matters contained in said petition, and also, as to the value of said real estate in said petition mentioned:

And the court having examined said petition, files and exhibits, and heard the testimony adduced in support of said petition, and the argument of counsel; and being now sufficiently advised and satisfied in the premises, doth find, that said petition and each and every allegation thereof are true, and that the prayer of said petition should be granted; and that the interest of said ward will be promoted by the sale of a part of said premises in said petition described, and that funds are needed for the support, maintenance and education of said ward.

It is therefore ordered, adjudged and decreed, by the court, that the said guardian have leave, and he is hereby authorized to sell all the right,

---

*Or, should the requisite notice have been given by posting notices, the following should be inserted within the brackets: "setting up written or printed notices thereof in three of the most public places in this county, more than three weeks before the first day of this term of the court."

title, claim and interest of said........., in and to the following described real estate, to-wit: [*Here describe the real estate.*] He having previously filed his bond with good and sufficient sureties, approved by the court, conditioned for the due and faithful accounting for, and disposition of real estate that may be sold by him, under this order, in double the amount of the value of said real estate, as ascertained by the court.

And it is further ordered, that said guardian advertise the time, terms and place of said sale, and a description of the premises sought to be sold, for at least three weeks prior to the day of said sale, by publication in some weekly newspaper published in said..........county, Illinois, and by posting up written or printed notices thereof, in at least four of the most public places in the county, in the vicinity of said real estate sought to be sold.

That said sale shall be made on the following terms: Ten per cent. of said purchase money to be paid cash in hand, and the residue thereof in two equal payments, one of which shall be payable in six and the other in twelve months from the day of said sale, the purchaser to give his notes with approved personal security, and a mortgage on the premises sold to secure the payment of the purchase money.

Said sale to be made at the...front door of the court house, in......Illinois, at the hour of one o'clock p. m., of the day of sale, to the highest and best bidder, at public outcry. *Provided*, however, no bid shall be received for less than.......dollars per acre.

And it is further ordered, that said guardian may, for good cause, postpone said sale at the time first fixed for the same, to some other time, on giving notice as in the first instance.

And it is further ordered, that this cause stand continued for report of said sale.

5. NOTICE AND TERMS OF SALE.—The court shall direct notice of the time and place of sale to be given, and may direct the sale to be made on reasonable credit, and require such security of the guardian or purchaser as the interest of the ward may require.([1])

The notice of the guardian's sale may be in form as follows:

NOTICE OF GUARDIAN'S SALE OF REAL ESTATE.

STATE OF ILLINOIS, } ss.
............County,

By virtue of a decretal order of the......court of said county, entered at the......term of said court, A. D. 18..., on the application of........., guardian of...... ... , minor, to sell the following described real estate, belonging to said minor, situate in the county of........., State of Illinois, to-wit: [*Here describe the real estate.*] I shall, on the...day of....., A. D. 18..., at the...door of the court house, in the town of........., ...county, Illinois, at the hour

---

(1) Hurd's R. S., Chap. 64, § 32; Hurd's R. S., Chap. 100, § 3.

of one o'clock, p. m., sell all the interest of said minor in and to the said real estate at public vendue.

Terms of Sale:

Ten per cent. of said purchase money to be paid cash in hand, and the residue thereof in two equal payments, one of which shall be payable in six and the other in twelve months from the day of said sale, the purchaser to give his notes with approved personal security, and a mortgage on the premises sold to secure the payment of the purchase money: *Provided*, however, no bid will be received for less than......dollars per acre.

A B,
By........., Attorney.   Guardian for.........

6. RETURN—SALE APPROVED—TITLE.—It shall be the duty of the guardian making such sale, as soon as may be, to make return of such sale to the court granting the order, which, if approved, shall be recorded, and shall vest in the purchaser or purchasers all the interest of the ward in the real estate so sold.(¹)

The report of the guardian may be in form as follows:

GUARDIAN'S REPORT.

STATE OF ILLINOIS, } ss.   *In the County Court,*
..................County, }   *To the............term, A. D.* 18....

In the matter of the application }
of A B, Guardian of........., }   Report of Guardian's Sale.
minor heir of........, deceased. }

To the Hon........., Judge of said Court:

The undersigned, guardian of..........., minor heir of..........., deceased, would respectfully report: That, in pursuance of the order and decree of this honorable court, made and entered of record at its.....term, A. D. 18..., on the petition of the undersigned for leave to sell the real estate in said order described, for the purposes therein mentioned, after having first advertised the time, terms and place of said sale, together with a description of the real estate sought to be sold, by posting four printed notices thereof, as follows: One at..., one at..., one at..., and one at..., the same being four of the most public places in the county and in the vicinity of said real estate, at least three weeks before the day of said sale; and by publishing a copy of said notice in the....., a weekly newspaper, published in the town of......, in said county of......, and State of Illinois, for three successive weeks, the first insertion being on the...day of......, A. D. 18..., and the last being on the...day of......, A. D. 18..., a copy of which notice with the affidavit of posting and the printer's certificate of publication is hereto attached, marked "Exhibit A," and made a part of this report, I did, on......, the...day of......A. D. 18..., at one o'clock p. m., of said day, at the.........front door of the court house

(1) Hurd's R. S., Chap. 64, § 33.

in.........., Illinois, offer said lands in said order of the court, and in said notices aforesaid specified, for sale at public vendue, and............bid the sum of........dollars for the said real estate described as follows, viz.: [*Here describe the real estate.*] And that being the highest and best bid offered at said sale, I struck off and sold the same to him for that sum.

And the said............having complied with all the terms of said sale, by paying ten per cent. cash in hand and executing his notes in two equal payments for the residue thereof, the first of said notes due and payable in six months, and the second payable in twelve months from the day of said sale, with good personal security and a mortgage on the premises so sold, I,........, as guardian of the said............, executed a deed of conveyance of the said real estate, and delivered the same to the said............, subject to the approval and ratification of the court.

All of which is respectfully submitted and an order of approval and confirmation of title in said purchaser prayed for.

Dated this....day of........, A. D. 18....

By............Attorney.

............, Guardian of...........

ORDER APPROVING SALE.

STATE OF ILLINOIS, } ss.
..................County, }

In the County Court,
To the........term, A. D. 18....

In the matter of..........., Guardian of............, minor heir of............., deceased. }

Order confirming report and sale of real estate by Guardian.

And now on this day, the same being the....judicial day of the present term of this court, comes the said............by............, his attorney, and made report of the sale of the real estate, described, in pursuance of an order of this court, made at the......term, A. D. 18...., which said report is in words and figures as follows, to-wit: [*Here copy the report in full.*] Which said report is received and approved, and ordered to be spread at large upon the records of this court, which is accordingly done; and all the acts and doings of said guardian in and about said sale confirmed; and all the interest or title of the said............in said real estate, confirmed in............, the purchaser, at said sale.

GUARDIAN'S DEED ON SALE OF REAL ESTATE.

This indenture, made this....day of........, A. D. 18...., between A B, of the county of........ , and State of Illinois, the duly appointed and qualified guardian of C D, minor, under letters issued from the county court of..........county, in the State of Illinois, as such guardian, party of the first part, and E F, of the.........., in the county of............, and State of............, party of the second part:

Witnesseth, that whereas, the said party of the first part, as such guardian, on the......day of........, A. D. 18...., more than ten days before the commencement of the term of court at which said application was made, filed.... petition in said court, praying, upon legal cause therein set forth, for an order to sell the real estate belonging to said ward, hereinafter described, and gave notice of such application, to all persons concerned, by publication in the............, (a newspaper published in said county of............,) once a week for three successive weeks, before the session of the court at which said application was made, and also served said ward with a copy of such notice ten days before the hearing of such application: And whereas, the said county court, after hearing said application, on the....day of........, A. D. 18...., did, by order duly entered, empower and direct the said A B, as such guardian, to sell at public vendue the real estate of said ward hereinafter described, as prayed in said petition:

And whereas, in pursuance of the said decretal order of the county court aforesaid, the said party of the first part, as such guardian as aforesaid, having given due public notice of the intended sale, together with a description of the real estate to be sold, to be previously posted for....weeks at.... of the most public places in the county where such real estate was sold, and also to be published for...successive weeks prior to said sale in the......., a newspaper published in said......county, agreeably to the order and direction of the said county court, did, on the....day of........, A. D. 18...., pursuant to the order and notice aforesaid, sell at public vendue, the real estate of the said ward hereinafter described, to E F, the said party of the second part, for the sum of........dollars, ...being the highest bidder therefor.

And whereas, the said party of the first part made return of his proceedings and sale under said order to said county court, and the said county court having carefully examined the same on the....day of........, A. D. 18..., finding the same correct, did approve and confirm the same, and ordered the said A B, as such guardian, to execute, acknowledge and deliver a deed of said real estate to said party of the second part, on...complying with the terms of said sale.

And whereas, the said party of the second part has in all things complied with the terms of said sale on...part to be performed; now, therefore, this indenture witnesseth, that the said party of the first part, in consideration of the premises and the sum of........dollars to....in hand paid by the said party of the second part, the receipt whereof is hereby acknowledged,...granted, bargained and sold, and by these presents do grant, bargain and sell unto the said party of the second part,....heirs and assigns forever, all the following described lot, piece, or parcel of land, situate in the county of......, and State of Illinois, and known and described as follows, to-wit: [*Here describe the land.*] Together with all and singular the hereditaments and appurtenances thereunto belonging, or in anywise, appertaining, and all the estate, right, title, interest, claim and demand whatsoever, at law or in equity, of the said ward.........., in and to the said premises. To have and to hold the same unto the said party of the second part,....heirs and assigns forever, as fully and effectually to all intents and purposes in law as he, the said party of the first part, might, could, or ought to sell and convey the same, by virtue of the said decretal order of the said county court above referred to.

In witness whereof, the said party of the first part, as guardian as aforesaid,....hereunto set....hand and seal the day and year first above written.

A B, [L. S.]
........., [L. S.]

State of Illinois, } ss.
County of............ }

I, G H, clerk of the county court in and for the said county, in the State aforesaid, do hereby certify that A B, guardian of C D, who is personally known to me to be the same person whose name is subscribed to the foregoing instrument, appeared before me this day in person, and, as such guardian, acknowledged that he signed, sealed and delivered the said instrument, as his free and voluntary act, for the uses and purposes therein set forth.

Given under my hand and official seal, this...day of......, A. D. 18...

G H,

[L. S.]   Clerk of the County Court.

7. Proceeds—Accounting for—Re-investment.—An account of all moneys and securities received by any guardian for the sale of real estate of his ward, shall be returned on oath of such guardian, to the county court of the county where letters of guardianship were obtained, and such money shall be accounted for, and subject to the order of the county court, in like manner as other moneys belonging to such minor.

In case of sale for re-investment in this state, the money shall be re-invested under the direction of the court.([1])

8. Sale of real estate by non-resident guardian.— Where any person residing in any other state of the United States, or any territory thereof, shall have been or may hereafter be appointed guardian, in the state or territory in which such person resides, of any infant or other person owning real estate within this state, not having any guardian in this state, it shall and may be lawful for every such guardian to file his or her petition in the circuit court of the county in which said real estate, or the major part thereof, may lie, for sale of said real estate, for the purpose of educating and supporting such infant, or other person under guardianship, or for the purpose of investing the proceeds of such real estate in such manner as the court which appointed such guardian, may order and direct; and the said circuit court is hereby fully authorized and empowered to order a sale of such real estate conformably to the prayer of said petition: *Provided*, that every such guardian applying for such sale, shall file with his or her petition, an authenticated copy of his or her letters of guardianship:

(1. Hurd's R. S., Chap. 64, ? 34.

And, Provided, further, that the said circuit court shall make no order for a sale under said petition, until the said guardian shall have executed and filed in the court which appointed said guardian, a bond, with sufficient security, approved by said last mentioned court, for the due and faithful application of the proceeds of every such sale, in such manner as the said last mentioned court may direct; an authenticated copy of which said bond, and the approval thereof, shall be deemed and taken by the circuit court as sufficient evidence of the execution and filing of the same.(1)

9. TERMS OF SALE.—Every guardian applying for an order of sale under the foregoing section, shall be required to give notice of his or her petition in the same manner as is now required by law in cases of application for sales of lands belonging to minors, by resident guardians; and in every order for the sale of real estate under this act, it shall be the duty of the court to prescribe the terms of said sale, and the notice which shall be given thereof, and the place where such sale shall be made.(2)

10. DEEDS—TITLE.—All sales of real estate, under the provisions of this act, are hereby declared to be good and valid; and all deeds executed by such guardian to the purchaser or purchasers under such sales, shall convey to and vest in such purchaser or purchasers all the estate, right, title and interest, in law or equity, of said infant or others in and to the land so sold.(3)

11. BOND FOR COSTS.—In all suits and petitions by non-resident guardians, they shall give a bond for costs, as in cases of other non-residents.(4)

12. THE PROCEEDING.—A proceeding to sell real estate by the guardian, is not adverse to the interest of his wards, nor against them; and it is not necessary they should have a day in court.(5) They need not be made parties to the proceeding, nor is the appointment of a guardian *ad litem* required.(6) It is a proceeding purely

---

(1) Hurd's R. S., Chap. 64, § 47.
(2) Hurd's R. S., Chap. 64, § 48.
(3) Hurd's R. S., Chap. 64, § 49.
(4) Hurd's R. S., Chap. 64, § 50.
(5) McClay vs. Norris, 4 Gilm., 372; Mason vs. Wait, 4 Scam., 127; Smith vs. Race, 27 Ill., 387; Gibson vs. Roll, 27 Ill., 88.
(6) Smith vs. Race, *supra;* Campbell vs. Harmon, 43 Ill., 18; Fitzgibbon vs. Lake, 29 Ill., 165; Rice vs. Parkman, 16 Mass., 326; Whitlock's case, 32 Barb., (N. Y.) 48; Berry vs. Young, 15 Texas, 369; Barnes vs. Hardeman, 15 Texas, 366.

in rem. No parties are necessary. It is *ex parte*, in the name of the guardian, on behalf of the ward, after notice to all concerned.(¹) He has no power to sell the real estate of his ward, unless authorized by the court, and the power then conferred, is a naked power, and must be strictly pursued.(²) And the provisions of the statute relating to guardians' sales under a decree of the court, must be strictly complied with, or the sale will be void.(³)

13. PETITION.—A guardian can not, on his own motion, apply for an order to sell his ward's real estate, but must follow the directions of the county court; if, on an order being made by that court, he finds he has no funds in his hands, he may then, but not sooner, file his petition, and apply for the sale.(⁴) The application in case of residents, should be made in the county where the ward resides, although the estate may be in a different county.(⁵) The petition should state affirmatively where the wards reside.(⁶) Where the guardian avers in his petition, that no personal property of the ward had ever come to his hands, it was held, although the expression was a departure from the statute, still it was not fatal to the jurisdiction of the court. The proper averment, however, would have been, that the guardian has faithfully applied all the personal estate.(⁷)

If the petition alleges that the application is made for the support and education of the ward, the necessity for a sale for that purpose must be shown.(⁸) So, too, where a guardian petitions the court to sell the real estate of his ward, to pay off a mortgage thereon, it should not be entertained, unless there is something more than the mere opinion of the guardian shown, by which the court can see that such a sale would be more advantageous to the

---

(1) Mulford vs. Beveridge, 78 Ill., 455.
(2) Mason vs. Wait, 4 Scam., 127; Moore vs. Hood, 9 Rich., (S. C.) Eq., 311; Worth vs. Curtis, 15 Me., 228; Dorr, Petitioner, etc., Walk., (Michigan) 145; Jackson vs. Todd, 25 N. J., L., (I. Dutch) 121; Antonidas vs. Walling, 4 (N. J.) Eq., (3 Green) 42.
(3) Cooper vs. Sunderland, 3 Iowa, 114; Frazier vs. Steenrod, 7 Iowa, 339; Shanks vs. Seamonds, 24 Iowa, 13; Wells vs. Cowherd, 2 Metc., (Ky.) 514; Barrett vs. Churchill, 18 B. Mon., 387; Pendleton vs. Trueblood, 2 Jones, (N. C.) 96.
(4) Loyd vs. Malone, 23 Ill., 43.
(5) Spellman vs. Dowse, 79 Ill., 66; Loyd vs. Malone, *supra*.
(6) Loyd vs. Malone, *supra*.
(7) Young vs. Lorain, 11 Ill., 624.
(8) Loyd vs. Malone, *supra*.

interest of the wards, than a sale upon the foreclosure of the mortgage.(¹)

Without legal authority of a court of competent jurisdiction, a guardian can not sell the property of his ward.

14. JURISDICTION.—In a guardian's sale of real estate, if the court acted within its jurisdiction, every presumption is in favor of its judgment, and nothing can be alleged against it in a collateral proceeding.(²) As a general rule, where a court has jurisdiction of the subject matter and of the parties, and proceeds to adjudicate, and render a judgment or decree, it can not be impeached in a collateral proceeding.(³) Enough must appear, either in the application or the order, or somewhere upon the face of the proceedings, to call upon the court to proceed to act, and where that does appear, then the court has properly acquired jurisdiction.(⁴) A sale without the notice required by law, is void for want of jurisdiction in the court ordering such sale. Where, however, the notice is merely defective, the jurisdiction is saved, and the proceeding can not be assailed collaterally.(⁵)

The proceedings will be void for want of jurisdiction, where a notice is given by publication, under the statute, that the guardian will apply to the court at a certain term, for an order to sell the land of his ward, and the application is made at a different term. And such will be the result, although the term of the court to which the notice was given, was not held, by reason of the absence of the judge, there being no petition filed within the time for which such term could have been held by law, nor any steps taken to give the court jurisdiction, either of the subject matter or the person, at that term.(⁶) Where, however, notice was given to the April term of the court, but the term was changed from April to March, by an act of the legislature, it was held the application was properly made

---

(1) Greenbaum vs. Greenbaum, 81 Ill., 367.
(2) Young vs. Lorain, 11 Ill., 624; Nichols vs. Mitchell, 70 Ill., 258; Mulford vs. Stalzenbach, 46 Ill., 303.
(3) Conover vs. Musgrave, 68 Ill., 58.
(4) *Ib.*
(5) Lyon vs. Vanatta, 35 Iowa, 521; Rankin vs. Miller, 43 Iowa, 11; Kenedy vs. Gains, 51 Miss., 625.
(6) Knickerbocker vs. Knickerbocker, 58 Ill., 399; Nichols vs. Mitchell, *supra.*

at the March term, the notice standing in the place and performing the office, of process.(¹)

The proceeding being statutory, and the statute requiring that the application for the sale of the real estate shall be made in the county where the ward resides, or, in case the ward does not reside in the state, in some county where the whole or a part of the real estate is situated, is jurisdictional, and any material deviation from these requirements, as to the court in which the proceedings must be had, is fatal to the jurisdiction of the court. So, an order made by a probate court, directing the sale of property in another state, would be an assumption of authority over a subject matter not within the jurisdiction of the court, and consequently void.(²) And it would be fatal if a person, having no letters of guardianship, were to apply for the sale of the land of a minor; as, it is only by the power conferred by the appointment of a guardian, that he becomes invested with authority to apply for, or the court with jurisdiction to pass such decree.

The want of jurisdiction of the subject matter, may be shown at any stage of the proceeding, and until every order or step required by the statute has been taken and completed.(³)

A proceeding by guardian to sell the land of his ward, for his maintenance, being *in rem*, and made on behalf of the owner, it is only necessary the court should have jurisdiction of the subject matter to make an order, to sustain a sale thereunder. And where the decree recites, that the proceedings of the guardian had in all respects been in conformity with law, etc., it was held, the court had jurisdiction to render the decree.(⁴)

15. SPECIAL BOND.—No title passes by a sale of real estate by a guardian, who fails to give the special bond required by law; and the purchase money may be recovered of him by the purchaser, by action for money had and received, or on the covenants of the deed.(⁵)*

(1) Pursley vs. Hays, 22 Iowa, 11; Gilmore vs. Rodgers, 41 Pa. St., 120;
(2) Price vs. Johnson, 1 Ohio St., 390.   [Spring vs. Kane, 86 Ill., 580.
(3) Spellman vs. Dowse, 79 Ill., 66.
(4) Spring vs. Kane, *supra*.
(5) Williams vs. Morton, 38 Me., 47.

*NOTE.—The authority of *Williams* vs. *Morton*, upon which this text is predicated, may well be doubted, where the court pronouncing the decree has jurisdiction. At most, the failure to give the special bond provided for in Section 28, is but an irregularity, of which a bidder, who is only bound to know that the court had jurisdiction, need not take notice. In *Wyman* vs. *Campbell*, 6 Porter, (Ala.) where it was sought to defeat a title in a collateral action, on account of the failure to give a special bond, such as is required in the above Section and in Section 23, Chap. 3, Hurd's Statutes, it was held, that such an omission could not affect an innocent purchaser.

Where a guardian makes a sale of property under a void decree of the court, if the ward, after arriving at maturity, receives the purchase money, it will amount to a confirmation of the sale by the ward, and work an estoppel.([1])

A sale made by a guardian of the estate of the ward, to pay off a claim allowed the mother by the guardian for their nurture, which is in fraud of the wards, and which enables the mother to get possession of the children's estate, will be set aside, even upon the motion of a stranger.([2])

Orders and decrees are final against minors subject to writs of error;([3]) but they may file an original bill to impeach the decree, either for fraud or for error appearing on its face, or for want of jurisdiction.([4])

The principle of *caveat emptor*, (Let the purchaser beware,) applies to guardian's sales; and a *suppressio veri*, (Concealment of truth,) on the part of the guardian, will not invalidate the sale, or enable the purchaser to rescind it. *Aliter*, (Otherwise,) of a *suggestio falsi*, (A statement of a falsehood).([5]) It is the rule in this state, that a purchaser under a judicial sale, is not bound to look beyond the decree, when executed by a conveyance, nor go further back than the order of the court, when the facts necessary to give the court jurisdiction, appear on the face of the record.([6]) While a guardian's sale should be closely scrutinized, yet, if it should be made to appear, on such scrutiny, that the substantial requirements of the law have been observed and pursued, persons claiming under such proceedings, have a right, and it is the policy of the law, no less than the dictates of justice, that protection should be afforded them([7]). Public policy requires stability in all sales, and that they

---

(1) Parmele vs. McGinty, 52 Miss., 476; Douglas vs. Bennett, 51 Miss., 680.
(2) Barnes vs. Hazleton, 50 Ill., 430; Hess vs. Voss, 52 Ill., 473.
(3) Enos vs. Capps, 15 Ill., 277; Loyd vs. Malone, 23 Ill., 44.
(4) Loyd vs. Malone, 23 Ill., 43; Kuchenbeiser vs. Beckert, 41 Ill., 177; Hess vs. Voss, *supra;* Reynolds vs. McCurry, 100 Ill., 356; Gooch vs. Green, 102 Ill., 507; Wright vs. Gay, 101 Ill., 233.
(5) Mason vs. Wait, 4 Scam., 127.
(6) Buckmaster vs. Carlin, 3 Scam., 104; *ante* page 165; Selb vs. Montague, 102 Ill., 446.
(7) Mulford vs. Stalzenback, 46 Ill., 303.

A notice in the following form was given:

Notice is hereby given, that a petition to sell the real estate belonging to the minor heirs of Martin Spellman, deceased, will be presented to the circuit court of Will county, Illinois, at the next term thereof, to be holden at the court house in Joliet, in said Will county, on the third Monday in December next, when and where all persons interested may appear and show cause, if any they have, why such petition should not be granted.

LOCKPORT, Oct. 27, 1853.   A. J. MATHEWSON, Guardian.

The notice was held sufficient. It is not necessary to state in the notice the special reasons why the order of sale should be asked. Neither will the court reverse the decree of sale, for the reason that the printer's certificate of the publishing the notice failed to show the county where such notice was published, it being otherwise in due form, presuming that the court below heard other evidence of that fact, as it could legally do.(¹)

After the lapse of twenty years from the date of a decree for the sale of a ward's land by his guardian, and the destruction of the court records, oral proof of the publication of notice by the guardian of his intention to present a petition for leave to sell, etc., coupled with the fact, that a copy of the original decree, recited that due proof of the time, place, and intention of presenting such petition, was made by publication in one of the public newspapers of the county, for six successive weeks, was held sufficient to show the requisite notice of the application to sell had been given.(²)

18. PURCHASER AT SALE.—To entitle one claiming to be the highest bidder at a guardian's sale, to the rights of a purchaser, payment must be tendered within a reasonable time.(³)

19. REPORT OF SALE.—Upon a sale by a guardian, the title is defective, unless the guardian shall make a report of his proceedings, and have the same confirmed by the court. The title does not vest in the purchaser until the report is made and approved by the order of the court authorizing the sale.(⁴) Where a statute says that a title to land may be transferred in a particular way, it must be done in the way prescribed, or it receives no sanction from the statute, and is void.(⁵)

(1) Spellman vs. Mathewson, 65 Ill., 306; Pierce vs. Carleton, 12 Ill., 364.
(2) Spring vs. Kane, 86 Ill., 580.
(3) People vs. Circuit Judge, 19 Mich., 296.
(4) Young vs. Keogh, 11 Ill., 642; Young vs. Dowling, 15 Ill., 481; Rawlings vs. Bailey, 15 Ill., 178; Ayres vs. Baumgarten, 15 Ill., 444; Mulford vs. Beveridge, 78 Ill., 455.
(5) Young vs. Dowling, *supra*.

The lapse of time will not prevent a present confirmation of the sale, where all the proceedings are regular and in compliance with the statute, it appearing that had the report been made soon after the sale, it would have been confirmed, even though seventeen years may have elapsed.(¹) Where a report of a guardian's sale is presented to the court, and a motion entered for an order approving the sale, seven or eight years after the sale, the motion and order form a part of the orignal proceeding under which the sale was ordered to be made, and on the hearing of the motion, any objection can be urged that could have been, had the motion been made at the next term after the sale.(²)

The account of moneys received on sale of real estate required to be made by the guardian to the county court under oath, is not conclusive upon the ward when assailed by him. The county court has the right to allow or reject the report, may require proofs, examine witnesses, and resort to all means necessary to ascertain the truth. This is its duty, and its powers in this respect are co-extensive with a court of chancery.(³)

After the lapse of many years, and the destruction of the records, where the validity of a guardian's sale is questioned collaterally, it will be presumed that the clerk of the court filed the guardian's petition, and that he also recorded the guardian's report of sale on its approval, as it was his duty to do so.(⁴)

20. GUARDIAN'S DEED.—The guardian can insert no covenants in the deed, which are binding upon the ward;(⁵) and hence there can be nothing in the deed which can operate by way of estoppel upon the ward. If the guardian choose to insert covenants in the deed, he may be held responsible upon them, and to him alone must the grantee look for redress.(⁶) So, where a guardian made a deed which contained ambiguities in the description of the grantees, and also omitting the number of the block, in describing the premises, it was held that parol evidence was competent in both cases to remedy the defect, and held, also, that a subsequent deed executed by the guardian for the purpose of explaining the deed and correct-

(1) Harvey, Guardian, In the matter of, 16 Ill., 127.
(2) Spellman vs. Dowse, 79 Ill., 66.
(3) *In Re* Steele, 65 Ill., 322.
(4) Spring vs. Kane, 86 Ill., 580.
(5) Mason vs. Caldwell, 5 Gilm., 196; Young vs. Lorain, 11 Ill., 624.
(6) Whiting vs. Dewey, 15 Pick., (Mass.) 428; Young vs. Lorain, *supra*.

ing mistakes therein, could not be admitted in evidence. The guardian's power ceases when he has made the sale and conveyance, and his acts are approved by the court.([1])

If, at the time of a guardian's sale, the infant has but an equitable title and subsequently acquires the legal title, equity will compel a conveyance to the purchaser of the subsequently acquired legal title, on the ground that the legal title was held as a trust;([2]) but, where a ward subsequently acquires from the government of the United States, a patent to the premises which had been sold by his guardian, at a guardian's sale, under the statute, his independent title, subsequently acquired, does not inure to the benefit of a previous purchaser at a guardian's sale; nor is he estopped by the guardian's deed from setting up such subsequent title.([3])

A guardian sold land, and executed a deed to be delivered to the purchaser upon his securing the purchase money, in accordance with the decree. The party who purchased at the guardian's sale, having failed to comply with the terms of the sale, under an arrangement with the guardian, conveyed the land to a third person by a deed absolute on its face, but to be held by such third person and by him to be re-sold. The land was afterwards re-sold for more money than the amount of the original bid by the purchaser at the guardian's sale, and the proceeds were accounted for to the guardian. Under these circumstances, it was held not material whether the deed from the guardian to the purchaser at the guardian's sale, was ever in actual possession of such purchaser or not, and that what occurred, was equivalent to a delivery, and the title acquired under these circumstances, was valid.([4])

A married woman, who is a guardian, can convey the real estate of her ward, without her husband joining in the deed.([5])

If a person should purchase at a guardian's sale for the benefit of the guardian, but take the deed to himself, afterward conveying to the guardian, the purchase will not be void at law, and even in equity, such sales are not *ipso jure*, void, but the trustee purchases subject to the equity of having the sale set aside, if the *cestui que*

(1) Young vs. Lorain, 11 Ill., 624.
(2) Young vs. Dowling, 15 Ill., 482.
(3) Young vs. Lorain, *supra*.
(4) Mulford vs. Beveridge, 78 Ill., 455.
(5) Palmer vs. Oakley, 2 Douglass, (Mich.) 433.

trust, within a reasonable time chooses to say he is not satisfied with it.([1])

21. CONFIRMATION OF SALE.—The approval of a guardian's sale of real estate, by the county court, is not a mere formality; it is an affirmation not merely of the deed, but of the sale or mortgage necessary to make it valid.([2]) The discretion to be used by the court in confirming sales of guardian's must conform to established principles; and as a general principle, mere inadequacy of price is not a sufficient cause for setting aside a sale. The English practice of opening sales before confimation of the report, on the offer of a reasonable advance upon the sum bid at a sale, and the payment of the expenses of the purchaser—the party applying to have the biddings opened being required to deposit the amount of such advance and expenses—has not been adopted in this country.([3])

The confirmation of a sale is a judicial act.([4]) Unless judicial, a court would have no power to perform it, for a court has no other functions than judicial.([5]) A void act can not be confirmed.([6])

An order entered by mistake, dismissing the proceeding after decree and before the confirmation of sale, would not vacate the order of sale, nor revoke the authority of the guardian.([7]) Where the statute requires the court to direct the time of sale, a sale at another time must be void.([8]) Where, however, the sale was ordered to be made, and was made on the 19th day of June, but was advertised for the 18th day of June, and no fraud was shown, the sale was not void as having been made without power, and not even voidable as against a purchaser having no notice of the irregularity.([9]) For, where the court has jurisdiction, and makes an order of sale, the fact that the guardian may proceed irregularly in the execution of the order, will not make the sale invalid.([10])

(1) Hoskins vs. Wilson, 4 Dev. & B., (N. C.) Law, 243; Patton vs. Thompson, 2 Jones, (N. C.) Eq., 285; Wyman vs. Hooper, 2 Gray, (Mass.) 141; Bostwick vs. Atkins, 3 Comst., 53.
(2) Wade vs. Carpenter, 4 Iowa, 361.
(3) Ayers vs. Baumgarten, 15 Ill., 444.
(4) Halleck vs. Guy, 9 Cal., 181.
(5) Ayers vs. Baumgarten, *supra*; *Ex Parte* Guernsey, 21 Ill., 443.
(6) Sinclair vs. Jackson, 8 Cowen, (N. Y.) 543.
(7) Fitzgibbon vs. Lake, 29 Ill., 165.
(8) Wellman vs. Lawrence, 15 Mass., 326; Reynolds vs. Wilson, 15 Ill., 394.
(9) Conover vs. Musgrave, 68 Ill., 58.
(10) Mulford vs. Beveridge, 78 Ill., 455.

22. PURCHASER NOT BOUND TO SEE TO APPLICATION.—The purchaser of real estate at a guardian's sale, is not responsible for the order of the court in appropriating the money realized from the sale; and, although it may have been mis-applied, the purchaser's title would not be affected thereby.(1)

Any agreement among parties not to bid against each other at a public sale of land, being designed and calculated to stifle competition, is such a fraud as to afford ground of avoiding the sale as against a purchaser participating in the fraud.(2)

Whether one of two guardians named in a will, had authority to apply for an order of sale, was for the court, where the application was made, to determine. And so of the regularity of the sale, that court would determine that question upon hearing.(3) Where land was sold by a guardian under authority of law, though the sale was not confirmed, and the purchase money paid and part applied to the support of the minors, and the residue invested in lands, which were received and appropriated by the ward, the minors will be estopped in equity, from proceeding to recover the land sold by the guardian, from an innocent purchaser, not immediately connected with the sale.(4) But the mere fact, that the guardian applied a part of the proceeds of such sale to the support of the ward, will not be an estoppel on him from disputing the validity of the sale.(5)

Where a sale is confirmed by the court, the confirmation cures all irregularities in the sale.(6)

Land subject to dower, should not be sold for the support of infant heirs, without first ascertaining and recognizing the rights of the widow.(7) And when a sale by a guardian of the ward's lands, in which the guardian herself has a right of dower, is avoided by the ward, because made to the guardian herself, the right of dower revives.(8)

(1) Fitzgibbon vs. Lake, 29 Ill., 165; Mulford vs. Stalzenback, 46 Ill., 303; Mulford vs. Beveridge, 79 Ill., 455.
(2) Loyd vs. Malone, 23 Ill., 43.
(3) Fitzgibbon vs. Lake, *supra*.
(4) Penn and wife vs. Heisey, 19 Ill., 295; Commonwealth vs. Sherman, 6 Penn. St., 346; Smith vs. Warden, 7 Penn. St., 424; Gibson vs. Roll, 27 Ill., 88; Conover vs. Musgrave, 68 Ill., 58; Favil vs. Roberts, 10 N. Y., 222.
(5) Schnell vs. Chicago, 38 Ill., 384.
(6) Anderson vs. Foulke, 2 Harris & Gill, 346; Bland vs. Muncarter, 24 Miss., 62; Doe vs. Harvey, 5 Blackf., (Ind.) 487; Garrett vs. Moss, 20 Ill., 550; Fitzgibbon vs. Lake, *supra*; Conover vs. Musgrave, *supra*.
(7) Loyd vs. Malone, *supra*; *Ex Parte* Guernsey, 21 Ill., 443.
(8) Walker vs. Walker, 101 Mass., 169.

Where a guardian proceeded by bill in circuit court for leave to sell his ward's land, and filed as an exhibit with the bill, an order showing her appointment as guardian, and that she had filed her bond, the court may properly presume that the bond mentioned in the order of the probate court, was such as the law requires.([1])

16. FIXING TIME OF SALE.—It was not intended under our statute, to require the court to fix the precise day or hour of sale. It is sufficient if the court in its order fixes certain reasonable limits, both as to the day and hour within which the sale shall be held, requiring the guardian to give due notice; and the guardian may exercise some discretion in a mode favorable to the ward's interests;([2]) and while it is the duty of the court, in authorizing a guardian's sale of real estate, to fix the day of sale, which admits of doubt, its omission to do so, can not vitiate the sale, as it does not affect the jurisdiction. It is a mere irregularity, at most.([3]) But a sale of land by a guardian, at a time other than that prescribed by the statute or the decree, is not only irregular, but void, even in the case of one holding a derivative title acquired in good faith, unless the sale is formally approved by the probate court.([4])

17. NOTICE OF APPLICATION.—A notice in due form, signed in the name of the guardian by her attorney, with the affidavit of the attorney showing that he posted it in the manner required by law, is sufficient; and the attorney is a competent person, not only to post the notice, but also to prove such posting.([5])

Where the statute requires the notice of the application of the guardian to sell the real estate, to be published in a public newspaper at least once in each week for three weeks successively, or to be posted in three public places at least three weeks before the session of the court at which the application is to be made, it is sufficient if the notice is published for three successive weeks in a newspaper, and the first publication is made only three weeks before the session of the court.([6])

(1) Campbell vs. Harmon, 43 Ill., 19.
(2) Ib.
(3) Spring vs. Kane, 86 Ill., 580.
(4) Brown vs. Christie, 27 Texas, 73.
(5) Campbell vs. Harmon, supra.
(6) Fry vs. Bidwell, 74 Ill., 381; Gilmore vs. Sapp, 100 Ill., 297.

should not be disturbed for slight cause, otherwise property can not be expected to bring its value at such sales.(¹)

(1) Conover vs. Musgrave, 68 Ill., 58.

NOTE.—The question often arises as to how far courts of equity have jurisdiction to order sales of the land of minors for the same purposes contemplated by the statute herein referred to, and has been the subject of some discussion. In a recent case,(1) following *Smith* vs. *Sacket*, 5 Gilm., 534, the supreme court of Illinois, hold, that a court of chancery, under its general powers over the estates of infants, lunatics or distracted persons, has jurisdiction to order the sale of the land of such persons for their support, upon application made, notwithstanding the statutory jurisdiction given the county court.

(1) Allman vs. Taylor, 101 Ill., 185 ; also, Dodge vs. Cole, 97 Ill., 338

ADDITIONAL NOTES.

1. Constitutionality of the act conferring jurisdiction on probate courts.
2. Guardian's deed must be based on decree.
3. Jurisdiction of city court to sell lands of ward by guardian.
4. Error in the decree not going to the jurisdiction.

1. CONSTITUTIONALITY OF ACT CONFERRING JURISDICTION.—There being no inhibition in respect thereto in the constitution, the legislature, by the act of 877, had power to create and establish probate courts, the jurisdiction of such courts to extend over and include all probate matters, as defined by the act of 1874, establishing county courts, and so include guardians' sales of real estate belonging to their wards (¹).

2. GUARDIAN'S DEED BASED ON DECREE.—A guardian has no power to sell his ward's land without an order of the court for the purpose of raising funds for the support and education of the ward. Without any petition for leave to sell the ward's land, and a decree granting leave, the guardian's deed is absolutely void.(²)

3. JURISDICTION OF CITY COURT TO SELL LANDS.—Where the act creating a city court invests it with the same jurisdiction possessed by circuit courts, a sale by the guardian of his ward's lands, under and by virtue of a decree rendered by such city court, will be sustained; and if the petition contain the requisite facts, and due notice was given, as required by law, the mere fact of lands belonging to the ward outside the city and in other counties will not deprive the court of its jurisdiction to order sale.(³) A petition for the sale of real estate of the ward, signed "Mary M. Olcott, guardian for Lizzie Olcott and Sue Olcott, by Levi Davis, her solicitor," was held a sufficient signing by the guardian.(⁴) A purchaser at such sale may have an order approving the same entered *nunc pro*

---

(1) Winch vs. Tobin, 107 Ill., 212.
(2) Cooter vs. Dearborn, 115 Ill., 509.
(3) Reid vs. Morton, 119 Ill., 118.
(4) *Ib.*

tunc to protect his title. For such purpose he is a *quasi* party to the suit.(¹)

4. ERROR IN DECREE.—The fact that a decree or order of the court authorizing a guardian's sale may fail to fix the time and place of sale may be erroneous, but this does not affect the jurisdiction and render the sale void.(²)

(1) Reid vs. Morton, 119 Ill., 118.
(2) Benefield vs. Albert, 132 Ill., 665.

CHAPTER VIII.

MORTGAGING AND LEASING REAL ESTATE OF WARD.

1. Statutory Power.
2. Petition—forms.
3. Foreclosures.
4. No strict foreclosures.
5. Forms used in foreclosure.
6. Remarks.
7. Leasing ward's real estate.

1. STATUTORY POWER.—The guardian may, by leave of the county court, mortgage the real estate of the ward for a term of years not exceeding the minority of the ward, or in fee; but the time of the maturity of the indebtedness secured by such mortgage, shall not be extended beyond the time of minority of the ward.(¹)

2. PETITION.—Before any mortgage shall be made, the guardian shall petition the county court for an order authorizing such mortgage to be made, in which petition shall be set out the condition of the estate, and the facts and circumstances on which the petition is founded, and a description of the premises sought to be mortgaged.(²)

The petition may be in form as follows:

PETITION TO MORTGAGE REAL ESTATE OF WARD.

STATE OF ILLINOIS, } ss. *In the County Court,*
..................County. }   *To the.........term, A. D. 18...*

To the Hon............, Judge of said Court:

Your petitioner, ..., by the appointment of this court guardian of the person and property of........., minor heir of.........deceased, would respectfully represent unto your honor, that he is desirous of mortgaging the lands of his ward for a term of five years.

That the condition of the estate of said ward is as follows: That the personal estate of said.........is entirely exhausted, and there is no money belonging to said ward whereby to pay taxes on said real estate, and said taxes now amount to......dollars. That said ward is not of sufficient health to enable him to earn a subsistence by manual labor, and your petitioner is

---

(1) Hurd's R. S., Chap. 64, § 24.   (2) Hurd's R. S., Chap. 64, § 25.

desirous of educating said ward, and believes that it would be of more interest to the estate to mortgage said real estate than to sell the same. That said real estate consists of one hundred and sixty acres, and is described as follows, viz: [*Here describe the real estate.*] And is worth some......dollars. That during the past year your petitioner has been unable to raise any crops on said lands, owing to the......and repairs necessary to be made, but your petitioner believes with the expenditure of......dollars, that he can put said place in such a condition as to enable him to not only pay taxes and make the necessary repairs, but also pay off said mortgage by the time the same will have matured. Your petitioner is desirous of raising......dollars thereon, and by and with the consent of your honor, can make said loan of one........., of said county. That his said ward is aged...years, on the...day of......, A. D. 18..., and your petitioner believes that it will be beneficial to the interest of said ward to so mortgage said estate and make said loan for the purpose of paying taxes, making said repairs and educating said ward; and respectfully prays an order authorizing him to make said loan.

And your petitioner will ever pray, etc.

By........., Attorney. ...., Guardian.

STATE OF ILLINOIS, } ss.
,..............County.

........., being duly sworn, on oath states, that the matters and facts set forth in said petition, are true.   ....

Subscribed and sworn to before me, this...day of......, A. D. 18...
....

ORDER ON PETITION TO MORTGAGE REAL ESTATE BY GUARDIAN.

STATE OF ILLINOIS, } ss.
.................County.

In the matter of........., Guardian } Application to mortgage the real
of............   }   estate of ward.

And now, on this...day of......, A. D. 18...., comes the said guardian by........., his attorney, and presents his petition herein, for leave to mortgage the real estate of his ward, ..., described therein; and this cause coming on now to be heard upon the petition and oral proofs heard by the court, and the court being now sufficiently advised in the premises, doth find that: [*Here set out the circumstances in evidence justifying the action of the court.*] It therefore, is ordered that said petition be allowed, and that said guardian be authorized to make said loan as prayed for in his said petition, for the sum of......dollars, and that he execute a mortgage on the real estate of his said ward, described as follows, viz: [*Here describe the real estate.*] That said mortgage be given for the term of......years, which said term does not exceed the minority of said ward, and provided, the interest on said mortgage shall not exceed the rate of...per cent. per annum.

And it is further ordered that said guardian report his actings and doing in the premises at the next term of this court, to which time this cause stands continued.

The report of the guardian may be in form as follows:

REPORT OF THE GUARDIAN.

STATE OF ILLINOIS, } ss. In the County Court,
................County. }   Of the............term, A. D. 18....

To the Hon........., Judge of said Court:

The undersigned, guardian of........., would respectfully report: That in pursuance of the order made and entered of record at the.....term, A. D. 18..., in this cause, he did, on...day of......, A. D. 18..., negotiate said loan for.....dollars, at...per cent. interest per annum, for...years, and on said day executed, acknowledged and delivered as guardian of the said........., a mortgage to the said............as security for said loan for the real estate described in said petition and order, viz.: [*Here describe the real estate.*] All of which actings and doings he prays may be confirmed and he be discharged from further consideration of this cause.

All of which is respectfully submitted.

By............, Attorney.

3. FORECLOSURES.—Foreclosures of mortgages authorized by this act shall only be made by petition to the county court of the county where letters of guardianship were granted, or in case of non-resident minors, in the county in which the premises, or some part thereof, are situated, in which proceeding, the guardian and ward shall be made defendants; and any sale made by virtue of any order or decree of foreclosure of such mortgage may, at any time before confirmation, be set aside by the court for inadequacy of price, or other good cause, and shall not be binding upon the guardian or ward until confirmed by the court.([1])

4. NO STRICT FORECLOSURE.—No decree of strict foreclosure shall be made upon any such mortgage, but redemption shall be allowed as is now provided by law in cases of sales under executions upon common law judgments.([2])

5. FORMS USED IN FORECLOSURE.—The petition for the foreclosure of mortgage authorized under this act may be in form as follows:

PETITION TO FORECLOSE MORTGAGE.

STATE OF ILLINOIS, } ss. In the County Court,
...............County. }   To the......term, A. D. 18...

To the Hon.........Judge of the County Court in and for said County:

Your petitioner........., would respectfully show unto your honor, that on or about the...day of......, A. D. 18..., one........., guardian of the person and property of........., a minor child.........of.........deceased, whose letters bear date...day of......, A. D. 18..., and were issued by this honorable court

---

(1) Hurd's R. S., Chap. 64, § 26.   (2) Hurd's R. S., Chap. 64, § 27.

at its......term, A. D. 18..., reference being had and made to the records of this court for greater certainty, became and was indebted to your petitioner in his capacity as guardian aforesaid, in the sum of.....dollars, and being so indebted, in consideration thereof, the said..........as guardian aforesaid, on the day and year aforesaid, made and executed under his hand a certain writing obligatory for the sum of.....dollars, due and payable in...years after the date thereof to your petitioner, with interest at the rate of....per cent. per annum from date until paid, the interest to be paid annually.

And your petitioner would further show unto your honor, that the said..........by.........., as guardian as aforesaid, on the...day of......, A. D. 18..., to secure the payment of the principal and interest mentioned in said note, made and executed under his hand and seal as guardian as aforesaid, and delivered to your petitioner, under and by virtue of an order of this honorable court, authorizing said loan, made and entered of record at its......term, A. D. 18..., a mortgage, conditioned for the payment of the said sum of...... dollars, and interest mentioned in said note according to the conditions of said note, by which said mortgage, the said..........by.........., as guardian as aforesaid, mortgaged to the said.........., your petitioner, certain lands and real estate, in..........county, Illinois, and described as follows, viz.: [*Here describe the lands.*] Which said mortgage was duly acknowledged, and afterwards recorded as a mortgage, in the office of the Recorder of Deeds, of the county of.........., in the State of Illinois, on the....dayof......, A. D. 18..., at....o'clock in the....noon, in book....of Mortgages, on page....; as by said mortgage and the certificate of acknowledgment, and recording indorsed thereon, and ready to be produced in court, and to which your petitioner prays leave to refer, will more fully appear.

And your petitioner believes and states that the sum of.....dollars, with interest from the....day of........, A. D. 18...., remains due and unpaid to your petitioner on the said note and mortgage. And your petitioner would further show unto your honor, and state upon information and belief that no other person has or claims to have any interest in the said mortgaged premises, or any part thereof, as purchaser, mortgagee or otherwise. Your petitioner therefore asks the aid of the court in the premises, and that the above named.........., guardian of.........., and............the defendants in this suit, may appear before the judge of our said county court at its........term, A. D. 18...., and answer this your petitioner's petition, according to the rules and practice of said court, without oath, their oaths to their answers being hereby waived, and that the usual decree may be made for the sale of the mortgaged premises aforesaid, for the payment of the amount due your petitioner for principal and interest in the said note and mortgage, and costs of suit, and that the said defendant and all persons claiming under them subsequent to the commencement of this suit, and all other persons not party to this suit, who have any liens, by judgment or decree upon the mortgaged premises subsequent to the said mortgage of your petitioner, or any liens or claims thereon by or under any such subsequent judgment or decree, either as purchaser, incumbrances or otherwise, may be barred and foreclosed of all equity of redemption in said premises, and that your petitioner may have such other and further relief as the nature of his case may require, and as to this court shall seem meet; that summons may issue under the seal of this court for..........guardian of..........., and........therein and thereby commanding them and each of them, on a certain day and under a certain penalty, to be inserted, that they personally be and appear before the judge of the county court of........county, Illinois, at the court room in......, then and there to answer all and singular, the premises, and to stand to and abide by and perform such order and decree therein as shall seem to your honor just. And your petitioner will ever pray, etc.

By.........., his Attorney.

The decree may be in form as follows:

STATE OF ILLINOIS, } ss.
..............County, }

In the County Court,
To the..........term, A. D. 18...

.... }
vs. }
.... }

Decree on bill to foreclose mortgage.

And now, on this day, come the petitioner, by............, his attorney, and it appearing to the court here, from the summons issued herein to the sheriff of..........county, Illinois, and the return thereon, that the defendants............, have each been regularly served herein at least ten days prior to the first day of the present term of this court. And the defendants..........., having been three times solemnly called, come not, but herein make default, and thereupon the petitioner's petition is taken for confessed against said........., and this cause coming on now for a final hearing on bill, exhibits the answer of..........., guardian *ad litem* for said............, infant, and default of..........., and the petitioner introduced the exhibits, the said note and mortgage, and ...., a witness, who testified............, and the court being fully advised in the premises, finds that one............, as guardian of............, under an order of this court, made and entered of record at the........term, A. D. 18...., made his certain promissory note of that date, due........, A. D. 18...., for the sum of........ dollars, together with interest at the rate of....per cent., and to secure said promissory note, the said............as guardian as aforesaid, on the....day of........, A. D. 18...., made and executed their certain mortgage deed of conveyance to the said..........., thereby then and there conveying in fee, subject, however, to be redeemed by the said..........., the real estate described as follows, to-wit: [*Here describe the real estate.*] Which said note and mortgage were signed by............, by............, his..........., guardian. Which said mortgage was recorded in the recorder's office of..........county, Illinois, on the....day of........, 18...., in book...., page.... And that there is now due on said note and mortgage, the sum of........

It is therefore ordered, adjudged and decreed, by the court, that said defendant............, pay said last sum of money, together with legal interest from the date of this decree and the costs of this proceeding, within....days from this date, and that in default thereof, said defendant............ be forever barred and foreclosed of and from the equity of redemption in said mortgaged premises, and that said mortgaged premises mentioned in the bill of complaint now on file in this cause, to-wit: [*Here describe the real estate.*] or, so much as may be necessary to realize the amount so due the complainant, principal and interest and costs in this suit, and which can be sold separately without material injury to the parties interested, be sold at public vendue, by............, who is hereby appointed a special commissioner in said cause to make said sale, and who is hereby authorized and empowered to execute this decree, and carry out the orders of this court, to the highest and best bidder at said sale, for cash in hand, subject to redemption under the statutes of this state, as in cases of sales under executions upon common law judgments. That, previous to making said sale, the said........... shall give notice of the time, terms and place of said sale, together with a description of the premises sought to be sold, by publishing an advertisement of said sale for at least....weeks in some newspaper published in said county, as directed by the petitioner or his attorney; or by posting up written or printed notices in three public places in said county, one of which shall be at the court house, for at least....days. That said...........as such special commissioner, shall execute a certificate of purchase to the purchaser of said premises, and file a duplicate thereof for record in the office of the clerk of the circuit court, and in case said premises are not redeemed from such sale in the time and manner prescribed by law, then said............shall make and execute a deed of conveyance of said premises to the owner of said certificate of purchase, and on demand of the grantee in said deed or any person claiming under him, the said defendant............, and all persons claiming under..........., shall be required to give up and surrender possession of said premises to such grantee, on the production of the deed of conveyance of said............, special commissioner, and in case of refusal so to do, be considered in contempt of this court. And it is further ordered, that said..........., special commissioner, report his action in the premises at the term of court succeeding said sale, and that this cause stand continued for report.

The report of the sale may be in form as follows:

To the Hon............, Judge of the County Court of............ county, Illinois:

The undersigned, a special commissioner, appointed by this honorable court, at its........term, A. D. 18...., reports, that in pursuance of a decree of the county court of........county, Illinois, rendered at the........term, A. D. 18...., in case of............against............, to foreclose mortgage, after having duly advertised the land mentioned in said decree, according to law and the decree, I did, on the....day of........, A. D. 18...., between the hours of ten o'clock, a. m. and five p. m. of said day, at the door of the court house in........, in........county, Illinois, strike off and sell at public sale, the following described real estate, in separate tracts, lying in......county, Illinois, to-wit: [*Here describe the real estate.*] to.........., subject to the equity of redemption, for the sum of........dollars, being the amount of debt, interest and costs, ...being the highest and best bidder.

Dated this...day of......, A. D. 18...

................,
Special Commissioner.

ORDER CONFIRMING SALE.

STATE OF ILLINOIS, } ss.
.................County, }   *In the County Court,*
                                 To the.........term, A. D. 18....

A B ⎫
vs. ⎬   Foreclosure.
C D. ⎭

And now comes............, special commissioner, appointed by this court in said cause, and files his report in court of said sale, made in said cause, and the court being sufficiently advised of and concerning the same, it is ordered, adjudged and decreed, by this court, that said report be in all things confirmed and approved, and this cause continued.

6. REMARKS.—The mortgage provided for in the foregoing statute, as well as that permitted to executors by the statute,(¹) are purely statutory, and to be effectual against the devisee or ward, all the proceedings must be in strict conformity to the statutes under whose authority they are made. Any material departure from the conditions made essential, will render the mortgage void,(²) and covenants entered into by the guardian in such a mortgage, purporting to be made in his official capacity, are void, unless such covenants contain an express undertaking on the part of the guardian. In which case the guardian only is bound.(³)

(1) Hurd's R. S., Chap. 3, § 119.
(2) Merritt vs. Simpson, 41 Ill., 391.
(3) Webster vs. Conley, 46 Ill., 14; *Ante* page, 188.

ADDITIONAL NOTES.

1. Defenses accorded to the ward on foreclosure.
2. Bill of review by a ward in respect to an order mortgaging the ward's land.
3. Mortgaging ward's real estate—Duty of guardian with respect to interests.

1. DEFENSES ACCORDED WARD ON FORECLOSURE.—On a proceeding in the county court to foreclose a mortgage given by a guardian on his ward's lands, the guardian and the ward are both necessary parties; and any sale made on a decree of foreclosure may, at any time before confirmation, be set aside for good cause shown, and will not be binding on the guardian or ward until confirmed by the court. In such a suit the ward may have the entire proceeding, including the authority to give the mortgage, reviewed by the court.(1)

2. BILL OF REVIEW BY WARD, ETC.—A ward may, before a bill is filed to foreclose a mortgage given by his guardian, maintain a bill of review, to review the order granted by the county court, authorizing the guardian to mortgage his lands, and thereby take advantage of every objection that might be allowed on writ of error, if one were allowed.(2)

3. MORTGAGING WARD'S REAL ESTATE—DUTY OF GUARDIAN.—The probate court may, where it becomes necessary to protect the ward's estate, empower the guardian to mortgage the real estate of the ward. And where he does so, it is his duty to pay interest as it falls due.(3) Borrowing money to improve ward's estate is a proper purpose to authorize the guardian to procure a loan.(4) There can be no strict foreclosure against the ward; the right of foreclosure is implied, even though not mentioned in the mortgage.(5)

Upon a bill filed to foreclose a mortgage given to secure a note made by the guardian of a minor, and payable to his successor on a

---

(1) Kingsbury vs. Sperry, 119 Ill., 279; Kingsbury vs. Powers, 131 Ill., 182; Kingman vs. Harmon, 32 Ill. Ap., 529.
(2) Kingsbury vs. Sperry, *supra*.
(3) Kingsbury vs. Powers, *supra*.
(4) U. S. Mortgage Co. vs. Sperry, 138 U. S., 313.
(5) *Ib.*

promise by the latter to credit the guardianship account of the maker and to procure an order from the county court to that effect, it is *held:* That an answer setting up said promise, a failure of performance, and the pendency of a suit against the maker for the entire balance of said guardianship account, was pertinent; that the promise of the payee did not bind him personally or as guardian, the note being void for want of consideration.[1]

[1] DeLand vs. Metzger, 21 Ill. Ap., 89.

CHAPTER IX.

NON-RESIDENT GUARDIANS.

1. Non-resident guardians—power to collect.
2. Transfer of estate to non-resident guardians.
3. Conditions.
4. Manner of procedure—forms.
5. Rules governing non-resident guardians.

1. NON-RESIDENT GUARDIANS—POWER TO COLLECT.—When there is no guardian in the state of a non-resident minor, his guardian appointed and qualified according to the law of the place where the minor resides, having first obtained the authority of the county court of the county in this state where any of the personal estate of such minor may be, so to do, may collect, by suit or otherwise, receive and remove to such place of residence of the minor, any personal estate of such minor.([1])

2. TRANSFER OF ESTATE TO NON-RESIDENT GUARDIANS.—When there is a guardian in this state of a non-resident minor, the court may authorize such guardian to pay over and transfer the whole or any part of the ward's property to the non-resident guardian of such ward, appointed and qualified according to the law of the place where the ward resides, upon such terms as shall be proper in the premises, requiring receipts to be passed; and when the whole estate in the hands of the resident guardian shall be so transferred, may discharge him.([2])

3. CONDITIONS.—But the court shall not grant the authority mentioned in sections forty-four and forty-five, except upon petition of such foreign guardian, signed by him and verified by his affidavit, and unless he shall file with the court properly authenticated copies of his letters of guardianship and bond, with security in double the amount of the value of the property and estate sought, which shall have been executed and filed in the court which appointed such guardian. And unless it shall appear to the court,

(1) Hurd's R. S., Chap. 64, § 44.   (2) Hurd's R. S., Chap. 64, § 45.

that a removal of such estate will not conflict with the interest of the ward or the terms of limitation attending the right by which the ward owns the same, or the rights of creditors, the resident guardian shall have ten days' previous notice of such application.([1])

4. PROCEEDINGS TO TRANSFER ESTATE, ETC.—In order to transfer property held by a resident guardian into the hands of a non-resident guardian, it is necessary that such non-resident guardian shall be appointed and qualified according to the law of the place where the ward resides. We give below the record of such an appointment made in the State of Texas, as an example:

THE STATE OF TEXAS, } ss.
   Collin County,

   Be it remembered, that there was begun and holden at the court house in the city of McKinney, on Monday, May 21st, 1877 (it being the 3rd Monday), a regular term of the county court of Collin county, for civil and probate business. Present and presiding:

                    Hon. T. C. GOODNER, County Judge,
                    W. W. MERRITT, Sheriff, and
                    J. M. BURGE, Clerk,

When the following proceedings were had, to-wit:

John Havill
   vs.   }
John F. Havill.   Monday, May 19th, 1877.

   Now, on this day comes on to be heard the application of John Havill to be appointed guardian of the person and estate of John F. Havill, a minor, and it appearing to the court, that notice of the same has been given according to law: It is ordered, that said prayer be granted and that letters of guardianship issue to him, upon his filing a bond with good and approved security, in the sum of twelve hundred dollars, and taking the oath as the law requires.

                              BOND.

THE STATE OF TEXAS, } ss.
   Collin County,

   Know all men by these presents, that we, John Havill as principal, and T. W. Garrett, W. C. Stanford and J. W. Williams as sureties, are held and firmly bound unto the County Judge of Collin county, and his successors in office, in the sum of twelve hundred dollars, for the payment of which well and truly to be made, we bind ourselves, our heirs, executors and administrators. Signed and dated May 21st, A. D. 1877.

   The condition of this obligation is such, that whereas, the above bound

(1) Hurd's R. S., Chap. 64, § 46

en John Havill has been appointed by the County Judge of Collin county, guardian of the person and estate of John F. Havill, a minor of said county. Now, should the said John Havill faithfully discharge the duties of guardian of the person and estate of such minor according to law, then this obligation to be void.

JOHN HAVILL,
T. W. GARRETT,
W. C. STANFORD,
J. W. WILLIAMS.

Approved, May 21st, A. D. 1877.

T. C. GOODNER, County Judge.

OATH OF OFFICE.

I, John Havill, do solemnly swear that I will faithfully discharge and perform all the duties as guardian of the person and estate of John F. Havill, a minor, according to law, to the best of my skill and knowledge.

JOHN HAVILL.

Sworn to before me, May 21st, A. D. 1877.

J. M. BURGE, County Clerk,
Collin County, Texas.

CERTIFICATE OF CLERK AS TO PROCEEDINGS.

THE STATE OF TEXAS, } ss.
Collin County,

I, J. M. Burge, Clerk of the county court of Collin county, Texas, do hereby certify that the above and foregoing is a true copy of all proceedings had in the matter of John F. Havill, a minor, as appears of record and on file in my office.

[Seal] Witness may hand and seal of office, this June 15th, A. D. 1877.

J. M. BURGE, Clerk.

CERTIFICATE OF THE COUNTY JUDGE AS TO CLERK.

THE STATE OF TEXAS, } ss.
Collin County,

I, T. C. Goodner, Judge of the county court of said county, do hereby certify that J. M. Burge, whose genuine signature is affixed to the above certificate, is now, and was at the above date thereof, the duly elected clerk of said court, qualified and commissioned, according to law. That said certificate is in due form of law, and that his official acts are entitled to full faith and credit. In witness whereof, I have hereunto set my hand officially at office in McKinney, this June 15th, A. D. 1877.

T. C. GOODNER, Judge
County Court, Collin County, Texas.

One of the conditions required of the foreign guardian under Section 3 above, is that he file a petition, signed by him, verified by his affidavit, together with certified copies of his letters of guardianship and bond, with security in double the amount of the value of the property and estate sought, which shall have been executed and filed in the court which appointed the guardian. In Texas, a certified copy of the appointment of guardian and bond, constitute and are the only letters of guardianship required by the laws of that state.

The petition required under Sections 1 and 2 above, are similar in form, and the non-resident guardian, having first filed an authenticated copy of his appointment, and obtained an order to have the same recorded and placed on file, may file his petition, which may be in form as follows:

STATE OF ILLINOIS, } ss.
....................County. }

In the County Court,
To the........term, A. D. 18...

To the Hon.......Judge of the County Court of ..... County, in the State of Illinois:

Your petitioner, John Havill, a resident of the county of Collin, and State of Texas, by........., his attorney, would respectfully represent and show unto your honor, that John F. Havill is a minor, aged...years on the...day of......, A. D. 18..., and resides in the said county of Collin, and State aforesaid. That your petitioner has been duly appointed guardian of said minor by the county court of said Collin county, both of the person and property of the said minor aforesaid. A certified copy of the same being now on file in this honorable court, duly recorded, reference being had thereto for greater certainty.

And your petitioner would further show unto your honor, that said minor has an estate coming to him from one..........., who is the guardian legally appointed by this honorable court, for the said John F. Havill, as will more fully appear by his appointment, a record of the same being now on file in this honorable court, in book "C," page 22, Record of Guardians.

And your petitioner would further show, that at the last settlement made with this court by the said guardian aforesaid, there was in the hands of said guardian belonging to said minor, the sum of $500, which said settlement bears date...day of......, A. D. 18, and is on file in this court.

And your petitioner having fully complied with the laws of the said State of Texas, and having filed authenticated copies of his letters of guardianship and bond, with security in the sum of twelve hundred dollars, a certified copy of which said letters and bond he herewith files, marked exhibit "A," prays that a citation may issue to the said..........., guardian as aforesaid, commanding him to be and appear before this honorable court at its next......term, to be held at the court house in......, on the...day of......, A. D. 18...

And your petitioner prays that on a final hearing hereof, your honor will cause to be entered an order of record, authorizing the said..........., guardian aforesaid, to pay over to and deliver up, and transfer the property aforesaid to your petitioner, upon his giving him a receipt therefor, according to the statute in such case made and provided, and your petitioner, as in duty bound, will ever pray, etc.

By............, his Attorney.   JOHN HAVILL.

STATE OF TEXAS, } ss.
  Collin County, }

John Havill, whose genuine signature appears to the foregoing petition, personally appeared before me, and having heard the same read over, states upon oath that all the facts set forth in said petition, are true in substance and in fact.   JOHN HAVILL.

Subscribed and sworn to before me, this 15th day of......, A. D. 18...

                            J. M. BURGE, Clerk
                     County Court, Collin County, Texas.

[*Add certified copy of appointment as exhibit " A.".*]

Unless it shall appear to the court, that a removal of the estate will not conflict with the interest of the ward, or the terms of limitation attending the right by which the ward owns the same, or the rights of creditors, and the resident guardian has had the ten days' notice required, the petition should be refused; if, however, the conditions imposed in Section 3, shall have all been obviated, the guardian will be entitled to a decree, which may be in form as follows:

In the Matter of the Guardianship of............, minor.

STATE OF ILLINOIS, } ss.
...................County. }

And now, on this day, the same being the...judicial day of the present term of this court, comes the said........., by........., his attorney, comes also, the said........., by........., his attorney, and it appearing from the return of the officer, that due notice has been given to the defendant........., of this proceeding, by service made by the sheriff of......county, Illinois, on the... day of......, A. D. 18..., and this cause coming on now to be heard upon the petition of the said........., petitioner, and the answer of the said........., defendant, and the replication of the said.........thereto, and the exhibits, files and oral proofs, and the court being sufficiently advised and satisfied in the premises, finds, that all the allegations of the said petitioner's petition, are true as therein stated, and doth order and adjudge, that the said........., resident guardian of .....county, Illinois, pay over and transfer to John Havill, guardian of John F. Havill, of Collin county, in the State of Texas, the sum of $512, the amount found due in the hands of the said..........., resident guardian, and that he take his receipt therefor.

And it is further ordered, that the said John Havill, guardian as aforesaid, pay the costs of this proceeding.

5. RULES GOVERNING NON-RESIDENT GUARDIANS.—The power of a guardian is local to the state in which he receives his appointment. He is competent, however, upon proof of his guardianship, to receive the property or the custody of the ward, when placed in his hands, by the courts of another state, to be taken to the state where either or both belong, and in which he received his appointment.[1]

And a court of chancery will order the funds of an infant under its control to be paid to a guardian appointed, and residing in another state.[2]

The transcript, which a foreign guardian, making application for the removal of his ward's property, is required to produce, must not only show that he has given bond with security for the performance of his trust, but must set out a copy of it, in order that the court authorizing the removal, may see that it is sufficient to protect the ward's estate.[3]

Where one acting in the capacity of a guardian of minors, but not by appointment of any court, came into the possession of their property in another state and removed to Illinois, where he died, his administrator was held to account in a court of equity, as if the deceased had been in fact the guardian of such minors.[4]

(1) Warren vs. Hofer, 13 Ind., 167; Martin vs. McDonald, 14 B. Mon., (Ky.) 544; Swayzee vs. Miller, 17 B. Mon., (Ky.) 564.
(2) *Ex Parte* Smith, 1 Hill, S. C. Ch., 140; *Ex Parte* Heard, 2 Hill, S C. Ch., 54; *Ex Parte* Baker Andrews, 3 Hump., (Tenn.) 592.
(3) Carlile vs. Tuttle, 30 Ala., 613.
(4) Davis vs. Harkness, 1 Gilm., 173.

ADDITIONAL NOTES.

1. A foreign guardian has a right to take steps to collect his ward's money.

1. Foreign guardian has a right to collect his ward's money.—A foreign guardian will have the right to compel the citation of a former resident guardian who has failed to make settlement or account to his ward. Nor is it necessary to obtain an order first for that purpose. It is sufficient if such order be obtained to collect the money due to his ward before he institutes suit. Where suit is instituted on the guardian's bond, the amount found due on citation, which was afterward appealed from, and judgment by consent rendered in the circuit court, affirming the amount found due by the county court, such amount is conclusive in any action brought on the guardian's bond.[1] A foreign guardian has no authority over the person or property of the ward in another state, except by the comity of the latter.[2]

(1) McCleary vs. Menke, 109 Ill., 294.
(2) Lamar vs. Micou, 112 U. S., 452.

CHAPTER X.

RESIGNATION OF GUARDIANS.

1. Resignation of guardians—forms.
2. Rules.

1. RESIGNATION OF GUARDIANS.—When it shall appear proper, the court may permit the guardian to resign his trust, if he first settles his accounts and delivers over the estate as by the court directed.([1])

A guardian having fully settled and discharged his duty, may file his petition to resign, and for good reasons shown, it is the duty of the court to accept it, and relieve him from any further burden, upon his filing the receipt of his successor in office.

The petition may be in form as follows:

STATE OF ILLINOIS, } ss. *In the County Court,*
..............County.   *To the......term, A. D. 18...*

In the Matter of the Guardianship of.........

To the Hon........., Judge of the County Court of said County:

Your petitioner, ..., by appointment of this court, made on the... day of......, A. D. 18..., guardian of the person and estate of........., and........ minor heirs of........, late of said county, deceased, would respectfully represent and show unto your honor: That your petitioner at, to-wit: the........ term, A. D. 18...., filed his settlement as guardian aforesaid, which said settlement was approved by the court, and he hereby tenders his resignation as guardian aforesaid, and prays the court to accept the same.

And your petitioner assigns as a reason for his said resignation, that he desires to remove from the State of Illinois, and without the jurisdiction of this court, and that it will be impossible for him longer to look after and care for the interests of his said wards.

Your petitioner therefore prays that he may be finally discharged from his said trust, upon filing the receipt of his successor in office, of the amount ascertained to be due from him on settlement made and approved as aforesaid.

And your petitioner will ever pray, etc.

By............, his Attorney.

---

(1) Hurd's R. S., Chap. 64, § 39.

STATE OF ILLINOIS, } ss.
............County.

........., the above named petitioner, states on oath, that he has heard the foregoing petition read over, and that the matters and things therein stated, are true and correct.

Subscribed and sworn to before me, this...day of......, A. D. 18...
........., Clerk County Court

The guardian may also tender his resignation in the settlement filed with the court, and it is usual to simply insert at the close of the settlement filed for approval, the words:

"And the said........., guardian as aforesaid, having filed this, his settlement, respectfully asks the approval of the same, and hereby tenders his resignation of the office of guardian, and prays the court to accept the same; and that he may be discharged upon filing the receipt of his successor in office.

And your petitioner assigns as a reason for so asking to resign his trust as aforesaid, That he is old and unable longer to attend properly to the duties of his said office, being now above the age of seventy, and hence asks to be relieved from said trust.

And your petitioner, as he is in duty bound, will ever pray, etc."

Upon the filing, presenting and acceptance of the petition by the court, the clerk shall enter an order, which may be in form as follows:

STATE OF ILLINOIS, } ss.
............County,

In the Matter of the Guardianship of.........., Guardian of.........., minor heirs of.........., deceased.

And now, on this day, the same being the....judicial day of the present term of this court, comes the said.........., by appointment of this court guardian of.........., minor heirs of.........., late of........county, deceased, by.........., his attorney, and presents his petition for resignation of said trust; and the court having considered thereof, and being now sufficiently advised and satisfied concerning the same, orders that said resignation be accepted, and that said..........be discharged from said trust upon the filing of the receipt of his successor in office for the amount found due in his hands on final settlement made and approved by the court at its present term.

And now, to-wit: it being the....judicial day of the present term, comes again the said.........., by.........., his attorney, and files herewith the receipt of.........., by appointment of this court, guardian of the person and estate of.........., minor heirs of.........., deceased, and the successor in office to the said.........., for the sum of......dollars, in full of the amount found due in his hands by the court, at his settlement at the present term of this court, which said receipt is ordered filed, approved and credited, and said guardian finally discharged from further service in and about said trust.

2. RULES.—The validity of the revocation of letters of guardianship, and the appointment of another guardian, can not be collaterally called in question.([1])

His resignation will not be accepted by the court, and he be discharged from his trust, on his own petition, unless for good reasons shown.([2])

(1) Young vs. Lorain, 11 Ill., 624.
(2) *Ex Parte* Crumb, 2 Johns. Ch., (N. Y.) 439.

CHAPTER XI.

REMOVAL OF GUARDIANS.

1. Power of court.
2. Notice to guardian—petition, etc.
3. Successor in office.
4. Rules governing the removal of guardians.
5. Appeals.

1. POWER OF COURT.—The county court may remove a guardian for his failure to give bond or security, or additional or counter security, when required, or for failure to make inventory, or to account and make settlement, or support or educate the ward, or when he shall have become insane, or have removed out of the state, or become incapable or unsuitable for the discharge of his duties, or for failure to discharge any duty required of him by law or the order of the court, or for other good cause.(¹)

2. NOTICE TO GUARDIAN.—Before removing a guardian, the court shall summon him to show cause why he should not be removed for the cause alleged. If the guardian has left the state, or can not be served with process, he may be notified in the same manner as non-resident defendants in chancery.(²)

The petition for the removal of a guardian may be in form as follows:

STATE OF ILLINOIS, }   *In the County Court,*
...............County. } ss.   *To the............term, A. D. 18....*

To the Hon............, Judge of the County Court:

Your petitioner............, of the county of........, and State of Illinois, by..........., his attorney, would respectfully represent and show unto your honor, that on to-wit: the....day of........, A. D. 18...., one............was appointed by this honorable court guardian of............, a minor, aged....years, as will more fully appear by reference to the records of said appointment now on file in this court.

Yout petitioner would further show, that he is a brother of said minor, and that he is desirous of watching the interest of his estate; and that the said guardian aforesaid since his said appointment, has wholly mismanaged the estate of his said ward, in this: That he has failed to file an inventory

---

(1) Hurd's R. S., Chap. 64, § 37.   (2) Hurd's R. S., Chap. 64, § 38.

of the estate of said ward; and has converted a portion of the estate of said ward to his own use; and has wholly failed to give additional or counter security, although required to do so, by an order of this honorable court, made and entered of record at its........term, A. D. 18...., and has, in other and many respects, mismanaged the estate of his said ward.

Your petitioner, therefore, prays that a summons may issue against the said............, and that he may be cited to be and appear before this honorable court, at the......term thereof, to show cause, if any he has, why he should not be removed; and upon a final hearing hereof, in case of the failure of the said............to justify or show cause why he should not be removed, your petitioner prays that he may be removed, and his letters revoked, and the guardianship of said minors be committed to some other person.

And your petitioner will ever pray, etc.

By........., Attorney.

Dated this....day of........., A. D. 18....

STATE OF ILLINOIS, } ss.
...............County.

............being duly sworn, states, that he has heard the foregoing petition read and knows the contents thereof, and that the same is true in substance and in fact.   ....

Subscribed and sworn to before me, this...day of......, A. D. 18...
........., Clerk.

Upon filing the petition, it is the duty of the clerk to issue a summons or citation, which may be in form as follows:

STATE OF ILLINOIS, } ss.
...............County,

The People of the State of Illinois, to the Sheriff of said County, Greeting:

Whereas, it has been represented to the county court of said county, by petition of............, that............, guardian of............, minor, has been guilty of mismanaging and wasting the estate of his ward, and has failed to file an inventory of his said ward's estate, and to give additional or counter security as required by the court: You are therefore commanded to summon the said............to be and appear before the county court of..........county, Illinois, on the....day of........., A. D. 18...., at the court house in............, Illinois, and show cause why, if any he has, his letters of guardianship should not be revoked, and he be removed from his office of guardianship of............

Witness,............, clerk of the county court of............county, Illinois, and the seal thereof, at his office, in........., in said county, this....day of......, A. D. 18....
........., Clerk of the County Court.

The clerk should deliver the citation to the sheriff, whose duty it is to see that the same is served within a reasonable time before the court convenes.

The return of the officer may be in form as follows:

STATE OF ILLINOIS, } ss.
................County,

I have duly served the foregoing summons by reading and delivering a true copy of the same to............, as I am therein commanded. This....day of........, A. D. 18.....   ...., Sheriff.

On the day of the return, if service be had or due notice given, the court will proceed to hear and determine the petition. In case the allegations are not true, the same will be dismissed at the costs of the petitioner filing the same. If, however, the court be satisfied sufficient cause exist for the removal of the guardian, it will cause an order to be so entered of record.

The order may be in form as follows:

STATE OF ILLINOIS, } ss.   *In the County Court,*
................County, ...*term, A. D.* 18....

Present: Hon............, Judge.   Attest : ...., Clerk.

In the matter of the Guardianship
of............, minor heir of............,   Removal of Guardian.
    deceased.

And now, on this day, the same being the....judicial day of the present term of this court, comes the said............, by his attorney, ..., comes also, the said............ by............, his attorney, and the said...........having filed his answer herein, denying each and every allegation of said petition, and the said...........having filed his replication thereto, and this cause coming on now to be heard, and the court having heard all the testimony adduced and the argument of counsel, and having considered thereof, and being satisfied in the premises, finds each and every allegation of said petition true, as stated in said petition, viz.: [*Here set out the facts.*] The court doth therefore order, adjudge and decree: That said letters of guardianship issued to said............, be revoked; and that said guardian's accounts be closed; and that he forthwith render to this court, a full settlement of said guardianship, and that upon the same being approved, he pay and deliver over to his successor in office, all of the estate of the said............, now remaining undisposed of in his hands, and exhibit his receipt therefor.

That said............shall fully comply with this order and decree of the court at its present term, and in default thereof, he stand committed as in contempt of court.

3. SUCCESSOR IN OFFICE.—Upon the removal, resignation or death of a guardian, another may be appointed, who shall give bond and security and perform the duties prescribed by this act.

And the court shall have power to compel the guardian so removed or resigned, or the executor or administrator of a deceased guardian, or the conservator of an insane person, or other person, to deliver up to such successor, all the goods, chattels, moneys, title papers, and other effects in his custody or control, belonging to such minor; and upon failure to so deliver the same, to commit the person offending to jail, until he shall comply with the order of the court.([1])

4. RULES GOVERNING THE REMOVAL OF GUARDIANS.—The court of probate has power to remove the guardian for good and sufficient reasons.([2])

The proper proceeding for the removal of a guardian, is by petition.([3]) Where the removal is sought on the ground of the "notoriously bad conduct of the guardian," the petition should allege particular facts of which the defendant was guilty, in order to enable the court to determine whether such facts constituted notoriously bad conduct.([4]) Conduct of a guardian tending to alienate the affection of his infant ward from its mother, who is a person of good character, is a sufficient cause for his removal from the trust.([5])

He may be removed for misconduct in investing the funds of his ward;([6]) and for his failure to file his inventory, verified by oath, of the real and personal estate of his ward, within the time required by law.([7])

The removal of a guardian beyond the limits of the state, is a sufficient reason for severing the relation of guardian and ward, and revoking the appointment.([8]) Where he acts corruptly and collusively, to defraud his wards, it will not only justify his removal, but damages will be awarded against him, on proof of the damages sustained by his fraudulent conduct.([9])

(1) Hurd's R. S., Chap. 64, § 40.
(2) Young vs. Lorain, 11 Ill., 624; Pickens vs. Clayton, 7 Blackf., (Ind.) 321; Simpson vs. Gonzales, 15 Fla., 9.
(3) Disbrow vs. Henshaw, 8 Cow., (N.Y.) 349.
(4) Edwards vs. Morrow, 12 La. Ann., 887; Whitney vs. Whitney, 15 Miss., 740; (7 Smedes & Marshall.)
(5) Perkins vs. Finnegan, 105 Mass., 501.
(6) O'Neil's Case, 1 Tuck., (1 N. Y. Surr.) 34.
(7) Barnes vs. Powers, 12 Ind., 341; Kimmel vs. Kimmel, 48 Ind., 203.
(8) Eiland vs. Chandler, 8 Ala., 781; Speight vs. Knight, 11 Ala., 461; Cockrell vs. Cockrell, 36 Ala., 673; Nettleton vs. State, 13 Ind., 159; Cooke vs. Beale, 11 Ired. (N. C.) Eq., 36.
(9) Marks vs. Whitkouski, 16 La. Ann., 341.

His insolvency, together with the insolvency of one of his sureties, is a sufficient cause for his removal,[1] unless upon notice he files a sufficient bond.

Ignorance or imprudence on the part of the guardian, resulting in the injury of his ward's estate;[2] drunkenness;[3] abandonment of the trust;[4] in fact, where the county court deems it best for the interest of the ward, it has authority to displace the guardian.[5]

A large discretion is necessarily left to the courts having original jurisdiction, of removing guardians, for a breach of their duties, and their decision will not be interfered with, unless their discretion has been grossly abused.[6]

A father, who was guardian for his children, and received an annual income from their estate of $2,000, and who, for a period of several years, refused to support and educate them, was removed, as being a person unsuitable to have the care and management of their person and estate.[7]

It is no ground for the removal of a guardian, that he has retained the funds of his ward, instead of investing them, admitting his liability for interest.[8]

Letters of guardianship create a trust coupled with an interest, and where one of two guardians dies, or is removed, the trust survives or remains to the other.[9]

A guardian can not be removed without notice or a citation to show cause.[10]

Where his authority is revoked, he is required by his bond to pay over the money in his hands to the person appointed to receive it.[11]

It has been held, that where a guardian is removed, that he can not claim compensation for his services.[12]

---

[1] Matter of Cooper, 2 Paige, (N. Y.) 34.
[2] Nicholson's Appeal, 20 Penn. St., 50.
[3] Kettletas vs. Gardner, 1 Paige, 488.
[4] Lefever vs. Lefever, 6 Md., 472.
[5] *Ex Parte* Crutchfield, 3 Yerg., (Tenn.) 336.
[6] Young vs. Young, 5 Ind., 513; Nicholson's Appeal, *supra*.
[7] In the Matter of Swifyts, 47 Cal., 629.
[8] Sweet vs. Sweet, Spears (S. C.) Ch., 309.
[9] Pepper vs. Stone, 10 Vt., 427.
[10] Montgomery vs. Smith, 3 Dana, (Ky.) 599; Eddy vs. People, 15 Ill., 386; Dibble vs. Dibble, 8 Ind., 307.
[11] United States vs. Nichols, 4 Cranch., Cir. Ct., 191.
[12] Trimble vs. Dodd, 2 Tenn. Ch., 500.

Where the court removes a guardian, the order should state the grounds on which the court proceeded.(¹)

The guardianship may be also determined by the majority of the wards, which in males, is twenty-one years, and females, eighteen. And the ward, when he arrives at the age of fourteen, may determine the guardianship, by his election and selection of another guardian.(²)

The guardianship may also be determined by the death of the ward and by the death of the guardian.(³)

The marriage of a female ward terminates the guardianship, as to her person; it is otherwise of the marriage of a male ward.(⁴)

5. APPEALS.—Appeals shall be allowed to the circuit court from any order or judgment made or rendered under this act, upon the appellant giving such bond and security as shall be directed by the court; but no appeal from an order removing a guardian, shall in any wise affect such order, until the same be reversed.(⁵)

(1) Pepper vs. Stone, 10 Vt., 427.
(2) Dibble vs. Dibble, 8 Ind., 307.
(3) Johnson vs. Carter, 16 Mass., 443.
(4) Bricks' Estate, 15 Abb., (N. Y.) Pr., 12; Holmes vs. Field, 12 Ill., 424; Shutt vs. Carloss, 1 Ired. (N. C) Eq., 232; Burr vs. Wilson, 18 Texas, 367.
(5) Hurd's R. S., Chap. 64, § 43.

CHAPTER XII.

RIGHTS AND LIABILITIES OF SURETIES ON GUARDIANS' BONDS

1. Defenses to suits upon guardians' bonds.
2. Counter security—petition—order of court.
3. Proceedings under the order.

1. LIABILITY OF THE SURETY.—Sureties of a guardian can not set up in defense, during the ward's minority, that the guardian and ward have together, and with the consent of the ward, squandered the estate. A ward can not, during minority, give a consent which will excuse a misappropriation.([1])

The estate of a surety upon a guardian's bond, is liable for a default which occurred subsequent to the death of the surety.([2])

While a decree rendered against a guardian on final account, is conclusive against him, it is not so against a surety not a party to that suit, and he may show, when sued, that the guardian failed to charge his wards with boarding, tuition or commissions, or that he made improper charges in their favor against himself.([3]) A final settlement made by a guardian, with the court, showing the amount of his indebtedness to the wards, is conclusive alike on the guardian and his sureties, unless they can impeach it for fraud or collusion.([4])

Where a ward, after the death and distribution of the estate of a surety on the guardian's bond, obtains a decree against the guardian, upon which execution is issued and returned no property found, a court of equity will entertain jurisdiction of a bill filed by the ward against personal and legal representatives of the deceased surety, to enforce satisfaction of the demand.([5]) If the estate of the guardian of a minor is insolvent and his sureties irresponsible, it is not necessary for the ward to institute proceedings at law before he can file a bill in equity to recover such part of the estate as he can trace.([6]) Where several bonds, with different sets of sureties have

---

(1) Judge of Probate vs. Cook, 57 N. H., 450.
(2) Voris vs. State, 47 Ind., 345.
(3) State vs. Hall, 53 Miss., 626.
(4) Chilton vs. Parks, 15 Ala., 671; Meyer vs. Rives, 11 Ala., 769; Ammons vs. People, 11 Ill., 6; Ralston vs. Wood, 15 Ill., 159; Stone vs. Wood, 16 Ill., 177; Gilbert vs. Guptil, 34 Ill., 140; Ream vs. Lynch, 7 Bradwell, 161.
(5) Moore vs. Wallis, 18 Ala., 458.
(6) Hill vs. McIntire, 39 N. H., 410.

been given by a guardian, so long as the principal is confessedly solvent, the remedy at law on the bonds is ample, notwithstanding the different liabilities of the sureties.([1])

Bonds that are void at law, are sometimes enforceable in equity.([2]) Where an order of the court directed that the guardian give bond in a certain sum, and give for security certain persons, and the bond was executed in such a form as to be void, upon the ward becoming of age, a bill was filed, and the bond was corrected as against the surety.([3]) So, too, where the bond was void at law, on the ground that the sureties were justices of the county, and were, therefore, both obligors and obligees, the bond was enforced in equity.([4])

It is not necessary before an action can be maintained at law, upon a guardian's bond, that the accounts must have been adjusted, and a specific sum decreed to be paid over.([5])

Until the removal of a guardian from his trust, the statute does not authorize a suit by his infant wards on his bond for the recovery of money in his hands;([6]) for, whilst the relation of guardian and ward subsists, an action can not be maintained against a guardian or his sureties, on his official bond.([7])

Where an administrator becomes guardian to a minor interested in the estate, he must do some act in his hands, as administrator, in order to charge himself and sureties under the guardian's bond, such as passing an account charging himself as guardian.([8]) But, where a person sustains the dual relation or trust of administrator and guardian, he will be chargeable as guardian, if the estate is virtually settled up, and a reasonable time has elapsed for settling, and he has charged himself in a private book with the funds belonging to the heir who is the sole distributee, his sureties as administrator will be released, and his sureties as guardian will be liable for the funds which came into his hands in the capacity

(1) McDougald vs. Maddox, 17 Ga., 52.
(2) Butler vs. Durham, 3 Ired. (N. C.) Eq., 589.
(3) Armistead vs. Bozman, 1 Ired. (N. C.) Eq., 117.
(4) Butler vs. Durham, *supra*.
(5) State vs. Strange, 1 Ind., 538; Stillwell vs. Mills, 19 Johns., (N. Y.) 304; Barrrett vs. Munroe, 4 Dev. & B. (N. C.) L., 194; Wann vs. People, 57 Ill., 202; McIntyre vs. People, 103 Ill., 142.
(6) Ely vs. Hawkins, 15 Ind., 230.
(7) Erland vs. Chandler, 8 Ala., 781.
(8) Burton vs. Tunnell, 4 Harr., (Del.) 424.

of administrator. An order of the county court transferring the funds in his hands as administrator, is not indispensable in such case to charge the sureties on the guardian's bond.(¹)

Upon the death of the principal in a guardian's bond, the trust is thereby terminated, and the sureties become liable for the amount of money in the guardian's hands, belonging to the ward at the time of his death, and it is not necessary that the ward should first resort to a suit against the legal representatives of the guardian;(²) for, an action will lie upon the bond of a guardian, against the surety, without any previous suit against the principal.(³)

Where a guardian neglects to account, a citation from the judge of probate requiring him to render his account, is a necessary preliminary, in order to charge the guardian on his bond for refusing to account.(⁴)

An action on a guardian's bond for a failure to pay over money to a subsequently appointed guardian, can not be sustained, if the declaration fails to allege the due appointment of the plaintiff as successor,—as the plaintiff shows no right to sue, under the conditions in the bond. Mere profert of letters attached to the declaration, is no averment of appointment.

It is not a sufficient allegation of the breach of the bond, that the guardian had failed to make report to the court when thereunto required, without further alleging that the guardian was required by the court to make such report.(⁵)

2. COUNTER SECURITY.—Upon the application of the surety of any guardian, and after summoning the guardian, the court may, if it believes him insolvent or in doubtful circumstances, require him to give counter security to his sureties.(⁶)

The application should be made by petition to the court, and may be in form as follows:

STATE OF ILLINOIS, } ss.   In the County Court,
.................County, ...term, A D. 18....

To the Hon............, Judge of said Court:

Your petitioners, ..., would respectfully show unto your honor, that

(1) Bell vs. People, 94 Ill., 2 0.
(2) State vs. Thorn, 28 Ind.,306.
(3) Call vs. Ruffin, 1 Call, (Va.) 333; Foster vs. Maxey, 6 Yerg., (Tenn.) 224.
(4) Bailey vs. Rodgers, 1 Me., (1 Greenlf.) 186.
(5) People vs. Steele, 7 Bradwell, 20.
(6) Hurd's R. S., Chap. 64, § 36.

on or about the....day of........, A. D. 18...., they became the sureties of one........ on his bond as guardian of............, minor heir of............, deceased; which said bond was afterwards approved and accepted by this honorable court as the official bond of the said............, guardian as aforesaid, and still remains on file in the office of the clerk of this honorable court, and in full force and effect. Your petitioners further show unto your honor, that since the said bond was accepted and approved by the court as aforesaid, the said............ has, as your petitioners are informed and believe, become insolvent; that he is in doubtful circumstances, and your petitioners have cause to fear, and do fear, that they will suffer loss as sureties on the bond of the said............, guardian as aforesaid.

Your petitioners, therefore, pray that the said...........may be summoned to appear before this honorable court at the....term thereof, to be holden the.... day of......, A. D. 18..... And your petitioners pray that on a final hearing of this petition, the said............may be required to give to your petitioners, counter security as surety on said guardian's bond, according to the form of the statute in such case made and provided, and that your petitioners may have such other and further relief in the premises as the nature of their case may require. And your petitioners will ever pray, etc.

By........., Attorney.

Subscribed and sworn to before me this...day of......, A. D. 18....

A B, Clerk.

The order of the court granting the prayer of said petition, may be as follows:

STATE OF ILLINOIS, } ss.
...................County,

In the County Court,
Of the........term, A. D. 18....

Present: Hon............, Judge.

Attest:............, Clerk.

In the matter of........., Guardian
of............, the minor child........
of............, deceased.

On the application of..........,
sureties on said guard-
ian's bond for counter security.

And now, on this day, come the petitioners, by............, attorneys, none appearing for the said............, guardian of............, and it appearing to the satisfaction of the court that the said............, guardian as aforesaid, has been duly served with a summons to answer said petition more than ten days before the first day of the present term of this court: It is ordered that the said........., guardian, be called, and he being three times called by the sheriff comes not, but makes default herein. It is ordered, that the petition of said petitioners be taken for confessed by the said guardian ; and this cause coming on to be heard upon said petition taken for confessed, oral proofs heard by the court, and the court having heard all the proofs in support of said petition, and being now sufficiently advised and satisfied in the premises, finds that said guardian is insolvent or in doubtful circumstances: It is ordered and adjudged, that the said............, guardian as aforesaid, do, within...days from the date of this order, execute and deliver to the petitioners a good and sufficient bond in the penal sum of...dollars, with at least two sureties to be approved by the court, or accepted by the petitioners, conditioned that the said........., guardian as aforesaid, shall save harmless the said petitioners as sureties on the bond of said guardian, or that he give to the petitioners such other counter security as may be agreed upon by the parties and be acceptable to said petitioners. It is further ordered, that the said guardian report his action in the premises to the next term of this court, and that he pay the costs of this proceeding to be taxed by the clerk, that execution issue therefor, and that this proceeding stand continued for report.

3. PROCEEDINGS UNDER THE ORDER.—The guardian may give the bond and security named in the order, or if he and the petitioners should agree upon some other security, such as a pledge or a mortgage, acceptable to the surety, that would be a sufficient compliance with the order of the court.

The bond to be given may be in form as follows:

Know all men by these presents: That........., as principal, and........., as sureties, are held and firmly bound unto........., in the penal sum of...dollars, lawful money, for the payment of which well and truly to be made, we bind ourselves, our heirs, executors and administrators, jointly, severally and firmly by these presents. Sealed with our seals, and dated on this...day of......, A. D. 18....

The condition of the above obligation is such, that whereas on the....day of......, A. D. 18...., the above named.........became one of the sureties of the above bounden.........on his bond as the guardian of........., minor child...... of.........deceased, in the penal sum of......dollars; and whereas, the county court of.........county, in the state of Illinois, at the......term thereof, A. D. 18...., by its order made and entered of record, required the above bounden........., guardian as aforesaid, to give to the said........., surety on said guardian's bond as aforesaid, counter security, in the said sum of......dollars. [*Penalty of the bond.*]

Now, if the above bounden.........shall so execute and discharge the duties of his said guardianship as to save the said.........entirely harmless as surety on the bond of said guardian, then this obligation shall be void, but otherwise shall remain in full force and effect.

........., [Seal.]
Signed, sealed and delivered in ...., [Seal.]
    presence of......... ...., [Seal.]

STATE OF ILLINOIS, } ss.
...............County,

I........., in and for said county and state, do hereby certify that........., who are each personally known to me to be the same persons whose names are subscribed to the foregoing instrument, appeared before me this day in person and acknowledged that they signed, sealed and delivered said instrument as their free and voluntary act, for the uses and purposes as therein set forth.

Given under my hand and.........seal, this....day of........., A. D. 18....

........., County Clerk.

The report required of the guardian, may be as follows:

STATE OF ILLINOIS, } ss.
...............County,

In the County Court,
To the......term, A. D. 18....

To the Hon.........., Judge of said Court:

The undersigned, by appointment of this court guardian of the person and property of.........., minor child....of.........., deceased, would respectfully report unto your honor, that in pursuance of an order of this court, made at its......term, A. D. 18...., "In the matter of.........petitioners, to require.........guardian.......of.........., to give counter security," an order was made requiring the undersigned, guardian, as aforesaid, to give to the said ....counter security, and report herein at the present term of this court. The undersigned would therefore respectfully report that in pursuance of said order, he has executed and delivered to the said..........a bond, with.......... and..........as sureties, in the penal sum of......dollars, which said bond has been accepted by the..........as a good and sufficient bond for counter security, as required by the order of the court aforesaid.

The undersigned would further report that he has paid the cost of this proceeding, and prays hence to be discharged.

All of which is respectfully submitted for the approval of the court.

Dated this....day of........, A. D. 18....

........, Attorney.

As has been already stated, should the guardian refuse to give such counter security, it will be cause for his removal.([1])

A ward can not be prejudiced by an unauthorized alteration made in the bond of his guardian.([2])

(1) Hurd's R. S., Chap. 64, § 37.
(2) McIntyre vs. People, 103 Ill., 142.

ADDITIONAL NOTES.

1. Alteration of guardian's bond will not affect ward.
2. Guardian's bond—Action lies on, without first fixing guardian's liability.
3. Grounds of liability on a guardian's bond—No devastavit need be established.
4. A release obtained by the guardian from the ward under influence.
5. Subrogation—Right of surety.
6. In case of several wards and only one bond, several liability to the wards.
7. A guardian owes his ward a duty, which can be discharged only by the performance of all the conditions of his bond.
8. Citation of a surety.
9. Security may recover from co-security—When.
10. The finding of amount due ward conclusive—When.
11. A failure to make settlement on arrival of age, a breach of guardian's bond.

1. ALTERATION OF GUARDIAN'S BOND WILL NOT AFFECT WARD.—The adding of another name as security in the body of a guardian's bond, and the signing and sealing of such bond by the new surety, under an order of the court requiring additional security, even if unlawful, will not affect the security of the ward in the bond as originally made, or defeat a recovery thereon; and if lawfully made, the ward may treat the bond as that of all the sureties named in it after its alteration, and may sue any one of such sureties separately.(1)

2. GUARDIAN'S BOND—ACTION LIES ON, WITHOUT FIRST FIXING LIABILITY.—Nor will it be necessary, before bringing suit upon the bond, to have the liabilities of the guardian ascertained and fixed; the damages may be ascertained in the suit on the bond.(2)

3. GROUNDS OF LIABILITY—NEED NOT ESTABLISH DEVASTAVIT.—An action will lie on a guardian's bond given prior to the act of 1874, without first establishing a *devastavit*. A declaration on such bond containing two breaches: First, that the guardian was on a certain day required to account and failed to do so; and, second, that one of the wards became of age on a certain day, etc., and the guardian failed to account and pay over to her a certain sum of

(1) McIntire vs. The People, for the use of Alice Wilkey, 103 Ill., 142.
(2) *Ib.*

money, which was due to the ward, and which the ward was entitled to receive from the guardian, but which sum was converted by the guardian to his own use, and not paid over by him, is sufficient to authorize the rendition against the surety upon the guardian's bond.(1) It is no defense to an action on a guardian's bond to allege and show that no adjustment was ever had of the accounts of the guardian by the probate court.(2)

4. RELEASE OBTAINED BY GUARDIAN FROM WARD UNDER INFLUENCE.—A release obtained by a guardian and his sureties, after her arrival of age, she being a daughter of the guardian, and ignorant of her rights, the receipt amounting to a gift, will be invalid, and she may file a bill within ten years after she arrives of age, against her guardian and his sureties on his bond, for an account and the payment of moneys due the ward, and to set aside a release given without consideration and in ignorance of the ward's rights, the sureties having full notice that such release was fraudulently obtained. A release obtained by the father, the guardian of his minor child, and his sureties, in ignorance of her rights, amounts to constructive fraud on the ward.(3)

5. SUBROGATION.—A surety has a clear right, in equity, upon paying the debt of his principal, to be substituted in the place of the creditor, as to all the securities held by the latter for the debt, and to have the same benefit therein as the creditor would have.(4)

6. SEVERAL WARDS AND ONE BOND—LIABILITY.—Where one is appointed guardian for three wards and gives but one bond, he will be the separate guardian of each ward, and the death of one will not relieve the guardian from responsibility as guardian of the survivors, and an action may be maintained on his bond, in the name of The People, for the use of the surviving wards.(5)

7. GUARDIAN'S DUTY—HOW DISCHARGED.—A guardian owes his ward a duty, which can be discharged only by a performance of all the conditions of his bond, and no one but the ward has power to release the guardian or his surety. A surety on a guardian's bond undertakes for the fidelity and honesty of his principal toward his

(1) Winslow vs. The People, for use of Walrath, 117 Ill., 152.
(2) Ib.
(3) Carter vs. Tice, 120 Ill., 277.
(4) Rice vs. Rice, 108 Ill., 199.
(5) Winslow vs. The People, for the use of Walrath, 117 Ill., 152; Ib., 17 Ill. Ap., 222.

ward, and when the guardian, by means of fraud and circumvention, procures his ward to execute an instrument in writing as an acquittance, in the belief it is something else, whereby the guardian is enabled to defraud his surety, the doctrine of estoppel cannot be invoked by such surety to prevent the ward from asserting his legal rights.([1])

8. CITATION OF SURETY.—The citation of a surety twenty-one years after the ward became of age, to state a knowledge of the guardian's accounts, the guardian having died, will not revive a right of recovery against the surety for any balance remaining due and unpaid.([2])

9. SECURITY MAY RECOVER FROM CO-SECURITY—WHEN.—The insolvency of one security cannot operate to increase the amounts recoverable against those who are solvent, where sureties bring suit against a co-security for contribution. The security who is compelled to pay judgment in full may recover from each of his several co-securities a *pro rata* share of the sum so paid, with interest from the time of payment.([3])

10. FINDING AMOUNT DUE WARD CONCLUSIVE—WHEN.—In a suit upon a guardian's bond, as against the sureties, a judgment of the county court finding the amount due from the guardian to his ward on final settlement is, in the absence of fraud, conclusive upon the sureties and their privies.([4])

11. FAILURE TO MAKE SETTLEMENT ON ARRIVAL OF AGE, A BREACH OF GUARDIAN'S BOND.—A failure to make a settlement immediately upon the ward's arrival of age is a breach of the guardian's bond, and action arises at once against the sureties under the statute.([5]) A condition in a guardian's bond that settlement shall be made in the county court does not bind the surety thereon to a settlement in the probate court ([6]) But the transfer of said cause from the county court to the probate court in conformity to the act of 1877 did not void such bond as to other conditions therein. [7])

(1) Gillett vs. Wiley, 126 Ill., 310.
(2) The People, for use, vs. Stewart, 29 Ill. Ap., 441.
(3) Moore vs. Bruner, 31 Ill. Ap., 400.
(4) Brooks vs. The People, for use, 15 Ill. Ap., 570; Seago vs. The People, for use, 21 Ill. Ap., 283.
(5) The People, for use, vs. Brooks, 22 Ill. Ap., 594.
(6) Seelye vs. The People, 40 Ill. Ap., 449.
(7) *Ib.*

CHAPTER XIII.

THE LAW OF TRUSTS AS APPLIED TO EXECUTORS, ADMINISTRATORS AND GUARDIANS.

1. Definition.
2. When a trust is not implied.
3. Duties of trustees.
4. Disabilities of trustees.
5. Duty to act in good faith.
6. Remedy against trustees.
7. Settlements between trustee and *cestui que* trust.
8. Relations of trustee to the court.

1. DEFINITION.—A trust is a right of property, real or personal, held by one party for the benefit of another. The party holding, is the trustee; the one for whom he holds, is the *cestui que* trust.

A trustee is a person in whom some estate, interest or power in or affecting property of any kind or description is vested for the benefit of another: hence, executors, administrators, guardians, conservators and assignees are trustees, and the law of trusts is applicable to them.

2. WHEN NOT IMPLIED.—Trusts, however, will not be implied merely from the fact that parties are related; and the mere fact of relatives trading with one another, does not impose upon them the duty of disclosing their knowledge of the value of property, or the sum for which it could be sold, any more than where mutual friends trade, and the purchaser fails to disclose his superior knowledge of the value of the property. The rule would be different, however, if the relative were acting as the vendor's agent; or had been the confidential business adviser; or had been entrusted with or interested in the management of the business affairs; or had agreed to ascertain the value of the property in question for the party selling; or had been told by the vendor, that he was relied upon, owing to his relationship, to truly disclose the facts, and that the sale was made in consequence only of such confidence reposed in him.(¹)

3. DUTIES OF TRUSTEES.—Frequently questions of interest

(1) Fish vs. Clelland, 33 Ill., 238; Clelland vs. Fish, 43 Ill., 282.

arise as to the duty which a trustee owes to the trust property and to the beneficiary; and we have deemed it not inappropriate here to give a brief outline or synopsis of the law of trusts in relation to the duties of the trustee, with respect to the trust property and the *cestui que* trust.

From the very sacredness of the obligation, to apply the property faithfully, and for the purpose to which it was intended, and in accordance with the confidence reposed, it follows as a general rule, that the trustee shall not be allowed to deal with the *cestui que* trust, nor with the trust property.([1]) This was so by the rules of the common law, and persons who were acting in a fiduciary capacity, were bound to act for their principals alone.([2]) Trustees and others sustaining a fiduciary and confidential relation, can not deal on their own account with the thing or person falling within the trust or relationship;([3]) hence, it follows, as we have seen, that if at sales made by them in such capacity, they become purchasers, no matter by what means, open or covert, their purchases are voidable.([4]) The reason is apparent, for a party can not legally be allowed to purchase on his own account, that which his duty or trust requires him to sell on account of another.([5]) A deed of trust property from the trustee to himself, however, is not *ipso facto* void; and, if relieved from suspicious circumstances, is at least sufficient to give color of title.([6]) And, while voidable at the option of the *cestui que* trust, it can not be questioned by third parties.([7])

(1) Thorp vs. McCullom, 1 Gilm., 614; Michoud vs. Girod, 4 How, 503; Hitchcock vs. Watson, 18 Ill., 289; Wickliff vs. Robinson, 18 Ill., 145; Robbins vs. Butler, 24 Ill., 387; Lockwood vs. Mills, 39 Ill., 602; King vs. Cushman, 41 Ill., 31; Miles vs. Wheeler, 43 Ill., 123; Ringo vs. Binns, 10 Peters, 269.
(2) Pensoneau vs. Bleakley, 14 Ill., 15; Wickliff vs. Robinson, *supra*.
(3) Dennis vs. McCagg, 32 Ill., 429; Davoue vs. Fanning, 2 Johns. Ch., 252; Thorp vs. McCullom, *supra;* Switzer vs. Skiles, 3 Gilm., 529; Casey vs. Casey, 14 Ill., 112.
(4) Worthy vs. Johnson, 8 Ga., 236; Wickliff vs. Robinson, *supra;* Tatum vs. McLillan, 50 Miss., 1; Clark vs. Deveaux, 1 S. C., 172; *ante* page, 163.
(5) De Caters vs. Leray De Chaumont, 3 Paige, (N. Y.) 178; Child vs. Brace, 4 *Id.*, 309; Campbell vs. Johnson, 1 Sandf. (N. Y.) Ch., 148: Boyd vs. Hawkins, 2 Ired. (N. C.) Eq., 304; Saltmarsh vs. Beene, 4 Port., (Ala.) 283; Renew vs. Butler, 30 Ga., 954; Remick vs. Butterfield, 31 N. H., (2 Frost) 70; Den vs. Hileman, 7 N. J., L., (2 Hals.) 180; Obert vs. Hammel, 18 N. J., L., (3 Har.) 73; Bank of Orleans vs. Torrey, 7 Hill., (N. Y.) 260.
(6) Veasey vs. Graham, 17 Ga., 99.
(7) Baldwin vs. Allison, 4 Minn., 25; McKinley vs. Irwin, 13 Ala., 681; Woelper's Appeal, 2 Pa. St., 71; Painter vs. Henderson, 77 *Il.*, 48; McNish vs. Pope, 8 Rich. (S. C.) Eq., 112.

But as the trustee is not allowed to deal with the *cestui que* trust as with a third person, purchases of trust property made by him will not be sustained, unless the court is satisfied he has acted throughout with the most perfect fairness, and no advantage taken of his peculiar relation.(¹)

If he purchases, it must be upon a full and fair disclosure of everything that relates to it, or, that may, in any material degree, affect its value. Should he have an advantageous offer for the property, it is his duty to make this known to the *cestui que* trust before purchasing from him.(²)

4. DISABILITY OF TRUSTEES. — Executors, administrators, guardians or trustees, entrusted with the selling of real estate, can not purchase the same, because the seller and purchaser would constitute one person, and a valid contract requires two parties. Every man is partial to his own interest; and this maxim is one not required to be proved, for the law will not allow it to be controverted. An administrator appointed to sell real estate, because of his fiduciary relation, can not purchase it, either directly and openly, or secretly and covertly, through a sale to another person, whom he employs for the purpose. It is not enough for a trustee in such case, to say: "The sale was a public one, and you can show no fraud;" for it is in his power to conceal it. Every such sale must be considered absolutely void in a court of common law, because it has not the power of converting the purchaser into an accountable trustee; whereas, a court of equity will sometimes affirm the sale, and give a remedy for the fraud, by making the purchaser give up all the profit he has made by it.(³)

On bill filed by the heirs of a deceased intestate, to set aside a sale of lands made by the administrator of their father, under an order of the circuit court, it is sufficient to show, that the administrator was himself the purchaser at his own sale, though he may have used the name of another, and observed the forms of a conveyance to and from such other party, as a means of vesting the title in himself, and may even have paid what at the time was a fair

---

(1) Schwartz vs. Wendell, Walk. Ch., (Mich.) 267; Puzey vs. Senier, 9 Wis., 370; Staats vs. Bergen, 17 N. J. Eq., 554, 297.
(2) Ward vs. Armstrong, 84 Ill., 151.
(3) Den vs. Hammel, 18 N. J., L., (3 Har.) 73; Dyer vs. Shurtleff, 112 Mass., 165; Brown vs. Cowell, 116 Mass., 461.

price, entertaining no intent to defraud,(¹) as the law will not permit an administrator, or any kind of a trustee or person acting in a representative capacity, to be both seller and buyer, or *vice versa*, in the same transaction. The act is fraudulent, whatever the intent.(²) So, too, a sale by a trustee, directly or indirectly, to a corporation of which he is a member and large owner, is as fraudulent as an outright transfer to himself.(³) Nor will a trustee be permitted to lease a railroad to another company of which he is a stockholder and a director.(⁴)

Directors of a railroad company are the trustees of the stockholders, and it is regarded as a breach of duty to transfer the trust, or assume obligations inconsistent with that relation—as becoming members of a company to build and equip the road, so that they may share in the profits—and they will be compelled in equity to account for the profits so realized.

The *cestui que* trust has an election to ratify or avoid contracts, in which the trustee has a private interest.(⁵)

It is a rule of equity, that no person who is interested, with the power to sell or dispose of trust property, can become a purchaser at his own sale, even though he may employ another to conduct the formal part of it. This applies to sheriffs, masters, marshals, constables, or other officers employed to sell for another.(⁶) The fact that the person interested by law to make the sale, becomes the purchaser, whether by direct or indirect means, creates such a presumption of fraud as requires the sale to be vacated, if application is made within a reasonable time.(⁷) Where no actual fraud appears in the sale to the administrator, the proceeding to set aside the sale must be had in a court of equity;(⁸) and this, too, whether a loss has resulted to the owner or not.(⁹) At law, a different rule pre-

(1) Miles vs. Wheeler, 43 Ill., 123.
(2) *Id.*
(3) Robbins vs. Butler, 24 Ill., 387.
(4) Ashuelot Railroad vs. Elliott, 57 N. H. 397.
(5) Gilman C. & S. R. R. Co. vs. Kelly, 77 Ill., 426.
(6) Mapps vs. Sharpe, 32 Ill., 13; Dempster vs. West, 69 Ill., 613.
(7) Pensoneau vs. Bleakley, 14 Ill., 15; Wickliff vs. Robinson, 18 Ill., 145; Robbins vs. Butler, 24 Ill., 387; Dennis vs. McCagg, 32 Ill., 429; Patten vs. Pearson, 60 Me., 220.
(8) Lockwood vs. Mills, 39 Ill., 602.
(9) Thorp vs. McCullom, 1 Gilm., 614.

vails. There, a fraudulent deed may be invalidated, if the fraud can be sufficiently proved.(¹)

If a trustee exchanges trust property for other real estate, and takes the title thereto in his own name, such property so acquired, will be considered trust property to the extent of the value of the trust property exchanged therefor. And if no deed has been made by the trustee, and the trust property is afterwards forfeited and given back to the trustee for breach of conditions, it will inure to the benefit of the trust fund, and not to the benefit of the trustee.(²)

An agent or trustee for another, can not speculate in the execution of his fiduciary duties or employment, and if he, by compromise or otherwise, liquidates or pays off a debt of his principal or *cestui que* trust at less than he received for that purpose, he is accountable for the residue.(³) Nor will an agent be permitted to purchase the property of his principal at a sale of lands for taxes; for a trustee can not buy in an outstanding title, or purchase the lands for taxes, and in equity set up title thus acquired, to defeat the title of the *cestui que* trust.(⁴)

A trustee will never be permitted to obtain a personal benefit for himself, at the expense of his *cestui que* trust.(⁵) Should the trustee loan the money of his *cestui que* trust at an usurious rate of interest, the profits will inure to the beneficiary.(⁶) And where a trustee speculates with the trust funds, he may be held to account for profits if the investment has been successful, or for interest, if disastrous.(⁷)

Nor can a trustee purchase a title adverse to his beneficiary; a purchase so made, will be considered as made for the benefit of the *cestui que* trust.(⁸) And, should the trustee purchase lands or other

(1) Den vs. Hammel, 18 N. J., L., (3 Har.) 73; Thorp vs. McCullom, 1 Gilm., 614; Lockwood vs. Mills, 39 Ills., 602.
(2) Blauvelt vs. Ackerman, 5 C. E. Gr. Ch., 141.
(3) Trenton Banking Co., vs. Woodruff, 1 Gr. Ch., 117; Switzer vs. Skiles, 3 Gilm., 529; Hitchcock vs. Watson, 18 Ill., 289.
(4) Morris vs. Joseph, 1 W. Va., 256; O'Halloran vs. Fitzgerald, 71 Ill., 53.
(5) Sloo vs. Law, 3 Blatchf., 459; Page vs. Naglee, 6 Cal., 241; Buell vs. Buckingham, 16 Iowa, 284; Richardson vs. Spencer, 18 B. Mon., (Ky.) 450; Emerson vs. Altwater, 7 Mich., 12; Jones vs. Smith, 33 Miss., 215; Jamison vs. Glascock, 29 Mo., 191; Davis vs. Wright, 2 Hill, (S. C.) 560.
(6) Barney vs. Sanders, 16 How., 535.
(7) Norris's Appeal, 71 Pa. St., 106; Blauvelt vs. Ackerman, 20 N. J. Eq., 141.
(8) Brantley vs. Key, 5 Jones (N. C.) Eq., 332; Crutchfield vs. Haynes, 14 Ala., 49; McClanahan vs. Henderson, 2 A. K. Marsh., (Ky.) 388.

property with the money of the estate, and afterwards re-sell it at a profit, the benefit of the purchase inures to the estate, and not to himself individually;([1]) or, the *cestui que* trust may claim an equity upon the property, for the money. A vendee from such purchaser, with notice, stands as trustee. The trust can be enforced against all persons who come into possession of the trust property with notice of it;([2]) and the *cestui que* trust has his election to follow the trust property in the hands of the purchaser, or sue the trustee for his breach of trust.([3]) But a party acquiring the legal title to either real or personal estate, by purchase from a trustee, in good faith, and for value, without notice, will be protected against the *cestui que* trust.([4])

The *cestui que* trust, in prosecuting a suit in equity, to compel the trustee to convey the legal title to him, may, in the same suit, recover of the trustee, the rents and profits, which the trustee has received to the use of the *cestui que* trust, while the trustee was in possession of the land.([5])

Should the trustee sell the trust property and receive money, a court of equity will nevertheless retain jurisdiction to enforce the payment.([6])

Where a trustee purchases in an outstanding title, independent of any agreement, a court of equity will consider money advanced by a trustee, as money advanced for the benefit of his *cestui que* trust, and not for his own use, giving to him a lien on the property, until he is reimbursed for the advancement.([7]) A trustee has no right to derive any advantage or benefit from the trust fund, but all his skill and labor in the management of it, must be directed to the advancement of the interest of his *cestui que* trust.([8]) And,

---

(1) Mozely vs. Lane, 27 Ala., 62.
(2) Wood vs. Stafford, 50 Miss., 370; Shibla vs. Ely, 2 Hal. (N. J.) Ch., 181; Johns vs. Norris, 12 C. E. Green (N. J.) Ch., 485.
(3) Isom vs. First Nat. Bank, 52 Miss., 902; Durling vs. Hammar, 20 N. J. Eq., 220; Treadwell vs. McKeon, 7 Baxter, (Tenn.) 201; McLeod vs. First Nat. Bank, 42 Miss., 99; National Bank vs. Hyde Park, 101 Ill., 595.
(4) Wyse vs. Dandridge, 35 Miss., 672; Prevo vs. Walters, 4 Scam., 35; Christmas vs. Mitchell, 3 Ired. (N. C.) Eq., 535; Hadnul vs. Wilder, 4 McCord, (S. C.) 294.
(5) Hill vs. Cooper, 8 Oregon, 254.
(6) Nease vs. Capehart, 8 West Va., 95.
(7) King vs. Cushman, 41 Ill., 31.
(8) Arnold vs. Brown, 24 Pick., (Mass.) 89; Meyres vs. Meyres, 2 McCord (S. C.) Ch., 214.

should he purchase an incumbrance upon the trust estate; or, purchase or pay off a debt due from his *cestui que* trust, to a third person, at a discount, he will be treated as having purchased them for the benefit of the *cestui que* trust.(¹) Where a trustee buys lands in his own name, and pays for them out of the trust money in his hands, a court of equity will fasten a trust upon the lands in favor of the person beneficially entitled to the money, and the *cestui que* trust has a right to the estate,(²) and may sell it to satisfy the trust fund.(³) Property so purchased by the trustee, with the trust funds, will not be liable to a judgment against him, merely because he took the title in his own name, if he always treated it as trust property, and it is not shown that the creditor considered it as the estate of the trustee, and contracted with him on the faith of it.(⁴) If a trustee trades with himself upon the trust fund, the *cestui que* trust may repudiate the act,(⁵) and always has the option to take the benefit of any purchase which the trustee may make, of claims or titles adverse to the estate, upon reimbursing the trustee to the extent of his outlay.

While this is true, it is a general rule, he should signify his election to do so within a reasonable time;(⁶) as equity will not relieve a *cestui que* trust, who, with full knowledge of the misconduct of the trustee, has for a long time either acquiesced in it, or slept on his rights.(⁷)

A sale by a trustee to his *cestui que* trust stands on the same footing as a purchase by a trustee from his *cestui que* trust, and is void, especially, if the trustee has taken advantage of the necessities of the *cestui que* trust, or, from the nature of the case, such advantage may be presumed.(⁸)

A trustee can not, by the failure of the object of the trust, be-

---

(1) Hawley vs. Mancius, 7 Johns. (N. Y.) Ch., 174; Green vs. Winter, 1 Johns. (N. Y.) Ch., 27; Boyd vs. Hawkins, 2 Dev. (N. C.) Eq., 195; Matter of Oakley, 2 Edw., (N. Y.) 478; Hitchcock vs. Watson, 18 Ill., 289; Phelps vs. Reeder, 39 Ill., 172.
(2) Pugh vs. Pugh, 9 Ind., 132; Durling vs. Hammar, 20 N. J. Eq., 220.
(3) Treadwell vs. McKeon, 7 Baxter, (Tenn.) 442; Pugh vs. Pugh, *supra;* Durling vs. Hammar, *supra.*
(4) Hancock vs. Titus, 39 Miss., 224.
(5) Boyd vs. Clements, 14 Ga., 639.
(6) Wiswall vs. Stewart, 32 Ala., 433.
(7) Hume vs. Beale, 17 Wall., 336.
(8) McCants vs. Bee, 1 McCord (S. C.) Ch., 383.

come the beneficial owner of the trust property;(¹) nor can he divest himself of his fiduciary character, by converting the trust fund into money, and the money into land.(²) Nor will he be permitted to deny the title of the *cestui que* trust, and retain the property discharged of the trust.(³) Nor can he use the trust fund in the payment of his own debts.(⁴)

We have seen that executors and administrators cannot purchase at their own sales, and, generally, all trustees, except those appointed to preserve contingent remainders, or otherwise to stand merely nominally as such, are incapable of purchasing or dealing in the trust property.(⁵)

A contingent remainder, is one which is limited to take effect on an event or condition which may never happen or be performed, or which may not happen or be performed, until after the determination of the preceding particular estate; while a vested remainder, is one by which a present interest passes to the party, though to be enjoyed in the future, and by which the estate is invariably fixed to remain to a determinate person, after the particular estate has been spent. Hence, we have a remainder-man, or one who is entitled to the remainder of the estate, after a particular estate carved out of it has expired. Now, let us suppose, A should convey property over to B, in trust for C, with remainder over to D, would B be allowed to take advantage of his trust, and purchase from the remainder-man D? Let us suppose C, to be a person *non compos mentis*, B, his conservator, would the law tolerate B, in in making purchases of the estate in remainder from the remainder-man? If such practice were tolerated, the grossest outrages might be perpetrated—the object of the trust defeated—the beneficiary be deprived during his life of the proper enjoyment of that to which he is rightfully entitled, in order that the remainder, thus purchased, might be carefully preserved for the trustee, who becomes a dealer in the trust property. While such sales are not absolutely void, they are certainly voidable, in the fullest extent of that term,

---

(1) Fox vs. Harrah, 1 Ired. (N. C.) Eq., 358.
(2) Pierce vs. McKeehan, 3 Watts & S., (Pa.) 280.
(3) Sweet vs. Jacobs, 6 Paige, (N. Y.) 355; Van Horne vs. Fonda, 5 Johns. Ch., 388.
(4) Graff vs. Castleman, 5 Rand., (Va.) 195; McConnell vs. Hodson, 2 Gilm., 640.
(5) Wright vs. Campbell, 27 Ark., 637; *Ante* page 163.

upon the petition of the *cestui que* trust, but not upon the application of the trustee.(¹)

The rule in chancery, is, that the purchaser of a reversion must prove that he gave a full price, and this rule applies with greater force to a purchaser who bore the relation of trustee to those in remainder.(²) Where, however, the title of a *cestui que* trust, mortgagor or remainder-man is destroyed, the trustee, mortgagee, or tenant for life, may acquire the real title, provided, his condition and conduct are free from fraud.(³)

5. DUTY OF TRUSTEE TO ACT IN GOOD FAITH.—The rule in regard to trustees, extends to all cases where confidence has been reposed, and applies as strongly to those who have gratuitously or officiously undertaken the management of another's property, as to those who are engaged for that purpose and paid for it.(⁴) Thus, where a party voluntarily interferes with and manages an estate in behalf of heirs, as their representative, and as such acquires information to which a stranger would not have access, he assumes the obligation to his principals which properly appertain to the character of an agent. In treating with them for the purchase of an interest in an estate, he is bound to disclose how he has acted, and every matter to them which it is important for them to know, unless such disclosures were distinctly dispensed with. An agent can not deal for his own advantage with the thing purchased for his principal; or become the seller, or buyer, to or of them, because of his confidential relation, and his duty to disclose to his principal every fact, circumstance or advantage, in relation to the purchase, which may come to his knowledge.(⁵) Where confidence is reasonably reposed, that confidence must not be abused. The party relied upon, whether he be a paid servant or an assumed friend, must see that he meets fully and fairly the responsibilities of his position, and does not take advantage, either to the injury of another, or for his own gain.(⁶) The rule is applied to all persons

(1) McClure vs. Miller, 1 Bailey Eq., 107.
(2) May vs. May, 7 Fla., 207.
(3) Price vs. Evans, 26 Mo., 30.
(4) Wright vs. Smith, 123 N. J. Eq., 106; Rankin vs. Porter, 7 Watts, (Pa.) 387.
(5) Casey vs. Casey, 14 Ill., 112; McDonald vs. Fithian, 1 Gilm., 269; Fish vs. Cleland, 33 Ill., 238.
(6) Casey vs. Casey, *supra*.

in whom there is a trust and confidence reposed, which would bring in conflict the interest of the trustee and *cestui que* trust.(¹)

The temptation of self-interest is too powerful and insinuating to be trusted; and it must be removed, by taking away every relation in which there may, by any possibility, arise a conflict between the duty to the person with whom the trustee is dealing, or on whose account he is acting, and his individual interest, and thus provide against the probability, in many cases, and the danger, in all cases, that the dictates of self-interest will exercise a predominant influence and supersede that of duty.(²

A court of equity will not usually aid any one against a voluntary act in fraud of the law. It is equally averse to allowing a person to profit by any instrument which is extorted by exciting false alarms or threats of legal consequences, when there is such a relation of confidence as gives one a special power over another.(³)

6. REMEDY AGAINST TRUSTEES.—Where one assumes to act as an agent or in a fiduciary capacity, and by concealment of facts, which the party was entitled to know, and which should, in good faith, have been disclosed, and which, if known at the time, would have prevented the party selling for a grossly inadequate price, equity will afford relief. Where, on bill to redeem, filed by a principal against one, who, assuming to act as agent, has paid the money and redeemed his principal's land from a decree of foreclosure, taking a conveyance to himself, and where the agent has sold and conveyed the lands to a *bona fide* purchaser, for value, he will be compelled to indemnify the principal for the loss sustained by his having placed the title beyond reach, either by requiring him to pay over the purchase money he received for the land with interest thereon, or the present value of the land, as may seem most equitable.(⁴) But where there is no peculiar relation of trust or confidence between the parties, the undue concealment which a court of equity will relieve, is the non-disclosure of those facts and circumstances, which one party is under some legal or equitable obligation to communicate to the other, and which the latter has a

---

(1) Davoue vs. Fanning, 2 Johns. Ch., (N. Y.) 252; Hewitt vs. School District, 94 Ill., 528.
(2) Thorp vs. McCullom, 1 Gilm., 614; Switzer vs. Skiles, 3 Gilm., 529; Michoud vs. Girod, 4 How., 503.
(3) Barnes vs. Brown, 32 Mich., 146.
(4) Dennis vs. McCagg, 32 Ill., 430; Smith vs. Frost, 70 N. Y., 65.

right not merely, *in foro conscientiæ,* but *juris et de juri,* to know.([1])

A trustee will not be held for any loss accruing in the management of the trust property, where he acts with good faith in the exercise of a fair discretion, and in the same manner he would ordinarily do in regard to his own property,([2]) as the measure of care required for trustees, is the care which a prudent man would take on his own behalf, in making like investments for himself.([3]) Acts of trustees, done in good faith, without selfish motives, and especially under the advice of counsel, are to be viewed indulgently by a court of equity.([4]) Trustees are not responsible for wrongs to the trust estate in which they had no agency ;([5]) nor are they liable for the title or soundness of property sold by them at public sale, except upon their own express warranty, or where fraud exists.([6])

7. SETTLEMENT BETWEEN TRUSTEE AND CESTUI QUE TRUST.—Parties acting in fiduciary relations, may make amicable settlements of their accounts with the *cestui que* trust, and there is no rule of law or justice which will prevent it, nor are they obliged to have their accounts passed through the probate court ;([7]) but a trustee can not be permitted to set up a fraudulent acquittance, obtained by willful misrepresentations from his *cestui que* trust.([8]) While public policy and fair dealing will not allow a trustee, either directly or indirectly, to become a purchaser of property at his own sale, yet, after the sale is made, and the property has passed beyond his control, he will have the same right to purchase it as a stranger, if the transaction is in good faith.([9])

In the absence of any proof of collusion, the fact that property was sold by a trustee for a sum less than half its value, and was shortly afterwards sold back to him by the purchaser for the same amount, is insufficient to charge him with speculation in violation of his duty.([10]) Nor will the fact that the relation of guardian and

(1) Fish vs. Cleland, 33 Ill., 238.
(2) Knowlton vs. Bradley, 17 N. H., 458; Finley vs. Merriman, 39 Texas, 56.
(3) Roosevelt vs. Roosevelt, 6 Abb., (N. Y.) N. Cas., 447; Neff's Appeal, 57 Pa. St., 91; Higgins vs. Whitson, 20 Barb., (N. Y.) 141.
(4) Ellig vs. Naglee, 9 Cal., 683.
(5) Hestor vs. Wilkinson, 6 Hump., (Tenn.) 215.
(6) Northy vs. Johnson, 8 Ga., 236.
(7) Hooper vs. Hooper, 26 Mich., 435.
(8) Berryhill's Appeal, 35 Pa. St., 245.
(9) Bush vs. Sherman, 80 Ill., 160; Watson vs. Sherman, 84 Ill., 263.
(10) Bochlest vs. McBride, 48 Mo., 505.

ward has existed, preclude the making of contracts between the two after the fiduciary relation has terminated, and the accounts fully and fairly settled.([1])

8. RELATIONS TO THE COURT.—A trustee appointed, becomes an officer of the court, acting under its direction and authority, and, so far as concerns matters of equitable jurisdiction, as to what he does, or ought to do, in discharge of his duties, is responsible to that court alone.([2]) And as letters of administration have no extra territorial force, such as would give administrators appointed in one state control over lands lying in another state, an agreement between Michigan administrators and another party, that they should buy for their joint interest and benefit, the claim of the estate to certain lands in Illinois, and fixing the price relatively at which such claims should be sold, is not on its face presumptively fraudulent and consequently void, on the ground that it places the administrators in relations where their self-interests conflict with their duty, since, as to these Illinois lands, said administrators, as such, could not have occupied at once the two positions of seller and purchaser.([3])

It will be thus seen, that the policy of our laws, prohibits the trustee from dealing with the *cestui que* trust, or the trust property; and the rule which prohibits a trustee or agent, private or public, from assuming a position tending to produce a conflict between his individual interests and a faithful discharge of his fiduciary duties, *is so strict*, that no question will be allowed to be raised as to the fairness of the transaction, and no actual injury to the *cestui que* trust, need be shown.([4])

(1) Wickiser vs. Cook, 85 Ill., 68.
(2) Penn vs. Brewer, 12 Gill. & J., (Md.) 113.
(3) Sheldon vs. Rice, 30 Mich., 296.
(4) Gilman C. & S. R. R. Co., vs. Kelly, 77 Ill., 426.

ADDITIONAL NOTES.

1. Cestui que trust may pursue trust fund into property into which it is converted.
2. Agent of a trustee or guardian—When to be held as a trustee.
3. Speculating in trust fund.
4. Trustee cannot purchase at his own sale.
5. Making profit out of the trust fund.

1. CESTUI QUE TRUST MAY PURSUE FUND.—Should the guardian invest the money of his ward in the purchase of land, taking the title to himself, a resulting trust arises, and the ward may either follow the money into the land and hold it as a trust estate, or sue upon the guardian's bond.(¹)

2. AGENT—WHEN HELD AS TRUSTEE.—An agent of a trustee, when he acts fraudulently and collusively, may be treated as a trustee by construction, and as such held liable to the *cestui que trust*. If he secures any benefit by a breach of his trust, he will be responsible to the beneficial interest. Should he obtain possession of trust property, the *cestui que trust* may proceed against him as a trustee.(²) If one uses trust funds in his own private business, he will be chargeable with interest on same.(³) And should he willfully violate his trust, and a loss occur, he will be chargeable with compound interest.(⁴)

3. SPECULATING IN TRUST FUND.—A court of equity will not permit a trustee to speculate in the subject-matter of his trust. Should he purchase an outstanding claim against the trust fund, the transaction will be treated as a payment only, and he will be allowed only what he paid for it.(⁵)

4. TRUSTEE CANNOT PURCHASE AT HIS OWN SALE.—A trustee, or one acting in a fiduciary capacity, cannot become a purchaser at his own sale, either directly or indirectly, and hold to his own use;

---

(1) Rice vs. Rice, 108 Ill., 199.
(2) Lehmann vs. Rothbarth, 111 Ill., 185.
(3) *Ib.*
(4) Hughes vs. The People, for use of Kerrick, 111 Ill., 457.
(5) Rankin vs. Barcroft, 114 Ill., 441.

and it matters not whether the sale is made by himself or under a decree of court, or whether there was any fraud, in fact, intended.

The general rule is, when a trustee of any description, or a person acting as agent for others, sells a trust estate, and becomes himself interested, either directly or indirectly, in the purchase, the *cestui que trust* is entitled, as a matter of course, at his election, to have the sale affirmed or set aside.

An executor, under a decree of court authorizing the sale of lands of the estate to pay debts, sold one hundred and sixty acres of land to his son and partner for the sum of one dollar, subject to a mortgage then held and controlled by the executor. The son testified that his object was to secure the rents, about falling due, to apply on the debt held by his father. It was *held*, that the heirs of the testator were entitled to have the sale set aside, and have an account for the rents and profits received by the purchaser.[1]

5. MAKING PROFIT OUT OF TRUST FUND.—A trustee, or a person standing in a fiduciary relation, will not, in equity, be allowed to so exercise his trust as to speculate or make profit out of the trust fund.[2]

(1) Borders vs. Murphy, 125 Ill., 578.
(2) Roseboom vs. Whitaker, 132 Ill., 81

CHAPTER XIV.

ADOPTION OF CHILDREN.

1. Humane provisions of the law—who may adopt.
2. What the petition shall contain—forms.
3. What must be found by court—decree.
4. When consent of child is necessary—form.
5. Rights of child adopted.
6. Rights of parents of adopted children.
7. Former adoptions.
8. Effect as to natural parents.

1. HUMANE PROVISIONS OF THE LAW—WHO MAY ADOPT.—An act of the General Assembly was approved February 27th, 1874, and went into effect July 1st, 1874, giving concurrent jurisdiction to the circuit and county courts in the adoption of children.([1])

The county court, from its large jurisdiction over the domestic relations, is naturally the court, it would seem, in which to transact such business. It is open twelve terms a year. It is convenient alike to the attorney and client, and were the humane provisions of this chapter more generally made known, and the ease and facility for the adoption of children, better understood, many poor and orphaned children would find comfortable homes and foster parents, who would care and provide for them.

Any resident of this state may petition the circuit or county court, of the county in which he resides, for leave to adopt a child, not his own, and, if desired, for a change of the child's name, but the prayer of such petition, by a person having a husband or wife, shall not be granted, unless such husband or wife joins therein, and when they so join, the adoption shall be by them jointly.

2. PETITION—FORM.—The petition shall state the name, sex and age, of the child sought to be adopted; and, if it is desired to change the name, the new name; the name and residence of the parents of the child, if known to the petitioner, and of the guardian, if any,

---

(1) Hurd's R. S., Chap. 4, § 1.

and whether the parents or the survivor of them, or the guardian, if any, consents to such adoption.(¹)

The petition, under Section two of this Act, may be in form as follows:

STATE OF ILLINOIS,⎱ ss. *In the County Court,*
...............County,⎰   ....*term, A. D.* 18...

To the Hon............, Judge of said Court:

Your petitioners, A B and C B, his wife, of........., in said county, would respectfully show unto your honor: That they are residents of said county, and are desirous of adopting a child, so as to render it capable of inheriting their estate. That the name of said child is E F, that it was of the age of... years, on the...day of......last, and is a male child. And your petitioners would further show unto your honor, that the mother of said child is dead, but the father, C F, is still living, and consents to the adoption of said child by your petitioners, as will appear from written consent filed herewith. And further, that the said E F has resided with them for the space of four years now last past; that the father of said child is wholly unable to provide for him and educate him in a suitable manner, and that your petitioners have ample means so to do, and that it would, therefore, be to the interest of said child to become the adopted child of your petitioners.

Your petitioners would further show, that the father of said child has had due notice of the time when, and the place where, this application would be made, as will appear by a copy of such notice, with proof of service filed herewith. Your petitioners, therefore, pray this honorable court, to make an order declaring said child to be the adopted child of your petitioners, and capable of inheriting their estate, and that the name of said child be changed to that of E B, according to the Statute in such case made and provided, and your petitioners will ever pray, etc.

By............J, Attorney.   A B,
                                                                    C B.

STATE OF ILLINOIS,⎱ ss.
................County.⎰

A B and C B, the above named petitioners, being duly sworn, depose and say, that the facts contained in the above petition by them subscribed, are true, according to the best of their knowledge, information and belief.
                                                                    A B,
                                                                    C B.

Subscribed and sworn to before me, this...day of......, A. D. 18...
                                        ...., County Clerk.

Notice to parent or guardian of application for adoption of child, may be in form as follows:

To Mr........, Please take notice: That we will, on the...day of......, A. D.

(1) Hurd's R. S., Chap. 4, § 2.

18..., and at the hour of......o'clock......m., of said day, or, as soon thereafter as counsel can be heard, present to the county court of.........county, in the State of Illinois, our petition, asking for an order of said court, declaring your minor child, E F, to be our adopted child, and also changing its name to that of E B, as is provided by Act of the General Assembly of the State of Illinois, approved February 27, 1874, when and where you can appear and file objections to such application, if you desire so to do.

Dated this...day of......, A. D. 18...

A B,
C B.

STATE OF ILLINOIS, }
....................County, } ss.

.........being first duly sworn, on his oath says, that on the...day of......, A. D. 18..., he delivered to the above named C F, a true copy of the foregoing notice.

....

Sworn to and subscribed before me, this...day of......, A. D. 18...

........., County Clerk.

CONSENT OF PARENT TO ADOPTION OF CHILD.

I, C F, of........., in the county of........., and State of Illinois, father of E F, a minor child, do hereby consent to the adoption of said child by A B and C B, in manner and form as provided by an Act of the General Assembly of the State of Illinois, approved February 27, A. D. 1874.

Dated this....day of........, A. D. 18....

C F.

Said petition shall be docketed by the clerk when filed, in form as follows:

In the Matter of the Application of A B and C B, for an Order Declaring a Child Adopted.

3. WHAT MUST BE FOUND BY COURT—DECREE.—If the court is satisfied that the parents of the child, or the survivor of them, has deserted his or her family, or such child, for the space of one year next preceding the application, or, if neither is living, the guardian, or, if there is no guardian, the next of kin, in this state, capable of giving consent, has notice of the presentation of the petition, and consents to such adoption, or that such child has no father or mother living, and no next of kin living in this state, capable of giving consent, or is a foundling, and that the facts stated in the petition are true, and that the petitioner is of sufficient ability to bring up the child and furnish suitable nurture and education, and that it is fit and proper that such adoption should be made, a decree shall be made, setting forth the facts, and ordering that from the

374 ADOPTION OF CHILDREN [CH. XIV.

date of the decree the child shall, to all legal intents and purposes, be the child of the petitioner or petitioners, and may decree that the name of the child be changed according to the prayer of the petition.(¹)

The decree may be in form as follows:

STATE OF ILLINOIS, } ss. In the County Court of..........
..............County,   County,..........term, A D. 18....

In the Matter of the Petition of A B }
 and C B, for an Order Declaring
 E F to be their Adopted Child.

And now, on this day, the above cause coming on to be heard upon the petition filed in the above cause, and proofs adduced in support of the facts therein stated; and it appearing to the court from the petition and evidence herein, that said petitioners are residents of said county, and desire to adopt said child; that said child is a male, and of the age of...years, on the...day of......, A. D. 18... And further, that said petitioners desire the name of said child changed to that of E B. That the mother of said child is dead, but the father is living, and consents to the adoption of said child by said petitioners; and further, that the father of said child is not a suitable person to bring up said child. That said A B and C B, are proper persons, and have sufficient ability to bring up said child, and furnish it suitable nurture and education, and that all the other matters and facts in said petition as therein stated, are true, and that it would, therefore, be to the interest of said child to be the adopted child of said petitioners. And it further appearing, that the father of said child has had due notice of the time when, and the place where, said petitioners would make the application for an order in this cause, It is therefore ordered and adjudged by the court, that the said E F, be, from henceforth, the adopted child of said petitioners and capable of inheriting their estate; that the name of said child be changed to that of E B, and that said petitioners pay the costs of this proceeding.

Approved.   ...., Judge of the
                                County Court of......County, Illinois.

Or, the decree may be in form as follows:

STATE OF ILLINOIS, } ss. In the County Court of..........County,
..............County.   To the..........term, A. D. 18...

In the Matter of the Petition of A B }
 and C B, for an Order Declaring   Final Order.
 E F to be their Adopted Child.

And now, on this...day of......, A. D. 18..., the same being the...judicial day of the present term of this court, comes the said petitioners, by.........., their attorney, and this cause coming on now to be heard, upon said petition, and the consent of.........., the child to be adopted.

(1) Hurd's R. S., Chap. 4, § 3.

And it appearing to the court that the father of said child has had due notice of the time when, and the place where, said petitioners would make application for an order in this cause, and has filed his written consent herein to the application, and the court being now sufficiently advised and satisfied in the premises, and having heard the testimony of..........and.........., witnesses, who were produced and sworn, and all the evidence adduced in support of said petition, finds: That the petitioners, who are residents of the county of......, and State of Illinois, desire to adopt E F, a male child, aged... years on the...day of......, A. D. 18..., and desire the name of said child to be changed to that of E B. That the mother of said child is dead, and the father is not a suitable person to bring up said child, and that he has also filed his written consent herein, to the adoption of his child by said petitioners. That said A B and C B, are proper persons, and have sufficient ability to bring up said child, and furnish suitable nurture and education; and that all the matters and facts in said petition as therein stated are true.

It is therefore ordered, adjudged and decreed, by the court, that the said E F be the adopted child of the said petitioners, and capable of inheriting their estate. And it is further ordered and decreed, that the name of the said child be changed to that of E B, and said petitioners pay all the costs of this proceeding, within...days from this date, and that in default thereof, execution may issue.

Approved.   ...., Judge of the
                                        County Court of......County, Illinois.

4. WHEN CONSENT OF CHILD IS NECESSARY.—If the child is of the age of fourteen years or upwards, the adoption shall not be made without his consent.[1]

The form of consent to be used when the child is fourteen years old and upwards, may be as follows:

STATE OF ILLINOIS, } ss.
...............County,

I, E F, a minor child of G F, the child for whose adoption A B and C B, his wife, have filed in the county court a petition, which is now pending and undetermined, and is entitled of the......term, A. D. 18..., of said court, being aged...years on the...day of......, A. D. 18..., do hereby request that the prayer of said petition may be granted, and consent to become the adopted child of the said A B and C B, the petitioners, and be known and called by the name of E B.   E F.

5. RIGHTS OF CHILD ADOPTED.—A child so adopted, shall be deemed, for the purpose of inheritance by such child, and his descendants and husband or wife, and other legal consequences and incidents of the natural relation of parents and children, the child

(1) Hurd's R. S., Chap. 4, § 4.

of the parents by adoption, the same as if he had been born to them in lawful wedlock, except that he shall not be capable of taking property expressly limited to the body or bodies of the parents by adoption, nor property from the lineal or collateral kindred of such parents by right of representation.([1])

Under this statute, which, being in derogation of the common law, is strictly construed, an adopted child can take by descent only from the person or persons adopting him, and not from the lineal or collateral kindred of the adopting parents. Therefore, such child can not, by inheritance, take from a child of the adopting parents, born in wedlock, the adopted child not being a brother or sister in fact.([2])

The rights of inheritance acquired by an adopted child under the laws of another state, where, and under whose laws he was adopted, will be recognized and upheld in this state, only so far as they are not inconsistent with our laws of descent: so, that, if such child can not take by descent by our statute, it can not take at all, no matter what may be the law of the state where the adoption was made, as the laws of this state must govern the descent of real property situated within its limits.([3])

6. RIGHTS OF ADOPTED PARENTS, ETC.—The parents by adoption and their heirs shall take by descent, from any child adopted under this or any other law of this state for the adoption of children, and the descendants, and husband or wife, of such child, only such property as he has taken or may hereafter take from or through the adopting parents, or either of them, either by gift, bequest, devise or descent, with the accumulations, income and profits thereof; and all laws of descent and rules of inheritance, shall apply to and govern the descent of any such property, the same as if the child were the natural child of such parents; but the parents by adoption and their heirs, shall not inherit any property which such child may take or have taken, by gift, bequest, devise or descent, from his kindred by blood.([4])

7. FORMER ADOPTIONS.—The preceding section shall apply to any case where a child has heretofore been declared by any court to

---
(1) Hurd's R. S., Chap. 4, § 5.
(2) Keeghan vs. Geraghty, 101 Ill., 26.
(3) *Ib.*
(4) Hurd's R. S., Chap. 4, § 6.

have been adopted, or where such adoption has been declared or assumed in any deed or last will and testament, giving, bequeathing or devising property to such child, as the adopted child of the grantor or testator, and the wife or husband of such adopted parent shall be capable of inheriting from such child the same as if she or he had become the adopted mother or father of such child, pursuant to this act.(¹)

8. EFFECT AS TO NATURAL PARENTS.—The natural parents of a child so adopted, shall be deprived, by the decree, of all legal rights, as respects the child, and the child shall be freed from all obligations of maintenance and obedience as respects such parents.(²)

(1) Hurd's R. S., Chap. 4, § 7. (2) Hurd's R. S., Chap. 4, § 8.

ADDITIONAL NOTES.

1. Of the petition.
2. Jurisdiction of the county court—Presumption.
3. Witness—Competency of party as against one suing as heir.
4. Adoption of child so as to confer the right of inheritance.

1. PETITION.—A petition by a party to enable him to adopt a child under the act of 1867, in order to give the court jurisdiction to act, need not recite any jurisdictional facts, except those the statute specifies shall be recited. The law does not require the petition to state the name of the father of the child, and that he consents, whether he is dead, or, if he be alive, that he has abandoned the child. In such case it will be sufficient to state the mother's name, and that she consents. The failure to allege in the petition the death of the father, or his abandonment, will not go to the jurisdiction of the court. Where the father is not named, the presumption will be, he was dead or had abandoned his child.

2. JURISDICTION OF COUNTY COURT—PRESUMPTION.—Where an order of the county court, made in 1870, for the adoption of a child, is shown, it will be presumed the court had jurisdiction, unless it appears from the record itself that it could not have had jurisdiction in any contingency, or unless the statute authorizing the court to act requires the record affirmatively to show, precedent to its decree, some fact which it fails to show. Decree cannot be questioned collaterally. A decree of the court declaring a child adopted and to be the adopted heir of another, if the court had jurisdiction to act at all, however erroneous it may be, must stand until reversed in some direct proceeding.

3. WITNESS—COMPETENCY.—On a bill by a minor adopted heir for the partition of lands of which his adopted father died seized, and for the assignment of dower, the widow of the deceased ancestor is not a competent witness to prove advances made by her to her husband, to discharge the incumbrances on the land, and have such advances made a lien on the premises in her favor.[1]

---

[1] Barnard vs. Barnard, 119 Ill., 92.

4. To confer right of inheritance.—Under the statute, where there are husband and wife, the wife's interest, as respects herself or her children in the right of inheritance, cannot be affected by any act of adoption by the husband alone of another's child than their own, giving it the right of inheritance, but there must be the consent of the wife thereto.(¹)

The welfare of the child is of prime importance, and the caprice, obstinacy or opposition of non-consenting parents should not be regarded.(²) And appeal to the circuit court will not lie from an order entered by the county court for the adoption of a child hereunder.(³)

(1) Wallace vs. Rappleye, 103 Ill., 229.
(2) Baker vs. Strahorn, 33 Ill. Ap., 59.
(3) Meyers vs. Meyers, 32 Ill. Ap., 189.

CHAPTER XV.

Proceedings as Conservator.

1. Appointment of—form of a petition for the appointment of a conservator.
2. Summons—notice—form of notice to person alleged to be insane.
3. Bond—counter security.
4. Suit on bond.
5. Care of estate—custody of person—children.
6. Inventory.
7. Form of inventory.
8. Settlements.
9. Final settlement.
10. Manner of accounting.
11. Collections.
12. Performance of contracts.
13. Legal proceeding.
14. What contracts void.
15. What contracts voidable.
16. Swindling idiot, lunatic, etc.
17. Management of estate.
18. Investment of money.
19. Leasing real estate.
20. Mortgaging real estate.
21. Petition to mortgage.
22. No strict foreclosure.
23. Sale of real estate provided for.
24. Petition for sale.
25. Notice of application.
26. Docket—practice.
27. Sale.
28. Return of sale—approval—record—title.
29. Proceeds of sale.
30. Sufficiency of sureties.
31. Counter security.
32. Removal of conservator.
33. Summons to show cause—notice.
34. Resignation.
35. Successor appointed—delivery to successor
36. Compensation.
37. Restoration to reason—form of a petition to remove the conservator.
38. Notice.
39. Trial—judgment—form of order removing conservator.

40. Appeals.
41. Suits, collection, etc., by non-resident conservator.
42. Sale of real estate by non-resident conservator.
43. Notice of petition.
44. Bond.
45. Bond for costs.

1. APPOINTMENT—PETITION FOR—FORM OF.—An act to revise the law in relation to idiots, lunatics, drunkards and spendthrifts, was approved March 26, 1874, and went into force July 1, 1874. Almost all that has been written in relation to guardian and ward is applicable to this relation, for a conservator is simply a guardian, appointed by the court to look after the person and estate of certain persons under disability.

The conservator is the guardian of the idiot, the lunatic or distracted, the drunkard or the spendthrift—they are, when appointed, the wards of the conservator. Many, if not all the forms used under the head of guardian and ward, are suitable to be used here, for the course to be pursued by the guardian of the minor, is the same to be pursued by the conservator. Both are officers of the court, which, in the exercise of its jurisdiction, appoints them to look after and care for those, who, by reason of their disability, are unable to look after and care for themselves, their estates and property. The chapter of the statute is a full and complete code, and not unlike the chapter in relation to guardian and ward, and we give here its various provisions at large: Whenever any idiot, lunatic or distracted person has an estate, real or personal; or when any person, by excessive drinking, gaming, idleness or debauchery of any kind, so spends, wastes or lessens his estate, as to expose himself or his family to want or suffering, or any county, town or incorporated city, town or village to any charge or expense for the support of himself or his family, the county court of the county in which such person lives, shall, on the application of any relative or creditor, or if there be neither relative or creditor, then any person living in such county, order a jury to be summoned to ascertain whether such person be idiot, lunatic or distracted, a drunkard or such spendthrift; and if the jury return in their verdict that such person is idiot, lunatic or distracted, or drunkard, or so spends, wastes or lessens his estate, it shall be the duty of the court to appoint some fit person to be the conservator of such person.(¹)

The validity of the appointment of a conservator, as in the case of an administrator, can not be inquired into in a collateral proceeding, as in case of a bill filed to set aside a sale of the lunatic's land, made by his conservator.(²)

The petition may be in form as follows:

In the Matter of the Estate of.........., alleged to be..........

STATE OF ILLINOIS, } ss.
...............County,

To the Hon.........., Judge of the...... Court of...... County, in the State of Illinois:

The petition of the undersigned respectfully represents, that.........., of the county of......, and state aforesaid, is..........; that he has real property, known and described as follows, viz.: [*Here describe the realty.*] That his personal property consists of the following, to-wit: [*Here describe the personalty,*] and is reasonably worth about......., and that he the said.........., is, by reason of.........., unfit properly to manage or control his property.

Your petitioner, being a...of......., therefore prays that your honor will appoint.........., or some other fit person to be conservator of the said..........

Dated this....day of........, A. D. 18....

By.........., Attorney. ....

Subscribed and sworn to before me, this...day of......, A. D. 18..., by A B, the petitioner aforesaid.

.........., Clerk.

2. SUMMONS—NOTICE.—On an application for the appointment of a conservator of any person being filed, summons shall be issued and served upon the person for whom a conservator is sought to be appointed, in the same manner as summons is issued and served in cases in chancery. When the application is against an idiot or lunatic, the clerk of the court in which the application is filed, shall also give not less than ten days' notice thereof, by at least one insertion in some newspaper published in the county.(³)

The notice may be in form as follows:

In the Matter of the Estate of.........., alleged to be..........

STATE OF ILLINOIS, } ss.   *In the County Court,*
.............County,   *To the...........term, A. D.* 18....

To.........., alleged to be......   Take Notice:
That A B has filed in the county court of said county, a petition against

(1) Hurd's R. S., Chap. 86, § 1.   (3) Hurd's R. S., Chap. 86, § 2.
(2) Dodge vs. Cole, 97 Ill., 338.

you for the appointment of a conservator, which said petition will be heard at the...term, A. D. 18..., when and where you can appear and defend.

........., Attorney.   ...., Clerk of the County Court.

3. BOND.—The conservator so appointed, shall, before entering upon the duties of his office, give bond payable to the people of the State of Illinois, with at least two sufficient sureties, to be approved by the court, in double the amount of his ward's real and personal estate, with such conditions as near as may be, as provided in the case of the bonds of guardians of infants. Additional bonds and counter security may be required, as hereinafter provided.([1])

4. SUIT ON BOND.—Bonds given in pursuance of this act, may be put in suit in the name of the people of the State of Illinois, to the use of any person entitled to recover on the breach thereof, and damages adjudged on proceedings had thereon as in other cases of penal bonds.([2])

Mere informalities in the execution of a conservator's bond, will not avail as a defense thereto.([3])

5. CARE OF ESTATE—CUSTODY OF PERSON—CHILDREN.—Such conservator shall have the care and management of the real and personal estate of his ward, and the custody of his person, unless otherwise ordered by the court, and the custody and education of his children, where no other guardian is appointed, unless the court orders otherwise; but this act shall not be so construed, as to deprive the mother of the custody and education of the children without her consent, if she be a fit and competent person to have such custody and education.([4])

6. INVENTORY.—The conservator shall, immediately upon his appointment, take charge of the estate of his ward, and within sixty days after such appointment, or, if the court is not in session at the expiration of that time, at the next term thereafter, return to the court a true and perfect inventory of the real and personal estate of the ward, signed by him and verified by his affidavit. As often as other estate shall thereafter come to his knowledge, he shall return an inventory thereof within sixty days from the time the same shall come to his knowledge.([5])

(1) Hurd's R. S., Chap. 86, § 3.
(2) Hurd's R. S., Chap. 86, § 4.
(3) Richardson vs. People, 85 Ill., 495.
(4) Hurd's R. S., Chap. 86, § 5.
(5) Hurd's R. S., Chap. 86, § 6.

7. FORM OF INVENTORY.—The inventory shall describe the real estate, its probable value and rental, and state whether the same is encumbered, and if encumbered, how, and for how much; what amount of money is on hand, and contain a list of all personal property, including annuities and credits of the ward, designating them as "good," "doubtful," or "desperate," as the case may be.([1])

8. SETTLEMENTS.—The conservator shall, at the expiration of a year from his appointment, settle his accounts as conservator with the county court, and at least once each year thereafter, and as much oftener as the court may require.([2])

9. FINAL SETTLEMENT.—Such conservator, at the expiration of his trust, shall pay and deliver to those entitled thereto, all the moneys, estate and title papers, in his hands as conservator, or with which he is chargeable as such, in such manner as shall be directed by the order or decree of any court having jurisdiction thereof.([3])

10. MANNER OF ACCOUNTING.—On every accounting or final settlement of a conservator, he shall exhibit and file his account as such conservator, setting forth specifically, in separate items, on what account expenditures were made by him, and all sums received and paid out since last accounting, and on what account each was received and paid out, and showing the true balance of money on hand—which account, shall be accompanied by the proper vouchers, and signed by him and verified by his affidavit.([4])

11. COLLECTIONS.—The conservator shall settle all accounts of his ward, and demand and sue for and receive in his own name, as conservator, all personal property of and demands due the ward, or with the approbation of the court, compound for the same, and give a discharge to the debtor upon receiving a fair and just dividend of his estate and effects.([5])

12. PERFORMANCE OF CONTRACTS.—The conservator, by the permission and subject to the direction of the court which appointed him, may perform the personal contracts of his ward, made in good faith and legally subsisting at the time of the commencement of his

---

(1) Hurd's R. S., Chap. 86, § 7.
(2) Hurd's R. S., Chap. 86, § 8.
(3) Hurd's R. S., Chap. 86. § 9.
(4) Hurd's R. S., Chap. 86, § 10.
(5) Hurd's R. S., Chap. 86, § 11.

disability, and which may be performed with advantage to the estate of the ward.([1])

13. LEGAL PROCEEDINGS.—He shall appear for and represent his ward in all suits and proceedings, unless another person is appointed for that purpose, as conservator or next friend; but nothing contained in this act shall impair or affect the power of any court to appoint a conservator or next friend to defend the interest of said ward impleaded in such court, or interested in a suit or matter therein pending, nor its power to appoint or allow any person, as next friend for such ward, to commence, prosecute or defend any suit in his behalf, subject to the direction of such court.([2])

14. WHAT CONTRACTS VOID.—Every note, bill, bond or other contract, by an idiot, lunatic, distracted person, or spendthrift, made after the finding of the jury, as provided in Section 1 of this act, shall be void as against the idiot, lunatic, distracted person, drunkard or spendthrift, and his estate; but the person making any contract with such idiot, lunatic, distracted person or spendthrift, shall be bound thereby.([3])

15. WHAT CONTRACTS VOIDABLE.—Every contract made with an idiot, lunatic or distracted person, before such finding, or with a drunkard or spendthrift, made after the application for the appointment of a conservator, may be avoided, except in favor of the person fraudulently making the same.([4])

16. SWINDLING IDIOT, LUNATIC, ETC.—Whoever, by trading with, bartering, gaming, or any other device, possesses himself of any property or valuable thing belonging to any idiot, lunatic or notoriously distracted person, drunkard or spendthrift, shall be deemed guilty of swindling, and upon conviction thereof, be fined in a sum not exceeding $2,000, or confined in the county jail not exceeding one year, or both.([5])

17. MANAGEMENT OF ESTATE.—The conservator shall manage the estate of the ward frugally and without waste, and apply the income and profit thereof, so far as the same may be necessary, to the comfort and suitable support of his ward and his family, and the education of his children.([6])

(1) Hurd's R. S., Chap. 86, § 12.
(2) Hurd's R. S., Chap. 86, § 13.
(3) Hurd's R. S., Chap. 86, § 14.
(4) Hurd's R. S., Chap. 86, § 15.
(5) Hurd's R. S., Chap. 86, § 16.
(6) Hurd's R. S., Chap. 86, § 17.

18. INVESTMENT OF MONEY.—It shall be the duty of the conservator to put and keep his ward's money at interest, upon security to be approved by the court, or invest the same in United States bonds or other United States interest-bearing securities. Personal security may be taken for loans not exceeding $100. Loans in larger amounts shall be upon real estate security. No loan shall be made for a longer time than three years, unless authorized by the court: *Provided,* the same may be extended from year to year, without the approval of the court.([1])

19. LEASING REAL ESTATE.—The conservator may lease the real estate of the ward, upon such terms, and for such length of time, as the county court shall approve.([2])

20. MORTGAGING REAL ESTATE.—The conservator may, by leave of the county court, mortgage the real estate of the ward for a term of years, or in fee.([3])

21. PETITION TO MORTGAGE.—Before any mortgage shall be made, the conservator shall petition the county court for an order authorizing such mortgage to be made, in which petition shall be set out the condition of the estate, and the facts and circumstances on which the petition is founded, and a description of the premises sought to be mortgaged.([4])

22. NO STRICT FORECLOSURE.—No decree of strict foreclosure shall be made upon any such mortgage, but redemption shall be allowed, as is now provided by law in cases of sales under executions upon common law judgments.([5])

23. SALE OF REAL ESTATE.—On the petition of the conservator, the county court of the county where the ward resides, or if the ward does not reside in the state, of the county where the real estate or some part of it is situated, may order the sale of the real estate of the ward for his support and that of his family, when the court shall deem it necessary, or to invest the proceeds in other real estate, or for the purpose of otherwise investing the same, or for the purpose of paying the debts of the ward or the education of the children of said ward.([6])

The right to order a sale of the real estate of a lunatic, is inher-

(1) Hurd's R. S., Chap. 86, § 18.
(2) Hurd's R. S., Chap. 86, § 19.
(3) Hurd's R. S., Chap. 86, § 20.
(4) Hurd's R. S., Chap. 86, § 21.
(5) Hurd's R. S., Chap. 86, § 22.
(6) Hurd's R. S., Chap. 86, § 23.

ent in courts of chancery in this state, and does not depend upon the existence of a statute specifically giving such authority to the court.(¹)

24. PETITION FOR SALE.—The petition shall set forth the condition of the estate and the facts and circumstances on which the petition is founded, and shall be signed by the conservator and be verified by his affidavit, and shall be filed at least ten days before the commencement of the term of court at which the application shall be made.(²)

25. NOTICE OF APPLICATION.—Notice of such application shall be given to all persons concerned by publication in some newspaper published in the county where the application is made, at least once in each week for three successive weeks, or if no newspaper is published in such county, by setting up written or printed notices in three of the most public places in the county at least three weeks before the session of the court at which such application shall be made. The ward shall be served with a copy of such notice at least ten days before the hearing of such application. Such service may be proved in the same manner as the service of a copy of a bill in chancery.(³)

26. DOCKET—PRACTICE.—Such application shall be docketed as other causes, and the petition may be amended, heard or continued for further notice, or for other cause. The practice in such cases shall be the same as in other cases in chancery.(⁴)

27. SALE.—The court shall direct notice of the time and place of sale to be given, and may direct the sale to be made on reasonable credit, and require such security of the conservator or purchaser as the interest of the ward may require.(⁵)

28. RETURN OF SALE—APPROVAL—RECORD—TITLE.—It shall be the duty of the conservator making such sale, as soon as may be, to make return of such sale to the court granting the order, which, if approved, shall be recorded, and shall vest in the purchaser or purchasers, all the interest of the ward in the estate so sold.(⁶)

29. PROCEEDS OF SALE.—An account of all moneys and securities received by any conservator for the sale of real estate of his

---

(1) Dodge vs. Cole, 97 Ill., 338; Allman vs. Taylor, 101 Ill., 185.
(2) Hurd's R. S., Chap. 86, § 24.
(3) Hurd's R. S., Chap. 86, § 25.
(4) Hurd's R. S., Chap. 86, § 26.
(5) Hurd's R. S., Chap. 86, § 27.
(6) Hurd's R. S., Chap. 86, § 28.

ward, shall be returned on oath of such conservator to the county court of the county where letters of conservatorship were obtained, and such money shall be accounted for and subject to the order of the county court in like manner as other moneys belonging to such ward. In case of sale for re-investment in this state, the money shall be re-invested under the direction of the court.([1])

30. SUFFICIENCY OF SURETIES.—It shall be the duty of the county court, at each accounting of the conservator, to inquire into the sufficiency of his sureties, and if at any time it has cause to believe that the sureties of a conservator are insufficient or in failing circumstances, it shall, after summoning the conservator, if he be not before the court, require him to give additional security.([2])

31. COUNTER SECURITY.—Upon the application of the surety of any conservator, and after summoning the conservator, the court may, if it believes him to be insolvent or in doubtful circumstances, require him to give counter security to his sureties.([3])

32. REMOVAL OF CONSERVATOR.—The county court may remove a conservator for his failure to give bond or security or additional or counter security when required, or for a failure to make inventory or to account and make settlement, or support the ward, or when he shall have become insane, or have removed out of the state, or become incapable or unsuitable for the discharge of his duties, or for failure to discharge any duty required of him by law or the order of the court, or for other good cause.([4])

33. SUMMONS TO SHOW CAUSE—NOTICE.—Before removing a conservator, the court shall summon him to show cause why he should not be removed for the cause alleged. If the conservator has left the state, or can not be served with process, he may be notified in the same manner as non-resident defendants in chancery.([5])

34. RESIGNATION.—When it shall appear proper the court may permit the conservator to resign his trust, if he first settles his accounts and delivers over the estate as by the court directed.([6])

35. SUCCESSOR APPOINTED—DELIVERY TO SUCCESSOR.—Upon the removal, resignation or death of a conservator, another may be appointed, who shall give bond and security, and perform the

---

(1) Hurd's R. S., Chap. 86, § 29.
(2) Hurd's R. S., Chap. 86, § 30.
(3) Hurd's R. S., Chap. 86, § 31.
(4) Hurd's R. S., Chap. 86, § 32.
(5) Hurd's R. S., Chap. 86, § 33.
(6) Hurd's R. S., Chap. 86, § 34.

duties prescribed by this act. The court shall have power to compel the conservator so removed or resigned, or the executor or administrator of a deceased conservator, to deliver up to such successor, all the goods, chattels, moneys, title papers and other effects in his custody or control belonging to the ward ; and upon failure to so deliver the same, to commit the person offending to jail, until he shall comply with the order of the court.(¹)

36. COMPENSATION.—Conservators on settlement shall be allowed such fees and compensation for their services, as shall seem reasonable and just to the court.(²)

37. RESTORATION TO REASON.—When any person, for whom a conservator has been or may be appointed, under the provisions of this act, shall be restored to his reason, or in case such drunkard or spendthrift shall have become so reformed as to be a proper and safe person to have the care and management of his estate, such person may apply to the county court of the county in which such conservator was appointed, to have said conservator removed, and the care and management of his property, or so much thereof as shall remain, restored to him.(³)

It is usual to file a petition addressed to the court, which may be in form as follows:

STATE OF ILLINOIS, } ss.
...............County, }

In the County Court,
To the......term, A. D. 18....

To the Hon........., Judge of the County Court of said County:

Your petitioner, ..., of the county of......, and State of Illinois, would respectfully represent unto your honor, that at the...term of this honorable court, one.........was appointed as his conservator, and from that time on until the present, has continued to act as such conservator. That your petitioner was adjudged insane, and on to-wit: the...day of......, A. D. 18..., sent to the Insane Asylum at Anna, Illinois, to be cared for and treated, and that on to-wit: the...day of......, A. D. 18.., your petitioner, having fully recovered from said insanity, was, by the superintendent of said hospital, discharged as fully restored to reason. Wherefore, in consideration of the premises aforesaid, your petitioner prays that the said.........may be removed as conservator of your petitioner, and that all the estate, both real and personal, belonging to your petitioner, may be restored to him.

To that end your petitioner prays that a summons may issue for the said........., conservator, whom he makes defendant to this petition, return-

(1) Hurd's R. S., Chap. 86, § 35. (3) Hurd's R. S., Chap. 86, § 37.
(2) Hurd's R. S., Chap. 86, § 36.

able at the......term of this honorable court, and on the...day thereof, A. D. 18..., and that upon a final hearing hereof your honor will cause a jury to be impanneled to try the question whether your petitioner is a fit person to have the care, custody and control of his property, and that upon such final hearing, your honor will cause to be entered an order, fully restoring your petitioner to all the rights and privileges enjoyed before the appointment of said conservatorship.

And your petitioner, as he is in duty bound, will ever pray, etc.

By........., Attorney.

Subscribed and sworn to before me this...day of......, A. D. 18...., by the said ...., petitioner as aforesaid.

........., County Clerk.

38. NOTICE.—Notice of such intended application shall be given to the conservator ten days before the commencement of the term of the court to which the application shall be made.([1])

A precipe for a summons should be filed with said petition, and it will then be the duty of the clerk to issue a summons to the sheriff to execute.

39. TRIAL—JUDGMENT.—It shall be the duty of the court to which any such application, as provided in the foregoing section, is made, on proof that said conservator has been duly notified of such application, to cause a jury to be summoned to try the question whether said applicant is a fit person to have the care, custody and control of his or her property, and if the jury return in their verdict, that such person is a fit person to have the control of such property as aforesaid, then the court shall enter an order fully restoring such person to all the rights and privileges enjoyed before said conservator was appointed: *Provided*, that such conservator, so removed, shall be allowed a reasonable time to settle his accounts as such, and to pass over the money or property in his hands, and such removal shall not invalidate any contracts made in good faith by such conservator while acting as such: *Provided further*, that no application shall be entertained for the removal of any conservator appointed for any person under the provisions of this act, within less than one year from such appointment, unless for neglect of duty or mismanagement of his trust.([2])

(1) Hurd's R. S., Chap. 86, § 38.   (2) Hurd's R. S., Chap. 86, § 39.

ORDER REMOVING CONSERVATOR.

STATE OF ILLINOIS, }
.................County, } ss.
Of the.........term, A. D. 18....
Of the......County County Court.

In the matter of the Conservator-
ship of........., alleged to be } Petition for Removal of Conservator.
Insane.

And now on this day, comes the said........., the petitioner, by........., his attorney, and the said........., conservator, by........., his attorney, and this cause coming on now to be heard, it is ordered that a jury be called, whereupon comes a jury of twelve good and lawful men, who having been duly examined, impanneled and sworn, and having heard all the evidence adduced in this cause, and the arguments of counsel and the instructions of the court, retire to consider of their verdict, and having duly considered thereof, return into open court their verdict, signed by the jurors in words and figures as follows, to-wit: "We, the jury, in the case of.........vs.........., conservator of the said........., find that the said.........is a fit person to have the care and custody and control of his property." It is therefore ordered: That said verdict be received and recorded, and that said jury be discharged, and that said.........be removed as conservator, and that the property of the said.........be restored to his care, custody and control, and that he be fully restored to all the rights and privileges enjoyed before said conservator was appointed.

And it is further ordered, that said........., as conservator as aforesaid, have until......to settle up his accounts as such conservator, and that upon a final settlement of the same, he pay the costs of this proceeding.

40. APPEALS.—Appeals shall be allowed to the circuit court from any order or judgment made or rendered under this act, upon the appellant giving such bond and security as shall be directed by the court; but no appeal from an order removing a conservator shall in any wise affect such order until the same be reversed.(¹)

41. SUITS, COLLECTIONS, ETC., BY NON-RESIDENT CONSERVATORS.—The conservator, guardian, curator or committee, of any non-resident idiot, lunatic, insane or distracted person, spendthrift or drunkard, appointed in any of the United States or territories, or any foreign country, in pursuance of the laws of any such state, territory or country, may commence and prosecute in his name as such conservator, guardian, curator or committee, suits for the recovery of any real or personal property, or any interest therein in this state, belonging to any idiot, lunatic, insane or distracted person, spendthrift or drunkard, or for any injury to such property,

(1) Hurd's R. S., Chap. 86, § 40.

in any of the courts of record in this state having jurisdiction in similar cases by persons in their own rights, and may collect, receive and remove to his place of residence, any personal estate of his ward.(¹)

42. SALE OF REAL ESTATE BY NON-RESIDENT CONSERVATOR.— It shall be lawful for any such conservator, guardian, curator or committee, of any non-resident idiot, lunatic, insane or distracted person, spendthrift or drunkard, who shall obtain an order from the proper court in the state, territory or country in which such conservator, guardian, curator or committee was appointed, authorizing him to make application for the sale of his ward's real estate or personal property in this state, upon filing a certified copy of such order for record in the office of the clerk of the circuit court of the county in this state, in which the property or the major part thereof is situated, by petition to such court to obtain an order authorizing such conservator, guardian, curator or committee, to sell and transfer any such property or interest therein, belonging to any such idiot, lunatic, insane or distracted person, spendthrift or drunkard, and to make deeds and conveyances thereof; which deeds and conveyances, executed and acknowledged in pursuance of the laws of this state, or of the state, territory or country in which such conservator, guardian, curator or committee was appointed, shall be effectual in law and equity to pass to the grantee or grantees therein all the right, title and interest of such idiot, lunatic, insane or distracted person, spendthrift or drunkard therein. The court ordering the sale, may authorize any person to act as auctioneer of the property, but the deed shall be executed by the conservator, guardian, curator or committee.(²)

43. NOTICE OF PETITION.—Notice of the time and place of presenting said petition to said circuit court shall be given by publication in the nearest newspaper for four successive weeks, the first of which publications shall be at least forty days before the time fixed for the presentation of said petition, requesting all persons interested to show cause why the prayer of said petition should not be granted.(³)

44. BOND.—The said circuit court may, in its discretion, re-

---

(1) Hurd's R. S., Chap. 86, § 41.
(2) Hurd's R. S., Chap. 86, § 42.
(3) Hurd's R. S., Chap. 86, § 43.

quire such conservator, curator, guardian or committee, to file a bond, with sufficient securities, conditioned for the faithful application of the moneys which may be received for any such property, for the benefit, and to the use of such idiot, lunatic, insane or distracted person, spendthrift or drunkard.(¹)

45. BOND FOR COSTS.—In all suits by non-resident conservators, guardians, curators or committees, they shall give a bond for costs as in cases of other non-residents.(²)

As before remarked, the provisions of this chapter are very similar to that of guardian and ward, and the forms will answer for both, substituting the word conservator for that of guardian. The form for settlement given for the use of the guardian, see page 272, may be used by the conservator; so, too, the forms for inventorying the estate, see page 230, and for mortgaging real estate, see page 297; and for selling real estate, see page 275; and for security and counter security, see page 321; and for removal of conservator for cause, etc., see page 313; and resignation of conservator, see page 310. The forms of procedure are similar, and by reference to those already given, a necessity for repeating them here will be obviated.

The conservator, if he discharge his duties well, finds that he has a task somewhat difficult, but it may be materially lessened, by always obtaining an order of the court in the transaction of his various duties, and in keeping an account of all he pays out and all that he receives, and by always giving, and especially always taking, receipts for any amount which he pays out. His duties are almost identical with those of the guardian, and, therefore, his compensation should be the same. But the compensation is discretionary with the court, and every case should be determined by the attending circumstances.

He should file his reports at least once every year, at which time the work of the year is open to the inspection of the court, for its approval or rejection.

(1) Hurd's R. S., Chap. 86, § 44.   (2) Hurd's R. S., Chap. 86, § 45.

CHAPTER XVI.

PROCEEDINGS IN INSANITY.

1. Petition—form of petition.
2. Writ—service—order of the county judge to the clerk—form of writ.
3. Subpœnas—form of precipe for witnesses—form of subpœnas for witnesses.
4. Jury—trial—form of a venire for jury.
5. Verdict—form—form of the verdict of the jury.
6. Verdict recorded—order of committal—application—form of final order.
7. To which hospital—application.
8. Warrant to commit.
9. Form of warrant.
10. Indorsement—return.
11. Who not admitted—idiots discharged.
12. Temporary commitment.
13. Costs.
14. Who to pay expenses—sheriffs' fees.
15. Bond to furnish clothing—form of a bond to trustees of hospital.
16. Clothing.
17. Paupers—Duty of the county judge in regard to clothing.
18. Discharge of patient—notice—removal.
19. Non-resident patients.
20. Restoration to reason—discharge.
21. County hospital.
22. Trial by jury necessary.
23. Penalty.

1. PETITION.—When any person is supposed to be insane or distracted, any near relative, or in case there be none, any respectable person residing in the county, may petition the judge of the county court for proceedings to inquire into such alleged insanity or distraction. For the hearing of such application and proceedings thereon, the county court shall be considered as always open.([1])

The petition may be in form as follows:

STATE OF ILLINOIS, } ss.   *In the County Court,*
..............County, }   ....*term, A. D.* 18...
To the Hon..........., Judge of said Court:

    Your petitioner, ..., of said county, respectfully represents that.........,

(1) Hurd's R. S., Chap. 85, § 1.

of said county, is supposed to be insane or distracted; that your petitioner is......of said........., and respectfully asks for proceedings to inquire into...... alleged insanity or distraction, according to law.

By............, his Attorney.   A B.

A B, being duly sworn, according to law, says that the matters and facts stated in said petition are true, in substance and in fact, as he verily believes.

.........., County Clerk.

2. WRIT—SERVICE.—Upon the filing of such petition, the judge shall order the clerk of the court to issue a writ, directed to the sheriff or any constable, or to the person having the custody or charge of the alleged insane or distracted person, unless he shall be brought before the court without such writ, requiring the alleged insane person to be brought before him at a time and place to be appointed for the hearing of the matter. It shall be the duty of the officer or person to whom the writ is directed, to execute and return the same, and bring the alleged insane person before the court as directed in the writ.([1])

ORDER OF THE COUNTY JUDGE TO THE CLERK.

STATE OF ILLINOIS, } ss.   *In the County Court.*
................County.

In the Matter of.........., alleged to be Insane.

Whereas,.........., of the county aforesaid, has duly filed in the county court of said county a petition, asking the judge of said court for proceedings to inquire into the alleged insanity or distraction of.........., of said county and state aforesaid. It is therefore, hereby ordered by the undersigned, judge of said court, that the clerk of said court issue a writ under the seal of said court, directed to.........., requiring the said person alleged to be insane or distracted, to be brought before said judge, at the office of the clerk of said court, in......, in said county, at the hour of...o'clock in the...noon, on the...day of......, A. D. 18..., which time and place are appointed by said judge for the hearing of said matter.

It is also ordered, that you cause to be issued a venire for a jury, as directed by the law, returnable at the same time and place, directed to the sheriff to execute.

Witness my hand, this...day of......, A. D. 18...

.........., Judge.

WRIT—INSANE.

In the Matter of.........., alleged to be Insane.

STATE OF ILLINOIS, } ss.   *In the County Court.*
..................County.

The People of the State of Illinois, to.........., of said County, Greeting:

Whereas, a petition has been duly filed in the office of the clerk of the

(1) Hurd's R. S., Chap. 85, § 2.

county court of said county, by........., of said county, asking the judge of said court for proceedings to inquire into the alleged insanity of........., of said county and state aforesaid.

And whereas, upon the filing of said petition, the judge of said county court did order the clerk of said court to issue a writ requiring said person alleged to be insane, to be brought before him, the said judge, at the office of the clerk of said court, in........., at the hour of...o'clock in the...noon, on the...day of......, A. D. 18...

You are therefore, hereby commanded and required to bring said......... before said judge at the day, hour and place aforesaid. Hereof fail not.

     Witness, ..., Clerk of the said County Court, and the
[Seal.] seal thereof, this...day of......, A. D. 18...
          ...., Clerk County Court.

3. SUBPŒNAS.—The clerk shall also issue subpœnas for such witnesses as may be desired on behalf of the petitioner, or of the person alleged to be insane, to appear at the time fixed for the trial of the matter.(¹)

The precipe to be filed for the witnesses, may be in form as follows:

STATE OF ILLINOIS, } ss.   *In the County Court.*
..................County,

In the Matter of........., alleged to be Insane.

The clerk of said court will please issue subpœnas for.........and........., witnesses for and on behalf of........., in said proceeding, directed to the sheriff to execute.

By........., his Attorney.
  To........., Clerk of the County Court.

The form of subpœna may be as follows:

STATE OF ILLINOIS, } ss.
..................County,

The People of the State of Illinois to the Sheriff of said County, Greeting.

We command you to summon.........to appear before the county court of said county, at......, on the...day of..., A. D. 18..., at...o'clock in the...noon, to testify and the truth to speak, in behalf of the People of said state, concerning the facts in the case of........., alleged to be insane,.........a cause now pending in said court, at the clerk's office, in the court house, at......... .

And have you then and there this writ, with a return thereon, showing in what manner you have executed the same.

     Witness, ..., Clerk of said court, and the seal thereof, at his
[Seal.] office in........., in said county, this....day of........, A. D. 18....
          ...., Clerk.

(1) Hurd's R. S., Chap. 85, § 3.

4. JURY—TRIAL.—At the time fixed for the trial, a jury of six persons, one of whom shall be a physician, shall be impanneled to try the case. The case shall be tried in the presence of the person alleged to be insane, who shall have the right to be assisted by counsel, and may challenge jurors as in civil cases. The court may, for good cause, continue the case from time to time.(¹)

The clerk may issue his venire for a jury in form as follows:

STATE OF ILLINOIS, }
................County,   } ss.

The People of the State of Illinois to the Sheriff of said County, Greeting:

You are commanded forthwith to summon six suitable persons, at least one of whom shall be a physician, and the others lawful jurors, to assemble before the county court of said county, at.........., on the...day of......, A. D. 18..., at...o'clock in the...noon, to serve as jurors in the case hereinafter named, and as a jury to be sworn to try the fact of the sanity or insanity of.........., of said county, alleged to be insane, in the matter of the application of.........., to have said alleged insane person committed to the Illinois State Hospital for the Insane, now pending in said court. Hereof fail not, and of this writ make due service and return.

        Witness, ..., Clerk of said court, and the seal thereof, at
[Seal.]   .... aforesaid, this...day of......, A. D. 18...
                                                       ...., Clerk.

5. VERDICT—FORM.—After hearing the evidence, the jury shall render their verdict in writing, signed by them, which shall embody the substantial facts shown by the evidence, which verdict may be substantially in the following form:

STATE OF ILLINOIS, }
................County,   } ss.

In the Matter of.........., alleged to be Insane.

We, the undersigned, jurors in the case of.........., alleged to be insane, having heard the evidence in the case, are satisfied that said..........is insane, and a fit person to be sent to the Illinois State Hospital for the Insane; that..he is a resident of the State of Illinois, and county of.........., that h... age is....., that h...disease is of......duration; that the cause is supposed to be....;......., that the disease is, with h... ...hereditary; that..he is not subject to epilepsy, and that..he is free from vermin or any infectious disease, and that..he is...a pauper.

Given under our hands, this...day of......, A. D. 18...(2)
                                                    ...., M. D.
                                                    .....,
                                                    ......,
                                                    ......,
                                                    ......,
                                                  ....,

(1) Hurd's R S., Chap. 85, § 4.   (2) Hurd's R S., Chap. 85, § 5.

6. VERDICT RECORDED—ORDER OF COMMITTAL—APPLICATION.—Upon the return of the verdict, the same shall be recorded at large by the clerk, and if it appears that the person is insane, and is a fit person to be sent to a state hospital for the insane, the court shall enter an order that the insane person be committed to a state hospital for the insane, and thereupon it shall be the duty of the clerk of the court to make application to the superintendent of some one of the state hospitals for the insane for the admission of such insane person.([1])

The order may be in form as follows:

STATE OF ILLINOIS, } ss.   *In the County Court,*
..................County, ..., *A. D.* 18....

In the Matter of........., alleged to be Insane.

And now on this day, came the said petitioner, ..., by A B, his attorney, also comes the said........., alleged to be insane, in charge of the......., and the court appoints.........., an attorney of said court, to defend the interest of the said........., alleged to be insane, and to make for h...a suitable defense. Whereupon comes the sheriff of.........county, Illinois, with a jury of six good and lawful men, to-wit: [*Here insert the jurors' names.*] One of whom is a physician, and this cause coming on now to be heard, before the court and jury impanneled as aforesaid, the evidence was all submitted, argument of counsel heard, and instructions given by the court, whereupon the jury retired to consider their verdict, and after due consideration thereof, returned into open court, their verdict, in form as follows: [*Here insert copy of the verdict of the jury in full.*] Whereupon said verdict is received and ordered to be recorded, and said jury discharged.

It is, therefore, ordered by the court, that.........who has been found to be a fit person for the insane hospital, be committed to the insane hospital of the State of Illinois, at..........., and that the clerk of this court make application to the superintendent thereof immediately.

It is further ordered, that.........pay the costs of this proceeding, to be taxed at......dollars.

7. TO WHICH HOSPITAL—APPLICATION.—If such insane person is a pauper, the application shall be first made to the nearest hospital, but if he be not a pauper, application shall be made to such one of the state hospitals for the insane, as the relatives or friends of the patient shall desire. In any case, if, on account of the crowded condition of any one of the hospitals, or for other good reason, the patient cannot be received therein, or it is not desirable

(1) Hurd's R. S., Chap. 85, ? 6.

to commit him thereto, he may be committed to any other of said hospitals. Upon receiving any such application, the superintendent shall immediately inform the clerk whether the patient can be received, and if so, at what time; and if not, shall state the reason why.([1])

The application made by the clerk usually consists in sending a certified copy of the order made and entered in the proceeding, with a request that the patient may be admitted to the hospital to which said application is made.

8. WARRANT TO COMMIT.—Upon receiving notice at what time the patient will be received, the clerk shall, in due season for the conveyance of the person to the hospital by the appointed time, issue a warrant, directed to the sheriff or any other suitable person, preferring some relative of the insane person when desired, commanding him to arrest such insane person and convey him to the hospital; and if the clerk is satisfied that it is necessary, he may authorize an assistant to be employed.([2])

9. The warrant may be substantially as follows:

STATE OF ILLINOIS, } ss.
................County,

The People of the State of Illinois, to..........

You are hereby commanded forthwith to arrest.........., who has been declared to be insane, and convey h...to the..........Illinois Hospital for the Insane, and you are hereby authorized to take to your aid an assistant, if deemed necessary, and of this warrant make due return to this office with an endorsement thereon, in what manner you shall have executed the same.
                  Witness my hand and the seal of our said County Court,
  [Seal.]   at.........., this...day of......, A. D. 18...
                              ...., Clerk County Court.([3])

10. INDORSEMENT—RETURN.—Upon receiving the patient, the superintendent shall indorse upon said warrant a receipt as follows:

..........ILLINOIS HOSPITAL FOR THE INSANE.
      Received, this...day of......, A. D. 18..., the patient named in the within warrant.   ...., Superintendent.

This warrant, with a receipt thereon, shall be returned to the clerk, to be filed by him with the other papers relating to the case.([4])

(1) Hurd's R. S., Chap. 85, § 7.   (3) Hurd's R. S., Chap. 85, § 9.
(2) Hurd's R. S., Chap. 85, § 8.   (4) Hurd's R. S., Chap. 85, § 10.

11. WHO NOT ADMITTED—IDIOTS DISCHARGED.—No person having any contagious or infectious disease, and no idiot, shall be admitted to either of the state hospitals. When the trustees and superintendent shall find that an idiot has been received into the hospital, they may discharge him.(1)

12. TEMPORARY COMMITMENT.—If the court shall deem it necessary, pending proceedings and previous to verdict, or after verdict and pending admission to the hospital, temporarily to restrain of his liberty, the person alleged to be insane, then the court shall make such order in that behalf as the case may require, and the same being entered of record, a copy thereof certified by the clerk, shall authorize such person to be temporarily detained by the sheriff, jailor or other suitable person, to whom the same shall be directed.(2)

13. COSTS.—When a person, not a pauper, is alleged to be insane, and is found by the jury not to be insane, the costs of the proceeding, including the fees of the jury, shall be paid by the petitioner, and judgment may be awarded against him therefor. If such person is found to be insane, such costs shall be paid by his guardian, conservator, or relatives, as the court may direct. If the person alleged to be insane is a pauper, the costs of the proceeding, including the fees of the jury, shall be paid out of the county treasury. *Provided*, if such pauper is found not to be insane, the court may, in its discretion, award the costs against the petitioner.(3)

14. WHO TO PAY EXPENSES—SHERIFF'S FEES.—The expense of conveying a pauper to the hospital, shall be paid by the county in which he resides, and that of any other patient, by his guardian, conservator or relatives; and in no case, shall any such expense be paid by the state, or out of any funds for the insane. The fees of the sheriff for conveying any person to a hospital, shall be the same as for conveying convicts to the penitentiary.(4)

15. BOND TO FURNISH CLOTHING.—If the person be not a pauper, then one or more persons, relatives or friends of the patient, shall, upon his admission into the hospital, become responsible to the trustees for finding the patient in clothes, and removing him

---

(1) Hurd's R. S., Chap. 85, § 11. (3) Hurd's R. S., Chap. 85, § 13.
(2) Hurd's R. S., Chap. 85, § 12. (4) Hurd's R. S., Chap. 85, § 14.

when required; and shall execute a bond conditioned as follows, viz.:

Know all men by these presents, that we, ...and.........., of the county of.........., and State of Illinois, are held and firmly bound unto the Trustees of the..........Hospital for the Insane, in the sum of one hundred dollars, for the payment of which we jointly and severally bind ourselves firmly by these presents.

The condition of this obligation is such, that whereas.........., an insane person, of the county and state aforesaid, has been admitted as a patient into the..........Hospital for the Insane: Now, therefore, if we shall find said patient in suitable and sufficient clothing, while..he may remain in said institution, and shall promptly pay for such articles of clothing as it may be necessary to procure for said.........., at the hospital.........., and shall remove h...from said hospital, when required by the trustees to do so, then this obligation to be void, otherwise to remain in full force.

Witness our hands and seals, this...day of......, A. D. 18...

.........., [Seal.]
.........., [Seal.]

STATE OF ILLINOIS, } ss.
..............County,

I, ..., Clerk of the County Court for said county, do certify that.........., who are named in, and whose names are, in their own proper handwriting, subscribed to the foregoing bond, have been approved as sureties therein, and as being good and sufficient, to meet and duly respond to the conditions of said bond, by said..........court, as appears by the order of said court, duly entered on the records of said court in my office remaining.

[Seal.] Given under my hand and the seal of said court, at my office in.........., this...day of......, A. D.

.........., Clerk.

16. CLOTHING.—The clothing to be furnished each patient, upon being sent to the hospital, shall not be less than the following:

For a Male:—Three new shirts, a new and substantial coat, vest, and two pairs of pantaloons of woolen cloth, three pairs of woolen socks, a black or dark stock or cravat, a good hat or cap, and a pair of new shoes or boots, and a pair of slippers to wear within doors.

For a Female:—In addition to the same quantity of undergarments, shoes and stockings, there shall be two woolen petticoats or skirts, three good dresses, a cloak or shawl, and a decent bonnet. Unless such clothing be delivered in good order to the superintendent, he shall not be bound to receive the patient.([1])

([1]) Hurd's R. S., Chap. 85, § 16.

17. PAUPERS—DUTY OF THE COUNTY JUDGE IN REGARD TO CLOTHING.—If the insane person be a pauper, it shall be the duty of the judge of the county court to see that he is furnished with the necessary amount of substantial clothing at the time he is sent to the hospital, and from time to time while he remains a patient in the hospital, and that he be removed therefrom when required by the trustees; the expense of such clothing and removal, shall be paid out of the county treasury, upon the certificate of the judge of the county court.[1]

18. DISCHARGE OF PATIENT—NOTICE—REMOVAL.—Whenever the trustees shall order any patient discharged, the superintendent shall at once notify the clerk of the county court of the proper county thereof, if the patient is a pauper, and if not, shall notify all the persons who signed the bond required in section 15 of this act, and request the removal of the patient. If such patient be not removed within thirty days after such notice is received, then the superintendent may return him to the place from whence he came, and the reasonable expenses thereof may be recovered by suit on the bond, or in case of a pauper, shall be paid by the proper county.[2]

19. NON-RESIDENT PATIENTS.—Whenever application shall be made for a patient not residing within the state, if the superintendent shall be of the opinion that from the character of the case it is probably curable, and if there be at the time room in the hospital, the trustees, in their discretion, may order the patient to be admitted, always taking a satisfactory bond for the maintenance of the patient, and for his removal, when required. The rate of maintenance in such cases, shall be fixed by the trustees, and two months' pay in advance shall be required. But no such patient shall be detained without the order of a court of competent jurisdiction, or a verdict of a jury.[3]

20. RESTORATION TO REASON—DISCHARGE.—When any patient shall be restored to reason, he shall have the right to leave the hospital at any time, and if detained therein contrary to his wishes, after such restoration, shall have the privilege of a writ of habeas corpus at all times, either on his own application, or that of any

---

[1] Hurd's R. S., Chap. 85, § 17.
[2] Hurd's R. S., Chap. 85, § 18.
[3] Hurd's R. S., Chap. 85, § 19.

other person in his behalf. If the patient is discharged on such writ, and it shall appear that the superintendent has acted in bad faith or negligently, the superintendent shall pay all the costs of the proceeding. Such superintendent shall moreover be liable to a civil action for false imprisonment.([1])

21. COUNTY HOSPITAL.—This act shall not be construed to prevent the committing of any insane pauper to the hospital for the insane of the county in which he may reside, where such a hospital is provided.([2])

22. TRIAL BY JURY NECESSARY.—No superintendent, or other officer or person connected with either of the state hospitals for the insane, or with any hospital or asylum for insane or distracted persons, in this state, shall receive, detain, or keep in custody, at such hospital or asylum, any person who shall not have been declared insane by the verdict of a jury, and authorized to be confined by the order of a court of competent jurisdiction; and no trial shall be had of the question of the sanity or insanity of any person before any judge or court, without the presence of the person alleged to be insane.([3])

23. PENALTY.—If any superintendent, or other officer or person connected with either of the state hospitals for the insane, or with any hospital or asylum for insane or distracted persons, in this state, whether public or private, shall receive or detain any person who has not been declared insane by the verdict of a jury, and whose confinement is not authorized by the order of a court of competent jurisdiction, he shall be confined in the county jail not exceeding one year, or fined not exceeding $500, or both, and be liable civilly to the person injured for all damages which he may have sustained; and if he be connected with either of the insane hospitals of this state, he shall be discharged from service therein.([4])

(1) Hurd's R. S., Chap. 85, § 20.
(2) Hurd's R. S., Chap. 85, § 21.
(3) Hurd's R. S., Chap. 85, § 22.
(4) Hurd's R. S., Chap. 85, § 23.

ADDITIONAL NOTES

1. Appointment of conservator.
2. Bond--Powers and duties.
3. Removal of conservator upon the restoration of lunatic to health.
4. Notice of application for removal.
5. Trial by jury—Verdict—Settlement of accounts of convervator.
6. Costs taxed against conservator.
7. Appeals.
8. Superintendent of hospital for the insane to make semi-annual report to county clerk of the number of patients confined in hospital from such county.
9. Penalty for failure to comply with act.

1. APPOINTMENT OF CONSERVATOR.—When it shall appear to the court, upon any trial wherein any person may be adjudged insane under the act of 1874, that any such person is the owner or possessed of any property, either real or personal, which, in the opinion of such court, is in danger of waste or depreciation, it shall be the duty of the court to appoint some fit person to be the conservator of such insane person; or, in case there is a probate court in the county, then the court shall transmit to said probate court a duly certified copy of the record of the verdict of the jury finding said person insane, and upon presentation of the same said probate court shall, in its discretion, appoint some fit person to be conservator of such insane person: *Provided,* that the petition for an inquest shall also apply for the appointment of a conservator, and the necessity for the appointment of such conservator shall first be found by the jury, and such trial shall be had before a jury composed of twelve jurors.([1])

2. BOND—POWERS AND DUTIES.—Said conservator, when so appointed, shall give bond, qualify, have the same power and discharge the same duties as are now required by law of conservators in other cases.

3. REMOVAL OF CONSERVATOR.—When any person for whom a conservator has been appointed as aforesaid shall be discharged from any hospital [in] which he or she may have been confined,

([1]) Hurd's R. S., Chap. 85, § 24, 929.

and shall be restored to reason, so as to be able to manage and control his or her property, such person may file his petition, in writing, in the county court of the county in which such conservator was appointed, to have such conservator removed, and the care and management of his property restored to him.

4. NOTICE OF APPLICATION FOR REMOVAL.—Notice of such application shall be given by service of summons as in other cases, ten days before the commencement of the term of court to which application shall be made.

5. TRIAL BY JURY—VERDICT—SETTLEMENT.—It shall be the duty of the court to which any such application is made, on proof that such conservator has been duly notified of such application, to cause a jury to be summoned to try the issue whether such applicant is so far restored to reason as to be a fit person to have the custody and control of his property, and if the jury return in their verdict that such person is fit to have the custody of his property as aforesaid, the court shall enter an order removing such conservator and fully restoring such person to all rights and privileges enjoyed by him before the appointment of such conservator: *Provided*, that such conservator so removed shall be allowed a reasonable time to settle his accounts as such, and pay all debts contracted by him, and pass over the money or property remaining in his hands, and such removal shall not invalidate any contracts made in good faith by such conservator while acting as such.

6. COSTS TAXED AGAINST CONSERVATOR.—The costs of proceedings under this act for the removal of conservators, including the fees of the jury, shall be taxed against such conservator, to be paid by him out of the money or property in his hands.

7. APPEALS.—Appeals shall be allowed to the circuit court from any order or judgment made or rendered under this act, upon the applicant giving such bond and security within such time as the court may direct.([1])

8. SUPERINTENDENT OF HOSPITAL TO REPORT TO COUNTY CLERKS.—Each superintendent of any hospital for the insane in this state shall, on the first day of January and July, of each year, furnish the clerk of the county court of the proper county thereof

---

(1) Hurd's R. S., Chap. 85, § 30, 930.

with a full and complete list of all insane patients confined in said hospital from said county, stating the date of admission of each, whether said patients be paupers, the present physical and mental condition of each; also giving the names of such as may have died or been discharged since last report, with date of such death or discharge.

9. PENALTY FOR FAILURE TO COMPLY WITH ACT.—Any such superintendent failing to comply with the foregoing section shall be liable to a fine of one hundred dollars for each failure, to be collected by suit before a justice of the peace of the county wherein such hospital is situate, on complaint of such clerk of the county court, or other person having relatives or friends confined in said hospital.([1])*

(1) Hurd's R. S., Chap. 85, § 31-32, 930.

---

*NOTE.—Prior to this amendment (§ 30) there was no right to appeal given to the person adjudged insane. Remedy held to be by habeas corpus.(1)

(1) People ex. rel. Fullerton vs. Gilbert, 115 Ill., 59.

CHAPTER XVII.

PROCEEDINGS IN INSANITY AND AS CONSERVATOR.

1. Inquisition of lunacy and appointment of conservator.
2. Can not be questioned collaterally.
3. Liability when appointed.
4. Liability for interest.
5. How insanity is ascertained.
6. Who are deemed insane.
7. Evidence.
8. Effect of finding.
9. Powers.
10. Custody and support.
11. Claims against the estate of the insane.
12. Commissions.
13. Voluntary support.
14. Suits affecting the person and property of lunatics.
15. Sale of real estate by conservator.
16. Contracts.
17. Criminal responsibility.
18. Liability for torts.

1. INQUISITIONS OF LUNACY AND APPOINTMENT OF CONSERVATOR.—Inquisitions of lunacy must be taken in court, unless it appears by affidavit that the subject of it can not be controlled, or that his health forbids it.([1]) In such proceedings under the statute for the appointment of a conservator, the lunatic must have reasonable notice, or the inquisition will be set aside.([2]) And the want of sufficient notice to the alleged lunatic of the taking of an inquisition of lunacy, is not aided by his appearing and attempting a defense.([3]) An insane person can not appear in court by attorney.([4])

The county where an alleged lunatic is domiciled, and well known, and all his property situated, is the only proper place for the inquisition.([5]) The father has preference, he being a suitable

([1]) McApee vs. Commonwealth, 3 B. Mon., (Ky.) 305.
([2]) Eddy vs. The People, 15 Ill., 386.
([3]) Matter of Whitenack, 2 Green Ch., 252; *Ex Parte* Van Auken, 10 N. J. Eq., (2 Stock.) 186.
([4]) Elliott vs. Elliott, 1 Ind., 119.
([5]) Castleman vs. Castleman, 6 Dana, (Ky.) 55.

person, and should be appointed conservator ;(¹) a husband is entitled to be preferred to a third person as guardian of his insane wife, where he is otherwise suitable ;(²) and the wife is entitled to preference, she being a suitable person, to be appointed as the conservator of the insane husband.(³)

That a person makes unprofitable and improvident bargains, and is generally unthrifty in his business or unsuccessful in his enterprises, does not *per se* prove himself to be *non compos mentis*, though it may tend to show that fact ;(⁴) and to warrant an appointment of a guardian for a spendthrift, there must be evidence of bad habits, of excessive drinking, gaming, idleness, debauchery, or the like. Proof of weak minded habits in the management of money, is not enough.(⁵)

The physician who sits upon an inquisition of insanity, must be one licensed by the board of physicians of the state.(⁶)

A court of equity has no authority to make an order for an inquisition by a jury, as to the lunacy or idiocy of a party ;(⁷) but where the husband of an insane wife was unable to support her, it was held, that a court of chancery might appoint a conservator for her estate, held in her own right.(⁸)

Upon the application for the appointment of a guardian to one represented as *non compos mentis*, the court is not confined to a trial by the inspection and examination of such person, but may admit other evidence.(⁹)

A verdict in proceedings upon a commission of lunacy, may be set aside as against the weight of evidence, and a new commission ordered.(¹⁰)

An inquisition of lunacy is *prima facie* evidence only of mental incapacity, as to one who was not a party to the proceedings.(¹¹) It

---

(1) Coleman vs. Commissioners of Lunatic Asylum, 6 B. Mon. (Ky.) 239.
(2) Drew's Appeal, 57 N. H., 181.
(3) Grant vs. Green, 41 Iowa, 88.
(4) *Re* Carmichael, 36 Ala., 514.
(5) Morey's Appeal, 57 N. H., 54.
(6) Norwood vs. Hardy, 17 Ga., 595.
(7) Dowell vs. Jacks, 5 Jones, N. C. Eq., 417.
(8) Davenport vs. Davenport, 5 Allen, 464.
(9) Brigham vs. Brigham. 12 Mass., 505.
(10) Matter of Lawrence, 28 N. J. Eq., 331.
(11) Hirsch vs. Trainer, 3 Abb., (N. Y.) Cas., 274 ; Field vs. Lucas, 21 Ga., 447 ; Hopson vs. Boyd, 6 B. Mon., (Ky.) 296 ; Clark vs. Trail, 1 Metc. (Ky.) 35; Lucas vs. Perkins, 23 Ga., 267.

is never conclusive against any person not a party to it;(¹) for sanity is triable anew as often as the question arises, as the verdict is effective only in the suit in which it is rendered.(²)

Under the statutes of Illinois, and even before the married woman's act of 1861, the county court may appoint a conservator for the estate of a married woman.(³)

2. CAN NOT BE QUESTIONED COLLATERALLY.—Letters of guardianship of a lunatic, when issued by a probate court, can not be questioned in a collateral proceeding.(⁴) And where a guardian of an insane person has been appointed by the county court, and under the sanction of the court, has sold the land of such insane person, the validity of this sale can not be questioned in a collateral proceeding, on the ground that notice of the inquisition was not given to the alleged lunatic.(⁵) The findings of the county court are conclusive in all collateral proceedings.(⁶)

3. THEIR LIABILITY WHEN APPOINTED.—A guardian, appointed under the act relative to common drunkards, is not liable to an action upon a note made by the drunkard before the guardian's appointment.(⁷)

4. LIABILITY FOR INTEREST.—A guardian of an insane person, who allows his ward's money to lie idle in his hands for an unreasonable time, or mingles the same with his own money, is chargeable with interest thereon.(⁸)

5. HOW INSANITY IS ASCERTAINED.—The only legal test of insanity is delusion; and this consists in a belief of facts which no rational person would believe.(⁹) The law presumes that every adult man is sane, and possessed of the absolute right to sell and dispose of his property in whatever way he may choose; his will in every case standing as the reason of his conduct, and the burden of

---

(1) Den vs. Clark, 10 N. J. L., (5 Hals.) 217.
(2) Emery vs. Hoyt, 46 Ill., 258.
(3) Gardner vs. Maroney, 95 Ill., 552.
(4) Warner vs. Wilson, 4 Cal., 310; Wing vs. Dodge, 80 Ill., 564.
(5) Dutcher vs. Hill, 29 Mo., 271; Gardner vs. Maroney, *supra;* Dodge vs. Cole, 97 Ill., 338.
(6) Wing vs. Dodge, *supra.*
(7) Coombs vs. Janvier, 31 N. J. L., 240.
(8) Stumph vs. Pfeiffer, 58 Ind., 472.
(9) Matter of Forman, 54 Barb., (N. Y.) 274.

proving insanity lies on the party who asserts it.(¹) Even in the case of suicide, insanity will not be presumed.(²) But evidence of hereditary taint is competent to corroborate direct proof.(³) Every man will be presumed to be sane, until the contrary is proved, and the burden then of proof lies upon the party who alleges insanity;(⁴) and this presumption will continue until inquest found, when, perhaps, the presumption is reversed until rebutted by evidence that sanity has returned.(⁵) Never until the disease manifests its presence, can we infer its existence.(⁶)

6. WHO ARE DEEMED INSANE.—So long as a person is possessed of the requisite mental faculties to transact rationally the ordinary affairs of life, he will be deemed sane, and will not be relieved from the responsibilities that rest on the ordinary citizen.(⁷) A person deaf and dumb from birth, is not, on that account, to be deemed *non compos mentis*;(⁸) as it does not follow necessarily that a deaf mute is an idiot or *non compos mentis*.(⁹)

Occasional oddity or hypochondria, does not amount to insanity.(¹⁰)

7. EVIDENCE.—The fact of insanity is established by the opinions of those, who, from habits of daily or common intercourse with, or observation of such person, can make an intelligent comparison of his mental manifestations with his conduct when he was admitted to enjoy the full use of his natural faculties, together with the facts upon which such opinions are founded;(¹¹) and in proving insanity of a party making a contract, evidence of the state of his mind before, at, and after, such time, is admissible.(¹²) The law presumes sanity, and, when insanity has been once proved, it pre-

---

(1) Hall vs. Unger, 2 Abb., (U. S.) 507.
(2) Coffey vs. Home Life Ins. Co., 44 How., (N.Y.) Pr., 481.
(3) Smith vs. Kramer, 5 Pa. Law. J. Rep., 226.
(4) Menkins vs. Lightner, 18 Ill., 282; Jackson vs. Van Dusen, 5 Johns., 154; Grabill vs. Barr, 5 Penn. St. R., 441.
(5) Titcomb vs. Vantyle, 84 Ill., 371.
(6) Snow vs. Benton, 28 Ill., 306.
(7) Titcomb vs. Van Tyle, *supra*.
(8) Brower vs. Fisher, 4 Johns. (N. Y.) Ch., 441; Markle vs. Markle, 4 Johns. (N. Y.) Ch., 168.
(9) Christmas vs. Mitchell, 3 Ired., N. C. L., 535.
(10) Hawe vs. State, 11 Neb., 537.
(11) Beller vs. Jones, 22 Ark., 92.
(12) Grant vs. Thompson, 4 Conn., 203; Peaslee vs. Robbins, 3 Metc., (Mass.) 164.

sumes its continuance.(¹) But it can not be presumed against proof that a person is insane, from the fact that his mother was so.(²) The conversations of a party upon any subject tending to show the state of his mind, are admissible in evidence on the question of sanity.(³) And the opinion of a non-professional witness in relation thereto, derived from personal observations of, and conversations with, such person, is admissible in evidence in connection with the facts upon which the opinion is based.(⁴) But, the opinion of a witness that the defendant was incompetent to manage his own affairs and take care of himself, is inadmissible,(⁵) for the reason, that it fails to state the grounds upon which the opinion was formed.(⁶) Witnesses who are not experts, may testify to their opinions concerning sanity, based on their own observations;(⁷) but, whether experts or not, they must always state the facts upon which their opinions are based.(⁸)

8. EFFECT OF FINDING.—After a person has been found to be of unsound mind, he should, so long as the unsoundness exist, be regarded as civilly dead.(⁹) And while the law presumes every man to be sane, when insanity is once proved to exist, the law presumes it still to continue.(¹⁰) A discharge from the insane asylum, because the officers adjudged the patient restored, would be at least *prima facie* evidence of such restoration.(¹¹) And, so a person under guardianship, as *non compos mentis*, if his reason be restored, is competent to make a will, although the letters of guardianship are unrepealed.(¹²)

After a person has been found insane, and a conservator has

---

(1) Myatt vs. Walker, 44 Ill., 485; Achey vs. Stephens, 8 Ind., 411; Cook vs. Cook, 53 Barb., (N. Y.) 180.
(2) Snow vs. Benton, 28 Ill., 306.
(3) Mollins vs. Cottrell, 41 Miss., 291.
(4) Cram vs. Cram, 33 Vt., 15.
(5) *Re* Carmichael, 36 Ala., 514.
(6) Jones vs. Perkins, 5 B. Mon., (Ky.) 222.
(7) Beaubein vs. Cicotte, 12 Mich., 459.
(8) White vs. Bailey, 10 Mich., 155.
(9) McNees vs. Thompson, 5 Bush., (Ky.) 686.
(10) Menkins vs. Lightner, 18 Ill., 282; State vs. Reddick, 7 Kansas, 143; Carpenter vs. Carpenter, 8 Bush., (Ky.) 283; Aurentz vs. Anderson, 3 Pittsb., (Pa.) 310; Haynes vs. Swann, 6 Heisk., (Tenn.) 560; Chicago West Div. R. R. Co. vs. Mills, 91 Ill., 39.
(11) Haynes vs. Swann, *supra*.
(12) Stone vs. Damon, 12 Mass., 488; Leonard vs. Leonard, 14 Pick., (Mass.) 280; Breed vs. Pratt, 18 Pick., 115.

been appointed, such conservator will not be discharged from his trust, on his own application, as of course, merely because the execution of the trust has become unpleasant to him.(¹)

9. POWERS.—The guardian of a lunatic, under the statute, has the same powers, is subject to the same restrictions and duties as are required of, and granted to, the guardian of a minor, so far as the same are applicable.(²)

The conservator has a right to enter the dwelling house of his ward, without his permission, and against his will, to take an inventory of the property of the ward, or to attend to any other duties of his office that require such entry.(³) One of two guardians of a spendthrift is competent to receive payment of a debt due to the ward, and his receipt is *prima facie* evidence of the payment.(⁴)

Where a trust is already created by a lunatic, the committee of his person and estate has no right to the control of his property;(⁵) but they have a right to demand and receive the annual interest and income thereof from the trustees.(⁶)

Guardians of spendthrifts, have no control of the persons of their wards.(⁷)

A guardian of an idiot appointed in another state, is but the guardian of the person and estate of the idiot within that state; he has no power over the estate of the infant in this state, by virtue of such appointment.(⁸)

10. CUSTODY AND SUPPORT.—The guardian of an insane person has general power to determine and to change the domicile of his ward.(⁹)

A man of wealth, and having no family dependent upon him, under guardianship as insane, should be allowed those luxuries which he desires and can enjoy, which are unobjectionable in themselves,

---

(1) Matter of Lytle, 3 Paige, (N. Y.) 251.
(2) Alexander vs. Alexander, 8 Ala., 796; Dearman vs. Dearman, 5 Ala., 202; Stumph vs. Pfeiffer, 58 Ind., 472.
(3) State vs. Hyde, 29 Conn., 564.
(4) Raymond vs. Wyman, 18 Me., 385.
(5) Wilson's Estate, 2 Pa. St., 325.
(6) Earp's Estate, 2 Pars., (Pa.) Sel. Cas., 178.
(7) Boyden vs. Boyden, 5 Mass., 427.
(8) Rodgers vs. McLean, 31 Barb., (N. Y.) 304; Boyce vs. Warren, 2 Dev. & B., (N. C.) L., 152.
(9) Anderson vs. Anderson, 42 Vt., 350.

and would be proper and reasonable expenditures for a sane man in a similar position.(¹)

An insane person having property adequate to his support, is not a pauper, and the county is not liable for the support of such person, nor is the city in which he resides, liable for his support.(²)

11. CLAIMS AGAINST THE ESTATE OF THE INSANE.—The fact that one has been adjudged a lunatic, or of unsound mind, does not abate any right of action against him upon his contracts previously made; but actions may be commenced and prosecuted against him as against other persons, and equity will not interfere.(³) No claim can be allowed against the estate of an insane person in the hands of his conservator, by the county court, as the proper remedy of the creditor is by suit against the conservator as his representative, under which the creditor may have any property of the insane person sold under execution.(⁴) Nor do the creditors of a lunatic, who obtain judgment after inquisition found, thereby acquire any right of priority over other creditors.(⁵)

12. COMMISSIONS.—The question of compensation of the committee of a lunatic, is not governed by the statute prescribing commissions of executors and guardians, but is to be determined by the court having custody of the estate, in view of its value and situation, and of the attending circumstances.(⁶) When charged with annual interest on money in his account with the ward, he is entitled to his commissions upon such interest.(⁷) A wife appointed conservator of her insane husband, can not recover compensation for her services in that capacity from his estate.(⁸)

13. VOLUNTARY SUPPORT.—One who voluntarily expends money in the support of a lunatic, can not recover for such expenditure, either against the lunatic or his committee.(⁹)

14.—SUITS AFFECTING THE PERSON AND PROPERTY OF LUNATICS.—All suits affecting the person or property of a lunatic,

(1) May vs. May, 109 Mass., 252.
(2) The City of Alton vs. County of Madison, 21 Ill., 115; Smith vs. The People *Ex Rel*, 65 Ill., 375.
(3) Stigers vs. Brent, 50 Md., 214.
(4) Morgan vs. Hoyt, 69 Ill., 489.
(5) Wright's Appeal, 8 Pa. St., 57.
(6) Matter of Colah, 6 Daly, (N. Y.) 51.
(7) Bird vs. Bird, 21 Gratt., (Va.) 712.
(8) Grant vs. Green, 41 Iowa, 88.
(9) Hehn vs. Hehn, 23 Pa. St., 415.

must be prosecuted in his name, except those which are authorized by statute to be brought in the name of his conservator.(¹) The guardian of a lunatic is authorized and may sue in his own name as guardian, in trover, for the property of the lunatic;(²) and where a promissory note is given to a guardian of an insane person as guardian, he may institute suit upon it in his own name.(³)

A lunatic whose interests are sought to be affected by a decree, must be made party to a suit, and, if a defendant, must answer by a conservator; and if he has none, the court will appoint a guardian *ad litem* to defend the suit, and answer for the lunatic.(⁴)

The guardian of a lunatic can not bring an action of ejectment, nor any other action at law, in his own name;(⁵) but a suit on behalf of a lunatic, brought in the name of his guardian, as follows, viz: "A B, Guardian of B C," (the lunatic,) was held to be regular.(⁶) When the guardian of an insane person sues in his own name, the complaint should show that the right of action is in the insane person, and should not allege the cause of action to be in the guardian.(⁷)

Until the appointment and qualification of a conservator for an insane person, a suit may be maintained in such insane person's name for the recovery of a debt due him.(⁸)

Where a conservator of an idiot, on his removal from office and settlement with the court, is ordered to pay over the balance in his hands to his successor, and the latter is also removed before the money is paid, and another appointed in his place, the latter may maintain an action on the bond of the first for non-payment, as the latter is authorized to receive the money.(⁹)

Where a party is unable, in consequence of mental weakness, to protect himself, equity will lend its aid to see that no injustice may be done. It will protect such party against his own acts, as well

---

(1) McKillip vs. McKillip, 8 Barb., (N. Y.) 552; Reed vs. Wilson, 13 Mo., 28.
(2) Field vs. Lucas, 21 Ga., 447.
(3) Nickerson vs. Gilliam, 29 Mo., 456.
(4) Harrison vs. Rowan, 4 Wash., 202; Sunday vs. Gordon, Blatchf. & H., Adm., 569.
(5) Brooks vs. Brooks, 3 Ired. (N. C.) L., 389.
(6) Shaw vs. Burney, 1 Ired. (N. C.) L., 148
(7) Bearss vs. Montgomery, 46 Ind., 544.
(8) Chicago & Pacific R. R. vs. Munger, 78 Ill., 300.
(9) Richardson vs. People, 85 Ill., 495.

as those of others, done in his name. A bill filed in the name of an insane wife against her husband for a divorce, while she is in close confinement, she not being capable of giving consent, the proceedings under it are void, and may all be set aside on bill filed by her conservator. Whether there be fraud, in fact, or not, the law will presume it, and that will vitiate the decree.[1]

15. SALE OF REAL ESTATE BY CONSERVATOR.—The petition to be filed by a conservator of this state, must show the facts and specify the purposes for which the sale is sought, and these must be for one or more of the objects named in the statute. But where the application is made by a non-resident conservator or guardian of an insane person, the law does not require the petition to state the purposes for which the property is to be sold. It is deemed sufficient to confer jurisdiction for the petition to show that the court of the state where the conservator resides, has required the sale, without reference to the application of the proceeds.[2]

Notice published in a daily newspaper, three insertions in each successive week, the first being not less than thirty days before the presentation of the petition, of the time and place of presenting the petition, requesting all persons interested to show cause why the prayer of the petition shall not be granted, is sufficient to give the court jurisdiction on an application by a non-resident conservator for the sale of real estate.[3]

Conveyances by conservators, are, in no sense, to be regarded as conveyances by the lunatic. They are conveyances made by the law for the benefit of the lunatic, and are analogous to conveyances by guardians and administrators.[4] The acts in regard to conveyances by married women, have no relation whatever to conveyances by conservators. The latter are governed entirely by the statute in relation to idiots and lunatics.[5]

16. CONTRACTS.—After the finding of an inquisition, declaring the incompetency of a lunatic or habitual drunkard, and until he is permitted by the court to assume control of his property, all gifts,

(1) Bradford vs. Abend, 89 Ill., 78.
(2) Wing vs. Dodge, 80 Ill., 564.
(3) Ib.
(4) Gardner vs. Maroney, 95 Ill., 552.
(5) Ib.; Guardianship of Eliza Fegan, 45 Cal., 176; Drew's Appeal, 57 N. H., 181.

bonds, or contracts, made by him are void.[1] And this is true, even though proved to be at the time perfectly sober, and competent to transact business.[2]

In many forms of insanity, the capacity to transact is entirely unaffected, and in such cases, the fact of insanity can not be set up to avoid business transactions.[3] If the party alleged to be insane, has received all the benefit from a sale, and had sufficient capacity to comprehend the act, he is estopped from denying its validity.[4]

Where no conservator has been appointed, although the person may have been adjudged insane, if he is in the management of his business, and there is nothing about his appearance to indicate his incapacity to contract, if he purchases an article at a fair and reasonable price, necessary and useful in his business, and the seller have no notice of his being adjudged insane, he will be liable to pay the price he agreed to pay, and it will be error to enjoin a judgment on a note given for the price.[5] And so, a contract made in good faith, by one apparently in sound mind, will not be set aside by him or his representative, after the subject matter thereof can not be restored.[6] Where a conveyance is set aside on the ground of insanity or lunacy of the grantor, and an account taken, the grantee, having purchased in good faith, without the knowledge of the alleged insanity, will be entitled to be reimbursed that which he has paid on the same. The consideration must be returned before the conveyance can be avoided. And if the contract was fair and made in good faith, and is executed and completed, and the property which is the subject matter of the contract can not be restored, so as to put the parties in the same place, courts have held, that such contracts can not be set aside, either by the alleged lunatic or those who represent him.[7] A court of equity, when its jurisdiction is invoked to set aside deeds and contracts of a person on the ground of insanity, acts upon equitable principles. It is

---

(1) L'Amoureaux vs. Crosby, 2 Paige, (N. Y.) 422; Griswold vs. Miller, 15 Barb., (N. Y.) 520.
(2) Wadsworth vs. Sherman, 14 Barb., 169.
(3) Searle vs. Galbraith, 73 Ill., 269.
(4) Miller vs. Craig, 36 Ill., 109; Searle vs. Galraith, *supra*.
(5) McCormick vs. Littler, 85 Ill., 62.
(6) Scanlan vs. Cobb, 85 Ill., 296.
(7) *Ib.*

by no means a matter of course for a court of equity to set aside and declare void the act of a lunatic, executed during lunacy. It does so in no case, except on equitable terms. He who seeks equity, must do equity.(¹) A great many of the acts done, and contracts made, by lunatics, are void, while others are only voidable: Thus a contract for the sale of land, made by one who had been adjudged a lunatic, is absolutely void, and no action can be maintained to enforce it.(²) So, too, a power of attorney to sell lands, given by a lunatic, is void, and not merely voidable.(³) A deed, executed by a person under conservatorship, is void, even though it be executed with the consent of the conservator;(⁴) and it is the duty of the conservator to take measures to set aside a deed made by his insane grantor, after his appointment.(⁵) But the deed of an insane grantor, not under guardianship, is voidable only.(⁶) The evidence showing the insanity at the time of the execution of the deed, must preponderate, or the legal presumption in favor of sanity, will sustain the act;(⁷) for sanity being the rule, and insanity the exception, to destroy the binding effect of the deed, the evidence showing insanity, must decidedly preponderate. In chancery cases, involving questions of insanity, an issue should be formed upon the question and submitted to a jury.(⁸) The want of absolute and perfect soundness of mind, does not necessarily affect the capacity to make a valid conveyance, provided the mind is still capable of fully comprehending the import of the act.(⁹) A deed can not be impeached on the ground that the grantor, at the time of the execution, was a monomaniac on the subject of religion.(¹⁰)

Where a person, subject to temporary insanity, in a lucid interval, sold property for a full price, for the payment of urgent debts, he acting under the advice and counsel of friends, the sale will not

(1) Canfield vs. Fairbanks, 63 Barb., (N. Y.) 461.
(2) Fitzhugh vs. Wilcox, 12 Barb., (N. Y.) 235.
(3) Dexter vs. Hall, 15 Wall., 9
(4) Griswold vs. Butler, 3 Conn., 227; Van Dusen vs. Sweet, 51 N. Y., 378; Elston vs. Jasper, 45 Texas, 409; Nichol vs. Thomas, 53 Ind., 42; Mohr vs. Tulip, 40 Wis., 66.
(5) Kilber vs. Myrick, 12 Florida, 419.
(6) Wait vs. Maxwell, 5 Pick., (Mass.) 217.
(7) Lilly vs. Waggoner, 27 Ill., 395; Myatt vs. Walker, 44 Ill., 485.
(8) Myatt vs. Walker, *supra;* Titcomb vs. Vantyle, 84 Ill., 371.
(9) Miller vs. Craig, 36 Ill., 109; Speers vs. Sewell, 4 Bush., (Ky.) 239; Harvey vs. Hobson, 55 Maine, 256; Dennett vs. Dennett, 44 N. H., 531.
(10) Burgess vs. Pollock, 53 Iowa, 273.

be set aside;[1] for a contract entered into during the lucid intervals of one who is a lunatic, is valid.[2]

The term lucid interval, implies that the normal condition of the person is insanity; and the burden of proving that a contract was made during a lucid interval, is on the party seeking performance of the contract.[3]

When the mind is so deranged, that a person can not comprehend and understand the effect and consequences of an act, or business in which he may be engaged, the law will relieve him from his acts.[4] The voluntary conveyance by a father, of all his property to a person not his relative, the father being old and in a state of dotage, may be set aside at the instance of his children after his death;[5] and the party signing a deed or other instrument, or any person claiming under him, may show that, at the time such deed, or instrument was signed, he was of insane mind.[6]

Promissory notes will be set aside on the ground of mental incapacity of the maker, where there appears such weakness of mind as to incapacitate the party to guard himself against imposition and undue influence.[7] And where the consideration is very inadequate, a court of equity or an impartial jury will closely scrutinize the facts, and will give weight to slight evidence of imposition and circumvention, when one of the parties is of weak intellect.[8]

An insane person is not bound by his contract of suretyship, even though the creditor accepted him as surety without knowledge of his incapacity.[9] A lunatic can not make a note.[10] So, too, the transfer of negotiable paper by him is void.[11] Contracts with lunatics are not all absolutely void; but such as are fairly made

---

(1) Jones vs. Perkins, 5 B. Mon., (Ky.) 222.
(2) Lilly vs. Waggoner, 27 Ill., 395; McCormick vs. Littler, 85 Ill., 62.
(3) Emery vs. Hoyt, 46 Ill., 258.
(4) Titcomb vs. Vantyle, 84 Ill., 371.
(5) Keible vs. Cummings, 5 Hayw., (Tenn.) 43; Parris vs. Cobb., 5 Rich., S. C. Eq., 450.
(6) Ballew vs. Clark, 2 Ired. (N. C.) L., 23; Bensell vs. Chancellor, 5 Whart., (Pa.) 371.
(7) Johnson vs. Chadwell, 8 Humph., (Tenn.) 145; Beller vs. Jones, 22 Ark., 92.
(8) McFadden vs. Vincent, 21 Texas, 47; Hale vs. Brown, 11 Ala., 87; James vs. Langdon, 7 B. Mon., (Ky.) 193; Wilson vs. Oldham, 12 B. Mon., 55.
(9) Van Patton vs. Beals, 46 Iowa, 62.
(10) Taylor vs. Dudley, 5 Dana, (Ky.) 308.
(11) Hannahs vs. Sheldon, 20 Mich., 278.

with them for necessaries, or things suitable to their condition and habits of life, will be sustained.(¹) And where no undue advantage is taken, contracts with a person of unsound mind, are held valid.(²) But if it appear that one of the parties was so overreached while in such a mental condition from the use of alcoholic spirits, as to make him an easy victim, the settlement will not be conclusive upon the party so overreached.(³) For a party will be protected against his own acts, while in a state of insanity, even if brought on by drunkenness.(⁴)

Mental incapacity at the time of contracting, produced by drunkenness or any other cause, is a good defense against the contract, whether it be by deed or parol;(⁵) and relief may be granted against acts done by a party who is so inebriated as to be incapable of contracting, or who, from the effects of inebriation, continues incapable.(⁶)

17. CRIMINAL RESPONSIBILITY.—The law presumes persons of full age to be sane and responsible agents, and this presumption stands until overcome by evidence.(⁷) The old rule was, that it must be shown that the defendant was insane, and not responsible for his acts at the time the deed was committed; for, the presumption being, that all men are of sufficient capacity to be responsible for crime, therefore, the defendant must establish his insanity.(⁸) And, in some states, it has been held, that if a defendant sets up insanity as a defense, he must establish it beyond a reasonable doubt.(⁹) The burden of proof, to establish the insanity of one who has committed a criminal act, is upon the accused;(¹⁰) but in Illinois, as well as in quite a number, if not majority of all the states,

(1) Pearl vs. McDowell, 3 J. J. Marsh, (Ky.) 658; Skidmore vs. Romaine, 2 Bradf., N. Y.) 122; Crouse vs. Holman, 19 Ind., 30.
(2) Sims vs. McClure, 8 Rich., S. C. Eq., 286; Dods vs. Wilson, 1 Treadw., S. C. Const., 448.
(3) Murray vs. Carlin, 67 Ill., 286.
(4) Menkins vs. Lightner, 18 Ill., 282.
(5) Jenners vs. Howard, 6 Blackf., (Ind.) 240.
(6) Menkins vs. Lightner, 18 Ill., 282.
(7) Commonwealth vs. Heath, 11 Gray, (Mass.) 303; State vs. McCoy, 34 Miss., 531; Newcomb vs. State, 37 Miss., 383; Water vs. People, 32 N. Y., 147; Fisher vs. People, 23 Ill., 283.
(8) Graham vs. Commonwealth, 16 B. Mon., (Ky.) 587; Fisher vs. People, *supra*.
(9) State vs. Brinyea, 5 Ala., 241; State vs. Marler, 2 Ala., 43; People vs. Coffman, 24 Cal., 230.
(10) State vs. Lawrence, 57 Me., 574.

it need not be established beyond a reasonable doubt—it is enough if the jury be satisfied by the preponderance of the evidence.(¹) Where a defendant, charged with crime, sets up insanity as a defense to the act, he does not thereby assume the burden of proof upon that question—such a defense being only a denial of one of the essential allegations against him.(²) In Kansas, it has been held, that in a criminal action, where the defense of insanity is interposed, it does not devolve upon the defendant to prove that he is insane by a preponderance of the evidence; but if, upon the whole of the evidence introduced on the trial, together with all the legal presumptions applicable to the case, under the evidence, there should be a reasonable doubt as to whether the defendant is sane or insane, he must be acquitted.(³) This seems to be the rule in Illinois.(⁴)

The same doctrine is held in Michigan, that where any evidence is given, which tends to overthrow the presumption of sanity, the burden of proof then falls upon the prosecution to establish the insanity.(⁵)

In California, it was held, that where insanity was relied upon as a defense, the burden of proof is on the defendant; and the proof must be such in amount that, if the issue of sanity or insanity of the defendant, were submitted to a jury in a civil case, they would find he was insane.(⁶)

In order for insanity to constitute a defense, the evidence must show, that, at the time of committing the act charged, the defendant was laboring under such a defect of reason from disease of the mind, as not to know the nature and quality of the act he was doing; or, that if he did know, he did not know that what he was doing, was wrong. For, if the party indicted, had, at the time of the offense, capacity and reason sufficient to enable him to distinguish between right and wrong, and to understand the nature, character and consequences of his act, and his relation to the party

(1) Fisher vs. People, 23 Ill., 283; State vs. Klinger, 43 Mo., 127.
(2) Hopps vs. People, 31 Ill., 385.
(3) State vs. Crawford, 11 Kansas, 32.
(4) Chase vs. People, 40 Ill., 352; Hopps vs. People, *supra*.
(5). People vs. Garbutt, 17 Mich., 9; *Contra*, Boswell vs. State, 63 Ala., 307; See, also, note to the above case, 35 American Rep., 32.
(6) People vs. Hamilton, (Supreme Court of Cal., May, 1882) 14 *Reporter*, 46.

injured, the defense of insanity is not made out.([1]) To constitute a defense, the insane delusion must be shown to have existed to such an extent as to blind its subject to the consequences of his acts, and deprive him of all freedom of agency.([2])

Where hereditary insanity is offered as an excuse for crime, it must appear that the kind of insanity proposed to be proven, as existing in the prisoner, is no temporary malady; but that it is notorious, and of the same species as that with which other members of the family have been afflicted.([3])

While voluntary intoxication is no excuse for crime, still insanity produced by continued drunkenness, is a good defense in a criminal action.([4]) Delirium tremens, is a species of insanity, and, like insanity from other causes, affects the responsibility for crime.([5]) But when set up as a defense, the prisoner must show that he was under the influence of delirium at the time the act was perpetrated.([6]) A fixed, habitual madness, which is the result of long continued drunkenness, will excuse a crime; but insanity, which is the immediate result of intoxication, affords no excuse for crime,([7]) where the person, when sane, of his own volition, became intoxicated.([8])

It is as much the duty of a conservator of the peace, to order into custody an insane man, who is committing a breach of the peace in his presence, as to order the arrest of a sane person under like circumstances; for, although an insane person may not be guilty of crime, he may lawfully be prevented from doing harm.([9])

18. LIABILITY FOR TORTS.—A lunatic or insane person is liable, in a civil action, for any tort he may commit, though he is not punishable criminally.([10]) Generally, insanity is no defense to an action of tort,([11]) but it may be shown as a defense to an action for slander.([12])

(1) People vs. Pine, 2 Barb., (N. Y.) 566; Hopps vs. People, 31 Ill., 385; State vs. Brandon, 8 Jones, N. C. L., 463; People vs. Montgomery, 13 Abb., (N. Y. Pr.) N. S., 207; Commonwealth vs. Rodgers, 7 Metc., (Mass.) 500; Fisher
(2) Commonwealth vs. Mosler, 4 Pa. St., 264.   [vs. People, 23 Ill., 283.
(3) State vs. Christmas, 6 Jones, N. C. L., 471; People vs. Smith, 31
(4) Bradley vs. State, 31 Ind., 492.   [Cal., 466.
(5) Maconnehey vs. State, 5 Ohio St., 77.
(6) State vs. Sewell, 3 Jones, N. C. L., 245.
(7) Cornwell vs. State, Mart. & Y. (Tenn.) 147.
(8) Bennett vs. State, Mart. & Y., (Tenn.) 133; People vs. Lewis, 36
(9) Lott vs. Sweet, 33 Mich., 308.   [Cal., 531.
(10) Cross vs. Kent, 32 Md., 581.
(11) Morse vs. Crawford, 17 Vt., 499.
(12) Bryant vs. Jackson, 6 Humph., (Tenn.) 199.

ADDITIONAL NOTES.

1. Liability for torts.
2. Evidence in action for injury by tort of a lunatic.
3. Measure of damages.
4. Judgment cannot be attacked collaterally.
5. Insanity produced by intoxication, as a defense.
6. Presumption of sanity—Degree of proof to overcome presumption.
7. Instruction construed.
8. Evidence of defendant's previous habits of intoxication.
9. Restraining violence of the prisoner pending motion for a new trial.
10. Opinion of persons not experts as to sanity.
11. Evidence to overcome presumption of sanity.
12. Judgment—How far conclusive.
13. Remedy where a lunatic is sued.
14. Proper court in which to review a decree.
15. Statute construed.
16. Parties in chancery—Bill against a lunatic.
17. Insanity of partner—Effect upon partnership.
18. Relation of partner—Both principal and agent.
19. Accounting by conservator.
20. Appeal.
21. Recovery of insane person.

1. LIABILITY FOR TORTS.—Although a lunatic or insane person is not punishable criminally, he is liable in a civil action for any tort he may commit.

2. EVIDENCE IN ACTION FOR INJURY.—In an action by the personal representatives of a person wrongfully killed, against the estate of the party killing, to recover compensation for the death, evidence of the insanity of the latter party at the time of his wrongful act causing the death, is inadmissible when offered in defense of the action.

3. MEASURE OF DAMAGES.—A lunatic having no will of his own, and his acts lacking the element of intention, the only proper measure of damages in an action against him for a wrong is the mere compensation of the party injured. Punishment is not the object of the law when persons unsound in mind are the wrongdoers.(1)

4. JUDGMENT CANNOT BE ATTACKED COLLATERALLY.—The

---

(1) McIntyre, Adm'r, vs. Sholty, Adm'r, 121 Ill., 660.

force and effect of a decree of a sister state, when set up as an estoppel to deny a fact necessarily found by it, cannot be avoided by showing that the defendant in such former suit, and against whom the finding is offered, was insane at the time such proceedings were had therein. The effect of such decree can be obviated only by a direct proceeding in the courts of such state to impeach or set it aside.(1)

5. INSANITY PRODUCED BY INTOXICATION.—Temporary insanity produced by intoxication furnishes no excuse for the commission of a homicide or other crime, but a fixed insanity does. Whether a party committing a crime is under the influence of a fixed insanity, or a temporary one induced immediately by intoxication, is a question of fact for the jury, and their verdict will not be disturbed, unless it is clearly against the evidence.

While it is true there must be a union of act and intention, or criminal negligence, to constitute a criminal offense, yet, when without intoxication, the law will impute to the act a criminal intent, as in the case of a wanton killing of another without provocation, voluntary drunkenness is not available to disprove such intent, so as to reduce the crime from murder to manslaughter.(2)

Voluntary intoxication furnishes no excuse for crime committed under its influence, even if the intoxication is so extreme as to make the author of the crime unconscious of what he is doing, or to create a temporary insanity.(3)

6. PRESUMPTION OF SANITY—PROOF TO OVERCOME.—On the trial of one for murder, where insanity was relied on as a defense, the court instructed the jury that the law presumed every man to be sane until the contrary was shown, and that when insanity was set up as a defense, before the accused could be acquitted on that ground it must appear from the evidence that at the time of the commission of the crime he was not of sound mind, but affected with insanity to such a degree as to create an uncontrollable impulse to do the act charged, by overriding his reason and judgment, etc.: *Held*, that the instruction stated the law correctly, and there was no error in giving the same.(4)

The presumption of the sanity of one accused of crime obtains

(1) Hanna vs. Read, 102 Ill.. 596.
(2) Upstone vs. The People, 109 Ill., 169.
(3) *Id.*
(4) Dacey vs. The People, 116 Ill., 555.

and holds at and during every stage of the trial, until it is overcome by evidence. This presemption, in this state, may be overcome by evidence tending to prove insanity which is sufficient to raise a reasonable doubt of the sanity of the accused at the time of the commission of the act charged. When this is done, the presumption of sanity ceases, and the burden is shifted upon the prosecution to prove his sanity, as any other element necessary to constitute crime, beyond a reasonable doubt.

7. INSTRUCTION CONSTRUED.—An instruction in a criminal case, that before the jury can acquit on the ground of insanity it must appear from the evidence in the case that at the time of the commission of the crime the accused was not of sound mind, but affected with insanity to such a degree as to create an uncontrollable impulse to do the act, etc., is not liable to the objection that it imposes on the defendant the burden of proving his insanity by a preponderance of the evidence. It does not state to what extent insanity must be made to appear—whether beyond a reasonable doubt, by a preponderance of the evidence, or to an extent only sufficient to raise a reasonable doubt of sanity.([1])

8. DEFENDANT'S PREVIOUS HABITS.—On the trial of a defendant for murder, when insanity is set up as a defense, and he is shown to have been intoxicated at the time of the homicide, evidence of his previous intoxication will be properly received from the prosecution, as bearing upon the question of intoxication at the time of the killing, and of the conduct of the defendant while in that state.

9. RESTRAINING PRISONER.—After the trial and conviction of a prisoner upon a charge of murder, upon the hearing of a motion for a new trial, which had been continued to a subsequent term, the prisoner broke out in manifestations of rage and violence toward the officers, and attempted to break away. Thereupon handcuffs were placed upon his wrists to restrain him. It was *held*, that there was no error in preserving order and protecting the sheriff and his bailiffs from violence, and that it could not affect the justness of the verdict at the preceding term, nor the sentence following the overruling the motion for a new trial.([2])

10. OPINION OF PERSONS NOT EXPERTS.—On the trial of one for crime, the opinion of neighbors and acquaintances of the defend-

(1) Dacey vs. The People, 116 Ill., 555.
(2) Upstone vs. The People, 109 Ill., 169.

ant, who are not experts, may be given as to his sanity or insanity, founded on their actual observations.(¹)

11. SANITY—EVIDENCE TO OVERCOME PRESUMPTION.—As the law presumes the sanity of all persons, the burden is cast upon the party alleging the insanity at a particular time to establish it by a preponderance of the proof. No rule can be laid down as to the quantum of evidence necessary to establish insanity, except that it must be sufficient to overcome the legal presumption of sanity, and to overbalance the testimony tending to sustain such presumption.(²)

12. How FAR JUDGMENT CONCLUSIVE.—Where an insane person is properly brought before the court by personal service, the judgment or decree rendered against him will be valid and binding, and is said to be neither void nor voidable.

13. REMEDY WHERE A LUNATIC IS SUED.—Where a lunatic or insane person is sued at law, the proper remedy for the lunatic is to apply to a court of chancery to restrain the proceedings, and to compel the plaintiff to go there for justice. But a judgment against a lunatic, until set aside in chancery, or otherwise, is as valid and binding as any other judgment. It seems, however, that the mere fact of insanity alone is not sufficient ground to set aside the judgment. It should further be shown that the judgment is inequitable.(³)

14. PROPER COURT TO REVIEW DECREE.—Where a decree of strict foreclosure has been rendered in the circuit court of the United States against a lunatic or insane person, that court is the proper forum in which to apply for relief against the decree. The state courts have no power or authority to review, revise and correct such decree.

15. STATUTE CONSTRUED.—The provision of section 6 of the chancery code, that in any cause in equity it shall be lawful for the court to appoint a guardian *ad litem* to any insane defendant in such cause, is not made jurisdictional, and can have no application where a conservator has been appointed and is acting, or when the complainant has no knowledge of the insanity.

16. PARTIES IN CHANCERY—BILL AGAINST LUNATIC.—After inquisition and the appointment of a conservator for a lunatic, a

---

(1) Upstone vs. The People, 109 Ill., 169.
(2) Green vs. The Phœnix Life Ins. Co., 134 Ill., 310.
(3) Maloney vs. Dewey, 127 Ill., 395.

party filing a bill to enforce the contracts of a lunatic should make the conservator a party; but until such appointment it is competent to commence suit against the lunatic. The complainant is not bound to ascertain the mental capacity of the defendant before he can bring his suit.(1)

17. INSANITY OF PARTNER—EFFECT.—The insanity of a partner does not, *per se*, work a dissolution of the partnership, but may constitute sufficient grounds to justify a court of equity in decreeing its dissolution. But this doctrine is applied in equity with appropriate limitations and restrictions. For, while curable, temporary insanity will be sufficient, upon an inquisition, to sustain an adjudication of insanity in the county court, the appointment of a conservator, and commitment of the ward to an insane asylum, yet it will not authorize a court of chancery to decree a dissolution of the partnership if the malady be temporary only, with a fair prospect of recovery in a reasonable time. An adjudication of insanity by the county court can have no effect in determining the partnership, and upon a bill to dissolve the partnership it will have no other effect than to establish the insanity. Courts of equity will, as between the partners, look to the effect produced upon the partnership relations and business, and refuse to dissolve the partnership and apply its assets unless the insanity materially affects the capacity of the partner to discharge the duties imposed by his contract relation.

18. RELATION OF PARTNER—The relation of a partner embraces the character of both principal and agent. As to the partnership concerns, for himself he acts as principal, and as agent for his partners. His power to act for them is coupled with an interest in all that pertains to the firm business. Therefore, if, for any reason, one member of the firm should assume control and management of the business and affairs of the partnership, he should, while so controlling it, manage it for all, and in the interest of all the partners. He will not be allowed to derive personal advantage from the use of the partnership assets, or business or good will of the firm. So where, after one of two partners had been adjudged insane, but his insanity was considered only temporary, and curable, and the other, without objection or notice to any one, continued the business precisely as before, it was *held* that the presumption was

(1) Maloney vs. Dewey, 127 Ill., 395.

that he did not intend a dissolution of the firm, and, in the absence of evidence to the contrary, that he waited to determine whether the incapacity of his partner would prove temporary merely, and it become practicable for him to resume business. In such a case, as long as the same partner continued thus to carry on the business without taking steps to dissolve the partnership, there could be no dissolution, or he be excused from afterward accounting for the profits actually derived by him from the business of the firm.(¹)

19. ACCOUNTING BY CONSERVATOR.—A. and B. were partners in this state in the business of brokers, and the former was adjudged insane, and the latter appointed his conservator, and continued the business precisely as before. The conservator did not inventory the partnership matters, and the profits of the business thereafter were not embraced in the final account of the conservator. Upon his recovery, a bill was filed in chancery by A. for an accounting of the partnership matters and profits: *Held*, that the final accounting of the conservator partner in the county court was no bar to the relief sought by the bill.

The judgment of the county court approving a conservator's account and discharging him without any notice, actual or constructive, to the ward, who was at that time in a lunatic asylum, is not conclusive upon the latter or his personal representatives. A claim cannot be barred by a proceeding in which it was in no wise involved, and of which the party to be estopped had no kind of notice.(²)

20. APPEAL.—No appeal will lie from the finding and order of the county court in a proceeding to inquire into the alleged insanity of a person had under the act to revise the laws in relation to the commitment and detention of lunatics, approved March 21, 1874.

21. RECOVERY OF INSANE PERSON.—If a person adjudged insane and committed to the hospital for the insane shall be restored to reason, he will be entitled to be discharged, and if he shall afterward be detained against his wishes, the law gives him a remedy by the writ of *habeas corpus*.(³)

(1) Raymond vs. Vaughn, 128 Ill., 256.
( ) *Id.*
(3) The People vs. Gilbert, 115 Ill., 59.

CHAPTER XVIII.

ASSIGNMENT FOR THE BENEFIT OF CREDITORS.

1. Definition.
2. How made.
3. Notice to creditors to present claims.
4. Assignee to file inventory under oath.
5. Report of claims made and list of creditors.
6. How claims may be contested.
7. Dividends—final account and settlement.
8. Power of court over assignee.
9. Want of list or inventory not to void assignment.
10. When additional inventory and bond.
11. When claim not due—limitation.
12. Power of assignee to sell property, collect debts, etc.
13. Death or failure of assignee to act.
14. Preferences void.
15. Jurisdiction of county courts.
16. Discontinuance of proceedings.
17. Forms of a deed of assignment and schedules.
18. Inventory of the estate of assignor—bond.
19. Assignee's notice to creditors—form.
20. List of creditors and their claims to be filed.
21. Manner of presenting claims—form.
22. Exceptions to claim—forms and service of notice.
23. Order of distribution.
24. Final report of assignee.
25. Who may make assignments.
26. Construction given to deeds.
27. What assignments are fraudulent.
28. Modifications subsequently made.
29. Preference of creditors.
30. Trustees—rights of creditors.

1. DEFINITION.—The student should distinguish between bankruptcy and insolvency—or, bankrupt laws, and those relating to insolvents. By the provisions of the Federal Constitution, the power of enacting bankrupt laws is given to congress; hence, the several states have no power to pass bankrupt laws. Such laws necessarily impair the obligation of contracts.([1]) Yet, the legisla-

---

([1]) Sturgis vs. Crowningshield, 4 Wheat., 125; McMillan vs. McNeill, *Id*., 209.

CH. XVIII] ASSIGNMENT FOR BENEFIT OF CREDITORS. 429

tures of the several states may, in the absence of a federal bankrupt law, pass laws providing for, and regulating assignments for the benefit of creditors; and may even provide that a discharge under state insolvent laws, shall bar actions for debts contracted between citizens of that state after the passage of the act; but can not, by such legislation, affect obligations due to citizens of another state, nor those antedating the law.([1])

An assignment is a transfer to another of real or personal property in possession or in action, or of any estate or interest therein.

Assignments are either *voluntary*, as where the debtor voluntarily makes an assignment for the benefit of his creditors; or, *involuntary*, as when made by an imprisoned debtor, upon his application for discharge.

These are mostly regulated by statutes, and the reader should consult these for details. The purpose of this chapter is to give the law relating to voluntary assignments as it now exists in the State of Illinois. Prior to the act of May 22d, 1877, there was no statute regulating assignments in this State, except such as are contained in the insolvent debtor's act, which will be treated in another chapter. The act passed May 22d, 1877, which went into force and effect July 1st, 1877, we shall give here in detail.

2. How MADE.—In all cases of voluntary assignments hereafter made for the benefit of creditors, the debtor or debtors shall annex to such assignment an inventory under oath or affirmation, of his, her or their estate, real and personal, according to the best of his, her or their knowledge; and also a list of his, or their creditors, their residence and place of business, if known, and the amount of their respective demands; but such inventory shall not be conclusive as to the amount of the debtor's estate, but such assignment shall vest in the assignee or assignees, the title to any other property not exempt by law, belonging to the debtor or debtors, at the time of making the assignment, and comprehended within the general terms of the same. ' Every assignment shall be duly acknowledged and recorded in the county where the person or persons making the same, reside, or where the business in respect of which the same is made, has been carried on; and in case said assignment

(1) Mather vs. Bush, 16 Johns., 233; Hicks vs. Hotchkiss, 7 Johns. Ch., 742; Vanuxem vs. Hazelhurst, 1 Southard, (N. J.) 192; Norton vs. Cook, 9 Conn., 314; See, also, note to the above case, 23 Am. Decisions, 346.

shall embrace lands, or any interest therein, then the same shall also be recorded in the county or counties in which said land may be situated.(¹)

Where one partner transfers and delivers to another, all the assets of the firm, to collect the debts due the firm, and pay and discharge its liabilities, giving such managing partner all the powers possessed by both, for the purpose of settling the partnership affairs, and a division of proceeds after the payment of debts, this is not an assignment for the benefit of creditors of the firm, and will not prevent the partner taking the assignment, from securing one creditor to the prejudice of others.(²)

3. NOTICE TO CREDITORS TO PRESENT CLAIMS.—That the assignee or assignees named in such assignment, shall forthwith give notice thereof by publication in some newspaper published in the county, if any; and if none, then in the nearest county thereto, which publication shall be continued at least six weeks, and shall also forthwith send a notice thereof by mail to each creditor, of whom he or they shall be informed, directed to their usual place of residence, and notifying the creditors to present their claims under oath or affirmation to him within three months thereafter.(³)

4. ASSIGNEE TO FILE INVENTORY UNDER OATH—GIVE BOND TO PERFORM TRUST.—That the assignee or assignees shall also forthwith file with the clerk of the county court where such assignment shall be recorded, a true and full inventory and valuation of said estate, under oath or affirmation, so far as the same has come to his or their knowledge, and shall then and there enter into bonds to the People of the State of Illinois, for the use of the creditors, in double the amount of the inventory and valuation, with one or more sufficient sureties, to be approved by said clerk, and the said clerk shall give a receipt therefor, and the assignee or assignees may thereupon proceed to perform any duty necessary to carry into effect the intention of said assignment as respects the collection of debts and the sale of real or personal estate. Which said bond shall be taken in the name of the People of the State of Illinois, and the condition shall be as follows:

The condition of this obligation is such, that if the above bound.........,

(1) Hurd's R. S., Chap. 10*a*, § 1. (3) Hurd's R. S., Chap. 10*a*, § 2.
(2) Smith vs. Dennison, 101 Ill., 531.

assignee of........., shall, in all things, discharge his duty as assignee of........., aforesaid, and faithfully execute the trust confided to him, then the above obligation to be void, otherwise to remain in full force.(1)

Such an assignment, if valid, passes all the property, real and personal, which the debtor owns at the time to the assignee.(2)

5. REPORT OF CLAIMS AND LIST OF CREDITORS.—That at the expiration of three months from the time of first publishing notice as before provided, the assignee or assignees shall report and file with the clerk of the county court, as aforesaid, a true and full list, under oath or affirmation, of all such creditors of the assignor or assignors, as shall have claimed to be such, with a true statement of their respective claims, and also an affidavit of publication of notice, and a list of the creditors, with their places of residence and the date of mailing, to whom notice has been sent by mail, duly verified.(3)

6. HOW CLAIMS MAY BE CONTESTED—BOND FOR COSTS.—That any person interested as creditor or otherwise, by himself or attorney, may appear within thirty days after filing such report, and file with said clerk any exceptions to the claim or demand of any creditor's exhibit as aforesaid, and the clerk of said court upon such person, by himself or attorney, filing in said court, good and sufficient bond for cost, to be approved by the clerk, and executed in the same manner and to like effect in law as is now required in *qui tam* actions as provided in sections one and two of an act entitled, "An Act to Revise the Law in Relation to Costs," approved February 11, 1874, shall forthwith cause notice thereof to be given to the creditor, which shall be served as in case of an original notice in the county court, and shall be returnable at the next term of the county court in said county; and the said county court, shall, at the next term, proceed to hear the proofs and allegations of the parties in the premises, and shall render such judgment thereon as shall be just, and may allow a trial by jury thereon.(4)

7. DIVIDENDS—FINAL ACCOUNT AND SETTLEMENT—COMMISSIONS.—That at the first term of the said county court after the expiration of the three months, as aforesaid, should no exceptions

(1) Hurd's R. S., Chap. 10a, § 3.
(2) Freydendall vs. Baldwin, 103 Ill., 325.
(3) Hurd's R. S., Chap. 10a, § 4.
(4) Hurd's R. S., Chap. 10a, § 5.

be made to the claim of any creditor, or, if exceptions have been made, and the same have been adjudicated and settled by the court, the said court shall order the assignee or assignees, to make from time to time, fair and equal dividends (among the creditors) of the assets in his or their hands, in proportion to their claims, and as soon as may be, and within one year thereafter, to render a final account of said trust to said county court, and said court may allow such commissions and allowances to said assignee or assignees, in the final settlement, as may be considered by the court just and right.([1])

8. POWER OF COURT OVER ASSIGNEE.—That the assignee or assignees, in the execution of assignments, shall, at all times, be subject to the order and supervision of the county court, when in session, or the judge of said court, when not in session, and the said court or the said judge, may, by citation and attachment, compel the assignee or assignees from time to time, to file reports of his or their proceedings, and of the situation and condition of the trust, and to proceed in the faithful execution of the duties required by this act, and to obey the order of such court when in session, or the said judge, when not in session, in relation to the complete and final settlement, distribution and paying over of the proceeds derived from said trust or any part thereof, until a final settlement and distribution is made.([2])

The whole management of the estates of insolvent debtors, under voluntary assignments, is committed to the jurisdiction of county courts. How the trust funds, in the hands of the assignee, are to be paid over and distributed, are matters for the determination of the county court, where such proceedings are pending, and its judgments and orders in that respect, can only be reviewed as the judgments and decrees of other courts of competent and original jurisdiction are reviewable by appellate courts. In supervising the administration of these estates, this court will determine the priority of creditors claiming to have judgment or execution liens against the property of the assignor, as well as all other questions that may arise, during the period of its administration. This jurisdiction being given by statute to the county court, a court of equity can

---

(1) Hurd's R. S., Chap. 10*a*, § 6.   (2) Hurd's R. S., Chap. 10*a*, § 7.

not, in any manner, interfere with the estate while it is being administered by that court.(¹)

9. WANT OF LIST OR INVENTORY NOT TO VOID ASSIGNMENT.—That no assignment shall be declared fraudulent or void for want of any list or inventory, as provided in the first section of this act. The county court of the county may, upon application of the assignee or assignees, or any creditor, compel the appearance in person of the debtor or debtors before such court, by citation returnable forthwith, or at the next term thereof, and by attachment to answer, under oath, such matters as may then and there be inquired of him, her or them; and such debtor or debtors may then and there be fully examined under oath, as to the amount and situation of his, her or their estate, and the names of the creditors, and amounts due to each, with their places of residence; and may compel the delivery to the assignee or assignees, of any property or estate embraced in the assignment.(²)

10. WHEN ADDITIONAL INVENTORY AND BOND.—That the assignee or assignees, shall, from time to time, file with the clerk of the county court, an additional inventory and valuation of any additional property or estate, which may come into his or their hands under said assignment, after the filing of the first inventory, and the clerk may thereupon require additional security by bond, as upon the filing a first inventory.(³)

11. WHEN CLAIM NOT DUE—LIMITATION.—That any creditor may claim debts to become due as well as debts due, but on debts not due, a reasonable abatement shall be made when the same are not drawing interest, and all creditors who shall not exhibit his, her or their claim within the term of three months from the publication of notice as aforesaid, shall not participate in the dividends until after the payment in full of all claims presented within said term, and allowed by the county court.(⁴)

12. POWER OF ASSIGNEE TO SELL PROPERTY, COLLECT DEBTS, ETC.—That any assignee or assignees as aforesaid, shall have as full power and authority to dispose of all estate, real and personal, assigned, as the debtor or debtors had at the time of the assignment,

(1) Freydendall vs. Baldwin, 103 Ill., 325.
(2) Hurd's R. S., Chap. 10a, § 8.
(3) Hurd's R. S., Chap. 10a, § 9.
(4) Hurd's R S., Chap. 10a, § 10.

and to sue for and recover in the name of such assignee or assignees, every thing belonging or appertaining to said estate, real or personal, and generally to act and do whatsoever the said debtor or debtors might have done in the premises; but no sale of any real estate belonging to said trust, shall be made only on notice published as in case of sales of real estate on execution, unless the county court shall order and direct otherwise.(¹)

13. DEATH OR FAILURE OF ASSIGNEE TO ACT—COURT TO APPOINT A SUCCESSOR—REMOVAL—BOND.—That in case any assignee shall die before the closing of his trust, or in case any assignee shall fail or neglect for the period of twenty days after the making of any assignment, to file any inventory and valuation, and give bonds as required by this act, it shall be the duty of the county judge of the county where such assignment may be recorded, on the application of any person interested as creditor or otherwise, to appoint some one or more discreet and qualified person or persons to execute the trust embraced in such assignment; and such person or persons on giving bond with sureties as required of the assignee or assignees named in such assignment, shall possess all the powers thereby, and by this act conferred upon such assignee or assignees, and shall be subject to all the duties hereby imposed, as fully as though he or they are named in the assignment, and in case any security shall be discovered to be insufficient, or on complaint before the county court, it shall be made to appear that any assignee or assignees, are guilty of wasting or misapplying the trust estate, said county court may direct and require the giving additional security, and may remove such assignee or assignees, and may appoint others in their stead to fulfill the duties of said trust; and such person, so appointed, on giving bond, shall have full power to execute such duties, and to demand, and sue for all the estate in the hands of the person or persons removed, and to demand and recover the amount and value of all moneys and property or estate so wasted and misapplied, which he or they may neglect or refuse to make satisfaction for, from such person or persons, and his or their sureties.(²)

14. PREFERENCES VOID.—Every provision in any assignment

---

(1) Hurd's R. S., Chap. 10a, § 11. (2) Hurd's R. S., Chap. 10a, § 12.

hereafter made in this state, providing for the payment of one debt or liability in preference to another, shall be void, and all debts and liabilities within the provisions of the assignment, shall be paid *pro rata* from the assets thereof.(¹)

15. JURISDICTION OF COUNTY COURTS.—Full authority and jurisdiction is hereby conferred upon county courts and the judges thereof, to execute and carry out the provisions of this act, and said courts shall be and remain open at all times for the transaction of business, under this act.(²)

16. DISCONTINUANCE OF PROCEEDINGS.—All proceedings under the act of which this is amendatory, may be discontinued upon the assent, in writing, of such debtor, and a majority of his creditors in number and amount; and in such case, all parties shall be remitted to the same rights and duties existing at the date of the assignment, except so far as such estate shall have already been administered and disposed of; and the court shall have power to make all needful orders to carry the foregoing provision into effect.(³)

17. FORMS.—The date of this act is so recent, that it has not yet become the subject of judicial construction to any considerable extent. No statutory forms have been provided for the proceedings under the act, and thus far each one has used such forms as his own skill could construct. The following forms meet all the requirements of the act:

FORM FOR DEED OF ASSIGNMENT.

Know all men by these presents: That I, ..., of the county of.........., in the State of Illinois, in consideration of one dollar to me paid by.........., of the same county and state, the receipt whereof I hereby acknowledge, and of the uses, purposes and trusts hereinafter mentioned, have granted, bargained, sold, assigned, transferred and set over, and by these presents, do grant, bargain, sell, assign and set over, to the said.........., and to his successors in trust, all my lands, tenements and hereditaments, goods, chattels and effects, and all accounts, debts and demands due, owing or belonging to me, together with all securities for the same, which said lands, goods, chattels, debts and demands, are particularly enumerated and described in the schedules hereto annexed, marked "Schedule A" and "Schedule B." To have and to hold the same to the said.........., and to his successors in trust, should any be appointed; in trust, nevertheless, that the said..........shall forthwith take possession of the premises, estate and property hereby assigned, and file an inventory thereof, with the clerk of the

(1) Hurd's R. S., Chap. 10*a*, § 13. (3) Hurd's R. S., Chap. 10*a*, § 15.
(2) Hurd's R. S., Chap. 10*a*, § 14.

county court of.........county, in the State of Illinois, and with all reasonable diligence, sell and dispose of the same, for the benefit and use of the creditors of the said........., the grantor, under the order and direction of the county court of the said county of........., and of the judge of said court, and in conformity with the statute of the State of Illinois, concerning voluntary assignments.

In witness whereof, the said.........has hereunto set his hand and affixed his seal, this...day of......, A. D. 18...

........., [Seal.]

STATE OF ILLINOIS, } ss.
.............County,

I, ..., in and for the said county, in the state aforesaid, do hereby certify that........., who...personally known to me to be the same person.. whose name...subscribed to the foregoing instrument, appeared before me this day in person, and acknowledged that..he..signed, sealed and delivered the said instrument as...free and voluntary act, for the uses and purposes therein set forth.

Given under my hand and......seal, this...day of......, A. D. 18...

........., Clerk of the County Court.

It has been usual to insert in the deed of assignment a power of attorney to the assignee. Under the statute this is not necessary, as the statute confers upon the assignee, acting under the order of the county court, or the judge thereof, all the power necessary.

SCHEDULE "A."—INVENTORY OF THE ESTATE OF ASSIGNOR.

STATE OF ILLINOIS, } ss.
...............County,

Inventory and Valuation of the Estate of........., Assignor, as the same existed on the...day of......, A. D. 18...

REAL ESTATE.	
Description.	Value.

CHATTEL PROPERTY.	
Articles.	Value.

CH. XVIII.] ASSIGNMENT FOR BENEFIT OF CREDITORS. 437

NOTES, ACCOUNTS, AND CHOSES IN ACTION.					
From Whom Due.	*Date.*	*Interest.*	*Principal.*	*Amount.*

Cash on hand,..$...........
Amount of Real Estate brought forward,..................................... ....
Amount of Chattel Property brought forward,.............................. ....
Amount of Notes, &c.,.. ....
   Total Value of Estate,..$...........

STATE OF ILLINOIS, }
..................County, } *ss.*

   ...., the above named assignor, being first duly sworn, on oath deposes and says, that the above and foregoing schedule embraces all of his property, real and personal, as well as all notes, accounts, cash on hand and evidences of indebtedness, and that the values therein placed upon the above named property, are true and just valuations, according to his best knowledge and judgment.

                                             ...., Assignor.

   Subscribed and sworn to before me, this...day of......, A. D. 18....
                                               ...., County Clerk.

SCHEDULE "B."—LIST OF CREDITORS OF THE ASSIGNOR.

List of Creditors of........., the grantor in the assignment, hereto attached, with their residence and place of business, so far as known, and the amount of their respective demands:

Names.	Residence and Place of Business.	Demand.

STATE OF ILLINOIS, }
. ...County, } *ss.*

   ...., the assignor, being duly sworn, on his oath, states that the foregoing is a true list of all his creditors, with the residences and place of business of each of them, and the amount of their respective demands, to the best of his present knowledge, information and belief.

                                             ...., Assignor.

   Subscribed and sworn to before me, this...day of......, A. D. 18...
                                               ...., County Clerk.

The name of a person being included in the list of creditors, in making a deed of assignment, as a creditor, the assignor will be estopped from afterwards denying that he is a creditor; and in like manner will other creditors be estopped by such statement, from denying he is a creditor, unless it can be shown that such statement was falsely made for the purpose of defrauding the other creditors, or reducing their *pro rata* share.(¹)

18. INVENTORY TO BE FILED.—The first duty of the assignee is to file with the clerk of the county court where the assignment is recorded, a full inventory and valuation of the estate assigned to him, in form as follows:

STATE OF ILLINOIS, } ss.
....................County,

In the Matter of the Assignment of..........

The following is a true, full and perfect inventory of all the real and personal estate of the said.........., so far as the same has come to the knowledge of the undersigned,..........assignee of said..........:

Description of Real Estate.	Value.

No.	Chattel Property.	Value.

Cash on hand..$..............

NOTES AND ACCOUNTS.						
No.	Name of Debtor.	Date of Note or Acc't.	Am't.	Accrued Interest.	Good. D'btful or Desperate.	Total.

Total amount of Personal Estate,...$..............

STATE OF ILLINOIS, } ss.
....................County,

.........., assignee, as aforesaid, being duly sworn, deposes and says, that the above is a true and full inventory of all the real and personal estate

(1) McCracken vs. Milhous, 7 Bradwell, 169.

of.........., so far as the same has come to....knowledge, and that....believes the foregoing to be a fair and just valuation of the same.

.........., Assignee of..........

Subscribed and sworn to before me, this...day of......, A. D. 18...

.........., Clerk of the County Court.

Having filed his inventory in the county court, the assignee is required then and there to enter into bond to the People of the State of Illinois, for the use of the creditors, in double the amount of the value of the property inventoried, with one or more sufficient securities, to be approved by the clerk.

ASSIGNEE'S BOND.

Know all men by these presents, that we,.........., of the county of.........., and State of Illinois, are held and firmly bound unto the People of the State of Illinois, for the use of the creditors of.........., in the penal sum of......dollars, current money of the United States, which payment, well and truly to be made and performed, we, and each of us, do hereby bind ourselves, our heirs, executors and administrators, jointly, severally and firmly, by these presents.

Witness our hands and seals, this...day of......, A. D. 18...

The condition of this obligation is such, that if the above bounden,.........., assignee of.........., shall in all things discharge his duty as assignee of.......... aforesaid, and faithfully execute the trust confided to him, then the above obligation shall be void; otherwise to remain in full force and virtue.

.........., [Seal.]
.........., [Seal.]
.........., [Seal.]

STATE OF ILLINOIS, }
................County, } ss.

I,.........., do hereby certify that.........., personally known to me to be the same persons whose names are subscribed to the foregoing instrument, appeared before me this day in person, and acknowledged that they signed, sealed and delivered the said instrument as their free and voluntary act, for the uses and purposes therein set forth. Given under my hand and...... seal, this....day of......, A. D. 18....

[Seal.] ...., Clerk of the County Court.

Having executed his bond, and the clerk having endorsed thereon an approval of the same, the assignee is authorized to perform any and all duties necessary to carry into effect the assignment, as respects the collection of debts, and the sale of real and personal estate.

19. NOTICE TO CREDITORS—FORM.—The assignee should forth-

with give notice of his appointment and qualification in some newspaper published in the county, and if there is no newspaper published in the county, then in the nearest county thereto. This publication must be continued for six weeks. He is also required to send a copy of such notice by mail to each creditor of whom he shall be informed, directed to their usual place of residence. The notice may be in form as follows:

Notice is hereby given, that the undersigned ha..been appointed assignee of.........., and all persons holding any claim or claims against said........., are hereby notified to present the same to me under oath or affirmation, within three months from this date, whether said claims are due or not. All persons indebted to said assignor..are requested to make prompt payment of the same. Dated this.....day of......... A. D. 18....

.........., Assignee.

AFFIDAVIT—PUBLICATION IN ASSIGNMENT.

STATE OF ILLINOIS, } ss.
...............County,

..........being duly sworn, on oath depose and say, that on the...day of......, A. D. 18..., ..he..caused to be published in the.........., a newspaper published in said county of..........., a notice, of which the annexed is a true copy. That the first publication thereof was made on the...day of......, A. D. 18..., and said publication was continued for six consecutive weeks, the last publication having been made on the...day of......, A. D. 18...

....
....

Subscribed and sworn to before me, this...day of:......, A. D. 18...
.........., Clerk of the County Court.

Annex a copy of the notice published, and file with the clerk.

20. LIST OF CREDITORS.—At the expiration of three months from the first publication of this notice, the assignee is required to file with the clerk of the county court, a true and full list, upon oath or affirmation, of all persons who have claimed to be creditors of the assignor, with a true statement of their respective claims. He must also file an affidavit of the publication of the notice to creditors, and a list of the creditors, with their places of residence, and the date of mailing, to whom notice has been sent by mail. This also must be verified by oath or affirmation. The following are the forms to be used:

STATE OF ILLINOIS, } ss.
................County, }

In the Matter of the Assignment of............

List of Persons who have claimed to be Creditors of the said........., Assignor.., and a Statement of their respective Claims:

Name.	Nature of Claim.	Amount.

.........., Assignee.

STATE OF ILLINOIS, } ss.
................County, }

.........., Assignee of........., being duly sworn, on oath depose.. and say.. that the foregoing is a true and full list of all persons who have claimed to be creditors of said........., assignor, together with a true statement of their respective claims.

.........., Assignee.

Subscribed and sworn to before me, this...day of......, A. D. 18...

.........., County Clerk.

The form following contains a list of creditors of the assignor notified by mail, which should also be filed with the clerk :

ASSIGNEE'S LIST OF CREDITORS NOTIFIED BY MAIL.

In the Matter of the Assignment of.........

List of Creditors of the said........., to whom notices have been sent by mail by........., Assignee, together with the places of residence of said Creditors, and the date of mailing such notice:

Name.	Residence.	Date of Mailing Notice.

.........., Assignee.

STATE OF ILLINOIS, } ss.
................County. }

.........., assignee of........., being duly sworn, on oath depose..and say.. that the foregoing is a true and full list of all creditors of said.........to whom notices have been sent by mail, together with their places of residence and date of mailing of said notices; and affiant..further say..that the said notices so sent, notified said creditors to present their claims to.........within three months, and that the postage on said notices was prepaid. Affiant further say..that the said.........list contains the names and residence of all the creditors of the said........., of whom affiant has been informed.

....
....

Subscribed and sworn to before me, this...day of......, A. D. 18...

........., County Clerk.

21. MANNER OF PRESENTING CLAIMS.—Claims should be presented to the assignee, verified by the oath of the claimant. A copy of the note or account which constitutes the basis of the claim, should be attached to the affidavit, which may be in form as follows:

STATE OF ILLINOIS, } ss.   *In the County Court of.........County,*
...............County.   ......*Term, A. D.* 18...

In the Matter of........., Insolvent.   ...., Assignee.

Claim of........., ...being duly sworn, says that the demand of the said.........against the above named insolvent, a copy of which is hereto attached, is for.........[*Here state the nature of the demand*], and that there is due to the said.........from the said insolvent, after allowing to...all payments, deductions and offsets,......dollars. Deponent further says, that the said claimant......resident of said.........county.

........., Attorney.   ....

Subscribed and sworn to before me, this...day of......, A. D. 18...

........., County Clerk.

22. EXCEPTIONS TO CLAIMS.—Any person interested as a creditor or otherwise, at any time within thirty days after the report of the assignee is filed, may file exceptions to the claim or demand of any creditor, and upon giving a bond for costs, the same as in *qui tam* actions, the clerk is required to cause notice thereof to be given to the creditor, which shall be served as in case of an original notice in the county court. This notice is returnable to the next term of the county court, when the exceptions shall be tried either by the court or a jury.

EXCEPTIONS TO A CLAIM.

STATE OF ILLINOIS, } ss.   *In the County Court,*
...............County.   *To the......Term, A. D.* 18 ..

In the Matter of........., Assignee of.........

Exceptions of........., a Creditor of the said........., Assignor, to the Claim of........., filed with said assignee and included in his report to this court.

First Exception:—For that said claim is not founded upon any consideration good and sufficient in law.

Second Exception.—[*Here insert all the grounds of exception.*] Wherefore the said........., does except to the said claim and demand, and prays that such exceptions may be heard and determined by the court in pursuance of the statute in such case made and provided.

By........., Attorney.

NOTICE TO CREDITOR OF EXCEPTIONS.

STATE OF ILLINOIS. }
................County. } ss.

In the County Court,
...... *Term, A. D.* 18...

To........,
............: You are hereby notified that.........has filed exceptions to your claim against........., presented by you to........., assignee of the said........., and that such exceptions have been set for a hearing at a term of our said county court, to be begun and holden at the court house, in........., in said county of........., on the....Monday of......, A. D. 18...

Now, unless you shall then and there appear and defend against such exceptions, the same will be heard and determined by the court in your absence. Given under my hand and the seal of said court, this...day of......, A. D. 18....

[Seal.]
........., Clerk County Court.

This notice is required to be "served as in case of an original notice in the county court." The meaning of this statute is not clear. It is copied from section 2121, of the Iowa code, with the words, "in the county court,'" added. It is reasonable to conclude that the service should be made in the same manner as notices are served upon creditors by the assignee, that is by publication and by mail. Any personal service would be sufficient, and if the creditor resides within the state, it would be safe practice, to have the notice served by a sheriff by reading and delivering a copy of the notice to the creditor.

23. ORDER OF DISTRIBUTION.—Should there be no exceptions to the report of the assignee, or if there are exceptions, as soon as the same are settled and adjudicated, the court should order the money in the hands of the assignee to be paid out equally among the creditors, who have proven their claims, and should require the assignee to render a final account of his trust in one year thereafter. The assignee is at all times, subject to the order and supervision of the county court, when in session, and of the county judge, when not in session. The court has complete jurisdiction of the subject, and has power to compel the attendance of the debtor, for the purpose of compelling him to answer under oath, all such matters as may be required of him; and may, by attachment, compel the delivery to the assignee of any property or estate embraced in the

assignment. No preference can be given to one creditor over another. Every provision of any assignment having that effect, is void.([1])

Provision is made for carrying out the trusts of the assignment in case of death of the assignee, or of his refusal to act. The act is so full as to leave but little to construction, and all persons who may become interested in any assignment, must necessarily consult and be governed by the provisions of the statute.

24. REPORT OF ASSIGNEE.—The report of the assignee is similar to the report of a guardian. It is simply an exhibit of the amount of moneys received and amount paid out, showing the court the remainder, if any, in his hands for distribution among creditors.

The form of an assignee's report may be as follows:

STATE OF ILLINOIS, } ss.   *In the County Court,*
............County.   *To the......term, A. D. 18...*

To the Hon.........., Judge of the County Court of said County:

The undersigned, by appointment assignee of the estate of.........., assignor, would respectfully report his acts and doings as such assignee, from his appointment to the....day of......., A. D. 18...

He charges himself as follows, to-wit:

To amount of cash on hand at the time of said assignment,.........$..............
To amount realized from the sale of the real estate of said assignor, heretofore reported as sold to...................... ....
To amount realized from the sale of chattel property, of said as- ....
    signor, heretofore reported to the court,............... ....
To amount realized from the collection of the notes and accounts
    belonging to said assignor, as follows:
From note of... ....
From account of... ....
    (*Giving in detail all the amounts received from any source.*)
He asks to be credited as follows:
By commissions to Assignee,.......................................$..............
By paid A. & B., Attorney's fees,................................... ....
By paid.........., Assignor, amount allowed as exempt, ...
By paid C. D., Clerk's fees,.. ....

RECAPITULATION.

Total amount Received,......................................$..............
Total amount Paid Out,...................................... ....
Balance in the hands of the Assignee for distribution,... ....$..........

(1) Section 14, *ante.*

And your petitioner would respectfully ask that this his report may be approved, and he ordered to pay out the balance found remaining in his hands to the creditors entitled to the same, and be discharged upon filing their receipts for the same.

By..........., Attorney. ...., Assignee.

Subscribed and sworn to before me, this...d>v of......, A. D. 18...

... ., County Clerk.

25. ASSIGNMENT—WHO MAY MAKE.—A debtor may make an assignment for the benefit of his creditors, and, if fairly done, it passes the title to his property to the assignee. The question of fairness of the transaction, is one of fact for the finding of a jury: and whether certain facts would have the legal effect of an abandonment of an assignment, may or may not be conclusive. They should be accompanied with an intention to abandon, and that intention should be left to the jury for decision.[1]

The power to make an assignment exists independent of statutory provisions, yet it may be affected or modified by such provisions.[2]

One partner can not make a general assignment for the benefit of creditors of the firm, except in the absence of the other partners, or when for some valid reason there can be no consultation had.[3]

Corporations are in law, for civil purposes, deemed persons, and may make assignments for the benefit of creditors.[4]

An assignment which covers only personal property, need not be recorded, if possession accompanies the assignment.[5]

26. DEED OF ASSIGNMENT—CONSTRUCTION TO BE GIVEN TO.— The covenant of the assignor to the assignee, in the first part of the deed, that the assignee shall not be held liable to the assignor, except for actual receipts and willful defaults, when construed in connection with the covenant of the assignee in the last part of the deed to all the parties interested, that he will faithfully execute the trusts, does not invalidate the assignment.[6] An assignment, like any other instrument in writing, should be so construed as to render it legal and operative, rather than illegal and void,[7] and

---

(1) Wilson vs. Pearson, 20 Ill., 81; Myers vs. Kinzie, 26 Ill., 36.
(2) Dehner vs. Helmbacher Forge and Rolling Mills, 7 Bradwell, 47.
(3) Lieb vs. Pierpont, (Sup. Court of Iowa, June 1882) 14 Reporter, 77.
(4) Shockley vs. Fisher, (Sup. Court of Miss., March 1882) 14 Reporter, 89.
(5) Wilson vs. Pearson, *supra*.
(6) Grover vs. Wakeman, 11 Wend, (N. Y.) 187; Brigham vs. Tillinghast, 15 Barb., (N. Y.) 618; jacobs vs. Allen, 18 Barb., (N. Y.) 549.
(7) Grover vs. Wakeman, *supra*; Brigham vs. Tillinghast, *supra*.

whenever the law will imply a discretion, a discretion may be given in the assignment.([1])

A clause in a deed of assignment, that the assignee covenants and agrees to execute the trust faithfully, according to the stipulations therein contained, being responsible only for his actual receipts and willful defaults, makes the deed fraudulent and void.([2]) But where the deed of assignment contained a clause providing that the assignees should be responsible only for their actual benefits and willful or neglectful defaults, it was held, that this language only expressed the legal liability of the assignees, and did not invalidate the deed.([3])

A clause in an assignment which provides that any surplus remaining, after the claims of the creditors have been satisfied, shall be paid over to the assignor, does not invalidate the assignment.([4])

The validity of a deed of assignment of property, although executed in another state, so far as it attempts to convey real estate situate in this state, must be determined by laws of this state.([5])

An assignor has no power to change the terms and conditions of the assignment after he has made it, without the consent of the assignee and the creditors.([6])

A deed of assignment, which purports to include all creditors and make provisions for them, embraces all the individual creditors of the assignor, even should some names be omitted in the schedule subsequently filed.([7])

A verbal assignment of both real and personal property, is invalid under the statute of frauds.([8])

When an assignment is made, the assignee of the assignors is simply a trustee, for the purpose of converting their estate into money and paying the proceeds out to the creditors.([9])

(1) Sackett vs. Mansfield, 26 Ill., 21.
(2) McIntyre vs. Benson, 20 Ill., 500; Robinson vs. Nye, 21 Ill., 592; Finlay vs. Dickerson, 29 Ill., 9.
(3) Whipple vs. Pope, 33 Ill., 334.
(4) Conkling vs. Carson, 11 Ill., 503; Finlay vs. Dikerson, *supra*.
(5) Gardner vs. Commercial Nat'l Bank of Providence, 95 Ill., 298.
(6) Union Nat'l Bank of Chicago vs. Bank of Commerce, St. Louis, 94 Ill., 271.
(7) *Ib.*
(8) Lill vs. Brant, 6 Bradwell, 366.
(9) McCracken vs. Milhous, 7 Bradwell, 169.

27. WHAT FRAUDULENT AND VOID.—A clause in a voluntary assignment by failing debtors for the benefit of creditors, made to an attorney at law as assignee to pay himself commissions as assignee, and also counsel fees as an attorney, is in fraud of the creditors, as it places the assignee in a double position, and tends directly to the wasting of the trust fund.(1) So, too, a clause in an assignment for the benefit of creditors, authorizing the assignees to sell the assigned property on credit, renders it fraudulent and void as against creditors, as tending to hinder and delay them;(2) although such a clause is good as between the assignor and assignee.(3) And a clause, in a general assignment for the benefit of creditors, authorizing the trustee to compound with creditors, makes void the assignment.(4)

An assignment for benefit of creditors to an assignee who is known to be insolvent at the time, is *prima facie*, but not conclusive evidence of a fraudulent intent, but may be refuted by circumstances, as by showing consent of creditors.(5)

A voluntary deed of assignment for the benefit of creditors, containing authority to the assignee, to sell and dispose of the property with all convenient diligence at public or private sale, as he may deem most beneficial to the interests of the creditors, and with all reasonable dispatch to collect the debts assigned, is not therefore fraudulent and void as to creditors,(6) no discretion being given to such a clause but such as the law would imply.(7)

The employment of the debtor to assist in the settlement of the business after assignment made by the assignor to the assignee, is not a badge of fraud. Nor is the appropriation to the general fund of goods purchased in contemplation of an assignment, where the right of stoppage in transitue was not exercised by the seller, a badge of fraud. Fraud on the part of a debtor in making an assignment must be proved, and as there is no rule of law requiring

(1) Heacock vs. Durand, 42 Ill., 230.
(2) Bowen vs. Parkhurst, 24 Ill., 257; Pierce vs. Brewster, 32 Ill., 268; Whipple vs. Pope, 33 Ill., 334; Gardner vs. Commercial Nat'l Bank of Providence, 95 Ill., 298.
(3) Chickering vs. Raymond, 15 Ill., 362.
(4) Hudson vs. Maze, 3 Scam., 578.
(5) Reed vs. Emery, 8 Paige's Ch., 417.
(6) Sackett vs. Mansfield, 26 Ill., 21; Finlay vs. Dickerson, 29 Ill., 9; Pierce vs. Brewster, *supra;* Whipple vs. Pope, *supra*.
(7) Finlay vs. Dickerson, *supra*.

a debtor to give notice of his failure, the simple fact that purchases are made on credit, when the debtor knows that he is unable at the time to pay his debts, does not necessarily render such purchases fraudulent.(1)

The question of fraud being a question of fact, the verdict of a jury, as to the good faith of an assignment, will not be disturbed, unless the proof shows clearly that the assignment was fraudulent.(2) Where partnership property is appropriated to the payment of individual debts by deed of assignment by an insolvent firm, such assignment is fraudulent and void as to the firm creditors.(3) The fact of an injudicious selection of an assignee, nor his lack of pecuniary responsibility, is not conclusive evidence of fraud.(4)

Where an assignment is made without any preference, or indication of fraudulent intent, a few days before the recovery of a judgment against the assignor, it will be sustained, and pass the title to the assignee, and he may maintain replevin for the same as against the sheriff levying an execution upon the same.(5)

Where an assignment is made for the purpose of paying a particular debt, the balance of the proceeds to be returned to the debtor, it is fraudulent and void, because of the reservation to the debtor, and as hindering and delaying creditors.(6)

So, an assignment for the benefit of creditors, which requires creditors to release the assignor from all liability before receiving any benefit under the deed, with a further provision that after paying in full the creditors who should release the assignor, the creditors who should not release him, should be paid *pro rata*, is fraudulent and void.(7)

28. SUBSEQUENT ADDITIONAL AGREEMENT.—A deed of assign-

---

(1) Blow vs. Gage, 44 Ill., 208; but see, further, Schweizer vs. Tracy, 76 Ill., 345.
(2) Wilson vs. Pearson, 20 Ill., 81; Clark vs. Groom, 24 Ill., 316; Nimmo vs. Kuykendall, 85 Ill., 476.
(3) Keith vs. Funk, 47 Ill., 272; Wilson vs. Robertson, 21 N. Y., 587; Lester vs. Abbott, 28 How., (N. Y. Pr.) 488.
(4) Clark vs. Groom, *supra*.
(5) Nimmo vs. Kuykendall, *supra*.
(6) Lill vs. Brant, 6 Bradwell, 366; Selz, Schwab & Co. vs. Evans, 6 Bradwell, 466.
(7) Hubbard vs. McNaughton, 43 Mich., 220; Duggan vs. Bliss, 4 Col., 223; Grover vs. Wakeman, 11 Wend., (N. Y.) 187; *Contra*, see Clayton vs. Johnson, 36 Ark., 40, and cases there cited (38 Am. Rep., 40.)

ment being voidable only at the instance of judgment creditors of the assignor, may be made good by matter *ex post facto;* and when an assignment is so modified and changed as to divest it of its objectionable features, by consent of all parties thereto, prior to the time that any of the creditors are in a position to attack the original assignment, it must stand, and the rights of creditors must be governed by it.([1]) But a subsequent additional agreement to a deed of assignment, to be valid, must be with the consent of all parties to the instrument.([2])

29. PREFERENCE OF CREDITOR.—It has been held that a debtor may prefer one creditor, pay him fully, and thus exhaust his whole property, leaving nothing for others equally meritorious. He may also partially pay a portion of his creditors, and neglect others, and the law will not disturb such disposition of his property.([3]) But, since the passage of our statute, the same is expressly prohibited, and now, where an assignor makes an assignment for the benefit of his creditors, he can not make any preferences, even though they be ever so fairly and honestly made.([4])

A voluntary assignment is not vitiated because it delays creditors. It must appear to have been collusively designed so to do, and the intent is a question of fact. The good or bad faith of the transaction, stamps its character.([5])

The mere assent of a creditor that his debtor may make an assignment for the benefit of his creditors, does not have the effect to release the debt.([6])

Where a party has funds deposited with a banker, who holds the promissory note of the depositor, the latter may insist that his note shall be satisfied out of the deposit, although the banker, before the note became due, had voluntarily assigned all of his effects for the benefit of his creditors.([7])

Property, in the hands of an assignee for the purpose of paying

---

(1) Conkling vs. Carson, 11 Ill., 503.
(2) Ramsdell vs. Sigerson, 2 Gilm., 78; Murray vs. Riggs, 15 Johns., 571; Pierce vs. Brewster, 32 Ill., 268.
(3) Cross vs. Bryant, 2 Scam., 36; Howell vs. Edgar, 3 Scam., 417; Cooper vs. McClun, 16 Ill., 435; Gibson vs. Rees, 50 Ill., 383; Ramsdell vs. Sigerson, *supra;* Conkling vs. Carson, 11 Ill., 503; Blow vs. Gage, 44 Ill., 208.
(4) H. R. S., Chap. 10a, § 13; Lill vs. Bryant, 6 Bradwell, 366.
(5) Sackett vs. Mansfield, 26 Ill., 21.
(6) Howlett vs. Mills, 22 Ill., 341.
(7) McCagg vs. Woodman, 28 Ill., 84.

creditors, can not be reached by attachment or garnishee process.(¹) Nor can money due the defendant in attachment, after he has made an assignment for the benefit of his creditors, be reached by garnishment at the suit of an individual creditor.(²)

The law allows charges, costs, expenses and disbursements attending the execution of the trust, but requires them to be reasonable; and they are always subject to review by a court of equity.(³)

30. TRUSTEES—TRUST PROPERTY—RIGHTS OF CREDITORS.— Where a debtor makes an assignment of his property for the benefit of his creditors, preferring none of them, the creditors all become vested with an equitable lien on the property so assigned for the satisfaction of their debts in *pro rata* proportions; and the fraudulent acts of the trustees of the debtor of other creditors or strangers to the transaction, would not deprive them of the right to participate in the fund. That can only be done by the acts of the creditors on the judgment or decree of a court of competent jurisdiction, or the legal acts of the trustees; and while all the acts of trustees within the scope of their authority conferred by the deed, and within the duties imposed by law, bind the creditors, the debtors and themselves, the unauthorized acts do not, and they may be required to account for the misapplication of the fund or omission of duty. They are under no obligation to accept, but having done so, they must perform their duty in good faith to all parties in interest. Such trustees may control the fund and convert it into money in the mode prescribed; may sue for property or money, and the determination of the court in such cases binds them and the creditors; and a judgment against such trustees who have sued for property embraced in the assignment, is binding upon the trustees and creditors, unless it can be shown to have been the result of fraud and collusion, when it may be set aside and canceled in equity.(⁴)

Where an assignment is made to a claim of money then in suit, it is sufficient to pass all the interest of the debtor, and he can not

---

(1) Kimball vs. Mulhern, 15 Ill., 205; Lupton vs. Cutter, 8 Pick., 298; Gore vs. Clisby, 8 Pick., 555; Tucker vs. Clisby, 12 Pick., 22; Sandford vs. Bliss, 12 Pick., 116.
(2) Dehner vs. Helmbacher Forge and Rolling Mills, 7 Bradwell, 47.
(3) Blow vs. Gage, 44 Ill., 208.
(4) Field vs. Flanders, 40 Ill., 470.

apprropriate private proceeds differently, and if he does, he becomes liable in equity for its repayment to his creditors.(¹)

An assignee to pay debts, can not be sued at law by a creditor to recover his proportionate part of the estate, until a dividend has been declared, and then there must be either a refusal or neglect upon the part of the assignee to pay.(²)

The assignee of the partnership effects of an insolvent firm, has no power to bring suits against the partners of the firm for the purpose of securing debts due the firm, or in any other manner to enforce their payment, as his duty is confined to the distribution of the proceeds of the property assigned to him.(³)

(1) Nichols vs. Pool, 89 Ill., 491.
(2) Hexter vs. Loughry, 6 Bradwell, 362.
(3) Lund vs. The Skanes Ensklider Bank, 96 Ill., 181.

ADDITIONAL NOTES.

1. Definitions.
2. How made.
3. Notice to creditors to present claims.
4. Dividends, final accountings and settlements.
5. Power of county court over assignee.
6. Power of assignee to sell property, collect debts, etc.
7. Death or failure of assignee to act.
8. Preference of creditors void.
9. Preference of creditors—When permitted.
10. Jurisdiction of county court.
11. Jurisdiction of circuit court and court of chancery.
12. Partnership property assigned.
13. What assignments are fraudulent.
14. Compensation of assignee.
15. Appeal from county court.
16. Foreign assignments.

1. DEFINITIONS.—A voluntary assignment is an instrument in writing executed by a failing debtor, by which he assigns or transfers to some third person, as assignee or trustee, the whole, or sometimes the bulk, of his estate, to be by the trustee distributed among the assignor's creditors, in satisfaction of their demands. The act relating to voluntary assignments cannot, by construction, apply to any other subject than to voluntary assignments. It has nothing to do with chattel mortgages. A mortgage is a mere security for a debt, the equity of redemption remaining in the mortgagor, while an assignment is more than a security for a debt, and is an absolute appropriation of the property to its payment. It does not create a lien in the creditors, but passes both the legal and equitable title to the property, absolutely beyond the control of the assignor, and leaves no equity of redemption.([1])

2. HOW MADE.—As to a debtor and his creditors, an assignment takes effect at the time of the delivery of the deed to the assignee, and no lien attaches against such property because of an execution issued after that time, but before the recording of the deed by the assignee. Filing the deed of assignment for record gives notice of the

(1) Weber vs. Mick, 131 Ill., 520.

assignment, and gives the court jurisdiction of the subject-matter.(¹) The deed of assignment is to be recorded in the recorder's office of the proper county, and its record in the county court is not a necessary condition to the validity of the assignment, and the taking jurisdiction thereof by that court.(²)

A valid assignment can be made only under the statute, and when so made the estate must be administered and distributed substantially in conformity with its provisions.(³)

An assignment shall not be void for want of an inventory and list of creditors, and a conveyance of property in trust for the use of particular creditors, though the assignor does not annex an inventory or list of creditors, nor purport to convey all his property, is an assignment for the benefit of all his creditors. An assignment for the benefit of creditors gives the county court jurisdiction, although the instrument was not acknowledged or recorded.(⁴)

3. NOTICE TO CREDITORS.—It is the object of the statute to fix a time at which the estate of the assignor shall be placed in process of final settlement, and after which distributions may be made, without the risk of uncertainties arising from the allowance of subsequently-presented claims. The courts will give effect to the express language of the statute, making it apply to all creditors, and not merely to those who were known to the assignee, and to whom notice was mailed.(⁵)

4. DIVIDENDS, FINAL ACCOUNTINGS AND SETTLEMENTS.— Where the assignee of an insolvent debtor fails to make any dividend, or to render any account to the creditors of his acts and doings, or make settlement, the creditors may compel a settlement by bill in chancery(.⁶)

It is the duty of the assignee to keep an account of all money received and paid out by him. Where the assignee mixes the trust funds with his own, and neglects to settle his account, a decree in equity requiring him to pay interest is proper.(⁷) The assignee takes the estate in trust for the benefit of all the creditors, notwith-

(1) Myer, assignee, vs. Fales' Sons, & Co., 12 Ill. Ap., 351.
(2) Osborne vs. Williams, 34 Ill. Ap., 422.
(3) Milligan vs. O'Conor, 19 Ill. Ap., 487.
(4) Farwell vs. Cohen, 28 N. E. Reporter, 35.
(5) Suppiger vs. Seybt, Adm'r, 23 Ill. Ap., 468.
(6) Asay vs. Allen, 124 Ill., 391.
(7) *Id.*

standing some of the creditors may have their debt secured by deed of trust or otherwise; and such secured creditors are entitled to share equally with unsecured creditors, in all dividends, and should the property be encumbered the assignee will take subject to the incumbrance. He would take simply the equity of redemption. The mortgagee may foreclose his mortgage, or sue at law on the mortgage debt; and where the mortgagor makes a general assignment, the mortgagee may claim his dividend on his whole debt, out of the general assets of the estate assigned. The amount of the dividend should then be credited on the debt, and the mortgage be foreclosed for the balance.[1]

The assignee takes as a volunteer, and hence can have no greater right than the assignor.[2] The assignee should allow the creditor to prove his whole debt, without regard to any collateral security he may have; and if the dividend so reduces the whole debt that the collateral security will more than pay it, then the assignee must redeem for the benefit of other creditors.[3]

A creditor of an insolvent debtor, who has made a voluntary assignment for the benefit of creditors, by proving his debt against the estate, will not waive or lose his lien on the assigned property acquired by levy of an attachment before the assignment.[4]

5. POWERS OF COUNTY COURT OVER THE ASSIGNEE.—Where the property of an insolvent debtor, under a voluntary assignment, has passed into the hands of an assignee, the county court has ample power to direct and control the disposition of such property, and in so doing to adjudicate upon the conflicting legal rights of claimants therefor, arising in that court.[5]

The county court has power to determine what property has passed to the assignee, and the nature and extent of his interest therein under the assignment. It does not follow that the county court is given jurisdiction in cases of purely equitable nature, or that it may adjudicate on property not in possession or control of assignee.[6]

(1) *In re* Bates, 118 Ill., 524; O'Hara vs. Jones, 46 Ill., 288; Eames vs. Mayo, 6 Ill. Ap., 334.
(2) Hardin vs. Osborne, 94 Ill., 571; Jenkins vs. Pierce, 98 Ill., 646; *In re* Bates, *supra*.
(3) Paddock vs. Stout, 121 Ill., 571; Paddock vs. Bates, 19 Ill. Ap., 471; *In re* Bates, *supra*.
(4) Yates vs. Dodge, 123 Ill., 50.
(5) Preston vs. Spaulding, 120 Ill., 208.
(6) *Id.*

While the county court has power to direct the assignee in all matters pertaining to the estate, and to settle all controversies relating to the property in possession of the assignee, yet, if the assignee seeks to recover possession of property, he must resort to some court having jurisdiction of the appropriate remedy, and competent to afford adequate relief.(¹)

6. POWER OF ASSIGNEE TO SELL PROPERTY, COLLECT DEBTS, ETC.—The assignee, in cases of voluntary assignment for the benefit of creditors, is not the representative of the creditors, but the agent of the assignor for the distribution of the property, and the agreement with one creditor by the assignee will not bind another creditor(²). The assignee of an insolvent debtor, having due regard to the administration of the estate and to the rights of the creditors, may do whatever his assignor might have done, in respect to the assigned property. The assignee must act under the supervision and control of the county court, and may, under its direction, do whatever is necessary to make complete settlement and distribution of the trust estate.(³)

The assignee of an insolvent debtor takes the property assigned subject to all valid pre-existing liens; and where such property is subject to the lien of an execution issued upon judgment entered by confession, and such judgment is opened to let the defendant interpose a defense, the county court should wait until the defense is heard and decided before determining upon the lien of such execution.(⁴)

7. DEATH OR FAILURE OF ASSIGNEE TO ACT.—Where the assignee died before completing the trust of assignment, a creditor of the assignor holding a claim unpaid, which he had not probated against the assignee's estate, may maintain a bill in equity in the circuit court against the personal representatives of the assignee for an accounting and enforcement of the trust.(⁵)

8. PREFERENCE OF CREDITORS VOID.—The act in regard to assignments for the benefit of creditors does not attempt to regulate the conduct of creditors; its object is to regulate the conduct of the

---

(1) Davis vs. Chicago Dock Co., 129 Ill., 180.
(2) Hanford Oil Co. vs. First Nat. Bank, 126 Ill., 584.
(3) Davis vs. Chicago Dock Co., *supra*.
(4) Hier vs. Kaufman, 134 Ill., 215.
(5) Howell vs. Moores, 127 Ill., 67.

debtor, and make void preferences given by the assignor in the assignment of his estate. Creditors procuring security, or payment in good faith, are not affected by the act.(¹)

If a failing debtor gives notes to certain of his creditors for the debt actually due them and fifteen per cent. of the amount of the debt in addition, as attorney fees, with a power of attorney to confess judgment on the notes, including the attorney fees, as to the other creditors not preferred the attorney fees were a gift to the preferred creditors, and as to non-preferred creditors fraudulent and void. The normal obligation resting upon a debtor to see that his creditor gets all his money, without the deduction of fees, is a sufficient consideraiton for a contract between a solvent debtor and his creditor to have judgment confessed for a reasonable attorney fee, in addition to the debt, but this cannot be done to the prejudice of other equally meritorious creditors.(²)

After a debtor has made up his mind to make an assignment of his property for the benefit of creditors, all conveyances made in view of his intended general assignment, whereby any preference is given, will, in a court of equity, be declared void and set aside. And if a debtor, being aware of his hopeless insolvency, and having determined to make a disposition of his estate among his creditors, makes preferential payments and conveyances of his estate to relatives, in satisfaction of alleged indebtedness, and then, without solicitation, made and delivered judgment notes for the purpose of preferring certain other of his creditors, and then make a deed of assignment for the benefit of all of his creditors, such preference is void, and will be set aside in a suit by the creditors not preferred.(³)

9. PREFERENCE OF CREDITORS—WHEN PERMITTED.—The act relating to voluntary assignments does not interfere with the action of the debtor while he retains dominion of his property. He may in good faith sell his property, or mortgage or pledge it to secure a *bona fide* debt, or create a lien upon it by confession of a judgment in favor of a *bona fide* creditor.(⁴) The act in regard to voluntary

---

(1) Preston vs. Spaulding, 120 Ill., 208.
(2) Hulse vs. Mershon, 125 Ill., 52.
(3) Hanford Oil Co. vs. First Nat. Bank, 126 Ill., 584; Hide and Leather Nat. Bank vs. Rahm, 126 Ill., 461; Preston vs. Spaulding, *supra;* Heuer vs. Schaffner, 30 Ill. Ap., 337.
(4) Hanford Oil Co. vs. First Nat. Bank, *supra;* Preston vs. Spaulding, *supra;* Farwell vs. Nillson, 35 Ill. Ap., 164; Field vs. Geoghan, 125 Ill., 68.

assignments does not prohibit preferences among creditors generally, but only preferences in the assignment. It is not preference of a creditor itself that the statute condemns, as the act regulates the conduct of the assignment, not that of the assignor.(1)

Before the debtor has determined to make a general assignment, he may, in good faith, sell or mortgage any part of his property, or give warrants of attorney for the confession of judgments, and the transaction will be valid. But after he has determined to make a general assignment he can do no act preferring any creditor. To allow this would be to permit a fraudulent evasion of the statute. The creditor, if he does not know that the debtor has determined to make an assignment, may take from him a mortgage or other security for his debt and enforce the same, and the subsequent assignment by the debtor will not affect such security. The law gives the creditor the advantage he may secure by his superior diligence, when he is guilty of no fraud or collusion to evade the statute.(2)

The statute relating to voluntary assignments does not prohibit the debtor from giving his creditor a judgment note or other security, unless it is made after he has made up his mind to assign, with a view thereby to give a preference, in fraud of the act. If the debtor has no intention of ceasing business when he gives a judgment note or other security, and expects to continue in business, such security will be valid and binding.(3) To render a lien acquired by confession of judgment and the issue of execution before the making of a general assignment fraudulent, it must appear, first, that at the time the judgment was entered, execution issued and levy made, the debtor had made up his mind to make an assignment; and, second, that he had some agency in bringing about the entry of the judgment. When the lien of the execution is apparently superior to the assignment, the burden will rest upon the party seeking to defeat such lien to establish both of the foregoing propositions.(4)

JURISDICTION OF COUNTY COURT.—When a voluntary assignment is made under the statute, and the property has passed into the hands of the assignee, the property is thereby brought under the

---

(1) Farwell vs. Nillson, 35 Ill. Ap., 164.
(2) The Home Nat. Bank of Chicago vs. Sanchez & Haya, 131 Ill., 330.
(3) Hier vs. Kaufman, 134 Ill., 215; Hulse vs. Mershon, 125 Ill., 52.
(4) Hanford vs. Prouty, 133 Ill., 339; Hulse vs. Mershon, *supra*.

control of the county court, and that court is vested with ample power to make all orders in respect thereof necessary to the distribution under the law, and to that end to adjudicate upon and determine the conflicting rights of claimants thereto. The county court has power to determine whether certain executions have or have not prior liens, and entitled to be first paid out of the debtor's estate.[1]

The county court cannot be required to wait and try and determine intricate and conflicting claims on property before authorizing the assignee to sell whatever interest the estate possesses therein. What to order the assignee to dispose of is within the discretion of the county court.[2] The county court is invested with full power to control the trust fund and the assignee until the property is disposed of and the proceeds distributed to those entitled to share therein, and has power to determine the priority of the liens of the several creditors.[3] Where the assignee has been appointed and is proceeding to execute the trust, under the supervision of the county court, another person claiming to own part of the property assigned cannot bring an action of replevin therefor. The county court has exclusive jurisdiction, and all conflicting claims should be settled thereby.[4] The county court is not a court of equity for the disposition of all incidental disputes between creditors of insolvents and third persons, growing out of antagonistic claims of dividends.[5]

When the voluntary assignment is properly made, and the assignee accepts the trust and takes possession of the property, the county court will have acquired complete jurisdiction of the property assigned. After the county court has acquired jurisdiction of the property assigned, an execution cannot be levied upon the property. If the assignment is void, from any cause, or a party has a prior lien upon the property which he wishes to assert, it is his duty to go before the county court and there seek relief, and in case of a levy on the property the county court may order a return of the property so levied on to the assignee.[6]

(1) Hanford Oil Co. vs. First Nat. Bank, 126 Ill., 584; Farwell vs. Crandall, 120 Ill., 70.
(2) Osborne vs. Gibbs, 27 Ill. Ap., 246; Boyden vs. Frank, 20 Ill. Ap., 169.
(3) Mersinger vs. Yager, 16 Ill. Ap., 260.
(4) Colby vs. O'Donnell, 17 Ill. Ap., 473.
(5) Webster vs. Judah, 27 Ill. Ap., 294.
(6) Wilson vs. Aaron, 132 Ill., 238.

11. JURISDICTION OF CIRCUIT COURT AND COURT OF CHANCERY.—The circuit courts have original jurisdiction in all cases in law and equity, and where property is assigned in trust to secure payment of debts, and the circuit court obtains jurisdiction by bill to enforce the trust, the circuit court will not yield jurisdiction of the property to the county court. In case of concurrent jurisdiction, the court which first obtains jurisdiction will have precedence.(¹)

The circuit court has no jurisdiction to entertain an action of replevin against an assignee in possession of the property sought to be replevied under a valid deed of assignment.(²) The circuit court is not divested of its jurisdiction to enforce a mechanic's lien by the voluntary assignment of the property subject to the lien for the benefit of creditors; all that the assignee takes is the equity of redemption.(³)

The county court is not invested with general chancery powers, such as to entertain a bill to set aside a sale for fraud, or to remove a cloud from the title of property. In matters purely of an equitable character, resort must be had to a court of chancery. If the assignee has not reduced the property assigned to possession, and the property should come into the hands of a receiver who had been appointed by a court of chancery, the fund in the receiver's hands, arising from a sale of the property so in his hands, should not be surrendered to the assignee, but should be retained by the receiver, subject to the control of the court of chancery. It being the duty of the assignee to sue for and take possession of the property assigned, and upon his refusal or neglect so to do the right of a creditor to come into a court of equity and there seek protection cannot be denied.(⁴)

County courts have no general chancery powers, and none are conferred by the assignment act; they may, however, exercise both legal and equitable powers to carry out the provisions of that act. If an insolvent debtor, after making up his mind to make a general assignment, should prefer one creditor by conveyance of part of his property to such creditor, and then make a general assignment of

(1) Howell vs. Moores, 127 Ill., 67.
(2) Osborne vs. Williams, 34 Ill. Ap., 422.
(3) Paddock vs. Stout, 121 Ill., 571.
(4) Preston vs. Spaulding, 120 Ill., 208.

balance of his property, the remedy of the creditor sought to be defrauded must be sought in a court of chancery.(1)

12. PARTNERSHIP PROPERTY ASSIGNED.—Under a general voluntary assignment of all the property of a firm and of the several partners, the interest of the firm or of an individual member of the firm in real estate, will pass to the assignee, although not included in the schedule of assets.(2) Where co-partners make an assignment of their individual and firm property for the benefit of creditors, the assignee will be justified, in the absence of any statutory regulations, in making such distribution as the assignment calls for, there being no proof of fraud in the assignment.(3)

Although the members of a partnership sign a note with their individual names, and not by the name of the firm, if it is in fact for a partnership object it will be treated as a partnership debt, as between firm and individual creditors. Such note may be shown by parole evidence to have been given for a firm debt, and a description of such note in a deed of assignment as a firm debt, will be sufficient evidence of that fact to warrant the assignee in distributing such funds accordingly.(4)

13. WHAT ASSIGNMENTS ARE FRAUDULENT.—A mere shift or evasion to defeat the voluntary assignment by attempting to make an unequal distribution of the estate of the insolvent is voidable at the instance of the other creditors.(5) All assignments made in which an attempt is made to give preference to any creditor are void, and where the debtor enters upon a course of conduct having for its object the disposition of all his estate for the benefit of his creditors, and as part of the plan by which to effect that object he executes a general assignment, if he has taken steps whereby to give one creditor preferment over another, his action will be fraudulent and void.(6)

14. COMPENSATION OF ASSIGNEE.— The assignee should be allowed for his services such reasonable amount as is allowed by law to administrators and executors for like services.(7)

(1) Ide vs. Sayer, 129 Ill., 230.
(2) Davis vs. Chicago Dock Co., 129 Ill., 180.
(3) Howell vs. Moores, 127 Ill., 67.
(4) Id.
(5) Heuer vs. Schaffner, 30 Ill. Ap., 337.
(6) Hanford Oil Co. vs. First Nat. Bank, Chicago, 126 Ill., 584.
(7) Howell vs. Moores. supra.

15. APPEAL FROM COUNTY COURT.—Where a petition is filed by a person claiming property held by an assignee, an appeal will lie to the circuit court from an order of the county court granting such petition.([1])

16. FOREIGN ASSIGNMENTS.—It is the policy of the law in this state to give resident creditors priority over foreign creditors, as to assets situated in this state.([2]) It is not against the policy of the statute in this state to recognize foreign assignments, although such foreign assignment provides for the preference of some creditors over others, such preference being permitted by the law where such foreign assignment is made. At common law a debtor in failing circumstances had the right to prefer one creditor over another, and the provision in our statute against preferring creditors has no reference to any assignments made out of this state.([3])

A voluntary assignment made in another state by a non-resident debtor in conformity with our statute will not be enforced here to the detriment of our citizens; but for all other purposes, if the assignment be valid by the *lex loci*, it will be carried fully into effect. The provision in our statute prohibiting all preferences in assignments by debtors applies to those only made in this state, and not to those made in another state. A non-resident debtor may execute voluntary assignments, with or without preferences, among foreign creditors, so long as creditors in this state are not injuriously affected thereby.([4])

In the absence of domestic creditors, the assignee under a valid foreign assignment may reduce to his possession the property and collect the debts assigned to him situated in this state, and debtors here owing the assignor will be compelled to pay the assignee. But in case the foreign assignment, if made here, would be set aside as fraudulent, our courts will not enforce it, as against attaching creditors, whether foreign or domestic, although it may be valid in the state where made. It is contrary to the policy of our laws to allow the property of a non-resident debtor to be withdrawn from this state, and thus compel creditors to seek redress in a foreign jurisdiction.([5])

(1) Traver vs. Rogers, 16 Ill. Ap., 372.
(2) Webster vs. Judah, 27 Ill. Ap., 294.
(3) Lipman vs. Link, 20 Ill. Ap., 359.
(4) May vs. First Nat. Bank, 122 Ill., 551; Juilliard & Co. vs. May, 130 Ill., 87.
(5) Woodward vs. Brooks, 128 Ill., 222.

CHAPTER XIX.

PROCEEDINGS IN INSOLVENCY—INVOLUNTARY ASSIGNMENT.

1. Jurisdiction.
2. Release of debtor.
3. Notice of intended application required.
4. Duty of officer.
5. Traverse of fraud or refusal—jury—forms.
6. Schedule.
7. Contesting schedule.
8. Adjournments—bond.
9. Assignment—assignee—exemption—bond.
10. Effect of assignment—form.
11. Discharge of debtor—form of discharge.
12. Liberation by officer.
13. Recording assignment.
14. Proving demands—notice.
15. What proof required.
16. Further assignment.
17. Collection and disposition of estate.
18. Conveyances.
19. Keeping account.
20. Removal—new assignment.
21. Settlement—dividends.
22. Compensation of assignee.
23. Fees.
24. Insolvency of judge.
25. Effect of discharge—evidence.
26. Appeal—bond.
27. Filing record.
28. Proceedings on appeal.
29. Stay during appeal.
30. Jail fees.
31. Further jail fees—unexpended fees.
32. Jail fees—costs.
33. Effect of discharge of debtor.
34. Satisfaction by imprisonment.
35. False oath—penalty therefor.
36. Rules governing—sufficiency of affidavit.
37. Effect of arrest.
38. Debtor can not be compelled to schedule
39. Fraud—presumption as to.
40. Jurisdiction.
41. Appeal.
42. Bond on appeal.

1. JURISDICTION.—The county courts shall have exclusive original jurisdiction in their respective counties in all applications for discharge from arrest or imprisonment under the provisions of this act, and shall be held to be always open and in session for the hearing of such applications.(¹)

2. RELEASE OF DEBTOR.—When any person is arrested or imprisoned upon any process issued for the purpose of holding such person to bail upon any indebtedness, or in any civil action, when malice is not the gist of the action, or when any debtor is surrendered or committed to custody by his bail in any such action, or is arrested and imprisoned upon execution in any such action, such person may be released from such arrest or imprisonment, upon complying with the provisions of this act.(²)

3. NOTICE OF INTENDED APPLICATION REQUIRED.—When any such debtor shall desire to make application to be discharged under the provisions of this act, he shall give reasonable notice of his intended application, to the creditor, at whose instance he was arrested or imprisoned, or to his agent or his attorney, if in the county, if not, to the officer who made the arrest. Reasonable notice shall be not less than one hour before such application, and time for travel at the rate of not less than one day for every twenty-four miles' travel.(³)

NOTICE TO THE CREDITOR OF APPLICATION FOR DISCHARGE.

STATE OF ILLINOIS, } ss. *In County Court,*
............County. *At Chambers, ...day of......, A. D. 18...*

In the Matter of the Insolvency of.........

Notice of Application to be Discharged.

To.........., of the......., County of.........., and State of Illinois:

You are hereby notified, that I will, on the...day of......, A. D. 18..., apply to the Hon......., Judge of the County Court of......county, Illinois, at his chambers, at.........., Illinois, for a trial by jury of the question of fact, whether I am guilty of a refusal upon execution to surrender my estate for the payment of any judgment rendered against me, with which I now stand charged, upon affidavit filed by you, and for a discharge from arrest and imprisonment; when and where you may appear and contest such discharge, if you see fit so to do.

By........., Attorney. ....

(1) Hurd's R. S., Chap. 72, § 1.   (3) Hurd's R. S., Chap. 72, § 3.
(2) Hurd's R. S., Chap. 72, § 2.

RETURN—SHOWING SERVICE.

STATE OF ILLINOIS, } ss.
................County.

I,........., Sheriff of.........county, State of Illinois, have duly served the within notice on........., by reading the same to him and at the same time delivering to him a true copy thereof, this...day of......, A. D. 18...

.........., Sheriff.

The petition to the county judge for such discharge, may be made in form as follows:

STATE OF ILLINOIS, } ss.   *In the County Court,*
................County.   *At Chambers,* ...day of......, *A. D.* 18...

In the Matter of the Insolvency of.........

To the Hon............, the Judge of the County Court of.......... county, Illinois:

Your petitioner........., of the county of........., and State of Illinois, would respectfully represent and show unto your honor, that he was on the...day of......, A. D. 18..., by virtue of a *capias ad satisfaciendum*, issued out of the office of the circuit court of.........county, Illinois, on the...day of......, A. D. 18..., at the suit of........., committed to the common jail of said county, and that he is now held in custody, and is desirous of being released from imprisonment.

Your petitioner would further represent, that he has given notice to........., the creditor, at whose instance he was so arrested and imprisoned, of this his intended application for discharge from such imprisonment, and that on the...day of......, A. D. 18..., your petitioner would apply unto your honor, at chambers, in........., for a trial by jury of the question of fact, whether your petitioner was guilty of a refusal upon execution to surrender his estate for the payment of a judgment rendered against him, with which your petitioner now stands charged upon affidavit filed against him by the said......... Which said notice so given as aforesaid, was duly served as the law directs, and is ready to be now here shown to the court.

Your petitioner, therefore, prays that a jury may be summoned, that proper proceedings may be had, and that he may be discharged from said imprisonment, upon his complying with the terms of, and provisions of the statute in relation to insolvent debtors. And your petitioner will ever pray, etc.

By........., Attorneys.   ....

Subscribed and sworn to before me, this...day of......, A. D. 18...
.........., Clerk County Court.

4. DUTY OF OFFICER.—At the time appointed in such notice, it shall be the duty of the officer in whose custody the debtor shall

be, to convey him before the judge of the county court of the county in which the debtor is arrested or imprisoned.(¹)

5. TRAVERSE OF FRAUD OR REFUSAL—JURY.—When any debtor is arrested or imprisoned for debt upon charge of fraud, or upon execution on the charge of refusal to surrender his estate for the payment of any judgment, he shall be entitled, upon giving notice as provided in section 3 of this act, to have the question, whether he is guilty of such fraud, or has refused to surrender his estate, tried by a jury, who may be summoned, tried and selected for that purpose. If the jury shall find the debtor "not guilty" of such fraud, or refusal, as the case may be, the debtor shall be discharged from the arrest or imprisonment, and the creditor, at whose instance he was arrested or imprisoned, shall be adjudged to pay the costs of the arrest or imprisonment and of such proceeding. If the debtor shall be found "guilty" of such fraud or refusal, he shall be remanded to the custody of the proper officer; but such finding shall not prevent his availing himself of the other provisions of this act.(²)

The form of a venire for jury may be as follows:

STATE OF ILLINOIS, } ss.
..............County.

The People of the State of Illinois, to the Sheriff of said County, Greeting:

We command you forthwith to summon twelve lawful men of your county, to appear before the Hon.........., Judge of the County Court of........ county, Illinois, on the...day of......, A. D. 18..., at...o'clock..m., (or forthwith) at chambers, at the court house, in.........., Illinois, to make a jury to try a question of fact, whether..........is guilty of a refusal to surrender his estate upon execution for the payment of a judgment rendered against him, with which he now stands charged upon affidavit filed against him by.......... And have you then and there the names of the jury and this writ.

               Witness, ..., Clerk of the County Court, and the seal there-
[Seal.] ·   of, at.........., in said county, this...day of......, A. D. 18...
                                         ...., Clerk.

FINAL ORDER ON PETITION TO BE DISCHARGED AS AN INSOLVENT DEBTOR.

STATE OF ILLINOIS, } ss.
..............County.

In the Matter of the Petition of......, to be Discharged under the Insolvent Laws. Order entered...day of......, A. D. 18...

And now, on this...day of......, A. D. 18..., comes the said.........., in

---

(1) Hurd's R. S., Chap. 72, § 4.   (2) Hurd's R. S., Chap. 72, § 5.

custody of......, sheriff of......county, Illinois, on a *capias ad satisfaciendum*, issued out of the circuit court of said county, on the...day of......, A. D. 18..., at the suit of......... And this cause coming on now to be heard, upon the question of fact before the court, viz.: whether the said.........was guilty of a refusal to surrender his estate upon execution for the payment of a judgment rendered against him, with which he now stands charged upon affidavit filed against him by........., it is on motion ordered that a jury be called, and the clerk having issued his venire to........., sheriff of.........county, Illinois, it is ordered by the court, that this cause stand continued until one o'clock for said jury.

And now, at this time, the same being the hour to which this cause was continued, comes again the said petitioner........., by........., his attorney, also comes the said........, by........, his attorney, and it appearing to the court that the said.........has had sufficient notice hereof, as required by law, and the sheriff having returned a jury into court, it is ordered that a jury be impanneled, and the jury having been duly called, impanneled and sworn, and having heard all the evidence, the arguments of counsel, and the instructions of the court, retired to consider their verdict, and having duly considered thereof, returned into open court their verdict in words as follows, to-wit: We, the jury, find the said.........guilty of such refusal to surrender his estate upon execution for the payment of a judgment against him. [*Signed by all the jurors.*]

It is therefore ordered that said verdict be received and recorded, and that said jury be discharged, and that said.........be remanded to the custody of ...., sheriff of.........county, Illinois, the officer having him in charge.

6. SWORN SCHEDULE.—When a debtor is brought before the judge of the county court, and is not discharged pursuant to the preceding section, the judge shall require of him a full, fair and complete schedule of all his estate, real or personal, including money, notes, bonds, bills, obligations and contracts for money or property of any and every description or kind, name or nature whatsoever, together with a true and perfect account of all the debts which he shall or may be owing at the time; which schedule shall be subscribed by the debtor, who shall also take and subscribe the following oath or affirmation, to-wit:

SCHEDULE IN INSOLVENCY.

STATE OF ILLINOIS, } ss. *In the County Court,*
...............County, }   *At Chambers,* ...., *A. D.* 18...

In the Matter of the Insolvency of.........
   Schedule of Insolvent.

A full, fair and complete Schedule of all the estate, real and personal, including money, notes, bonds, bills, obligations and contracts for money and property of every description and kind, name and nature whatsoever, of the said.........., together with a true and perfect account of all debts which he owes at this time:

SCHEDULE OF REAL ESTATE.

The northwest quarter of the northwest quarter of section twenty, township six, north, in range twelve, west, forty acres.

SCHEDULE OF PERSONAL PROPERTY.

Cash on hand,..$100 00
Seven horses, five head of cattle.

SCHEDULE OF NOTES AND ACCOUNTS ON HAND.

One note on.........., dated June 21st, 1875, due one year after date, with ten per cent. interest,..$500 00
Accounts on.........., for cattle sold,.. 9 00

DEBTS OWING AT THIS TIME BY..........

Judgment owing.........., rendered at the...term of ....., A. D. 18..., $1000, etc. Given under my hand, this...day of......, A. D. 18....

....

I do solemnly swear that the schedule now delivered and by me subscribed, contains, to the best of my knowledge and belief, a full, true and perfect account and discovery of all the estate, lands, tenements, hereditaments, goods, chattels and effects unto me in any wise belonging, and such debts as are unto me owing, or unto any person or persons for me, or in trust for me, and of all securities and contracts whereby any money may become due or payable, or any advantage or benefit accrue to me or to my use, or to any person or persons for me or in trust for me; that I have not lands, money, or other estate, real or personal, in possession, reversion or remainder, which is not set forth in this schedule; nor have I, at any day or time, directly or indirectly, sold, lessened in value, or otherwise disposed of, all or any part of my lands, money, goods, stock, debts, securities, contracts or estate, whereby to secure the same, or to receive, or expect to receive, any profit or advantage therefrom, to defraud any creditor or creditors, to whom I am indebted in anywise whatsoever; and also, that this schedule contains a true and perfect account of all the debts that I owe to any and every person whatsoever.(1)

....

Subscribed and sworn to before me, by the said.........., this...day of......, A. D. 18...
[L. S.] ...., Clerk County Court.

7. CONTESTING SCHEDULE.—Any creditor of such debtor shall have the right to appear before the court and contest the truth of such schedule, and may, for that purpose, examine the debtor and call such witnesses as he shall deem necessary; and the court shall issue subpœnas and compel the attendance of witnesses as in other cases.(2)

(1) Hurd's R. S., Chap. 72, § 6.   (2) Hurd's R. S., Chap. 72, § 7.

8. ADJOURNMENTS—BOND.—The court may adjourn any hearing from time to time, not exceeding thirty days at any time, and may remand the debtor into the custody of the officer, or allow the debtor to give bond for his appearance in such demand upon such security as shall be approved by the court, which bond shall be payable to the People of the State of Illinois, and be conditioned that the debtor will appear at the time to which the hearing is adjourned, and from time to time until the same is concluded, and will make due assignment of all his estate, lands, tenements, hereditaments, goods, chattels and effects, not exempt from execution, and deliver the same to his assignee, if one shall be appointed by the court; or, in case he shall not be allowed to make such assignment, will surrender himself to the officer into whose custody he may be ordered by the court, and abide the order of the court. Upon a breach of such bond, it may be put in suit by any person interested therein, for his use, and at his expense.(¹)

The bond to be given may be in form as follows:

Know all Men by these Presents: That we, ...and........., are held and firmly bound unto the People of the State of Illinois, in the penal sum of...dollars, for the payment of which, well and truly to be made, we bind ourselves, our heirs, executors and administrators, jointly and severally and firmly by these presents.

Witness our hands and seals, this...day of......, A. D. 18...

The condition of the above obligation is such, that whereas the said........ who has been arrested by virtue of a writ of *capias ad satisfaciendum*, issued out of the office of the circuit court of.........county, Illinois, on the...day of......, A. D. 18..., at the suit of.........against.........; and.........having filed in the county court of said county, a schedule of all his property, both real and personal, together with an account of all debts owing by him, for the purpose of procuring his discharge from such arrest and imprisonment, under the provisions of the statute in such case made and provided, and......... having filed his objections to the approval of said schedule, and the court having granted a continuance of the hearing in respect thereto until...day of......, A. D. 18..., at the hour of...o'clock..; now, if the said.........will appear at the time to which the hearing hereof is adjourned, and from time to time until the same is concluded, and will make due assignment of all his estate, lands, tenements, hereditaments, goods, chattels and effects, not exempt from execution, and deliver the same to his assignee, if one shall be appointed by the court, and in case he shall not be allowed to make such assignment, will surrender himself to the officer into whose custody he may

---

(1) Hurd's R. S., Chap. 72, ? 8.

be ordered by the court, and abide any further order of the court, then the above obligation to be void, otherwise to remain in full force and effect.

..........., [Seal.]
..........., [Seal.]

9. ASSIGNMENT — ASSIGNEE — EXEMPTION—BOND.—If, after full investigation, it shall appear to the court, that the debtor has made a full, fair and complete schedule of all his estate, and all debts which he may be owing at the time, as required by section five of the act to which this is an amendment, and has not fraudulently conveyed, concealed or otherwise disposed of, some part of his estate, with a design to secure the same to his own use, or defraud his creditors, or has not willfully misused or expended his goods and estate, or some part thereof, for the purpose of defrauding his creditors, it shall be the duty of the court to designate and set out to the debtor such property mentioned in the schedule as is exempt from execution, and to appoint some fit person to act as assignee of the debtor; and such debtor shall, immediately by indorsement upon such schedule, and otherwise, as the court may direct, assign to such person, all his said estate, except such as shall have been designated as exempt from execution, as aforesaid, or so much of said estate as may be sufficient to pay all the debts, interest, costs and charges, in such schedule mentioned. Said assignee shall be required by the court to give a bond for the faithful performance of his trust as such assignee; the conditions of said bond, and the security and the penal sum of the bond to be such as the court shall direct and approve.([1])

FINAL ORDER OF DISCHARGE OF INSOLVENT DEBTOR AND APPOINTMENT OF ASSIGNEE BY THE COURT.

STATE OF ILLINOIS, } ss. *In the County Court,*
...............County.   *At Chambers, ...day of......, A. D.* 18...

In the Matter of the Insolvency of..........

Order of Discharge and Appointment of Assignee.

And now, on this day comes the said.........., by.........., his attorney, and the said.........., by.........., his attorney, and this being the day to which this cause was continued by the court, and the said..........having appeared and filed his exceptions to the approval of said schedule, and it appearing to the court, that the said..........has filed a fair and complete schedule of all his estate, lands, tenements, hereditaments, goods, chattels and effects, not

(1) Hurd's R. S., Chap. 72, § 9.

exempt from execution, together with a true and perfect account of all the debts which he shall or may be owing at the time; and it further appearing to the court, after a hearing of said cause, that the said.........has in all respects conducted himself fairly in making said assignment, and that said schedule of the said.........is just and fair in every respect. It is therefore ordered by the court, that.........be and he is hereby appointed assignee of the said......... And it further appearing to the court, that the said.........is the head of a family, and residing with the same, it is ordered, that the said assignee set apart to him the amount of property exempt by law from execution and sale.

And it further appearing to the court, that the said.........has, by his endorsement on said schedule, assigned all the property therein mentioned to........., the assignee, and that the said.........assignee, has receipted him for the same, and that he has taken and subscribed the oath required by the statute. It is ordered by the court that he be discharged from said arrest and imprisonment, and that a certificate thereof issue to him in accordance with the statute in such case made and provided.

And it is further ordered, that the said.........assignee as aforesaid, pay the cost of this proceeding out of the funds belonging to said estate.

10. EFFECT OF ASSIGNMENT.—Such assignment shall absolutely vest in such assignee all the interest of such debtor in and to the estate so assigned, for the use of the creditors of such debtor, and such assignee shall have full right to sue for and recover the same in his own name as such assignee, and redeem all mortgages, conditional contracts, pledges and liens of or upon any goods or estate of the debtor, so assigned, or sell the same subject to such mortgage or other incumbrance.([1])

The assignment may be in form as follows:

STATE OF ILLINOIS, } ss.
.............County,

I, ..., an insolvent debtor, having filed my schedule as the law directs, and made application to the county court to be discharged from arrest and imprisonment under the insolvent laws of the State of Illinois, I being confined by virtue of a *capias ad satisfaciendum* issued out of the circuit court of.........county, Illinois, at the suit of.........and against myself, and the court having examined and approved said schedule and application, appointed.........assignee of my said estate. I, ..., in consideration of the premises aforesaid, do hereby assign, convey and make over to the said........., all my property, both real and personal, not exempt from levy and sale, and mentioned in the within schedule, to have and to hold the same unto the said........., for the use of my creditors, under the provisions of the insolvent laws of the State of Illinois.

Witness my hand and seal, this...day of......, A. D. 18...

........., [Seal.]

(1) Hurd's R. S., Chap. 72 § 10.

11. DISCHARGE OF DEBTOR.—Whenever the said debtor shall produce to the court the receipt of the assignee of such debtor, certifying that he has received all the estate so assigned to him, together with the evidences of indebtedness to, and the books of account of, such debtor, if any, showing the accounts owing to such debtor, the court shall enter an order discharging such debtor from arrest or imprisonment.(1)

The certificate of discharge may be in form as follows:

STATE OF ILLINOIS, } ss.
................County,

The People of the State of Illinois, to the Sheriff of said County, Greeting:

Whereas, ..., who was on the...day of......, A. D. 18..., adjudged an insolvent debtor under the laws of this state, by the county court of........ county, Illinois, and.........appointed assignee of his said estate, having produced the receipt of said assignee for the property mentioned in his schedule, and the same having been accepted by the court, it was ordered by the court that the said.........be discharged from imprisonment and forever released for and on account of any debts by him owing in said schedule mentioned, according to the statute in such case made and provided.

You will therefore release the said.........from imprisonment immediately upon receipt of this order.

[Seal.] In testimony whereof, I have hereunto set my hand and affixed the seal of said court, at my office in......Illinois, this...day of......, A. D. 18....

.........., Clerk of the County Court.

12. LIBERATION BY OFFICER.—On the production of a copy of such order, certified under the seal of the court, the officer having the custody of such debtor, shall forthwith liberate such debtor from arrest or imprisonment.(2)

13. RECORDING ASSIGNMENT.—The assignee shall forthwith cause the assignment, or such other conveyance as shall be made to him on such assignment, to be recorded in the recorder's office of every county in which there may be real estate of the debtor on which it may operate.(3)

14. PROVING DEMANDS—NOTICE.—If the estate so assigned, shall, in the opinion of the court, be of sufficient value to justify further proceedings in regard thereto, an order shall be entered

---

(1) Hurd's R., S. Chap. 72, § 11. (3) Hurd's R. S., Chap. 72, § 13.
(2) Hurd's R., S. Chap. 72, § 12.

fixing a time when demands may be proved against the estate of such debtor, and requiring the assignee to give notice to the creditors of such debtor of such assignment, and of the time and place when and where they may appear and prove their demands, which notice shall be given by personal service, or by mail or otherwise, as the court shall direct.([1])

The order fixing the time when demands may be proved against the estate of such debtor, may be in form as follows:

STATE OF ILLINOIS, } ss.   *In the County Court,*
................County,   *At Chambers,......, A. D. 18...*

It appearing to the court, that the estate assigned by.........., an insolvent debtor, is of sufficient value to justify further proceedings therewith; it is therefore ordered that the said.........., assignee of said estate, give notice to the creditors thereof, which said notices may be either printed or written, or partly printed and partly written, or both, and shall be served by personal service upon all those who are residents of said county, and by mailing to all those who reside out of said county, notifying them that they may appear at.........., in.........., Illinois, and prove their demands against said estate, on the...day of......, A. D. 18..., the time and place fixed by this court for the hearing thereof, to which time this cause stands continued.

ASSIGNEE'S NOTICE TO PROVE CLAIM.

Notice is hereby given, that the undersigned has been appointed assignee of........, and all persons holding any claim or claims against said........, are hereby notified to be present and present the same under oath or affirmation, at the court house, in.........., Illinois, on the...day of......, A. D. 18..., the time fixed by order of the court for the adjustment thereof. All persons are hereby notified who are indebted to said.........., assignor.., that they must come forward and make immediate payment of such indebtedness to the undersigned. Dated at........, this...day of......, A. D. 18...

                                              ...., Assignee.

To......
        ...., Illinois.

Where notices are sent by mail, the affidavit used in the chapter on assignment for the benefit of creditors and list of creditors so notified, the form there given, may be used by the assignee.([2])

If the service was made by an officer, the return may be in form as follows:

I have duly served the foregoing and within notice upon.........., a creditor of said estate, by reading, and at the same time delivering him a true copy of the same, as I am therein commanded, on this...day of......, A. D. 18...

                                              ...., Sheriff.

(1) Hurd's R. S., Chap. 72, § 14.   (2) *Ante* page, 396.

Any person of lawful age may make the service, but he should file an affidavit that he served the same, or in other words, make a sworn return. Where the court directs the notice to be published, obtain a printer's certificate of publication, and file affidavit of publishing the same for the length of time, and in the manner directed by the court.

15. WHAT PROOF REQUIRED.—If any creditor shall, at or before the time appointed, file with the clerk of the court his demand, verified by the affidavit of some person knowing the facts, stating the nature and amount of the demand, and that the amount claimed is justly owing to him by the debtor, after allowing all payments and offsets, the same shall be allowed, unless it shall be contested by some person interested in such estate, when further evidence may be required.(¹)

AFFIDAVIT OF CLAIM AGAINST ESTATE OF INSOLVENT DEBTOR.

In the County Court, at Chambers, ...day of......, A. D. 18...

In the Matter of the Insolvency of.................., Assignee.

STATE OF ILLINOIS, } ss.
..................County,

Claim of........., who being duly sworn, says that the demand of the said.........against the estate of the above named insolvent, a copy of which is hereto attached, is for [*here state the nature of the demand*], and that there is due to the said.........from the said insolvent, after allowing to........ all payments, deductions and offsets, ...dollars. Deponent further says, that the said claimant....resident of........, in said........county.

........., Attorney.

Subscribed and sworn to before me, this...day of......, A. D. 18...

........., Clerk of the County Court.

Should there be any exceptions filed against any claim, the form found on page 397, of Chapter 18, may be used.

16. FURTHER ASSIGNMENT.—Any creditor who shall not have been notified of the intended application of his debtor to take the benefit of this act, may, at any time within one year after the discharge of the debtor under the provisions of the foregoing sections, petition the court, under oath, for permission to re-examine the debtor touching the fairness of his schedule; and if the court shall be satisfied, from such petition, that there is good reason to believe

(1) Hurd's R. S., Chap. 72, § 15.

that the debtor had other estate which he ought to have assigned, it shall cause the debtor to be cited to appear before the court at a time to be fixed in the citation, to show cause why he should not make a further assignment of his estate. Upon the hearing, like proceedings may be had as in the case of the original assignment. In case that the court shall find that the debtor has other property which he ought to have assigned, it shall enter an order requiring the debtor to make an assignment thereof; and if the debtor shall fail to obey such citation, or to make such assignment, and deliver such property to the assignee, he may be proceeded against as for a contempt, and shall be liable to arrest at the suit of any creditor, notwithstanding the original discharge.([1])

17. COLLECTION—DISPOSITION OF ESTATE.—The assignee shall forthwith proceed to collect such demands as may have been assigned to him, and as soon as may be, consistently with the interest of the creditors, sell all the estate so assigned, both real and personal, including such claims as are not collectible by reasonable diligence. He may make such sale in the manner and upon such terms as he shall deem most for the interests of the creditors; but the court may make such order concerning the time, place and manner of sale of the whole or any part of such estate, as will, in its opinion, promote the interests of the creditors.([2])

18. CONVEYANCES.—It shall be the duty of the assignee who shall sell any lands or tenements under authority of this act, upon payment of the purchase money being made by the purchaser, to make and execute to such purchaser, his heirs, executors, administrators or assigns, a deed of conveyance for the same, which shall be acknowledged in the same manner as deeds are acknowledged by sheriffs, and such deed shall vest in the purchaser all the rights of the assignor in such lands and tenements.([3])

The deed may be in form as follows:

This indenture witnesseth, that whereas, I, ..., assignee of the estate of.........., an insolvent debtor, under and by virtue of an order of the county court of........county, Illinois, made and entered of record on the...day of......, A. D. 18..., in record..., of the records of said........county, appointing me assignee as aforesaid, and by virtue of a certain assignment made to me as

(1) Hurd's R. S., Chap. 72, § 16.   (3) Hurd's R. S., Chap. 72, § 18.
(2) Hurd's R. S., Chap. 72, § 17.

such assignee by the said........., insolvent debtor as aforesaid, which said assignment among other property, included the lands hereinafter described, and which were assigned to me for the use and benefit of the creditors of the said........., on the...day of......, A. D. 18..., as directed by order of the said county court, recorded in the recorder's office of the county of........., and state aforesaid, I, the said........., assignee, in pursuance thereof, did advertise the same as directed by law, by posting notices of said sale in...... of the most public places in the county, one of which said notices I posted on the..door of the court house, and one at..., one at..., one at..., which said advertisements contained a description of the land to be sold and the time, terms and place of said sale; and whereas, also, on to-wit: the...day of......, A. D. 18..., at the court house, in........., Illinois, I, as assignee as aforesaid, (the same being the time and place advertised for said sale,) did, between the hours of..o'clock a. m. and..o'clock p. m., of said day, sell the lands to........., for the sum of......dollars, for cash in hand, and the said.........having paid to me the full amount of said purchase money, I therefore, as assignee as aforesaid, and in consideration of the premises above recited, do grant and convey unto the said........., his heirs and assigns, the following described lands and tenements, to-wit: [*Here describe the lands.*] To have and to hold the same unto the said party of the second part, his heirs and assigns forever.

In testimony whereof, I, as assignee as aforesaid, have hereto set my hand and affixed my seal, this...day of......, A. D. 18...

........., Assignee, [Seal.]

STATE OF ILLINOIS, } ss.
..............County,

I,........., Clerk of the County Court, in and for the county aforesaid, do hereby certify, that........., who..personally known to me to be the identical person..whose name.. ...subscribed to the foregoing instrument as having executed the same, appeared before me this day in person, and acknowledged the signing, sealing and delivery thereof to be his own voluntary act, done in his official capacity as assignee of.........

Given under my hand and official seal, this...day of......, A. D. 18...
[Seal.]   ...., Clerk County Court.

19. KEEPING ACCOUNT.—The assignee shall keep a regular account of all money received by him as assignee, to which all persons interested therein, shall, at all reasonable times, have access, and the court may call upon him to account to it as often as it shall think for the interest of the estate.([1])

20. REMOVAL—NEW ASSIGNEE.—The court, after due notice and hearing, may remove an assignee if it is made to appear, upon the complaint of any person interested in the estate, that the as-

(1) Hurd's R. S., Chap. 72, § 19.

signee has fraudulently received, concealed, embezzled or conveyed away any of the money, goods, effects, or other estate, assigned to him, or in any manner misbehaved in regard thereto, and may appoint another in his stead, or in the place of any deceased assignee, and may, at any time, when it shall think best for the interests of the estate, require the assignee to give bond with sufficient security, and remove the assignee for a failure to comply with such requirement. In all cases of the appointment of a new assignee, the court may compel all necessary conveyances and transfers to be made to him.(1)

21. SETTLEMENTS—DIVIDEND.—It shall be the duty of every assignee of any insolvent debtor, within eighteen months after such assignment, to make a settlement of the estate of such insolvent debtor before the court, giving thirty days' public notice of the time of making such settlement—and the court shall make such order concerning the distribution thereof as is made in cases of insolvency of deceased persons; and such assignee shall pay the creditors of such insolvent debtor the amount of their several dividends, within thirty days after such settlement. And if the whole amount of debts shall not have been collected at the time of making such settlement, then such assignee shall continue to collect such outstanding debts, and from time to time make dividends of such sums as shall come to his possession, until the whole is collected and paid, first deducting such charges and fees as are by law allowed; and if anything shall remain in the hands of any such assignee, after paying all such debts as shall have been proved, as hereinbefore provided, together with the cost thereon, then such assignee shall pay over the same to the said debtor, his heirs, executors, administrators or assigns.(2)

22. COMPENSATION OF ASSIGNEE.—The court may allow every assignee, who shall be appointed under the provisions of this act, such compensation as shall be reasonable and just for the services which he shall be necessarily called upon to perform in the discharge of his duties as assignee.(3)

23. FEES.—The clerk of the county court, and other officers,

(1) Hurd's R. S., Chap. 72, § 20.
(2) Hurd's R. S., Chap. 72, § 21.
(3) Hurd's R. S., Chap. 72, § 22.

shall be allowed the same fees for services rendered by authority of this act, as are allowed for like services in other cases.(¹)

24. INSOLVENCY OF JUDGE.—In case of the insolvency of the judge of a county court, the same proceedings may be had in regard to him in the circuit court as are prescribed for other debtors in the county court.(²)

25. EFFECT OF DISCHARGE—EVIDENCE.—Any debtor who shall be discharged under this act, upon assignment, and who shall have acted honestly and without fraud, shall, so long as the order of discharge shall remain in force, and not vacated according to law, be discharged and exempted from arrest or imprisonment upon the demand or judgment upon which he was arrested or imprisoned, and upon all debts that he may owe at the time of obtaining such discharge, and are mentioned in the schedule hereinbefore required to be made or proved against him. The certified copy of the order of discharge shall be evidence in all courts and places.(³)*

26. APPEAL—BOND.—Any debtor or creditor who may feel himself aggrieved by any final order or judgment of the county court under the provisions of this act, may, at any time within ten days from the entering of such order or judgment, appeal to the circuit court of the county, upon giving bond in such amount and with such security as shall be approved by the county court. If the appeal is taken by the creditor, the bond shall run to the debtor, and be conditioned to prosecute such appeal with effect, and pay

(1) Hurd's R. S., Chap. 72, § 23.
(2) Hurd's R. S., Chap. 72, § 24.
(3) Hurd's R. S., Chap. 72, § 25.

*NOTE.—The repeal of the National Bankrupt Law, gives to this and the insolvent laws of the several states, an importance which can not attach to them when inoperative, by reason of the existence of the Federal law, and makes it important to inquire how far the courts will give effect to a discharge granted under this section of the statute.
The Supreme Court of the United States held, in *McMillan* vs. *McNeill,* 4 Wheaton, 209, that insolvent laws have no extra territorial operation upon the contracts of other states. The same court also held, in *Ogden* vs. *Saunders,* 12 Wheaton, 213, that a certificate of discharge, under a state law, can not be pleaded in bar of an action brought by a citizen of another state in the courts of the United States, or of any other state than that where the discharge was obtained. The same principle was affirmed in *Snydam* vs. *Broadnax,* 14 Peters, 75, and may be considered as the settled doctrine of the courts. In *Cook* vs. *Moffatt,* 5 Howard, 308, the same court say, that such laws "can have no effect upon contracts made before their enactment or beyond their territory." Many of the state courts have, in the same manner, limited the effect and operation of state insolvent laws.
In accordance with the above principles, we may be justified in anticipating the effect to be given a discharge issued to an insolvent debtor under this law. Other state courts and the federal courts, will give such a discharge no effect whatever, except where the question arises between suitors who were citizens of this state during the pendency of the proceedings. Our own courts must hold the discharge no bar to a debt contracted in another state or with a citizen of another state, and, also, that such a discharge is no bar to a debt contracted before the date of the statute, in any case, unless, perhaps, in cases where the creditor proved his claim and participated in the distribution of the effects of the insolvent. To hold that such a discharge is a general acquittal of all debts, would be to hold, that a state may enact a law "impairing the obligation of contracts."

30

all costs and damages that may accrue to the person seeking such discharge. If taken by the debtor, the bond shall run to the People of the State of Illinois, and be conditioned that he will prosecute his said appeal with effect, and in case the appeal is dismissed, or the order or judgment of the county court is affirmed, in whole or in part, he will perform the same and will appear before and abide whatever decision the circuit court shall make in the premises, and pay all costs that may be awarded against him; and also, that he will not sell or dispose of any of his estate pending such appeal, but that the same shall be forthcoming and subject to the order of the county court. Upon a breach of such bond, it may be put in suit by any person interested therein, for his use and at his expense.(¹)

The appeal bond may be in form as follows:

Know all men by these presents, that we,..........and.........., of the county of........., and State of Illinois, are held and firmly bound unto the People of the State of Illinois, in the penal sum of...dollars, for the payment of which well and truly to be made, we bind ourselves, our heirs, executors and administrators, jointly, severally and firmly by these presents.

Witness our hands and seals, this...day of......, A. D. 18...

The condition of the above obligation is such, that whereas the said........ on the...day of......, A. D. 18..., was brought before the county court of........ county, by........., sheriff of said county, on a......issued out of the circuit court of said county, on the...day of......, A. D. 18..., at the suit of........., and made application to said court to be discharged from arrest and imprisonment on complying with the statutes in such case made and provided, and on the...day of......, A. D. 18..., a trial was had thereon, and the court refused the prayer of said petition, and remanded said.........back into the custody of said sheriff, from which said order of the county court the said.........prays an appeal.

Now, if the said.........will prosecute his appeal with effect; and in case his appeal is dismissed, or the order or judgment of the county court is affirmed, in whole or in part, he will perform the same, and will appear before and abide whatever decision the circuit court shall make in the premises, and pay all the costs that may be awarded against him; and also, that he will not sell or dispose of any of his estate, pending such appeal, but that the same shall be forthcoming, and subject to the order of the county court, then this obligation to be void, otherwise to remain in full force and virtue.

.........., [Seal.]
...., [Seal.]

Taken and approved by me, this...day of......, A. D. 18....
.........., judge of the County Court.

(1) Hurd's R. S., Chap. 72, § 26.

27. FILING RECORD.—The appellant shall file in the office of the clerk of the circuit court a certified copy of the record of proceedings and order, or judgment appealed from, on or before the first day of the succeeding term of the circuit court: *Provided*, ten days shall intervene between the time of praying such appeal and the sitting of such court; but if that time shall not so intervene, then by the tenth day of the same term. If the record shall not be so filed, the appeal shall be dismissed, unless further time is given therefor by the court, upon good reason shown why the same could not be filed in the time aforesaid.(1)

28. PROCEEDINGS ON APPEAL.—The circuit court shall, at the term to which the appeal is taken (unless for good cause), proceed to hear and determine the matter, and, at the request of either party, impannel a jury to find the facts. The circuit court may affirm or reverse the order or judgment of the county court, in whole or in part, and give such directions to the county court, in the premises as shall be according to equity and justice, and make all necessary orders in the premises. Upon the filing of a certified copy of the order of the circuit court, directing further proceedings in the county court, the cause shall proceed therein in conformity therewith.(2)

29. STAY DURING APPEAL.—No assignee shall sell any property assigned to him by any debtor as aforesaid, during the pendency of any appeal to the circuit court, unless the same be of a perishable nature, and such as will be materially injured in its value by delay.(3)

30. JAIL FEES.—In all cases where any person is committed to the jail of any county upon any writ of *capias ad respondendum* or *capias ad satisfaciendum*, issued in any suit, it shall be the duty of the creditor in such writ to pay the keeper of the jail or sheriff his fees for receiving such person and his board for one week at the time the debtor is committed to jail, and before the jailer shall be bound to receive the debtor, and in default of such payment, the debtor may be discharged: *Provided*, the officer having such debtor in charge, shall give reasonable notice to the creditor or his agent

---

(1) Hurd's R. S., Chap. 72, § 27.
(2) Hurd's R. S., Chap. 72, § 28.
(3) Hurd's R. S., Chap. 72, § 29.

or attorney, if within the county, that such debtor is about to be committed to jail on such writ.(⁴)

31. FURTHER JAIL FEES—UNEXPENDED FEES.—Should the debtor be detained in jail under such writ for more than one week, it shall be the duty of the creditor, at the commencement of each week, to advance to such jailer the board of the debtor for the succeeding week, and in default of such payment in advance, the debtor may be discharged by such jailer. In case the debtor shall not be detained in such jail for any week for which his board may have been paid in advance, the jailer shall return to the creditor, or his agent or attorney, the amount so advanced for and unexhausted in boarding.(²)

32. JAIL FEES—COSTS.—The amount paid by any creditor (under the provisions of this act) to the jailer, shall be indorsed by the same on the writ on which the debtor was committed, and shall be charged against and collected of the debtor as part of the costs in the suit in which the writ is issued.(³)

33. EFFECT OF DISCHARGE OF DEBTOR.—The discharge of any person under the foregoing provision of this act, shall be no discharge or satisfaction of the demand, judgment or costs upon which he was arrested or imprisoned, or any debt mentioned in such schedule, but the same may be inforced against the property of such discharged person.(⁴)

34. SATISFACTION BY IMPRISONMENT.—In any case where the defendant arrested upon final process shall not be entitled to relief under the provisions of this act, if the plaintiff will advance the jail fees and board in manner hereinbefore provided, the defendant may be imprisoned at one dollar and fifty cents per day, until the judgment shall be satisfied, and the officer making the arrest shall indorse the execution "satisfied in full by imprisonment."(⁵)

35. FALSE OATH.—Any person who shall be convicted of taking a false oath in any proceeding under this act, shall be deemed guilty of willful perjury, and on conviction, shall suffer the pains and penalties inforced by law therefor.(⁶)

36. RULES GOVERNING INVOLUNTARY ASSIGNMENTS—SUFFI-

---

(1) Hurd's R. S., Chap. 72, § 30.
(2) Hurd's R. S., Chap. 72, § 31.
(3) Hurd's R. S., Chap. 72, § 32.
(4) Hurd's R. S., Chap. 72, § 33.
(5) Hurd's R. S., Chap. 72, § 34.
(6) Hurd's R. S., Chap. 72, § 35.

CIENCY OF AFFIDAVIT.—An affidavit of a plaintiff in execution to obtain a *ca. sa.*, which declares that the debtor has refused, and still does refuse to surrender his property and estate in satisfaction of an execution, is insufficient. The affidavit should aver that the defendant had estate, lands and tenements, goods and chattels, liable to be seized and sold, specifying them, and that he refuses to surrender them after a personal demand made, if a demand is practicable.(¹) If an officer should refuse to execute a *ca. sa.*, issued upon an insufficient affidavit, he will be protected, nor is he liable for an escape under it, although where he executes it he may protect himself by pleading it.(²)

37. EFFECT OF ARREST—AT COMMON LAW AND UNDER OUR STATUTE.—Imprisonment for debt, strictly speaking, is abolished, and the effects and consequences of imprisonment for debt at the common law must fail. At common law, seizing the body of a defendant in execution operates as a satisfaction of the debt, and the plaintiff can have no further process under his judgment; but, where a defendant is arrested under a *ca. sa.*, and a trial had under our insolvent laws, even though the verdict may be in favor of the defendant and he be discharged and released from imprisonment, still the debt is not discharged. Nor will the debt be discharged where the jury fail to agree, and by agreement of parties the defendant is released and discharged from imprisonment.(³)

38. INSOLVENT DEBTOR CAN NOT BE COMPELLED TO SCHEDULE.—A debtor arrested on a *ca. sa.*, if found guilty, can not be compelled to schedule, even though found guilty of fraud, upon a trial of that question, although if he desire to do so, he may, in the cases allowed.(⁴)

39. FRAUD—PRESUMPTION AS TO FRAUD.—Fraud can not be shown without proof of the facts. No fraud can be presumed. An insolvent debtor has the right to sell his property to pay his debts, and where the design of such an act may be traced to an honest and legitimate source, equally as well as to a corrupt one, fraud can not be presumed, but must be shown, although it is suffi-

(1) Tuttle vs. Wilson, 24 Ill., 553.
(2) *Ib.;* Howard vs. Crawford, 15 Ga., 424.
(3) Strode vs. Broadwell, 36 Ill., 419.
(4) Bowden vs. Bowden, 75 Ill., 143.

ciently proven if the facts and circumstances shown are strong enough to justify the jury in inferring a fraudulent intent.(¹)

40. JURISDICTION.—In passing this act, it was the intention of the legislature to place tort feasors upon the same footing as contract debtors, in relation to imprisonment for debt, where the injury complained of results from mere inadvertance and from no bad design. So, where judgment is obtained against one for a tort not resulting from malice, and such debtor is imprisoned under a writ of *capias ad satisfaciendum*, he may be discharged from imprisonment the same as a contract debtor.(²) It is otherwise, however, where the wrong complained of, and on account of which the judgment was rendered, had its origin in an intentional wrong. In such a case, this law affords no relief to the imprisoned debtor.(³)

A judge of the county court has no authority to entertain an insolvent proceeding and discharge an insolvent, except when sitting as a court. In such a proceeding, the plaintiff in the writ, or his attorney, is entitled to notice of the proceeding, so that the right to a discharge may be contested.(⁴) The rule in this case has been changed by statute. (*See Section* 1.) County court is always open for the transaction of such business. The statute was passed in 1861. (See laws 1861, page 105.)

41. APPEAL.—Appeal lies from the county to the circuit court, in an insolvent proceeding. Where a party is arrested on a *ca. sa.*, and denies the grounds for his arrest stated in the plaintiff's affidavit, and demands a jury to try the question in the county court, and they find against him, and the court remands him back to the officer having him in custody, the order thus made is not a ministerial, but a judicial act, and is for all purposes, final; and an appeal lies therefrom.(⁵)

Where an insolvent debtor appeals from the order of the county court refusing his discharge from arrest for debt, he is not required to appear in person in the circuit court before a trial is had and a verdict found against him. And it is error to dismiss his appeal merely for want of such appearance, where he appears by attorney

(1) Bowden vs. Bowden, 75 Ill., 143.
(2) People vs. Greer, 33 Ill., 213.
(3) First National Bank of Flora, vs. Burkett, 101 Ill., 391.
(4) The People *ex. rel.* Loomis vs. Williamson, 13 Ill., 660.
(5) Bowden vs. Bowden, *supra*.

and demands a trial of the issues as to fraud or refusal to surrender his property in execution.(¹)

42. BOND ON APPEAL.—The condition required in the bond given by a debtor on an appeal from the order of the county court refusing to release him from arrest was as follows: "That he will prosecute his said appeal with effect; and in case appeal is dismissed, or the order or judgment of the county court is affirmed, in whole or in part, he will perform the same, and will appear before and abide whatever decision the circuit court shall make in the premises, and pay all costs that may be awarded against him ; and, also, that he will not sell or dispose of any of his estate, pending such appeal, but the same shall be forthcoming, and subject to the order of the county court." It was held, this bond does not require a personal appearance before the court, until the case has reached a stage at which it is the province of the court to make a decision which the debtor is required to perform. He is not bound to personally appear until the appeal is dismissed, or the order of the county court is affirmed, in whole or in part.(²)

(1) Cooley vs. Culton, 20 Ill., 40; Maher vs. Huette, 89 Ill., 495.
(2) Maher vs. Huette, *supra*.

ADDITIONAL NOTES.

1. Imprisonment for debt—Satisfaction.
2. County court given exclusive jurisdiction.
3. Who may have relief—When malice is not the gist of action.
4. Bail—Imprisonment.
5. Continuance.
6. Verdict—How far conclusive on appeal.
7. Appeal.
8. Credit for imprisonment.

1. IMPRISONMENT—SATISFACTION.—In any case where the defendant arrested upon final process shall not be entitled to relief under the provisions of the act of 1887, if the plaintiff will advance the jail fees and board in manner hereinbefore provided, the defendant may be imprisoned at $1.50 per day, until the judgment shall be satisfied, and the officer making the arrest shall endorse the execution, "Satisfied in full by imprisonment:" *Provided*, that no person heretofore or hereafter imprisoned under the provisions of this act shall be imprisoned for a longer period than six months from the date of arrest; and all persons imprisoned under the provisions of this act for the period of six months or more at the time this act takes effect shall thereupon be immediately discharged: *Provided, however,* that no person shall be released from imprisonment under this act who neglects or refuses to schedule in manner and form as provided by this act.(¹)

2. COUNTY COURT GIVEN EXCLUSIVE JURISDICTION.—The county court is given exclusive original jurisdiction in applications for discharge from imprisonment hereunder.(²)

3. WHO MAY HAVE RELIEF—WHEN MALICE IS NOT THE GIST OF ACTION.—Malice is determinable from pleadings, where expressly charged and either admitted or proved, and judgment based on such proof.(³) Malice is the gist of action in action of trespass for assault and battery.(⁴) A wrong done a creditor and an intention to commit

(1) Hurd's R. S., Chap. 73, § 34, 809.
(2) Kitson vs. Farwell, 132 Ill., 327.
(3) Mahler vs. Sinsheimer, 20 Ill. Ap., 401; **Flora Nat. Bank vs. Burkett,** 101 Ill., 391.
(4) *In re* Murphy, 109 Ill., 31.

the injury are necessary to deprive the debtor of the right to discharge from arrest and imprisonment.(¹) Where malice is the gist of action, an insolvent debtor is not entitled to discharge under this section.(²)

Before petitioner rested his case, the court permitted respondent to offer in evidence the record and files in the case in which the judgment was rendered, for the purpose of proving that malice was the gist of action. This putting in part of respondent's case in advance was not error.(³)

4. BAIL—IMPRISONMENT.—Enlargement of insolvent debtor to bail by county court, pending his application for discharge, is not escape voluntary or negligent so as to prevent his again being imprisoned for the same debt.(⁴)

5. CONTINUANCE.—With defendant's express or implied consent, the court may grant continuance for more than thirty days without losing jurisdiction of defendant's person or of the subject-matter.(⁵)

6. VERDICT—HOW FAR CONCLUSIVE ON APPEAL.—A verdict on a trial of a person imprisoned for debt on a charge of fraudulently disposing of his property, and a charge of unjustly refusing to surrender his property, which finds him not guilty of fraud, but guilty of the other ground, is conclusive upon an appeal from an order of remandment upon the question of fraud, *expedit reipublicæ ut sit finis litium*.(⁶)

7. APPEAL.—On appeal to the circuit court in proceeding to schedule, the finding in the county court being that malice was the gist of action on which defendant was arrested, and denial of permission to schedule, the judgment in the circuit court reversing this, and remanding with directions to allow debtor to schedule, is final and appealable.(⁷)

8. IMPRISONMENT—CREDIT.—The defendant is entitled to the credit of $1.50 for every day he is imprisoned under execution, irrespective of whether the duration of imprisonment is sufficient to satisfy the writ in full or not.(⁸)

(1) Mahler vs. Sinsheimer, 20 Ill. Ap., 401; Flora Nat. Bank vs. Burkett, 101 Ill., 391.
(2) *In re* Mullin, 118 Ill., 551; *In re* Murphy, 109 Ill., 551.
(3) Kitson vs. Farwell, 30 Ill. Ap., 341.
(4) People vs. Hanchett, 111 Ill., 90.
(5) *Id.*
(6) *In re* Ennor, 105 Ill., 105.
(7) Mahler vs. Sinsheimer, 20 Ill. Ap., 409.
(8) Hanchett vs. Weber, 17 Ill. Ap., 114.

CHAPTER XX.

BASTARDY.

1. Complaint by mother—form.
2. Warrant—form.
3. Examination—bail—forms.
4. Trial in the county court.
5. Continuance—form of recognizance.
6. Parties may testify.
7. When judgment is for the defendant.
8. When judgment is against defendant—forms.
9. Refusal to give security.
10. Money—how used.
11. Quarterly installments—default in payment—forms.
12. Contempt—lien of judgment.
13. Custody of child.
14. Child not born alive, or dying.
15. Marriage of parents.
16. Limitation.
17. Rules governing the action of bastardy.
18. Pleadings.
19. Annuity.
20. Birth of twins.
21. Escape of defendant.
22. Acquittal of defendant.
23. Marriage of mother.
24. Venue.
25. By next friend.
26. Exceptions.
27. Instructions.
28. Defendant as witness.
29. New trial.
30. Verdict.
31. Fees of State's Attorney.
32. Period of gestation.
33. Evidence.
34. Continuance.
35. Depositions.
36. Action on bond.
37. Appeals and writ of error.

1. COMPLAINT BY MOTHER.—When an unmarried woman who shall be pregnant, or delivered of a child which by law would be

deemed a bastard, shall make complaint to a justice of the peace of the county where she may be so pregnant or delivered, or the person accused may be found, and shall accuse, under oath or affirmation, a person with being the father of such child, it shall be the duty of such justice to issue a warrant against the person so accused, and cause him to be brought forthwith before him, or in case of his absence, any other justice of the peace in such county.(1)

The complaint must be in writing, and may be in form as follows:

FORM OF COMPLAINT.

STATE OF ILLINOIS, } ss.
...............County,

On this......day of........., A. D. 18..., personally appeared before me, the undersigned, a justice of the peace, within and for said county, C. D., of the county and state aforesaid, who, being duly sworn according to law, upon her oath says, that she is an unmarried woman, and that she [is pregnant with child], which by law would be deemed a bastard. [*Or, if the child had already been born, insert within the brackets as follows:* "*Was, on to-wit: the......day of........., A. D. 18..., delivered of a ...male child.*"] That E. F., of the county and state aforesaid, is the father of such child; and she prays that a warrant may issue against him, and that he may be dealt with according to law. C. D.

Subscribed and sworn to before me, this......day of........., 18...
A. B., Justice of the Peace.

2. WARRANT.—The warrant shall be directed to all sheriffs, coroners and constables in the State of Illinois, and may be executed by any such officer in any county.(2)

WARRANT FOR BASTARDY.

STATE OF ILLINOIS, } ss.
...............County,

The People of the State of Illinois, to all Sheriffs, Coroners and Constables in said State, Greeting:

Whereas, C D, of.........county, and State of Illinois, has this day made complaint on oath before me, A B, a justice of the peace, in and for said county, that she is pregnant with child, [*or, that she on, etc., gave birth to a ..male child,*] which by law would be deemed a bastard, and that E F is the father of said child.

We, therefore, command you that you arrest the said E F, and bring him before the said A B, Esq., a justice of the peace of said county, or in

(1) Hurd's R. S., Chap. 17, § 1; Drennan vs. Douglas, 102 Ill., 341.
(2) Hurd's R. S., Chap. 17, § 2; Pease vs. Hubbard, 37 Ill., 257.

case of his absence, before any other justice of the peace of the said county, te answer said charge, and be dealt with according to law.

Given under my hand and seal, this...day of......, A. D. 18...

A B, Justice of the Peace.

3. EXAMINATION—BAIL.—Upon his appearance, it shall be the duty of said justice to examine the woman, upon oath or affirmation, in the presence of the man alleged to be the father of the child, touching the charge against him. The defendant shall have the right to controvert such charge, and evidence may be heard as in cases of trial before the county court. If the justice shall be of opinion that sufficient cause appears, it shall be his duty to bind the person so accused, in bond, with sufficient security to appear at the next county court, to be holden in such county, to answer to such charge; to which court said warrant and bond shall be returned, except that in the county of Cook, where said warrant and bond shall be returned to the criminal court of Cook county. On neglect or refusal to give bond and security, the justice shall cause such person to be committed to the jail of the county, there to be held to answer the complaint.(¹)

BOND FOR APPEARANCE AT THE COUNTY COURT.

Know all men by these presents, that we, E F, G H and I J, of the county of........., and State of Illinois, are held and firmly bound unto the People of the State of Illinois in the penal sum of...dollars, to be paid to the said people, for which payment well and truly to be made, we bind ourselves, our heirs, our executors and administrators, jointly and severally, firmly by these presents. Sealed with our seals, and dated this...day of......, A. D. 18...

Whereas, complaint has been made before A B, one of the justices of the peace in and for the said county of........., by C D, of said county, that she is an unmarried woman and is now pregnant with child, [*or has been delivered of a child,*] which by law would be deemed a bastard, and that E F is the father of said child: Whereupon the said justice issued a warrant and caused the said E F to be brought before him to answer the charge and to be further dealt with according to law; and upon the examination of said justice, of the said C D, touching the said charge, and upon due consideration thereupon had, the said justice was of the opinion, that sufficient cause appeared, and did adjudge and determine that the said E F enter into bond with a good and sufficient security to appear at the next county court, to be held in and for the said county of........., and State of Illinois, to answer such charge.

(1) Hurd's R. S., Chap. 17, § 3.

Now, therefore, the condition of this obligation is such, that if the above bounden E F shall appear at the next county court, to be held in and for the said county of........., [after the birth of said child,] (*if the facts show the child to have been already born, the words in brackets may be omitted,*) and answer to the said charge, and not depart the court without leave, then this obligation to be void, otherwise to remain in force.

Signed, sealed and delivered in }
presence of .... }

E F, [L. S.]
G H, [L. S.]
I J, [L. S.]

COMMITMENT ON NEGLECTING OR REFUSING TO GIVE BOND.

STATE OF ILLINOIS, } ss.
................County, }

The People of the State of Illinois, to any constable of said county; and to the sheriff or keeper of the county jail of said county:

Whereas, complaint has been made before A B, one of the justices of the peace of the said county, by C D, of said county, an unmarried woman, that she is pregnant with child; which by law would be deemed a bastard, and that E F is the father of said child. Whereupon the said justice issued a warrant, and caused the said E F to be brought before him, to answer to the said complaint, and to be dealt with according to law, and, upon examination of the said C D, upon oath, in the presence of the said E F, touching the said charge, and upon due consideration thereupon had, the said justice was of opinion that sufficient cause appeared, and did adjudge and determine that the said E F enter into a bond to appear at the next county court, to be held in and for the said county of........., to answer such charge, and the said E F having refused to give such bond and security, you, the said constable, are therefore, hereby commanded forthwith to convey the said E F to the common jail of the said county, and deliver him to the sheriff or keeper thereof, together with this precept; and you, the said sheriff or keeper, are hereby required to receive the said E F into your custody, in the said jail, there to be held to answer such complaint until he shall give such bond and security, or until he shall be discharged by due course of law.

Given under my hand and seal, this...day of......, A. D. 18...

A B, justice of the Peace, [L. S.]

4. TRIAL IN THE COUNTY COURT.—The county court or the said criminal court of such county, at its next term, shall cause an issue to be made up, whether the person charged, as aforesaid, is the real father of the child or not, which issue shall be tried by a jury. When the person charged, appears and denies the charge, he shall have the right to controvert, by all legal evidence, the truth of such charge.(¹)

(1) Hurd's R. S., Chap. 17, § 4.

Any term of the court, whether for probate business alone or otherwise, has jurisdiction to try a complaint for bastardy. A recognizance taken in accordance with the provisions of Section 3, is forfeited if the defendant fails to appear at the first term thereafter.

5. CONTINUANCE.—If, at the time of such court, the woman be not delivered, or is unable to attend, the court shall order a recognizance to be taken of the person charged as aforesaid, in such an amount, and with such securities as the court may deem just, for the appearance of such person at the next court, after the birth of her child; and should such mother not be able to attend at the next term after the birth of her child, the recognizance shall be continued until she is able.(¹)

The form of such recognizance may be as follows:

Know all men by these presents, that we, E F, G H and I J, of the county of........., and State of Illinois, are held and firmly bound unto the People of the State of Illinois, in the penal sum of...dollars, to be paid to the said People, for which payment, well and truly to be made, we bind ourselves, our heirs, executors and administrators, jointly and severally, firmly by these presents.

Sealed with our seals, and dated this...day of......, A. D. 18...

The condition of the above obligation is such, that whereas the above bounden E F, was, on the...day of......, A. D. 18..., before A B, one of the justices of the peace in and for the county of........., and State of Illinois, examined on a charge of bastardy preferred against him, by C D, the complaining witness, and was, by such justice of the peace, recognized to appear before the county court of the said county of........., and State of Illinois, at the present term thereof, to answer unto said charge; and whereas, the child of the complaining witness, C D, which by law would be deemed a bastard, is not yet delivered, and said cause has been continued in accordance with the provision of the statute in such case made and provided, until the first term of said court after the birth of said child; and said E F, has, by the said county court, been required to enter into a recognizance for his appearance at that term, to answer unto such charge, in the sum of...dollars.

Now, if the said E F shall well and truly be and appear before the said county court, at the next term after the birth of said child, and shall not depart the court without leave, and obey its orders in the premises, then the above obligation shall be void, otherwise to remain in full force and effect.

Signed, sealed and delivered in }
    presence of......... }
                                E F, [L. S.]
                                G H, [L. S.]
                                I J, [L. S.]

Approved by me, this...day of......, 18...

..........., Judge of the County Court.

(1) Hurd's R. S., Chap. 17, § 5.

6. PARTIES MAY TESTIFY.—On the trial of every issue of bastardy, the mother and defendant shall be admitted as competent witnesses, and their credibility shall be left to the jury.([1])

7. WHEN JUDGMENT IS FOR THE DEFENDANT.—If, upon trial of the issue aforesaid, the jury shall find that the child is not the child of the defendant, or alleged father, then the judgment of the court shall be that he be discharged. The woman making the complaint shall pay the costs of the prosecution, and judgment shall be entered therefor, and execution may thereupon issue.([2])

8. WHEN JUDGMENT IS AGAINST DEFENDANT.—In case the issue be found against the defendant, or reputed father, or whenever he shall, in open court, have confessed the truth of the accusation against him, he shall be condemned by the order and judgment of the court, to pay a sum of money not exceeding one hundred dollars for the first year, after the birth of such child, and a sum not exceeding fifty dollars yearly, for nine years succeeding said first year, for the support, maintenance and education of such child, and shall moreover, be adjudged to pay all the costs of the prosecution, for which costs execution shall issue as in other cases. And the said reputed father shall be required by said court to give bond with sufficient security, to be approved by the judge of said court, for the payment of such sum of money as shall be ordered by said court as aforesaid, which said bond shall be made payable to the People of the State of Illinois, and conditioned for the due and faithful payment of said yearly sum, in equal quarterly installments, to the clerk of said court, which bond shall be filed and preserved by the clerk of said court.([3])

In case the issue be found against the defendant, the following is a form of final order:

STATE OF ILLINOIS, } ss.
................County, }

In the County Court,
To the......Term, A. D. 18...

The People of the State of Illinois,
on the Relation of C D,
vs.
E.........F.........

Bastardy.

And now, on this day, the same being the...judicial day of the present

(1) Hurd's R. S., Chap. 17, § 6.
(2) Hurd's R. S., Chap. 17, § 7.
(3) Hurd's R. S., Chap. 17, § 8.

term of this court, come the said plaintiff, by.........., attorney, also, come the said defendant, by.........., his attorney, and this cause coming on now to be heard, before the court and a jury: It was ordered, that a jury be called; whereupon, come the following jurors, to-wit: [*Here insert the names of the jurors*], twelve good and lawful men, who were duly empanneled, tried and sworn to try the cause and a true verdict render, according to the evidence: Whereupon, the parties plaintiff and defendant, introduced evidence to the jury, and the jury having heard the evidence, the arguments of the counsel, and received the instructions of the court, retired in charge of an officer to consider of their verdict, and having duly considered thereof, the said jury returned into open court with their verdict, in words and figures as follows, to-wit:

We, the undersigned, jurors, in the case of the people of the State of Illinois, on the relation of C D vs. E F, find the said E F, the defendant, to be the father of the said bastard child, of the said C D. [*Signed by all the jurors.*]

Which said verdict is received and ordered to be recorded, and said jury discharged from any further consideration of this cause: Whereupon the said defendant, by his counsel, moves the court to set aside said verdict, and grant the said defendant a new trial herein, and ask the time until......, to file the specific reasons why said motion should be allowed; which said time is granted by the court as asked. And afterwards, to-wit: on the... day of this term, come again the parties, by their respective attorneys, and the said defendant having filed his reasons for a new trial, the same came on now to be heard by the court, and the court having heard the arguments of counsel and having duly considered thereof, and being now sufficiently advised and satisfied in the premises, overrules said motion; to which decision of the court in overruling said motion, the defendant by his counsel, then and there excepted. Whereupon the counsel for the plaintiff, moves the court for judgment upon the verdict of the jury; and the court being now sufficiently advised and satisfied in the premises, as to what order and judgment should be made and entered in this cause, doth order and adjudge: That the said E F do pay to the clerk of this court, for the support, maintenance and education of the bastard child of the said C D, the sum of one hundred dollars, for the first year after the birth of said bastard child, which was born on the...day of......, A. D. 18...; and fifty dollars for each year for nine years thereafter; such payments to be made in equal quarterly installments, to-wit: on the first days of......, ..., ..., and......, of each year.

And it is further ordered, that said defendant give bond in the sum of...dollars, with security to be approved by the court, for the payment of the several sums of money hereinbefore ordered to be paid by the said defendant, conditioned for the due and faithful payment of said yearly sums in equal quarterly installments, to the clerk of this court, according to the statute in such case made and provided, and that the said defendant be committed to the custody of the sheriff until he complies with this order.

And it is further ordered by the court, that if the said defendant shall neglect or refuse to give said bond and security so ordered by the court, he shall be committed to the common jail of the county, there to remain until he shall comply with such order, or until otherwise discharged by due course of law.

The defendant shall be placed in the custody of the sheriff, until he gives bond on final judgment. The constitutional prohibition of imprisonment for debt, has reference only to debts arising *ex contractu*, and has no reference to torts or to a proceeding under the bastardy act.([1])

The bond may be in form as follows:

STATE OF ILLINOIS, } ss.
..................County, }

Know all men by these presents, that we, E F, G H and I J, of the county of........., and State of Illinois, are held and firmly bound unto the People of the State of Illinois, in the penal sum of...dollars, to be paid to the said People, for which payment, well and truly to be made, we bind ourselves, our heirs, executors and administrators, jointly and severally, firmly by these presents. Sealed with our seals, and dated this...day of......., A. D. 18...

The condition of the above obligation is such, that whereas, the above bounden E F, was, at the......term, A. D. 18..., of the county court of......... county, and on to-wit: the...judicial day of said term, before the Hon........., judge, presiding, and a jury, found guilty of being the father of a...male bastard child, on a charge of bastardy preferred against him by C D, the mother of said child: Whereupon the court did order and adjudge that the said E F do pay to the clerk of this court for the support, maintenance and education of the bastard child of the said C D, the sum of one hundred dollars for the first year after the birth of said child; which was born on the...day of......, A. D. 18..., and fifty dollars for each year, for nine years thereafter, such payments to be made in equal quarterly installments, to-wit: on the first days of......, ..., ..., and......, of each year.

Now, therefore, the condition of this obligation is such, that if the above bounden E F shall well and truly pay or cause to be paid, the said installments of money as they may become due, to the clerk of this court, for the uses and purposes set forth in the order and judgment of this court; and shall fully comply with the order and judgment of this court rendered in said cause; and with all the terms and conditions thereof, then this obligation to be void, otherwise to remain in full force and effect.

Signed, sealed and delivered in } E F, [L. S.]
   the presence of......... } G H, [L. S.]
                                      I J, [L. S.]

Taken and approved by me, this...day of......, A. D. 18...

........., Judge of the County Court.

(1) Rich vs. People, 66 Ill., 514.

9. REFUSAL TO GIVE SECURITY.—In case the defendant or reputed father shall refuse or neglect to give such security as may be ordered by the court, he shall be committed to the jail of the county, there to remain until he shall comply with such order, or until otherwise discharged by due course of law.

10. MONEY, HOW USED.—The money, when received, shall be laid out and appropriated for the support of such child in such manner as shall be directed by the court; but when a guardian shall be appointed for such bastard, the money arising from such bond, shall be paid over to such guardian.(¹)

11. QUARTERLY INSTALLMENT—DEFAULT IN PAYMENT.— Whenever default shall be made in the payment of a quarterly installment, or any part thereof, mentioned in the bond provided for in the foregoing section, the county judge of the county, or the judge of the criminal court in Cook county, wherein such bond is filed, shall, at the request of the mother, guardian, or any other person interested in the support of such child, issue a citation to the principal and sureties in said bond, requiring them to appear, on some day in said citation mentioned, during the next term of the county court of said county for probate business, or of the said criminal court, and show cause, if any they have, why execution should not issue against them for the amount of the installment or installments due and unpaid on said bond, which said citation shall be served by any sheriff or constable of the county in which such principal or sureties reside or may be found, at least five days before the term day thereof, and if the amount due on such installment or installments, shall not be paid at or before the time mentioned for showing cause as aforesaid, the said county judge shall render judgment in favor of the People of the State of Illinois, against the principal and sureties who have been served with said citation, for the amount unpaid on the installment or installments due on said bond, and the costs of said proceeding; and execution shall issue from said county court against the goods and chattels of the person or persons against whom said judgment shall be rendered, for the amount of said judgment and costs, to the sheriff of any county in the state where the parties to said judgment, or either of them, reside, or have property subject to such execution.(²)

(1) Hurd's R. S., Chap. 17, § 10.   (2) Hurd's R. S., Chap. 17, § 11.

The request or petition for a citation above referred to, may be in form as follows:

STATE OF ILLINOIS, } ss.   *In the County Court,*
..............County,   *To the.......Term, A. D.* 18...

To the Hon............, Judge of said Court:

Your petitioner, C D, by her attorney, would respectfully represent and show unto your honor, that at to-wit: the......term, A. D. 18..., of this honorable court, one E F was found guilty of being the father of a...male bastard child of your petitioner, and required to give bond to be approved by your honor, in the sum of...dollars, with..........and........., as his sureties, conditioned for the faithful payment of the order and judgment of this court, rendered in said cause upon the trial thereof. And your petitioner would further show, that by the order of said court, and the terms and conditions of said bond, the said E F was condemned to pay one hundred dollars for the first year after the birth of said child, and fifty dollars for each year, for nine years thereafter; commencing from the day of the birth of said child, to-wit: ......, 18..., in equal quarterly installments, to the clerk of this honorable court. Your petitioner would further show, that by the terms and conditions of said bond, (the same being now on file in this honorable court, and reference being had and made thereto for greater certainty,) the second installment of twenty-five dollars, due for the support, maintenance and education of said bastard child, was due and payable on the...day of....., A. D. 18..., but that the same has not been paid by the said E F, nor by any one for him, to the clerk of this court or to your petitioner: Wherefore, she prays that a citation may issue for the said E F, as well, also, for the said G H and I J, the sureties on his bond; commanding them and each of them, to appear before this honorable court at its next......term, A. D. 18...; and on the...day thereof, to show cause, if any they have, why execution shall not issue against them for the amount of the installment or installments, due and unpaid on said bond.

And your petitioner will ever pray, etc.

By........., her Attorney.   C D.

The statute provides, that upon the filing of such request or petition, the judge of the county court shall order the clerk to issue a citation against the said principal and his sureties. The citation may be in form as follows:

STATE OF ILLINOIS, } ss.
..............County,

The People of the State of Illinois, to the Sheriff or any Constable of said County, Greeting:

Whereas, C D has represented by petition, filed in the county court of said county, at the......term, A. D. 18..., that E F, as principal, and G H and

I J, as sureties upon the bastardy bond given by the said E F, at the......
term, A. D. 18..., upon his being found guilty of being the father of the
...male bastard child of the said C D, have made default in the payment of
the...installment, due for the support, maintenance and education of said
bastard child, and have violated the terms and conditions of said bond:

You are therefore, hereby commanded to cite and give notice, to the
said E F, G H and I J, as aforesaid, that they be and appear before our
county court of..........county, Illinois, at the next......term thereof, to be
holden at the court house, in.........., on the...day of......, A. D. 18, then and
there to show cause, if any they have, why execution shall not issue against
them, for the amount of the installment due and unpaid on said bond. And
hereof make due service and return as the law directs.

    Witness.........., Clerk of said County Court, at........., Illinois, this
[L. S.]   ...day of......, A. D. 18...
                ...., County Clerk.

The sheriff or other officer having the same, will serve the citation, and then return the same back into the office of the county clerk. The service should be at least five days before the term day thereof. The return may be in form as follows:

STATE OF ILLINOIS, | ss.
..............County, |

I have duly served the within citation, by reading the same, to the within named E F, G H and I J, as I am therein commanded, this...day of......, A. D. 18...
         ...., Sheriff of.........County, Illinois.

At the term to which the citation is issued, the judge shall proceed to hear and determine the cause, and if the amount due on such installment or installments, shall not be paid at or before the time mentioned for showing cause as aforesaid, the county judge shall render judgment in favor of the people of the State of Illinois, against the principal and sureties who have been served with said citation, for the amount unpaid on the installment or installments, due on said bond and the costs of this proceeding, and execution shall issue therefor. The judgment may be in form as follows:

The People of the State of Illinois, ⎫
  for the use, etc.,   ⎬ Judgment on an Installment
    vs.   ⎪ Due on a Bastardy Bond.
  E F, G H and I J.   ⎭

And now, on this day, comes the said People of the State of Illinois, by.........., attorney, and the said E F, G H and I J, by.........., attorney, and this cause coming on now to be heard before the court, and the court having heard all the evidence and the argument of counsel, and being now sufficiently advised and satisfied in the premises, it is ordered, that the said plaintiff have and recover of the said defendants, the sum of twenty-five dollars, the same being the amount of the...installment due on the...day of......, 18..., of the bastardy bond given by the said E F, as principal, and G H and I J, as sureties, to the People of the State of Illinois aforesaid, for the support, education and maintenance of the bastard child of the said C D.

And it is further ordered, that the defendants pay all the costs of this proceeding, and that execution may issue for the amount of the judgment and costs so rendered as aforesaid in this cause.

12. CONTEMPT—LIEN OF JUDGMENT.—And said county judge shall also have power, in case of default in the payment, when due, of any installment or installments, or any part thereof, in the condition of said bond mentioned, to adjudge the reputed father of such child guilty of contempt of said court, by reason of the non-payment as aforesaid, and to order him to be committed to the county jail of said county, until the amount of said installment or installments, so due, shall be fully paid, together with all costs of said commitment, and in the obtaining and enforcing of said judgment and execution, as aforesaid. But the commitment of such reputed father, shall not operate to stay or defeat the obtaining of judgment and the collection thereof by execution as aforesaid: *Provided*, that the rendition and collection of judgment, as aforesaid, shall not be construed to bar or hinder the taking of similar proceedings for the collection of subsequent quarterly installments on said bond, as they shall become due and remain unpaid: *And, Provided, further*, that if the county judge, or any other person interested in the support of such child, shall deem it necessary, in order to secure the payment or collection of such judgment, that the same should be made a lien on real estate, a transcript of said proceedings and judgment shall be made by the clerk of said county court, and filed and recorded in the office of the clerk of the circuit court of said county, in the same manner and with like effect as transcripts of judgments of justices of the peace are filed and recorded, to make the same a lien on real estate; and execution and other process shall thereupon issue for the collection of said judgment, as in case of other judgments in said circuit court; and the provisions of this section shall, as far as applicable, apply to all bonds which have

heretofore been taken in pursuance of the statutes in regard to bastardy.(¹)

13. CUSTODY OF CHILD.—The reputed father of a bastard child, shall not have the right to the custody or control of such child, if the mother is living and wishes to retain such custody and control, until after it shall have arrived at the age of ten years, unless, upon petition to the circuit court of the county in which the mother resides, it shall, on full hearing of the facts in the case, after notice to the mother, be made to appear to the judge of said court, that said mother is not a suitable person to have the control and custody of such child.(²)

14. CHILD NOT BORN ALIVE OR DYING.—If the said child should never be born alive, or being born alive, should die at any time, and the fact shall be suggested upon the record of the said court, then the bond aforesaid shall from thenceforth be void.(³)

15. MARRIAGE OF PARENTS.—If the mother of any bastard child, and reputed father, shall, at any time after its birth, intermarry, the said child shall, in all respects, be deemed and held legitimate, and the bond aforesaid be void.(⁴)

16. LIMITATION.—No prosecution under this act shall be brought after two years from the birth of the bastard child: *Provided*, the time any person accused shall be absent from the state shall not be computed.(⁵)

17. RULES GOVERNING THE ACTION OF BASTARDY.—A prosecution for bastardy, is a civil proceeding.(⁶) A writ of error may be sued out by the people, and were it a criminal proceeding, this could not be allowed.(⁷) So far as the arrest and trial are concerned, the form is criminal;(⁸) and it may be tried at a criminal term.(⁹) In the means of coercing a compliance with the order and judgment of the

(1) Hurd's R. S., Chap. 17, ¿ 12.
(2) Hurd's R. S., Chap. 17, ¿ 13.
(3) Hurd's R. S., Chap. 17, ¿ 14.
(4) Hurd's R. S., Chap. 17, ¿ 15.
(5) Hurd's R. S., Chap. 17, ¿ 16.
(6) The People vs. Starr, 50 Ill., 52; Mann vs. The People, 35 Ill., 467; Maloney vs. The People, 38 Ill., 62; Allison vs. The People, 45 Ill., 37; Davis vs. The People, 50 Ill., 199; The People vs. Christman, 66 Ill., 162: Peak vs. The People, 76 Ill., 289; Holcomb vs. The People, 79 Ill., 409; Lewis vs. The People, 82 Ill., 104; McElhaney vs. People, 1 Bradwell, 550; Rawlings vs. People, 102 Ill., 475
(7) The People vs Noxon, 40 Ill., 30.
(8) Holcomb vs. The People, *supra*.
(9) Kelley vs. The People, 29 Ill., 287.

court, or having execution of the judgment, it is essentially criminal in form and effect. The public has such an interest in the prosecution and the support of the child, as to declare or treat it as a misdemeanor, and thus enforce the judgment by imprisonment, until the order is complied with, precisely as in cases of fines recovered for misdemeanors, or similar offenses against the public. Although a prosecution under the bastardy act is civil, as distinguishable from a criminal prosecution, the constitutional provision relating to imprisonment for debt, has reference only to debts arising *ex contractu*. It has no reference to torts or to a prosecution under the bastardy act.([1]) Though criminal in form, it is not essential to a conviction that the evidence of guilt should exclude every reasonable doubt, a mere preponderance of evidence is sufficient.

The sole power of originating proceedings against the reputed father, rests with the mother,([2]) and she may settle and dismiss the complaint.([3]) If she be an infant, however, at the time the settlement was made, it does not bar her action.([4])

18. PLEADINGS.—The complaint is required to be in writing;([5]) and it is a sufficient allegation of time in a bastardy proceeding, if it is stated that the mother was between the first and fifteenth days of July, 1853, made pregnant; or, if she alleges, that on or about a certain day, the child was begotten, it is sufficient.([6])

Formal pleadings are not necessary, where there is a sworn complaint which shows the character of the charge against the defendant, and the record shows a plea of not guilty, the issue thus made, is sufficient.([7])

A non-resident female may prosecute the putative father in the courts of this state, as our statute is not limited in its operation to residents of the state. And where a suit is instituted by a mother, who at the time is a non-resident, no bond for costs is required to

---

(1) Kelly vs. The People, 29 Ill., 287; Rich vs. The People, 66 Ill., 513; State vs. Palin, 63 N. C., 471; Reynolds vs. Lamount, 45 Ind., 308; Paulk vs. State, 52 Ala., 427.
(2) Burgen vs. Straughan, 7 J. J. Marsh, (Ky.) 583; Harter vs. Johnson, 16 Ind., 271; jones vs. The People, 53 Ill., 366.
(3) Coleman vs. Frum, 3 Scam., 378; Holcomb vs. The People, 79 Ill., 409; Baker vs. Roberts, 14 Ind., 552; McElhaney vs. People, 1 Bradwell, 550.
(4) State vs. Wilson, 21 Ind., 273.
(5) Constitution, Art. I, § 6, page 54.
(6) Beals vs. Furbish, 19 Me., 496.
(7) People vs. Woodside, 72 Ill., 407.

be filed, as our statute in regard to costs, does not apply to such cases.(¹)

County courts are vested with full power and jurisdiction to hear and determine a case of bastardy, and this in addition to the jurisdiction conferred by the county court act, nor is any section of the county court act, in conflict with, or repugnant to the bastardy act.(²)

Where the evidence shows the child was born alive, the proceedings are not abated by its death. And, where the suit was instituted while living, in case the reputed father is found guilty, the court should order the payment of so much of the amount fixed by the statute as shall have accrued between the birth and death of the child.(³) Nor will the death of the mother abate a bastardy proceeding commenced during her life.(⁴)

19. ANNUITY.—The annuity allowed for the support of the bastard, should commence at its birth.(⁵)

20. TWINS.—Where the complaint charges the defendant of being the father of a child, which, when born, will be a bastard, and, subsequently the woman making the complaint, gives birth to twins, it is not erroneous to render judgment, upon conviction, for the payment of the same amount as if only one child had been born.(⁶) The father of two bastard children, born at one birth, is chargeable for the maintenance of both.(⁷)

21. ESCAPE.—An officer who negligently permits the escape of a prisoner, arrested for bastardy, is liable to the prosecutrix for damages.(⁸)

22. ACQUITTAL.—Where a justice discharged a person accused of being the father of an illegitimate child, it was held to be no bar to a subsequent prosecution for the same offense.(⁹) So, if the time of the child's birth is wrongly stated in the warrant, an acquittal of the defendant will not be a bar to a subsequent proceeding, on a warrant which avers the time truly. Nor will a judgment on a

---

(1) Kolbe vs. People, 85 Ill., 336.
(2) People vs. Woodside, 72 Ill., 407.
(3) Meredith vs. Wall, 14 Allen, (Mass.) 155; Hinton vs. Dickenson, 19 Ohio St., 583; Hauskins vs. The People, 82 Ill., 193.
(4) The People vs. Nixon, 45 Ill., 353.
(5) Kelly vs. The People, 29 Ill., 287.
(6) Connelly vs. The People, 81 Ill., 379.
(7) Hall vs. Commonwealth, Hard., (Ky.) 479.
(8) Pease vs. Hubbard, 37 Ill., 257.
(9) Davis vs. State, 6 Blackford, (Ind.) 494.

recognizance, for failure to appear and answer be a bar to the same charge.(¹)

23. MARRIAGE.—It is improper to dismiss a proceeding in bastardy upon the prosecutrix's marriage with a man other than the defendant; for, the reputed father is nevertheless chargeable with the maintenance of the bastard child.(²)

24. VENUE.—The woman not being a party to a bastardy proceeding, but a witness, can not make application for a change of venue.(³)

25. PROCHEIN AMI.—It is proper for the county court, after a motion to dismiss a proceeding by the defendant, commenced by an infant, to allow a *prochein ami* to enter as prosecutor.(⁴)

26. EXCEPTIONS.—Exceptions to the rulings of the court must be made and entered in the lower court. The refusal to quash the affidavit and writ thereon, because the complaint was made by a person other than the mother, cannot be assigned for error. Nor can it be availed of on motion in arrest of judgment. So, too, objections to insufficiency of proof on formal questions, must be made in the lower court.(⁵)

27. INSTRUCTIONS.—An instruction which states that the defendant may be found guilty on a preponderance of evidence, is not erroneous.(⁶) Although an instruction may contain a correct proposition of law, if the substance has been given in other instructions and it can be seen that its refusal made no difference in the result of the trial, its refusal will not be any ground for a reversal of the judgment.(⁷) Where it is stated in an instruction that "it is not incumbent upon the people to show, by a clear preponderance of evidence, that the defendant is the father of the child charged to be his in the complaint; but it is sufficient, if the evidence creates probabilities in favor of that opinion, and the weight inclines to that side of the question," it is erroneous.(⁸) So, too, an in-

---

(1) Burnet vs. Commonwealth, 4 T. B. Mon., 108; Commonwealth vs. Thompson, 3 Litt., (Ky.,) 284.
(2) State vs. Ingram, 4 Hayw., (Tenn.) 221; Roth vs. Jacobs, 21 Ohio, 646.
(3) Duffries vs. State, 7 Wis., 672; State vs. Smith, 55 Ind., 385.
(4) Coomes vs. Knapp, 11 Vt., 543.
(5) Jones vs. The People, 53 Ill., 366; Cook vs. The People, 51 Ill., 143; Hauskins vs. The People, 82 Ill., 193.
(6) Lewis vs. The People, 82 Ill., 104.
(7) Holcomb vs. The People, 79 Ill., 409.
(8) Peak vs. The People, 76 Ill., 289.

struction that the maxim, false in one statement, false in all, should only be applied in cases where a witness willfully and knowingly gives false testimony, and if the jury believe from the evidence, that the defendant, or any other witness, has intentionally sworn falsely as to one matter, the jury may properly reject his whole statements and testimony as "unworthy of belief," was held to be erroneous, as being too broad, the words "unless corroborated," should have been added.([1]) An instruction to the jury that if they believed that the witness was mistaken as to the day, but, from all the evidence, that the defendant is the father, they should find for the complainant, was held to be correct.([2])

28. WITNESSES.—The putative father is a competent witness to testify in his own behalf.([3]) It is for the court to decide upon the competency of a witness, and for the jury to determine what credibility shall be given to his testimony.([4])

29. NEW TRIAL.—The rule is well established, that where the jury has been properly instructed, and where the testimony is contradictory and irreconcilable, a new trial will not be awarded.([5])

30. VERDICT.—A verdict of "guilty," is responsive to the charge in such a proceeding, and is substantially good. A more formal verdict would be guilty of being the father of the child.([6])

31. FEES OF STATE'S ATTORNEY.—The State's attorney is allowed the sum of ten dollars upon the trial of any person under the provisions of the laws concerning bastardy.([7])

32. GESTATION.—Writers upon medical jurisprudence, fix no definite period of gestation. Ten lunar months or forty weeks, equaling 280 days, to forty-three weeks, or 291 days, is considered by most authorities to be the usual period of gestation. Nine calendar months and one week is equal to ten lunar months. Instances have been given, however, of fully developed children, which were born after a gestation of only 251 days, while on the other hand, cases are reported where the period of gestation has ex-

---

(1) Peak vs. The People, 76 Ill., 289.
(2) Spivey vs. State, 8 Ind., 405.
(3) The People vs. Starr, 50 Ill., 52.
(4) Kelly vs. The People, 29 Ill., 287.
(5) Holcomb vs. The People, 79 Ill., 409; Connelly vs. The People, 81 Ill., 379.
(6) Davis vs. People, 50 Ill., 199.
(7) Hurd's R. S., Chap. 53, § 8.

tended to 296 days. Out of thirty well defined cases observed, the period of gestation varied from 283 days to one case where it extended to 313 days.([1])

33. EVIDENCE.—The defendant can not introduce evidence of his general good character.([2]) Where, however, other witnesses testify that the prosecutrix has made statements in reference to the paternity of the child, inconsistent with her testimony upon the stand, she may call witnesses to sustain her general good character for truth.([3])

Evidence showing a resemblance of the child to its alleged father, is not admissible.([4]) It is competent to show that the reputed father is impotent, and if true, and proven, it will be a complete and satisfactory defense.([5]) The statements or acknowledgments of the reputed father, as to the relations which he sustained to the mother, are competent.([6])

The day on which it is alleged the prosecutrix became pregnant, is no more material than in any other class of cases. She may be mistaken as to the date, yet if the jury believe from the evidence, that the defendant is the father, they should find him guilty, as it matters not on what day he became so.([7]) And, where the time and place at which the child was begotten, is supported, on a trial, by proof that intercourse took place between the parties, at the time and place named, and also at another time and place, and that the child was begotten by one of these acts of intercourse, it is sufficient, even if the prosecutrix does not know at which of these times the child was begotten.([8])

Neither is it essential, to support a verdict of guilty in a bastardy proceeding, that it shall appear that the period of gestation was for the usual length of time—the evidence being otherwise sat-

---

(1) Taylor's Med. Jur., C. 65, pages 639 to 657; Beck's Med. Jur., vol. 1, pages 595 to 602; Wharton & Stille's Med. Jur., Part 1, Book 2, Chap. 3, Secs. 41 to 73.
(2) Walker vs. State, 6 Blackf., (Ind.) 1; Low vs. Mitchell, 18 Me., 372.
(3) Sweet vs. Sherman, 21 Vt., 23.
(4) Young vs. Makepeace, 103 Mass., 50; United States vs. Collins, 1 Cranch., (Ct.) 592; Kennisten vs. Rowe, 18 Me., 38; *Contra*, Paulk vs. State, 52 Ala., 427.
(5) State vs. Broadwell, 69 N. C., 411.
(6) Sale vs. Crutchfield, 8 Bush., (Ky.) 636.
(7) Holcomb vs. The People, 79 Ill., 409.
(8) Bassett vs. Abbott, 4 Grey, (Mass.) 69.

isfactory in that regard.(¹) And, where it is shown the prosecutrix was delivered of a child, and there is no evidence to the contrary, it will be presumed it was born alive from the ordinary course of nature.(²)

It is not admissible to prove that the mother's general reputation for chastity was bad before her connection with the defendant, and that previously she had frequent intercourse with other men;(³) or that she was in the habit of associating with young men, whose reputation for chastity was bad; or that she had intercourse with other men more than ten calendar months before the birth of the child, unless there be evidence that the period of gestation was unusually protracted.(⁴) So, too, acts of intercourse with other men than the reputed father, twelve months before the birth, are inadmissible.(⁵) Such evidence is too remote.(⁶)

While the prosecutrix can not be asked generally whether prior to the time when she says she was begotten with child by the defendant, she had sexual intercourse with other men,(⁷) yet she having been examined on the trial as a witness for the state, may be asked, on cross examination, whether she had sexual intercourse with any other person than the defendant about the time when she said the child was begotten.(⁸) The rule is, that the time must be limited to a period, such as to admit of the possible inference that the child in question derived its paternity from such intercourse.(⁹) The inquiry being thus restricted to a proper time, it is competent.(¹⁰)

Thus, the mother having sworn to a single act of intercourse, and the child being born eight and one-half months thereafter, evidence of intercourse with other men during the fortnight before, and the fortnight after that act, is admissible; but, notwithstanding, the doubt which might be raised as to the paternity of the child by prosecutrix's connection with other men, at about the time

(1) Cook vs. The People, 51 Ill., 143.
(2) Mann vs. The People, 35 Ill., 467.
(3) Commonwealth vs. Moore, 3 Pick., (Mass.) 194.
(4) Ib.
(5) Eddy vs. Gray, 4 Allen, (Mass.) 435. [409.
(6) Sabines vs. Jones, 119 Mass., 167; Holcomb vs. The People, 79 Ill.,
(7) Townsend vs. State, 13 Ind., 357.
(8) Lowe vs. Mitchell, 18 Me., 372; Walker vs. State, 6 Blackf., (Ind.) 1.
(9) Bowen vs. Reed, 103 Mass., 46; Holcomb vs. The People, *supra*.
(10) Duffries vs. State, 7 Wis., 672.

it was begotten, yet other facts may be introduced sufficient to satisfy the jury of the defendant's liability.(¹)

Where the prosecutrix testified that the child was begotten in a certain month, or the next month following, and could not be any more definite as to the time, it appearing that about the date at which the child was probably begotten, allowing the ordinary period of gestation, being about the first of the former month designated by her, she had sexual intercourse with several men, and it not being shown that there was anything peculiar in one of the connections or attending circumstances, which enabled her to determine that the child was begotten at that time, the evidence was held not sufficient to authorize a finding that the defendant was the father of the child.(²)

Where the only proof of the charge was the unsupported testimony of the prosecutrix, who testified she gave birth to the child on the 15th day of August, 1871, the result of a single act of intercourse with the defendant, in the middle or latter part of November, 1870, and that this was the only act of intercourse she had ever had with either the defendant or any other person: Where the defendant denied the charge in all its parts, and proved by another witness that he himself had sexual intercourse with the complainant as often as once, and sometimes twice a week, during the months of October and November, 1870, and that during her pregnancy, she informed him of her condition, and inquired of him what he was going to do about it: Where two other witnesses testified to having seen the prosecutrix, and still another person in the direct act of sexual intercourse, in the months of October and November, 1870: Where it appeared that the prosecutrix had also informed her father, that the father of the child lived in another county from that the defendant lived in; that her father went there to see the person on the subject: The witnesses on the part of the defendant being unimpeached, the court held, taking all the testimony, it was too unsatisfactory to fix the paternity of the child upon the defendant.(³)

A prosecution for bastardy, being a merely civil proceeding, the

---

(1) O'Brien vs. State, 14 Ind., 469; State vs. Pratt, 40 Iowa, 631.
(2) Whitman vs. State, 34 Ind., 360.
(3) McCoy vs. The People, 65 Ill., 439; Jones vs. The People, 53 Ill., 366.

defendant may be found guilty on a preponderance of evidence.(¹)

The jury must determine from all the evidence, whether the prosecutrix is entitled to greater or less weight on any point in the case, than other witnesses. That depends upon the degree of fidelity with which she and they adhere to the truth. When the mother of a bastard child swears that the defendant is its father, and the defendant swears that he is not, and they are of equal credibility, the one offsets the other, and, unless there is other testimony given or circumstances proved, which give the preponderance to the plaintiff, the defendant should be acquitted.(²)

A jury may infer that the mother of a bastard child is an unmarried woman, from the fact appearing that the defendant paid his attentions to her as such.(³)

34. CONTINUANCE.—An affidavit for a continuance should show the witnesses are material, the facts expected to be proven by the witnesses, and that the affiant knows of no other witness by whom the same facts can be proven. It should show where the witnesses were at the time the application was made, so that the court could know that they were not within its jurisdiction, and either that efforts have been made to procure the attendance of the witnesses, or that such efforts would have been ineffectual for that purpose; that there is a reasonable prospect of obtaining the testimony of the witnesses at some future time, and that the application is not made for delay, but that justice may be done.(⁴)

35. DEPOSITIONS.—In cases of misdemeanors, the depositions of absent witnesses may be taken by consent.(⁵)

So, in a case of prosecution under the bastardy act, if it appear that the attendance of material witnesses on the part of the defendant can not be procured, he may offer to join in a commission with the opposite party to take their depositions, and, if it appear that due diligence has been employed, if such offer be not accepted, the court in its discretion, may grant continuances from term to term, until the other party will join in the commission. And in

---

(1) Lewis vs. People, 82 Ill., 104.
(2) McFarland vs. The People, 72 Ill., 368.
(3) Cook vs. People, 51 Ill., 143.
(4) Richardson vs. The People, 31 Ill., 170.
(5) King vs. Morphew, 2 Maule & Sel., 602; Roscoe's Crim. Ev., 55; Mariner vs. Dyer, 2 Me., (2 Greenl.) 172.

case the commission be joined in by both parties, then the court will continue the cause until the next term.(¹)

36. BOND.—A bond is defined to be a deed, and the words, *ex vi termini*, import a sealed instrument. Although it contains the words, "Sealed with my seal," etc., when there is no seal or scrawl attached, it will not make it a bond or sealed instrument.(²)

A recognizance to support a bastard child, though not taken conformably to the statute, may be good at common law.(³) So is a bond voluntarily given.(⁴)

A bond given by a father of an illegitimate child to its mother, in consideration of her agreement to dismiss a prosecution pending against him, is founded upon a valid consideration.(⁵)

An infant charged with bastardy, may be required to give bond with sureties, and his infancy is no defense, either for him or his sureties, to an action on such bond.(⁶)

The surety on a bastardy bond, upon the death of the reputed father, has a right to petition the county court for a discharge from the bond, and to support the same by affidavit.(⁷)

The surety on a bond, taken before a justice of the peace, is released by the appearance of the reputed father at the next term of the circuit court, and the continuance of the case. He is only bound that the defendant will appear at and during that term, and not depart without leave, and abide the judgment and order of the court in the premises.(⁸)

A bond without a seal is not a compliance with the laws, and is not binding on the obligors. And where an action of debt is brought upon an instrument declared to be a bond or sealed instrument, and the writing produced on oyer has no seal, the variance is fatal, and may be taken advantage of on demurrer.(⁹)

At common law, the conditions of a bond may be valid in part and void in part, if they are severable one from the other,(¹⁰) and the

(1) Richardson vs. The People, 31 Ill., 170.
(2) Chilton vs. the The People, 66 Ill., 501.
(3) State vs. Mason, 2 Nott & M. I., S. C., 425.
(4) Commissioners vs. Gilbert, 2 Strobh., (S. C.) 152.
(5) Coleman vs. Frum, 3 Scam., 378.
(6) McCall vs. Parker, 13 Met., (Mass.) 372.
(7) Hoch vs. Lord Thach, Mass. Cr. Cas., 263.
(8) Burr vs. Wilson, 50 Ind., 587.
(9) Chilton vs. The People, *supra*.
(10) Pigot's Case, 11 Coke, 27.

same principle is applicable to statutory bonds in cases where the statute is silent as to the effect of a departure from the statutory form.(¹)

If one charged with bastardy, enters into a recognizance before a justice of the peace for his appearance at the next term of the county court, to answer the charge, which recognizance provided that "he should not depart the court without leave," and after trial was had, finding him guilty and requiring him to give bond, he fled without leave, this was manifestly a breach of the bond.(²)

A justice has power to take recognizance, and declare it forfeited on the failure of the reputed father to appear according to the conditions of his recognizance.

Where a declaration in debt is brought on such a recognizance, and it fails to aver that there was a default in appearance before the justice of the peace, and that he certified the recognizance, with the record of default to the circuit court of the county, such declaration is bad on a general demurrer, as these are statutory requirements essential to a right of recovery. The recognizance being a statutory obligation, its provisions must be complied with, to authorize a recovery.(³)

A suit on a bastardy bond simply determines the liability of the obligors in the bond to the people of the State of Illinois. Hence, a suit instituted in the name of the mother, instead of for the benefit of the county judge, to the use of the infant child, can neither affect the rights of the county judge or any other person in reference to the money recovered.(⁴)

The fact that the instrument sued on in the declaration, is called a recognizance, is no error. An error in the appellation does not close the eyes of the court to the real character of the instrument—it is a bond.

Neither is it error that a judgment was rendered for the penalty of the bond, $600, to be discharged on the payment of $500 dam-

---

(1) Newman vs. Newman, 4 Maule & Sel., 70; Marlett vs. Wilson, 30 Ind., 240; Erlinger vs. The People, 36 Ill., 458; Anderson vs. Foster, 2 Bailey, 501; United States vs. Brown, Gilpin's Rep., 178; Vroom vs. Exr. of Smith, 2 Green, (N. J.) 480; Commonwealth vs. Pearce, 7 Mon. 317.
(2) Chilton vs. The People, 66 Ill., 501; Simmons vs. Adams, 15 Vt., 677; People vs. jayne, 27 Barb., (N. Y.) 58; Tracy vs. Howe, 119 Mass., 228.
(3) The People vs. Green, 58 Ill., 236.
(4) Erlinger vs. The People, *supra*.

ages and costs of suit, the bond not being given for the support of the child, but to secure the appearance of the obligors at court.(¹)

A judgment on a recognizance, for failing to appear and answer to a prosecution, is no bar to another prosecution for the same charge.(²)

37. APPEAL—ERROR.—Under the constitution, the supreme court have appellate jurisdiction: And Art. 6, Sec. 19, of the constitution, provides, that "Appeals and writs of error, shall be allowed from the final determination of county courts, as may be provided by law."

The statute having provided no appeal or writ of error from the judgment of the county court, in bastardy proceedings, to the circuit court, it follows, that such judgments may be reviewed by this court, on writ of error to the county court, to prevent a failure of justice.(³)

In Peak's case, *supra*, it was held, that by the county court act of 1872, no appeal was given to the circuit court in bastardy cases, but the right of appeal is given from the county court to the circuit court, by the act of 1874.(⁴)

And where the appeal is taken to the circuit court, the case will be tried *de novo*.(⁵)

A prosecution for bastardy, being a civil, and not a criminal proceeding, it is not embraced in the statute of 1879, relating to appeals in criminal cases, which provides that in criminal cases below the grade of felony, the appeal from the county court shall be taken directly to the appellate court.(⁶) But the sum which a defendant is condemned to pay in a bastardy case, is so much in the nature of a penalty, as not to be included in the class of cases not appealable from the appellate court to the supreme court, where the amount involved is less than $1,000.(⁷)

(1) Erlinger vs. The People, 36 Ill., 458.
(2) Commonwealth vs. Thompson, 3 Litt., (Ky.) 284.
(3) Peak vs. The People, 76 Ill., 289; Haines vs. People, 97 Ill., 162.
(4) Holcomb vs. The People, 79 Ill., 409; Lewis vs. The People, 82 Ill., 104; Rawlings vs. People, 102 Ill., 475; Stanley vs. People, 84 Ill., 212.
(5) Hauskins vs. The People, 82 Ill., 193; Stanley vs. People, *supra*.
(6) Rawlings vs. People, *supra*.
(7) *Ib.*

ADDITIONAL NOTES.

1. Bond for security.
2. Release from liability—Compromise—judge of the county court to consent.
3. Liability of the father when the mother marries another man.
4. Subsequent marriage of the mother—Effect upon her rights.
5. Bastardy maintainable by a non-resident.
6. Complaint.
7. Prosecution—C'vil proceedings—May be tried at probate terms.
8. No appeal lies from appellate to supreme court.
9. Evidence—What may be introduced.
10. What is inadmissible.
11. In bastardy proceedings.
12. Bond.
13. What an erroneous appeal.
14. When error to dismiss suit.
15. Appeal lies direct to appellate court from county court.

1. BOND FOR SECURITY.—The act of 1889, approved June 4, amends section 9 of the act of 1872 to read as follows:

"In case the defendant shall refuse or neglect to give such security as may be ordered by the court, he shall be committed to the jail of the county, there to remain until he shall comply with such order, or until otherwise discharged by due course of law. Any person so committed shall be discharged for insolvency or inability to give bond: *Provided*, such discharge shall not be made within six months after such commitment."(1)

2. RELEASE FROM LIABILITY—COMPROMISE.—At the same session, section 17 of the statute, by act approved June 3, 1889, was amended to read as follows:

"The mother of a bastard child, before or after its birth, may release the reputed father of such child from all legal liability on account of such bastardy, upon such terms as may be consented to by the judge of the county court of the county in which such mother resides: *Provided*, a release obtained from the mother in consideration of a payment to her of a sum of money less than four hundred dollars ($400), in the absence of the written consent of the county judge, shall not be a bar to a suit for bastardy against such father;

(1) Hurd's R. S., Chap. 17, § 9, 201.

but if, after such release is obtained, suit be instituted against such father, and the issue be found against him, he shall be entitled to a set-off for the amount so paid, and it shall be accredited to him as of the first payment or payments: *And provided, further,* that such father may compromise all his legal liability, without the written consent of the county judge, by paying to her any sum not less than four hundred dollars ($400)."(¹)

3. LIABILITY OF THE FATHER WHEN THE MOTHER MARRIES ANOTHER MAN.—The natural father of a child cannot be held for its support, under the bastardy act, if the mother, after the child was begotten, and during pregnancy, contracts a marriage with another man, who marries her with full knowledge of her condition. The man so marrying consents to stand in *loco parentis* to such child, and is presumed in law to be the father of the child, and this presumption is conclusive. This rule, however, can have no relation to actions where questions of heirship and inheritance are involved, but is confined to proceedings under the bastardy act.(²)

4. SUBSEQUENT MARRIAGE OF THE MOTHER—EFFECT UPON HER RIGHTS.—The complaint during pregnancy, and before delivery of the child, can only be made by an unmarried woman; but after delivery, while she is single, the subsequent marriage of the mother will not prevent her from making complaint against the reputed father of the child. The true construction of the statute is, that the mother shall be unmarried at the time the child is born; and the word "unmarried," in the law, does not properly relate to the time of making the complaint. But the marriage of the mother of an illegitimate, after delivery, to one not its father cannot affect the status of such child, and render the husband liable for its support.(³)

5. BASTARDY MAINTAINABLE BY NON-RESIDENT.—Bastardy is maintainable by a non-resident woman against the putative father of her child in the courts of this state.(⁴)

(1) Hurd's R. S., Chap. 17, § 17, 202.
(2) Miller vs. Anderson (Ohio), 3 N. E. Reports, 605; State vs. Romaine, 58 Iowa, 48; Rhyne vs. Hoffman, 6 jones' Eq., N. C., 335; Tioga Co. vs. South Creek Tp., 75 Pa. Stat., 433; Parker vs. Way, 15 N. H., 45; Vetten vs. Wallace, 39 Ill. Ap., 390; Davis vs. Houston, 2 Yeates, 289; State vs. Wilson, 10 Ired., N. C., 131; State vs. Herman, 13 Ired., 502; Page vs. Dennison, 1 Grant, Kas., 577; State vs. Shoemaker, 62 Iowa, 343; Glidden vs. Nelson, 15 Ill. Ap., 297.
(3) People *ex. rel.* vs. Volksdorf, 112 Ill., 292; Vetten vs. Wallace, *supra*.
(4) Mings vs. People, 111 Ill., 98.

6. COMPLAINT.—Under the revised statutes of Illinois, chapter 17, section 1, which provides that "When an unmarried woman, who shall be pregnant or delivered of a bastard child, shall accuse, under oath, a person with being the father of such child, such person shall be held to answer the charge," an affidavit in the following form: "The complaint of M. N., an unmarried woman, under oath, who says that she is now pregnant with a child, and that said child is likely to be born a bastard," is insufficient, as the affiant does not make oath therein that she is unmarried.([1])

7. PROSECUTION—CIVIL PROCEEDINGS.—A prosecution under the bastardy act is a civil proceeding, primarily within the jurisdiction of county courts at their probate terms.([2])

8. NO APPEAL.—A judgment against the putative father in a proceeding in bastardy is necessarily less than one thousand dollars, and in the absence of a certificate of importance, no appeal will lie from the decision of the appellate court.([3]) Bastardy being a civil proceeding, the court has power to permit amendments, and the complaint is amendable by virtue of chapter 7, section 1, Ill. R. S., which provides that "The court in which an action is pending shall have power to permit amendments to any process, pleading or proceeding in such action."([4])

9. EVIDENCE—WHAT MAY BE INTRODUCED.—It is within the discretion of the court to allow competent evidence to be introduced at any time before the case is submitted to the jury.([5])

10. WHAT IS INADMISSIBLE.—Evidence as to acts of impropriety on the part of the prosecuting witness, with parties other than the defendant, at times outside the period of gestation, should not be admitted.([6]) Writings that tend to show that at the time of the making thereof the defendant considered himself to be the father of the child in question are proper to be introduced.([7]) Evidence tending to prove the poverty of the mother, or that she named the child after the reputed father, is inadmissible.([8]) Nor is it proper

---

(1) Maynard vs. People, 135 Ill., 416.
(2) People *ex. rel.* vs. Stevens, 19 Ill. Ap., 405.
(3) Scharf vs. People, 134 Ill., 240; People vs. Stevens, *supra*.
(4) Maynard vs. People, *supra*.
(5) Guinea vs. People, 37 Ill. Ap., 450.
(6) Scharf vs. People, *supra*, overruling Rawlings vs. People, 102 Ill., 475.
(7) Miene vs. People, 37 Ill. Ap., 589.
(8) Corcoran vs. People, 27 Ill. Ap., 638.

to introduce the bastard child in evidence for the purpose of showing a resemblance between it and the defendant.(¹)

11. IN BASTARDY PROCEEDINGS.—Evidence is competent to show that the woman had been out late at night with other men and boys; that a witness had had sexual intercourse with the relatrix; and evidence to corroborate the testimony of a witness, as the fact of their being on friendly and intimate terms. And if it were shown in evidence that the defendant had made purchases for the relatrix, it would be proper to permit him to show that such purchases were made at the request of her brother. And where a witness for the defendant has testified that he was present where and at the time the defendant was said to have made certain admissions, and that he did not hear them, it would be error to refuse to allow him to testify whether he would have heard them had they been made.(²) If the issue be whether the defendant had sexual intercourse with a certain woman at a particular time, and the direct testimony is conflicting, evidence of corroborative circumstances is not rendered inadmissible by the fact that it also tends to prove seduction and attempt to produce abortion.(³) The admission of evidence as to the attention of other men is inadmissible.(⁴)

The precise time of the coition, if it be within the proper time of gestation, is immaterial, even though the complaining witness may have fixed the time definitely, except as affecting her credibility.(⁵) And where the child was born June 18, 1888, upon inquiry as to paternity of the child, questions for the purpose of ascertaining whether or not the relatrix had had illicit intercourse with other men than the defendant between August 14 and September 12, 1887, were proper.(⁶)

In a prosecution for bastardy, where the evidence was conflicting and a right to convict doubtful, the court, on the part of the People, instructed the jury that the People were not bound to prove, beyond a reasonable doubt, that the defendant was the father of the bastard child, and added: "If, upon a consideration of all the evidence,

---

(1) Robnett vs. People, 16 Ill. Ap., 299; *Contra*, State vs. Smith, 54 Iowa, 104.
(2) Maynard vs. People, 135 Ill., 416.
(3) *Ib.*
(4) Curran vs. People, *ex. rel.*, 35 Ill. Ap., 275.
(5) Ross vs. People, 34 Ill. Ap., 21.
(6) Pike vs. People, 34 Ill. Ap., 112.

you are inclined to believe he is the father of such child, then you should so find by your verdict." There was no other instruction in the record curing the error: *Held*, that the instruction was erroneous. Jurors are required to decide cases according to their conviction of the truth of the matter found by their verdict, and not their mere inclinations.(¹)

It is competent for the parties to make a settlement and release that will bar a prosecution, if the release is not vitiated by fraud in its procurement. In order to make false statements fraudulent, the party alleged to have been defrauded must have been ignorant of the truth, and must have relied upon the statements made.(²) An agreement on the part of the putative father in anticipation of the birth of the child, that he will adopt the child and make it his heir, will be no bar to a prosecution for bastardy, or to an action for damages with respect thereto.(³)

12. BOND.—A bond given in a bastardy proceeding conditioned that the defendant shall appear at the next term of the court and answer to the charge, and not depart the court without leave, is not met by the appearance of the defendant, a trial and a judgment against him. He must comply with the judgment, and should he flee the state the conditions of the bond would be broken, and an action will lie against the obligors. If the bond be regarded as a recognizance, then its conditions require the defendant to appear on the first day of the term, and from day to day, and from term to term, until the final sentence or order of the court. It is not extending the liability upon the bond for the parties and sureties to agree in open court by parol to continue the cause. Such an agreement is an agreement of record, and will operate as an estoppel.(⁴)

A judgment order entered which required the condition of the bond to be given by the defendant for the support of the child should make the installments payable to the county judge was error. The installments should be paid to the clerk of the court, as now required.(⁵)

The statute requiring that a person accused of being the father

(1) Cox vs. People, 109 Ill., 457.
(2) Hendrix vs. People, 9 Ill. Ap., 42; Hurd's R. S., Chap. 17, § 17, 202; Gurley vs. People, 31 Ill., Ap., 465.
(3) Wallace vs. Rappleye, 103 Ill., 229.
(4) People vs. Ogden, 10 Ill. Ap., 226.
(5) Moore vs. People, 13 Ill. Ap., 248.

of a bastard child, on a complaint by the mother before a justice of the peace, must give bond, with sureties, to appear and answer such complaint at the next term of the court, to abide the order of the court thereon, does not except infants, and in an action on such bond the infancy of the obligor is no defense.([1])

13. WHAT AN ERRONEOUS JUDGMENT.—A judgment in the circuit court in a bastardy proceeding affirming that of the county court and remitting the case to that court for execution is erroneous in form.([2])

14. WHEN ERROR TO DISMISS SUIT.—It is error to dismiss a suit brought under the bastardy act on account of the death of the prosecuting witness.([3])

Where the defendant shows due diligence in endeavoring to procure testimony of important witnesses, he should be granted a continuance.([4])

15. APPEAL LIES DIRECT TO APPELLATE COURT.—An appeal does not lie direct to the appellate court from the judgment of a county court in a bastardy proceeding.([5]) To the *contra*, see *Lee* vs. *The People*, where the supreme court held an appeal does lie direct to the appellate court.([6])

(1) McCall vs. Parker, 13 Metcalf, 372; People vs. Moores, 4 Denio, 518.
(2) Church vs. People, 26 Ill. Ap., 232.
(3) People vs. Smith, 17 Ill. Ap., 597.
(4) Common vs. People, 28 Ill. Ap., 230.
(5) Rodgers vs. People, 34 Ill. Ap., 448; Lee vs. People, 40 Ill. Ap., 79.
(6) Lee vs. People, 30 N. E. Reporter, 690.

CHAPTER XXI.

TRIAL OF THE RIGHT OF PROPERTY.

1. Proceedings for—Jurisdiction—forms.
2. Trial in county court—form of Judge's entry.
3. Notice to plaintiff in execution.
4. Service of notice—continuance.
5. Notice by publication.
6. Affidavit of complainant.
7. Time of giving notice—forms.
8. Entering appearance.
9. Trial—pleadings—jury.
10. Trial by jury—forms of venire, &c.
11. Subpœnas for witnesses.
12. Judgment—exempt property—costs.
13. Appeal—bond—trial *de novo.*
14. Judgment—indemnity.
15. Apportionment of costs—fees—form.
16. Rules governing the action of the trial of the right of property.
    a. Notice.
    b. Jurisdiction.
    c. Jury.
    d. Evidence.
    e. Title.
    f. Effect of judgment.
    g. Bailment.
    h. Competency of witnesses.
    i. Verdict.
    j. Appeal.

By an act of the General Assembly of 1875, approved April 9, 1875, taking effect July 1, 1875, jurisdiction was conferred upon the county court to try the right of property, whenever the execution or writ of attachment issued from any court of record.

1. JURISDICTION GIVEN.—Whenever an execution or writ of attachment, issued from any court of record, shall be levied by any sheriff or coroner upon any personal property, and such property shall be claimed by any person other than the defendant in such execution or attachment, or shall be claimed by the defendant in execution or attachment as exempt from execution or attachment,

by virtue of the exemption laws of the state, by giving to the sheriff or coroner notice, in writing, of his claim, and intention to prosecute the same, it shall be the duty of such sheriff or coroner to notify the judge of the county court of such claim.[1]

The notice under this section to be given the sheriff or coroner, may be in form as follows:

STATE OF ILLINOIS, } ss.
..................County, }

To........., Sheriff of......... County, Illinois:

Take notice: That I........., claim the following personal property, and intend to prosecute my claim to the same, to-wit: One bay horse, called "John," 5 years old last spring; one Wood's self-rake reaper and mower combined; one Milburn wagon, with side boards and spring seat, and one two-year old heifer, levied on by you on the...day of......, A. D. 18..., as the property of C D, by virtue of an execution issued out of the circuit court of.........county, Illinois, in favor of E F, plaintiff, and against the lands and tenements, goods and chattels of the said C D, defendant.

By........., Attorney.   A D.

After the notice has been given to the sheriff or coroner as aforesaid, it is the duty of that officer to notify the judge of the county court, which said notice may be in form as follows:

STATE OF ILLINOIS, } ss.
................County, }

To the Hon............, Judge of the County Court of.......... County:

I respectfully notify your Honor, that the following described personal property, to-wit: One bay horse, called "John," five years old last spring; one Wood's self-rake reaper and mower combined; one Milburn wagon, with side boards and spring seat, and one two-year old heifer, levied upon by me, on the...day of......, 18..., as the property of........., by virtue of an execution issued out of the circuit court of.........county, in favor of E F, plaintiff, against the lands and tenements, goods and chattels of the said C D, defendant, to me delivered, has been claimed by A D, who has given me notice in writing of h...claim, and of h...intention to prosecute the same according to the statute in such case made and provided.

Dated this....day of........, A. D. 18....

........., Sheriff of.........County.

2. TRIAL IN COUNTY COURT.—The judge of the county court shall thereupon cause the proceeding to be entered on the docket of

(1) Hurd's R. S., Chap. 140a, § 1.

518 TRIAL OF THE RIGHT OF PROPERTY. [CH. XXI.

the county court, and the claimant shall be made plaintiff in the proceeding before the county court, and the plaintiff in the execution or attachment shall be made defendant in such proceedings.(¹)

FORM OF JUDGE'S ENTRY.

In the Matter of A D vs. E F.

Goods levied on as the property of C D, and claimed by A D. Notice received by me, ...day of......, A. D. 18...

.... , Judge of the County Court.

The clerk will docket this proceeding, and notify the plaintiff in the execution that the trial will occur on the...day of ......, A. D. 18...

........., Judge of the County Court.

3. NOTICE TO PLAINTIFF.—The clerk of the county court shall thereupon issue a notice, directed to the plaintiff in the execution or attachment, notifying him of such claim, and of the time and place of trial, which time shall be not more than ten days nor less than five days from the date of such notice.(²)

The form of notice may be as follows:

STATE OF ILLINOIS, }
...............County, } ss.

The People of the State of Illinois, to........., Greeting:

Whereas, the following described personal property, to-wit: One bay horse, called "John," five years old last spring; one Wood's self-rake reaper and mower combined; one Milburn wagon, with side boards and spring seat, and one two-year old heifer, levied upon by........., sheriff of said county, as the property of ...., by virtue of an execution issued out of the circuit court of.........county, in favor of........., plaintiff, against the lands and tenements, goods and chattels of the said C D, defendant, has been claimed by A D, who has given said sheriff notice in writing of h... claim, and of h... intention to prosecute the same according to the statute in such case made and provided.

You are, therefore, hereby notified that said claim will be tried before the county court of said.........county, at the court house in........., in said county, on the...day of......, A. D. 18..., at...o'clock...m., when and where you can appear and contest said claim.

Witness, ..., Clerk of our said County Court, and the seal
[Seal.]   thereof, at his office in........., in said.........county, this...day of......, A. D. 18...

........., Clerk of the County Court.

(1) Hurd's R. S., Chap. 140a, § 2.   (2) Hurd's R. S., Chap. 140a, § 3.

The officer shall serve the same and make return thereof as follows:

STATE OF ILLINOIS, } ss.
............County,

I have duly served the within notice by reading and delivering a true copy of the same to the within named........., on this...day of......, A. D. 18...
........., Sheriff.

4. SERVICE OF NOTICE.—Such notice shall be served by the sheriff or coroner of any county where the plaintiff in execution or attachment may be found, in like manner as summonses in chancery are served, at least five days before the day of trial; and if such notice shall be served less than five days before the day of trial, the trial shall, on demand of either party, be continued for a period not exceeding ten days.[1]

5. NOTICE BY PUBLICATION.—In case the sheriff or coroner shall make return on such notice that the plaintiff in the execution or attachment can not be found, the proceeding shall be continued for a period not exceeding ninety days, and the plaintiff in the execution or attachment shall be notified of such proceeding by publication, in like manner as non-resident defendants are notified in chancery cases.[2]

6. AFFIDAVIT OF COMPLAINANT.—Whenever any complainant or his attorney, shall file in the office of the clerk of the court in which his suit is pending, an affidavit showing that any defendant resides or hath gone out of this state, or on due inquiry can not be found, or is concealed within this state, so that process can not be served upon him, and stating the place of residence of such defendant if known, or that upon diligent inquiry his place of residence can not be ascertained, the clerk shall cause publication to be made in some newspaper printed in his county, and if there be no newspaper published in his county, then in the nearest newspaper published in this state, containing notice of the pendency of such suit, the names of the parties thereto, the title of the court, and the time and place of the return of summons in the case; and he shall also, within ten days of the first publication of such notice, send a copy thereof by mail, addressed to such defendant whose place of resi-

(1) Hurd's R. S., Chap. 140*a*, § 4.   (2) Hurd's R. S., Chap. 140*a*, § 5.

dence is stated in such affidavit. The certificate of the clerk that he has sent such notice in pursuance of this section, shall be evidence.(¹)

7. TIME OF GIVING NOTICE.—The notice required in the preceding section may be given at any time after the commencement of the suit, and shall be published at least once in each week for four successive weeks, and no default or proceeding shall be taken against any defendant not served with summons, or a copy of the bill, and not appearing unless forty days shall intervene between the first publication, as aforesaid, and the first day of the term at which such default or proceeding is proposed to be taken.(²)

In case the return of the sheriff shows the defendant can not be found, or service can not be had for any cause shown under the above section, an affidavit may be made by the plaintiff in compliance with section 12 above. The affidavit may be in form as follows:

STATE OF ILLINOIS, } ss.   *In the County Court,*
............County,   *In Vacation after the......term, A. D. 18...*

A D
vs.   Trial of the Right of Property.
E F.

A D, the above named plaintiff, on oath states, that E F, the above named defendant, is not a resident of the State of Illinois, and that he resides in..........   ....

Subscribed and sworn to before me, this...day of......, A. D. 18...
                     ...., Clerk of the County Court.

As directed under section 6, the clerk shall thereupon give notice by publication, which may be in form as follows:

STATE OF ILLINOIS, } ss.   *In the County Court,*
............County,   *In Vacation after the......term, A. D. 18...*

A D
vs.   Trial of the Right of Property.
E F.

Affidavit of the non-residence of E F, the above named defendant, whose place of residence is.........., having been filed in the clerk's office of the county court, notice is, therefore, hereby given to you, the said E F, that the plaintiff, on the...day of......, A. D. 18..., filed her notice of claim to

(1) Hurd's R. S., Chap. 22, § 12.   (2) Hurd's R. S., Chap. 22, § 13.

the property, and of her intention to prosecute the same, levied upon by virtue of an execution issued out of the circuit court of.........county, Illinois, in favor of you, the said.........., as plaintiff in execution, and against the lands and tenements, goods and chattels, of C D, defendant in execution, and that thereupon a notice to you as plaintiff in such execution, issued out of said court, returnable on the...day of......, A. D. 18..., at...o'clock...m., of said day, at the court house, in.........., ...county, Illinois, as required by law, which said notice was duly returned in my office on the...day of......, A. D. 18..., with an indorsement thereon, that you, the said E F, can not be found in.........county, Illinois, whereupon said cause was continued to the... day of......, A. D. 18..., and publication ordered against you, as required by the statute in such case made and provided.

Now, unless you the said.........., shall be and appear before the said court on the said...day of......, A. D. 18..., at the court house in.........., ... county, Illinois, and defend said cause, a judgment will be entered against you, and in favor of the said plaintiff, for the possession of said property and costs of suit.

Dated...day of......, A. D. 18...

[L. S.]   ...., Clerk County Court.

By.........., Attorney.

The clerk shall, in all cases, where the post office address of the defendant has been shown by the affidavit on file, mail within ten days after the first publication of such notice, a copy of the notice to said defendant, addressed to him at his post office, and file a certificate of the same in his office, which may be in form as follows:

STATE OF ILLINOIS, } ss.
..................County,

A D
vs.   (Copy of Notice herein Referred to.)
E F.

I, ..., clerk of the county court of said county, in the state aforesaid, do hereby certify, that on the...day of......, A. D. 18..., being within ten days after the first publication of the notice hereunto appended, I sent by mail a copy of the annexed notice to.........., defendant, at.........., in pursuance of section 12 of an act of the general assembly of the State of Illinois, entitled "An Act Regulating the Practice in Courts of Chancery," approved March 15, 1872.

Witness my hand and the seal of said court, this...day of......, A. D. 18...

[L. S.]   ...., Clerk of the County Court.

8. ENTERING APPEARANCE.—If the plaintiff in the execution or attachment, or his attorney, shall, at least five days before the day of trial, file with the clerk of the county court a paper, enter-

ing his appearance in such proceeding, then it shall not be necessary to notify such plaintiff as above provided.(¹)

The form for entering the appearance of the plaintiff may be as follows:

STATE OF ILLINOIS, } ss.   *In the County Court,*
............County,   *In Vacation after the......term, A. D. 18...*

A D ⎫
vs.   ⎬   Trial of the Right of Property.
E F ⎭

E F, the defendant, in the above entitled cause, waives the issuing and service of process upon him, and hereby enters his appearance in this cause.

....

9. TRIAL—PLEADINGS—JURY.—The trial shall be had without written pleadings, before the county judge, in the same manner as other trials before the county court, and may be by a jury if either party demand one.(²)

10. TRIAL BY JURY.—If a jury shall be demanded by either party, the judge shall direct the county clerk to issue a venire for twelve competent jurors, unless the parties to such proceedings shall elect to have the same tried by six jurors, and deliver the same to the sheriff or coroner, who shall summon such jurors from the body of the county, to be and appear before such court at the time set for the return of such venire; and if, by reason of non-attendance, challenge or otherwise, said jury shall not be full, the panel may be filled by talesmen. Said court shall have the same power to compel the attendance of jurors and witnesses, as the circuit court has, and shall be governed by the same rules in impanneling a jury.(³)

FORM OF A VENIRE FOR A JURY.

STATE OF ILLINOIS, } ss.
............County,

The People of the State of Illinois, to the Sheriff of said County, Greeting:

You are hereby commanded, without delay, to summon *twelve* good and lawful men of your county, to be and appear before our county court, within and for the county of........., at the court house in the town of........., in said county, on the...day of......, A. D. 18..., at...o'clock...m., and so from

(1) Hurd's R. S., Chap. 22, § 6.   (3) Hurd's R. S., Chap. 140a, § 8.
(2) Hurd's R. S., Chap. 140a, § 7.

day to day, until discharged by the court, then and there to serve as jurors in a certain cause now pending in said court, wherein A D is plaintiff, and E F is defendant.

And have you then and there this writ, with an endorsement thereon in what manner you shall have executed the same.

      Witness.........., Clerk of said Court, and the seal thereof, at.........,
[L. S.]   this...day of......, A. D. 18...
              ...., Clerk County Court.

RETURN OF OFFICER.

In pursuance of the mandate of the within writ, I have executed the same by summoning, as directed in the said writ, the following named persons from the body of the county, to-wit: [*Here insert the names.*]
                  ...., Sheriff.

11. SUBPŒNAS FOR WITNESSES.—The county clerk shall issue subpœnas for witnesses on the demand of either party.(¹)

A præcipe filed with the clerk, is a demand which will entitle the parties to witnesses, and may be in form as follows:

STATE OF ILLINOIS,   *In the County Court,*
..............County, } ss. *In Vacation after the......term, A. D.* 18...

A D
vs. } Trial of the Right of Property—Præcipe for Witnesses.
E F.

The clerk of said court will issue subpœnas for.........., ..., ..., ..., witnesses in the above entitled cause, returnable....., ...A. D. 18..., at...o'clock...m. Directed to the sheriff of..........county, Illinois, to execute.
Dated this...day of......, A. D. 18...
By.........., Attorney.

12. JUDGMENT—EXEMPT PROPERTY—COSTS.—In case the property shall appear to belong to the claimant, when the claimant is any other person than the defendant in execution or attachment, or in case the property shall be found to be exempt from execution or attachment, when the claimant is the defendant in the execution or attachment, judgment shall be entered against the plaintiff in the execution or attachment for the costs, and the property levied on shall be released. If it shall appear that the property does not belong to the claimant, or is not exempt from execution or attachment, as the case may be, judgment shall be entered against the claimant for costs, and an order shall be made that the sheriff or coroner proceed to sell the property levied on.(²)

(1) Hurd's R. S., Chap. 140a, § 9. (2) Hurd's R. S., Chap. 140a, § 10.

VERDICT OF THE JURY—TRIAL OF THE RIGHT OF PROPERTY.

A D
vs.
E F.

We, the jury, called to try the right of property on a claim made by A D, to the following described goods and chattels, to-wit: One bay horse, called "John," five years old last spring; one Wood's self rake reaper and mower combined; one Milburn wagon, with side boards and spring seat, and one two-year old heifer, levied upon by........., sheriff, by virtue of an *execution* issued out of the circuit court of......... county, Illinois, in favor of E F, plaintiff, and against the goods and chattels, lands and tenements of C D, find that the property of the said goods and chattels so claimed, is in......... the said claimant.

Witness our hands, this...day of......, A. D. 18...

The verdict should be signed by all the jury, and conform to their finding; it may be for all of the property, or a part only, or it may be that, it is not in said claimant.

13. APPEAL—BOND—TRIAL DE NOVO.—An appeal may be taken to the circuit court, as in other cases: *Provided*, the same is prayed on the day of the entering of judgment, and the bond shall be given within five days from the time of entering judgment, and the trial in the circuit court shall be *de novo*.([1])

In order to take an appeal, the same must be prayed on the day of entering the judgment. The bond must be perfected in five days from the time of entering judgment. When these steps are properly taken, it is the duty of the clerk of the county court, to make out a transcript of the proceedings and certify the same to the clerk of the circuit court, when the trial shall proceed *de novo*.

The form of an appeal bond may be as follows:

Know all men by these presents, that we, E F, G H and I J, of the county of........., and State of Illinois, are held and firmly bound unto A D, in the penal sum of...dollars, for the payment of which, well and truly to be made, we bind ourselves, our heirs, executors and administrators, jointly and severally, firmly, by these presents. Sealed with our seals, and dated at........., this...day of......, A. D. 18...

The condition of the above obligation is such: That whereas, the said A D, did, on the...day of......, A. D. 18..., at a term of the county court then being holden within and for the county of........., and State of Illinois, obtain a judgment against the above bounden E F, for the sum of...dollars, costs of suit, in a trial of the right of property, from which said judgment the said

---

(1) Hurd's R. S., Chap. 140*a*, § 11.

E F has prayed for and obtained an appeal to the circuit court of said county.

Now, if the said E F shall prosecute his said appeal with effect and pay whatever judgment may be rendered against him by said court upon trial of said appeal, or by consent, or, in case the appeal is dismissed, will pay the judgment rendered against him .by said county court, and all costs occasioned by said appeal, then the above obligation to be void, otherwise to remain in full force and effect.

E F, [L. S.]
G H, [L. S.]
I J, [L. S.]

Taken and approved by me in open court, this...day of......, A. D. 18...

.........., Judge of the County Court.

14. JUDGMENT—INDEMNITY.—The judgment in such cases shall be a complete indemnity to the sheriff or coroner in selling or restoring any such property, as the case may be.(¹)

15. APPORTIONMENT OF COSTS—FEES.—If the judgment shall be for the claimant as to part of the property, and for the plaintiff in execution or attachment as to part, then the court shall apportion the costs in his discretion; and the sheriff, coroner and county clerk shall have the same fees as are allowed by law for similar services.(²)

The final order or clerk's entry, in trials of the right of property, may be in form as follows:

A D }
vs. } Trial of the Right of Property.
E F. }

And now on this...day of......, A. D. 18..., the day set for the hearing of this cause, comes the said plaintiff, A D, by........., her attorney, comes also, the said E F, by........., his attorney, and this cause coming on now to be heard, the said defendant demands that the same be tried by a jury—ordered: That a venire be issued to the sheriff of this county for a jury of twelve men, returnable at...o'clock...m., of this day:

Comes now the said sheriff, with an indorsement on said venire, and returned the same into open court, that he had executed said writ, by summoning from the body of the county, [*names of the jurors*] twelve good and lawful men as jurors. Said jury were thereupon called; empanneled, tried and sworn to try the cause, and after hearing the evidence both for the plaintiff and the defendant, the arguments of the counsel, and having received the instructions of the court, retired in charge of an officer to consider of their verdict, and after due consideration thereof, returned into open court their verdict, in words and figures as follows, to-wit: [*Copy the verdict in full.*] Which said verdict is ordered to be recorded, and the jury discharged

(1) Hurd's R. S., Chap. 140*a*, § 12.   (2) Hurd's R. S., Chap. 140*a*, § 13.

from any further consideration of this cause. It is therefore, ordered and adjudged, that the said plaintiff, A D, have judgment against the said defendant, E F, for the costs of this suit, and that execution may issue therefor.

It is further ordered, that the property in controversy in this suit be released by the officer having the same in charge and restored to the possession of said A D, the plaintiff in this suit: From which said judgment the defendant prays an appeal to the circuit court, which is granted upon condition that said defendant file his bond in the sum of...dollars, with good and sufficient security to be approved by the judge of this court, within five days from the time of the entry of the judgment in this cause.

16. RULES GOVERNING TRIAL.—The object of a trial of the right of property, under the statute, is merely to furnish an imdemnity to the officer in case he disposes of the property in conformity with the verdict, but the officer may, notwithstanding the verdict be for the claimant, retain and sell the property at his peril, if he choose to do so. The only safe course, however, is for the officer to surrender it.[1] The only question for trial, is, whether the property levied on belongs to the claimant; for, unless he shows affirmatively that it belongs to him, and is not subject to sale on execution, the verdict must be against him,[2] and title acquired subsequently to the commencement of the proceedings can not be shown.[3]

a. It is exclusively the duty of officer to give the notice for the trial, and for any neglect in case damage ensue, he will be held responsible.[4] The court acts upon his return, and it matters not whether it be true or false.[5] Claiming the property which has been levied upon is merely an act *in pais*, and may be performed by an ordinary agent.[6] The statute does not require the claimant of property taken on execution, to state on whose execution the levy has been made, in the notice he serves upon the officer. Notice that he claims the goods levied upon, intends to prosecute his claim, and forbids the sale, is sufficient.[7]

b. To authorize the inquiry, it is necessary there should be a taking of personal property, by a writ of execution regularly issued

(1) Foltz vs. Stevens, 54 Ill., 180.
(2) Marshall vs. Cunningham, 13 Ill., 20.
(3) Graff vs. Fitch, 58 Ill., 373.
(4) Ice vs. McLain, 14 Ill., 62.
(5) *Ib.*
(6) Webber vs. Brown, 38 Ill., 87.
(7) Pearce vs. Swan, 1 Scam., 266.

at the suit of a plaintiff, against a defendant, and a claim interposed by a third person.(¹) The claimant can not object to the execution. By giving notice of the trial of the right of property, he admits the validity of the execution. For, the remedy would be, were the execution a nullity, by an action of trespass, replevin, or trover against the officer.(²)

c. The statutory provision requiring a jury, is not to be construed as prohibiting the parties from agreeing upon a less number than six, nor to prevent their excusing a juror by consent after the trial had commenced, or waiving a jury altogether.(³)

d. On the trial of the right of property levied upon by attachment, the writ of attachment and return thereon, are admissible in evidence.(⁴) A recital in the execution of the rendition of the judgment, is sufficient proof of the judgment, as the claimant by giving notice, admits the regularity and existence of the proceedings against the defendant.(⁵) Where a plaintiff has evidence tending to make out his case, it is error for the court to exclude it all on motion of the other party.(⁶) And if there be evidence tending to show property in the claimant, it is erroneous to instruct the jury that he fails to show any right, and they must find against him.(⁷)

e. A landlord who has distrained upon the goods of his tenant, has a sufficient interest in them to enable him to be the claimant of the same, if they are subsequently taken in execution.(⁸)

In an action of trespass *de bonis asportatis*, against others than the officer who made the levy and sale, the plaintiff should show title to the property sold. It is not a legal presumption, because the property was seized and sold under an execution against him, that it was his property.(⁹)

Where the owner of an elevator had money advanced to him by a third party, with which to buy and hold for such party a lot of corn, the fact that such agent received corn in payment of debts

---

(1) Mason vs. The State Bank, Breese, 141.
(2) Harrison vs. Singleton, 2 Scam., 21; Merricks vs. Davis, 65 Ill., 319; Thompson vs. Wilhite, 81 Ill., 356.
(3) Kreuchi vs. Dehler, 50 Ill., 176.
(4) Sheldon vs. Reihle, 1 Scam., 519
(5) Dexter vs. Parkins, 22 Ill., 144
(6) Merricks vs. Davis, *supra*.
(7) Craig vs. Peake, 22 Ill., 185.
(8) Grimsley vs. Klein, 1 Scam., 343
(9) Ice vs. McLain, 14 Ill., 62.

due him, as a means of collecting the same, and for that purpose paid more than the market value, but only charged his principal with the market value, will not necessarily render the transaction fraudulent as to creditors, and subject such corn to execution subsequently issued against the agent.([1]) And where ground is leased for a share of the crops raised, to be divided after the same is gathered, the title to the whole of the crops raised, will be that of the tenant until divided and possession given, and after the levy of an execution against the tenant, an agreement between him and the landlord, that the latter shall receive his share in the field, will not be allowed to defeat the levy.([2]) But where growing wheat and corn are sold in good faith, and the purchaser takes all the possession that is practicable before harvesting, and after it is cut down, and before a sufficient time elapsed for him to remove it, it is seized on execution against the seller, the purchaser will be entitled to hold it.([3])

f. The judgment is conclusive only between parties and privies.([4]) And a trial which results in a judgment against the claimant, does not establish or confirm a right to the property in the defendant in execution.([5]) But such a trial and judgment would be a bar to an action of trover subsequently brought by the claimant against the officers for the same property.([6])

Where a levy has been made upon property to which the debtor has no title, sold at public sale to the plaintiff in execution, from whom it is subsequently taken by the rightful owner, the court may, on motion, vacate the levy and satisfaction as shown by the return of the sheriff, under its power to correct its own records. In the same proceeding a new execution may be awarded.([7])

g. Where an officer has levied an execution upon personal property, and placed the same in the hands of a third person merely as bailee, the fact that a person other than the defendant in execution procures a trial to be had, under the statute, which results in favor of the claimant, will not justify such bailee in refusing to deliver

(1) Cool vs. Phillips, 66 Ill., 216.
(2) Sargent vs. Courrier, 66 Ill., 245.
(3) Thompson vs. Wilhite, 81 Ill., 356.
(4) Arenz vs. Reihle, 1 Scam., 340.
(5) Cassell vs. Williams, 12 Ill., 387.
(6) Kreuchi vs. Dehler, 50 Ill., 176.
(7) Zeigler vs. McCormick, Sup. Ct. Nebraska, 14 Legal News, 375.

the property to the officer who placed it in his custody, according to the terms of the bailment. In such case, the finding on the trial would not authorize the bailee to surrender the property to the claimant, but he should, notwithstanding such finding, return the property to the officer.(¹)

h. It was formerly held, that the wife of a defendant in execution on a trial of the right of property, was not a competent witness to testify;(²) but the rule is now changed, and in an action of assumpsit, brought by the husband to recover the value of certain articles, belonging to the wife which were lost in transportation, the wife was held to be a competent witness to testify.(³) So, where a defendant in replevin, pleaded that the property replevied from him was the separate property of his wife, it was held, that the wife, under the act of 1867, was a competent witness to prove execution of a bill of sale of the property by the plaintiff to her, and to the fact and manner of payment by her, as the fifth section of February 19th, 1867, relating to witnesses, making the husband and wife competent witnesses for and against each other in litigation concerning the wife's separate property, is not restricted to cases where she is plaintiff or defendant, and where her title is admitted, but is general—extending to all cases where the litigation shall concern her separate property, whether her title is admitted or controverted.(⁴)

i. A verdict against the claimant, is a complete indemnity to the sheriff, but does not conclude the contesting parties, nor does it protect any person who intermeddles with the property.(⁵)

And a verdict of a jury which found the title in the defendant in the attachment, is sufficiently formal and explicit, as it negatived the title set up by the claimant.(⁶)

But a verdict for the claimant would not authorize a bailee to surrender the property to the claimant. He should, notwithstanding such finding, return the property to the officer.(⁷)

(1) Foltz vs. Stevens, 54 Ill., 180.
(2) Dexter vs. Parkins, 22 Ill., 143.
(3) Northern Line Packet Co. vs. Shearer, 61 Ill., 263.
(4) McNail vs. Ziegler, 68 Ill., 224.
(5) Rowe vs. Bowen, 28 Ill., 117.
(6) Sheldon vs. Reihle, 1 Scam., 519.
(7) Foltz vs. Stevens, *supra.*

j. Where an appeal is taken to the circuit court, all the proceedings should be transmitted; if they are not, the circuit court can not exercise jurisdiction.([1])

An appeal may be properly dismissed, upon a motion founded on the affidavit of the sheriff, stating that the property in question had been sold with the assistance of the claimant, (who was the appellant,) and that the proceeds thereof remained in his hands, subject to the order of such claimant.([2])

(1) Sheldon vs. Reihle, 1 Scam., 519.
(2) Morgan vs. Griffin, 1 Gilm., 565.

ADDITIONAL NOTES.

1. Suit on official bond—Judgment—Costs.
2. Measure of damages.

1. SUIT ON OFFICIAL BOND—JUDGMENT—COSTS.—The levy by a sheriff upon the property of A., by virtue of a writ against B., is a breach of the sheriff's bond. Judgment in favor of intervening claimant on trial of the right of property is not of itself conclusive that he has the right to recover in action against the sheriff on his bond.([1])

2. MEASURE OF DAMAGES.—As a general rule, the true measure of damages will be the value of the property and interest.([2]) The plaintiff and defendant, in an execution issued, pending a trial of the right of property between the latter as claimant and the judgment creditors of a third person, in goods levied upon as the property of such third person, are in such privity of relation that both will be alike bound by a judgment finding the right of property against the claimant.([3])

(1) Jones vs. People, 19 Ill. Ap., 300.
(2) *Ib.*
(3) Hill vs. Reitz, 24 Ill. Ap., 391.

CHAPTER XXII.

CONTESTED ELECTIONS.

1. Jurisdiction of County Courts.
    a. Exceptional cases in the circuit court.
    b. Other officers to contest in county court.
    c. To include officers of certain cities and villages.
    d. Does not include alderman of any city.
    e. Jurisdiction and practice statutory.
    f. May try at any term of the court.
2. Powers of chancery courts to inquire into elections.
    a. Statute does not prohibit the use of the common law writs of *mandamus* and *quo warranto*.
    b. Cases in which courts of chancery may inquire.
3. Who may contest elections in the county court.
4. Manner of proceeding—pleading.
    a. Summons.
    b. Taking of evidence.
    c. Proceeding like a suit in chancery—amendments.
5. Matters to be considered on trial.
    a. Adjournment does not vitiate election.
    b. Holding open after legal hour for closing.
    c. Closing the polls before the legal hour.
    d. Election held by unauthorized officers.
    e. Rules designed to effect a free and fair election.
    f. Who may vote.
    g. Presumptions of law as to those voting.
    h. Permanent abode.
    i. Declarations of a voter as affecting his right to vote.
    j. Paupers and persons of unsound mind.
    k. Registration of voters constitutional.
    l. Right of such to vote.
    m. Receiving ballots.
6. Custody of ballots—examination.
    a. Rejection of ballots.
    b. Ballots as evidence.
7. Intention of voter to govern.
8. Bribery by candidates.
9. In case of a tie vote.
10. Void election.
11. Judgment of the court.
    a. Form of decree.
12. Certified copy of judgment.
13. Appeal.
    a. Lies only to supreme court.

1. JURISDICTION.—The statute of 1872 confers upon the county court exclusive jurisdiction in cases of the contest of the election of all county officers, except that of the judge of that court, of all township, precinct and city officers, in cities organized under the general law.

a. The circuit courts of the respective counties shall hear and determine contests of the election of the judges of the county court of their counties, and in regard to the removal of county seats, and in regard to any other subject which may by law be submitted to the vote of the people of the county.(1)

b. The county court shall hear and determine contests of election of all other county, township and precinct officers, and all other officers for the contesting of whose election no provision is made.(2)

c. The manner of conducting and voting at elections to be held under this act, (*act to provide for the incorporation of cities and villages,*) and contesting the same, the keeping of poll lists and canvassing the votes, shall be the same, as nearly as may be, as in the case of the election of county officers, under the general laws of this state.(3)

The section last quoted, confers jurisdiction to contest the elections of city and village officers of only those cities and villages which are organized under the general law providing for their incorporation.(4) This also includes school officers.(5)

d. Notwithstanding this sweeping language, it has been held, that this court has no authority to consider a contest involving the election of an alderman of a city, even though organized under the general law—that power being alone in the city council, under the statute which makes it the "judge of the election and qualification of its own members."(6) Such council has, however, no power to pass upon the election of the mayor.(7)

e. The jurisdiction of the court, the mode of trial, and the

---

(1) Hurd's R. S., Chap. 46, § 97.
(2) Hurd's R. S., Chap. 46, § 98.
(3) Hurd's R. S., Chap. 24, § 57.
(4) Brush vs. Lemma, 77 Ill., 496; Young vs. Adam, 74 Ill., 480; Winter vs. Thistlewood, 101 Ill., 450; Talkington vs. Turner, 71 Ill., 234.
(5) Misch vs. Russell, 136 Ill., 22.
(6) Hurd's R. S , Chap. 24, § 34; Linegar vs. Rittenhouse, 94 Ill., 208; Cooley's Constitutional Limitations, 624.
(7) Winter vs. Thistlewood, *supra.*

whole contest, is purely statutory, and is not regulated or governed by the common law.(¹) Elections belong to the political branch of the government, and are beyond the control of the judicial power. It was not designed, when the fundamental law of the state was framed, that either department of the government should interfere with, or control the other, and it is for the political power of the state, within the limits of the constitution, to provide the manner in which elections shall be held, and the manner in which officers thus elected, shall be qualified, and their elections contested. Until the courts are empowered to act, by the constitution or legislative enactment, they must refrain from interference.(²)

f. The jurisdiction of the court to hear and determine contested election cases, being restricted by the statute to no particular term of the court, it may hear such cases at any term in the year, whether the term is held for probate business alone, or for both probate and common law business.

2. POWERS OF A COURT OF CHANCERY IN SUCH CASES.—Courts of chancery, both in this country and in England, have never claimed nor exercised the right of trying a contested election case, unless in cases where the power has been given by statute.(³) Nor can a court of equity interfere by injunction to restrain the holding of an election provided for by statute.(⁴) Should such an injunction be allowed, it is the plain duty of the officer enjoined, to disobey the writ, and perform the legal duty imposed by the statute; and such disregard of the writ of injunction, will be no contempt of the court ordering it.(⁵) The fact that the law has prescribed no manner of contesting an election, will not confer jurisdiction upon a court of equity to interfere.(⁶)

Where the law provides a mode for contesting elections, as in this chapter of the statute, it must be followed, and courts of equity have no power to interfere—the remedy at law being complete.(⁷)

(1) Lineger vs. Rittenhouse, 94 Ill., 208.
(2) Dickey et al. vs. Reed, 78 Ill., 261.
(3) *Ib*; Moore vs. Hoisington, 31 Ill., 243.
(4) Darst vs. People, 62 Ill., 306; Walton et al. vs. Develing et al., 61 Ill., 201; People vs. City of Galesburg, 48 Ill., 485; Harris et al. vs. Schryrock et al., 82 Ill., 119.
(5) Walton et al. vs. Develing, *supra;* Darst et al. vs. People, *supra;* Dickey vs. Reed, *supra*.
(6) Moore vs. Hoisington et al., *supra*.
(7) People vs. City of Galesburg, *supra*.

a. The existence of such a statute, does not in any manner interfere with the right to proceed by *quo warranto* against one claiming to exercise an office, for the purpose of inquiring into the legality of his election.([1]) Nor does the fact, that a branch of the general assembly is, by a provision of the constitution, made the judge of the election and qualification of its members, debar the courts of their jurisdiction to compel, by *mandamus*, a board of canvassers to issue to a successful candidate his certificate of election.([2])

b. It is true, courts of equity in Illinois, have entertained jurisdiction of proceedings prosecuted to inquire into elections held for the purpose of voting upon the removal of county seats, and have ascertained and declared the results of such elections; but this interference is placed expressly upon the ground that the constitution provides that county seats should not be removed, except on a vote resulting in a majority for removal; and that the statute was silent upon the subject of contesting such elections. To prevent the obstruction and a defeat of the rights of the majority, conferred and intended to be secured to them, it was held, that the fundamental law by implication conferred the power to interfere on courts of chancery. Such cases have been tolerated upon the express ground, that they were exceptions to all other cases.([3])

3. WHO MAY CONTEST ELECTION.—The election of any person declared elected to any office other than governor, lieutenant governor, secretary of state, auditor of public accounts, treasurer, superintendent of public instruction, attorney-general, senator or representative, may be contested by any elector of the state, judicial division, district, county, town or precinct in and for which the person is declared elected.([4])

4. MANNER OF PROCEEDING—PLEADING.—The person desiring to contest such election, shall, within thirty days after the person whose election is contested is declared elected, file with the clerk of the proper court, a statement, in writing, setting forth the points on which he will contest the election, which statement shall

(1) Stephens vs. People, 89 Ill., 338; Rafferty vs. McGowan, 136 Ill., 621.
(2) Fuller vs. Hilliard, 29 Ill., 413.
(3) Turley vs. Logan Co., 17 Ill., 151; Board of Supervisors vs. Keady, 34 Ill., 293; Boren vs. Smith, 47 Ill., 482; Knox Co. vs. Davis, 63 Ill., 405; Dickey et al. vs. Reed et al., 78 Ill., 261; People vs. Smith, 51 Ill., 177.
(4) Hurd's R. S., Chap. 46, § 112; Talkington vs. Turner, 71 Ill., 234.

be verified by affidavit in the same manner as bills in chancery may be verified.(¹)

a. Upon the filing of such statement, summons shall issue against the person whose office is contested, and he may be served with process, or notified to appear, in the same manner as is provided in cases in chancery.(²)

b. Evidence may be taken in the same manner and upon like notice as in cases in chancery.(³)

c. The whole proceeding under this act, from its incipiency, by filing a statement verified by affidavit, followed by summons against the defendant to appear and answer, to final judgment, has all the incidents of a regular bill in chancery. Like a chancery proceeding, amendments may be allowed to the petition, and the contestant may, in such amendments, assign any new points necessary to bring before the court, the real points in the case, and meet the tactics of his opponent.(⁴) The contestant may, clearly, place his contest on any ground he chooses, and the opposite party may interpose, by answer, any matters which show that the contestant is not entitled to the relief he seeks.(⁵) The petition, like a bill in chancery, should charge facts sufficient to bring the case within the statutory jurisdiction of the court, and show the contestant, if the matters charged are true, entitled to prevail.* So, in a contest for the office of mayor of a city, the petition filed in the county court should show, by apt averment, that such city was duly organized under the general incorporation act, or had legally adopted it, and and this, too, notwithstanding the act provides that "all courts in this state, shall take judicial notice of the existence of all villages and cities organized under this act, and of the change of the organization of any town or city from its original organization to its organization under this act."(⁶)

As special replications are now out of use in chancery practice,

(1) Hurd's R. S., Chap. 46, § 113.
(2) Hurd's R. S., Chap. 46, § 114.
(3) Hurd's R. S., Chap. 46, § 115.
(4) Dale vs. Irwin, 78 Ill., 171; Kingery vs. Berry, 94 Ill., 515.
(5) Talkington vs. Turner, 71 Ill., 234.
(6) Brush vs. Lemma, 77 Ill., 496; Rafferty vs. McGowan, 136 Ill., 621.

*Note.—Without giving forms for the guide of the practitioner, it will be sufficient to say, that the forms in common use in chancery suits will be found adapted to this practice.

the same object may be met in this proceeding, by an amendment to the petition.(¹)

5. MATTERS TO BE CONSIDERED ON TRIAL—TIME AND PLACE OF HOLDING ELECTION.—The case shall be tried in like manner as cases in chancery.(²)

Where the bill and answer make an issue as to which side had the majority of votes, evidence is admissible to show that a voter whose ballot was rejected by the board of canvassers, for the reason that a ballot was found folded within the ballot cast, cast such double ballot by mistake. And where the evidence shows such double voting to have been done by mistake, the vote should be counted, as intended.(³)

When the time and place of an election are fixed by law, an omission to give the notice directed, of the election, will not vitiate an election held on the day and at the place appointed by law; but where the time and place are not fixed by law, but the election is only to be called, and the time and place fixed by some authority named in the statute, after the happening of some condition precedent, it is essential to the validity of such an election, that it be called, and the time and place thereof fixed, by the very agency designated by law, and none other.(⁴) If an election is held without warrant of law, or if ordered by a person or tribunal having no authority, there could be no doubt that the whole proceeding would be absolutely void and incapable of ratification;(⁵) but one who has participated in the election as a candidate or a voter, will not be permitted to disturb the public welfare by having such an election declared void.(⁶)

Where an election was called at the store of an individual, and upon the appearance of voters, permission to hold the election at the place designated was refused, and an adjournment had to a place near by where the election was held, it was held to be legal, no fraud appearing, and it not appearing that any voter had been thereby prevented from casting his ballot.(⁷)

(1) Dale vs. Irwin, 78 Ill., 171.
(2) Hurd's R. S., Chap. 46, § 116.
(3) City of Beardstown vs. City of Virginia, 81 Ill., 541.
(4) Stephens vs. People, 89 Ill., 337.
(5) Clark vs. Board of Supervisors, 27 Ill., 305; Marshall Co. vs. Cook, 38 Ill., 44; Force vs. Town of Batavia, 61 Ill., 99; Marshall vs. Silliman, 61 Ill., 218; Lippincott vs. Town of Pana, 92 Ill., 24.
(6) People vs. Waite, 70 Ill., 26.
(7) Dale vs. Irwin *supra*.

a. An adjournment of the election an hour for dinner, it not appearing that thereby any voter was prevented from voting, and no fraud appearing in the proceeding, was held not to vitiate an election, although the statute forbids any adjournment. The voters who have voted in good faith, are not to be disfranchised by such a mistake of the judges of election.([1])

b. So, also, where votes were received after five o'clock, that being the hour at which the law required the polls to be closed, such fact will not vitiate the election, although, upon a contest of the election, the ballots received after the legal hour for closing the polls, might be excluded.([2])

c. And where the evidence showed the closing of the polls an hour earlier than the hour fixed by statute, but no legal voter being thereby deprived of his right to vote, it was held not to affect the result of the election.([3])

d. An election is not void where it is held by persons who are not officers *de jure*, but are officers *de facto*, and act in good faith, under colorable authority.([4])

e. As applicable to all elections, it may be said, that the rules prescribed, by law for conducting an election, are designed chiefly to afford an opportunity for the free and fair exercise of the elective franchise, to prevent illegal voting, and to ascertain, with certainty, the result. Such rules are directory merely—not jurisdictional or imperative. If an irregularity, of which complaint is made, is shown neither to have deprived a legal voter of his right, nor to have admitted a disqualified person to vote—if it casts no uncertainty on the result, and has not been occasioned by the agency of the party seeking to derive a benefit from it—it may well be overlooked, in a contest where the only question is, which vote was the greatest.([5])

f. The right of voting at an election in Illinois, is confined to those included within this statutory provision: Every person having resided in this state one year, in the county ninety days, and in the election district thirty days next preceding any election therein, who was an elector in this state on the first day of April,

(1) Du Page Co. vs. People, 65 Ill., 360.
(2) Piatt vs. People, 29 Ill., 54; Knox Co. vs. Davis, 63 Ill., 405.
(3) Cleland vs. Porter, 74 Ill., 76; Cooley's Const. Lim., 617.
(4) Lippincott vs. Town of Pana, 92 Ill., 24.
(5) Piatt vs. People, *supra;* Du Page Co. vs. People, *supra*.

in the year of our Lord, 1848, or obtained a certificate of naturalization before any court of record in this state prior to the first day of January, in the year of our Lord, 1870, or who shall be a male citizen of the United States, above the age of twenty-one years, shall be entitled to vote at such election.(¹)

A permanent abode is necessary to constitute a residence within the meaning of the preceding section.(²)

g. The presumption of law is, that each voter voting at an election is a legal voter in the township or precinct where the election is held, which presumption continues until the contrary is proven.(³) So, the presumption is, that the vote cast at an election held according to law, is the vote of the whole number of legal voters.(⁴)

Where a person who has voted at an election, testifies that he is of foreign birth, and that neither he nor his father, so far as he knows, has ever been naturalized, this will be sufficient to rebut the presumption of the legality of the vote.(⁵)

In an election, where those not voting at all, are counted in the negative, no presumption is indulged as to the fact of such persons being voters or not; but in order to have such persons counted in the negative, in a contest of the election, the proof must show them not to be voters.(⁶)

h. A "permanent abode," in the sense of the statute, means nothing more than a domicile, a home, which the party is at liberty to have, as interest or whim may dictate, but without any present intention to change it.(⁷) Under-graduates of a college, having homes elsewhere to which they expect to return, when the purposes which brought them to the seat of the college have been met, and no interests to attach them to the town in which the college is situated, are not entitled to vote at its elections, although they may have paid a poll tax in labor The payment of such a tax does not necessarily determine the right to vote—as residence in a given township, is not a test of such liability, but simply inhabitancy. Yet such persons who are entirely free from parental control, and

(1) Art. 7, § 1, Constitution of Illinois; Hurd's R. S., Chap. 46, § 65;
(2) Hurd's R. S., Chap. 46, § 66.
(3) Webster vs. Gilmore, 91 Ill. 324; Clark vs. Robinson, 88 Ill., 498.
(4) Melvin et al. vs. Lisenby et al., 72 Ill., 63.
(5) City of Beardstown vs. City of Virginia, 81 Ill., 541.
(6) *Ib.*
(7) Dale vs. Irwin, 78 Ill., 171.

regard the seat of the college as their home, and have no other to which they expect to return in case of sickness or domestic affliction, are unquestionably as much entitled to vote as any other resident of the town, pursuing his usual avocation. It is the home of such students—their permanent abode, in the sense of the statute, as clearly so, as that of any other resident. As a general fact, however, the under-graduates of a college, are no more identified with the residents of the town in which they are pursuing their studies, than the merest strangers.(¹)

The fact of residence in a given place, depends largely upon the intention of the individual in coming to or remaining in such place, and not upon the length of time occupied in such residence. Where one went from Illinois to Tennessee, removing his family thereto, with an intention to remain if found to be profitable, but after a residence in the latter state of seven months, finding the experiment not to his taste, returned to Illinois, it was held that he did not thereby change his residence, but remained all the time a citizen of Illinois.(²) So, where one sold his property and went to Texas, with the intention of locating there if he found a place to suit him, but upon arriving there, without unloading his goods, returned to his former home in Illinois, after an absence of twenty-eight days, it was held that he did not thereby lose his residence in the latter state.(³)

i. The declarations of a person, made some time after having voted at an election, admitting or stating facts, showing that he was not a legal voter, are inadmissible as evidence to show his disqualification to vote. But where the person, when sought after to vote, stated that he was an alien born, and had no right to vote, such declarations, made immediately before or shortly after the act of voting, may be shown in evidence as a part of the *res gestœ*.(⁴)

j. Paupers, who are inmates of any county poor house, insane asylum or hospital in Illinois, are not, by virtue of such residence, deemed residents or legal voters in the town, city, village or election district or precinct in which such institution may be situated, but such persons are considered residents of the towns from which they

---

(1) Dale vs. Irwin, 78 Ill., 172; Fry's Election Case, 71 Penn. St., 302. As to what constitutes domicile, see *ante* page 238.
(2) Smith vs. People, 44 Ill., 16.
(3) City of Beardstown vs. City of Virginia, 81 Ill., 541.
(4) *Ib.*

were removed.(¹) When such persons become a public charge, and while they remain so, they cease to be free agents, but in the hands and under the control of the public authorities, are removed to the county poor house. As there must be an act of volition to accomplish a change of domicile or residence, such persons do not lose their residence.(²)

A person who is of weak mind, but capable of managing his business, and not laboring under any hallucination in political matters, is entitled to vote at an election.(³)

k. Laws providing for the registration of voters, if they do not amount to a denial or invasion of the constitutional right of voting, are valid.(⁴)

In all cases, where the constitution has conferred a political right or privilege, as the right to vote at elections held under it, and where the constitution has not particularly designated the manner in which that right is to be exercised, it is clearly within the just and constitutional limits of the legislative power to adopt any reasonable and uniform regulations in regard to the time and mode of exercising that right, which are designed to facilitate the exercise of such right, in a prompt, orderly and convenient manner.(⁵)*

l. On the contest of an election, it is error to reject the vote of an unregistered person, whose vote was received without challenge or objection, without proof showing that he was not entitled to vote, the presumption being, that he was a legal voter, and entitled to

---

(1) Hurd's R. S., Chap. 46, § 65*a*; Freeport vs. Board of Supervisors, 41 Ill., 495; Clark vs. Robinson, 88 Ill., 498.
(2) Clark vs. Robinson, *supra*.
(3) *Ib.*
(4) Edmonds vs. Baubnry, 28 Iowa, 267; State vs. Lean, 9 Wis., 279.
(5) Capen vs. Foster, 12 Pick., (Mass.) 485; See, also, note to same case, 23 American Decisions, 642. *Per contra*, see Dells vs. Kenedy, Sup. Ct. of Wisconsin, 12 Legal News, 363.

*NOTE.—Section 55, of the Chapter of the Illinois Statute on Elections, requires the judges of election to place upon the ballot of each voter a number corresponding to the number of the voter on the poll list. A similar law exists in the State of Indiana; but the supreme court of that state, in the case of *Williams* vs. *Stein*, 38 Ind., 89, declared the requirement in violation of a provision of the constitution, which declares, that "all elections by the people shall be by ballot." See, also, *Brisbin* vs. *Cleary*, by supreme court of Minnesota, 11 *Legal News*, 365, to the same effect.

No case involving this question, has yet come before the supreme court of Illinois, where all elections are required by the constitution to be by ballot. It is doubtful if that court would say, should the question come before them, that the ticket deposited by an elector is no ballot, for the reason that the judges, after it passes from the hand of the elector, place upon it a mark by which it may be identified, and the elector protected from the frauds of others in his right to vote and to an honest and a fair count. The circuit court of Cook county, in the case of *Hammer* vs. *Swift et al.*, 7 *Legal News*, 167, following the case of *Williams* vs. *Stein*, *supra*, held the statute unconstitutional. See, also, opinion by Judge Jameson, 8 *Legal News*, 69, to the same impor ;.

vote at that election.(¹) So, also, in the case of an unregistered voter, whose vote was received by the election board upon his affidavit, supported by the affidavit of one who was not a householder and a registered voter, as the statute requires. The statute, in this respect, is directory.(²)

The officers, whose duty it is, as a canvassing board, to canvass the returns of an election and certify the result, have no power to pass upon the qualifications of voters, nor decide as to what ballots shall be counted.(³)

m. Where a sick person is brought in a carriage to the polls, reaches out his ballot to one of the judges, who, not being able to receive it from his place, a person standing by, hands it to the judge, in whose sight it is, until received by him, such person's vote can not be rejected on the ground of not having been personally given.(⁴)

Where the evidence showed beyond all controversy, that stupendous frauds were committed at the election, by allowing persons to vote more than once; by adding names to the registry as application was made on the day of election, without inquiry as to the qualifications of the voter, and it appeared that the vote was double that ever was before; that the judges and clerks of the election, knowingly participated in such frauds, instead of using all reasonable and proper means to keep the ballot box pure and uncorrupted, it was held, that the court upon trial of a contest of such an election, properly rejected the poll lists and returns as impeached and so tainted with fraud, as to be unworthy of credit.(⁵)

6. EXAMINATION OF BALLOTS.—In all cases of contested election, the parties contesting the same shall have the right to have the said package of ballots opened, and said ballots referred to by witnesses for the purpose of such contest. But said ballots shall only be so examined and referred to in the presence of the officer having the custody thereof.(⁶)

(1) Kuykendall vs. Harker, 89 Ill., 126; Dale vs. Irwin, 78 Ill., 171; DuPage Co. vs. People, 65 Ill., 361.
(2) Clark vs. Robinson, 88 Ill., 498.
(3) Brewster vs. Kilduff, 15 Ill., 492.
(4) Clark vs. Robinson, *supra.*
(5) Knox Co. vs. Davis, 63 Ill., 405.
(6) Hurd's R. S., Chap. 46, § 60.

a. It is illegal for a board of canvassers to reject a numbered ballot found in the box, because an unnumbered ballot is found folded with it, and in a contest of such an election, the ballot so rejected, will be counted according to the intention of the voter;([1]) but a vote for a candidate on a separate slip of paper, folded within a numbered ballot deposited, not attached to it in any way, is properly rejected, the statute requiring the names of all the candidates voted for, to be upon the same ballot.([2])

The fact of the loss of the ballots and affidavits made at an election in a particular precinct, where such loss is accidental, affords no ground for rejecting the entire return from such precinct.([3])

b. Where ballots were illegally opened by the custodian and handled by a contestant and his friends, out of the presence of the other contestant, it was held, that the ballots thereby lost their value as evidence upon the trial, notwithstanding the testimony of those participating in the unlawful count, was offered to the effect that no changes were made in the ballots.([4])

It was held to be manifest error for the county court, when trying a contested election case, to allow one of the contestant's votes not in fact received, although offered to and rejected by the election board; and this, whether the proffered votes were properly or improperly rejected.([5])

So, where an ineligible candidate for a public office receives a plurality of the votes cast at the election, the next highest candidate is not entitled to the office if the ineligibility does not appear upon the ballots, and his lack of legal qualifications for the office is thus brought home to the knowledge of the voters.([6])

7. INTENTION OF VOTER TO GOVERN.—In determining contested election cases, after having ascertained who of the voters were legal electors, it becomes a matter of first importance to determine what was the intention of such voters in casting their ballots; for that intention, if ascertained, must control the court in its decision of the case. No informality in designating the office, as designating

---

(1) Clark vs. Robinson, 88 Ill., 488; Dale vs. Irwin, 78 Ill., 171.
(2) Webster vs. Gilmore, 91 Ill., 324.
(3) Beardstown vs. Virginia, 76 Ill., 34.
(4) Kingery vs. Berry, 94 Ill., 515.
(5) Webster vs. Byrnes, 34 Cal., 273.
(6) Barnum vs. Gilpin, 27 Minn., 426; People vs. Clute, 50 N. Y., 451.

the office as "magistrate," when the officer to be elected was that of police magistrate, can be allowed to defeat the intention of the voter, when it is apparent what office he intended to vote for.(¹) Where ballots omit a part of a candidate's name, or contain but one initial, or misspell the name, or omit the initials altogether; where the intention of the voter to vote for one of the contesting candidates is apparent, the ballot will be counted according to the intent of the voter.(²)

8. BRIBERY BY CANDIDATES.—It has been held, that where candidates for office, prior to the day of election, as an inducement for electors to vote for them, by printed circulars or in speeches from the stump, offer to accept election to office and perform the duties thereof for a sum less than the legal salary, leaving the balance in the treasury to the credit of the general public, in the absence of any statute declaring ineligibility to office a consequence of bribery at the election, will, when proven in a contested election case or in a *quo warranto*, justify a judgment against a candidate securing his election by such means.(³)

9. TIE.—If it appears that two or more persons have, or would have had, if the legal ballots cast or intended to be cast for them had been counted, the highest and an equal number of votes for the same office, the persons receiving such votes shall decide by lot, in such manner as the court shall direct, which of them shall be declared duly elected; and the judgment shall be entered accordingly.(⁴)

10. WHEN ELECTION ADJUDGED VOID.—When the person whose election is contested is found to have received the highest number of legal votes, but the election is declared null by reason of legal disqualification on his part, or for other causes, the person receiving the next highest number of votes, shall not be declared elected, but the election shall be declared void.(⁵)

11. JUDGMENT.—The judgment of the court, in cases of contested election, shall confirm or annul the election according to the

(1) People vs. Matteson et al., 17 Ill., 167.
(2) Talkington vs. Turner, 71 Ill., 234; Clark vs. Robinson, 88 Ill., 498.
(3) State vs. Newell, 36 Wis., 213; State vs. Church, 5 Oregon, 375; State vs. Collier, 72 Mo., 13; See, also, note to last named case, 37 American Rep., 422.
(4) Hurd's R. S., Chap. 46, § 120.
(5) Hurd's R. S., Chap. 46, § 122.

right of the matter; or, in case the contest is in relation to the election of some person to an office, shall declare as elected the person who shall appear to be duly elected.(¹)

a. The form of the judgment of the court should follow the usual form of a decree in chancery, and should not only show jurisdiction of the persons of the contestants, but the rule in chancery practice should be applied here, that to uphold the decree, it must appear from the record that the findings of the court are supported by the evidence.(²)

12. CERTIFIED COPY OF JUDGMENT.—A certified copy of the judgment of the court shall have the same effect as to the result of the election, as if it had been so declared by the canvassers.(³)

13. APPEAL.—In all cases of contested elections in the circuit courts or county courts, appeals may be taken to the supreme court in the same manner, and upon like conditions as is provided by law for taking appeals in cases in chancery from the circuit courts.(⁴)

a. Appeals from the decrees of the county court in cases of contested elections, lie to the supreme court direct. Section 8 of the act creating appellate courts, and giving jurisdiction thereto must not be understood as repealing this section of the statute.(⁵)

(1) Hurd's R. S., Chap. 46, § 119.
(2) Kingery vs. Berry, 94 Ill., 515.
(3) Hurd's R. S., Chap. 46, § 121.
(4) Hurd's R. S., Chap. 46, § 123.
(5) Webster vs. Gilmore, 91 Ill., 324.

ADDITIONAL NOTES.

1. Time of filing the petition.
2. Time in which to issue summons.
3. What constitutes a day.
4. Office hours of clerks of courts.
5. Requisites of a petition, as to the qualifications of petitioner.
6. Citizenship defined—Whether it includes the right to vote.
7. Failure to take oath of office and give bond during a contest.
8. Proceeding not a suit at law.
9. Can be tried at a probate term.
10. County court has no jurisdiction to determine the qualifications of an incumbent.
11. Practice same as in chancery—Chancery court has no jurisdiction.
12. Petition and proceedings to ascertain true vote.
13. Contest of town officers.
14. What the petition should contain.
15. The answer.
16. Answer not conclusive on the court.
17. Of matters that may be shown on a recount, irregularities, etc.
18. Quo warranto proceedings used—When.
19. Decree may be set aside—When.
20. Council to determine contest of members, under special charter.
21. Summons returnable—When.
22. Form of petition.
23. Form of answer.
24. Form of general replication.

1. TIME OF FILING PETITION.—Under section 113 of chapter 46, R. S., 1874, entitled "Elections," providing that in the case of the proposed contesting of an election, the person desiring to contest such election shall, within thirty days after the person whose election is contested is declared elected, file with the clerk of the proper court a statement, in writing, of the grounds upon which he will contest the election, the contestant is not restricted, as to the time of the day in which he may file such statement, to the hours during which the clerk is required by statute to keep his office open— that is, from eight o'clock A. M. to six o'clock P. M.—but the "day" contemplated by the statute is an ordinary day of twenty-four hours, which does not expire until twelve o'clock, midnight. So, where it was proposed to contest the election of a person who had been declared elected to the office of county treasurer, and the statement

in writing of the grounds of contest was filed with the clerk of the proper court on the last day limited by the statute, but not until after six o'clock P. M. of that day, it was held, the filing of statement was in apt time.

2. TIME IN WHICH TO ISSUE SUMMONS.—In a proceeding to contest such an election, the filing with the clerk of the statement in writing, as required by the statute, is the commencement of the suit, so that it is not essential, in order to preserve the right of the contestant to proceed, that the summons shall be issued within the thirty days limited for the filing of the statement, but it may as well be issued after that time has expired.

3. WHAT CONSTITUTES A DAY.—Where a person is required to take action within a given number of days in order to assert or secure a right, the "day" is to consist of twenty-four hours—that is the popular and the legal sense of the term—so that if the act be done on the last day limited, if it be done at any time before twelve o'clock at midnight, that will be sufficient.

4. OFFICE HOURS OF CLERKS OF COURTS.—The sixth section of chapter 25, R. S., 1874, entitled "Clerks of Courts," provides that the clerks of certain courts therein named shall keep their offices open, and attend to the duties thereof, from eight o'clock A. M. to six o'clock P. M. of each working day. This is to be understood as requiring such clerks to keep their offices open at least during the hours thus designated, but not in any way affecting their right or power to transact official business during any other hours in the day.([1])

5. REQUISITES OF PETITION, AS TO QUALIFICATIONS OF PETITIONER.—A petition for the contest of an election by one to the office of town clerk, or other town office, should aver that the petitioner was an elector of the town, or it will be fatally defective on demurrer. An averment that the contestant was a citizen and resident of the town is not sufficient.

6. CITIZENSHIP DEFINED.—A citizen, in the popular and appropriate sense of the term, is one who, by birth, naturalization or otherwise, is a member of an independent political society called a state, kingdom or empire, and who, as such, is subject to its laws and entitled to its protection in all his rights incident to that rela-

---

(1) Zimmerman vs. Cowan, 107 Ill., 631.

tion. The term includes females and minors. The right of suffrage is not coextensive with the right of citizenship.(¹)

7. FAILURE TO TAKE OATH OF OFFICE AND GIVE BOND—The statute requiring a town collector to take the oath of office and file his bond within the time prescribed applies only to the person declared elected by the canvassing board, and to whom the certificate of election has been given. In case of the contest of the election, it will be sufficient if the contestant qualifies within the same time after a judgment is rendered in his favor to entitle him to the fees and emoluments of the office which may have been received by his unsuccessful opponent.(²)

8. PROCEEDING NOT A SUIT AT LAW.—A proceeding to contest an election is not a suit at law.(³)

9. MAY BE TRIED AT PROBATE TERM.—Such a proceeding may be tried at the probate terms of the court.(⁴)

10. COUNTY COURT HAS NO JURISDICTION.—The county court has no jurisdiction to hear and determine the qualifications of an incumbent.(⁵)

11. PRACTICE—CHANCERY COURT HAS NO JURISDICTION.—The practice is the same as the practice in chancery courts, but courts of chancery have no jurisdiction to hear and determine contested election cases.(⁶)

12. PETITION AND PROCEEDINGS.—The petition and the proceedings under it should be directed to the matter of ascertaining the true vote of the people, and not to a mere amendment of the canvass.(⁷)

13. CONTEST OF TOWN OFFICERS.—The right to contest as to town officers is confined to electors of the town.(⁸)

14. WHAT THE PETITION SHOULD CONTAIN.—The petition should show the names of the persons whose ballots have been improperly counted, if known; but this is not indispensable.(⁹)

(1) Blanck vs. Pausch, 113 Ill., 60.
(2) Farwell vs. Adams, 112 Ill., 57.
(3) Kreitz vs. Behrensmeyer, 125 Ill., 141.
(4) *Ib.*
(5) Greenwood vs. Murphy, 131 Ill., 604.
(6) Jennings vs. Joyce, 116 Ill., 179; Kreitz vs. Behrensmeyer, *supra.*
(7) County of Lawrence vs. Schmaulhausen, 123 Ill., 321.
(8) Blanck vs. Pausch, *supra.*
(9) Kreitz vs. Behrensmeyer, *supra.*

15. THE ANSWER.—Less particularity is required in the answer of the defendant than in the petition. Where contestant alleges he was elected, and this is denied by the answer, it is competent for the defendant to show that persons voted for the contestant who were not legal voters, and whose names are not given in the answer.([1])

16. ANSWER NOT CONCLUSIVE ON THE COURT.—The answer of the defendant admitting the petitioner was elected is not conclusive upon the court.([2])

17. WHAT MAY BE SHOWN ON A RECOUNT.—As to what may be shown on a recount of ballots in a contested election case, what evidence is properly admissible, the rules applicable thereto, questions of irregularities, etc., the cases cited will be found to be very full.([3])

18. QUO WARRANTO PROCEEDINGS.—Quo warranto proceedings and judgment of ouster are not contemplated in proceedings to contest an election.([4]) Lack of qualifications for holding the office should be contested by quo warranto, and not under the act in relation to the contest of elections.([5])

19. DECREE MAY BE SET ASIDE.—A decree obtained by fraud may be set aside at any time during the term at which it was rendered.([6])

20. COUNCIL TO DETERMINE.—Where a special charter of a city authorizes the city council and invests it with the power to hear and determine all contested elections of its own members, no other tribunal than the city council has jurisdiction to determine the matter.([7])

21. SUMMONS RETURNABLE—WHEN.—A summons issued out of the county court in a proceeding to contest an election, made returnable to a term of the court beyond the second term after the *teste* of the writ, is void.([8])

(1) Kreitz vs. Behrensmeyer, 125 Ill., 141.
(2) Bahe vs. Jones, 132 Ill., 134.
(3) Kreitz vs. Behrensmeyer, *supra;* McKinnon vs. People, 110 Ill., 305; County of Lawrence vs. Schmaulhausen, 123 Ill., 321; Kreitz vs. Behrensmeyer, 131 Ill., 591; Moffitt vs. Hill, 131 Ill., 239; Blankenship vs. Israel, 132 Ill., 314.
(4) Simons vs. People, 18 Ill. Ap., 588.
(5) Greenwood vs. Murphy, 131 Ill., 604.
(6) Bahe vs. Jones, *supra*.
(7) Keating vs. Stack, 116 Ill., 191.
(8) Cavanaugh vs. McConochie, 134 Ill., 516.

22. FORM OF PETITION TO CONTEST AN ELECTION.

STATE OF ILLINOIS, } ss.   *In the County Court,*
.........County,   *To the.........term, A. D. 18...*

A. B.   }
  vs.   } Petition to Contest Election.
C. D.   }

To the Hon. J. K., judge of the county court, in and for.........county, Illinois:

A. B., your petitioner, would respectfully represent and show to your honor, that your petitioner had been, and on that day was, and from thence hitherto has been, and still is an elector of.........county, Illinois; that he was an elector of said county at the date of the election next hereinafter mentioned; that on the......day of........., A. D. 18..., in pursuance of law, an election was held in said county for, among other offices, [*here state name of the office,*] of said county; that the said election was held at the various election precincts and voting districts in said county, the polls having been opened at each one of said precincts according to law; that in said several and respective precincts and districts ballots were, at said election, received for said office of.........; that after the polls were closed a count was made by the judges of election of and at the respective precincts and districts aforesaid of the votes and ballots at each of said election precincts and districts cast; that upon such count the judges of the respective precincts and districts aforesaid made certificates of the number of votes cast for the several and respective persons voted for, for the different offices, including therein the said office of.........of said county, as said votes were counted by said judges, and said judges of said respective precincts and districts thereupon caused the ballot boxes containing the ballots voted in the respective precincts and districts, with their said certificate of the number of votes cast last above named, to be forwarded to the clerk of the county court of.........county, Illinois, who, together with two justices of the peace of said county, within four days of said election, opened the returns of said election and canvassed the same, as required by law.

And your petitioner would further represent, that at said election he was the candidate of the Democratic political party, and that one C. D. was the candidate of the Republican political party, and that one E. F. was the candidate of the Prohibition political party, for the office of.........of said county aforesaid, and that said C. D. had......votes at said election, and that said E. F. had......votes at said election, and your petitioner had......votes at said election for the office of.........aforesaid, as the result was declared by said canvassing board, and that upon the result as last named the county clerk of said.........county issued and delivered to the said C. D. a certificate of election to the office of.........aforesaid.

Your petitioner would state, on information and belief, that the canvassing board reached that result by adding together the votes for candidates for.........as the same were stated in the certificate of the judges of the respective precincts and districts aforesaid, and that any errors in the count of the election judges entered into the result as declared by said canvassing board.

Your petitioner would further show, that the names of the various townships in said county of........., Illinois, are as follows, viz: [*here name the townships*]; that the township of........., containing the city of........., was divided into.......election precincts or districts, numbered from.......to......, inclusive; that the other portions of said county were divided into election precincts or districts, as follows, viz: [*here name the precincts or districts*]; that at the election precinct or district in the city of.........numbered......, ...votes were cast for the contestant which should have been counted for him, but which were counted by the said judges of said precinct or district for the said C D., his opponent; that at the election precinct or district of ...., in said county, the judges counted one ballot for the said C. D. that was included within another; that at said voting precinct or district one G. H. voted, and was an illegal voter; that at said election precinct or district of ...., in..........township, ...persons voted who were not naturalized citizens of the United States, and......who were not residents of the State of Illinois; that at the election precinct or district of........., in the said township of........., ...legal votes were cast for the contestant which were counted by the judges of said election against him; that at the election precinct or district of........., in the said township of........., more ballots were in the ballot box than were on the poll list; that at the election precinct or district of........., in the said township of........., one J. K. voted, who was under the age of twenty-one years; that at the election precinct or district of........., in said township of........., one L. M., a convicted felon, was permitted to vote, and his vote was counted for said C. D., his opponent; [*and in like manner proceed and state every legal objection that can be urged.*]

Your petitioner therefore prays that a summons may issue for the said defendant, C. D., commanding him to personally be and appear before the county court of.........county, Illinois, then and there to fully answer this petition, at its.........term thereof, A. D. 18..., and on the......day of said term; that upon a final hearing hereof the ballots cast at said election may be recounted, and the correct count duly ascertained and found by and under the direction of the court, and if, upon a recount thereof under the direction of the court, it shall appear that your petitioner has received more legal votes than the said C. D., then that the certificate of election issued to the said C. D. may be declared null and void, and a proper certificate of election may issue to your petitioner, and he may be ordered, adjudged and decreed to be the duly authorized and legally elected.........of said county of........., and State of Illinois. And your petitioner will ever pray, etc.

By N. & O., Attorneys.   A. B.

AFFIDAVIT TO PETITION.

STATE OF ILLINOIS, } ss.
.........County,

On this......day of........., A. D. 18..., before me personally appeared the above named A. B., and made oath that he is the petitioner in the above and foregoing petition, and knows the contents thereof, which have been read over to him, and that the same is true of his own knowledge, except as to matters which are therein stated to be on his information and belief, and that as to those matters he believes the same to be true.

J. L., Clerk of the.........Court.

23. FORM OF ANSWER.

STATE OF ILLINOIS, } ss.　　　　In the County Court,
.........County,　　　　　　　　To the.........term, A. D. 18...

C. D.
vs.　　} Answer.
A. B.

The answer of C. D., the defendant, to the petition of A. B., the petitioner:

This defendant, reserving to himself all right of exceptions to the said petition, for answer thereto says: That he denies that the petitioner, on the ......day of....... ., A. D. 18..., was an elector of.........county, Illinois; admits an election on.......... ......, A. D. 18..., in said county, and that at said election the polls were open at each of the voting precincts and districts of said county, and that ballots were cast and received thereat; admits that after the polls were closed a count was made by the judges of the different precincts and election districts of the votes cast thereat, and that upon such count being made in each precinct and election district the judges thereof certified the number of votes cast for the different persons voted for, for the different offices, including therein the office of county........., as the votes were counted by said judges; admits that said judges of said precincts and election districts thereupon caused the ballot boxes containing the ballots voted at said respective precincts and polling places, with their said certificate of the number of votes cast thereat, to be forwarded to the county clerk of.........county, and that said clerk and two justices afterward, and within four days of said election, opened the returns of said election from all said precincts and polling places, and canvassed the same; admits that at such election.........was the candidate for..........of the.. ......party; that ....was the candidate for.........of the.........party; and respondent was the candidate for.........of the.........party, and that the result of the election, as declared by said canvassing board, was......votes cast for........., the contestant, and......for........., the candidate of the.........party, and......for the respondent, and that said county clerk issued to respondent a certificate of election; that the said canvassing board merely added together the result as certified by the judges of the different precincts or polling places, as to the office of.........of said county.

This respondent expressly denies that any errors or vices entering into the result as certified by the judges were preserved in the result as announced by the canvassing board, but avers the truth to be there were no errors or irregularities in said returns as certified by the election judges, except as hereinafter stated; admits that the precincts and election districts of the county of.........are as set out in the petition of the contestant; denies that at the election precinct or district in the city of.........numbered......, ...votes were cast for the contestant which should have been counted for him, but which were counted by said judges of said precinct or election district for your respondent; denies that at the election precinct or district of........., in said county, the judges counted one ballot for the respondent that was inclosed within another, but states the truth to be neither ballot was counted; denies that at said voting precinct or district one G. H. voted, and was an illegal voter; [*denying each and every allegation of the petition.*]

[*The answer may then aver and specify any and all irregularities in regard to the voting or conduct of the election, and all irregularities that would be of benefit or advantage to the respondent.*]

This respondent, further answering, shows that a recount of said ballots would give to the respondent......majority for the office of........., and expressly denies that the said contestant was ever legally elected by a majority of the legal votes of said county to said office of........., and that he is entitled to the relief prayed—all of which he is ready to maintain.

And having fully answered, this respondent prays hence to be dismissed, with his reasonable costs by him made in this behalf, most wrongfully sustained. C. D.

By R. & S., Attorneys.

To this answer a general replication may be filed, as in chancery; or, the contestant may file exception to the answer, the practice being precisely the same as in chancery cases.

24   FORM OF A GENERAL REPLICATION.

STATE OF ILLINOIS, } ss.   *Of the..........term, A. D. 18...,*
..........County, ...*County Court.*

A. B.
vs.   } Replication to answer.
C. D.

The replication of A. B., repliant, to the answer of C. D., defendant:

The said repliant, saving and reserving to himself all, and all manner of advantage of exception to the manifold insufficiencies of said answer, for replication thereunto says, that he will aver and prove his said bill to be true, certain and sufficient in the law to be answered unto; and that the said answer of the defendant is uncertain, untrue and insufficient to be replied unto by A. B., repliant, without this, that any other matter or thing whatsoever in the said answer contained, material or effectual in the law, to be replied unto, confessed and avoided, traversed or denied, is true, all which matters and things repliant is and will be ready to aver and prove, as this honorable court shall direct, and humbly prays as in and by his said bill he has already prayed.   ....Solicitors for Compl't.

CHAPTER XXIII.

NATURALIZATION OF FOREIGNERS.

1. Definition.
2. Who are subjects of this jurisdiction.
3. How an alien may be admitted to citizenship.
    a. Declaration of intention.
    b. Oath of allegiance—renunciation of allegiance.
    c. Facts to be proven.
    d. Renunciation of titles of nobility.
    e. Exceptions.
4. Congress alone may prescribe rules of naturalization.
5. Jurisdiction of county courts.
6. Aliens who have served in the army of the United States.
7. Aliens who have resided within the United States.
8. Widow and children of one who has declared his intention.
9. African aliens.
10. Term of residence.
11. Subjects of countries at war with the United States.
12. Children of naturalized citizens.
13. Foreign seamen.
14. Power to admit to citizenship judicial.
15. Declaration.
16. Perjury.
17. Record not to be contradicted by parol.
18. Effect upon children.

1. DEFINITION.—A citizen of the United States is one who is in the enjoyment of all the rights to which the people are entitled, and bound to fulfil the duties to which they are subject; this includes men, women and children. In a more limited sense, a citizen is one who has a right to vote for public officers; for example, representative in congress, and who is eligible to offices under the constitution and laws. Citizens are natives or naturalized.([1])

2. WHO ARE SUBJECTS OF THIS JURISDICTION.—The subject of a foreign government who has made the United States his permanent home, may become a citizen by complying with the act of Congress which is embodied herein.

3. HOW AN ALIEN MAY BE ADMITTED TO CITIZENSHIP.—An

---

(1) 1 Bouvier's Inst., 64.

alien may be admitted to become a citizen of the United States in the following manner, and not otherwise:

a. First—He shall declare on oath, before a circuit or district court of the United States, or a district or supreme court of the territories, or a court of record of any of the states having common law jurisdiction, and a seal and clerk, two years, at least, prior to his admission, that it is *bona fide* his intention to become a citizen of the United States, and to renounce forever all allegiance and fidelity to any foreign prince, potentate, state, or sovereignty, and, particularly, by name, to the prince, potentate, state, or sovereignty of which the alien may be at the time a citizen or subject.

b. Second—He shall, at the time of his application to be admitted, declare, on oath, before some one of the courts above specified, that he will support the constitution of the United States, and that he absolutely and entirely renounces and abjures all allegiance and fidelity to every foreign prince, potentate, state, or sovereignty, and, particularly, by name, to the prince, potentate, state, or sovereignty of which he was before a citizen or subject; which proceedings shall be recorded by the clerk of the court.

c. Third—It shall be made to appear to the satisfaction of the court admitting such alien, that he has resided within the United States five years at least, and within the state or territory where such court is at the time held, one year at least; and that during that time he has behaved as a man of a good moral character, attached to the principles of the constitution of the United States, and well disposed to the good order and happiness of the same; but the oath of the applicant shall in no case be allowed to prove his residence.

d. Fourth—In case the alien applying to be admitted to citizenship, has borne any hereditary title, or been of any of the orders of nobility in the kingdom or state from which he came, he shall, in addition to the above requisites, make an express renunciation of his title or order of nobility in the court to which his application is made, and his renunciation shall be recorded in the court.

e. Fifth—Any alien who was residing within the limits and under the jurisdiction of the United States before the twenty-ninth day of January, one thousand seven hundred and ninety-five, may be admitted to become a citizen, on due proof made to some one of the courts above specified, that he has resided two years, at least, within the jurisdiction of the United States, and one year, at least, immediately preceding his application, within the state or territory where such court is at the time held; and on his declaring on oath that he will support the constitution of the United States, and that he absolutely and entirely renounces and abjures all allegiance and fidelity to any foreign prince, potentate, state, or sovereignty, and, particularly, by name, to the prince, potentate, state, or sovereignty whereof he was before a citizen or subject; and, also, on its appearing to the satisfaction of the court, that during such term of two years he has behaved as a man of good moral character, attached to the constitution of the United States, and well disposed to the good order and happiness of the same; and where the alien, applying for admission to citizenship, has borne any hereditary title, or been of any of the orders of nobility in the kingdom or state from which he came, on his, moreover, making in the court an express renunciation of his title or order of nobility. All of the proceedings, required in this condition to be performed in the court, shall be recorded by the clerk thereof.

Sixth—Any alien who was residing within the limits and under the jurisdiction of the United States, between the eighteenth day of June, one thousand seven hundred and ninety-eight, and the eighteenth day of June, one thousand eight hundred and twelve, and who has continued to reside within the same, may be admitted to become a citizen of the United States without having made any previous declaration of his intention to become such; but whenever any person, without a certificate of such declaration of intention, makes application to be admitted a citizen, it must be proved to the satisfaction of the court, that the applicant was residing within the limits and under the jurisdiction of the United States before the eighteenth day of June, one thousand eight hundred and twelve, and has continued to reside within the same; and the residence of the applicant within the limits and under the jurisdiction of the United States, for at least five years immediately preceding the time of such application, must be proved by the oath of citizens of the United States, which citizens shall be named in the record as witnesses; and such continued residence within the limits and under the jurisdiction of the United States, when satisfactorily proved, and the place where the applicant has resided for at least five years, shall be stated and set forth, together with the names of such citizens, in the record of the court admitting the applicant; otherwise the same shall not entitle him to be considered and deemed a citizen of the United States.([1])

4. CONGRESS ALONE MAY PRESCRIBE RULES OF NATURALIZATION.—Since the adoption of the constitution of the United States, which gave to congress the power "to establish a uniform rule of naturalization,"([2]) the right to pass laws providing for the naturalization of such subjects of a foreign power as might from choice take up their homes within any of the states, and to confer jurisdiction upon state courts to naturalize, has alone been vested in congress; and no state has authority to legislate upon that subject.([3])

5. JURISDICTION OF COUNTY COURTS.—It is now settled by the decisions of the supreme court of Illinois, that the county courts of the state are within the definition, as "having common law jurisdiction," and may, under the authority of the federal statute, admit aliens to citizenship;([4]) although, for a time, following the rulings of courts of other states, to the effect that the common law jurisdiction must be general, and not limited, it was held in Illinois, that its county courts could not exercise that jurisdiction.([5]) It is held, that it is the fact of having a jurisdiction which belonged to the common law courts of England, and not the amount or extent of that jurisdiction, which gives the right. So, the right to take cognizance of any case at law, be it never so limited, brings the court within the definition of those having jurisdiction.([6])

The county courts of Illinois, from the date of their origin, have had common law jurisdiction, larger since 1871, than before, and have always been invested with jurisdiction to admit aliens to citizenship. Whenever legally convened for any business, these courts may grant certificates of naturalization; and the right to exercise a common law jurisdiction at the time, is not essential to confer this right.

(1) U. S. Statutes, Title 30, § 2165; Matter of Hawley, 1 Daley, 531.
(2) U. S. Constitution, Art. 1, § 8.
(3) Chirac vs. Chirac, 2 Wheaton, 259; State vs. Penney, 10 Ark., 621.
(4) People vs. McGowan, 77 Ill., 644; Dale vs. Irwin, 78 Ill., 171; City of Beardstown vs. City of Virginia, 81 Ill., 541.
(5) Mills vs. McCabe, 44 Ill., 194; Knox Co. vs. Davis, 63 Ill., 405; In the Matter of Martin Connor, 39 Cal., 98; Mills vs. McCabe, *supra;* Beardstown vs. Virginia, 76 Ill., 34.
(6) People vs. McGowan, *supra.*

6. ALIENS WHO HAVE SERVED IN THE ARMY OF THE UNITED STATES.—Any alien, of the age of twenty-one years and upward, who has enlisted, or may enlist, in the armies of the United States, either the regular or the volunteer forces, and has been, or may be hereafter, honorably discharged, shall be admitted to become a citizen of the United States, upon his petition, without any previous declaration of his intention to become such; and he shall not be required to prove more than one year's residence within the United States previous to his application to become such citizen; and the court admitting such alien shall, in addition to such proof of residence and good moral character, as now provided by law, be satisfied by competent proof of such person's having been honorably discharged from the service of the United States.([1])

7. ALIENS WHO HAVE RESIDED WITHIN THE UNITED STATES.—Any alien, being under the age of twenty-one years, who has resided in the United States three years next preceding his arriving at that age, and who has continued to reside therein to the time he may make application to be admitted a citizen thereof, may, after he arrives at the age of twenty-one years, and after he has resided five years within the United States, including the three years of his minority, be admitted a citizen of the United States, without having made the declaration required in the first condition of section twenty-one hundred and sixty-five; but such alien shall make the declaration required therein at the time of his admission; and shall further declare, on oath, and prove to the satisfaction of the court, that, for two years next preceding, it has been his *bona fide* intention to become a citizen of the United States; and he shall in all other respects comply with the laws in regard to naturalization.([2])

The right to apply for and be received to the privileges of citizenship, is not limited to males, but may be availed of by females, upon complying with the law.([3])

8. WIDOW AND CHILDREN OF ONE WHO HAS DECLARED HIS INTENTION.—When any alien, who has complied with the first condition specified in section twenty-one hundred and sixty-five, dies before he is actually naturalized, the widow and the children

---

(1) U. S. Statutes, Title 30, § 2166.
(2) U. S. Statutes, Title 30, § 2167.
(3) Priest vs. Cummings, 16 Wend., (N. Y.) 616.

of such alien shall be considered as citizens of the United States, and shall be entitled to all rights and privileges as such, upon taking the oaths prescribed by law.([1])

9. AFRICAN ALIENS.—The provisions of this title shall apply to aliens of African nativity and to persons of African descent.([2])

10. TERM OF RESIDENCE.—No alien shall be admitted to become a citizen who has not for the continued term of five years next preceding his admission, resided within the United States.([3])

11. SUBJECTS OF COUNTRIES AT WAR WITH THE UNITED STATES.—No alien who is a native citizen or subject, or a denizen of any country, state, or sovereignty with which the United States are at war, at the time of his application, shall be then admitted to become a citizen of the United States; but persons resident within the United States, or the territories thereof, on the eighteenth day of June, in the year one thousand eight hundred and twelve, who had before that day made a declaration, according to law, of their intention to become citizens of the United States, or who were on that day entitled to become citizens without making such declaration, may be admitted to become citizens thereof, notwithstanding they were alien enemies at the time and in the manner prescribed by the laws heretofore passed on that subject; nor shall anything herein contained, be taken or construed to interfere with or prevent the apprehension and removal, agreeably to law, of any alien enemy at any time previous to the actual naturalization of such alien.([4])

12. CHILDREN OF NATURALIZED CITIZENS.—The children of persons who have been duly naturalized under any law of the United States, or who, previous to the passing of any law on that subject, by the government of the United States, may have become citizens of any one of the states, under the laws thereof, being under the age of twenty-one years at the time of the naturalization of their parents, shall, if dwelling in the United States, be considered as citizens thereof; and the children of persons who now are, or have been citizens of the United States, shall, though born out of the limits and jurisdiction of the United States, be considered as citizens thereof; but no person heretofore proscribed by any state, or who has been legally convicted of having joined the army of

---

(1) U. S. Statutes, Title 30, § 2168. (3) U. S. Statutes, Title 30, § 2170.
(2) U. S. Statutes, Title 30, § 2169. (4) U. S. Statutes, Title 30, § 2171.

Great Britain during the Revolutionary War, shall be admitted to become a citizen without the consent of the legislature of the state in which such person was proscribed.(¹)

13. FOREIGN SEAMEN.—Every seaman, being a foreigner, who declares his intention of becoming a citizen of the United States in any competent court, and shall have served three years on board of a merchant-vessel of the United States subsequent to the date of such declaration, may, on his application to any competent court, and the production of his certificate of discharge and good conduct during that time, together with the certificate of his declaration of intention to become a citizen, be admitted a citizen of the United States; and every seaman, being a foreigner, shall, after his declaration of intention to become a citizen of the United States, and after he shall have served such three years, be deemed a citizen of the United States for the purpose of manning and serving on board any merchant-vessel of the United States, anything to the contrary in any act of Congress notwithstanding; but such seaman shall, for all purposes of protection as an American citizen, be deemed such, after the filing of his declaration of intention to become such citizen.(²)

14. POWER TO ADMIT TO CITIZENSHIP JUDICIAL.—The power to naturalize, is judicial.(³) Being judicial, and not ministerial or clerical, clerks of courts have no power to pass upon applications for naturalization and grant certificates;(⁴) but the act of receiving the preliminary declaration of intention is ministerial and not judicial, and may be performed before the clerk of the court.(⁵)

Courts must examine the petitions for naturalization, and be satisfied of the truth of all facts necessary to entitle the alien to citizenship. The applicant should submit common law proof of the facts which entitle him to admission to citizenship.(⁶)

15. DECLARATION.—A declaration of intention to become a citizen, need not give the name of the sovereign to whom allegiance is renounced, but may designate him or her as the king,

(1) U. S. Statutes, Title 30, § 2172.
(2) U. S. Statutes, Title 30, § 2174.
(3) *Ex Parte* Knowles, 5 Cal., 300.
(4) *In Re* Clark, 18 Barb., (N. Y.) 444.
(5) Butterworth's Case, Woodb. & M., 323.
(6) Spratt vs. Spratt, 4 Peters, 4061.

emperor, queen, etc., as the case may be, of such a country.(¹)

The fact that no declaration was made, as required by law, before the final action of the court, admitting the alien to citizenship, can not be used to impeach the right of the voter to vote, for the reason that the final action of the court imported regularity in the proceedings antedating the action of the court.(²)

16. PERJURY.—Swearing to a false affidavit relative to an application made in a state court for naturalization, under the laws of the United States, is perjury, and indictable in the courts of the state.(³)

17. RECORD NOT TO BE CONTRADICTED BY PAROL.—The record of the naturalization of an alien, like any other record of a court, imports verity, and can not be impeached for fraud, unless that defense has been specially pleaded, setting forth in what the fraud consists. Such a record can not be impeached, in a collateral proceeding, when made by a court having jurisdiction, by showing by parol that the preliminary steps required by law, had not, in fact, been taken. All that it was necessary for the alien or the court to have done before the entry of the order admitting him to citizenship, will be presumed to have been done.(⁴) Where, however, a certificate of naturalization recites the person as P. W. D., whose real name is P. P. W. D., he may prove, by his own oath, that he was the person to whom it was issued, and that he is the person naturalized thereby.(⁵)

18. EFFECT UPON CHILDREN.—By the express terms of the statute, the children of naturalized citizens, under the age of twenty-one years at the time of the admission to citizenship of the parent, become, *ipso facto*, if dwelling within the United States, citizens thereof.(⁶) Where the foreign born bastard son of the wife of one admitted to citizenship, was, at the time, living with the family of the person so admitted, it was held, that the above named section would include such child, and that the admission of the reputed father would operate to naturalize the child.(⁷)

(1) *Ex Parte* Smith. 8 Blackf., (Ind.) 395.
(2) People vs. McGowan, 77 Ill., 644.
(3) State vs. Whittemore, 50 N. H., 245.
(4) People vs. McGowan, *supra*.
(5) City of Beardstown vs. City of Virginia, 81 Ill., 541.
(6) Sec. 2172, *ante;* Matter of Morrison, 22 How., 99; West vs. West, 8
(7) Dale vs. Irwin, 78 Ill., 170.   [Paige, 433.

ADDITIONAL NOTES.

1. Whether certain persons are citizens.
2. Form of certificate of filing declaration.
3. Form of petition for final papers of naturalization.
4. Form of naturalization final oath.
5. Form of final certificate of naturalization.

1. WHETHER CERTAIN PERSONS ARE CITIZENS.—Any woman who might be lawfully naturalized under the existing laws, married, or who shall be married to a citizen of the United States, shall be deemed and taken to be a citizen; and the children of such a woman, under the age of twenty-one years, become citizens by virtue of her citizenship.[1]

2. FORM OF CERTIFICATE OF FILING DECLARATION.

UNITED STATES OF AMERICA,
   STATE OF ILLINOIS, } ss.
        ....County,

I, ..., do solemnly declare on oath to........., clerk of the.........court of the county of........., State of Illinois, that it is *bona fide* my intention to become a citizen of the United States, and to renounce forever all allegiance and fidelity to any foreign prince, potentate, state or sovereignty whatever, and particularly to........., whereof I was heretofore a citizen or subject.

Subscribed and sworn to before me, this......day of........., A. D. 18...
                                   ....Clerk.

STATE OF ILLINOIS, } ss.
   ....County,

I, ..., clerk of the.........court of the county of........., in the State of Illinois, do hereby certify that the above is a true copy of the declaration of ...., an alien, duly made before me, and filed in my office, on this......day of........., A. D. 18...

Given under my hand and the seal of said court, at........., in said county, the day and year aforesaid.   ....Clerk.

3. FORM OF PETITION FOR FINAL PAPERS OF NATURALIZATION.

STATE OF ILLINOIS, } ss.   *In the*.........*Court of said county,*
   ....County, ...*term, 18...*

To the Hon........., *presiding judge of the*.........*court of the county of*........., *in the State aforesaid:*

The undersigned, ..., your petitioner, respectfully represents, that

---

(1) Kreitz vs. Behrensmeyer, 125 Ill., 141.

he is an alien-born male person above the age of twenty-one years; that he has resided within the limits and under the jurisdiction of the United States for the space of five years last past, and for one year last past within the State of Illinois; that heretofore, to-wit, on the......day of........, A. D. 18..., (the same being two years and upward before the date hereof,) he declared on oath before the.........court of the county of........., and State of........., (the same being a court of record, having common law jurisdiction, and a seal and clerk,) that it was *bona fide* his intention to become a citizen of the United States, and to renounce forever all allegiance and fidelity to any foreign prince, potentate, state or sovereignty whatever, and particularly to ...., whereof he was heretofore a citizen or subject, as will more fully appear from the certificate under the seal of said court herewith presented.

Your petitioner therefore prays that he may be admitted to become a naturalized citizen of the United States of America, pursuant to the several acts of Congress heretofore passed on that subject.

........., being duly sworn, deposes and says that the facts averred in the above petition are true and correct.

Subscribed and sworn to before me, this......day of........., 18...
.........Clerk.

4. FORM OF NATURALIZATION FINAL OATH.

STATE OF ILLINOIS, } ss.   .... *Court*,
.........County, ...*term, A. D. 18...*

We, ...and........., lawful witnesses, and residents of the county of ...., and State of Illinois, having first been duly sworn, depose and say that we have been personally acquainted with........., an alien, who has applied to the.........court of said county of........., to be admitted as a naturalized citizen of the United States, for the space of five years last past; that during that time he has resided within the limits and under the jurisdiction of the United States, and one year at least in the State of Illinois, immediately preceding the day of the date hereof; and that, as far as our knowledge extends, has behaved himself as a man of good moral character, and appears to be attached to the principles contained in the Constitution of the United States, and well disposed to the good order, well being and happiness of the same.

Subscribed and sworn to in open court, this......day of........., A. D. 18...
.........Clerk.

STATE OF ILLINOIS, } ss.
.........County,

I, ..., do solemnly swear, in the presence of Almighty God, that I will support the Constitution of the United States, and that I do absolutely and entirely renounce and abjure all allegiance and fidelity to every foreign prince, potentate, state or sovereignty whatever, and more particularly the allegiance and fidelity which I may in anywise owe to........., whereof I was heretofore a citizen or a subject.

Sworn to and subscribed in open court, this......day of........., A. D. 18...
.........Clerk.

5. FORM OF FINAL CERTIFICATE OF NATURALIZATION.

UNITED STATES OF AMERICA,⎫
    STATE OF ILLINOIS,   ⎬ ss.
         ....County,   ⎭

Be it remembered, That on the.......day of........., in the year of our Lord One Thousand Eight Hundred and Ninety.........personally appeared before ...., presiding judge of the circuit court of the county of........., and State aforesaid, (the same being a court of record, having and exercising common law jurisdiction, a seal and a clerk,) and sitting judicially for the dispatch of business at the court house in........., A. B., an alien-born, free white male person, above the age of twenty-one years, and applied to the said court to be admitted to become a naturalized citizen of the United States of America, pursuant to the several acts of Congress heretofore passed on that subject, entitled "An Act to establish a uniform rule of Naturalization and to repeal the Acts heretofore passed on that subject," approved the 14th day of April, 1802; an act entitled "An Act in addition to an Act entitled 'An Act to establish a uniform rule of Naturalization and to repeal the Acts heretofore passed on that subject;'" approved on the 26th day of March, 1804; an act entitled "An Act supplementary to the Acts heretofore passed on the subject of a uniform rule of Naturalization," passed the 30th day of July, 1813; the act relative to evidence in cases of naturalization, passed the 22d day of March, 1816, and an act in further addition to an act to establish a uniform rule of naturalization and to repeal the acts heretofore passed on that subject, passed May 26th, 1824; and the said.........having thereupon produced to the court record testimony showing that he has heretofore reported himself and filed his declaration of his intention to become a citizen of the United States, according to the provisions of the said several acts of Congress, and the court being satisfied, as well from the oath of the said ....as from the testimony of.........and........., who are known to be citizens of the United States, that the said.........has resided within the limits and under the jurisdiction of the United States for at least five years last past, and at least one year last past within the State of Illinois, and that during the whole of that time he has behaved himself as a man of good moral character, attached to the principles contained in the Constitution of the United States, and well disposed to the good order, well being and happiness of the same, and two years and upward having elapsed since the said......... reported himself and filed his declaration of his intention aforesaid, *it was ordered,* that the said.........be permitted to take the oath to support the Constitution of the United States, and the usual oath whereby he renounces all allegiance and fidelity to every foreign prince, potentate, state and sovereignty whatever, and more particularly to........., whereof he was heretofore a subject, which said oath having been administered to the said.........by the clerk of said court, *it was ordered* by the court that the said.........be admitted to all and singular the rights, privileges and immunities of a naturalized citizen of the United States, and that the same be certified by the clerk of this court, under the seal of said court accordingly.

        In testimony whereof, the seal of the said court is hereto affixed at the clerk's office in........., this......day of.........,
[SEAL]   A. D. 18..., and of the Independence of the United States the One Hundred and.........
    By order of the court.
        Attest: ....
                Clerk of the Circuit Court of.........County.

APPENDIX—FORMS.

FORMS.

No. 1.
Form of Proof of Death and Petition for Letters of Administration.

Petition of.........., In the Matter of the Estate of.........., deceased, for Letters of Administration.

To the Hon..........., Judge of the County Court of......County, in the State of Illinois:

The petition of the undersigned,.........., respectfully represents, that.........., late of the county of.........., aforesaid, departed this life at.........., in said county, on or about the...day of......, A. D. 18...., leaving no last will and testament as far as your petitioner..know..or believe......

And this petition further shows that the said.........., died, seized and possessed of real estate and also personal property, consisting chiefly of..............; all of said personal estate being estimated to be worth about......dollars. That said deceased left surviving him.........., his widow, and........., ..., ..., his children, as heirs. That your petitioner (being......of said deceased, and) believing that the said estate should be immediately administered, as well for the proper care and management of said goods and chattels, as for the prompt collection of the assets, by virtue of h...right under the statute......, therefore pray that your honor will grant letters of administration to.........., in the premises, upon..h...taking the oath prescribed by the Statute, and entering into bond in such sum, and with securities, as may be approved **by your** honor.(1)

....

STATE OF ILLINOIS, } ss.
..............County,

..........being duly sworn, deposes and says that the facts averred in the above petition are true, according to the best of...knowledge, information and belief.

Sworn and subscribed to before me,
.........., Clerk of the County Court of........
County, this...day of......, A. D. 188...
.........., Clerk.

No. 2.
Form of Petition for Letters Testamentary.

Petition of.........:., In the Matter of the Last Will and Testament of.........., deceased, for Probate of Will and Letters Testamentary.

See pages 14 and 15.

To the Hon............, *Judge of the County Court of............County, in the State of Illinois:*

The petition of the undersigned............., respectfully represents, that........., late of the county of........., aforesaid, departed this life at........., in said county, on or about the...day of......, A. D. 18...., leaving a last Will and testament, duly signed, published and attested, as believed by your petitioner, and which by...is herewith presented to your honor for probate. That said Will is subscribed by........., ..., as witnesses to the execution thereof..............

That said testat...in...said last Will nominated and appointed........., your petitioner, execut...thereof, and that your petitioner......willing and ready to accept and undertake the office and trust confided to......

And this petition further shows, that the said.........died seized and possessed of real and personal estate, consisting chiefly of..............; all of said personal estate being estimated to be worth about.......dollars.

In consideration whereof, and to the end that said Will may be proved, established and performed, your petitioner..pray..that the subscribing witnesses aforesaid, may be summoned to be and appear before this court, at the next......term thereof, then and there to testify in the matter of said Will, as it may please your honor to direct; and that probate of said Will may be thereupon granted, and the same ordered for record.

And your petitioner..further pray..that it may please your honor to grant...letters testamentary of said last Will and testament, upon...taking the oath prescribed by the statute, and entering into bond in such sum and with such securities as may be approved by your honor.

STATE OF ILLINOIS, } ss.
.................County, }

.........being duly sworn, deposes and says, that the facts averred in the above petition are true, according to the best of h...knowledge, information and belief.

Sworn to and subscribed before me,
........., Clerk of the County Court of.........
County, this...day of......, A. D. 188..
........., Clerk.

No. 3.
Form of Clerk's Record of the Appointment of Administrator.

STATE OF ILLINOIS, } ss.   *In the......County Court—In Probate,*
.............County, }   ......*Term,* 18....

Present: Hon..........., Judge.   Attest: ...., Clerk.

And now on this...day of......, A. D. 188.., it being one of the days of said term, comes........., and duly files..h..petition to the Judge of said court in probate, representing that on the...day of......, A. D. 18...., ..., late of the county of........., and State of Illinois, departed this life intestate, and so far as petitioner knows or believes, no last Will or testament, or other writing, relating to the disposal or distribution of the estate of said deceased, or of any part thereof has been found or discovered by petitioner, or by any other person or persons, and [*Here insert in the record any other averments contained in the petition, showing that the petition should be granted, such as the right of the petitioner by virtue of relationship, or if he petitions as creditor, such fact,*] which petition is duly sworn to by the petitioner............ And it is thereupon ordered that said petition be filed by the clerk of this court.

And now on this day, said petition coming on to be heard by the court, the court doth find that by the filing thereof herein, the court has jurisdiction to hear and determine the same, and the application for letters therein made, and no one appearing to oppose the grant of letters of administration as therein prayed, the court doth find from said petition and oral proofs heard, that the matters set forth in said petition, are true, and that the said.........is entitled to receive letters of administration upon the estate of said........., deceased, upon filing in this court h...bond as such administrator, in the form prescribed by law, in the penal sum of......dollars.

And now on the same day comes the said........., and presents to the court, for the approval and acceptance of the court h...bond as such administrator of........., deceased, in the penal sum of......dollars, signed and sealed, and legally acknowledged by himself as principal, and.........and ...., as securities, and the said bond appearing to be in due form of law, and it being shown to the court that the securities therein are sufficient, it is thereupon ordered that the same be and it is hereby approved and accepted, and that the clerk of this court issue to the said........., under the seal of this court, letters of administration upon the estate of said........., deceased, upon the said.........taking the oath, and that he be appointed administrator of all and singular the goods and chattels, rights, credits and effects of........., deceased.(1)

No. 4.

Form of a Relinquishment by Widow or Next of Kin, of the Statutory Right to Administer.

STATE OF ILLINOIS, } ss.   In County Court of said County,
...............County, }   In Probate.

To the Hon......... Judge:

The undersigned being......of........, late of said county, deceased, hereby relinquishes and waives h...right under the statute to have letters of administration granted to h...upon the estate of said deceased.(2)

(1) See pages 15 and 16.
(2) *Ante* page 14.

No. 5.

Form of a Record to be made showing an Examination of Bonds by the Court at the January and July terms in each year.

STATE OF ILLINOIS, } ss.   *In County Court,*
..........County,   *January (or July) Term, A. D. 18....*

In the Matter of Bonds on file in the office } Examination by the Court.
of the Clerk of the County Court.

And now upon this...day of January (*or July*), A. D. 18...., it being the first day of said term, and the matter of the sufficiency of the official bonds required by law to be filed in the office of the clerk of this court, including the bonds of executors, administrators, guardians and conservators, coming before the court upon motion of.........., Esq., State's Attorney, and the court having made examination of each bond so on file, and being satisfied from such examination, that* each and every bond so on file, is amply sufficient for the security of all persons interested, it is ordered that each of said bonds be approved, and that the clerk of this court make a record of these proceedings.

Should any bond be found upon examination insufficient, then let there be inserted in said record following the (*), as follows:

[*The bond filed in this court and approved on the...day of......, 18...., by.........., as administrator of the estate of.........., deceased, is insufficient for the security of those interested in said estate.*]

In like manner the record should show at this point, the insufficiency of all bonds by the court deemed insufficient, and an approval of all other bonds. In case a bond or bonds are found insufficient, let the record conclude with this order:

It is further ordered by the court, that the clerk issue a summons (*or summonses*) to the said..........and.........., requiring them and each of them to appear before the court on the...day of......, 18...., to show cause why he (*or they*) should not be required to give a new bond as such administrator with sufficient surety.(1)

No. 6.

Form of a Petition to Require an Executor to Give Bond where the Testator in his Will directs that no Bond shall be Required of the Executor Nominated.

STATE OF ILLINOIS, } ss.   *In County Court,*
..........County,   To the...... *Term, A. D.* 18....

In the Matter of the Last Will and } Petition to Require Bond
Testament of.........., deceased.

To the Hon.........., *Judge of said Court—In Probate:*

Your petitioner, ..., would respectfully show unto your honor, that

(1) See page 31, *ante.*

one........., late of this county, departed this life on or about the...day of....., 18...., leaving a last Will and testament, in and by which last Will, one......... was nominated as the executor thereof, with directions in said Will that said.........should not be required to give any bond for the faithful performance of his trust as required in cases of other estates administered in the courts; that on the...day of......, 18...., said Will was presented for probate in this court, and upon being proven as required by law, was admitted to probate according to law; that thereupon letters testamentary were issued upon said Will to the said........., so nominated as executor, who entered upon the discharge of the duties devolving upon him as such, without having first given bond, and thenceforth to this day continued to act as such executor.

Petitioner would further show unto your honor, that said........., so appointed as executor, is insolvent, [*or, is a person of small means,*] and unable to make good to those interested in said estate any loss which may occur to the estate by reason of his waste or mismanagement; that said........., has, by virtue of his office as such executor, come in possession of all of the personal estate which was of said deceased, consisting of [*here set forth the personal estate of the testator*]; that said..........has converted to his own use in part said personal estate, (*or has wasted said estate, setting out at length in what the waste or conversion consists; or is about to commit a waste so as to endanger those interested in said estate; or, that the personal estate of said testator will be insufficient to pay the debts due from the estate*).

Petitioner would further show unto your honor, that by the provisions of the will of said deceased, he is made a legatee (*or is entitled to a distributive share in said estate; or that he is a creditor of said deceased, and his claim has been allowed by this court and ordered to be paid out of said estate*); that by the mismanagement of said estate by said........., petitioner fears a loss to himself and others interested in said estate. Wherefore, in consideration of the premises, your petitioner prays that said.........may be required by the court to execute and file in this court his bond, in a sum sufficient to indemnify all persons interested against loss as required by law, and to this end, that a summons may issue commanding him to appear at the next term of this court, to show cause, if any there be, why the prayer of this petition should not be granted.(1)

By........., Attorney.

No. 7.
Form of Record Revoking Letters of Administration on account of Fraud Practiced in Obtaining the same.

STATE OF ILLINOIS,} ss.   In the County Court—In Probate,
............County, ... Term, A. D. 18....

Present: Hon............, Judge.   Attest: ...., Clerk.

In the matter of the estate of........., } Petition for the removal of........., deceased, upon the relation of......... } Administrator.

And now upon this...day of......, A. D. 18...., it being one of the days of

---

(1) *Ante* page 26.

said term, comes the relator.........., by.........., his attorney, and comes also ...., heretofore appointed administrator of the estate of.........,deceased, and this cause coming on to be heard upon the petition and charges of the said.........., relator, the answer of the said.........., the replication thereto and oral proofs, and the court having heard the argument of counsel, and being fully advised in the premises, doth find that the said............, so appointed administrator of the estate of.........., deceased, in his petition for letters of administration filed in this court, and upon which said letters were issued as aforesaid, falsely and fraudulently represented himself to be the next of kin to said.........., deceased, (*or a creditor of said deceased, or that said deceased left no last Will and testament; or that said.........., administrator, has squandered the estate which came to his hands as such administrator: or that said..........has removed from this state; or that said.........., after due notice has refused to file additional bond, as required by an order of this court; or any other fact charged in the petition and proven to the court*).

It is therefore ordered and adjudged by the court, that the letters of administration heretofore issued by order of the court, to the said............, upon the estate of the said......., deceased, be and they are hereby revoked; that said........pay all costs of this proceeding, that execution issue therefor and that the said.........., on or before the...day of......next, file in this court his account, showing the condition of said estate, together with all vouchers which he may have; until which day this cause stands continued.(1)

No. 8.

Form of Record to be made when Letters are Revoked for the reason that a Will has been produced.

STATE OF ILLINOIS, } ss.   In the County Court—In Probate,
...........County, ... Term, A. D. 18....

Present: Hon..........., Judge.   Attest: ...., Clerk.

And now upon this...day of......, A. D. 18...., it being one of the days of said term, and the matter of the estate of.........., deceased, coming now again before the court, and it appearing to the court that said..........left a last Will and testament, which was on, to-wit: the...day of......, 18..., duly admitted to probate in this court, it is ordered that the letters of administration heretofore granted upon said estate to........., be, and they are hereby revoked. It is further ordered that said............ forthwith render an account to the court of his acts as such administrator, and turn over to........, the executor named in the Will of said deceased, all the personal estate of said deceased now in his hands.(2)

No. 9.

Form of Record to be made when Letters are Revoked by reason of the Insanity, &c., of the Administrator.

STATE OF ILLINOIS, } ss.   In the County Court—In Probate,
...........County, ... Term, A. D. 18....

Present: Hon..........., Judge.   Attest: ...., Clerk.

And now upon this...day of......, A. D. 18..., it being one of the days of

(1) See pages 20 and 21.   (2) *Ante* page 21.

said term, comes the relator.........., by.........., his attorney, and comes also,..........., heretofore appointed administrator of the estate of.........., deceased, and this cause coming on to be heard upon the petition and charges of the said.........., relator, the answer of the said.........., the replication thereto, and oral proofs, and the court having heard the argument of counsel, and being fully advised in the premises, doth find that the said.........., so appointed administrator of the estate of.........., deceased, has since his said appointment as such administrator (*or executor,*) become insane (*or habitual drunkard; or convicted of an infamous crime; or has wasted the estate of said deceased in his hands; or has mismanaged said estate; or conducts himself in such manner as to endanger, etc.*)

It is therefore ordered and adjudged by the court, that the letters of administration (*or testamentary,*) heretofore issued to said..........by order of this court, upon said estate, be and they are hereby revoked; and that said..........forthwith turn over to his associate executor.........., all property, choses in action, vouchers or money held by him as such executor (*or administrator*): (*Or where it is the sole executor or administrator,*) that he render an account to this court of his acts as such, and turn over to his successor, to be appointed by the court, all property, choses in action and moneys remaining in his hands, as such executor (*or administrator.*(1)

No. 10.
Form of Record to be made when knowledge comes to the Court of the Removal or contemplated Removal from the State, of an Executor or Administrator.

STATE OF ILLINOIS, } ss.
..........County, }

In the County Court—In Probate,
......*Term, A. D.* 18...

Present: Hon.........., Judge.   Attest: ...., Clerk.

In the matter of the estate of..........., deceased.

And now upon this day, it being made to appear to the satisfaction of the court, that.........., administrator of the estate of.........., deceased, is about to remove (*or has removed,*) beyond the limits of this state, it is therefore ordered, that the clerk of this court publish for four successive weeks in some newspaper in this county, a notice directed to said.........., administrator as aforesaid, notifying him to appear in this court within thirty days after the date of such notice, and make settlement of his accounts as required by law.

No. 11.
Form of Notice to be Used.

STATE OF ILLINOIS, } ss.
..........County, }

In County Court
of said County.

To.........., *Administrator of the Estate of*.........., *deceased:*

You are hereby notified, that on this day an order was entered of record in said court, requiring you to appear therein within thirty days of this date and make settlement of your accounts as such administrator.(2)

Dated at......., this...day of......, 18...   ...., Clerk.

(1) *Ante* page 21.   (2) *Ante* page 21.

574   APPENDIX—FORMS.

No. 12.

Form of Record to be made upon Removal of Executor or Administrator after above Notice.

STATE OF ILLINOIS, } ss.   *In the County Court—In Probate,*
.........County, ...*Term, A. D.* 18...

Present: Hon........., Judge.   Attest: ...., Clerk.

In the matter of the estate of........., deceased.

And now upon this...day of......, A. D. 18..., it being one of the days of said term, and the matter of the estate of........., deceased, coming now again before the court, and it appearing that........., administrator, has been notified by notice published for four successive weeks in the......, a weekly newspaper published in this county, said publication having been made by the clerk of this court in pursuance to an order heretofore entered, to appear upon this day and make settlement of his accounts as such administrator; and the said........., having been three times solemnly called comes not, but makes default. It is therefore ordered and adjudged, that the said.........be and he is hereby removed as such administrator (*or executor,*) of the estate (*or last will*) of........., deceased. It is further ordered, that said........pay the costs of this proceeding, and that execution issue therefor.(1)

No. 13.

Form of Petition to require Executor or Administrator to give other and Sufficient Security.

STATE OF ILLINOIS, } ss.   *In the County Court,*
.........County,   *To the......Term, A. D.* 18...

To the Hon........., Judge of said Court—In Probate:

Your petitioner,............, of said county, would respectfully show unto your Honor, that heretofore, to-wit: on the...day of......18..., in the matter of the estate of........., deceased, letters of administration (or testamentary) were, by order of this court granted to........., as administrator (or executor), he having under the order of the court, filed his bond in the sum of $......, with.........and.........as his securities thereon, which bond was approved by this court. Your petitioner would further show unto your Honor, that since the approval of said bond, both of said securities have become insolvent (*or........., one of said securities has become insolvent, and the remaining security........., is insufficient security; or that the assets of said estate are much larger than was represented to the court in the petition for letters, to-wit: the sum of $......,*) wherefore your petitioner, who is an heir of said ...., deceased, (or a creditor) and entitled to distribution from the assets of said estate, prays that said.........may be cited to appear before the court at an early day, and required by order of the court to give other and sufficient security for the performance of the trust committed to him.(2)

By........., Attorney.   ....

(1) *Ante* pages 21 and 22.   (2) *Ante* page 28.

STATE OF ILLINOIS,⎱ ss.
..........County, ⎰

..........being duly sworn, on his oath says, that the matters set forth in the above petition are true, as therein set forth.

Subscribed and sworn to before me, this...day of......, 18...
.........., Clerk.

No. 14.

Form of an Order of the Court requiring other and Sufficient Security in pursuance of the foregoing Petition.

STATE OF ILLINOIS,⎱ ss.   In the County Court—In Probate,
..........County, ⎰   ......Term, A. D. 18...

Present: Hon.........., Judge.   Attest: ...., Clerk.

In the matter of the application of.......... to require other security from.........., Administrator of the estate of.........., deceased.

And now upon this...day of......18..., it being one of the days of said term, comes the petitioner,.........., by.........., his attorney, and it appearing to the satisfaction of the court that the said..........has been duly served with a citation to appear and answer the petition of the said.........., more than ten days before this day; and the said........having been duly called, comes not, but makes default, it is ordered that said petition be taken for confessed by said......... And this cause coming on to be heard, upon said petition so taken as confessed, and oral proofs in support thereof, the court finds that..........and ...., securities upon said bond, are insolvent, &c. It is therefore ordered that the said.........., administrator as aforesaid, within...days from this day, execute his bond as such administrator, conditioned as required by law, in the penal sum of $......, with two good and sufficient securities, to be approved by the court, and file the same with the clerk, to which day this cause stands continued.(1)

In the event of the failure of the administrator to execute and file a bond, as required by the order, he may be removed, in which case a record similar to No. 12 *ante*, may be made.

Counter security may be required by the court to be given to the securities of an administrator, (2) in which case the forms given in Chap. 12 *ante*, in case of guardians, may be used.

RESIGNATION OF EXECUTORS AND ADMINISTRATORS.—The forms given upon pages 339 and 340 for the resignation of guardians and the record of the acceptance of the same by the court may, with such changes as will be manifestly necessary, be used in case of the resignation of executors and administrators.(3)

(1) *Ante* page 28.   (3) See page 22, *ante*.
(2) *Ante* page 29.

PETITION OF SECURITY FOR RELEASE.—The petition to b filed by any one desiring to be released from liability upon the bond of an executor or administrator may be in form similar to that given upon page 350 for a security upon a guardian's bond.

No. 15.

Form of Inventory to be filed by Executor or Administrator or surviving Partner.

STATE OF ILLINOIS, } ss.
.........County,

In the matter of the Estate of........., deceased—Inventory.

INVENTORY OF REAL ESTATE.

North-east quarter of Sec. No. 8, Township 19 North, of Range No. 9 East of the 3d p. m., held by warranty deed from........., of date the...day of ......, 18... Said real estate is subject to the right of homestead in the family of said deceased, to the right of dower of........., widow of said deceased, and to a mortgage made by the deceased and his wife, on the... day of......A. D. 18... to one........., to secure the payment of one principal note of $1000, due two years after date, and two annual interest notes of $80 each, one of which has been paid.

PERSONAL ESTATE.

No.	Chattels.	No.	Chattels.
1	Two Horse Wagon—new.	1	Bay Horse, "Archey," 9 years old.
1	One " Phæton.	1	" Mare, "Pet," 5 " "
1	Lyon & Healy Piano—new.	1	Red Cow,
1	Stack Hay—5 tons.	20	Head of Hogs.

PERSONAL ESTATE—MONEYS AND CREDITS.

					Am'nt.
Money on hand at Time of Decease,	-	-	-	-	$250 00

NOTES AND ACCOUNTS DUE DECEASED, AND DESCRIPTION OF THE SAME.

Name of Debtor.	Kind of Indebtedness.	Date of Note or Account.	Principal.	Accrued Int.	Good, Doubtful or Desperate.		
James Felton,	Note.	Dec. 25 1881	100 00	8 00	Good.	108	00
Henry Squires,	"	Sept. 1 1874	40 00	32 00	Doubtful.	72	00
Joseph Booker,	"	Mar. 10 1870	25 00	30 00	Desperate.	58	00
Samuel Gray.	Acc't.	Aug. 1 1882	55 20		Good.	55	20
Total Pers. Estate,						$543	20

.........do certify that the foregoing is a full and correct Inventory of all the real and personal estate or the proceeds of the same, which was of........, deceased, which has been committed to.......superintendence and management, or which has come to......hands, possession or knowledge, and that the notes and accounts above described are in quality as above indicated. Dated this...day of......18....

The same form may be used by a surviving partner, with the addition of a list and amounts of debts and liabilities due from the late firm. So, also, the following form of an appraisement bill, with slight change, may be used in such case.(¹)

No. 16.
Form of Warrant to Appraisers and Oath to be taken by them. This may be used in cases of Deceased persons and in the Settlement of Partnership Estates.

Estate of........., deceased.

STATE OF ILLINOIS, } ss.   *In County Court,*
.........County, ...*Term, A. D. 18...*

The People of the State of Illinois, to........., of the County of........., and State of Illinois, Greeting:

This is to authorize you, jointly, to appraise the goods, chattels, and personal estate of........., late of the county of........., and State of Illinois, deceased, so far as the same shall come to your sight and knowledge, each of you having first taken the oath hereto annexed; a certificate whereof you are to return, annexed to an appraisement bill of said goods, chattels and personal estate, by you appraised in dollars and cents; and in the said bill of appraisement you are to set down in a column or columns, opposite to each article appraised, the value thereof. You are also authorized in like manner to make out and certify to the court, an estimate of the value of each of the several items of property allowed to the widow (*or children*) by law, known as the "Widow's Award"—awarding to her (*or them*) a gross sum in lieu of articles given by law and not found upon the inventory.(2)*

Witness, ..., Clerk of the County Court of......County, and the seal
[SEAL.]   of said Court, this...day of......, A. D. 18...
                                                                                                             ...., Clerk.

No. 17.
Oath of Appraisers.

We, and each of us, do solemnly swear, that we will well and truly, without partiality or prejudice, value and appraise the goods, chattels and personal estate of........., deceased, so far as the same shall come to our sight and knowledge; and that we will in all respects perform our duties as appraisers, to the best of our skill and judgment.

Subscribed and sworn to, this...day of......, A. D.
18..., before me.
                  ...., Justice of the Peace.

---

*NOTE.—The last clause is not required by statute, but in order to acquaint the appraisers with their whole duty, it might not be inappropriate to add it.

No. 18.

Form of Appraisement Bill.

Estate of........., deceased.

STATE OF ILLINOIS, } ss. ....County, }

In County Court, ...*Term, A. D.* 18...

An Appraisement Bill of the Goods, Chattels and Personal Estate of........., late of said County, deceased, made by virtue of the annexed warrant:

No.	ARTICLES.	VALUE.	
		Dolls.	Cts.
1	Two Horse Wagon,	65	00
1	One " Phæton,	100	00
1	Lyon & Healy Piano,	500	00
1	Stack of Hay, estimated at 5 tons,	40	00
1	Bay Horse, called "Archey,"	100	00
1	" Mare, " "Pet,"	100	00
1	Red Cow, 7 years old,	50	00
20	Head Hogs—fat,	300	00
	Total,	$1255	00

We, the undersigned, appointed by the Honorable County Court of said County, to appraise the goods, chattels and personal estate of........., late of said County, deceased, do hereby certify that the foregoing is a true and correct Appraisement Bill of said goods, chattels and personal estate, so far as the same have come to our sight and knowledge; that we have appraised each article at its true value according to the best of our skill and judgment, having first taken the oath required by law.

Given under our hands and seals, this...day of......, A. D. 18...

........., [Seal.] }
........., [Seal.] } Appraisers.
........., [Seal.] }

We, the appraisers above named, do certify that we have attended and served...day..each, in appraising the estate of said deceased.

......, }
........., } Appraisers.
......, }

No. 19.

Form of a return of the Widow's or Children's Award by the Appraisers.

We, the undersigned, appraisers appointed by the judge of the County Court of......County to appraise and value the goods, chattels and personal estate of........., deceased, do hereby make and certify to said Court the following estimate of the value of each article of specific property allowed by law to the widow, for herself and family, to-wit :(1)

ITEMS.	Dolls.	Cts.
The Family Pictures and the Wearing Apparel, Jewels and Ornaments of the widow and minor children......................		
School Books and Family Library...	100	00
One Sewing Machine..		
Necessary Beds, Bedsteads and Bedding for widow and family,		
The Stoves and pipe used in the family, with the necessary Cooking Utensils...		
Household and Kitchen Furniture	100	00
.........Milch Cow.. and Cal... (being one for every four members of the family)...		
.........Sheep and Fleeces, (being two for each member of the family)		
One Horse, Saddle and Bridle		
Provisions for widow and family for one year.........................		
Food for the stock above specified for six months....................		
Fuel for the widow and family for three months......................		
Other property..	100	00
TOTAL...$		

Given under our hands.

..........,
.........., } Appraisers.
..........,

No. 20.

Form of Widow's Relinquishment and Selection.

Estate of........., deceased.

STATE OF ILLINOIS, } ss.
.........County,

I,........., widow of........., deceased, do hereby relinquish all my claim to the following articles mentioned in the "Appraisers' estimate of specific property," allowed me for myself and family, to-wit:.

[*Items same as above in No.* 19.]

The aggregate value of which, as estimated, is.............dollars ($......), and in lieu of the same I desire to retain the following articles named in the "Appraisement Bill of Personal Property" of said........., deceased, viz:

ARTICLES.	VALUE.	
(*)	Dolls.	Cts.

(*When the personal chattels are appraised at the same or at an amount less than the amount of the widow's or children's award, and the property is all taken in satisfaction of the claim, it will be sufficient here to say: "All the articles named in the appraisement bill, to which reference is made.")

The total value of which, as appraised, is........dollars, ($........,) and the balance, ...dollars ($........), I prefer to have in money.(1)

Witness my hand and seal, this...day of......, A. D. 18...

........., [Seal.]

(1) *Ante* page 89.

No. 21.

Form of Advertisement of Administrator's Sale of Personal Property.

ADMINISTRATOR'S SALE.

Notice is hereby given, that on......, the...day of......, next, between the hours of 10 o'clock in the forenoon and 5 o'clock in the afternoon of said day, at the late residence of........., deceased, in the town of......, county of......, and State of Illinois, the personal property of said decedent, consisting of........., and other articles, will be sold at public sale, in accordance with an order of the county court of......county.(1)

Terms of Sale:—......... ...., Administrator.
........., 18...

No. 22.

Form of a Report by Administrator that the Assets of the Estate do not Exceed the Widow's Award.

STATE OF ILLINOIS, } ss.   *In the County Court,*
.........County, ...*Term, A. D.* 18...

To the Hon..........., Judge of said Court:

The undersigned having heretofore been appointed by this court administrator of the estate of........., deceased, would respectfully report unto your honor, that after being so appointed, he entered upon the duties of his trust and made a careful inventory of all the estate of every character of which the said deceased died seized, filed the same as directed by law, and the same has been duly approved by the court; that the appraisers appointed by the court have appraised the personal chattels embraced in said inventory, and have made out and certified to the court an estimate of the value of each and every item of property allowed by law to........., widow of said deceased, known as the "widow's award," which report of the appraisers has likewise been approved by the court.

The undersigned would further show unto your honor, that the value of all the property of which the deceased died seized, including personal chattels, money on hand at the time of decease, and notes and accounts, amounts to the sum of......dollars, as shown by the inventory and appraisement bill now on file in said court, to which reference is made for greater certainty; that the amount of the widow's award as fixed by said appraisers and approved by the court, is......dollars (reference also being had to the report of the appraisers); that the whole assets of the estate do not exceed the amount of said award after deducting the necessary expenses already incurred; that there is no other property, real or personal, belonging to said estate known to the undersigned.(2)

........., Administrator.

STATE OF ILLINOIS, } ss.
.........County,

.........being first duly sworn, on his oath declares that the matters set forth above are true to the best of his knowledge.

Subscribed and sworn to before me, ..., this...day of ......, 18...

........., Clerk.

(1) *Ante* page 80.   (2) *Ante* page 63.

No. 23.

Form of Record to be Entered of the Finding of the Court upon said Report.

STATE OF ILLINOIS,⎫ ss.   *In County Court—In Probate,*
............County, ⎭   ....*Term, A. D.* 18....

Present: Hon............, Judge.   Attest: ...., Clerk.

In the matter of the estate of ⎫
............, deceased.   ⎭   Report of Administrator.

And now upon this day comes........, administrator of the estate of........, deceased, and comes also, ..., widow of said deceased; and now said administrator files with the court his report, showing that he has caused an inventory and appraisement of all the property of which the said.........died seized, to be made and filed in the court, and that the personal property and assets of the said estate do not exceed the amount of the widow's award, after deducting the necessary expenses of administration already incurred. And the court having inspected said report and heard the suggestions of parties, doth find said report to be true.

It is therefore ordered, that said.........., administrator, as aforesaid, first pay out of said property the costs of administration already incurred by him, and the residue of said assets and property he deliver forthwith to.........., widow of said.........., deceased, as provided by law, to be hers absolutely and forever, subject only to the payment of the funeral expenses of the deceased; that upon the report of said..........., with vouchers showing a compliance with this order being filed with the court, the said.........shall be discharged from further service as such administrator.(1)

No. 24.

Form of Notice to be Given by an Executor or Administrator of a term for Adjustment of Claims Against the Decedent.

ADMINISTRATOR'S NOTICE.

Estate of.........., deceased.

The undersigned, having been appointed administrat...of the estate of.........., late of the county of......, and the State of Illinois, deceased, hereby give..notice that..he..will appear before the county court of......county, at the court house in.........., at the......term, on the third Monday in......next, at which time all persons having claims against said estate are notified and requested to attend for the purpose of having the same adjusted. All persons indebted to said estate are required to make immediate payment to the undersigned.(2)

Dated this...day of......, A. D. 18...

.........., Administrat...

(1) *Ante* page 63.   (2) *Ante* page 97.

No. 25.

Form of a Record of Allowance of Claims at the Adjustment Term.

STATE OF ILLINOIS, } ss.   *In County Court—In Probate,*
.........County, ...*Term, A. D.* 18...

    Present: Hon........., Judge.   Attest:.........Clerk.

In the matter of the estate of }   Adjustment of Claims.
........., deceased,

And now on this day, it being the...day of said term, comes............., administrator of the estate of........., deceased, and produces to the court proof of the due publication of notice given by him appointing this term of the court for the settlement of claims against said estate; whereupon the following described claims were presented by the respective claimants, who appeared in person; and the court being sufficiently advised by evidence heard upon each of said claims, finds each of said claims just and unpaid, and it is Ordered that said claims be severally allowed and classified as follows, to-wit:

No.	NAMES OF CLAIMANTS.	CLASS.	AMOUNT.

It is further ordered that said administrator pay to each of said claimants, in the order of the classification of their respective claims, the amount thereof from the moneys and assets of said estate, in due course of administration.(1)

No. 26.

Form of a Record of Allowance of Claims Presented and Allowed after the Adjustment Term.

STATE OF ILLINOIS, } ss.   *In......County Court—In Probate,*
.........County, ...*Term, A. D.* 18...

On......, the...day of......, in the year of our Lord one thousand eight hundred and...

    Present: The Hon........., Judge, ..., Clerk, and........., Sheriff.

In the matter of........., ⎫
    vs.   ⎬
.................,   ⎪
of the........., deceased.   ⎭

This day come..the plaintiff.., by........., and also come..the said defendant.., by........., and by their agreement in open court, the said parties waive process, service, notice, etc., join issue herein, and submit this cause to the court for hearing and trial. And the court having heard and maturely considered the allegations and proofs of said parties respectively, for and against the allowance of said claim, and being fully advised thereon, finds for the said plaintiff.., and assesses the amount due said plaintiff..at the

(1) *Ante* page 117.

sum of ($......) . ....dollars and...cents, against said defendant..and the estate of said deceased. It is, therefore, considered and ordered by the court, that the said plaintiff..have and recover against the said defendant..,administrat..., ..., as aforesaid, the said sum of......dollars and...cents, assessed as aforesaid by the court against said administrat..., ...and said estate, to be paid by said administrat..., ...from the moneys and assets of said estate [*in due course of administration*].*

And the said plaintiff..having presented and filed in this court......said claim against said estate after the term fixed upon and advertised pursuant to the statute in such case, by said administrat..., ...for the presentation of claims against said estate for examination and allowance, it is further ordered by the court, that the costs of this proceeding be taxed against the said plaintiff.., and that the said defendant..have and·recover of the said plaintiff.........., costs and charges by..........about this suit expended, and that..........have execution therefor.(1)

No. 27.

Form of Suggestion by Administrator of the Insolvency of Debts due the Estate.

STATE OF ILLINOIS, } ss.
..........County,

In County Court—In Probate,
......*Term, A. D.* 18...

In the matter of the estate of.........., deceased.

To the Hon.........., Judge:

Your petitioner, ..., administrator of the estate of said deceased, would respectfully show unto your Honor, that there appears upon the inventory of claims and debts due the estate of said deceased, filed in this court by petitioner on the...day of......18..., debts due said deceased in amounts as follows, to-wit:

BY WHOM DUE.	DATE.	HOW INVENTORIED.	AMOUNT.
		(Good, Doubtful or Desperate.)	

That petitioner has reduced each of said claims to judgment in this court, caused executions to be at once issued to the sheriff of this county, but without realizing the amounts of said claims or any of them; that neither of said debtors have any estate, real or personal, known to your petitioner, out of which said claims or any part of them can be made, nor have they had any property since the date of his letters, not exempt from execution; that said claims accrued in the lifetime of the deceased and at his death were in no manner secured.

Your petitioner would further show that said claims as inventoried, amount to the sum of $......and form so much of the assets of said estate

(1) *Ante* page 104.

---

*If the claim is presented and allowed after the expiration of two years from the grant of letters, then the words, "hereafter discovered and inventoried," should take the place of those within the brackets.(1)

(1) Ante page 103.

shown by the records of this court to be in the hands of your petitioner as administrator. Wherefore, your petitioner prays that he may have leave of the court to file said claims for the benefit of such of the heirs, devisees, or creditors of the deceased as will sue for and recover the same, (or that the court will order said debts to be compounded or sold,) and he be credited with the amount in his next account current.(1)

..........., Admr.

STATE OF ILLINOIS, } ss.
..........County,

..........., the petitioner, being first duly sworn, on his oath says, that the matters set forth in the above petition are true.

Subscribed and sworn to before me, this...day of......18...
..........., Clerk.

No.-28.
Form of a Notice to be Given of the Presentation of said Petition.

Estate of..........., deceased.

To whom it may concern:

Take notice that the undersigned, as administrator of the estate of said deceased, has filed in the county court of...........county, Illinois, his petition, showing to the court the insolvency of certain creditors of said estate, and asking an order of the court directing him to sell or compound the same; and that the...day of......, 18..., has been set for the hearing of said petition.(2)

Dated this...day of......, 18...

[3w.]

..........., Administrator.

No. 29.
Form of Order of the Court upon the Suggestion of the Insolvency of Debtors of the Estate.

STATE OF ILLINOIS, } ss.
..........County,

In County Court—In Probate,
......Term, A. D. 18...

In the matter of the estate of } ...., deceased.

Petition on Insolvent Claims.

And now upon this day comes..........., administrator of the estate of..........., deceased, and presents his petition, showing that certain of the debts and claims by him inventoried as due to said deceased in his lifetime, are worthless and uncollectible; and it appearing to the court that said..........has given notice to the heirs of said deceased and to all persons interested in said estate, in the manner directed by the court of his intention to present his final account at this term of the court for approval; and the court having inspected said petition, and heard oral proofs on the part of the petitioner in support of said petition, and no one appearing to object to the allowance thereof, the court doth find from the evidence, that A B and C D, the parties whose debts to the said deceased were inventoried by said ...., as a part of the assets of said estate, were at the time of the grant of

(1) *Ante* page 76.   (2) *Ib.*

letters to said.........., insolvent, and that suits would have been unavailing (*or without the State of Illinois; or that their residences were and are unknown; or that said claims were at said date barred by the statute of limitations*), and that they have continued to be so to this date. (*Or that the said.........., as such administrator, within a reasonable time reduced said claims to judgments and caused executions to issue thereon without effect*). It is, therefore, ordered and adjudged by the court, that upon filing said claims with the court, for the benefit of such of the heirs (if the estate is insolvent, the word *creditors* should be inserted, instead of *heirs*, or if there be a Will, and the estate is solvent, the word *devisees* should be used,) of said deceased, as will sue for and recover the same, have credit in his next account filed herein for the sum of $......, the total amount of said claims.

With slight changes, the same petition and order may be used in cases where the debt is due at so remote a period as to prevent its collection within the time required for a final settlement of the estate.

No. 30.
Form of Petition to Sell Personal Property at Private Sale.

STATE OF ILLINOIS, } ss.
..........County,

In the matter of the estate of.........., deceased.

To the Hon..........., Judge of the County Court of........... County:

The undersigned, ..., your petitioner.., by appointment of this court,.........of the estate of.........., deceased, respectfully represent..that..he.. ha..heretofore duly returned to this court the inventory and appraisement of the personal estate of said deceased; that the following items of the personal property, goods and chattels of said estate, to-wit :.........., are.........., that it is necessary for the proper administration of said estate, that the same be sold, and that it will be to the best interest of said estate, that they be sold at private sale. Your petitioner..therefore respectfully pray..for an order of this court directing......to sell said personal property at private sale.(1)..........

STATE OF ILLINOIS, } ss.
..........County,

.........., the above named petitioner.. being duly sworn, depose.. and say..that the facts averred in the above petition are true to the best of... knowledge and belief.

Subscribed and sworn to before me, this...day of......, 18...
.........., County Clerk.

(1) *Ante* page 78.

No. 31.
Form of a Record Granting a Petition for a Private Sale of Personal Property.

STATE OF ILLINOIS, } ss.   In County Court—In Probate,
.........County,   of the...... Term, A. D. 18...

Present: Hon..........., Judge, ..., Sheriff. Attest: ...., Clerk.
In the matter of the estate of.........., deceased.

And now on this day come..........., of the.........of said deceased, and present.. to the court...petition, praying that the court order that......certain personal property of the estate of said deceased therein mentioned be sold at private sale. And it appearing to the court that the inventory of the personal property of said estate has been heretofore filed and approved in this court, and that said property has been legally appraised, the court proceeds to consider said petition. And it appearing to the court from the allegations in said petition contained, and from other satisfactory evidence, that it is necessary, for the proper administration of said estate, that said property be sold, that none of said property is reserved to the widow or included in specific legacies and bequests, and it further appearing that it will be to the interest of said estate that the property named in said petition be sold at private sale, it is therefore ordered that said.........., as aforesaid, proceed to sell at private sale, upon the best terms possible, the following named property :.............

It is further ordered, that said property be sold at.. price.. not less than..........

And it is further ordered, that said sale be upon the following terms :......., and that as soon after making said sale as possible, the said..........make due report to this court of ..h.. acts under this order, as required by law.

And it is further ordered that said petition be filed and recorded.

No. 32.
Report of Sale of Personal Property at Private Sale.

Estate of.........., deceased.

STATE OF ILLINOIS, } ss.   Sale Bill of the estate of.........., Deceased.
.........County,

To the Hon.........., Judge of the County Court of..........County.

The undersigned, ..., of the.............of............, deceased, would respectfully report the following bill of the sale of.........., of the personal estate of the said deceased, which sale was made at the date.. herein stated, at private sale, in accordance with an order of this court.
....

Terms of Sale :..........

WHEN SOLD.	ARTICLES SOLD.	NAME OF PURCHASER.	Am't of Sale.
		Total Amount of Sales,	$

STATE OF ILLINOIS, ⎱
.........County, ⎰ ss.   *In County Court—in Probate.*

Estate of........., deceased.

.................., being duly sworn, depose.. and say.. that the foregoing is a true and correct bill of the sale.. made by ...... at private sale of .... of the said personal property, goods and chattels of........., deceased; that said sale was, in all respects, regular, according to the requirements of law and the order of this Court, pursuant to which it was made, and was fairly conducted, and that each article was sold to the person, and at the price stated, and that......believe.. that the prices obtained were fair market prices at the date of sale,...................

Subscribed and sworn to before me, ⎱
this...day of......, 18... ⎰
........., Clerk of the County Court.

No. 33.
Form of Sale Bill of Personal Property at Public Sale.

Sale Bill of the Estate of........., deceased.

STATE OF ILLINOIS, ⎱ ss.   *To the Hon........., Judge of the County Court*
.........County, ⎰   *of.........County.*

The undersigned,..........., of the......of........., deceased, would respectfully report the following bill of the sale of the personal estate of said deceased, which sale was made at........., on the...day of......, A. D. 18..., in accordance with an order of this court, and was first duly advertised by..... notice........., a copy of which notice is hereunto appended and made a part of this report.

Terms of Sale:.........

ARTICLES SOLD.	NAME OF PURCHASER.	AM'T OF SALE.
	Total Amount of Sales,	

We do hereby certify that the above Sale Bill in the estate of............, deceased, is true and correct.(1)

Given under our hands, this...day of......18   ...., Clerk.
                                                     ...., Crier.

STATE OF ILLINOIS, ⎱ ss.   *In County Court, In Probate.*
.........County, ⎰

Estate of........., Deceased.

.............., being duly sworn, depose.. and say.., that the foregoing is a true and correct bill of the sale made by...as aforesaid, of the said personal

(1) *Ante* page 80.

property, goods and chattels of........., deceased; that said sale was in all respects regular, according to the requirements of law and the order of this court, pursuant to which it was made, and was fairly conducted, and that each article was sold to the person and at the price stated.

Subscribed and sworn to before me, this...day of......18...
........,Clerk of the County Court.

Copy of Notice referred to in Caption of within Sale Bill.

............SALE.

Notice is hereby given, that on......, the...day of......, next, between the hours of ten o'clock in the forenoon and five o'clock in the afternoon of the said day, at the late residence of........., deceased, personal property of the said decedent, consisting of............, and other articles, will be sold at public sale, in accordance with an order of the county court of.........county.

Terms of Sale:............
............, 18...

No. 34.

Form of Order of Court Directing a Distribution in kind of Personal Property.

STATE OF ILLINOIS, } ss.   *In the County Court—In Probate,*
............County, ... *Term, A. D.* 18...

Present: ...., Judge.   Attest: ...., Clerk.

In the Matter of the Estate of........., Deceased.

And now upon this...day of ......18..., it being one of the days of said term, and the matter of said estate coming again before the court upon the motion of........., administrator of the estate of said deceased, for a distribution in kind of the personal property of said deceased, among those by law entitled to share in said estate, and it appearing to the court that a sale of the personal effects of said deceased is not necessary for the payment of debts or legacies, nor for the proper distribution of the said effects, it is ordered that said administrator preserve the personal chattels which were of said deceased and distribute the same to the heirs (or legatees) in kind, share and share alike.(1)

No. 35.

Form of a Citation to be used in any case where, upon Petition or Information of any person, or upon the Determination of the Judge himself, it becomes necessary to bring the Administrator before the Court for any purpose.

STATE OF ILLINOIS, } ss.
............County,

The People of the State of Illinois
    to the Sheriff of said County—*GREETING:*

Whereas, complaint has been made to the county court of said County by one........., that (*here the clerk will insert an explanation of the reason moving the court to order the issue of the writ.*)

You are, therefore, hereby commanded that you cite and give notice to

(1) *Ante* page 151.

the said ...., as aforesaid, that ..he.. be and appear before the county court of ....county, at a ....term thereof, to be holden at the court house, in ...., on the...day of......, A. D. 18..., then and there to......................and further to do and perform what shall then, by the said court, be required and adjudged. And hereof make due service and return as the law directs.

      Witness,..........clerk of the said county court, and seal thereof,
 [SEAL] at.........., in said county, this...day of...... A. D. 18...
         ...., Clerk of the County Court.

No. 36.
Form of Petition for Sale of Real Estate.

STATE OF ILLINOIS, } ss.   *In County Court,*
.........County, ...*Term, A. D.* 18...

  Estate of........., Deceased.

To the Hon.........., Judge of the County Court of said County—In Probate.

Your petitioner..................., of the........., of.........late of said county, deceased, respectfully represents:

That the said........., departed this life at.........., on or about the.....day of......, 18...

That your petitioner w... on the...day of......, 18..., duly appointed by the county court of said county (*administrator or executor*) of the (*estate or last Will and testament*) of said deceased, aforesaid, as will appear by the records of this court.

That the inventory, appraisement bill, and sale bill, in said estate, have been duly filed in the office of the clerk of this court, as required by law, and that the undersigned, as such administrator, has rendered to said court a just and true account of the personal estate and debts of said deceased, a copy of which account is hereto attached, and made part of this petition, for reference and evidence, and marked " Exhibit......"

That the personal estate of said intestate is insufficient to pay the just claims against the said estate, as will appear by reference to said account and Exhibit, and amounts to...........dollars, including doubtful and desperate claims, in the hands of your petitioner.., amounting to........dollars, of which ...h... will probably collect or receive the sum of........dollars.

That the debts and demands allowed against and the liabilities of the said estate amount to.........dollars.

That there is the further sum of.........dollars of just claims to be presented and allowed against said estate, as will more particularly appear from said account, marked "Exhibit......" of which he has paid......dollars.

That your petitioner......applied all the proceeds of said personal estate which have come to ...possession toward the payment of said debts, as by .....account and vouchers on file in this court will more particularly appear, and that there is a deficiency of personal property to pay the debts of the said deceased.

And your petitioner.. further represent.. that the said.........died having some claim or title to certain real estate in the county of......, and state of

590   APPENDIX—FORMS.

Illinois, described as follows, to-wit: (*Here carefully describe the real estate by the legal subdivisions or other sufficient description,*) which your petitioner believes the said ....owned in fee simple at the time of his death, subject to the right of dower of........., his widow. That said real estate was occupied by said........as a homestead for himself and the family, consisting of the said........., his widow and his children hereinafter named, and is still the homestead of the survivors.

That the said real estate is reasonably worth the sum of......dollars.

That the said deceased left bim surviving the said...........as his widow, having a dower interest in his real estate as above set forth, and the following named children...........having no guardian.. resident in said......county; the said......... being under fourteen, the said.........female... minor.. under eighteen, and the said.........male minor.. under twenty-one years of age.

That said land is occuped by........., all of whom, to-wit :...............are hereby made parties hereto, and are interested herein.

Wherefore, in consideration of the premises, your petitioner.. pray.. that the said.........may be summoned and required to answer all the matters herein stated and charged, but not under oath, the necessity for answer under oath being hereby expressly waived, and that this court may appoint some discreet person as guardian *ad litem* for said minor heir.. to appear for ...and defend ...interest herein.

And that this court will first ascertain the right of dower or homestead remaining in any of said defendants by reason of their relationship to the deceased, and having set off and assigned the same, will order and direct your petitioner.. to sell the remaining real estate according to law, or so much thereof, as may be necessary to pay the debts of said intestate, and to make such further order or decree in the premises as may be deemed necessary, pursuant to the statute in such case made and provided. And your petitioner will ever pray, etc.(1)   ....,
                                                  ....,
                                                  ......of........., deceased.

STATE OF ILLINOIS, } ss.
.........County,

........., ...as aforesaid, being duly sworn, depose.. and say.. that the statements contained in the foregoing petition are true according to the best of...knowledge and belief.

   Subscribed and sworn to before me, }   ....
this...day of ....., 18....
                    ...., County Clerk.

No. 37.

Form of a Cross Petition to be Filed by Widow where Petition of Administrator does not Develope the Right of Dower and Homestead.

STATE OF ILLINOIS, } ss.   *In the County Court of said County,*
.........County, ... *Term, A. D.* 18....

To the Hon........., *Judge of the County Court of......County :*

   The petition of........., repectfully represents : That your petitioner, on

(1) *Ante* page 154.

or about the...day of......, A. D. 18..., intermarried with..........; that her said husband afterwards, on or about the...day of......, A. D. 18..., departed this life intestate, leaving your petitioner his widow, and......, ..., his children and only heirs at law.

That the said..........died seized in fee of the following described real estate, situate, lying and being in the county of.........., and State of Illinois, to-wit: ...., being the same lands named in said petition.

Your petitioner would further show unto your honor, that at the time of and before his death, her said husband, with his family, including petitioner, dwelt in the dwelling house situated upon the following named real estate, part of that above named, to-wit:............, and that your petitioner, by virtue of her relationship to the said.........., upon his death.........., became, and was entitled to dower and homestead of the value of $1000 in the lands above described, which said dower and homestead, nor either of them have never been assigned or set off to your petitioner, and she has never received any compensation or equivalent therefor, or for any part thereof.

Your petitioner therefore prays the aid of this honorable court in the premises, that the said petitioner and those named therein as defendants, may be made defendants to this application, and required to answer its various charges and allegations, (*but not under oath, their respective oaths thereto being specially waived*,) and that upon the hearing hereof, a decree may be made by this honorable court; that your petitioner recover dower and homestead of the value of $1000 in the premises above described, and that such dower and homestead may be assigned and set off to her in the manner and according to the provisions of the statute in such case made and provided, and that your petitioner may have such other, further and different relief, as the nature of her case requires, and your petitioner will ever pray, etc.(1)

By.........., Solicitor.

STATE OF ILLINOIS, } ss.
..........County,

On the..........day of......, A. D. 18..., before me, the undersigned, ..., personally appeared the above named.........., who being first duly sworn, did make oath and say that she had read the foregoing petition and knows the contents thereof, and that the same are true of her own knowledge in substance and in fact, except as to such matters as are therein stated to be on information and belief, and as to such matters, she believes them to be true.

Subscribed and sworn to before me, }
this...day of......, 18...   ....

No. 38.
Form of Guardian's Answer on Petition to Sell Real Estate.

STATE OF ILLINOIS, } ss.   In the County Court of said County,
..........County, ...Term, A. D. 18....

.... }
      vs. }   Petition to Sell Land.
.... }

And now at this time come.. the said minor..............., by their guardian

---

(1) *Ante* page 164.

ad litem........., and for answer to said petition, say that they are not advised of the matters and things in said petition contained, and neither admit or deny them, and respectfully demand that said petitioner be required to prove the same.(1)

........., Guardian Ad Litem.

No. 39.
Form of Answer of Adult Defendants to Petition to Sell Land.

STATE OF ILLINOIS, } ss.   *In the County Court of said County,*
.........County, }   ...... *Term, A. D.* 18...

The answer of........., the adult defendants named in the petition of........., administrator of........., deceased, for leave to sell the real estate of said deceased for the payment of debts and liabilities alleged to be unprovided for by the personal estate of said deceased.

And the said defendants, by........., their solicitor, now come, and for answer to said petition, or to so much thereof as they are advised it is material for them to make answer to, say: They admit the death of........., as alleged, and the appointment of the said.........as.........of the.........of said deceased; admit the filing of an inventory, appraisement bill and sale bill as alleged, but deny that said inventory was a true inventory of the personal estate of said deceased; but on the contrary these defendants say that, &c. (*Here may be set out any facts impeaching the truthfulness of the inventory.*) These defendants deny that the account of the personal estate and debts of said deceased, filed with this court, a copy of which appears attached to said petition as "Exhibit.......," is a just and true account of said personal estate, debts and liabilities; but aver that there was other and further personal estate, moneys, notes and accounts, which was of said deceased, and which, or the proceeds thereof, should appear upon the credit side of said account, to-wit: (*Here may be set forth in detail the property, debts, etc., which have not been reported.*) These defendants further answering to said petition deny that the personal estate which was of said deceased has been faithfully applied or was insufficient to pay the just claims against said estate, but say that said........., deceased, left ample personal estate, all of which was within the reach of the said administrator, and by diligence and care might and should have been recovered and applied to the extinguishment of the debts and liabilities: that the debt of........., amounting to the sum of...... dollars, part of said pretended deficit, is fraudulent and not a legal liability against said estate (*or was, at the time of its allowance by the court, barred by the statute of limitations*) and should not have been allowed.

And these defendants further answering, say that said petitioner has by want of diligence and care wasted said personal estate (*or has converted to his own use the personal estate*), without which all the legal liabilities of said estate would have been paid and no apparent necessity have existed for a sale of the patrimony of these defendants. And having fully answered, they pray to be hence discharged with their reasonable costs and charges, etc.(2)   ....

By........., Solicitor.

(1) *Ante* page 163.   (2) *Ante* pages 169, 170, 171.

No. 40.

Form of a Decree in Probate to Sell Real Estate to Pay Debts.

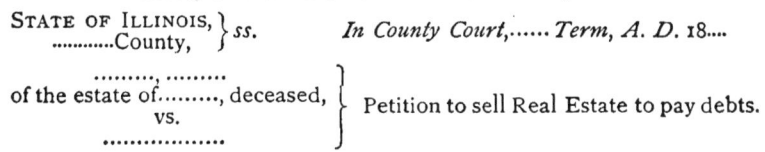

STATE OF ILLINOIS, } ss.   *In County Court,*...... *Term, A. D.* 18....
............County,

..........., ...
of the estate of........., deceased,   } Petition to sell Real Estate to pay debts.
vs.
....

And now........ come.. the petitioner.., by..........., solicitor.., and present ..... petition herein, asking for leave to sell the real estate of said deceased, described therein, to pay the debts of said deceased, and it satisfactorily appearing to the court that the defendant........., ha.. been duly served with summons herein by the sheriff of..... county, and that the defendant..........., who...... shown by affidavit to be non-resident.. of the state of Illinois, and ha.. been duly notified of this proceeding by publication as required by law; that publication has been made in the........., a weekly newspaper, published in said county, once in each week for four successive weeks, containing a notice of the filing of the petition, the names of the parties thereto, the title of the court, and the time and place of return of the summons in the case, and a description of the premises described in said petition; the first publication having been made in the paper dated the... day of......, A. D. 18..., and the last publication on the... day of......, A. D. 18..., those being the regular days for the publication of said paper; and that a copy of said notice was, within ten days of the first publication of said notice, and on the...day of......, A. D. 18..., sent by mail, addressed to the said defendant..........., at ... place of residence; and forty days having intervened between the first publication as aforesaid and the first day of the...... term, A. D. 18..., of this court, and it appearing from the foregoing that the court has full and complete jurisdiction of the persons of each and every of said defendants, to hear and adjudicate upon the matters presented in said petition, and said defendant.. having failed to appear and plead, answer or demur to said petition, it is therefore ordered by the court that the said adult defendant.. not answering be called. And......being three times solemnly called, the said .....who are shown to be adult defendants, came not, nor any one for......, but herein fail.. and make.. default; which is ordered to be entered of record, and a decree *pro confesso* entered against them herein respectively; and it further appearing to the court that the said............., are minor.. and have... guardian; and the court having appointed........., guardian *ad litem* for said infant defendant.. and afterwards the said........., as such guardian...... comes and files his answer herein, neither admitting nor denying the allegations in said petition contained, but reserving the right.. of said minor.. by requiring proof. And this cause having been brought on to be heard upon the petition herein taken as confessed by the adult defendant.. which the court finds was filed on the... day of...... 18..., the answer of said guardian......, and replication thereto, and the exhibits, records of this court and proofs, and the testimony of........., witness.. duly sworn, who testified herein in open court,......... and it satisfactorily appearing to the court from the evidence that the said.........departed this life on or about the... day of

594   APPENDIX—FORMS.

......, A. D. 18..., leaving........., his widow and............ his child... and only heirs at law; that the petitioner.. herein... duly appointed......... of the.......... of said........., deceased, and that letters..........duly granted to...... by this court, bearing date on the... day of......, A. D. 18..., and the court having ascertained that said petitioner, ..., as aforesaid, ... made a just and true account of the condition of the estate of said deceased to this court, and that the personal estate of said deceased is not sufficient for the payment of the debts of the said........., deceased; and the court having found the amount of the deficiency aforesaid to be the sum of........dollars, besides interest and costs, and it further appearing to the court that the said......... died seized of the following described real estate, situate in the county of ......and state of Illinois, to-wit:......... That at the time of his death, the said......... was the head of a family, residing with the same upon the........ parcel of said real estate, which was at his decease, the homestead of said ....; that ...., one of the defendants, was the wife of the said........., at the time of his decease, and is entitled to recover a homestead of the value of one thousand dollars out of said last named tract, if found to be of that or greater value, and if of less value than one thousand dollars, then from said last named tract and contiguous tracts or lots, and also to recover dower out of the whole of said lands.

And the court having ascertained that it will be necessary to sell.......... the said real estate, not subject to the homestead and dower right, to pay the deficiency aforesaid, with the expenses of administration now due and to accrue, it is therefore ordered, adjudged and decreed that the prayer of said petition be granted, and that ...., ... and ...., who are not connected with any of the parties, and are disinterested, be and they are hereby appointed commissioners, whose duty it shall be, after having taken the oath prescribed by statute, to go upon said lands and assign, out of the last named tract and contiguous tracts, to the said........., a homestead of the value of one thousand dollars, to include the dwelling house, and dower out of the residue, and report their action to the court, after the approval of which said petitioner.. shall proceed, according to law, to advertise and make sale of the residue of the real estate above described, or so much thereof as may be necessary to pay the debts now due from said estate, and the costs of administration now due and to accrue. And it is ordered and decreed by the court, that said sale shall be made on the following terms, viz: ....which terms shall be distinctly set forth in all the advertisements of said sale.

It is further ordered, that upon such sale being made, that said......... make and execute to the purchaser or purchasers of said real estate, good and sufficient deed or deeds to convey the interest of said deceased therein at the time of... decease, and that said......... report... action in the premises with all convenient speed. And it is further ordered, that this cause stand continued for said report.(1)   ...., judge.

Where, in the opinion of the court, the lands of the deceased

(1) *Ante* pages 164, 165, Selb vs. Montague, 102 Ill., 446.

sought to be sold will realize a larger sum upon sale by subdividing them into smaller lots, the decree, in addition to the above, should direct that the administrator first cause the lands to be surveyed, subdivided, and a plat of the same made and submitted to the court for its approval. After this has been done and the survey approved by a further decree, the sale may proceed.(¹)

No. 41.
Form of Warrant of Commissioners to Assign Dower and Homestead.

Estate of.........., deceased.

STATE OF ILLINOIS, }
..........County, } ss.
In County Court,
...... *Term, A. D.* 18....

The People of the State of Illinois to..........., of the County of.........., and State of Illinois, Greeting:

You are hereby commanded, jointly, to allot and set off to Mrs..........., a homestead, to include the dwelling house lately occupied by.........., deceased, of the value of one thousand dollars out of the following lands, to-wit: ...., if the same be found to be of that or greater value; and if of less value than one thousand dollars, then out of said land and contiguous lands of said estate; and further, that you allot and set off to the said.........., by metes and bounds, according to quality and quantity, her dower out of the residue of the real estate named below, after you have so assigned to her, her homestead as aforesaid, to-wit:............., each of you having first taken the oath required by law; a certificate whereof you are to return, annexed to an assignment of homestead and dower.

Witness,.........., Clerk of the County Court for the said county of.........., at his office, in.........., this...day of......., A. D. 18...,
[SEAL.] and the seal of said court hereunto affixed.(2)

.........., Clerk.

No. 42.
Form of Oath of Commissioners.

We, ..., ...and.........., do solemnly swear, that we will fairly and impartially allot and set off to Mrs..........., surviving widow of.........., her homestead and dower, out of the lands and tenements described in the order of the court for that purpose, (if the same can be done consistently with the interest of the estate,) according to the best of our judgment: so help us God. ....

....

Subscribed and sworn to before me, this...day of......, A. D. 18...
.........., justice of the Peace.

(1) *Ante* page 165.   (2) *Ib.*

No. 43.
Form of Report of Commissioners.

In the matter of the Estate of........., deceased.

To the Hon.........., Judge of the County Court of..........County:

We, the undersigned commissioners, appointed by your honor at the.....term of the........county court of said county, to assign, allot, and set off to Mrs.........., her homestead and dower in the estate of her late husband,......, deceased, respectfully report to your honor, as follows:

After having been sworn as required by law, which oath signed by us respectively is hereto attached, we went upon the premises described in the decree of the court, and have allotted and set off to the said........., as her homestead, the following lands, to-wit:.........., which includes the dwelling house of the late........., deceased, all of which is of the value of one thousand dollars.

We would further report unto your honor, that we also, in obedience to the mandate of the court, further set off and allotted to the said........., as her dower out of the residue of said lands, the following named lands, to-wit:............ All of which is respectfully submitted by us, this... day of......, 18...

..........,
.........., } Commissioners.
......,

No. 44.
Form of a Decree Approving the Report of Commissioners Setting Off Homestead and Dower.

STATE OF ILLINOIS, } ss. *In County Court, ...Term, A. D.* 18...
..........County,

And now again comes the petitioner, by.........., his solicitor, and the adult defendants, by........., their solicitor, and the minor defendants, by........., guardian *ad litem;* and come also,............, commissioners, heretofore appointed by the court to set off and allot to Mrs.........., widow of........., deceased, her homestead and dower in the lands of said deceased, named in the decree heretofore entered in this case, and make report of their action under said decree, which report is ordered filed, and is as follows, to-wit: [*Here copy the report in full*]. And said cause again coming on for hearing, upon the motion of petitioner for the approval of said report, and the court having examined the same, and listened to oral evidence and the argument of counsel, and being fully advised, doth further adjudge and decree herein, that said report be confirmed and approved by the court and entered of record by the clerk.

It is further ordered, adjudged and decreed by the court, that the said ...., be confirmed in her right to the premises so set off to her as her homestead, so long as she shall continue to occupy the same as such, and until the youngest child of said........., deceased, becomes twenty-one years of age; and further, that the said.........be confirmed in her right to the premises so set off to her as dower during her natural life.

It is further ordered, that the petitioner proceed as provided in the decree herein to make sale of the residue of said lands, to-wit:............, in accordance with all the requirements of said decree, and that he make report to the court of his action thereunder at a future day. ...., Judge.

No. 45.

Form of Advertisement of Sale of Real Estate.

ADMINISTRATOR'S (OR EXECUTOR'S) SALE OF REAL ESTATE.

By virtue of an order and decree of the county court of.........county, Illinois, made on the petition of the undersigned, ...of the.......of........., deceased, for leave to sell the real estate of said deceased, at the......term, A. D. 18..., of said court, to-wit: on the...day of......, 18..., ...shall, on the ...day of......, next, between the hours of ten o'clock in the forenoon and five o'clock in the afternoon of said day, sell at public sale, at the......, in......, in said county, the real estate described as follows, to-wit:............, in.........county, Illinois, on the following terms, to-wit: ...., the purchaser to give approved security and mortgage on the premises sold, to secure the payment of the......purchase money.(1)

Dated this...day of......, A. D. 18...   ...., ...
                                    of the.......of........., deceased.

No. 46.

Form of Report of Sale of Real Estate.

STATE OF ILLINOIS, ⎱ ss.   In the........County Court—In Probate,
.........County,   ⎰   ......Term, A. D. 18...

.........., ...
of the estate of........., deceased, ⎱ Petition to sell Real Estate to pay debts.
            vs.   ⎰
.........., ...

To the Hon..........., *Judge of said Court:*

The undersigned,........., ...of the.......of........., deceased, would hereby report that by virtue of the decree heretofore entered in this court in the above entitled cause, ...did, on the...day of......, A. D. 18..., between the hours of 10 o'clock in the forenoon and 5 o'clock in the afternoon of said day, at...... ..., in.......county, in the State of Illinois, offer for sale at public vendue, the real estate described in said decree, and.........bid the sum of...... dollars for the...... ....., and the said.........being the highest and best bidder.. for said......described......real estate, ...the same...struck off to...... at the sum.. aforesaid, and......executed and delivered to......deed.. for said real estate, as......of the......of........., deceased. And...further report.. that previous to making said sale...caused a notice, of which the annexed is a true copy, to be published for four successive weeks in the........., a weekly newspaper, published at........., in said county, where said real estate is situate, and...also posted up similar notices in four of the most public places in said county four weeks previous to said day of sale.

.........further report.. that said.........executed to......note......therefor, together with mortgage.. on said premises in pursuance of said decree.........

All of which is respectfully submitted.(2)

Dated......., A. D. 18...   ...., ...
                                     of the estate of........., deceased.

(1) *Ante* page 172.   (2) *Ante* pages 173, 174, 175.
See, also, Greenwalt vs. McClure, 7 Ill. Ap., 153.

No. 47.

Form of Exceptions to a Report of the Sale of Real Estate by an Executor or Administrator.

STATE OF ILLINOIS,⎱ ss.   In County Court of said County,
.........County,   ⎰   ...... Term, A. D. 18...

.........., ...,
of the estate of.........., deceased, ⎱ Petition to sell Real Estate to pay debts.
vs.   ⎰
.........., ...,

Exceptions taken by.........., one of said defendants, to the report of sale of real estate, filed herein by the said petitioner.

First Exception.—For that the said petitioner hath not shown in and by his said report, that the sale of the said real estate was advertised as required by law.

Second Exception.—For that the said sale to the said.........., [*the name of purchaser*] was made in fraud of the rights of this and the other defendants, as well as of the creditors of the said estate, because he says that the said..........with the knowledge and fraudulent procurement of the said petitioner, did not buy in his own interest and right, but in the interest and right of the said petitioner—and at less than the reasonable value of said real estate.

Third Exception.—For that the bidders at said sale, including the said..........., [*the purchaser*], before and at the time of said sale, fraudulently combined together to prevent bidding and competition at said sale, and so said real estate was struck off and sold for a sum less than its fair value.

Fourth Exception.—For that, etc.

All which matters this defendant avers a readiness to prove to the satisfaction of the court, and insists that by reason thereof, he, with other defendants and creditors, is damaged: Wherefore this defendant doth except to said report, and prays that the same, upon consideration by the court, may be disapproved and said real estate ordered re-sold.

By.........., Solicitor.

No. 48.

Form of an Order Overruling Exceptions Approving the Report or Sale and Confirming Title in the Purchaser.

STATE OF ILLINOIS,⎱ ss.   In County Court. ...... Term, A. D. 18...
.........County,   ⎰

And now again comes the petitioner, by.........., his solicitor, and files his report of sale of real estate made under authority of the decretal order; come, also,.........., the minor defendants, by.........., guardian *ad litem*, and comes, also, ..., adult defendant, and files his exceptions to said report. And this cause coming on again for hearing upon the motion of the said petitioner for confirmation of said report, and the exceptions thereto of the said.........., and oral proofs, and the court having examined the said report and the said exceptions, and having listened to the argument of counsel, and being fully advised, doth overrule the said exceptions of the said........ to said report, and doth further sustain the motion of the petitioner for a confirmation of said report of sale. And the court thereupon doth further adjudge and decree that said sale of lands be and the same is hereby confirmed, and all the title in and to the said real estate so sold by petitioner, which was of the said.........., deceased, in his lifetime, declared to be forever fixed and confirmed in the said.........., purchaser.

No. 49.

Form of an Order Sustaining Exceptions to Report of Sale and Ordering a Further Sale.

STATE OF ILLINOIS, } ss.
..........County, }   In County Court, ... Term, A. D. 18...

And now again comes the petitioner, by.........., his solicitor, and files his report of sale of real estate made under authority of the decretal order; come, also, ... the minor defendants, by..........., guardian *ad litem*, and comes, also, ..., adult defendant, and files his exceptions to said report. And this cause coming on again for hearing, upon the motion of the said petitioner for confirmation of said report, and the exceptions thereto of the said.........., and oral proofs, and the court having examined the said report and the said exceptions, and having listened to the argument of counsel, and being fully advised, doth sustain the said exceptions of the said......... to said report, and doth overrule the motion of the petitioner for a confirmation of said report of sale. And the court thereupon doth further adjudge and decree that said petitioner proceed again to make sale of said real estate in conformity to the statute and the decree of sale herein, and make to the court further report of his action under said decree.

No. 50.

Form of Administrator's Deed of Real Estate Sold by Order of the County Court.

The grantor, ..., as administrator of the estate of.........., deceased, under and by authority of a decree of the county court of..........county, Illinois, rendered at the......term, 18..., of said court, in a certain cause wherein said.........., as such administrator was petitioner, and.........., were defendants, having sold the premises hereinafter named at public auction to.........., on this day, for and in consideration of......dollars in hand paid, conveys to.........., the interest of said.........., deceased, in the following described real estate, viz: ...., in the county of.........., and State of Illinois.(1)

Dated this...day of......, A. D. 18...   ....

STATE OF ILLINOIS, } ss.
..........County, }

I, ..., in and for the said county, do hereby certify that.........., as administrator aforesaid, personally known to me to be the same person..

(1) Hurd's R. S., Chap 309, § 12; *ante* page 177.

whose name.. ....subscribed to the foregoing instrument, appeared before me this day in person, and acknowledged that ..he.. signed, sealed and delivered the said instrument as...free and voluntary act, for the uses and purposes therein set forth.

Given under my hand and......seal, this...day of......, A. D. 18...
.........., [Seal]

No. 51.

Form of Bill for Account between Co-Executors.

STATE OF ILLINOIS, } ss.   *In Circuit Court, ... Term, A. D.* 18...
.........County,

To the Honorable the Judges of the......Judicial Circuit of Illinois, and of the Circuit Court of.........County—In Chancery Sitting:

Humbly complaining showeth unto your honors your orator, ..., of the county of........., and State of Illinois, that on the...day of......, 18..., one........., of said county and state, departed this life testate at the......, in said county, and that in and by his last Will and testament he nominated and appointed your orator and.........and........., the defendants hereinafter named, executors of said last Will and testament: That said last Will and testament was duly probated in the county court of said county, on the... day of......, 18..., and admitted to record therein, as the last Will and testament of said........., deceased, and letters testamentary thereon were duly issued by said county court to your orator and the said defendants as executors of said last Will and testament, and your orator and the said defendants duly qualified as such executors, and entered upon the administration of said estate.

Your orator further showeth unto your honors, that the said.........left assets to be administered under and by virtue of said last Will and testament, amounting in the aggregate to more than fifty thousand dollars, as shown by the inventory of said estate, filed by your orator and the said defendants in said county as executors of said last Will and testament, and that such assets consist mostly of money, United States interest bearing bonds, promissory notes, secured by mortgage on real estate, accounts, and other personal estate, and that all of said assets have been taken possession of by the said defendants to the exclusion of your orator, and are now in the hands of the said defendants, except about the sum of ten thousand dollars of the same, which sum has been paid to the legatees named in said last Will and testament by order of said county court of.........county.

Your orator further showeth unto your honors, that said defendants have hitherto refused to deliver any portion of said assets into the hands of your orator; that your orator has requested the said defendants to render an account to him, and to deliver to him as one of the executors of said last Will and testament, a just proportion of said assets, to be held by your orator as such executor, and that said defendants wholly refused, and still do refuse to comply with said request, and still retain in their hands and under their exclusive control, the whole of said personal assets.

Your orator, therefore, prays the aid of this honorable court in the premises, and to that end makes the said.........and.........defendants to this bill: That process of summons in chancery may issue against them, and that they may be compelled to answer all and singular the allegations of this bill, but the oath of said defendants to such answer, is hereby expressly waived; that an account may be taken of the personal assets of said estate in the hands of said defendants, and that a just proportion of such assets may be delivered to your orator as executor of said last Will and testament, and that your honors will grant unto your orator such other and further relief in the premises, as to equity shall appertain, and to your honors shall seem meet, and your orator will ever pray, etc.(1)

By:........., Solicitor.

No. 52.

Form of a Bond to be Given by a Legatee or Distributee to an Executor or Administrator before Payment of Legacies or Distributive Shares.

Know all men by these presents, that we, ..., principal, and............, securities, are held and firmly bound unto........., executor [*or administrator*] of the last Will and testament [*or estate*] of........., deceased, in the penal sum of......dollars, lawful money of the United States, for the payment of which well and truly to be made, we bind ourselves, our heirs, executors and administrators firmly by these presents. Witness our hands and seals, this...day of......, 18...

The condition of the above obligation is such that, whereas, heretofore, to-wit: on the...day of......, 18..., one........., late of the county of........, and State of........, died, leaving a last Will and testament, which said Will was on the...day of......, 18..., by order of the county court of........county, duly admitted to probate, in and by the provisions of which a legacy of......dollars is bequeathed to the said........., principal, as aforesaid; and whereas, under and by virtue of a further order of the said court entered of record on the...day of......, 18..., requiring the said legacy to be paid by the said........, as executor [*or administrator*] aforesaid, upon the execution by the said........ to the said......as executor [*or administrator*] aforesaid, of a refunding bond as required by Sections 116 and 117, of Chapter 3 of Hurd's Revised Statutes: Now, if the said........, principal, as aforesaid, shall well and truly refund to the said........, as executor [*or administrator*] of the last Will [*or estate*] of said......, deceased, from time to time within sixty days after demand lawfully...made, his due proportion of any debt which may hereafter appear and be allowed by any court having jurisdiction against the estate of said deceased, as apportioned by the order of said county court, including costs to accrue thereon, and fully indemnify the said.........to the extent of the amount of the legacy so paid, with interest, against loss, by reason of the payment by him to the said.........of said legacy before the final settlement of said estate, then this bond to be void, otherwise to remain in full force and effect.(2)

........., [Seal.]
........., [Seal.]
........., [Seal.]

(1) *Ante* page 135.   (2) *Ante* page 133.

The foregoing may be varied in its terms to suit the case of a payment to an heir or creditor.

No. 53.
Form of Administrator's Notice for Final Settlement.

STATE OF ILLINOIS, } ss.   Estate of........., deceased.
.........County,

To the Heirs of said........., deceased:

You are hereby notified that I have filed in the office of the county clerk of........county, State of Illinois, suggestion of the insolvency of certain of the debtors to said estate, and my final report of...acts and doings as...... of said said estate, and that I will, on the...day of......, A. D. 18..., apply to the judge of said court to have the same approved, and will at the same time and place ask an order of court for a discharge as such......, at which time and place you can appear and object if you see fit.(1)

Dated this...day of......, 18...   ...., .

No. 54.
Form of an Order of Court making a Final Distribution among Creditors, Heirs or Residuary Legatees.

STATE OF ILLINOIS, } ss.   *In the County Court—In Probate,*
.........County, ...*Term, A. D.* 18...

Present: Hon..........., Judge.   Attest: ...., Clerk.

In the matter of the estate of........., } Order on Final Settlement.
      deceased.

And now upon this...day of......, A. D. 18...., it being one of the days of said term, comes........., administrator of the estate of........., deceased, and files his final account, and asks a distribution of the residue of assets in his hands among the 7th class creditors of said estate, [*or the heirs of said deceased, or the residuary legatees under the last Will of said deceased*]. And it appearing from the certificate of the publisher of the........, a weekly newspaper, published in this county, that notice has been given to the creditors [*or heirs or legatees*] and all persons interested in the matters now to come before the court, that a final report would be presented to the court at this time, and an order of distribution made, by publication of a notice to that effect, in said newspaper, for *two* weeks, as required by an order of the court; and no one appearing to make objection to said account, it is ordered that said final account be approved. And it appearing to the court that the said administrator has paid in full all costs of administration, and all claims against said estate having preference over those classed as of the 7th class, and that after the payment of said preferred claims, there yet remains in the hands of said administrator the sum of $1000, subject to distribution among claimants of the 7th class; and it further appearing to the

---

(1) *Ante* page 149.

court, that claims amounting to the sum of $10,000 have been allowed against said estate as of the 7th class, by this court and the circuit court of this county, to be paid in due course of administration, it is therefore ordered that said administrator forthwith pay to each of said claimants a sum equal to ten per cent. upon the amount of his claim so allowed, and that upon the exhibition of vouchers therefor to the court, he be discharged from further service as such administrator.

Where the account shows the payment of all debts and specific legacies, then the last order will direct a distribution of the balance shown by the account among the widow and heirs, or residuary legatees, specifically naming each with the amounts to be paid. Should it be shown, that advancements have been made to any heir in the lifetime of the ancestor, that fact may be noticed, and the order so shaped, as to equalize the distribution.(¹) So, also, should it appear that one of the heirs is indebted to the estate, the order of distribution will provide for that contingency.(²)

No. 55.
Form of an Appeal Bond to be Given by an Administrator or Executor upon Appealing from an Order or Judgment of the County Court.

Know all men by these presents, that we, ..., principal, and.........., security, are held and firmly bound unto.........., in the penal sum of......dollars, lawful money of the United States, for the payment of which sum well and truly to be made, we bind ourselves, our heirs, executors and administrators firmly by these presents. Witness our hands and seals this...day of ......, 18...

The condition of the above obligation is such, that whereas on the...day of......, 18..., at a term of the county court of......county, then held, the above named [*the obligee*] recovered a judgment in said court in probate against the above named [*the principal*] as administrator of the estate of.........., deceased, for the sum of......dollars, to be paid in due course of administration, as of the...class, from which judgment the said.........., as administrator, has taken an appeal to the circuit court of said county. Now, if the said...... shall prosecute his appeal with effect and pay, in due course of administration, whatever judgment may be rendered against him as such administrator, by said court, upon the trial of said appeal, or by consent, or in case the appeal is dismissed, will, in like manner, pay the judgment rendered against him by said county court, and all costs occasioned by said appeal which may by order of said court be taxed against him as such administrator, then the above obligation to be void; otherwise to remain in full force and effect.(3) ...., [Seal.]
 ...., [Seal.]

(1) *Ante* page 143.   (3) *Ante* page 209.
(2) *Ante* page 149.

No. 56.

Form of Record to be made of Presentation of the Will of a Non-Resident for Probate where there are Non-Resident Attesting Witnesses.

STATE OF ILLINOIS, } ss.   *In the County Court—In Probate,*
..........County, ... *Term, A. D.* 18...

Present: Hon..........., Judge.   Attest: ...., Clerk.

In the matter of the Probate of the last Will of.........., deceased.

And now on this...day of......, it being one of the days of said term, comes.........., by.........., his attorney, and presents proof to the satisfaction of the court of the death of.........., who died on the...day of......, 18...; and the said..........also presents to the court a paper purporting to be the last Will and testament of the said.........., who, it appears, was at the time of his death, a non-resident of this State, who resided at......, in the State of..........; and it appearing to the court further, that the said..........at the time of his death, was the owner of certain real estate in this county, it is ordered that said supposed Will be filed by the clerk, and that said clerk forthwith give notice to all persons interested, by [*here insert the nature of the notice*] that on the...day of......, 18..., a *dedimus potestatem* or commission will issue from this court, for the purpose of taking the depositions of......and......the attesting witnesses to said Will, (who are also shown to be non-residents of this State,) and that all persons interested may file interrogatories or cross interrogatories to be attached thereto. It is further ordered, that on having given such notice, the clerk of this court shall, on the said...day of......, *proximo*, issue, under the seal of the court, a commission directed to some competent person to take the depositions of said witnesses, and that he attach thereto all interrogatories and cross interrogatories filed by any party interested.(1)

No. 57.

Form of Notice to be given by the Clerk to persons interested in the Probate of a Will of the Issue of a dedimus potestatem to take the Depositions of the attesting Witnesses.

Estate of.........., deceased.

To all persons Interested:

Notice is hereby given, that a paper purporting to be the last Will of said deceased has been filed in the county court of......county, Illinois, for probate, and an order entered in said court that a *dedimus potestatem* issue therefrom on the...day of......, A. D. 18..., to take the depositions of the attesting witnesses to said Will, touching the execution of the same. All persons interested, may file interrogatories or cross interrogatories to be attached to said commission, if they choose, before that date.

Dated the...day of......, 18...   ...., Clerk.
.........., Attorney.

(1) *Ante* page 194.

No. 58.
Form of Affidavit of Witnesses for Probate of Will.

STATE OF ILLINOIS, } In the County Court of said County—In Probate,
.........County, } ....term, A. D. 18...

Personally appeared in open court.........and........., subscribing witness.. to the foregoing instrument of writing, purporting to be the last Will and Testament of........., late of.........county, deceased, who, being duly sworn according to law, do...depose and say, each for...self, that..he...subscribed ......name..to the foregoing instrument as the attesting witness..at the request of the said testat. ., and in......presence, and in the presence of each other, on the......day of........., A. D. 18...; that..he...then and there subscribed...... name..thereto in......presence, and declared the same to be h...last Will and Testament; and that the said testat...at the time of executing the same as aforesaid was of full age, of sound mind and memory, and under no constraint.

....
....

Subscribed and sworn to in open court, this......day of........., A. D. 18...
.........County Clerk.

No. 59.
Form of Dedimus to Prove Will.

STATE OF ILLINOIS, } ss. In the County Court of said County.
.........County, }

The People of the State of Illinois, to.........:

Whereas, A writing. purporting to be the last Will and Testament of ...., deceased, has been produced in said court for probate of the same, upon which Will the name..of.........and.........appear as subscribing witness..thereto, which said Will is hereunto annexed, and it being represented to said court that the said subscribing witness..reside..at........., in the county of........., and State of........., and without the limits of said........., and that said witness .....unable to attend said court.

Now, therefore, We do hereby, in pursuance of the statute in such case made and provided, authorize and require you, the said........., to cause the said subscribing witness..to come before you, at such time and place as you may designate and appoint, and faithfully to take the deposition of such witness.., on the oath or affirmation of such witness.., upon all interrogatories enclosed with or attached to these presents, and none other, and the same, when so taken, together with this commission, and the said interrogatories, to certify into our said court, with the least possible delay.

Witness, ...,
Judge of the said county court of.........county, at........., in the county aforesaid, this......day of........., A. D. 18...
'.........Clerk. ....Judge.

No. 60.
Form of a Renunciation by a Widow or surviving Husband of a Testator of Claim to Legacies and Bequests in a Will, and by Widow of a Jointure in her favor.

To the Hon........., Judge of the County Court of.........County:

I, ..., widow [*or surviving husband*] of........., late of the county of ...., and State of........., do hereby renounce and quit all claim to the benefit of *any legacy or devise made to me by the last Will and Testament of said deceased husband [*or wife*], which has been exhibited and proved according to law [*or otherwise, as the case may be*],* and I do elect to take in lieu thereof my dower or legal share of the estate of my said husband [*or wife*].

  Dated at........., etc.

[*In case of a widow renouncing her jointure under the statute, insert between the asterisks* "*of the jointure provided in my favor by*" (*here describe instrument and state date and parties to it*).]

No. 61.

Form of Clerk's Entry of the Probate of Will and Grant of Letters Testamentary.

In the matter of the Probate of the last Will of........., deceased, and the Grant of Letters Testamentary thereon to.........

  And now, to-wit, ..., 18..., comes........., the executrix named in the last Will of ...., deceased, and presents the said Will to the court, together with her petition for the probate of the same and for letters testamentary thereon; and it appearing from the allegations of said petition (the same being under the oath of said petitioner) that said......... departed this life at........., on the......day of........., 18..., leaving said last Will [*here set forth all necessary jurisdictional facts—as the residence of the deceased, where his real and personal estate are situated, so as to show that the court has jurisdiction of the matter.*]

  And it further appearing to the court from the testimony of.........and ...., whose names are subscribed to said Will, as attesting witness..to the execution thereof, that they were present on the......day of........., 18..., at ...., and saw said.........sign his name to said Will [*or as the fact may be*], and that they believed him to be of sound mind and memory at that time; that he was of full age, and that they attested his Will in his presence, [*see form No. 2—if the testimony of both witnesses is not alike, the substance of that given by each may be recited; and if one of them is dead, that fact may be recited, as well as the proof of his handwriting, etc.*]; and it satisfactorily appearing to the court that said Will was in all respects executed and attested according to law,. and that said........., deceased, was, at the time of the attestation of the same, of sound mind and memory and of full age, [*if the Will is contested for fraud, add*, "and no proof of fraud, compulsion or other improper conduct having been exhibited, which, in the opinion of the court, is sufficient to invalidate or destroy said Will"], it is ordered and adjudged by the court that the said Will be deemed and taken as duly proven, and that the same, together with the testimony of the witnesses above named, be admitted to record.*

  And it further appearing to the court that the said........., the executrix named in said Will, is ready and willing to accept the office and trust therein confided to her, and that the real estate of the testator at the disposal of said executrix is of the value of.........dollars, and the personal estate of said testator is of the value of.........dollars, it is ordered by the court that she give bond as such executrix, with good security, in the penal sum of......... dollars; and the said executrix having made and presented her bond as above ordered, with.........and.........as sureties, the same is approved by the court and ordered to be filed and recorded; and the said.........having also taken the oath required by law to be taken by her as executrix, it is further ordered that letters testamentary upon said Will be granted to her.

And it is further ordered by the court that.........., ...and.........., of said county, be and are hereby appointed to appraise the goods, chattels and estate of said.........., deceased.

No. 62.
Form of Clerk's Entry when the Testator directs in the Will that Security be not Required of the Executrix.

Proceed as in form No. 61 to the asterisk, and add:

And the petitioner having taken the oath required by law to be taken by her as executrix of said Will, and it appearing to the court that the testator left visible estate more than sufficient to pay all of his debts, and directed in said Will that said..........be not required to give security as executrix of said Will, and the court perceiving no cause, from its own knowledge, or the suggestions of creditors or legatees of said.........., to suspect said .... of fraud, or that the personal estate will not be sufficient to discharge all the debts, it is ordered by the court that such security be dispensed with, and that letters tes·amentary on said Will be granted to said..........

No. 63.
Form of a Refusal of a Person named as Executor to accept the Executorship of the Will.

To the Hon.........., *Judge of the County Court of*.......... *County, in the State of Illinois:*

The undersigned, named in the Will of.........., deceased, as executor thereof, does herewith present the said Will to said court, and respectfully decline to act as such executor.

No. 64.
Form of Petition for Letters of Administration with Will Annexed.

Petition of.........., in the matter of the Estate of.........., deceased, tor Letters of Administration..........

To the Hon.........., *Judge of the County Court of*.......... *County, in the State of Illinois:*

The petition of the undersigned, ..., respectfully represents that ...., late of the county of..........aforesaid, departed this life at.........., in said county, on or about the........day of.........., A. D. 18..., leaving a last Will and Testament, and appointing..........execut...; that said..........

And this petition further shows that the said..........died seized and possessed of real and personal estate, consisting chiefly of.........., all of said personal estate being estimated to be worth about..........dollars; that said deceased left surviving..........as heirs; that your petitioner (being..........of said deceased, and) believing that the said estate should be immediately administered, as well for the proper management of said··········as for the prompt collection of the assets, by virtue of.......right under the statute, ... therefore pray that your Honor will grant Letters of Administration with Will annexed, to..........in the premises, upon......taking the oath prescribed by the statute, and entering into bond in such sum, and with securities, as may be approved by your Honor.

STATE OF ILLINOIS, } ss.
.........County,

........., being duly sworn, deposes and says, that the facts averred in the above petition are true, according to the best of h...knowledge, information and belief.   ....

Sworn to and subscribed before me, ..., Clerk of the County Court of.........County, this.......day of........., A. D. 18...   ....Clerk.

No. 65.
Form of Bond for Executors and Administrators with Will Annexed.

Know all Men by these Presents, That we, ..., ...and..... ..., of the county of........., and State of Illinois, are held and firmly bound unto the People of the State of Illinois, in the penal sum of.........dollars, current money of the United States, which payment, well and truly to be made and performed, we. and each of us, bind ourselves, our heirs, executors and administrators, jointly, severally and firmly, by these presents.

Witness our hands and seals, this...... day of........., A. D. 18...

The condition of the above obligation is such, that if the above bounden ...., ...and........., execut...of the last Will and Testament of. ......, deceased (or administrator with the Will annexed of........., deceased), do make, or cause to be made, a true and perfect inventory of all and singular the goods and chattels, rights and credits, lands, tenements and hereditaments, and the rents and profits issuing out of the same, of the said deceased, which have or shall come to the hands, possession or knowledge of the said........., or into the possession of any other person for......., and the same so made do exhibit in the county court for the said county of........., as required by law; and also make and render a fair and just account of...... actings and doings as such execut... (or administrator) to said court, when thereunto lawfully required; and to well and truly fulfill the duties enjoined upon......in and by the said Will; and shall, moreover. pay and deliver to the persons entitled thereto all the legacies and bequests contained in said Will, so far as the estate of the said testat...will thereunto extend, according to the value thereof, and as the law shall charge......; and shall in general do all other acts which may, from time to time, be required of......by law, then this obligation to be void, otherwise to remain in full force and virtue.

.........[SEAL]
.........[SEAL]
.........[SEAL]

STATE OF ILLINOIS, } ss.
.... County,

I, ..., hereby certify that........., ...and........., who are each personally known to me to be the same persons whose names are subscribed to the foregoing instrument, appeared before me this day in person and acknowledged that they signed, sealed and delivered said instrument as their free and voluntary act, for the uses and purposes as therein set forth.

Given under my hand and.........seal, this......day of........., A. D. 18...

No. 66.

Form of Oath of Executor or Administrator with Will Annexed, to be Attached to and form part of the Probate of the Will.

STATE OF ILLINOIS, }
..........County, } ss.

I do solemnly swear..........that this writing contains the true last Will and Testament of the within named.......... deceased, so far as I know or believe, and that I will well and truly execute the same, by paying first the debts and then the legacies mentioned therein, as far as his goods and chattels will thereunto extend, and the law charge me; and that I will make a true and perfect inventory of all such goods and chattels, rights and credits, as may come to my hands or knowledge, belonging to the estate of said deceased, and render a fair and just account of my executorship, when thereunto required by law, to the best of my knowledge and ability: so help me God.

Subscribed and sworn to before me, this.......day of.........., A. D. 18...
..........Clerk.

No. 67.

Form of Letters Testamentary.

STATE OF ILLINOIS, }
..........County, } ss.

The People of the State of Illinois, to all to whom these Presents shall come, Greeting:

Know ye, That whereas, ..., late of the county of.........., and State of Illinois, died on or about the.......day of.........., A. D. 18..., as it is said, after having duly made and published his last Will and Testament, a copy whereof is hereunto annexed, leaving, at the time of his death, property in this state, which may be lost, destroyed, or diminished in value, if speedy care be not taken of the same; and, inasmuch as it appears that..........has been appointed executor, in and by the said last Will and Testament, to execute the same:

And, to the end that said property may be preserved for those who shall appear to have a legal right or interest therein, and that the said Will may be executed according to the request of the said testator, we do hereby authorize him, the said.........., as such executor, to collect and secure, all and singular, the goods and chattels, rights and credits, which were of the said..........at the time of his decease, in whosesoever hands or possession the same may be found in this state, and well and truly to perform and fulfill all such duties as may be enjoined upon him by the said Will, so far as there shall be property, and the law charge him, and, in general, to do and perform all other acts which now are, or may hereafter be, required of him by law.

[SEAL] Witness.........., Clerk of the County Court of the said County of.........., and the seal of said court, this......day of.........., A. D. 18...
..........Clerk.

No. 68.

Form for Proof of Signature of Subscribing Witness to Will by one acquainted with Handwriting.

STATE OF ILLINOIS, }   *In the County Court of said County—in Probate,*
.... County,   } ss.   *............term, A. D. 18..., and on the......day*
                                    of........., A. D. 18...

In the matter of the last Will and Testament of........., deceased.

Personally appeared in open court........., competent and credible witness.., who, being duly sworn according to law, do..depose and say, each for ...self, that......personally know..the handwriting of........., subscribing witness..to the annexed instrument of writing, purporting to be the last Will and Testament of........., late of.........county, deceased, and that......well know..the signature of........., having frequently seen......write*........, and that ......verily believe..that the name..of the said........., subscribed as witness.. to the execution of the Will as aforesaid, ...thereto subscribed by the said ....as such subscribing witness..   ....
                                                                                                ....

Subscribed and sworn to in open court, this......day of........., A. D. 18...
                                                                                ....

                                                                Clerk of the County Court.

*State here such means of knowledge as the witness may have.

No. 69.

Form of Clerk's Entry of Order Appointing an Administrator to Collect.

In the matter of the Appointment of an Administrator to Collect and Preserve the Estate of........., deceased.

Now, to-wit, ..., 18..., it having been made to appear to the satisfaction of the court that great delay will be produced in the administration of the estate of........., deceased, by reason of the contest pending in relation to the probate of the last Will of said........., (or other cause,) and that an administrator to collect and preserve said estate ought to be appointed: It is therefore ordered by the court, that such administration be committed to........., upon his taking the oath prescribed by law, and giving bond, with good security, in the penal sum of.........dollars.

And the said.........now comes and takes his oath as administrator to collect, and presents his bond for the sum above mentioned, with.........and ....as his sureties, which is approved by the court, and ordered to be filed and recorded; and thereupon it is further ordered by the court that letters of administration to collect and preserve said estate be issued to said.........

No. 70.

Form of Bond of Administrator to Collect.

The bond is in the same form as that of executors (see form No. 65), but the condition is as follows:

The condition of the above obligation is such that, if the above bounden ....shall well and honestly discharge the duties appertaining to his appointment as administrator to collect the estate of........., late of the county of........., deceased, shall make, or cause to be made, a true and perfect inventory of all such goods, chattels, debts and credits of the said deceased as shall come to his possession or knowledge, and the same in due time return to the county court of the proper county; and shall also deliver to the person or persons authorized by said county court, as executors or administrators, to receive the same, all such goods, chattels and personal estate as shall come to his possession, as aforesaid, and shall, in general, perform such other duties as shall be required of him by law, then the above obligation to be void: otherwise to remain in full force and virtue.

.........[L. S.]
.........[L. S.]

STATE OF ILLINOIS, } ss.
.........County,

I, ..., hereby certify that........., ...and........., who are each personally known to me to be the same persons whose names are subscribed to the foregoing instrument, appeared before me this day in person and acknowledged that they signed, sealed and delivered said instrument as their free and voluntary act, for the uses and purposes as therein set forth.

Given under my hand and.........seal, this.......day of........., A. D. 18...

No. 71.
Form of Oath of Administrator to Collect.

STATE OF ILLINOIS, } ss.   In the County Court.
.........County,

I do solemnly swear (or affirm) that I will well and honestly discharge the trust reposed in me as administrator to collect the estate of........., deceased, according to the tenor and effect of the letters granted to me by the county court of.........county, to the best of my knowledge and ability: so help me God.

Subscribed and sworn to before me, this.......day of........, A. D. 18...
.........Clerk.

No. 72.
Form of Letters of Administration to Collect.

The People of the State of Illinois, to all to whom these Presents shall come, Greeting:

Know ye, That whereas, ..., late of the county of........., and State of Illinois, deceased, as it is said, had, at his decease, personal property within this state, the administration whereof cannot be immediately granted to the persons by law entitled thereto, but which, if speedy care be not taken, may be lost, destroyed or diminished; to the end, therefore, that the same may be preserved for those who shall appear to have a legal right or interest therein, we do hereby request and authorize........., of the county of........., and State aforesaid, to collect and secure the said property, wheresoever the same may be in this state, whether it be goods, chattels, debts or credits, and to make, or cause to be made, a true and perfect inventory thereof, and to exhibit the same, with all convenient speed, to the county court of the said county of........., together with a reasonable account of his collection, acts and doings in the premises aforesaid.

[SEAL] Witness........., Clerk of the County Court in and for said County of........., and the seal of said court, this.......day of........., A. D. 18...   ....Clerk.

No. 73.
Form of Letters of Administration—De Bonis Non.

STATE OF ILLINOIS, } ss.
..........County,

The People of the State of Illinois, to all to whom these Presents shall come, Greeting:

Know ye, That whereas, ..., of the county of.........., and State of Illinois, died intestate, as it is said, on or about the........day of.........., A. D. 18..., having, at the time of......decease, personal property in this state, which may be lost, destroyed or diminished in value, if speedy care be not taken of the same.

And, whereas, We have heretofore appointed..........administrat...of the goods and chattels, rights and credits of said deceased; *And, whereas*, the said..........ha...since such appointment.........., leaving the estate of said ...., deceased, not fully administered: to the end, therefore, that said property may be collected and preserved for those who shall appear to have a legal right or interest therein, we do hereby appoint.........., of the county of ...., and State of Illinois, administrat...*de bonis non* of all and singular the goods and chattels, rights and credits, which were of the said..........at the time of......decease, as yet unadministered; with full power and authority to secure and collect the said property and debts, wheresoever the same may be found in this state, and, in general, to do and perform all other acts which now are or hereafter may be required of......by law.

Witness.........., Clerk of the County Court in and for the County of.........., at his office in.........., this......day of ...., A. D. 18..., and the probate seal of said court hereunto affixed. ....Clerk.

STATE OF ILLINOIS, } ss.
..........County,

I, ..., clerk of the county court of..........county, in the state aforesaid, do hereby certify that the within is a true and correct copy of the letters of administration, *de bonis non*, issued to.........., now in form, and properly on file in my office.

In witness whereof, I have hereunto set my hand, and the probate seal of said county of.........., at my office in ...., this......day of........ , A. D. 18...
..........Clerk.

No. 74.
Form of Clerk's Entry of an Order Requiring a Surviving Partner who has Committed Waste of the Partnership Property to give Bond.

In the matter of the Application of.........., Administrator of the Estate of ...., deceased, for an Order Requiring.........., Surviving Partner of said.........., to give Security for the Faithful Settlement of the Affairs of the Partnership, etc.

And now comes.........., administrator of the estate of.........., deceased, and.........., surviving partner of said.........., in the late firm of..........; and this cause coming on to be heard upon the application of said.........., and the testimony of witnesses sworn and examined on behalf of both the said.......... and..........in open court; and it appearing to the satisfaction of the court that the said....... has committed waste of the property of said partnership, by converting the moneys of said partnership in his hands to his own use, and refusing to pay therewith the creditors of said partnership, and to pay over to said administrator moneys of said partnership rightfully applicable to that purpose: It is ordered by the court that the said..........give bond, with good security, to the People of the State of Illinois, in the penal sum of.......... dollars, conditioned for the faithful settlement of the affairs of said partnership, and that he will account for and pay over to the said administrator of the estate of said.........., deceased, whatever shall be found to be due, after paying partnership debts and costs of settlement of said partnership affairs; and that he have till..........next to comply with this order; to which time this cause is continued.

No. 75.
Form of Clerk's Entry of an Order Directing the Personal Representative to Sell the Personal Property.

In the matter of the Application of.........., Administrator of the Estate of ...., deceased, for an Order to Sell the Personal Property, etc., of said Estate.

This day comes.........., administrator of the estate of.........., deceased, and presents his petition for an order directing him to sell the personal property, goods and chattels of the decedent, and shows to the satisfaction of the court here that it will be necessary to sell all the said property, goods and chattels of said estate not awarded to the widow, or selected and taken by her, [*and if an executor applies, say,* " and not specifically bequeathed to the legatees in the last Will of the deceased," *or as the fact may be*]: It is therefore ordered by the court, that said administrator proceed to sell all of said personal property, goods and chattels not awarded to said widow, or selected and taken by her, or specifically bequeathed as aforesaid, at public sale, as provided by law, [*or at private sale, or a specified part at private sale, as the facts shown may require.*]

No. 76.
Form of Petition by an Administrator of a Deceased Partner for a Citation of a Surviving Partner who is Committing Waste, to give Security for the Faithful Settlement of the Affairs of the Partnership, etc.

STATE OF ILLINOIS. } ss.   *In County Court of said County,*
..........County,   *To the*..........*term, A. D. 18*...

To the Hon.........., *judge of the county court of*..........*county:*

The undersigned, ..., to whom letters of administration upon the estate of.........., late of the county of.........., deceased, were heretofore granted by this court, respectfully represents that, at the time of his death, to-wit, on the......day of.........., A. D. 18..., the said..........was a member of the partnership of.........., doing business in said county, and composed of the following members, to-wit: said.........., deceased, and one.........., the said ....being now the surviving partner of said ....; that, at the time of the death of said.........., the said partnership was the owner of certain real estate [*describing it*], of about the value of..........dollars, and of personal property and notes and accounts deemed good amounting in value to.......... **dollars; and** that said partnership was indebted to sundry individuals **in the**

614   APPENDIX—FORMS.

sum of.........dollars; that said.........has sold the personal property of said partnership of the value of.........dollars, and collected money from the debtors of said partnership amounting to.........dollars, in all.........dollars, yet the undersigned is informed and believes that said.........has not paid any portion of said debts, though he has often been requested by the partnership creditors so to do, nor has he accounted with the undersigned in any way for any part of the said partnership estate, or paid to him any of said moneys, notwithstanding there is a large sum thereof, to-wit, ...dollars, in his hands, in excess of the sum necessary to pay said debts, and has been frequently requested so to do. Wherefore, the undersigned says that the said.........has committed waste of said partnership property, by converting the same to his own use, and respectfully petitions your Honor to cause said ....to be cited to make answer in the premises, and that he may be ordered and required to give security, in such sum as the court may determine, for the faithful settlement of the affairs of the said partnership, and for his accounting for, and paying over to the undersigned, as administrator as aforesaid, whatever shall be found to be due, after paying the said partnership debts and costs of settlement; and that a receiver of the partnership property and effects be appointed by this court, in case the said.........shall refuse to give such security.   ....

Subscribed and sworn to before me, this......day of........., 18...
....
Clerk of the County Court.

No. 77.

Form of Certified Copy of Order of Court Declaring Estate Insolvent and Discharging Administrator

STATE OF ILLINOIS, ⎱ ss.   *In the County Court—In Probate,*
.........County,   ⎰   ....*term, A. D. 18...*

On.........day, the......day of........., A. D. 18...
Present: The Hon........., Judge.   Attest: ...., Clerk.
In the matter of the Estate of........., deceased.

And now on this day come........., administrat...of the estate of........., deceased, and submits to the court a report of the condition of the estate of said decedent; and the court having duly examined the same, and it appearing from said report that the allowance made to the widow of said decedent amounts to the sum of.........dollars and.........cents ($.........), and it further appearing that the personal property and assets belonging to said estate amount to the sum of.........dollars and.........cents ($.........); that there is no real estate belonging to said decedent; that the said personal property does not exceed the amount of the said widow's allowance, after deducting the necessary expenses of administration; and the court finding the statements as set forth in said report to be true, it is therefore ordered and adjudged by the court that the said estate be and is hereby declared to be insolvent; and further ordered, that the said administrat...turn over and deliver to ...., widow of said decedent, all the residue of said property and assets now in......hands, as set forth in......said report, after paying the costs and expenses of administration, and that the said administrat...be discharged from further duty, upon paying said costs and expenses and filing the receipt of the said widow for the residue of said property and assets.

It is further ordered, that this order be recorded, and that the report of said administrat...be approved and recorded.

.........Judge.

STATE OF ILLINOIS, } ss.
.........County,

I, ..., clerk of the county court within and for the said county, do hereby certify that the foregoing is a correct copy of an order made and returned in the matter of the above estate, as appears of record in said court, in Record of Insolvent estates, Book........., page.........

In witness whereof, I have hereunto set my hand, and affixed the seal of said court, at my office, in........., this ......day of........., A. D. 18...

......Clerk.

No. 78.
Form of Notice of Settlement Due—Administrator or Executor.

STATE OF ILLINOIS, ...County,
County Court Room, ..., 18...

M.........:

As.........of the estate of........., deceased, you are required to appear before the county court of said county, on........., the......day of........., A. D. 18..., to render an account current of your administration in said estate, in accordance with the following requirement of the statute:

"All executors and administrators shall exhibit accounts of their administration for settlement, to the county court from which the letters testamentary or of administration were obtained, at the first term thereof after the expiration of one year after the date of their letters, and in like manner every twelve months thereafter, or sooner, if required, until the duties of their administration are fully completed."

....

In sending this letter the object is to save costs, and if its requirements are not complied with, a citation will issue.

By order of Hon........., County Judge.

........., County Clerk.

No. 79.
Form of the Entry to be made by the Clerk of a Circuit Court, showing Proof made in that Court by a County Judge who is a Witness to the Execution of a Will.

In the matter of the Probate of the last Will and Testament of........., deceased.

And now, to-wit, ..., A. D. 18..., comes........., the executs...appointed as such in and by the last Will and Testament of........., deceased, by........., ...solicitor, and presents the said Will, together with......petition to the county court of.........county, for the probate thereof; and it appearing to the court that........., one of the witnesses to the execution of said Will, is at this time judge of the county court of said county, and that his testimony is necessary to the proof of said Will; and the said.........having appeared in open court, and upon his oath testified as follows: [*here insert testimony, as in form No. 58*]: It is ordered by the court that the proceedings in this cause, together with said Will and Petition, be certified by the clerk of this court to the county court of this county.

INDEX.

A.

ACCOUNTS OF CONSERVATOR,
When to be filed..384, 392
Items composing 384

ACCOUNTS OF EXECUTORS AND ADMINISTRATORS,
Administrators *de son tort* cannot render.................................... 56
When to be rendered 123
Order of distribution on... 123
May be required at any time 124
Order approving, conclusive..126, 127
But items of, omitted may appear in future account 127
Court will not go back of order approving................................... 127
To be rejected, when..130, 131
For monument to deceased.. 131
Order approving, several 131
Principles of equity to govern approval of................................... 138

ACCOUNTS OF GUARDIANS,
Required... 283
A stranger may be required to render... 283
Balance on, to be paid ward.. 283
What they should contain...283, 285
Vouchers to accompany.. 284
To be verified by affidavit... 284
When not final... 284
Mistakes in, how rectified 284
When to be filed...283, 285
      interest to be charged in... 285
May be rendered after ward's majority 285
Proof to be submitted in support of.. 285
Rule in stating..285, 286, 296
Charging in, no longer liable as administrator............................. 286
Allowances for education 286
      removal.. 286
Charge for goods 286
May be opened, when.. 291
Approval of but *prima facie*..291, 292
Presumption of law as to 292
Receipt based on erroneous 292
Form of..293, 294, 296
Order on as a final adjudication.. 348

INDEX.

ACTIONS,   **PAGE.**

    Of account, when 43
    Which survive 66
    Replevin, damages, etc... 66
    Do not abate by death of plaintiff 67
    Of trespass, in case of death of plaintiff................. 67
    To be continued.. 67
    Prosecuted in name of deceased, a nullity............. 67

ADMINISTRATION,

    Taken from the clergy 9
    Power of, formerly ecclesiastical, now civil 9
    May be granted to creditor...................................... 9
    When unnecessary.. 13
    Rule in determining right of.................................... 13
    Reason of granting, to next of kin.......................... 12
    When not granted to husband, wife, or next of kin ... 12
    Cannot be granted to corporation............................ 12
    Rules governing granting do not apply................... 12
    To others than next of kin, when............................ 13
    Upon the estate of living person void..................... 14
    Grant of may be delayed.. 15
    When act of granting ministerial or judicial 16
    On estates of non-residents, where......................... 18
    Revoked when false pretenses used......................... 20
            minor or non-resident appointed........................ 21
            Administrator becomes lunatic 21
    Grant relates back to death...............................45, 46
    Without it, heirs and devisees may be sued........... 106
    Unnecessary on estate of deceased infant 142
    Estate must pass through...............................141, 142
    Grant of, local in effect... 203
    Foreign 203

ADMINISTRATOR,

    What court may appoint 9
    Who to be appointed... 9
        not to be appointed... 12
    Surviving partner not to be appointed................... 12
    To collect, when appointed..................................... 19
    May be removed on refusal to perform duty........ 21
            if found to be a minor 21
                       non-resident... 21
    About to remove from state, to be summoned 21
    Resignation of... 22
    Not discharged until full settlement made............. 22
    To deliver assets to successor 22

ADMINISTRATOR—*Continued.*

	PAGE.
To pay costs of resignation	22
Removal, acts valid	28
on failure to give bond	30
Surviving, may complete administration	30, 31
Improper conduct of, bond to be sued	32
Diligence required of	32, 35
Guilty of *devastavit*, to make loss good	33
Duty to interpose statute of limitation	34
Debt due from	34
Liability for acts of co-administrator	35
Liable as principal, and not as surety	35
Not liable for torts of co-administrator	35
money stolen	36
Duty to redeem mortgaged lands	36, 50, 75
Order on, binds securities	37, 292, 293
Liable on his bond to administer *de bonis non*	38
Acting also as guardian	41, 51, 52, 286, 293, 349
An officer of the law	46
Title relates back	46, 47
One of two may sell personal estate	47
With the will annexed—powers	47, 179
Succeeds to title to personal estate	48
Represents estate	48
Holds title until order of distribution	48
Liable for abuse of trust	48
Care to be used to protect property	48
Should collect foreign debts	48
Not to put money into partnership	48
No power over real estate, except on failure of personal estate	49, 50
Not bound to pay taxes	49
May bind himself personally	49
Cannot give possession of real estate	49
execute a trust of deceased	49
When can maintain ejectment	50
No control over rents not due at death	50
Liable for fraud	50, 54
When liable as garnishee	50
Should not loan money	50
Nor apply to other uses	50
Accounts should be kept separately	51
Cannot bind heirs	51
purchase interest in estate	51
Acts of bind subsequent administrator	51
May compound suit for negligence	51
Cannot be joined in suit with another	52
When liable for interest	52

ADMINISTRATOR—*Continued.*   PAGE.
    Must account for profits 52
    Liable for not taking real estate 52
    To account for real estate sold 52
        perform contracts of deceased, when 53
    May assign note due deceased 53
        sell personal property and give title 53
    When fraud vitiates such sales 54
    Cannot bind estate by warranty 54, 176
    Not chargeable on account of mistakes 54
    To make inventory 59, 60
        return appraisement 61
    Liable for want of due diligence 35, 48, 63
    To be discharged when assets do not exceed widow's allowance.. 63
    May be attached 63
    Invested with large powers 65
    Representative of deceased 65
    Recover property fraudulently transferred 65, 66
    May maintain actions of trover, etc. 66
    Must sue and be sued jointly 66
    Substituted in place of deceased plaintiff 67
    To have notice before issue of execution 68
    Not a party to right of way proceeding 69
    May take measures to secure concealed goods 69
    When to take rents 71
    Legacy to deceased goes to 71
    May compel settlement by guardian 71
    When may take rails 72
    Suits by, when in representative capacity 72
    Title to personalty vests in 73
    May maintain covenant, when 74
    Must plead appointment 74
    Payment to, good acquittance 75
        by mistake 75
    Suggestion by, of desperate claims 76
    Report sale of 76
    Name may be used to collect 76
    Not to remove property 76
    May sell personalty when ordered 78
        not purchase at his own sale 78
    Interest in growing crops 79
    To return sworn bill of such 80
    Not to continue partnership 81
    Becomes personally liable 82
    Cannot join surviving partner in suit 84
    May compel surviving partner to settle 86
    Liable only for interest of deceased in partnership property 86

PAGE.

ADMINISTRATOR—*Continued.*
   To notify widow and set apart award................89, 92
      give notice of adjustment of claims 97
      attend term for adjustment............................ 97
      have notice before allowance of claims................ 98
   Not bound by contract of widow........................... 99
   Former, cannot maintain suit............................. 101
   To be summoned to answer claims 103
   Proceeding against, in another state 105
   Revival of judgment against.............................. 106
   To be vigilant in defending claims........................ 107
   In foreclosure suits, must be made a party................ 111
   Acknowledgment of claim by—limitations................ 111
   Not compelled to set off debts............................ 112
   Claim in favor of... 114
   Paying claims before allowance........................... 119
   Required to make proof of claims......................... 120
   May recover payments made by mistake 120
   To exhibit accounts...................................... 123
   No right to hold money in his hands 124, 125
   Entitled to interest, when................................ 125
   Charged with interest, when............................. 125
   To account for money paid by heirs...................... 125
   Entitled to assistance of an attorney................125, 126
   May not charge attorney's fees....................125, 137
      make contract for contingent fee.................... 126
   To be allowed to employ assistance, when.............. 126
   Discharge of, does not affect claims..................60, 128
   Payment of claims by, after final distribution 129
   May be attached 130
   Should procure order of distribution 130
   Failing to defend, heirs not bound 131
      pay on demand, suit on bond........................ 132
         to be imprisoned............................ 133
   Duration of imprisonment............................... 132
   May have citation....................................... 136
      deposit unclaimed money........................... 137
   Compensation of.. 137
   Additional allowances to................................ 137
   Must collect and distribute estate....................... 142
   To make just and true account......................... 154
      file petition for leave to sell real estate 155, 156
   Cannot maintain bill to correct title..................... 168
      create debts to charge real estate 170
      pay debts barred and charge real estate 170
   Judgment against, conclusive............................ 171
   No privity between, and heirs........................... 171

ADMINISTRATOR—*Continued.*

	PAGE.
Judgment against an, in another state	171
Not in privity with each other	171
Cannot delegate power to sell	174
purchase at his own sale	174, 358, 359, 364
Surviving, may complete sale	174
Invested with naked power	174
Sale by, with will annexed	179
Authority local	203, 206
Cannot be sued in foreign state	203, 204
May call foreign administrator to account	204
collect foreign debts without suit	205
execute power of sale in foreign state	205
Charging as guardian, not liable as	286
Cannot be seller and buyer	360
As trustees	368

ADMINISTRATORS AND EXECUTORS,

May be imprisoned	6
Must make prompt and honest settlement	7
May be removed for illegally preferring creditors	20
refusing to perform duty	21
Removing from state to be removed from office	21
Becoming non-resident	21
Resignation of	22
Not discharged until full settlement made	22
To deliver assets to successor	22
pay costs of resignation	22
Surviving, may complete administration	30, 31
Improper conduct of bond to be sued	32
Diligence required of	32, 35
Guilty of *devastavit* to make loss good	33
To interpose statute of limitations	34
Debts due from	34
Liability for acts of co-administrator	35
money stolen, etc.	36
Duty to redeem mortgaged lands	36
Order on, binds securities	37
Action of account between	43
One of two may sell personal property	47
Cannot be joined in suit with another	51
Suits between	57, 135
May have citation against each other	136
To deposit unclaimed money	137

See, also, "Administrators," "Executors."

ADMINISTRATOR AND GUARDIAN,

When the same person acts as both 41, 42, 51, 52, 296, 293, 350

ADMINISTRATOR DE BONIS NON,

	PAGE.
May be appointed without renunciation	11
To be appointed upon resignation or removal	22
When appointment void	22
Not liable for contract of predecessor	23, 74
Who may be	22
To be appointed when further security not given	28, 30
sole executor or administrator dies	30
Suit by, against former administrator	34, 38
In suits by, for property	74
May complete sales of real estate	174
execute conveyances	177

ADMINISTRATOR DE SON TORT,

Who is	55
Liability as	55
Acts of necessity do not constitute	55
Nor intermeddling with lands	56
Suits against	56
Not liable to legatees	56
When acts of, binding	56
Power of court over	56
How one may discharge himself	57
May pay debts	57
If he take letters, renders his acts legal	57
One who fraudulently purchases, is	66
Widow as	57
Title from	57

ADMINISTRATOR TO COLLECT,

Appointed during contest	19
Bond of	19
Powers of	54
May sell under order of court	54
Commissions of	55
May commence suits	55
Powers cease, when	55
Duty to turn over property	55
Penalty for failure	55

ADJUSTMENT OF CLAIMS,

Notice to be given of	97
Not due	105
Filed after two years	108
Form of notice for	581
Record of	582

ADOPTED CHILDREN,

Become legal heirs	147, 375, 379

ADOPTED CHILDREN—*Continued.*
    Do not inherit from natural heirs..................................147, 376
    Under the laws of other states.................................... 376

ADOPTION OF CHILDREN,
    Petition for...371, 372, 378
        must be by husband and wife................................. 379
    Notice of 371
    Decree for 373, 378
    When consent of child necessary................................. 375
    Rights of child.. 375
        parents by adoption 376
        natural 377

ADVANCEMENTS,
    Considered a part of estate....................................... 143
    Heir not required to refund....................................... 143
    Must be charged... 143
        proven in case of infants 143
    Presumptions in relation to....................................... 143
    Real estate advanced... 143
    Personal estate 143
    Must be expressed in writing 144
    To one who dies before ancestor 144
    Do not affect widow 144
    Debts of heir to estate, considered.............................. 149
    By guardian to build on ward's land.............................. 290

AFFIDAVIT,
    Of failure of administrator to turn over assets................. 63
        non-residence..159, 160
    May be made by any person having knowledge....................... 160
        on information and belief..................................... 160
    Contents of 160
    For arrest of insolvent debtor.................................... 481

AFRICAN,
    Aliens, may be naturalized 559

AGENCY,
    Terminated by death of principal................................. 99

ALDERMAN,
    Contest of election of 533

ALIENS,
    May be naturalized 547
    Declaration by...547, 560, 561
    Must have resided five years...................................... 555
        renounce title of nobility 555
    Who have served in the army...................................... 558
        came here under eighteen..................................... 558
    Widows and children of.....................................558, 559, 561

INDEX. 625

ALIENS—*Continued.*
 African born.. 559
 Who are enemies.. 559
   seamen 560

ALLOWANCE TO CHILDREN,
 When made—same as widow... 90
 Only in case of residents.. 90, 92
 Policy of the law... 90
 Cannot be cut off by will.. 91
       See "Widow's Award."

ANCILLARY ADMINISTRATION,
 What law governs distribution in............................... 9, 118
 In, what necessary to justify a sale of land to pay debts.. 170
 Different executors in different states........................... 195
 What is 203
 May be called to account... 204
 What debts to be paid in... 204
 Legacies not payable in.. 204

ANSWER,
 By guardian—form... 591
   adults.. 592

ANTE NUPTIAL CONTRACT,
 Effect of, on widow's award................................. 90, 91, 92

APPEAL,
 Regularity of appointment can only be questioned on...... 16
 Securities on administrator's bond, may.................. 42, 208
 In case of widow's award... 94
   claims in favor of executor or administrator............ 114
 From order approving account 131, 209, 210, 295
 Effect of such appeal.. 131
 From probate of will, evidence in.................................. 188
 May be had from probate of will................................... 190
 On, any competent evidence may be heard................... 190
 Will not lie from feigned issues..................................... 194
 From order allowing claim.. 114
 Bond in case of.. 208, 603
 Who may take... 208
 In case of petition to sell land...................................... 208
  condemnation proceedings...................................... 209
  whose name prosecuted 209
 Extent of the right in probate matters........................... 209
 In case of imprisonment 209
 Condition of bond in... 209
 What the circuit court may do on.................................. 210
 From an order removing administrator 210

PAGE.

APPEAL—*Continued.*
 From an order appointing guardian.. 242
       refusing to appoint 243
       finding lunatic restored.............. ....391, 405
 By insolvent debtor..461, 477, 479, 482, 484
 In bastardy proceedings.. 509
  trials of right of property...524, 530
  contested elections.. 545

APPRAISERS,
 How appointed 61
 Duty of...... 62
 Compensation of.. 62
 To certify appraisement.............. 62
  fix widow's award 89, 93
  consider her condition in life............ 93
 Form of warrant to... 577
  oath of... 577

APPRAISEMENT,
 Warrant for, to issue... 59
 To be made 61
 Return of............... 62
 As evidence................... 62
 Further, to be made.. 63
 Growing crops.. 79
 Of partnership estate.. 83
 Bill, averments in petition to sell real estate in relation to............ 157
  form 578

APPRENTICES,
 Matters relating to, cognizant in county courts............................. 4

ARBITRATION,
 Claims cannot be submitted to 106
 By guardian, infant not bound.. 272

ASSETS OF ESTATES,
 Money received for causing death.. 35
 Stolen by burglars.. 36
 Measure of liability, of securities................................. 38
 Real estate taken by administrator becomes................................ 52
 When do not exceed widow's award.. 62
 To be delivered to widow, when...... 62
 Upon discovery of, to be inventoried... 62
 Bound for payment of debts.. 65
 Property in another state.. 72
 Not applicable to payment of claims presented after two years...... 102
 Money paid by heirs, etc... 125
 Presumed to be paid out, when........................... 128

ASSETS OF ESTATES—*Continued*.

	PAGE.
Discovery of, after discharge of administrator	129
Recovery of, from a stranger	132, 133
Debts due from heirs	149
Money from sale of real estate	178
Where land devised	201

ASSIGNMENT FOR BENEFIT OF CREDITORS,

Definition	428, 429, 452
Power of states to pass laws for	428, 429, 460
Voluntary and involuntary	429
How made	429, 452
What is	430
Notice of	430, 453
Passes title	431, 445, 450, 470
Proceedings in, conclusive	432
Not void for irregularities	432
Preference of creditors void, in	434, 435, 449, 455, 456
Discontinuance of proceedings	435
Form of	435
Who may make	445
When one partner may make	445
By corporation	445
Of personal estate, need not be recorded	445
Construction of deed of	445, 446
Deed of, when void	446, 447, 448, 449
how determined	446
verbal, invalid	446
may be made good	550
By insolvent debtor	469
effect of	470
additional	473
Dividends in	453

ASSIGNEE,

To give notice to creditors	430
file inventory	430
enter into bond	430
report list of creditors	431
Power of court over	432, 454
May sell estate and collect debts	433, 474
Death of	434
Removal of	434
Bond of	439
To file list of creditors	441
Is trustee	446, 450
Death of, or failure to act	455
Insolvent, deed void	447, 448

INDEX.

ASSIGNEE—*Continued.*   PAGE.
  May employ debtor 447
         maintain replevin 448
  Property in hands of, exempt from execution 449
  Compensation of 450, 460, 476
  Cannot be sued at law 451
  Suit by 451
  For insolvent debtor 469
        shall collect, etc. 453, 474
        may convey 474
        keep account 475
        may be removed 475
        make settlement 453, 476
        fees of 476

ATTACHMENT,
  Suit does not abate upon death of defendant 68
  Of surviving partner 84
  Abates upon death, when 112
  On failure to pay dividends 132
        distributees 134
  To compel production of will 185
  Property held by assignee exempt from 449, 450

ATTORNEY,
  Administrator entitled to services of 126, 127
  Fees of, by administrator 125
        chargeable against estate 125
  Cannot have lien on assets of estate 126
        make sale of real estate for administrator ... 174
  No power to waive rights of infant 267
  Fees of, paid by guardian for ward 282, 290

B.

BALLOTS,
  Receiving, after hour for closing 538
  Examination of 542
  When to be rejected 543
  Tampering with 543

BANKRUPTCY,
  Discharge of principal in bond, under 239
  Of guardian, does not affect ward 258
  Distinguished from insolvency 428
  Discharge in 477

BASTARDY,
  Complaint in 486, 487, 512
  Trial in 489, 491
  Order of court in 491

PAGE

BASTARDY—*Continued.*
    Prosecution in, civil proceeding....................................498, 499, 509, 512
               rules governing..498, 499, 511
               pleadings in... 499
               may be compromised..499, 510
               not abated by death.. 500
                    barred by marriage of mother........................... 501
                    new trial in... 502
                    verdict in.. 502
    Bond of father in...493, 507, 508, 514
    Proceedings, infancy no bar to.. 507
    Appeals in...509, 512, 515
    Where mother marries another... 511

BASTARD,
    Right to property at common law.. 146
    Mother of, natural guardian... 214
    Support of 494
    Death of...498, 500
    Twins 500
    Son of a foreigner.. 561

BILL IN CHANCERY,
    Form of, may be used in contested elections.................................. 536

BILL OF SALE,
    To be returned by administrator..80, 587
           certified by crier and clerk... 80
           sworn to by administrator 80

BOND,
    Of public administrator 18
        administrator to collect.. 19
        executor... 25
            to be signed, sealed, etc... 26
    Special, to be given when necessary to sell real estate...............26, 27
    Of administrator—form 27
    New, to be given by administrators and executors............................ 29
        have relation back... 29
    Two may be given..29, 31
    Execution of new, effect on old..29, 30
    Joint and several..31, 355
    To be examined at January and July terms.............................31, 240
    New, failure to give, works removal.. 32
    May be put in suit.. 32
    Not void on first suit... 32
    Certified copy of, to be evidence.. 32
    Not signed by principal does not bind security............................... 32
    Liability on, for failure to plead defenses...................................... 34

BOND—*Continued*.

    PAGE.

Voluntary, binding......38, 240
Informalities no defense to......38, 41
Of administrator may be sued by adm'r *de bonis non*, when......39, 40
    testamentary guardian......219, 225, 235
    statutory guardian......235, 236
        should be approved...... 237
        when void...... 238
Not at variance with statute, valid...... 238
Given by wrong name...... 238
Of guardian liable for rents...... 238
        any breach...... 238
        suits on......239, 354
        covers any property of ward...... 239
        void at law, enforced in equity......239, 349
        when name of ward is incorrectly given...... 240
        not to be avoided for slight defects...... 240
Inartificially drawn, not avoided...... 240
Adding new name...... 354
Of infant voidable...... 266
    non-resident guardian...... 334
    conservator...... 383
    non-resident conservator...... 391
For costs, by non-residents......210, 309, 393
    clothing for insane persons...... 401
Of assignee...... 430
        additional...... 433
By father of bastard......493, 507, 510
        proceedings on......494, 495, 497
        when to be void......498, 507
    administrator...... 603
For costs, not jurisdictional...... 226

BOOKS OF ACCOUNT,
    Subject to inspection by any one interested...... 70
            See "Evidence."

C.

CANDIDATES,
    Ineligible...... 543
    Informality in naming......543, 544
    Bribery by...... 543
    Tie of voters between...... 543
            See "Elections."

CAVEAT EMPTOR,
    Applies to sales by executors and administrators......79, 176
        of real estate...... 176
        guardian's sales...... 319

INDEX 631

	PAGE.

CESTUI QUE TRUST,
    Duty of trustee to.. 358
    May ratify act of trustee... 360
    Profits of trustee inure to...361, 362
    May repudiate acts of trustee.. 363
    Acquiescence by... 363
    Sales to, by trustee.. 363
    Trustee cannot deny title of.. 364
    May pursue fund... 369

CHANCERY,
    See "Equity," "Equity Courts."

CHANGE OF VENUE,
    Allowed in probate matters..113, 114
    In bastardy proceedings... 501

CHILDREN,
    Means lawful offspring... 142
    Of the half blood... 142
    Born in wedlock, presumed legitimate..................................... 142
    May be disinherited... 184
    Effect of birth of, on will.. 196
    Who entitled to custody of...214, 215
    Abandonment of home by... 215
    Adoption of... 371
    Consent of, to be adopted... 375
    Of naturalized aliens, become citizens..................................... 561

CIRCUIT COURT,
    Claims may be sued in.. 106
    Cannot refer claims to arbitration.. 106
    Change of venue to...113, 114
    To classify claims.. 117
    May change order classifying claims....................................... 119
        grant probate of will... 187
    Appeal to, in probate of will... 190
    Contest of will in..191, 192
    Jurisdiction to order sale of real estate by non-resident guardian.. 308
        in contested elections... 533
            assignments.. 459

CITATION,
    To party charged with concealing goods..................................... 69
        surviving partner... 84
    Should run in the name of the people...................................... 134
    Abates on death of administrator.......................................134, 286
    Cannot run against personal representative........................134, 286
    May issue against one of two executors.................................. 136
    To minor to choose guardian...229, 230

CITATION—*Continued.*

	PAGE.
Not a suit at law	284
To father of bastard	494
form of	495
administrator—form	588

CITIZEN,

Native or naturalized	554
Defined	547

CIVIL LAW,

Rule of relationship derived from	10
As applied to descent	141

CLAIMS AGAINST ESTATES,

Allowance by courts of equity	5
Payment of, out of order, a *devastavit*	32
May be brought by securities of administrator	38
Must have been allowed to entitle claimant to sue admr's bond	41
To be paid with smallest amount possible	52
Lien upon all property of deceased	65
Not to be paid from rents	74
To be presented to county court	98, 102
in writing	98
sworn to	98
What is a	98
Must accrue in lifetime	98, 111, 348
Claim for monument by widow not	98, 99
Judgment, when	98
Covenant broken before death	98
Firm debts are, when	99
Of an equitable nature	100
Forfeiture enforcible as	101
Taxes due at death	101
Must be presented within two years	101
Presented after two years, how allowed	102
Exhibited to administrator	102
Sufficient exhibiting	102
When principal in note dies	102
presented after two years	102
Barred if not presented within two years	103
Filed within two years, statute does not run	103
Presented after administration completed	103
Practice when presented after adjustment	104
When presented, should be allowed or continued	104
Not to be allowed except on notice	104, 112
Amount of, not increased by oath of claimant	105
Not due, how allowed	106
May be sued in circuit court	**105**

CLAIMS AGAINST ESTATES—*Continued.*

	PAGE.
Form of judgment on revival of judgment	106
Must be defended vigilantly	107
Heirs, legatees and creditors may defend	107
Promissory note executed as a gift	108
Post mortem examination	108
Must be a present debt	108
Must not rest on contingency	108, 110
Never presented to deceased, suspicious	108
Not barred where no inventory is filed	108
When judgment on, is general	109
Filing, is not commencement of suit	109
Of wards, not barred in five years	110
choice of remedies	110
When statute of limitations need not be urged	109, 110
On foreclosure—balance	111
Contingent	111, 348
Not to be allowed for more than claimed	111
Prosecution of, not governed by technicalities	111
A judgment on, not a lien	111
Should be proven as alleged	111
Allowance of, is judgment	111, 114
Barred by two-year statute, good as set-off	113
In favor of administrator	114
Not exhibited within two years, barred	117
When allowed to be classed	117
For debts due school fund	118
Paid by administrator before allowance	119
Effect upon, of final settlement	128
Must all be paid before heirs have distribution	150
Of insane person—how prosecuted	425
Against bankrupt, contest of	431
not due	433
presentation of	442
exceptions to	442
insolvent debtor	472, 473

CLASSIFICATION OF CLAIMS,

At common law	116
By statute	116, 117
Controlled by law in force at death	116
To be made when allowed	117
Order of, may be changed	119

CLERK.

Of sale may be employed	80
Compensation of	80
To certify bill of sale	80
publish notice, when	160

INDEX.

CLERK—*Continued.*   PAGE.

    Of court, as guardian *ad litem* 224
                may examine under oath party applying for license...... 273
                not to issue license to minors without consent............ 273

CLOTHING,
    For insane persons..400, 401

CODICIL,
    Contest over.. 19
                                    See "Will."

CO-EXECUTORS AND ADMINISTRATORS,
    Endangered, administrator to be removed................................. 21
    Liability for acts of... 35
    Not liable for torts of associate.. 35
    Act of one is the act of both... 47
    Bill for accounting between—form.. 600

COLLATERAL PROCEEDINGS,
    When grant of administration may be questioned in................ 16
    Grant to public administrator, not questioned........................... 18
    Widow's award conclusive in... 94
    Order on approving accounts conclusive in 126
    In, decree may be questioned, when.. 161
    Presumptions of law in.. 161
    Failure to appoint guardian *ad litem*....................................... 161
    Decrees to sell land in...168, 409
    Orders admitting or rejecting wills in....................................... 189
            appointing guardians 242
            accepting resignation... 341
    Finding of courts upon question of insanity............................. 409
            county court in assignments................................... 431

COLOR OF TITLE,
    Deed from trustee to himself is... 358

COMMISSION,
    To issue to take testimony 186
    Notice of—form 604
    Order of court directing issue of—form................................... 604

CONCEALED GOODS,
    Proceedings to secure 69
    Not to collect debt... 70
    When power to be exercised... 70

CONFIRMATION,
    Of sale of real estate by administrator..................................... 172
                       guardian 317
        is a judicial act.. 317
    Combination among bidders will defeat.................................. 318

	PAGE.
CONFIRMATION—*Continued.*	
Of sale cures all irregularities in sale	318
May be made by ward	319
Of sale under decree of foreclosure	329

CONSERVATORS,
- Appointment of, given to county courts............ 4, 381, 388, 404, 451
- Law of guardians applicable to..................381, 392, 411
- Officers of court.................. 381
- Validity of the appointment of, how questioned............ 382
- Bond of 382, 404
- Suits on bond of 382, 414
- To have care of person and estate.................382, 412
- Inventory of.................. 382
- Shall collect property of ward.................383, 412
  - account.................383, 392
  - perform contract of ward.................. 383
  - represent ward in suits.................348, 413, 414
  - manage estate of ward.................385, 412
  - invest money.................. 386
  - sell real estate.................386, 415
  - lease real estate.................. 386
- May mortgage real estate.................. 386
- Removal of.................388, 404, 411
- Resignation of.................. 388
- Compensation of.................389, 413
- Who should be appointed.................. 408
- May be appointed for married woman.................. 409
- When liable on contract of ward.................. 409
  - chargeable with interest.................. 409
- One of two may act.................. 412
- Of spendthrift, have not custody of person.................. 412
- May change domicile of ward.................. 412
- Suits by.................. 414
  - to set aside conveyance.................. 417
- Accounts by.................. 427

CONSTITUTION,
- Provisions establishing county courts.................. 3
- Public administrator's oath to support.................. 18
- Prohibition of imprisonment for debt.................. 133
- Power under to pass bankrupt laws.................428, 477
  - registration laws.................. 541

CONSTRUCTION OF WILLS,
- Rules governing.................199, 200
- Words not taken in technical sense.................. 200
- Whole instrument considered.................. 200
- Intention of testator.................. 200

CONSTRUCTION OF WILLS—*Continued.*

	PAGE.
When court of equity will construe	200
In relation to land sold	201
When land to be charged	201
Where custody of children is disposed of	219

CONTESTED ELECTIONS,

Jurisdiction in	533, 534
Of officers of towns, etc	533
city and village officers	533, 534
Statutory power in	533, 534, 546
May be conducted at any term	534
Power of court of chancery in	534
Who may institute proceedings in	535, 537
Proceedings in	535, 536, 537, 538, 539, 540, 541, 547
Judgment of court in	544, 545

CONTINGENCY,

Claim against estate must not rest on	108

CONTINUANCE,

Of claim against estate	104
In bastardy cases	490

CONTRACT,

Of deceased, when to be performed	53
Not terminated by death	98
For purchase of land, descends	99
Made by widow does not bind administrator	99
Legal, may be enforced	100
Descent varied by	148
For contingent fee to attorney	126
Verbal, in sales of real estate	177, 178
Of infant voidable	265, 276
may be affirmed or disaffirmed	265
to sell real estate, voidable	265
for necessaries, binding	266, 277
ancestor, liability of heir upon	274, 275, 276
With infants, when avoidable	276
Of infant to pay interest, void	277
lunatic to be performed by conservator	384
when void and when voidable	385, 415, 416, 417, 418, 419
Laws impairing obligation of	429

CONTRIBUTION,

By legatees	135
distributees	135
sureties	356

CONVEYANCES,

May be executed by surviving executor	47
What may be shown to sustain	47
Cannot be executed by administrator with will annexed	47
By administrator on sale of real estate	177, 599
Attorney cannot execute	177
Which fail to recite decree	177
May be made to another than the purchaser	177
By infant, voidable	265
married woman, void	265
how ratified	266
Of real estate may be made to an infant	266
By guardian	309
non-resident guardian	309
Delivery of	316
By trustee to himself, not void	358
conservators	387, 415
Of lunatic—when set aside	415, 416, 417
By assignee of insolvent debtor	474

See "Deeds by guardian."

CORPORATION,

Cannot have letters testamentary	12
May assign for benefit of creditors	445

COSTS,

Of resignation to be paid by administrator	22
Judgment to be rendered for	20
Person for whose use suit is brought, liable	32
Security for	40, 226
When administrator liable for	51, 77
Of settling partnership	84
allowing claims	104
In the discretion of the court	104
Against insolvent estates	114, 115
Of administration to be paid before distribution	128
citation, etc., to be paid by administrator	130
Bond for, by foreign executors and administrators	205
Of guardian *ad litem*, how taxed	224
Bond for, by non-resident guardian	309
conservator	393
In insanity proceedings	391, 400
bastardy proceedings	491
Bond for, in bastardy proceedings	499
In trials of right of property	525

COUNTER SECURITY,

By administrator or executor	29, 352
guardians	352, 355
Petition for, on guardian's bond	352, 353
conservator's bond	353

INDEX.

COUNTY,   PAGE.

    When divided, probate matters not changed 6
    Letters granted in wrong, void 17
    Proper county in which to take letters 18

COUNTY COURTS,

    Established by constitutional provisions 3
    Statutory provisions in relation to 3, 5
    Terms of 4
    Always open for probate business 4
    Jurisdiction for probate matters general and not inferior 4
    Decrees of 4
                cannot be questioned 5
    Records of, cannot be contradicted or varied 5
    How far jurisdiction shared by courts of equity 5
    Jurisdiction continues 6, 100
    Equitable claims, may entertain 6, 100
    Cannot adjudicate conflicting interests 6, 100
                in case of resulting trust 6
    Power of, to enforce orders, etc. 6
    May issue attachments 6, 134
             fine and imprison 6
    Unlimited general jurisdiction of 7, 9
    May construe wills 7
    To exercise discretion in grant of letters 11
    Having jurisdiction, acts not void 17
    When to commit estate to public administrator 17
    What gives jurisdiction of estates to 17
    Has discretion when to appoint administrator to collect 19
    May revoke letters, when 19
    Duty of, to remove administrators who go from the state 21
             require security 25, 27
    Taking and approving security 27
    To examine condition of bonds at January and July terms .. 28, 31, 284
            direct notice, upon petition of securities 28
            compel adm'r to settle when securities petition to be released 28
            cause administrator to show cause 29
            remove executor or administrator, on failure 31
            appoint administrator *de bonis non* 31
    No power over trustees appointed by will 35
    Order of, conclusive on securities 37
    To direct performance of contracts 53
    No power over administrator *de son tort* 56
    May order sale of desperate claims 76
    To order sale of personal property 78
            surviving partner to account 84
    May protect estate of deceased partner 84
            appoint receiver 84

INDEX.

COUNTY COURTS—*Continued.*   PAGE.

To adopt equity rules..84, 100, 284, 315
May set aside award to widow.. 93
    not modify award... 93
Order of, allowing partnership debts.. 99
May give judgment for set-off.. 105
To classify claims... 117
May change order classifying... 119
Make entry of claims.. 119
    order of distribution.. 123
When it may vacate order made at prior term................................ 127
Shall enforce settlements.. 129
May imprison, etc.. 132
To order payment of legacies.. 133
    apportion deficiency among legatees.. 135
May grant injunctions, when.. 138
Duty to equalize legacies... 150
Cannot enforce payment of distributive share until after order
                                                    [of distribution, 150
May order distribution in kind.. 150
    coerce sale of real estate... 155
    order land platted.. 166
        sold to pay debts.. 167
Confirmation of sale by... 173
Has no discretion, where proof shows execution of will............... 189
Order of, admitting or rejecting will, when binding........................ 189
Cannot overrule a testamentary appointment of guardian............ 219
Jurisdiction over minors..228, 230
Should refuse to ratify unwise choice of guardian......................... 230
Duty of, to appoint guardian.. 232
Order of, conclusive on guardian... 238
To approve lease of lands of wards... 251
Approval of, not necessary to valid lease.. 251
May fix the amount of expenditures for ward................................ 257
May compel guardians to render account...................................... 284
Powers in report of sale by guardian... 315
May remove guardians... 342
A large discretion given to... 346
Order of, transferring assets to account as guardian not necessary 350
Jurisdiction of, in the adoption of children..................................... 371
                appointment of conservators...............381, 457
                insanity proceedings.. 394
To inquire into conservators' bonds... 388
Finding of, conclusive.. 409
Jurisdiction of, in assignments..429, 432, 435
                insolvency proceedings...........................463, 484
Always open.. 463

COUNTY COURTS—*Continued.*

	PAGE.
Adjournment by	489
Jurisdiction of, in bastardy	500, 516
right of property	516
contested elections	533, 534
naturalization	557

COUNTY SEATS,

Contest of elections in relation to 535

COUNTY TREASURER,

When assets of estates to be paid to 136
Money of unknown heir or claimant 137
Escheats to be paid to 151

COURT OF CHANCERY,

See "Equity," "Equity Courts."

COVENANT,

Action of, by executor or administrator 74
Breaches of, when claim against estate 99
    occurring after death 103
Entered into by administrator 176
    do not bind estate 176
Guardian not liable on implied 257
    may bind himself by 259, 315
By guardian in mortgage, do not bind ward 359

CREDITOR,

One who has paid funeral expenses is 13
When he may administer 10
His debt must be such as survives 13
Legatee not entitled to letters as 13
How deprived of right 13
One having claim for causing death, is not 13
Falsely pretending to be 20
May defend against claims 107, 285
Not prejudiced by mechanic's lien, when 110
    affected by order of distribution of which he has no notice ... 149
May maintain bill to correct title, when 168
Judgment on, conclusive 171
Of bankrupt 431, 440
Preference of, void 434, 435, 449
List of 316
May except to claims 323
    contest schedule of insolvent debtor 467

CREDITOR'S BILL,

Filing of, gives lien 119

CRIER OF SALE,
May be employed 80
Compensation of 80
To certify bill of sale 80

CRIMINAL RESPONSIBILITY,
Of infants 278
Of lunatics 419, 420, 421

CUSTODY,
Of minors 214, 263
By testamentary guardians 220
Of lunatics, etc. 382
    bastard child 498

D.

DAMAGES,
Actions to recover, survive 66
For opening public road, personal 71

DEATH,
Fact of, must exist, or letters void 14, 75
Reputation may be received to prove 14
Of sole executor or administrator 30
Money due for causing 35, 72
Of one of several executors 46
Suit for causing, may be compounded 51
Of sole plaintiff may be suggested 67
    plaintiff not to hinder collection of judgment 67
        does not defeat lien 68
        defendant, execution to issue 68
        owner of land, title vests in heirs 140
Money paid for causing, personal 72
Does not terminate any contract 98, 99
Terminates agency 99
Does not affect lien of creditor 119
Of bastard—effect on proceedings 498, 500, 507
    father of bastard—securities 507

DEBTS DUE ESTATES,
Failure to collect, *devastavit* 32
From executor or administrator 34
Payment of, in case of living person 75
Sold in good faith 77
May be compounded or sold 77
Due at remote period 77
Not released by appointing debtor executor 191

DECLARATION OF INTENTION,
By alien 555

DECLARATION ON BOND,

	PAGE.
To recover more than nominal damages, must allege and prove special damages,	33
Not necessary to aver and prove *devastavit*.	37
Breaches may be assigned	37
When demand to be averred	37, 38
May be against part or all the obligors	38

DECREE,

To sell land, what it must show	156
form of	593
None can be made until all parties are in court	157
Contradicted by record	159, 160
Showing notice, concludes defendants	160, 314
Void, when parties not served	161
A nullity as to minors, when	163, 164
Which directs land named in the petition to be sold	166
What amount of land may be sold	166
For sale of land should specify terms	171, 172
be strictly followed	174
homestead	166
Power given by, not exhausted by one sale	175
when exhausted	175
Effect of reversal of, on sale	176
By default, not to be taken against minors	222, 265
Against minors absolute	267
To sell ward's land—recitations in	312
Final against minors subject to writs of error	319
Judgment to have form of	245
Approving assignment of dower—form	596
Against infant may be impeached	281
See "Judgment."	
For adoption of child	378

DEED BY ADMINISTRATOR,
See "Conveyances."

DEED BY GUARDIAN,

What it shall contain	315
Must be based on decree	321

DEFAULT,

Cannot be entered against minor	164

DEFINITIONS,

Of *devastavit*	32
legal representatives	71
family	92
children	142
next of kin	10, 141

DEFINITIONS—*Continued.*

	PAGE.
Of heirs	146
will	181
perpetuity	184
ancillary administrator	203
guardian	213
orphan	233
domicile	252
trust	357
contingent remainder	364
assignment	428
permanent abode	539
citizen	554

DEGREES OF CONSANGUINITY,

How reckoned	10

DEMAND,

To be made upon principal in bond	37
When not necessary	38
To be made before attachment issue	132
A necessary element	133
On legatee to contribute	135

DESCENT,

Rules of	140
What will bar	142
Of estate of deceased infant	142
How illegitimates may take by	144
Of estate of illegitimates	144
Not defeated by naked trust	149
Of property, governed by law of domicile	150
may be varied by contract	148
to heir renders him liable for debts of ancestor	273, 274

DESPERATE CLAIMS,

See "Doubtful and desperate claims."

DEVASTAVIT,

Definition of	32
Taking inadequate security	33
Releasing or compounding debt	33
Removing property from the state	33
Exhibiting untrue account	33
Failure to file inventory	34
For admitting claim barred	34
Failure to pay over money as ordered	37
Not necessary to aver and prove	37
Administrator who loans money of estate	50
pays money as	75
As applied to guardian	354

DEVISEE,

	PAGE.
May have action for waste, when	74
compel redemption of land	75
When witness to will	189
title vests in	201
entitled to purchase money, of land devised	201
No claim on lands devised until debts are paid	202

DISCHARGE,

Of administrator may not terminate duties	60, 128
conservator	390, 411, 412
patient from hospital for insane	402
insolvent debtor from imprisonment	471, 480, 499
debts	477
What class of debtors entitled to	482
Can only be made by the court	482

DISTRIBUTIVE SHARE,

Heir owing amount of	74, 149
When offset against indebtedness	149
Payment of, cannot be enforced until order made	150

DISTRIBUTION,

What law governs	118, 150
Among creditors, when made	123
and heirs	123
May be ordered at any time	124, 144
Administrator should procure order of	130
What will bar	142
Court may make, of estate of deceased infant	142
Before, must pass through administration	142
Advancements in	143
May be delayed	144
Not made without notice	149
to heirs until all debts and charges are paid	150
Cannot be enforced until order of	150
Order of, conclusive	150
In kind, when made	150
Of bankrupt's effects	431, 443

DIVIDENDS,

Are personal estate	70
From assignor's estate	431

DOMICILE,

Of deceased	9
personal estate	150
testator to govern devise of personal property	198
Will to be proven at	198
Of administrator	204

DOMICILE—*Continued.*
    Of parent fixes that of child... 252
        child 244, 26
    Definition of... 252
    Remains while in transit... 252
    Not lost by conditional removal... 252
    There must be intention to change... 252
    Of wards may be changed, when.. 412
        person charged to be insane.. 407
        electors...538, 539, 540, 541

DOUBTFUL AND DESPERATE CLAIMS,
    To be inventoried..60, 61
    Prima facie uncollectable.. 61
    Suggestion of.. 76
    Compounded and sold.. 76
    Filed, etc... 76
    Avails of... 77
    Form of petition, on... 583
        notice 584
        order of court, on... 584

DOWER,
    Right to, when will renounced... 141
    Assignment of.. 164
    When cannot be assigned.. 165
    Guardian to institute proceedings for assignment of................. 251
    Real estate of infant subject to.. 318
    Petition for—form 590
    Report assigning—form... 596

DRUNKARD,
    Letters to one becoming, to be revoked.................................... 21
    Conservator for.. 377
    Contracts of, void and voidable...385, 415
    Swindling a... 385
    Reformation of.. 389
    Contract of..409, 419
    Criminal responsibility of..421, 423

E.

EJECTMENT,
    In suit of, appointment of administrator cannot be questioned, 17, 18
    When administrator may maintain.. 50
    By minors, when estoppel will apply....................................... 271
        lunatic. 414

ELECTION,
    Of widow.. 141
    Contest of.. 533
    Of alderman, how contested... 533

ELECTION—*Continued.*

	PAGE.
Of mayor, how contested	533
Cannot be enjoined	534
Not vitiated by change of place	536
Calling of	536
Who may question	536
Adjournment of, for dinner	537
Not void, when	537
Rules of—design	537
Void	544

ELECTOR,

Any, may contest election	535
Who is	538, 539
Presumptions of law in relation to	539
Intention of	540
Declarations of	540
Intention of, to govern	543

EMANCIPATION,

Of infant, when presumed	268

EQUITABLE CLAIMS,

County court may adjust	6, 100
By one administrator against another	135, 136

EQUITY,

To govern approval of accounts	138, 226
Will not interfere to relieve against a judgment in probate, where [there is a legal defense,	107
interfere to protect against fraud	107
Rules of, to be followed by probate judge	85, 100, 129, 284, 296, 315
Will enforce re-payment to administraror	129
Contest of will in	191, 192
Will not relieve against contract with infant	276
When it will open account of guardian	292
compel conveyance by ward	316
Infant may have relief in	348
Jurisdiction in, of trusts	362
Will protect interest of a lunatic	414, 415

EQUITY COURTS,

When will entertain jurisdiction of probate matters	5
All parties must be before it	6
Power over trustees appointed by will	35
Will adopt action of probate courts	35
Where several bonds have been given	43, 348
Will interfere to protect securities from fraud	43, 292
May decree sale where executor refuses	47
compel delivery of funds of estate	70

INDEX. 647

EQUITY COURTS—*Continued.* PAGE.
    Will not require heir to pay to administrator............................ 74
    May entertain suits to settle partnership.................................... 85
    When to settle estates 129
    May require heirs to refund... 134
    Power of, to order sale of lands of infants and lunatics...169, 320, 387
    Having obtained jurisdiction.. 169
    Contest of will in..191, 192
    When it will construe wills.. 200
    Will interfere to marshal assets.. 204
    Have jurisdiction over infant's estate..........................216, 217, 218
    Will always guard rights of infants.. 216
    Jurisdiction of, over infants' estates not affected by statutory
                                                                                  [provisions, 217
    May set aside answer of guardian *ad litem*............................. 217
        appoint a person to prosecute or defend for infants............ 218
    Jurisdiction over guardians.. 218
    When allow ward's estate to be sold... 288
    Will order property of infant into the custody of foreign guardian, 334
    Will vacate sales, when...360, 416
        enforce trusts.. 362
        fasten a trust upon lands.. 363
    Powers of, in insanity proceedings.. 408
    Invoked to set aside conveyance of lunatic..........................416, 417
    Cannot interfere with assigned property.................................... 432
    Power of, in contested elections.................................534, 535, 548

ERROR,
    In proceedings will not vitiate..17, 322
        accounting, not evidence of fraud...................................131, 132
    Failure to make guardian a party, is.. 157
    To order sale of real estate without proper notice...................... 160
    Failure to appoint guardian *ad litem*.................................163, 233
    In proceeding, cannot be urged in collateral proceedings........... 169
        appointment of guardian, corrected on appeal.................... 242
    Failure to fix time of sale of ward's land, is................................ 313
    Writs of, may be prosecuted by infant....................................... 319

ESCAPE,
    When officer not liable for.. 482
    Of father of bastard... 500

ESCHEATS,
    Property of bastard.. 146
        one having no heirs... 151
        to be paid county treasurer.. 151

ESTATES,
    When committed to public administrator................................... 18
        administrator to collect.. 19

ESTATES—*Continued.*

	PAGE.
Represented by administrator	48
Not liable for fraud or torts of administrators	50
contracts	51
bound by warranty of administrator	54
liable for monument	98
When insolvent, to be so entered	114, 115
insufficient to pay all debts	117
Not bound by covenants of administrator	176
Of minors under care of equity courts	216
Insolvency of—form of suggestion	583
To be declared insolvent	63, 115

ESTOPPEL,

Makers of bond cannot deny	42
Inventory as	61
Of infants, not within the rule	270, 271, 279
In pais, when not allowed	271
In equity, when enforced against infants	271, 272, 318
Fraud an element in	272
Deed of guardian no, on ward	315, 316
Of ward from claiming real estate sold	318
lunatic	416
assignor by recitation in deed	438

EVIDENCE,

Certified copies of bonds to be	32
In suit on bond	34
Inventory as	60
Appraisement as	62
Inventory not conclusive	62
In proceedings to secure concealed goods	69
Of representative character	74
Admissions as	74
Of claims against estates	98
Allowance of partnership debts against individual estate	100
Judgment as	105
against administrator in another state, as	105
estate, *prima facie*, as to heir	113
Of advancements	143
service of summons	159
publication	159, 161
To be preserved in the record	162, 222
Of debts against an estate in another state	170
Judgment on claim, *prima facie*	171
against foreign administrator	171
Of non-resident witnesses to a will	186
In probate of will	186

                                                                    PAGE.
EVIDENCE—*Continued.*
   On appeal from probate of will.. 180
   What must appear to establish will.. 188
   When it differs as to mental condition................................188, 189
         brings case within the rule.. 189
   Copy of will as.. 190
   Of will probated in foreign state 194
   Foreign will, as.. 195
   Nuncupative will, as... 196
   Of lost will... 198
   Not admissible in construction of will.. 200
   Foreign letters, as.. 206
   Incompetent, against infant to be excluded............................... 222
   Taken without notice to guardian *ad litem*, inadmissible........... 223
   Against infants, must be taken before proper officer................. 223
   Of infancy 224
   Against infants in *scire facias*... 268
   In suit against heir for debt of ancestor..................................... 269
   To prove authority of minor to contract..................................... 285
         account of guardian.. 291
   Approval of account of guardian, as... 367
   Of fraud by trustees... 408
   In insanity proceedings.. 408
   Of insanity..410, 411, 412, 417
   Under plea of insanity..419, 420
   In bastardy proceedings................491, 499, 501, 503, 504, 505, 506
      trials of right of property... 527
      contested elections.. 536
      naturalization of foreigners 560

EXCEPTIONS,
   To claim in case of assignment... 442
   Form of.. 442
   Notice of... 443
   To report of sale of real estate—form.. 598

EXECUTION,
   May be issued for costs.. 22
   Sales under, duty of administrator to redeem............................ 50
   May be sued out by foreign administrator................................. 68
      issued after death of plaintiff....................................... 68
                defendant... 68
   Notice before issue of, in case of death 68
   May be issued for judgment on set-off....................................... 105
      not be awarded against administrator....................112, 113
   Issued at suit of foreign administrators...............................68, 207
      against father of bastard... 494

EXECUTORS,

	PAGE.
Resignation of	22
Bond of	25
To be removed on failure to give new bond	30
Surviving, may complete administration	30
Death or disqualification of	30
Improper conduct of, bond to be sued	32
Guilty of *devastavit*, to made loss good	33
Duty to interpose all known defenses	34, 107
Liable as trustees	35
To cause will to be probated	45
May refuse to act	45
Before probate of will	46
Officers of the law	46
Death of one, survivor to act	46
Survivor may convey	46
One of two or more may sell personal property	47
To administer intestate estate *ex officio*	47
make inventory	59
return appraisement	60
Liable for want of due diligence	63
To be discharged where assets do not exceed widow's allowance	63
May be attached, when	63
maintain actions of trover, etc.	66
Must sue and be sued jointly	66
Surviving, may probate against estate of deceased	67
Substituted in place of deceased plaintiff	67
To have notice before issue of execution	68
May take measures to secure concealed goods	69
When to take rents	70
Suits by, when in representative capacity	71
Title to personalty vests in	73
May maintain covenant, when	74
Suggestion of desperate claims	76
Report sale of desperate claims	76
Authority at common law	76
Not to remove property	77
May sell personalty	78
not purchase at his own sale	79
Interest in growing crops	79
To return sworn bill of sale	80
Personally liable in partnership	81
Must act by authority of will	82
May compel surviving partner to settle	83
To notify widow and set off award	89, 92
give notice of adjustment of claims	97
attend term for adjustment	98

                                                                    PAGE.
EXECUTORS—*Continued.*
   Have notice of presentation of claims................................ 97
   Duty of burial is upon him.. 100
   May be compelled to pay funeral expenses........................ 100
   To be summoned to answer claims.................................... 103
   Revival of judgment against.. 106
   Claim in favor of.. 114
   To exhibit account.. 123
   May provide for minor children, when................................ 126
   Failing to pay on demand, suit on bond.............................. 132
               to be imprisoned................................ 132
   Duration of imprisonment of.. 133
   Being residuary legatee.. 136
   May have citation against co-executor................................ 136
   To deposit unclaimed money.. 137
   Compensation of 137
   Additional allowances to.. 137
   Having sold lands, may apply, etc...................................... 155
   To file petition.. 155
   Cannot purchase at his own sale................................174, 359
   Sale of real estate by, under power........................178, 179
   Survivor may execute will.. 179
   Devise to, to sell.. 179
   Cannot in part decline.. 191
   Who may be.. 191
   During disability of.. 191
   Married woman as.. 191
   Debtor of testator as.. 191
   In different states, may be nominated................................ 195
   Acting in two capacities.. 225

EXHIBITION OF CLAIMS,
   Must be made within two years.. 101
   What is.. 102
   Sufficient to file.. 106
   Not made within two years.. 117

EXPENSES OF ADMINISTRATION,
   Need not be probated.. 100
   What administrator allowed for.. 126

EXPENSES,
   Of caring for estate of non-resident, preferred claim............ 18

F.

FAMILY,
   What the term includes.. 92

INDEX.

	PAGE.
FATHER,	
Guardian by nature	214
Must support child	215, 230
When bond for necessaries of child	215
Court may allow for support of child	216, 287, 289
Of infant, entitled to custody	229
Emancipation of infant by	268
Not liable for unauthorized torts of child	278
If suitable, entitled to be conservator	407
Of bastard—examination of	488
to be committed	488, 489, 493, 494, 497
bond by	488, 493
citation against	494
in contempt, when	497
when to have custody of child	498
not to be discharged as an insolvent	499
escape of	500
competent as witness	491, 502
death of	507
FEES,	
Of clerk to be remitted	115
administrators, etc.	137
Not to exceed six per cent	137
Of trustees	202
guardian *ad litem*	224
guardian	284, 286, 287, 290, 291
conservator	389, 425
assignee	450, 476
clerk	476
jailor	479, 480
FINAL SETTLEMENT,	
Not to be made without notice	123
Before made, costs to be paid	126
Order approving, conclusive if parties are notified	127
Disposition of real estate	128
Conditional order of	128
Order of, a nullity, when	128
After, presumption	128
Order of, may be entered *nunc pro tunc*	128
Effect of, upon claims	128
When effected by chancery	129
Of guardians—conclusive	292, 293
Form, notice of	602
order in—form	602, 615
FORECLOSURE,	
In county court	199, 325

FORECLOSURE—*Continued.*
	PAGE.
No strict, allowed	199, 325, 386
Of mortgage of ward's real estate	325
made by conservator	386
Parties in	330
Form of bill for	325
decree for	327

See "Mortgage."

FOREIGN ADMINISTRATORS AND EXECUTORS.
May sue out executions	68, 207
Judgment against, not evidence here	105, 203
Balance found in favor of, conclusive here	107
Judgment against, no evidence	171
No privity between, and domestic	171
May be called to account here, when	204
When they may not release mortgage	204
Statutory powers in this state	205
Not bound to account here, when	205
May be supplanted by domestic	205
Common law powers	206
No privity between, and domestic administrator	206

FOREIGN DEBTS,
Administrator should collect	48
Not included in term "property"	72
In judgment against administrator	171

FOREIGN GUARDIAN,
Power in this state	244, 338

FOREIGN ASSIGNMENTS,
Preference over	461

FORFEITURE,
Enforcible	101
For swindling idiot	385

FORM,
Of oath of administrator	15
executor	15
bond of executor	25
administrator	27
new bond of administrator or executor	29
security for costs	40
warrant to appraisers	61, 577
oath of appraisers	62, 577
judgment on revival of judgment	106
account current by executor, etc	124
petition for appointment of guardian	234

41

	PAGE.
FORM—*Continued.*	
Of nomination by infant over fourteen	231
on becoming fourteen years of age	232
petition by relative of infant	232
citation to minor to choose guardian	233
return of officer on citation	235
petition where parents are unfit	236
guardian's bond	240, 241
letters of guardianship	241, 245
record of appointment of guardian	245
guardian's inventory	245, 246
order of court approving inventory	246
guardian's account	293, 294
petition for sale of real estate	299
notice of application	301
affidavit of service	301
special bond of guardian in case of sale of real estate	302
decree for sale of ward's real estate	303
notice of guardian's sale of real estate	304
report of sale by guardian	305
order approving sale by guardian	306
deed by guardian	306
petition for leave to mortgage real estate of infant	323
order to mortgage ward's lands	324
report by guardian of mortgage of ward's real estate	325
petition to foreclose	325
decree of foreclosure	327
report of sale under foreclosure	328
record of appointment of non-resident guardian	333
bond of non-resident guardian	333
certificate of clerk	334
judge to foreign record	334
petition for removal of property	335
order for removal of property	336
petition by guardian to resign	339, 340
order accepting guardian's resignation	340
petition for removal of guardian	342
summons to guardian	343
order for removal of guardian	344
petition for counter security on guardian's bond	350
record on petition for counter security	351
bond under order for counter security	352
report of giving counter security	353
petition for adoption of children	372
notice to parents of child	372
consent of parents	373
order of court for adoption of children	374, 375

INDEX. 655

FORM—*Continued.*
                     PAGE.
 Of petition for appointment of conservator 382
  summons in lunacy cases 382
  order of county judge on petition in insanity 395
  precipe 396
  subpœna 396
  venire 397
  verdict of jury in insanity 397
  order of court finding insanity 398
  warrant for committing lunatic 399
  bond to furnish clothing to lunatic 401
   of assignee 430, 439
  assignment for benefit of creditors 435
  inventory of assignee 438
  notice to creditors 440
  list of creditors 441
  claim against bankrupt 442
  exceptions to claim 442
  notice of exceptions 443
  assignee's report 444
  notice by insolvent debtor 463
  petition by insolvent debtor 464
  venire for jury 465
  final order discharging debtor 465, 469
  schedule of insolvent debtor 466
  bond by insolvent debtor 468
  assignment by insolvent debtor 470
  discharge of insolvent debtor 471
  order of court fixing term 472
  assignee's notice to creditors 472
  proof of claim 473
  deed by assignee 474
  appeal bond by insolvent debtor 478
  complaint in bastardy 487
  warrant in bastardy 487
  bond by father of bastard 488
  recognizance in bastardy 490
  order of court in bastardy 491
  petition for citation in bastardy 495
  citation in bastardy 495
  order of court on citation 496
  notice to sheriff of claim of property 517
  entry by judge in trials of right of property 518
  notice to plaintiff 518
  affidavit of non-residence 520
  notice to non-resident 520
  clerk's certificate of mailing 521

FORM—*Continued.*
                       PAGE.
 Of venire in trials of right of property 522
  appeal bond in trials of right of property 524
  judgment in trials of right of property 525
  to contest election 550
  answer 552
  proof of death 568
  petition for letters testamentary 568
  record of appointment of administrator 568
  relinquishment by widow 569
  petition to require executor to give bond 570
  record on examination of bonds 570
    revoking letters on account of fraud 571
      where will is found 572
      by reason of insanity 572
    removing administrator who has removed 573, 574
  petition to require further security 574
  record requiring further security 575
  inventory by executor or administrator 576
  warrant to appraisers 577
  oath of appraisers 577
  bill of appraisement 578
  widow's award 578
      relinquishment 579
  advertisement of sale of personal property 580
  report that assets of estate do not exceed widow's allowance... 580
  record giving widow personal property 581
  adjustment notice 582
  record of allowance of claims on adjustment day 582
           after adjustment day 582
  suggestion of insolvent debtors 583
  notice of petition on insolvent claims 584
  order of court on insolvent claims 584
  petition for leave to sell at private sale 585
  record granting leave to sell at private sale 586
  for naturalization 562, 563, 564
  report of private sale 586
  sale bill at public sale 587
  order of court for distribution in kind 588
  citation to administrator 588
  petition for sale of real estate 589
  cross petition by widow 590
  answer of guardian *ad litem* 591
    to petition to sell land 592
  decree for sale of real estate by administrator 593
  warrant to commissioners 595
  oath of commissioners 595

FORM—Continued.
  Of report of commissioners... 596
    decree approving report.. 596
    notice of sale of real estate... 597
    report of sale of real estate... 597
    exceptions to report... 598
    order overruling exceptions... 598
      sustaining exceptions... 599
    administrator's deed... 599
    bill for account between co-executors.. 600
    refunding bond... 601
    notice of final settlement.. 602
    order of court making final distribution.. 602
    appeal bond by an administrator.. 603
    record of the presentation for probate of the will of a non-resid't.. 604
    notice of the issue of a *dedimus*... 604
    affidavit of witnesses for probate of will... 605
    dedimus to prove will.. 605
    renunciation of widow, etc., of rights given by will............................. 605
    clerk's entry of probate of will... 606
      where bond is waived.. 607
    refusal to accept by person named as executor..................................... 607
    petition for letters with will annexed.. 607
    bond of executor and administrator with will annexed............................ 608
    oath of same.. 609
    letters testamentary... 609
    proof of signature of subscribing witness.. 610
    clerk's entry appointing administrator to collect................................. 610
    bond of administrator to collect... 610
    oath of administrator to collect... 611
    letters to administrator to collect... 611
      de bonis non... 611
    clerk's entry of order requiring surviving partner to give bond.. 612
      directing sale of personal property.. 613
    petition of administrator for citation to surviving partner...... 613
    order declaring estate insolvent... 614
    notice of final settlement...602, 615
    entry by clerk of circuit court in probate of will................................ 615

FRAUD,
  In procuring letters—revocation.. 20
    exhibiting account... 33, 348
  Of administrators, estate not liable.. 50
  Administrator to recover goods sold in...65, 66
  Property transferred in.. 66
  May be shown to defeat recovery on notes... 79
  Equity will protect against.. 107

FRAUD—*Continued.*

	PAGE.
Proof of, required	129
Will vitiate will	182, 193
In the appointment of guardian	243, 244
Infants liable for	277, 278, 280
As to securities	292, 348
Combination among bidders, is	318
Sale made in fraud of infant	319
Must be proven	481
In elections	542
assignments	460

FRAUDULENT CONVEYANCES,

Of deceased persons, how set aside	168
Wills, etc., when	201, 202
May be avoided at law	361

FUNERAL EXPENSES,

Payment of, entitles one to letters	13
Chargeable to widow, when	63
Widow's award subject to	89, 92, 94
Charge against estate	100
Implied promise to pay	100
Need not be probated	101
Headstone may be considered such	101
Contracts with minor for, binding	277

G.

GARNISHEE,

When administrator liable as	50
Assignee not liable	449

GENERAL ISSUE,

Plea of, admits capacity	73

GESTATION,

Period of	502

GROWING CROPS,

To be inventoried and appraised	79
May be sold	79
gathered	79
When they pass to devisee	80

GUARDIANS,

Appointment of, given to county courts	4
Courts always open for appointment of	4
Where administrator is	41, 51, 52, 286, 293, 349
May be compelled to settle	283
Claims against deceased—limitations	109
Of heirs made parties to petition to sell	155

INDEX. 659

GUARDIANS—*Continued.*
    PAGE.
Failure to make parties, error... 157
Appearance of, does not confer jurisdiction over wards.............. 163
What is 213
Various kinds of... 214
Who are by nature... 214
By nature not entitled to ward's property..................................... 214
        powers of..214, 215, 251, 337
        must support child, when............................215, 217, 287, 346
In chancery.. 216
        origin of.. 216
May file bill against executors... 217
As trustees for ward..217, 248
Liabilities of... 263
By statute—definition... 218
Testamentary, how constituted.. 218
        powers of...219, 286
        to be commissioned..219, 235
        bond of...219, 225, 235
        duties of.. 219
        must qualify... 219
        one of two may act...220, 235
        right to custody of ward..220, 337
Appointment of, by county court.. 220
May be ordered to pay fees of guardian *ad litem*........................ 224
Appointment of..228, 229
Who may be appointed..230, 233
Duty of, to surrender to successor papers, moneys, etc., of ward... 231
Of estate to one, custody to another....................................234, 263
A stranger may be appointed... 234
No power to act until bond be given....................................273, 312
Derive power from appointment... 238
When appointment void... 238
Order of court conclusive upon.. 238
Bonds, suits on 239
        can be maintained after his removal only............................ 239
        where name of ward incorrectly given................................... 240
Failing to give new bond, may be removed.................................. 240
Trustee in equity for ward... 248
Bound to manage estate of ward in person........................248, 249
Should render account........................248, 249, 253, 283, 284
If beneficial, his acts will be sustained.. 249
Petition court in his own name.. 249
May redeem estate from mortgage.......................................249, 261
Cannot act by attorney.. 249
        release a debt due ward..249, 261
Undertakes to be vigilant..249, 251

GUARDIANS—*Continued.*   PAGE.
  Powers local..244, 249, 252, 286, 337
  May control ward's associations....................................... 249
      accept deed for ward... 250
      appear for him in suits 250
      maintain action for seduction................................. 250
      lease ward's real estate....................................... 251
  In socage, has custody of lands....................................... 251
      no such relation in Illinois................................... 251
  Not liable on implied covenants....................................... 251
  To institute proceedings for assignment of dower...................... 251
  May change residence of ward....................................244, 252
  Shall manage estate frugally.. 252
      apply income to support of ward............................... 252
      demand and sue for estate................................253, 258, 261
  May take notes in his own name...................................253, 258
      sue in his own name... 253
      transfer promissory notes................................253, 254, 258
      sell personal estate of ward...............................253, 254
  Acts of, may be repudiated by ward...............................253, 281
  Estate of, answerable to ward for waste............................... 254
  Duty to loan funds of ward.. 254
  To pay interest, when...254, 255, 257
  Responsible for loans made without security......................254, 255
  Allowed reasonable time to make loans................................ 255
  When chargeable with compound interest............................... 256
      robbed... 256
  May retain sufficient money on hand for current expenses............. 256
  Duty to educate ward.. 256
      apply no more than income to education of ward................ 257
  Depositing money in his own name...................................... 257
  Not responsible for acts of co-guardian............................... 257
  Payment by, to ward... 257
  Investments in his own name... 258
  Assuming to act as...258, 337
  Bankruptcy of..239, 258
  Negligence of..258, 259
  Waste by.. 258
  Cannot bind ward by his contract....................258, 281, 315, 329
  Rights of, against estate of ward................................258, 259
  Liable for costs, when.. 259
  Insure ward's property.. 262
  Not allowed to make gain from ward.................................... 264
  May pay mortgage on ward's land....................................... 261
  Courts presume against, when.. 264
  Admissions by, do not bind ward....................................... 265
  To receive ward's money..267, 268

GUARDIANS—*Continued.*
Not prejudiced by lapse of time... 268
　liable on contract of ward.. 268
Action against, by ward—account..'... 269
Settlement with ward..270, 272
Advances by, not a charge on ward's land.. 270
Election by ward in settlement with... 272
Purchase of ward's real estate by... 272
Accounts to be verified by affidavit..283, 284
Fees of...283, 285, 286, 289, 290
May submit proof to support account... 284
Competency of, as witness.. 284
When may remove ward to another state................285, 334, 335, 345
Allowed for adverse claim.. 286
Compromise of claim by... 281
Interest adverse to ward... 281
Entitled to interest, when... 286
Not being father, to be allowed for board........................286, 289, 346
Should be allowed for necessary disbursements of ward's money
　　　　　　　　　　　　　　　　　　　　　　　　　[without consent, 286
Not allowed to break in upon principal..................................286, 287
Should keep wards employed 287
May furnish ward with articles suitable to condition.................... 288
Cannot retract a gratuity to ward... 289
Advancements by.. 289
Attorney's fees paid by... 289
Not allowed to charge costs of controversy caused by his neglect, 289
Who is step-father, not entitled to pay for maintaining wards, 289, 290
Not entitled to fees where he uses fund................................289, 290
Commissions of..283, 285, 286, 289, 290, 346
　　　not forfeited by failure to account.. 290
Accounts of, may be opened...290, 291
Form of account of..292, 293
Sale of real estate by... 298
Deed by.. 306
Shall account for money received on sale of real estate............. 308
Non resident, sales by.. 308
Proceedings by, for sale of ward's lands not adverse to him....... 309
Power of, to sell land a naked power... 310
No power to sell ward's real estate without order................310, 311
Must apply for sale, on order of court.. 310
Where to apply for sale of real estate...................................310, 312
May bind himself, but not ward, by covenants....................315, 329
Power to make deed, ceases after once having been exercised..... 315
Married woman who is, may convey alone... 316
Irregularity by, does not vitiate sale... 317
Petition by one of two.. 318

GUARDIANS—*Continued.*

	PAGE
May mortgage ward's land	323
Non-resident, powers in Illinois	332
sale of land by	332
One holding trust relation to infant, required to account	337
Resignation of	339
Removal of	342
Appointment of successor	344
Causes for removal of	345, 346
Insolvency of	346
When removed to turn over assets	346
No suit can be maintained against, until removal	349
Death of, terminates trust	350
Citation to, necessary to charge on bond	350
Cannot purchase at his own sale	359
May contract with ward after the relation ceases	368
Answer by—form	591
Public, to be appointed by governor	226

GUARDIAN AD LITEM,

In sales of land to pay debts	162
To appear and answer for minors	162, 220
Failure to appoint, error	162, 220, 280
Answer of	162
form	591
cannot give jurisdiction	162, 163
Appointment of, something more than a form	163, 220
Must appear and defend	163, 221
Answer by, may be set aside	217
Definition of	220
Appointment of	220
Power of, confined to the suit	220
None appointed in criminal cases	220
Not liable for costs	220
When appointed	220, 221
Order appointing, must name infants	221
Must be appointed for infants in petition to sell land	221, 222
None to be appointed in applications to sell real estate	222
Can waive no rights of infant	222, 265
Must submit to court questions involving rights of infant	222
Cannot withdraw plea	222
Court to require answer from	222
Must be notified of taking of evidence	223
Court may appoint without motion	223, 250
Appointment presumed	223
of clerk of court as	224
master in chancery as	224
Need not be appointed for female over eighteen	224

GUARDIAN AD LITEM—*Continued.*
    Appointment of, as evidence of infancy.. 224
    May employ counsel.. 224
    Fees of.. 224
    To be reimbursed for outlays... 224
    In suits for debt of ancestor.. 274
        proceedings to sell infant's real estate... 309
        suits against lunatics.. 414

GUARDIAN AND WARD,
    No suit at law can be maintained between... 349
    May contract after relation ceases.. 368
        See "Guardian," "Infant."

H.

HANDWRITING,
    To be proven... 105
    Of attesting witness, when proven... 188

HEIRS,
    Administrator cannot bind.. 51
    To have notice of issue of execution... 68
    Title to land vests in, on death of owner.. 69
    Policy payable to... 71
    Cannot be called on to account for rents.. 74
    May have action against widow for waste.. 74
        compel redemption of lands...75, 148
        Maintain suit on desperate claims... 77
    Contract for purchase of land descends to.. 99
    May not object to partnership debts... 99
    Suits against, where there is no administration.................................. 106
    May defend against claims.. 107
    Judgment in probate, not conclusive on..........................113, 171, 275
    Must have notice of final settlement................................123, 149, 150
    Entitled to distribution of surplus money.....................124, 125, 144
    Not bound by allowance of claim.. 131
    When they may sue a stranger... 133
        be required to refund.. 135
    May receive from ancestor in full.. 142
    Cannot recover estate of ancestor.. 142
    Advancements to... 143
        by ancestor charged... 143
    Distribution to, may be delayed... 144
    At law, definition.. 146
        effect of a devise to... 146
    Wife not included in devise to... 146
    Dowress cannot be.. 146
    Heirs of heirs included in.. 147
    Interest in lands not defeated by naked trust..................................... 149

HEIRS—*Continued.*
    Owing estate amount of distributive share............................... 149
    Not affected by order of distribution of which they have no notice... 149
    Made parties to petition to sell... 155
    What they may show in defense.. 169
    Concluded by judgment on claim, when.............................. 171
    Should contest in name of administrator............................... 171
    No privity between, and administrator................................. 171
    May contest will... 192
    Take title to real estate subject to debts of ancestor............153, 202
    Of infant may disaffirm acts... 266
    Liability of, for debt of ancestor...........................273, 274, 275
    Not liable for debts of ancestor when personal estate was sufficient.. 275
    Decree against, must be joint... 276
    Extent of liability for debt of ancestor................................. 276
    Disability no defense, when... 276
    By adoption, rights of..375, 376

HOMESTEAD,
    When it may be sold..165, 166
    Real estate being, will explain delay.................................. 172
    Right of infant to... 269
    Abandonment of, by widow does not prejudice rights of child...... 270
    Minors cannot abandon... 269, 270
    Sale of infants', will be set aside....................................... 270
    Report assigning — form 296
    Decree approving assignment of—form............................... 296

HOSPITAL FOR THE INSANE,
    Application to... 398
    Who not admitted to... 400
    Temporary commitment to.. 400
    Discharge from 402
    County 403

HUSBAND,
    Right of, to administer..9, 13
    When not to be appointed administrator.............................. 11
    If suitable, to be appointed conservator............................... 408

HUSBAND AND WIFE,
    Rights of, in each other's estate..................................147, 148
    Neither can disinherit the other..................................147, 148
    Effect of renunciation by..147, 148

HYPOCHONDRIA,
    Not insanity... 410

I.

IDIOT,
- Conservator to be appointed for 381
- Contracts of, void 385
-           voidable 385
- Swindling an 385
- Restoration to reason 389
- Not allowed in hospital for insane 400

ILLEGITIMATE CHILDREN,
- Not considered next of kin 12
- included in the term children 142
- Heirs to mother and maternal ancestor 144
- May transmit to heirs 145
- Dying without issue, estate vests in husband or wife 145
- Legitimatized 145
- Rights of, at common law 146
-           under laws of Illinois 146
-                   See "Bastard," "Bastardy."

IMPRISONMENT,
- Courts always open to hear applications for discharge from 4
- County court may punish by 6
- Of executor or administrator on failure to pay 132
- Discharge from 132
- What necessary before 132
- Order of, acts only upon the person of administrator 132, 133
- Duration of 133
- Of witness on failure to attend court 186
- Appeal from order of 209
- Cannot be inflicted on a child only guilty of vagrancy 278
- Release of debtor from 463, 484
- For debt, abolished 481
-           does not satisfy debt 481
- Of father of bastard 493, 494, 497, 499

INFANT,
- Estate of deceased, may be distributed 142
- Suits by, how prosecuted 217, 218
- Wards of court 218, 223, 279
- May file bill against guardian 218
- Heirs, must be brought in by notice, or they will not be bound by [decree 220, 221
- Can only appear and defend a suit by guardian 221, 267
- Judgment by default against, erroneous 222, 264
- Jurisdiction over, not lost for want of answer 223
- Female, of age at eighteen 224, 266
- Guardian *ad litem* may employ counsel for 224
- Appointment of guardian for 229

INFANT—*Continued.*

	PAGE.
Custody of, when given to mother	229, 230
Over fourteen, may nominate guardian	230, 231, 232
Residence must be in county	230, 232
Interest and wishes of, to be consulted	230
Domicile of	244, 261
May prosecute suit by next friend	225, 250
To recover for services in name of parent or guardian	250
Seduction of, action by whom	250, 269
Residence of, may be changed by guardian	252, 286
May repudiate change of property	253
Money of, to be loaned	254
To be educated by guardian	256, 257, 286
Care of estate of	256
Cannot consent to improper use of money	257, 348
Not liable for contract of guardian	258
Unable to take care of himself	264
Owes obedience to guardian	264
Negligence not imputed to	265, 279, 282
Cannot bring advancement into hotchpot	265
Acts of, voidable only	265, 266
may be affirmed or disaffirmed	265
Conveyances by, voidable	265
How, may avoid statute of limitations	266
Heirs of, may disaffirm acts	266, 282
Deed of, how ratified	266
Not bound by bond	266
Liable for necessaries	266
May take title by deed	266
Release by, void	267
Husband of female, no power to bind	267
Decree against, absolute	267
Grantees of, protected	267
May prosecute writ of error by next friend	267
Rights of, cannot be waived by next friend or attorney	267
May maintain trover by next friend	267
Not entitled to receive money	267
Evidence against in *scire facias*	268
May maintain action for slander	268
Only can rely on plea of infancy	268
Action by, for assault and battery	268
Contracts by	265, 266, 276, 277
Emancipation of	268
Action by, against third parties dealing with guardian	269
Female cannot consent to carnal intercourse	269
abortion	269
Has no action against guardian until after settlement	269

INFANT—*Continued.*

	PAGE.
Remedy against guardian by action of account	269
Homestead rights of	269, 270
Settlement of, with guardian looked upon with suspicion	270
Advances by guardian not a charge on land of	270
Not estopped	270, 274, 279, 316
Bill to enforce estoppel, not allowed	274
When estopped in equity	272, 274, 318
May elect to receive profits, or charge interest	272
Not bound by arbitration of guardian	272
Not bound by purchase by guardian	272
Must place guardian in *statu quo* to avoid a contract with him	272
Male, over seventeen, and female, over fourteen, may contract marriage,	273
Liability for debt of ancestor	273, 274
No lien lies against	276
May recover against an employer	276
One deals with, at his peril	276
Note of infant for necessaries	277
Is liable for his torts	277, 278
Is liable for his fraud	280
Not liable for tort of guardian	278
Under ten, not guilty of crime	278
Over fourteen, may be guilty of rape	278
Destitute of parental care, no cause for imprisonment	278
On death of guardian, may compel settlement	286
Claims against, how verified	287, 288
Expenses of, to be kept within income	288
Principal of estate of, when encroached upon	287, 288
What are necessaries for	289
Board of	290, 346
Gratuity to, from guardian	290
Attorney's fees for	282, 290, 295
Step-father not obliged to support	290
May open account of guardian	291, 292
Receipt by, when not conclusive	292, 355
Receiving money from guardian after maturity—presumption	292
To refund, when	295
Sale of real estate of	298
Proceedings for sale of real estate not adverse	309
Not concluded by report of sale by guardian	315
When title of, will inure to purchaser	316
May avoid conveyance by guardian to one in his interest	316
When estopped from claiming land	318
Real estate of, subject to dower	318
May confirm void sale	319
May file original bill to impeach a decree	319

INDEX.

INFANT—*Continued.*   PAGE.
    Remedy of, in chancery 348
    Being mother of a bastard 499
    May be held liable in bastardy 507
    Injunction, when county courts may grant 138

INSANE,
    Pauper 402
    Non-resident 402
    Restoration of 402, 405

INSANITY,
    Of widow, court will choose property 141
    Proceedings 394, 403, 407
    Committal in 399
    Superintendent to report 405
    Costs in 400
    Evidence of 408
    Test of 409, 418
    Presumption of law against 409, 418
    In criminal prosecutions 419, 420, 42
    No defense in actions for torts 421, 422

INSOLVENT DEBTORS,
    Courts always open to hear application for discharge of 4
    Administrator being 133
    Wholly under jurisdiction of county court 432
    Proceedings for discharge of 463
    How released 463, 471
    Shall give notice 463
    Petition by, for discharge 464
    To be taken before the court 464
    Issue on petition of 465
    Schedule of 466
    Bond by 468, 483
    Assignment by 469
    Discharge of 471, 475
        effect of 475
    Appeal by 477, 479, 482, 483
    Not required to appear in person 482, 483

INSOLVENT ESTATES,
    When assets do not exceed widow's allowance 63
    To be entered of record 115

INSTRUCTIONS OF COURT,
    In bastardy proceedings 501, 502

INTEREST,
    When administrator liable for 52, 53
    Probate of, on claims not due 105

INDEX. 669

INTEREST—*Continued.*
PAGE.
On probated claim 107, 111, 112
To administrator...... 125
Executor to pay..... 125
When may be charged in account............... 127
  administrator must pay.. 130
Ten per cent. to be charged, when............ 130
On ward's money, when guardian to pay................ ....254, 256, 257
  to be paid annually... 256
Compound, when to be charged guardian................................... 256
To keep trust funds separate........ 256
When applied to ward's education................................. 257
  charged to guardian... 261, 284
On money in guardian's hands... 286
To guardian, when payable... 287
When chargeable to conservators.. 413

INTESTACY,
Presumed 139

INTESTATE ESTATE,
Of testator to be administered by executor............................... 47
Property devised to "heirs at law".. 146
How distributed...................:... 141

INVENTORY,
Of real and personal property... 59
When to be filed 59
When notes and accounts described... 59
Not to include property out of the state..................................... 60
Co-partnership assets... 60
Additonal 60
  to be filed after discharge... 60
Protection to executor or administrator...................................... 60
As evidence... 61, 62
All property should be inventoried... 61
Without, two years statute does not run........................... 61, 102, 109
Not conclusive... 62
Growing crops.. 79
To be made by surviving partner.. 83
Of guardian, when filed.. 245, 246
  what to contain.. 245
  form of.. 245, 246
  order approving.. 246
  should embrace debt due from guardian........................ 247
 conservator 383
Form of conservator's... 384
Of assignee... 430
  want of, not to affect assignment.................................. 312

42

INVENTORY—*Continued.*
    Of assignee, additional 312
               form of 438
               administrator—form 476
    Investment of ward's funds 262

J.

JUDGE OF THE COUNTY COURT,
    To examine bonds at January and July terms 31
        cause record to be made 31
    Interested—change of venue 113, 114
    A witness to will 187
    Discretion of, in appointments 242, 243
    Verbal directions of 45, 259
    Order of, on petition in insanity 395
    No authority to discharge debtor 482
    To order citation in bastardy 495, 497
    Notice to, of claim to property 517
    To entertain jurisdiction of claims to property levied upon ... 517, 526

JUDGMENT,
    Void, when against a void administrator 17
    For costs against one fraudulently obtaining letters 20
    In suits upon administrator's bonds 43
    Must be joint and not several 67
    Collection of, not delayed by death of plaintiff 67
    Lien not defeated by death of plaintiff 68
                                defendant 68
    Need not be revived 68
    For value of property removed 78
    On claim, when a nullity 98
    When a claim against an estate 98
    On claim presented after two years 101, 102
    Right to, not barred by settlement of the estate 103
    As evidence in support of claim 105
    From another state 105, 422
    Against administrator in another state 105, 203
    For set-off 105
    Revival of, against administrator 106
    On claim is general 107
          not a lien 111, 114
    Where not a lien, collected as other claims 111
    Allowance of claim is 111, 113
                  no particular form 111
    Revival of, against administrator—form 111
    Against estate, *prima facie* only 113, 171, 275
                equitable lien 113
    Disallowing claim, conclusive 114
    On claims, being general 118

JUDGMENT—*Continued.*
 On claims, conclusive between creditor and administrator......... 171
  not conclusive on heir... 171
   when 171
 Against minors where no guard'n *ad litem* is appointed, erroneous.. 221
 On bastardy bond...494, 500, 508, 509
 In bastardy, when a bar... 500
  trials of right of property......................................523, 525
  contested elections 544, 545
   as evidence.. 545
 Form of, on claim... 582
     See "Decree."

JUDICIAL ACT,
 Of county court 4
 Granting administration is a.................. 16
 Admitting will to probate.. 189
 Confirming sale of real estate is...................................... 317
 Admission to citizenship is... 560

JURISDICTION,
 Court having, acts not void.....................................18, 319
 What gives, to county court................................... ....9, 19
  issue attachment 132
 Of circuit court over claims... 106
 In proceedings to sell land.. 156
 Court having, its adjudications binding...............................157, 176
 Of persons, by summons... 158
 Want of, where parties are not legally notified.......................... 159
 Failure to obtain, decree void.. 159
 Of subject matter and parties, effect of................................... 159
 Court of chancery having, may order sale of lands..................... 169
  having, effect of reversal of decree............................... 176
 Of ward not obtained by service on guardian............................ 221
  infants, not lost for want of answer........................ 223
  county court over minors................................228, 230
   to order sale of ward's land........................... 300
  circuit court in case of non-resident guardians..................... 308
 Court acting within, presumption...... 311
 Must appear in application or order............................... 311
 Sale without, void 311
 In case of defective notice.. 311
  no notice 311
 Application to sell must be made where there is............. 312
 Courts have none to order sale of land in another state................ 312
 Want of, may be shown at any stage..................... 312
 In proceedings to sell ward's land—subject matter..................... 312
  for the adoption of children............................. 371
  appointment of conservator 382
  sale of lunatic's real estate........................... 386

JURISDICTION—*Continued.* PAGE.
    In proceedings in insanity 349, 409
        assignments 429, 432, 435
    Of insolvency proceedings 463, 482
        trials of right of property 521
    In naturalization of foreigners 557

JURY,
    May be demanded on trial of claims 98
        had on appeal from probate of will 187
            contest of will in equity 192
    In cases of lunacy, etc 381, 390
        insanity 397, 417
    Necessary before declaring one insane 403
    In trials of the right of property 522, 527

JUST AND TRUE ACCOUNT,
    To be made by administrator 155

K.

KING OF ENGLAND,
    Power over estates of deceased persons 8
        of, conceded to clergy 8

L.

LACHES,
    Not imputable to an infant 265, 279

LAPSE OF TIME,
    In petition to sell real estate 172
    May be explained 172
    Will not prevent report of sale and confirmation 315

LARCENY,
    Of will 185

LEASE,
    By executor 198
    Of ward's lands, who may make 214, 251, 281
        valid, unless disapproved 251

LEGACIES,
    Payment of, before debts, *devastavit* 32
    May be garnisheed 50
    To deceased, payable to administrator 71
    Payment of, when to be made 133
    To be equalized in case of renunciation 149
    When chargeable on real estate 201
    Not payable under ancillary administration 204

LEGAL REPRESENTATIVES,
    Policy payable to 71
    Meaning of 71

LEGATEES,

	PAGE.
May defend against claims	107
To give bond	133, 134
in case of life estate	134
When they must refund	135
Notice to	135
Refusing to contribute	135
Demand on	135
Action of, against executor	136

LETTERS OF ADMINISTRATION,

Courts always open to grant	4
When revoked, acts done under not void	17
Not void when will discovered	17, 20
Revoked for fraud in obtaining	20
when will produced	20
administrator becomes lunatic	21
fails to give new bond or counter security,	29
To be filed, in case of death of plaintiff	67
When to be produced	73
Claims must be exhibited within two years from date of	117
With the will annexed	191
On nuncupative wills	197
Authentication of	206

LETTERS OF GUARDIANSHIP,

To be issued to testamentary guardian	219, 235
Without, guardian no power	237
When need not issue	238
Steps to procure	240
Form of	240, 241
Create a trust	230

LETTERS TESTAMENTARY,

Courts always open to grant	4
To be revoked, when will set aside	20
When to be produced	73
To issue upon probate of will	191, 192
On nuncupative wills	197
Authentication of	206
Petition for	567

LICENSE,

To marry, how issued	273

LIEN,

Debts of deceased, on property	65
Of judgment, not defeated by death	68
Mechanic's, barred after six months	110

LIEN—*Continued.*

	PAGE.
Judgment on claim, is not	111, 113
equitable	113
Not affected by death	119
Filing of creditor's bill, gives	119
Attorney cannot have, on assets	126
Statute reserves, on real estate	154
May be lost by laches	154
To be adjusted in proceedings to sell	162
Does not lie against infant	271, 276
Of judgment in bastardy	497

LIMITATION,

In appointment of administrator	23
Duty of administrator to urge as defense	34, 107
Two years, as to claims	101
occurring after death, does not run	103
if no inventory is filed, does not run	109
where will is discovered	109
not presumed	109
When it begins to run, it continues	109
When running, commences	109
as to wards	109, 239
Death of debtor does not arrest	109, 110
Part payment arrests	110
When plead, cuts off, etc	110
Need not be specially pleaded	110
Not arrested for filing claim	110
Statute of, in claims by wards	110, 239, 285
Claim twenty-seven years old presumed paid	110
Effect on, of acknowledgment by administrator	111
Bars claim on distributees	135
No statute of, concerning sale of real estate	172
Avoided where real estate is homestead	172
In contest of will	192
settlements by guardians	292
Of bastardy actions	498

LOANS,

By guardians, security	254, 255, 256, 295
conservator	386

LUNACY,

Of administrator, justifies removal	21
Jurisdiction in cases of	381
Proceedings in	382, 394
must be had in court	407

PAGE.

LUNATIC,
 Conservators of.. 381
 Contracts of, void and voidable.................385, 415, 416, 417, 418, 419
 Swindling a 385
 Restoration of.. 389, 402
 Who is a pauper.. 402
 Petition to have declared... 394
 Notice to... 407
 To be allowed luxuries... 412
 Guardian *ad litem* for... 414
 Ejectment may be brought in name of.. 414
 Liability for necessaries... 416
 Not bound on contract of suretyship... 418
 Liable for torts.. 421, 422
 Suits against... 425

M.

MANDAMUS,
 Remedy by, not abridged by statute.. 535

MARRIAGE,
 Of testator—effect on will.. 196
 Males of seventeen may contract... 273
 Females of fourteen may contract.. 273
 Parties to, may be examined under oath...................................... 273
 Of female ward, terminates guardianship................................... 347
  parents of bastard... 146, 498
  mother of bastard no bar to bastardy proceedings................ 501

MARRIED WOMAN,
 May execute will... 182
  be appointed guardian... 233
 Statute of limitations runs against... 266
 Husband of infant, no power to bind... 267
 Who is guardian, may execute deed.. 316

MASTER IN CHANCERY,
 May be appointed guardian *ad litem*... 227

MAYOR OF CITY,
 Contest of election of... 553

MENTAL CAPACITY,
 Necessary to make a will.. 182, 183, 192, 193
  responsibility for crime.. 419, 420, 421

MINOR,
 Appointed administrator, to be removed..................................... 21
 Guardian *ad litem* appointed for... 162
 To appear by guardian 163
 Nothing to be taken against... 164, 280, 282
 Domicile of... 261
    See "Heir," "Infant."

MISTAKE,

	PAGE.
Payment by, recovered back	75, 120
In account of guardian, how rectified	284
may be shown	285
Order dismissing proceeding entered by	317

MONUMENT,

To deceased, not allowed	101, 131

MORTGAGE,

Redemption from, by administrator	34, 48, 72
Administrator cannot, real estate	49
In sales of real estate	161
By executor, when	198
Foreclosure of mortgage in county court	199
strict, not allowed	199, 330
Not in fee	199
Release of, by foreign administrator	204
Guardian may redeem from	249
Of ward's lands by guardian	261, 323, 330
Foreclosure of—form	325
Decree of foreclosure—form	327
Of ward's real estate purely statutory	329
lands of idiots, etc	386
Petition for leave to, lands of idiot, etc	386
See "Foreclosure."	

MORTGAGED LANDS,

Of deceased, duty to redeem	36, 50
To be redeemed out of personal estate	75, 148

MOTHER,

When entitled to custody of child	214, 229, 230
Of bastard, entitled to custody	214
Given custody of child may dispose of by will	220
Entitled to be appointed guardian	233
Of bastard—complaint	486, 487
when to pay costs	491
to have custody of child	498
alone may enter complaint	499
may compromise	499, 507
being infant	499
non-resident	499
marrying, no bar	501
not entitled to change of venue	501
next friend of	501
character may be shown	503

N.

NATURALIZATION OF FOREIGNERS,
Who are subjects of this law..554, 557, 559
Process of..554, 555
Laws for... 555
Power to pass laws for.. 557
Jurisdiction in... 557
Power judicial.. 560
Right of a woman to... 562

NECESSARIES,
When father liable for...215, 287
              infant liable for.. 266
What are, for an infant... 289
Guardian has the right to judge what are................................ 289
For lunatic...416, 419

NEGLIGENCE,
Of guardian...258, 259, 260
Cannot be imputed to a young child....................................... 265
Controversy caused by neglect of guardian not chargeable to ward.. 290

NEXT FRIEND,
Infant may sue by...225, 250
Bond for costs by.. 226

NEXT OF KIN,
Right of, to administer.. 9
Who are...10, 141
Renunciation of right of, to administer................................... 12
Why administration granted to... 12
Preference over, of residuary legatee...................................... 12
Illegitimates not considered.. 12
May plead statute of limitations against administrator's claim..... 114
To take estate by descent.. 140

NON-RESIDENT,
Not to be appointed administrator, and why.......................9, 12
Estates of, where to be administered....................................... 18
On being appointed administrator, to be removed.................. 21
Conservator—suits by... 391
              sales of land by.. 392
Lunatic... 402

NON-RESIDENT GUARDIAN,
Sale of real estate by... 308
To make deeds.. 309
Power in Illinois.. 332
Transfer of estate by..332, 337
Proceedings by, to transfer.. 333
Evidence of appointment of...334, 337

678 INDEX.

NOTICE,

	PAGE.
To be given to administrators about to remove	21
before execution	68
In case of compounding claims	77
sale of personal property	78
Of adjustment of claims	97
Judgment on claim, without, a nullity	98
To administrator of filing of claims	104
Must be given of final settlement	123, 129, 149
To owners of unclaimed estate	136
By publication, in case of sale of real estate	159, 160, 313
Form and contents of	160
When sufficient	160, 314
Decree showing	160
Of sale of real estate, improper	175
To heirs of nuncupative will	197
infants essential to bind them by decree	221
Defective, will not bind infants	222
To relations of minor in appointment of guardian	229, 235
Possession is, of what	266
Of application to sell infant's real estate	300, 313
guardian's sale of real estate—form	304
Defective, jurisdiction saved	311
To guardian of petition to remove	342
Must be given guardian, before removal	346
Of trusts	362, 363
To parents of child to be adopted	372
Of application to sell real estate of lunatic	387
for removal of conservator	390
petition by non-resident conservator	391
assignment for benefit of creditors	430, 439
exceptions	443
application for discharge of debtor	463
claim of property	517, 518, 526
By publication	519, 520
To be mailed to plaintiff	520
Of adjustment—form	581
petition on insolvent claims—form	584
sale of real estate—form	597
final settlement—form	602
issue of commission—form	604

NUNCUPATIVE WILLS,

Good, for what	196, 197
How made	196, 197
proven	197
To be recorded	197

INDEX. 679

NUNCUPATIVE WILLS—*Continued.*
 Letters on, when to issue.. 197
 Notice to heirs.. 197
 Evidence must show compliance with statute.....................197, 198
 At common law... 197
 Conveys personal property only..196, 198

O.

OATH,
 Of administrator... 15
  executor... 15
 To be administered by clerk.. 15
 Of public administrator.. 18
  appraisers...61, 577
  executor or administrator to bill of sale.......................80, 587
  claimant to claims presented.. 105
  commissioners—form.. 596

ORDER OF COURT,
 To be obtained before encroaching upon principal of ward........ 288
 Approving account of guardian as evidence.....................291, 305
 Approving sale of real estate by guardian................................ 306
 For sale of ward's real estate must be strictly complied with..... 310
 Not having jurisdiction, void.. 310
 Are final against minors, subject to writs of error.................... 319
 Confirming sale under mortgage... 329
 Accepting guardian's resignation.. 340
 Removing guardian.. 344
  should state cause... 347
 Transferring assets to account of guardian not necessary........... 350
 Removing conservator... 391
 On petition in insanity.. 395
 Discharging debtor from arrest.. 465
 In bastardy.. 491
  trials of right of property.. 525
 Appointing administrator—form... 568
 On examination of bonds—form.. 570
 Revoking letters for fraud—form... 571
  where will is found—form.. 572
  administrator is insane—form................................ 572
  removes — form..........573, 574
 Requiring further security — form... 575
 Giving to widow personal property—form.............................. 581
 Allowing claims at adjustment term—form............................. 582
  after the adjustment term—form........................ 582
 On insolvent claims—form... 584
 Granting leave to sell at private sale—form............................. 586
 Directing distribution in kind—form.. 588

ORDER OF COURT—*Continued.*

    Overruling exceptions and approving sale—form...... 598
    Sustaining exceptions—form 599
    Making final distribution...... 602
    Upon presentation of will of non-resident...... 604

ORDER OF DISTRIBUTION,

    After, statute of limitations runs...... 42
    Necessary, to make garnishment possible...... 50
               entitle heirs to sue a stranger...... 133
    Conclusive on distributees...... 126, 150
               guardian 238
    Of assignee's estate...... 431, 443

ORPHAN,

    Defined 233

P.

PARENTS,

    Surviving, to take two shares...... 140
               of only child, takes the whole estate...... 142
    Natural guardian of child...... 214
    Right of, to custody of child...... 214
    Misconduct of 214
    Right of, to control child's estate...... 214
    Obligation of, to support child...... 215
    Separation of, custody of children...... 215
    Own the clothing of child...... 216
    Residing apart, court may give custody of children to another..229, 230
    May maintain action for seduction...... 250
               release homestead right of child...... 269
    Consent to marriage of child 273
    Of child to be adopted...... 371
    Adopted, rights as to child...... 376
    Natural, lose right to control adopted child...... 377
    Of bastard marrying...... 498
                      See "Husband and Wife."

PARTIES,

    To petition to sell land by administrator...... 155, 157
    Unknown 155
    Must be before the court...... 161
    To petition, to sell land by guardian...... 309, 310

PARTITION SUITS,

    In, a decree may be made to pay debts...... 162

PARTNERSHIP,

    Administrator of deceased partner may not continue business of.. 48
    Interest in, how inventoried...... 60
    Terminated by death of partner...... 81

PARTNERSHIP—*Continued.*
 Continuance of, beyond death.. 81
      must be authorized in will.............................. 82
 Articles of, may provide for continuance................................ 82
 Assets of 82
 Statutory 83
 Proceedings on dissolution... 83
 Effects of, to be first applied to pay joint debts..................... 85
 Account of, as at time of death.. 85
 When to be settled.. 85
 Real estate of 87
 Debts may be probated, when 99
  subject to individual debts.. 99
  what shown before allowance.. 99
  to allowance of, heirs may not object 99
  preferred to interest on individual debts........................ 99
  joint and several 100
  allowance of, evidence of exhaustion of partnership assets.. 100
 Effects, assignment of 445, 460
 Insanity of a partner.. 426

PAUPERS,
 Lunatic, who is 402
 Right of, to vote...540, 541

PAYMENT,
 To acting administrator 75
 Of claims to be made in order of classification 117
  what law governs... 118
  before allowance... 119
 For land sold to pay debts 171, 172
 Of money in bastardy 494

PENALTY,
 For not filing bill for probate... 45
  removing property of estate... 77
  failing to set off award... 89
 Recoverable against an estate 101
 For selling land irregularly.. 173
  withholding will.. 185
  changing will... 185
  issuing marriage license to minor 273
  receiving person to insane hospital illegally..................... 403
  taking false oath... 480
  being father of bastard..491, 500

PERJURY,
 In naturalization proceedings.. 561

682 INDEX.

	PAGE.
PERMANENT ABODE,	
What is	539
PERPETUITY,	
Not permitted	184
PERSONAL ESTATE,	
Of intestate, vests in administrator	48, 70, 73
To be inventoried	59
appraised	61
Primarily liable for debts	65, 75, 154
Will may relieve, and charge other	65
Administrator to collect	65
Transferred in fraud	66
What is	70
Legacy is	.
Life insurance, when	71
Certificate of sale is not	71
Mesne profits, when	71
Nursery stock is not	71
Money due from guardian of deceased	71
for causing death of deceased	72
Claim occupied by deceased, not	72
Situated in another state	72
Foreign debts	72
Rails, when	72
Liable for payment of mortgages	75
Not to be removed from state	77
Sale of	78
Growing crops	79
Liable for payment of taxes	101
Must pass through the hands of an administrator	142
Advanced to heir	143
Natural and primary fund for payment of debts	148
Domicile of	150
Averment in petition, in relation to	156
In cases of ancillary administration	170
Of ward under control of guardian	253
may be sold by guardian	253
not be changed to realty.	253
ancestors must be insufficient or heirs cannot be charged	275
PETITION,	
When security desires to be released	28, 576
conceives himself in danger	29
For sale of real estate by administrator.	155
appointment of guardian	229
sale of ward's land	299
by one of two guardians.	318

PAGE.

PETITION—*Continued.*
    For leave to mortgage ward's land.. 323
        foreclosure of mortgage 325
        removal of ward's property... 335
        resignation of guardian.. 339
        removal of guardian.. 342
        adoption of children.. 371
        appointment of conservator... 382
        leave to mortgage lunatic's real estate.................................... 386
                sell lunatic's real estate............ 387
    By lunatic, etc., for removal of conservator................................... 389
    To have person declared lunatic.................. 394
    By insolvent debtor for discharge.. 464
    On insolvent claims.. 583
    For leave to sell at private sale.. 585
        letters testamentary.. 567
    To require better bond...570, 574
        executor to give bond.. 570
    For sale of real estate... 586
    Cross, by widow... 590

PETITION FOR LEAVE TO SELL REAL ESTATE,
    To be filed by executor or administrator, when.............................. 155
    Parties to 155
    Contents of.. 155
    Form 589
    Verified by affidavit... 156
    Must contain proper averments... 156
    Filing of, gives jurisdiction... 156
    Averments in relation to debts... 157
    Description of land.................................... 158
    To be docketed... 161
    May be continued.. 162
    In partition suits... 162
    Hearing of.. 164
    Court no power to interpret will in......................... 167
    Power of court under.. ... 167
    Not a chancery proceeding.. 167
    Is a proceeding *in rem* 167
    No power to remove incumbrances... 168
    By guardian..300, 310
        averments in.. 310

PHYSICIAN'S BILL,
    For *post mortem* examination.. 109
        last illness, claim of third class.. 117

PLAT,
    Of land to be made... 166

INDEX.

PLEADING,   PAGE.
   In suits on administrators' bonds..................................33, 38
   Statute of limitation to be, specially................................. 109
   Plene administravit, burden of proof................................. 112
                 when not good plea............................... 113
   Claim barred by statute may be plead................................ 113
   General issue admits capacity... 207
   Character in which plaintiff sues, must be raised by special plea.. 207
   Rules of, in cases where foreign administrator sues............... 207
   Of infancy, not dilatory.. 268
   In suit against heir... 274
          in equity.. 292
   Declaration on guardian's bond, must show appointment of [successor, 350
   Averments in suits on guardian's bond............................... 350
   In bastardy proceedings... 499
        trials of right of property.. 522
        contested elections.......................................335, 336, 337

PLENE ADMINISTRAVIT,
   In plea of, burden of proof.. 112
   When not a good plea... 113

POLICY,
   Of life insurance, personal estate..................................... 71

POLL LISTS,
   As evidence in contested elections.................................... 542

POLL TAX,
   Payment of, does not confer the right to vote....................... 539

POSTHUMOUS CHILDREN,
   Rights of, as heirs... 146
   Title vests in... 146
   Decree against, void...146, 147
   Not bound..149, 158

PRACTICE,
   In suits by administrator.. 74
       settlement of partnerships.. 85
       setting off widow's award.. 92
   On trial of claims..104, 111, 112
             change of venue.. 113
             in favor of administrator................................... 114
   In proceedings to sell land of decedent.............................. 161
             contest will.. 193
             sell land of ward.. 302
               lunatic... 387
       bastardy proceedings........498, 499, 500, 501, 502, 503, 504, 505, 506
       trials of right of property.....................522, 526, 527, 528, 529, 530
       contested elections.............535, 536, 537, 538, 539, 540, 541, 542, 543

	PAGE.
PREFERRED CLAIMS,	
Expenses of caring for estate of non-resident	19
Among claimants of same class	119
Debts due school fund	118
Money in the hands of guardian	118
Do not embrace all trusts	118, 119
Judgment creditor, without lien, not	119
having execution, is	119
PREFERENCE,	
In granting letters	13
PRESUMPTION,	
Of life cases, when	14
When judgment on claim is general	109
Of payment not destroyed by act of administrator	111
After final settlement	128
Of intestacy	139
As to children born in wedlock	142
In relation to advancements	143
Of law in collateral proceedings	161
May be rebutted	161
Of the courts in proceedings to sell	167
appointment of guardian *ad litem*	223
That special bond was given	238
Against guardian	264
Of acceptance of deed by infant	266
emancipation of infant	268
As to settlements between guardian and ward	270
guardian's accounts	292
When ward after maturity receives money from guardian	292
Where court has jurisdiction	311
In proceedings to sell ward's real estate	312
Of sanity	409, 410, 411, 418, 419, 420, 423
insanity	411, 425
law as to electors	539
PRIVATE SALES,	
Of personal property	78
PRIVITY OF CONTRACT,	
None exists between administr'r *de bonis non* and predecessor	23, 75
and heirs	171
foreign administrator	206
PROBATE,	
Jurisdiction, given to county courts	3
Matters, what are	4
cognizable at law terms	4
Terms of county courts	4
Equity jurisdiction in	5

PROBATE—*Continued.*
 Court of equity will not admit will to... 5
 Of will, testator cannot waive.. 186
  in circuit court, when.. 187
  what evidence admissible.. 188
  executed out of the state... 194
 Bond not avoided for slight defects... 240

PROBATE COURTS,
 Peculiar office to admit claims 5
 Constituted 7
 When acts are ministerial...16, 7
 No power to render a money judgment..................................... 135
 Declared legal.. 231
       See "County Court."

PROBATE OF WILL,
 On, letters to be revoked.. 20
 Place of.. 185
 Witnesses to attend... 186
 Cannot be waived in will.. 186
 Appeals from... 190
       See "Wills."

PROMISSORY NOTE,
 May be assigned by administrator.. 53
 Executed as a gift.. 108
 Of infant, voidable... 277

PROOF OF DEATH,
 To be made before letters are granted.............................9, 13, 14
 If untrue, grant of letters void... 14
 From reputation.. 14
 Made upon information... 14
 Passing upon, a judicial act.. 16
 Form of... 568

PUBLIC ADMINISTRATOR,
 When administration shall be granted to...................................... 9
  application must be made... 13
 Only when no relative or creditor.. 13
 Appointed by the Governor.. 18
 Oath of... 18
 When he may take administration... 18
 Bond of.. 18
 What should appear before estate is committed to................... 18
 Duties of.. 18
 Administers by virtue of letters.. 19
 To give notice of unclaimed estate... 136
  pay into the treasury of county.. 137

PUBLIC GUARDIAN,

	PAGE.
To be appointed by the Governor	226
take oath	226
give bond	227
Duties of	227

PUBLIC POLICY,

Requires stability in all sales	319, 320

PUBLICATION,
See "Notice."

PURCHASER,

From administrator at private sale in good faith	79
At administrator's sale, not prejudiced by reversal of decree	176
only bound to know the court had juris-[diction,	176
Conveyance may be made to another	177
Where he refuses to consummate	177
From executor with power	179
At guardian's sale, must tender payment	314
not bound to see to application of proceeds of..	318
Not bound to look beyond decree	319
Of reversion, must pay full price	365

Q.

QUO WARRANTO,

Remedy of, not abridged by statute	535, 549

R.

REAL ESTATE,

Administrator's power over	49
may take on debts	52
To be inventoried	59
Certificate of sale is	71
Nursery stock	71
Partly paid for, goes to heirs	72
Surplus money on sale of	72
Rails, when	72
Of partnership	87
Taken by administrator	128
Advanced to heir	143
Title to, vests in posthumous child	146
When liable for payment of debts	154, 155
Descends to heir burdened	154
Will not be sold to pay debts barred	170
Of ward, when court will refuse sale in partition	217
cannot be changed to personalty	253
waste of, guardian liable	254
Purchased with ward's money	264, 369

PAGE.

RECEIVER,
    To be appointed of partnership.. 84
    Powers and duties of.. 84

RECORD,
    Of appoinment of adm'r must show next of kin to have waived.. 17
    Reasons for removal of administrator to appear of..................... 22
    Bonds to be spread upon.. 26
    Of examination of bonds to be made... 31
    Must show petition filed, or decree will be reversed................. 156
        that the court heard proof....................................163, 164
    Evidence to appear in..163, 222
    Of appointment of guardian—form................................241, 242
        naturalization, may not be contradicted............................. 561
            be explained... 561
                See "Order of Court."

REFUNDING BOND,
    When to be given..133, 134, 150
    Liability under such... 134
    In case of life estate in personalty.. 134
    Action on, to pay debts.. 135
    Form of... 601

REGISTRATION LAWS,
    Constitutionality of... 541

RELEASE OF SECURITIES,
    Petition for... 28
    Execution and approval of new bond, effects......................29, 30

REMOVAL,
    Of executor or administrator, on failure, etc...........................29, 32
        administration *de bonis non* to be [granted, 30
        property from the state..........................77, 333, 334, 335
        guardians 342
            must be for good reasons................................. 345
            by petition... 345
    Petition for, of guardian should set forth facts............................. 345
    Causes for, of guardian..345, 346
    Of guardian, not without notice... 346
        by majority of ward... 347
            death of ward... 347
            marriage of female ward..................................... 347
            on failure to give counter security........................ 353

RENUNCIATION,
    Of right to administer by next of kin.. 12
    Right of widow to award not affected by..................................... 90
    Of right of widow under will..141, 149
    Legacies to be equalized in case of.. 149

INDEX. 689

	PAGE.
RENTS,	
Where administrator may collect	50
To be inventoried	59
Falling due before death, personal	71
When real and when personal estate	71
Collected by guardians	238, 249
Of infant's land to be first applied to his education	257
REPLEVIN,	
Survives to administrator	66
REPORT,	
Of sale of real estate by administrator	173, 597
May be made at any term	175
What may be considered on	175
Of sale of real estate by guardian	305, 314
Lapse of time will not prevent	315
Of sale by guardian does not conclude ward	315
special commissioner	328
conservator	387
account by conservator	384, 392
assignee	431, 444, 476
That assets are insufficient to pay widow's allowance—form	580
Of private sale—form	586
assignment of homestead and dower—form	596
exceptions, to	598
RES ADJUDICATA,	
In proceedings to secure concealed goods	69
case of foreign administration	108
allowing or disallowing claims	114
approving accounts	126, 127, 129
Order on guardian	238, 348, 356
In approving accounts of guardian	291, 292, 293
final accounts	292, 293, 348
proceedings in insanity	408, 409
bastardy	500
trials of right of property	529
RESIGNATION,	
Of executors and administrators	22
Acceptance of, amounts to removal	23
Administrator to pay costs of	23
Of guardians	339
cannot be questioned in a collateral suit	341
not accepted except for good cause	341
RESULTING TRUST,	
County court cannot adjudicate in case of	6

REVOCATION OF LETTERS,

	PAGE.
County court may	20
Unauthorized preference of creditors justifies	21
On refusal to perform duty	21
When minor or non-resident appointed	21
administrator becomes lunatic	2L
drunkard	21
criminal	21
wastes estate	21
To appear of record	22
In case further security not given	28
Relieves securities from future liability	41
In case of removal of property	77

REVOCATION OF WILLS,

Possible in all cases	195
How effected	195
Not by obliteration	195
Nor by declarations of the testator	195, 196
By birth of children	196

S.

SALE OF PERSONAL PROPERTY,

At inadequate prices, *devastavit*	32
When to be made	78
Made on credit or for cash	78
at private sale by order	78
without order	79
Clerk and crier may be employed	80
Private sale of	78
Crops may be sold	79
When made	80
Bill to be returned	80
Notice of—form	580
Petition for, at private sale—form	585
Order of court for private—form	586
Report of, private—form	586
Sale bill, public—form	587

SALE OF REAL ESTATE,

Jurisdiction in, given to county courts	4
Appointment of administrator cannot be questioned in	16
Additional bond to be given	26
Administrator no power to sell privately	49
Order for, in relation to partnership debts	99
May be coerced	155
Power derived from statute	156, 167
to order judicial	167

SALE OF REAL ESTATE—*Continued.*

	PAGE.
Power limited	167
Infant defendants—guardian *ad litem*	162, 163, 221, 222
May be enjoined by heir, until title is corrected	168
Power of a court of chancery to order	169
What may be shown in defense	169
Will be made only to pay debts contracted by the deceased	170
In cases of ancillary administration	170
Not made to pay debts barred	170
When made to reimburse administrator	170
Special statutory powers concerning, strictly construed	171
Court ordering, no power to direct other than legal payment	171
Decree in, should specify terms	171
Limitation to	171
Delays in applying for, may be explained	171
At public vendue	172
May be completed by administrator *de bonis non*	174
survivor	174
Failure to advertise, does not vitiate	174
For less than value	174
Where deposit is required	174
Should be made in separate tracts	174
To administrator fraudulent	174, 359, 364
Irregularities in, will not invalidate	175
When power to make, exhausted	175
On report of, what questions may arise	175
Not invalidated by failure to report	176
Title held by deceased only passes	176
Effect on, of reversal of decree	176
Where debts were fraudulent	176
Not paid for	178
Under power in will	178
By foreign executors and administrators	205
Of ward	217
no guardian *ad litem* necessary	222
By guardian	298
non-resident guardian	308
Proceedings for, *in rem*	309, 310, 312
Power to make a naked power	310
By one having no letters, void	312
Time of, by guardians	313
At a time other than that fixed by decree, void	313, 317
Order dismissing proceeding after decree, void	317
Irregularities in, do not vitiate	317
Bill filed to set aside	359
By conservators	386, 415
Petition by conservator for	387

SALE OF REAL ESTATE—*Continued.*

	PAGE.
Notice of application by conservator.....387,	415
Court to direct time, etc.	387
Report of.	387
Proceeds of.	387
By non resident conservator.....392,	415
Petition for—form.	589
Cross petition in, for dower—form.	590
Notice of—form.	597
Report of—form.	597
Exceptions to report of—form.	598
Order approving—form	598
disapproving—form	599
Administrator's deed in—form.	599

SCHEDULE,

To be attached to deed of assignment.....436,	437
Of property by insolvent debtor.	466
Contest of.	467
When debtor cannot be compelled to.	481

SECURITIES,

Endangered, administrator to be removed.	21
When not required.	26
Court to examine at January and July terms.....28, 284,	388
Upon bonds to be taken.	28
Desiring to be released.	28
To be discharged from liability, when.	28
Conceiving themselves in danger—petition.....29,	575
Liable for money received for causing death.	35
Becoming administrator *de bonis non*.	35
Bound by order directing administrator or guardian to pay.....37,	348
Liable to the extent of assets only.	38
Not in fiduciary relation to estate.	38
When liable to administrator *de bonis non*.	40
Names may not be in body of bond.	41
Exempt from future liability in case letters are revoked.	41
Not liable to co-administrators	41
Liability of, where administrator acts also as guard'n..41, 51, 286, 293,	349
Where will is set aside.	42
May appeal from any order affecting administrator.....42,	208
to equity for protection.	43
Not liable for mistakes of principal.....54,	348
Liable for removal of property.	78
On note discharged, if not probated.	102
Not liable to one of the principals.	136
On guardian's bond, liable for rents.	238
Suit against, on guardian's bond.....238,	348

PAGE.

SECURITIES—*Continued.*
    Supplemental, on guardian's bond..238, 239
    Liability conditional 239
    Effect on, by discharge under bankrupt law........................... 239
    For loans of ward's money 254
    Loans without, guardian liable..254, 255, 259
    Of guardians to be inquired into... 284
    Equity will protect against fraudulent accounts....................... 292
    On guardian's bond, defenses by... 348
    Not bound by finding of court on guardn's interlocutory account... 348
    Bound by finding of court on guardian's final account............ 348
    Action against, may be maintained before adjustment of accounts.. 349
                  can be maintained only after guardian's removal.. 349
    Death of guardian renders, liable.. 350
    Principal's estate need not be exhausted.................................. 350
    Counter, on guardian's bond.. 350
              conservators 388
    Of conservators... 388
    On bond of one convicted of bastardy...............................494, 507

SECURITY,
    For goods sold at public sale... 78
                   private sale 78
    May be subrogated.. 355

SEDUCTION,
    Of infant, parent or guardian may sue for..........................251, 269
    Female infant no power to consent to....................................... 269

SET-OFF,
    Not allowed against debts due estate...................................75, 112
    Allowed against claim... 105
    Not allowed where purchased after death................................ 112
    Administrator not compelled to.. 112
    Claim barred may be.. 113
    Distributive share against debt... 149
    In case of assignment... 449

SETTLEMENT,
    To be required of administrators and executors about to remove
                                             [from state, 22
    Of estate does not bar claims... 104
                 enforced 129
                 guardian with ward.. 270
                 conservator with the court..................................... 384
    Final, by conservator 384
    Of estate of insolvent debtor.. 476

694   INDEX.

	PAGE.
SHERIFF,	
Duties of, in county court	7
Fees of	7
To serve all writs issued by county court	7
summons	104
in petition to sell	158
Return of	158
To serve citation in bastardy	496
Notice to, of claim to property levied on	517
Duty of, in trials of right of property	517, 526
SLANDER AND LIBEL,	
Actions for, do not survive	66
by infants	268
against lunatics	421
SPECIAL BOND,	
To be given by executors and administrators, when	26
guardians, when	295
Effect of not giving	312
Presumptions in relation to	313
SPECIFIC LEGACIES,	
Not to contribute	135
SPENDTHRIFT,	
Conservator may be appointed for	381
Custody of	412
STATUTE,	
Construction of, must be to enforce honest settlement, etc.	7
English, models for ours	9
Providing for grant of administration mandatory	11
Providing for sale of personalty, directory	78
settlement of partnerships declaratory	85
Conflict of	118
Allowing imprisonment, to be strictly complied with	132
Special powers of, strictly construed	171
Of frauds, in sales of real estate	177
Bankruptcy	428
STATUTE OF LIMITATIONS,	
Duty of executors and administrators to plead	34
Securities on bond may insist on	42
Two years, does not run, when	61, 109
General statute, when it begins to run	109, 267
death does not arrest	109, 110
arrested by part payment	109
where plead, cuts off, etc.	109

STATUTE OF LIMITATIONS—*Continued.*
    General statute, when to be specially pleaded............................ 109
        not arrested by filing claim.................................. 109
        in cases against a deceased guardian................ 110
        effect on, of acknowledgment by administrator... 111
    May be set up by next of kin.. 114
    Two years statute..117, 118
    On payments made by administrator by mistake........................ 120
    Bars claim for contribution.. 135
    Debts barred by, cannot be paid by sale of real estate................. 169
    None relating to sale of land to pay debts................................... 172
    Avoided by infants, how..266, 268
    Runs against married women.. 266
    Does not run against infants... 268

STEP-FATHER,
    Not entitled to compensation for maintaining infants............290, 291
    Bill by.. 280

SUIT ON BOND,
    In, not necessary to establish *devastavit*..................................... 33
    For not taking good security... 33
        releasing or compounding debt... 33
        removing property from state.. 33
        exhibiting untrue account... 33
        failure to file inventory... 33
            plead known defenses 33
            account for debt due from administrator................. 33
        money received for causing death... 35
            stolen from administrator, etc....................................... 36
        failure to use diligence 36
            redeem mortgaged lands... 36
            pay over money as ordered.....................................35, 37
    Breaches of condition may be assigned.. 37
    Demand necessary, when.. 37
    May be against part or all the obligors... 38
        by administrator *de bonis non*, when.................................. 40
    Security for costs in... 40
    May be dismissed for want of cost bond 41
        instituted by any person injured.. 41
    Irregularities in bond, no defense to.. 41
    In, securities may insist on statute of limitations to claim............ 42
    May be brought in chancery, when... 43
    On failure to pay on demand... 131
    Securities not liable to one of the principals................................ 136
    Of guardian 269
        conservator 383

SUMMONS,
 To show cause why new bond should not be given.................. 31
  administrator on claims 104
 In case of petition to sell land 158
 Informalities in... 158
 Service of 158
  on infant 280
 To guardian.. 343
  lunatics, etc 382
 On petition in insanity.. 394

SURVIVING PARTNER,
 Not to be appointed administrator.. 12
 Trustees of partnership property... 83
 To make inventory, etc... 83
 Liable to attachment... 84
 To continue in possession..84, 85
  pay debts 84, 85
  account with executor or administrator............................ 84
  pay over balances... 84
  render account... 84
 Must sue alone... 84
 Waste by... 84
 Required to give security.. 84
 Cannot purchase of himself.. 85
  have individual account allowed....................................... 85
 May purchase of legal representative...................................... 85
  be required to make sale... 86
   render account... 86
  set off debts due firm from estate..................................... 86
 When entitled to compensation.. 86

T.

TAXES,
 Proceedings for collection of, in county courts....................... 4
 Administrator not bound to pay.. 49
 Due at death, payable from personal estate............................ 101
 When not legitimate charge.. 101
 Sales for, to trustee 361

TIE,
 In elections, how determined.. 544

TITLE,
 To personal estate vests in administrator................................ 49
  real estate vests in posthumous child............................... 146
   to be quieted.. 161
   passes on sale by administrator................................. 176
 Not divested by reversal of decree... 176

TITLE—*Continued.*
 By purchase from executor.. 179
 On sale under decree, does not vest until report made and
                   [confirmed, 314
 Does not pass except by compliance with the statute................ 314
 Equitable, when a conveyance will be compelled......................... 316

TORTS,
 Infants are liable as others..277, 280
 Purchases through fraud are..277, 278
 Lunatic liable for...422, 427

TRIAL,
 Of claims 104
 On appeal from probate of will, to be *de novo*........................... 190
  contest of will in equity... 192
  question of sanity.. 390
 In insolvency proceedings... 465
  bastardy..489, 490
  contested elections 537

TRIAL OF THE RIGHT OF PROPERTY,
 Jurisdiction in 516
 Notice to sheriff... 517
    county judge 517
    plaintiff..518, 519
    service of... 519
    by publication 519, 520
    to be mailed by clerk.. 521
 Appearance of plaintiff to be entered... 521
 Trials in, by jury—venire... 522
 Judgment in... 523
 Verdict in 524
 Appeals from judgment—bond 524, 525
 Rules governing..526, 527, 528, 529
 Issue in 526
 Observations upon.........................526, 527, 528, 529, 530, 531

TROVER,
 May be maintained by administrator.. 66
 Action of survivors... 66

TRUSTEES,
 Executor liable as.. 35
 Probate court no power over... 35
 May be appointed to execute will... 47
 Administrator of, no power to execute trust............................. 49
    liable as, when 52
 De son tort, who is... 55
 Surviving partner is 83

	PAGE.
TRUSTEES—*Continued.*	
Compensation of	202
When title vests in	203
Guardians are, for wards	271
Who are	357
Duties of	357, 358, 359
May not deal with trust property	358, 361, 368, 369
Must act for principals alone	358, 365
May not purchase from themselves	358, 360, 367, 369
Disabilities of	359
Directors of a corporation, are	360
Acts of, inure to benefit of *cestui que trust*	361, 362
Accounts by, for profits	361, 362
Purchasers from, in good faith	362
Purchasing outstanding title	362
Cannot divest himself of his character	364
deny title of *cestui que trust*	364
Must act in good faith	365, 370
Voluntary	365
Remedy against	366
Acting in good faith, not liable for loss	367
An officer of the court	368
Assignees, as	446, 450
When agent becomes	369
TRUSTS,	
Not all are considered preferred	118, 119
Naked, do not affect descent	149
Court will advise in relation to	200, 201
Naked, title vests in *cestui que trust*	201
Enforced by ward against guardian	217
Of guardians cannot be assigned	248
delegated	248
Funds of, to be kept separate	255
One holding trust relation to infant	327
Created by letters of guardianship	346
Survives to surviving guardian	346
Defined	357
When implied	357
May be enforced against all having notice	362, 363

U.

UNCLAIMED ESTATE,	
Disposition of	136, 137
To be deposited	137, 297
How obtained by owner	137
UNDERGRADUATES,	
As voters	539, 540

INDEX 699

UNDUE INFLUENCE,
 To avoid a will.. 193
 What constitutes... 193

V.

VENUE,
 See "Change of Venue."

VERDICT,
 In lunacy proceedings... 390
   insanity... 397
    to be recorded.. 398
    may be set aside.. 405
    how far conclusive... 405

VOID,
 When letters not..9, 17
 Acts of administrator not, when.. 17
 Appointment, does not become valid by lapse of time......17, 18
    not, on probate of will... 21
 Private sale of real estate... 49
 Allowance of claims by arbitration..................................... 106
    without notice.. 112
 Sale of land not named in petition.................................... 173
 Bond of guardian, when.. 238
 Deed by infant married woman...............................265, 266
 Release of his share of estate by infant............................. 267
 Contract of infant to pay interest, is.................................. 277
 Without jurisdiction, proceedings are................................ 311
 Order of court, not having jurisdiction.............................. 312
 Decree obtained by a person having letters, is................... 312
 Sale of a ward's land at a time different from time fixed by decree.. 313
 Act, cannot be confirmed.. 317
 Sale at time not named in decree..................................... 317
  of ward's real estate may be confirmed by him................. 319
    unless statute be strictly followed...... 329
 Covenants by guardian, when.. 329
 Deed from trustee to himself, not..................................... 358
 Proceedings for divorce of lunatic.................................... 415
 Contracts of lunatics, etc.....................385, 415, 416, 417, 418, 419
 Preference of creditors.. 435
 When deed of assignment is..................446, 447, 448, 449
 Election.. 544

VOIDABLE,
 When letters are...18, 21
 Illegal sales of property... 80
 Sale of land to administrator...................................174, 175
 Erroneous decree... 223

VOIDABLE—*Continued.*

	PAGE.
Acts of infant	265, 266, 276
Purchase of ward's land by guardian	272
Arbitration by guardian is, by infant	272
Conveyance by guardian to one for himself	316
Sale by trustee to himself	358, 359
Contracts with lunatics, etc	385, 416, 417, 418, 419

W.

WARD,

Estate of, when liable for maintenance	215
Services of, who entitled to	215
May file bill against guardian	218
Must be in court before guardian *ad litem* is appointed	221
May ratify acts	280

See "Infant."

WARRANT,

To commit insane person	399
appraisers—form	577
commissioners—form	595

WIDOW,

Preference in administration	11
When not to be appointed administrator	13
To receive assets of estate, when	63
Liable for funeral expenses, when	63
Policy payable to	71
Liable for waste	74
May select in lieu of specific articles	89
No power to waive award	90, 91
Right to award fixed upon death of husband	91
Not permitted to seize and hold money	91
Preferred over creditors	93
Bound by relinquishment	94
May compel sale of real estate	83
Bound by acceptance	91
May probate claim	108
Not affected by advancements	144
Of childless husband, takes personal estate charged with debts	148
Accepting provisions in will	149
To be made party to petition to sell	149
Relinquishment by—form	579
Petition by, for dower—form	590

WIDOW'S AWARD,

When assets do not exceed	63, 92
Of what it consists	88
Allowed in exclusion of debts, etc	88

WIDOW'S AWARD—*Continued.*

	PAGE.
Appraisers to estimate	89
Penalty for failure to set off	89
When there is not property in kind	89
Right to, not affected by renunciation	90
Only made in case of residents	90, 92
Policy of the law	90
For benefit of children	90
Not affected by ante-nuptial agreement	90, 91
Right fixed upon death of husband	91
right cannot be cut off by will	91
Need not be presented and allowed as a claim	91
Legal title to, vests in widow	92, 94
Takes subject to funeral expenses	92
A preferred claim	93, 94
Appraisers to consider condition in life	93
No allowance made for family pictures	93
Court may set aside	93
Conclusive in proceeding to sell land	94
upon widow	94
Is a lien upon real estate	94
Homestead and dower exempt from	95
Husband not entitled to	147
Form of	578
Where widow is insane	141

WIFE,

Right of, to administer	11
Entitled to be conservator of husband	408
Claim by	108
See "Widow."	

WILL,

Courts of equity will not admit to probate	5
When discovered, effect on administration	18
During contest of, estate to be committed to administrator	19
On production of, letters revoked	21
Setting aside, does not render letters void	21
Power of administrator, under	31
To be filed for probate by executor or custodian	45
May direct payment of debts	65
Must be strictly followed in relation to partnership	83
Construction of, by court of chancery	169
Power in, to sell lands	178, 179
Construction of, in relation to power to sell	179
Power to make, statutory	181
Definition of	181
Who may make	182
Mental capacity to execute	182, 183

WILL—*Continued.*

                             PAGE.
 How made and declared.. 183
 To be recorded 183
 Signatures to 183, 184
 Publication of, not necessary... 184
 Change in, must be witnessed... 184
 Attestation in presence of testator................................... 184
 Foreign 184
 Can be no mutual... 184
 All property may be disposed of, by................................. 184
 May limit estate in property devised................................ 184
 Power to dispose of property by, is unlimited................. 185
 Custodian to deliver to county court............................... 185
 Where probated 185
 Probate of, cannot be waived.. 186
    in circuit court.. 187
    evidence in.. 188
 Order remitting or rejecting, how far binding................. 189
 Devise in, to subscribing witness.............................. 189, 190
 Contest of.. 190, 191, 192
 To remain with clerk... 190
 Letters to issue on... 191
 Who may contest 192
 Contested by bill in circuit court..................................... 192
 Part of, may be contested.. 192
 Executed out of the state.. 194, 195
 How revoked.. 195, 196
 Nuncupative.. 196
 Lost, how proven... 198
 Law of domicile to control.. 198
 Construction of 199
 Evidence inadmissible to explain.................................... 190
 Words of, not taken in technical sense............................ 190
 Whole instrument considered... 190
 Fraudulent as to creditors, when............................... 201, 202
 Disposition by, of children 218, 219
 Of divorced wife.. 220

WITNESSES,
 In bastardy.. 491

WITNESSES TO WILL,
 Must sign in presence of testator.................................... 183
 To appear before the county court.................................. 186
 Imprisonment of. 186
 Non-resident 186
 Where county judge is... 187
    they differ.. 188, 189

WITNESSES TO WILL—*Continued.*
 Where neither could write his name 189
 Interest of.. 189, 190
 Need not be called in contest of will.. 192
 To nuncupative.. 197

WRIT OF ERROR,
 From order of imprisonment.. 209
 When it lies from county court in probate...................................... 210
 Infant may prosecute... 267
 In bastardy proceedings.. 498

WOMAN,
 Right to naturalization.. 562

7

LAW LIBRARY
UNIVERSITY OF CALIFORNIA
LOS ANGELES

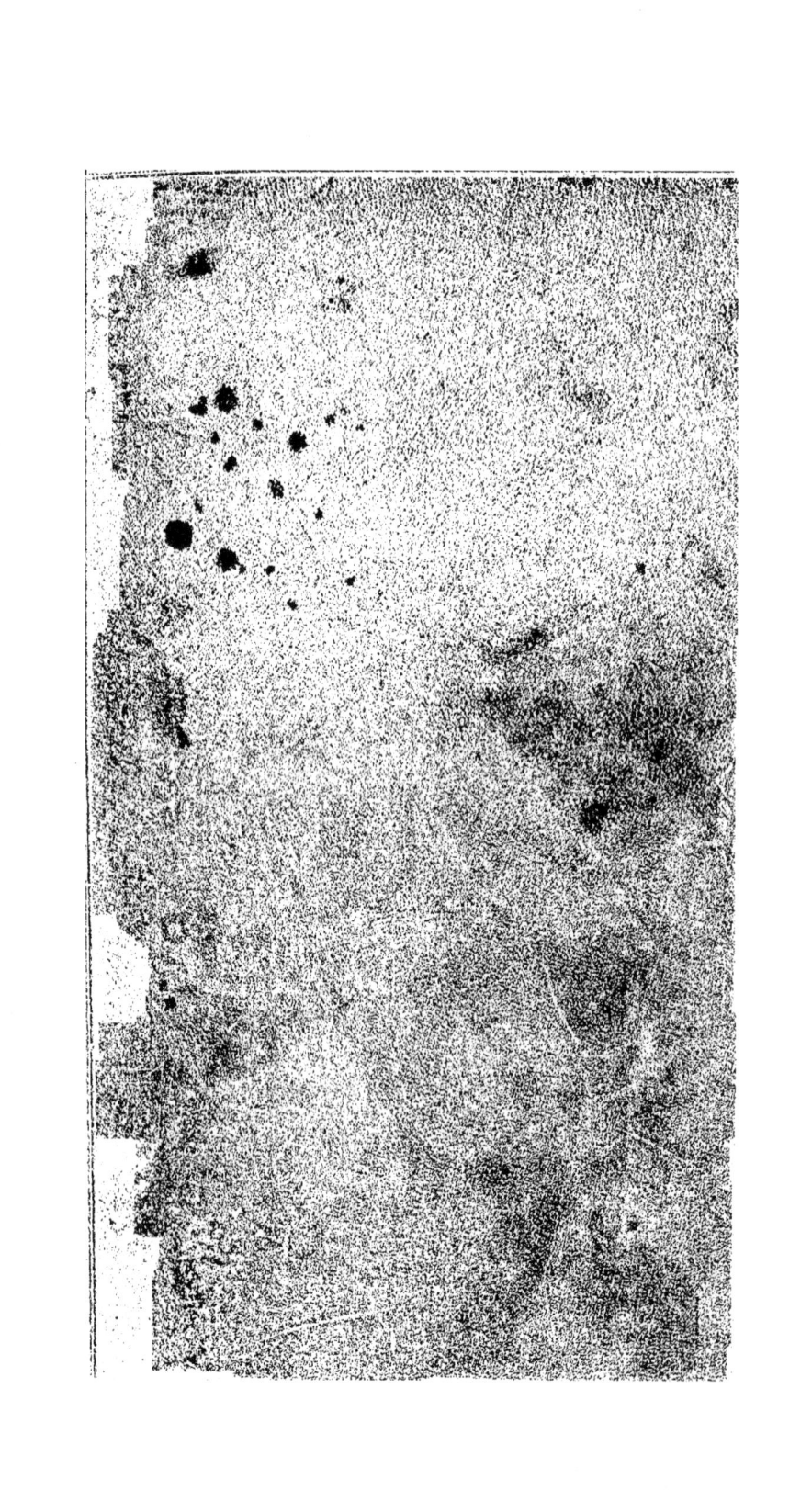

Lightning Source UK Ltd.
Milton Keynes UK
UKHW010721271118
333020UK00017B/270/P

9 781331 185277